Irish Taxation: Law and Practice

16th edition **2018/2019** **Volume 1**

Edited by Patrick Mulcahy

Authors:
Caitriona Gaynor
Raymond Holly
Pat Kennedy
Paul Murphy
Margaret Sheridan

Irish Tax Institute
South Block
Longboat Quay
Grand Canal Harbour
Dublin 2

Tel: +353 1 6631700
www.taxinstitute.ie

First Edition 2003
Sixteenth Edition 2018

A catalogue reference for this book is available from the British Library.

The object of this book is to explain in broad detail the principles and practice of taxation in the Republic of Ireland. The book is not intended as a detailed exposition of the extensive volume of statute and case law relating to taxation.

ISBN 978-1-84260-495-3

The legislation contained in Volume 1 and Volume 2 of *Irish Taxation: Law and Practice* has been updated to reflect Finance Act 2017.

Printed and bound in Ireland by Spectrum Print Logistics, Citywest Business Campus, Naas Road, Dublin 24.

PRESIDENT'S FOREWORD

I am very pleased to welcome readers to the sixteenth edition of *Irish Taxation: Law and Practice*, Ireland's leading third-level tax publication.

This educational text is divided into two separate volumes. In addition to an introduction to Irish tax principles and policy, Volume 1 provides analysis of the fundamentals of VAT, income tax, capital gains tax, corporation tax, capital acquisitions tax, stamp duty and local property tax, fully updated to Finance Act 2017. Volume 2 contains assignments, questions and solutions, which are also updated to current legislation.

As a supplement to the textbook, lecturers and tutors have access to an online teaching resource containing a complete set of teaching aids. These include customisable presentation slides for each tax head, solutions to revision questions, additional assignments and tax charts. Please contact us at cpd@taxinstitute.ie if you require access to this resource.

The Irish Tax Institute is the only professional body dedicated to tax and our Chartered Tax Advisers (CTA) are amongst 30,000 CTAs globally. The Institute is very committed to encouraging and supporting the study of tax in third-level institutions and I would encourage you to visit the dedicated careers area on our website, www.taxinstitute.ie. You will find interesting profiles of those working in tax, details on the Institute's scholarship programmes and other interesting competitions. Each year we promote a Fantasy Budget Competition for third-level students that is judged by some of Ireland's leading business commentators and economists. We are also delighted with the continuing interest in "*Your Take on Tax*", our dedicated annual competition for first and second year students at third-level. For further details on any aspect of the above please contact us at students@taxinstitute.ie.

I would sincerely like to thank all authors of this title, Caitriona Gaynor, Raymond Holly, Pat Kennedy, Paul Murphy, Margaret Sheridan and Martina Whyte for their immense contributions. Sincere thanks are also due to Laurence May (Editor, Volume 2) and Patrick Mulcahy (Editor, Volume 1), for their hard work and commitment.

David Fennell, FITI, Chartered Tax Adviser (CTA)
President
Irish Tax Institute

Contents

Volume 1

Section III Income Tax

TABLE OF CASES

LIST OF ABBREVIATIONS

AER	*All England Law Reports*
ATC	Annotated Tax Cases
CATCA 2003	Capital Acquisitions Tax Consolidation Act 2003
FA	Finance Act
HC	High Court (Ireland)
ICTA 1988 ..	Income and Corporation Taxes Act 1988 (UK)
ILRM	*Irish Law Reports Monthly*
ITA 1967	Income Tax Act 1967
ITC	Official Reports of Irish Tax Cases
ITR	*Irish Tax Reports*
JFL	*Irish Journal of Family Law*
KB	Law Reports, King's Bench Division (UK)
Para	Paragraph
PRSI	Pay-related social insurance
Pt	Part
QB	Law Reports, Queen's Bench Division (UK)
s	Section
SC	Supreme Court (Ireland)
Sch	Schedule
SDCA 1999	Stamp Duties Consolidation Act 1999
STC	*Simon's Tax Cases*
SW(Con)A ...	Social Welfare Consolidation Act 1993
TC	Official Reports of United Kingdom Tax Cases
TLR	*The Times Law Reports*
TCA97	Taxes Consolidation Act 1997
USC	Universal Social Charge
VATCA 2010	Value-Added Tax Consolidation Act 2010

LIST OF ABBREVIATIONS

AER	*All England Law Reports*
ATC	Annotated Tax Cases
CATCA 2003	Capital Acquisitions Tax Consolidation Act 2003
FA	Finance Act
HC	High Court (Ireland)
ICTA 1988	Income and Corporation Taxes Act 1988 (UK)
ILRM	*Irish Law Reports Monthly*
ITA 1967	Income Tax Act 1967
ITC	Official Reports of Irish Tax Cases
ITR	*Irish Tax Reports*
IJFL	*Irish Journal of Family Law*
KB	Law Reports, King's Bench Division (UK)
Para	Paragraph
PRSI	Pay-related social insurance
Pt	Part
QB	Law Reports, Queen's Bench Division (UK)
s	Section
SC	Supreme Court (Ireland)
Sch	Schedule
SDCA 1999	Stamp Duties Consolidation Act 1999
STC	Simon's Tax Cases
SW(C)A	Social Welfare Consolidation Act 1993
TC	Official Reports of United Kingdom Tax Cases
TLR	*The Times Law Reports*
TCA97	Taxes Consolidation Act 1997
USC	Universal Social Charge
VATCA 2010	Value-Added Tax Consolidation Act 2010

1 IRISH TAXATION – PRINCIPLES AND POLICY

Learning Outcomes

On completion of this chapter you will be able to:

- ✓ Understand the historical aspects of Irish taxation
- ✓ Describe sources of tax law and information
- ✓ Identify the objectives of taxation
- ✓ Discuss the tax base and methods of classifying taxes
- ✓ Identify the characteristics of an ideal tax system
- ✓ Recognise the stakeholders in Irish taxation policy and administration

The editor, Patrick Mulcahy, wishes to thank the former editors, Kieran Gallery, Gerardine Doyle and Moira O'Halloran for their contributions to the development of this publication.

1.1 Introduction

"To tax and to please, no more than to love and to be wise, is not given to men."

This quotation, attributed to Edmund Burke in a parliamentary address in 1774, sums up the difficulty associated with designing an ideal tax system. As you will see upon reading this chapter, a modern tax system must fulfil roles far beyond that of collecting tax!

Before delving into the intricacies of the principal Irish taxes, it is important to have some appreciation of the 'macro' aspects of Irish taxation. With this in mind, this chapter attempts to explain why taxation is necessary and to discuss some of the general principles of taxation and their application in the Irish context. The commentary is presented as follows:

- section 1.2 is concerned with the historical development of taxation, with particular reference to the Irish story,
- section 1.3 outlines the criteria that provide a framework within which specific tax measures and proposed reforms can be evaluated,
- section 1.4 explains the role of taxation in the economy,
- section 1.5 addresses the methods of classifying taxes, and

- section 1.6 is concerned with defining the tax base and explores the recommendations of the *Commission on Taxation* (2009) regarding the tax base, and
- section 1.7 summarizes the structure and roles of the key stakeholders in Irish tax policy and administration.

1.2 Historical Aspects of Taxation

1.2.1 General

Earliest forms of taxation consisted of the outright acquisition of men and goods when needed. For example, Réamonn (1981) refers to 'prisage' or 'prizage', a duty which dates from 1177 in Ireland. It was levied on ships importing wine and involved the requisitioning of one-ninth of the wine for the king's use. In general, more formal taxes involving the collection of cash were initially introduced as "war taxes". In ancient Rome, indirect taxes in the form of expenditure taxes on important goods such as slaves were a vital source of revenue for the expanding empire. In addition, the ancient Roman administration kept records of the property of each citizen, and a wealth tax known as the 'tributum' was levied on citizens in respect of their recorded property. This was abolished in 167 BC when "the spoils of war made it no longer necessary to raise large sums of money from Roman citizens" (James and Nobes, 2005 p. 212). In Britain, income tax was first introduced in 1799 to fund the Napoleonic wars.

The introduction of a formal system of taxation in Ireland to a large extent mirrors the British experience, as for much of its recent history, even prior to the Act of Union of 1800, Ireland was under British rule. In the Middle Ages, taxation generally took the form of feudal dues imposed on estates in territories under the English Crown and customs duties imposed on imports and exports. The administration and collection of customs and excise in Ireland was greatly formalised in 1662 with the enactment of two Acts, which provided for the establishment of an Office of Revenue Commissioners in Ireland and a system of accounting for revenues collected to the king.

Other taxes were introduced in Ireland on an *ad hoc* basis during the seventeenth and eighteenth centuries. A hearth tax was introduced by an Act of 1662 to compensate the Crown for the imminent abolition of the feudal dues referred to above. This was payable at a rate of 2s. per annum on every fire hearth or stove, with certain exceptions. Window taxes were introduced in Ireland in 1799 and probably explain why windows in many of the country's large 18th century houses were bricked up in the early part of the nineteenth century – an early example of tax planning. Window taxes were abolished in 1851. Stamp duties were introduced by the Stamp Act of 1774 and have remained an important source of tax revenues in Ireland to the present day. In 2006, they represented almost 6% of tax receipts – more than the total revenues from capital acquisitions tax and capital gains tax combined. However since the tax year 2007, stamp duties collected as a percentage of total gross taxes collected have been falling due to the downturn in the property market. For the tax year 2009, stamp duties collected amounted to 2% of the total taxes collected, equivalent to the aggregate of capital gains tax and capital acquisition tax. As stamp duty ceased to function as a property tax, it was expected that a property tax (an annual tax) would be introduced. This was a key recommendation of the *Commission on Taxation* (2009) [see section 1.6 below] as a mechanism to develop a more stable tax base and to reduce the economic distortion arising from transaction based property taxes. The government also committed to the introduction of a property tax as part of the terms of the EU/IMF Programme for Financial Support. The recommendation came to fruition (of a sort) in 2012, when a household charge was introduced for all residential property, with mixed success. The government introduced a more equitable property tax in 2013.

1.2.2 The introduction of income tax

While William Pitt introduced income tax in England in 1799, it was not extended to Ireland until Gladstone was Chancellor of the Exchequer in 1853. The interim period saw much debate on whether or not the same taxes should apply in both Ireland and England. Sir Robert Peel, on introducing his system of income tax in England in 1842, argued that the unique nature of Irish society meant that the efficient collection of income tax in Ireland would be "a matter of grave consideration" (Réamonn, 1981, p. 37). In dealing with a nation beset by famine, he felt that it was more appropriate to increase stamp duties and to introduce a special duty on spirits manufactured in Ireland.[1]

Gladstone argued that Peel's measures failed to yield an amount equivalent to that which an income tax would generate. As a firm advocate of the harmonisation of taxes in the UK and Ireland, he was adamant that exempting one country from taxation would lead to the "over-taxation" of another. In 1853, notwithstanding the social and economic problems that were the legacy of the Great Famine of 1845 – 49, Gladstone extended Peel's system of income tax to Ireland in the first of his 13 Budgets as Chancellor of the Exchequer. It should be noted that this tax had quite a high entry level: the first £150 of income was exempt from tax, and this effectively excluded a large portion of the population from the scope of income tax. Income above this level was taxed at 3%.

Ironically, Gladstone had originally intended income tax to be a temporary measure and had hoped to abolish it by 1860. However, rapid increases in public expenditure meant that this was not feasible. Thus, in 1923 – some 70 years later – Peel's system of income tax, subject to some amendments, was still broadly the basis for the income tax code. Following the formation of the Irish Free State in 1922, this code was taken over by the Irish Government in 1923. Together with the various adaptations necessitated by the establishment of the Irish Free State, by the Constitution of 1937 and by Irish Finance Acts from 1923 onwards, it formed the basis of the income tax legislation consolidated in the Income Tax Act 1967. This legislation was later incorporated into the Taxes Consolidation Act 1997 ("TCA97").

1 The onerous levy on whiskey contributed to the growth of illegal distilling in Ireland in the 19th century, an activity which required the Revenue Commissioners to provide their own dedicated police corps (*na ribhínigh*) for the period from 1824–1857 (Réamonn, 1981).

1.2.3 The introduction of value-added tax (VAT)

As well as inheriting an income tax code from our historical link with Britain, the Government of the Free State also adopted the system of indirect taxation that had applied prior to 1922. In fact, in the early years of the new State, the bulk of net receipts were derived from indirect taxation. Réamonn (1981) observes that, in 1924, direct taxes on the income of individuals and companies amounted to less than 24% of total receipts, estate and stamp duties accounted for approximately 6% of total receipts and more than 70% of revenues were collected from customs and excise duties and levies.

By the early 1960s, receipts from indirect taxation were derived mainly from duties imposed on a limited number of goods such as beer, spirits, tobacco and hydrocarbon oils. In 1962–63, tax receipts from this narrow base accounted for more than 40% of total government revenue. The dominance of this source of revenue meant that the public finances would be highly sensitive to a fall in the yield from any of these goods. In order to reduce the dependency of the Exchequer on these commodities, and also with a view to potentially reducing rates of income tax, the then Minister for Finance, Dr James Ryan, elected to introduce a turnover tax. This was a form of indirect taxation common in many Western European countries at that time. In Ireland, it involved a charge of 2.5% on all retail turnover and on receipts from the provision of services. To complement the turnover tax, a wholesale tax was introduced in 1966 at a rate of 5%. By 1969, the wholesale tax rate was increased to 10%, but certain "luxury" goods became chargeable at 15% in June of that year.

To facilitate Ireland's accession to the European Economic Community (EEC) in 1973, both of these taxes were replaced by value-added tax (VAT). VAT is an indirect tax applied at each stage in the production and distribution of goods and services. Although collected at each stage in the chain of supply on the basis of the value added by the trader, the cost is ultimately borne by the final consumer.[2] Two EEC Council Directives provided a loose framework for the new VAT legislation, which came into effect on 1 November 1972. However, with a view to increased harmonisation and integration across Member States, another Council Directive was agreed in 1977. This, the Sixth Council Directive, came into force on 1 January 1978 and forms the cornerstone of our current VAT legislation, the Value-Added Tax Consolidation Act 2010 ("VATCA").

1.2.4 The introduction of capital taxes

Stamp duties have been a feature of taxation in Ireland since 1774. Estate duties, or death duties, were first introduced in Ireland by Sir William Harcourt, Chancellor of the Exchequer, in 1894. However, it was not until 1974 that the introduction of other, more contemporary "capital taxes" in Ireland was proposed. In February of that year, the then Minister for Finance, Mr Richie Ryan, presented a White Paper to both Houses of the

2 It is not always possible, however, to attribute the burden of taxation to the final consumer. A supplier may alter his pricing mechanism so as to ensure his goods remain attractive to the final consumer, thereby absorbing the VAT cost and effectively enduring the burden of taxation.

Oireachtas outlining the Government's proposals in relation to capital gains tax (CGT), capital acquisitions tax (CAT) and wealth tax. All three taxes were introduced over the following three years. However, the wealth tax was very short-lived and was abolished with effect from 5 April 1978 – within three years of its original introduction.

CGT had been introduced in the UK in 1965 and the Irish Capital Gains Tax Act 1975 was, in most areas, essentially taken word for word from the existing UK legislation. The new legislation applied to both individuals and companies, and provided for the first time for the taxation of gains arising on the disposal of capital assets. Prior to this, capital receipts were, by and large, free of tax; generating increases in wealth via capital value growth as opposed to via income was much more tax efficient and presented considerable scope for tax planning. The 1975 Act and amendments provided for by subsequent Finance Acts and enactments were later incorporated into the TCA97.

The CAT provisions were legislated for in the Capital Acquisitions Tax Act 1976. This provided for both gift and inheritance tax on property passing from one individual to another. Ironically, the impetus for the gift tax, which survives today, was the short-lived annual wealth tax of 1975–78. In the absence of a gift tax to complement an annual wealth tax, wealth tax could be avoided or reduced where a donor made sufficient gifts to reach a lower wealth tax bracket. The introduction of inheritance tax coincided with the termination of estate duties arising on legacies and under succession law.

Drafting of the CAT Act 1976 was a somewhat more onerous task than that of drafting the CGT Act 1975. A capital transfer tax on the lifetime transfer of assets had been introduced in the UK in the previous year but, at the time, there was no example of a country with a common law legal system that had an inheritance tax in operation. Inheritance tax in its current form was not introduced in the UK until 1986.

The provisions of the CAT Act 1976 and subsequent Finance Acts were consolidated in 2003 and can now be found in the CAT Consolidation Act 2003 ("CATCA").

Probate tax, which involved an additional levy of 2% on estates of the deceased, was introduced by Finance Act 1993 but was later abolished in respect of deaths occurring on or after 6 December 2000.

1.2.5 The introduction of corporation tax

Prior to 1976, companies were subject to income tax and corporation profits tax on their income and CGT on their gains. In 1976, a single tax on companies' profits (which included both income and chargeable gains) was introduced. The new provisions were provided for in the Corporation Tax Act 1976 and the necessary amendments were made to the income tax and CGT legislation. The 1976 Act and amendments provided for by subsequent Finance Acts were later incorporated into the TCA97.

1.2.6 Sources of law

Legislation

The Acts referred to above and currently in force are the main statutory sources of law considered by tax practitioners. For the purposes of this text, readers will be most concerned with the provisions of the TCA97, the CATCA and the VATCA. These Acts are revised and updated on an annual basis in response to legislative amendments introduced by Finance Acts. The annual Finance Acts generally implement changes and new tax measures announced by the Minister for Finance in his Budget statement in December of each year (this statement outlines the Government's Budget plans for the year and how it proposes to finance these plans. See 1.7.1 for more details on the budgetary process).

Accordingly, when referring to any consolidated tax legislation (or any related commentary, such as this publication) it is important to ensure that it reflects the amendments as set out in the most recent Finance Act. The Irish Tax Institute's editions of consolidated tax legislation will state (normally on the cover) on which Finance Act they are based. With this in mind, it is worth noting that this publication is based on the TCA97, the CATCA and the VATCA, as amended by Finance Act 2017.

Case law precedent

In addition to understanding the statutory framework, given that our legal system is based on common law, knowledge of case law precedent is also essential. Decisions in cases heard in Irish courts form binding precedents, which must be followed in subsequent cases in the absence of distinguishing facts. Accordingly, an Irish taxpayer has a right to rely on such precedents and they constitute a vital source of law. Case law precedent is generally relied on in the absence of statutory legislation on specific issues and also in interpreting legislation where components may not be clearly defined.

Because of the similarities (which have evolved for historic and other reasons, as outlined above) between our tax code and that of the UK there is a wealth of UK case law pertinent to Irish tax law. However, decisions from other common law jurisdictions (such as the UK) do not form binding precedents that Irish courts are obliged to follow. They are, however, very persuasive and, accordingly, in most instances where a tax issue has already been the subject of judicial consideration in a UK court, it is not challenged again in the Irish courts. Nonetheless, there are exceptions (most notably in the area of tax avoidance) and caution should be exercised in relying on UK precedent.

The European influence

The European Union (EU) also represents an important source of tax law. In recent times, decisions of the Court of Justice of the European Union (CJEU) have become increasingly influential.

EU Directives also have a significant influence on Irish legislation. This is most notable in the area of VAT, where the provisions of EU Directives form the basis of domestic legislation in Member States. However, a number of Directives relating to direct taxation are also relevant. The "Parent/Subsidiary Directive" is concerned with implementing a common system of taxation where parent companies and their subsidiaries operate in different Member States. The "Mergers Directive" is concerned with facilitating cross-border mergers and transfers of assets between companies located in different Member States. The provisions of these Directives were introduced by legislative amendments contained in the Finance Acts of 1991 and 1992.

Two further Directives have been incorporated into Irish legislation by the provisions of Finance Act 2004. A Directive on the taxation of income and savings (the "Savings Directive") provides for information exchange between Member States. The "Withholding Tax Exemption Directive" aims to eliminate withholding taxes on interest and royalty payments between associated companies in different Member States[3].

Revenue practice

Finally, although not legally binding, documented details of Revenue practice in specific areas can throw light on the practical treatment of many technical statutory issues that require further explanation. Such information can be found in official *Statements of Practice*, in information leaflets issued by Revenue and in *Tax Briefing*, a bimonthly Revenue publication on technical issues. In general Revenue *Statements of Practice* are valid for five years after which time practitioners are advised to seek confirmation of any changes in tax practice. In addition, details of past rulings and concessions granted by Revenue can be obtained under the Freedom of Information Act 1997 and Freedom of Information Amendment Act 2003. To a lesser extent, details of UK Inland Revenue practice are also helpful.

1.3 Desirable Characteristics of Taxation

It is possible to evaluate systems of taxation and individual tax measures on the basis of clearly defined criteria. For example, in his landmark publication *The Wealth of Nations* (1776), Adam Smith proposed four canons of taxation:

- **Equity:** The tax should be fair.
- **Certainty:** It should be possible to determine the tax liability with reasonable exactitude and minimal subjectivity.
- **Convenience:** It should be possible to collect the tax with minimal effort on the part of the administrator and with minimal disruption to the taxpayer.
- **Efficiency:** The tax should minimise distortionary effects on consumer behaviour and the revenue collected from the tax should justify the costs of collection.

3 Not all EU countries are covered by the Withholding Tax Exemption Directive: Greece and Portugal may continue to apply withholding taxes to interest and royalties, while Spain reserves the right to withhold taxes on royalty payments.

The Irish *Commission on Taxation*, established in the 1980s, used a variation of this framework when it focused on issues of equity, efficiency and simplicity in assessing various aspects of the Irish regime. Effectively, this involved consideration of Smith's canons of "certainty" and "convenience" under the single heading "simplicity".

It should be borne in mind that Smith (1776) wrote at a time when the main function of taxation was to generate funds for public finance. While this is still the case, in more recent times taxation has also been used as an instrument of social and economic policy (see 1.4 below). Accordingly, the criterion of efficiency presented by Smith (1776) has been extended somewhat to also encompass the issue of incentives, i.e., a tax incentive may be perceived as efficient insofar as it encourages desirable social behaviour and economic activity. This can be specifically be seen in an opening comment by Minister for Finance, Paschal Donohoe in his Budget Speech on October 11 2016:

"Fairness is, of course, about the relative distribution of income in society, but it is also about improving services for our people, and treating all members of our community well. It is about investment in education for all children and improving our health services. It is about opportunities to work in a good job, run your own business if you choose to, live in a good home and in a safe community, whilst caring for your family, whatever shape that family may take"

The most recent *Commission on Taxation* (2009, page 2) adopted another variation of the *Canons of Taxation* in guiding their work; equity, flexibility, tax neutrality, simplicity, and an evidence based approach (Readers are referred to the *Report of the Commission on Taxation, 2009*).

Realistically, given the conflicts between individual canons of taxation, it may not be possible to design an ideal tax system. Nonetheless, the criteria are useful, as they provide a framework within which tax proposals may be considered. They also help to identify and highlight criticisms that might otherwise be overlooked.

1.4 The Role of Taxation in the Economy

As described at 1.2.1 above, many taxes were historically introduced to finance war. More recently, with the advent of the Welfare State, and the provision by most modern governments of certain services and public goods for the benefit of citizens, taxation has become a tool used by governments to generate public finance, to redistribute resources to the less well-off and to encourage certain desirable behaviour.

1.4.1 Tax as a source of public finance

The Government needs revenue to fund our infrastructure, our education system, our healthcare service, our public transport system, etc. There are a number of options available to it. For instance, it can simply charge for the goods or services provided. This is the method by which the Government funds our public transport system. It is also the method that some local authorities controversially implemented to fund the cost of refuse collection.

However, this method is not appropriate to the provision of certain public goods, where the beneficiaries are not clearly identifiable. For example, who should be charged for services provided by the Department of the Environment aimed at ensuring we have clean air? Who should be charged for the services of An Garda Síochána in policing our streets? It would be very difficult to charge a particular sub-group of the population for these services and even more difficult to prevent those who do not pay from benefiting. In addition, where additional individuals can benefit from the provision of a service at no extra cost to the provider, it would be inefficient to exclude them on the basis that they have not paid. For example, there are unlikely to be additional costs associated with allowing an extra child to sit in a classroom so, if there was not a system of free primary education in this country, it would be inefficient to exclude a child who could not afford to pay. In fact, there would undoubtedly be a benefit to society in granting that child a free education.

Thus, as an alternative to charging for certain goods and services that it provides, the Government must generate finance from some other source. A second option available to the Government is to create more money and use it to finance these goods and services. This tried and tested method invariably leads to devaluation of the currency and inflation. Another option is to simply borrow more money. However, there are limits on the amount that can be raised in this way, as can be seen from the current EU/IMF bailout package.

Taxation has proved to be the favoured method of raising public finance in most modern economies and usually represents the greater part of government revenue. Such reliance on taxation to raise public finance creates a phenomenon known as "the burden of taxation". At a household or individual level, this can be measured as the total tax paid expressed as a percentage of household or personal income. At a macro level, the burden of taxation is usually measured by expressing government tax receipts as a percentage of gross domestic product (GDP). The first table below shows the national tax burden (i.e., total tax revenues expressed as a percentage of GDP) for all OECD countries for a selection of years from 1965 to 2016.

Table 1.1: Total tax revenue as percentage of GDP

	1965	1975	1985	1995	2000	2007	2009	2010	2011	2012	2013	2014	2015	2016
Australia	20.606	25.35	27.688	28.195	30.422	29.636	25.765	25.584	26.285	27.288	27.50	27.85	28.22	n.a.
Austria	33.59	36.423	40.534	41.04	42.089	40.541	40.971	40.9	41.03	41.667	42.524	42.99	43.46	42.67
Belgium	30.625	38.794	43.548	42.778	43.777	42.435	41.997	42.366	42.898	43.954	44.641	44.66	44.81	44.18
Canada	25.21	31.415	31.883	34.874	34.909	32.271	31.421	30.544	30.371	30.687	30.558	30.82	31.94	31.68
Chile	..	..	..	18.371	18.772	22.779	17.207	19.529	21.221	21.385	20.228	19.82	20.70	20.39
Czech Republic	..	..	..	34.851	32.521	34.285	32.354	32.549	33.353	33.783	34.097	33.09	33.47	34.03
Denmark	29.492	37.762	45.378	47.998	48.137	47.665	46.387	46.457	46.606	47.162	48.575	50.88	46.62	45.94
Estonia	..	..	..	36.22	30.946	31.096	34.928	33.232	31.914	32.111	31.837	32.87	33.59	34.74

(Continued)

Table 1.1: Continued

	1965	1975	1985	1995	2000	2007	2009	2010	2011	2012	2013	2014	2015	2016
Finland	30.017	36.113	39.14	44.496	45.82	41.508	40.934	40.788	42.033	42.834	43.999	43.85	43.99	44.13
France	33.637	34.896	41.886	41.896	43.05	42.386	41.323	41.577	42.863	44.002	45.038	45.22	45.50	45.27
Germany	31.601	34.312	36.084	36.246	36.293	34.928	36.111	35.03	35.698	36.45	36.677	36.13	36.94	37.55
Greece	17.035	18.598	24.417	27.629	33.148	30.935	29.56	31.08	32.494	33.714	33.512	25.90	36.78	38.56
Hungary	..	..	..	40.999	38.67	39.602	39.019	37.559	36.858	38.454	38.923	38.48	39.40	39.41
Iceland	25.521	29.179	27.439	30.377	36.187	38.708	32.007	33.329	34.456	35.313	35.545	38.67	37.12	36.37
Ireland	24.512	27.924	33.654	31.803	30.886	30.428	26.997	26.761	26.671	27.263	28.29	29.90	23.59	23.03
Israel	..	..	..	35.219	35.555	34.666	29.767	30.581	30.871	29.643	30.518	31.12	31.37	31.25
Italy	24.662	24.513	32.504	38.569	40.58	41.681	41.858	41.541	41.37	42.746	42.64	43.64	43.34	42.87
Japan	17.783	20.376	26.719	26.413	26.648	28.506	26.959	27.587	28.641	29.524	30.31	32.04	30.74	n.a.
Korea	..	14.183	15.255	19.011	21.458	24.785	23.606	23.236	24.012	24.762	24.309	24.61	25.25	26.31
Luxembourg	26.35	31.169	37.546	35.295	37.236	37.162	38.973	38.003	37.501	38.492	39.335	37.79	29.00	37.07
Mexico	..	..	15.18	14.919	16.545	17.57	17.162	18.529	19.509	19.59	19.69	15.15	16.23	17.22
Netherlands	30.874	38.358	39.948	39.044	36.79	36.327	35.417	36.147	35.883	36.331	36.68	37.52	37.75	38.85
New Zealand	23.63	28.043	30.603	35.823	32.906	34.486	30.997	31.045	31.404	32.986	32.091	32.37	32.76	32.08
Norway	29.64	39.2	42.623	40.872	42.639	42.93	41.99	42.642	42.699	42.298	40.78	39.07	38.06	37.98
Poland	..	..	..	36.104	32.668	34.478	31.335	31.251	31.776	32.07	31.93	32.08	32.44	33.56
Portugal	15.668	18.854	24.122	28.894	30.575	31.328	29.492	30.039	32.016	31.191	33.439	34.44	34.49	34.38
Slovak Republic	..	..	..	39.562	33.632	28.816	28.447	27.728	28.339	28.082	29.627	31.01	32.25	32.73
Slovenia	..	..	..	38.36	36.629	37.065	36.212	36.733	36.281	36.547	36.812	35.55	36.60	36.98
Spain	14.294	17.953	26.837	31.294	33.376	36.413	29.834	31.436	31.222	32.055	32.579	33.20	33.85	33.48
Sweden	31.373	38.895	44.777	45.619	48.954	44.901	43.972	43.063	42.292	42.346	42.78	42.70	43.34	44.12
Switzerland	16.554	22.543	23.875	25.509	27.643	26.126	27.13	26.504	27.018	26.919	27.052	26.65	27.89	27.83
Turkey	10.565	11.883	11.487	16.785	24.159	24.082	24.636	26.199	27.83	27.638	29.306	28.72	30.03	25.46
United Kingdom	29.278	33.618	35.556	32.093	34.695	34.087	32.323	32.806	33.588	33.048	32.88	32.57	32.52	33.21
United States	23.5	24.595	24.614	26.712	28.407	26.915	23.295	23.705	24.008	24.382	25.444	26.00	26.36	26.02
OECD - Average	**24.834**	**28.598**	**31.665**	**33.643**	**34.315**	**34.163**	**32.658**	**32.825**	**33.265**	**33.727**	**34.16**	**34.18**	**34.27**	**34.26**

n.a. indicates not available.

The statistical data for Israel are supplied by and under the responsibility of the relevant Israeli authorities. The use of such data by the OECD is without prejudice to the status of the Golan Heights, East Jerusalem and Israeli settlements in the West Bank under the terms of international law.

Source: OECD (2018), Tax revenue (indicator). doi: 10.1787/d98b8cf5-en (Accessed on 18 June 2018).

Table 1.2: Taxes on income and profits as percentage of GDP

	1965	1975	1985	1995	2000	2007	2009	2011	2012	2013	2014	2015	2016
Australia	10.4	14.2	15.1	15.6	17.7	17.7	14.4	15.5	15.9	15.7	16.1	16.0	n.a.
Austria[1]	8.6	9.5	10.7	10.8	12.0	12.2	11.5	11.9	12.2	12.5	12.7	13.2	11.9
Belgium	8.5	15.3	17.6	16.3	16.9	15.2	14.2	14.9	15.2	15.8	16.1	16.0	15.7
Canada	9.7	14.8	14.1	16.2	17.5	15.8	14.9	14.3	14.5	14.4	14.7	15.2	15.1
Chile	..	..	..	4.6	4.4	10.4	5.4	8.5	8.3	7.2	6.5	7.5	6.8
Czech Republic	..	..	..	8.7	7.4	8.5	6.9	6.8	6.9	7.0	7.1	7.2	7.4

(Continued)

Table 1.2: Continued

	1965	1975	1985	1995	2000	2007	2009	2011	2012	2013	2014	2015	2016
Denmark[1]	13.8	22.3	26.2	29.6	29.0	28.6	28.3	28.4	29.2	30.7	33.2	29.2	28.7
Estonia	..	..	..	10.9	7.7	7.4	7.4	6.4	6.7	7.2	7.6	7.9	7.8
Finland	12.4	15.6	16.0	16.1	19.7	16.3	14.6	14.9	14.7	15.3	15.3	15.5	15.3
France[1]	5.3	5.5	6.7	6.8	10.7	10.1	8.6	9.8	10.4	10.9	10.5	10.7	10.6
Germany[2]	10.7	11.8	12.6	11.0	10.9	10.9	10.4	10.5	11.1	11.4	11.0	11.6	12.0
Greece[1]	1.6	2.5	4.3	6.2	8.9	7.2	7.3	7.0	8.2	7.7	8.7	8.7	9.1
Hungary	..	..	..	8.6	9.4	10.0	9.6	6.1	6.6	6.4	6.5	6.9	7.1
Iceland	5.5	6.7	6.2	10.4	14.4	17.6	15.1	15.7	16.0	16.4	18.0	17.5	17.8
Ireland	6.3	8.4	11.6	12.8	13.5	12.5	10.7	10.7	11.4	11.7	12.1	10.2	10.0
Israel	..	..	..	12.3	14.1	12.7	9.0	9.3	9.1	9.7	9.7	9.9	9.8
Italy	4.4	5.3	12.0	13.6	13.5	14.1	13.7	13.4	14.0	14.2	14.2	13.9	13.7
Japan	7.8	9.1	12.2	10.1	9.3	10.4	8.0	8.6	9.2	9.5	9.8	10.4	9.5
Korea	..	3.4	4.0	5.7	6.2	7.9	6.8	7.3	7.4	7.1	7.2	7.6	8.2
Luxembourg	9.5	13.4	16.2	13.9	13.4	12.9	13.8	13.4	13.6	13.9	13.1	13.4	13.7
Mexico	..	..	3.4	3.7	4.5	4.9	4.9	5.3	5.2	6.0	5.8	6.8	7.3
Netherlands	11.0	13.3	10.5	10.3	9.3	10.3	10.0	9.6	9.2	9.1	9.6	10.5	10.6
New Zealand	14.3	18.7	21.2	21.9	19.7	21.7	17.6	16.8	18.3	17.8	18.0	18.1	17.8
Norway	12.9	13.5	16.9	14.4	19.2	20.5	19.2	20.8	20.4	18.6	16.9	15.0	14.0
Poland	..	..	..	11.0	6.8	7.9	6.8	6.4	6.6	6.2	6.3	6.5	6.7
Portugal	3.9	3.3	6.2	7.6	9.1	8.8	8.3	9.1	8.5	10.9	10.7	10.5	9.9
Slovak Republic	..	..	..	10.1	6.9	5.7	5.1	5.1	5.2	5.3	6.3	6.9	7.3
Slovenia	..	..	..	6.4	6.8	8.7	7.5	7.2	6.9	6.6	6.5	6.6	6.9
Spain[1]	3.5	4.0	6.7	9.1	9.5	12.2	8.9	9.0	9.6	9.6	9.6	9.7	9.4
Sweden	17.2	19.6	18.9	17.9	20.0	17.4	15.5	14.8	14.5	14.8	14.8	15.5	15.7
Switzerland	6.8	10.7	11.0	11.1	12.2	12.1	12.7	12.5	12.3	12.3	12.3	13.0	13.0
Turkey	3.1	5.0	4.3	4.8	7.1	5.7	5.9	5.8	6.0	5.9	6.1	6.1	5.4
United Kingdom	10.8	15.0	13.7	11.8	13.5	13.4	12.4	12.3	11.8	11.7	11.4	11.5	11.9
United States	11.3	11.3	11.2	12.3	14.3	13.1	9.6	11.2	11.7	12.1	12.5	12.9	12.7
Unweighted average:													
OECD Total	**8.7**	**10.9**	**11.9**	**11.6**	**12.2**	**12.4**	**11.0**	**11.2**	**11.4**	**11.5[3]**	**11.5**	**11.5**	**n.a.**

n.a. indicates not available.

1.The total tax revenues have been reduced by the amount of any capital transfer that represents uncollected taxes.

2.Unified Germany beginning in 1991.

3.Calculated by applying the unweighted average percentage change for 2013 in the 30 countries providing data for that year to the overall average tax to GDP ratio in 2012.

Source: OECD *Revenue Statistics 2017* © OECD Publishing

The second table illustrates that the tax burden in Ireland is quite low, in fact lower than that of most of its European counterparts. This is surprising in view of our relatively high marginal rate of income tax of between 51%/52% (including Social security contributions (PRSI) and the universal social charge (USC) - these are included in the definition of income tax for the above purposes on the basis that they are mandatory payments). The relatively low burden of taxation in Ireland is not, it would appear, attributable to our rates of income tax, but rather to our narrow tax base. This was highlighted by the second *Commission on Taxation* (2009, page 2). The often-quoted rationale for a broad tax base is that it allows for taxes to be collected from a wider range of sources while enabling tax rates to be kept low. It will be interesting to evaluate the impact of the property tax, once figures become available.

1.4.2 Tax as a mechanism for redistributing income and wealth

In addition to being used to generate public finance, governments also endeavour to use the tax system to transfer resources from wealthy members of society to the less well-off in an equitable manner.

Effecting a redistribution of income can be accomplished to some degree by having a progressive income tax. A progressive tax system seeks to collect proportionately more tax from those on higher incomes. A very progressive income tax system will reduce disparity in after-tax income. A proportional income tax is one that is levied at the same rate on all income. Progressivity in the Irish tax system is attempted by taxing the a certain amount of income (depending on the taxpayer's personal circumstances) at a standard rate of 20% and the balance of income in excess of this band at a higher rate of 40%. The income tax system was made more progressive in the Supplementary Budget 2009 and subsequent Finance Acts whereby the marginal rate of income tax increases from 51% to 55% as income increases.

For most of the 1980s and early 1990s, there were three rates of income tax in Ireland. 1992 saw the removal of one of the bands and, since then, we have had just two rates of income tax. However, this does not necessarily infer that inequality in the distribution of after-tax income in Ireland has increased. Other tax measures, such as the replacement of the system of personal allowances with a tax credits system[4] and efforts to exclude those on the minimum wage from the tax net, may have compensated for the reduced number of bands. The universal social charge has had the effect of introducing four rates of tax on income, due to four possible rates of the charge, i.e., 1.5%, 3%, 7% and 8%.

The concept of progressivity is not confined to income tax. For example, our VAT system endeavours to be progressive by taxing luxury goods consumed more heavily than every day goods. Accordingly, a rate of VAT of 23% applies to "luxury" items such as jewellery, DVD players, etc., while essential goods such as basic foodstuffs, children's clothing and oral medicines are zero-rated. However, there is a view that, despite such

4 Readers are referred to Chapter 11 of Section II of this book, regarding the system of tax credits and personal allowances.

efforts to differentiate between luxury goods and essentials, VAT is a regressive tax. A regressive tax is a tax that takes a decreasing proportion of income as the level of income increases. To the extent that the less well-off in society consume a greater proportion of their incomes on goods/services, VAT may be regressive. The application of a more favourable system for the taxation of capital gains suggests that the interaction between income tax and capital gains tax is important in considering progressivity in the Irish tax system. Capital gains are subject to tax at a rate of 33%, whereas income can be taxed at effective rates of up to 51%/52% (including PRSI, and the USC). As investment in capital assets is generally confined to more affluent individuals, this discrepancy in rates may be perceived as inequitable and regressive. In addition, capital taxes and, in particular, wealth taxes, can be an important tool in the redistribution of wealth.

While increased taxes on the wealthy and other progressive tax measures can reduce disparity in after-tax income and wealth, they only truly have a redistributive effect where the revenues from such measures are used efficiently. Efforts to effect a redistribution of income cannot be considered without looking also at social welfare reforms and legal initiatives, such as the introduction of a minimum wage. Certainly, tackling poverty is not something that can be accomplished by reforming the tax system in isolation, since many of those who may be classified as poor in accordance with the generally accepted measures and benchmarks are outside the tax net.

Some of the more radical proposals for tax and welfare reform suggest that the two systems should be totally integrated. In Ireland, a working group led by the Department of the Taoiseach considered the implications of the introduction of a "Basic Income" scheme. In its purest form, this would involve the replacement of the existing system of welfare payments and personal tax credits with a single basic income payment paid unconditionally to everyone. While social welfare reforms and such radical schemes are outside the scope of this analysis, the reader should be aware of their importance as redistribution tools.

1.4.3 Tax as an instrument of economic and social policy

Tax is also used to encourage certain behaviour that might benefit society and the economy as a whole. For example, as mentioned previously, a number of tax reliefs were introduced in the past for expenditure on property development in certain clearly defined geographical areas. These measures were targeted at encouraging investment in areas most in need of economic development. Areas such as Temple Bar, which was transformed over 20 years from a state of fatigue to a hub of economic and social activity, appear to be tangible evidence of the success of these measures in accomplishing their stated objectives.[5]

5 Some research suggests that the success of Temple Bar is not specifically attributable to tax incentives. See the findings of a survey carried out by Indecon on behalf of Temple Bar properties in KPMG's *Study on the Urban Renewal Schemes* (Dublin: The Stationery Office, 1996). In addition, the 2005 Government studies into the incentive schemes highlighted some shortcomings. For example, Goodbody (2005) observed that the Rural Renewal Scheme had little direct impact on economic activity and resulted in an excess supply of housing in the scheme area.

All incentives require careful consideration from a cost/benefit perspective as there is clearly a cost to the Exchequer in terms of the tax foregone to incentivise certain behaviour or sectoral activity. Indeed, the expected cost to the Exchequer of a proposed introduction of or amendment to incentives/reliefs is set out as part of each year's Government budget documentation.

Encouraging desirable behaviour through the tax system does not necessarily have to cost the Government money in terms of revenues foregone. For example, heavy taxes on petrol and tobacco are targeted partly at discouraging their consumption, thereby improving the environment, but have the added benefit of generating substantial revenue[6]. Another example of such an effective measure is the plastic bag levy. The objective of this measure was "to educate the shopping public towards moving away from plastic packaging towards biodegradable and recyclable alternatives" (Revenue Commissioners 2002, p57).

Anecdotal evidence from a trip to the supermarket would suggest that the measure has been very successful in encouraging more environmentally-friendly shopping habits; it simultaneously yielded more than €154 million for the Exchequer from the date of its introduction on 4 March 2002 to 31 December 2010 (Revenue Commissioners, 2010b).

Not all tax measures accomplish their stated objectives and, very often, unforeseen results can arise. For example in 1997, in an effort to dampen booming property prices, the Government prohibited relief for interest expenses (on loans to purchase residential properties) in calculating taxable rental income. The objective of this measure was to dissuade investors from purchasing residential property, thereby making the market more "first-time buyer friendly". While the impact of this measure is difficult to gauge, it does not appear to have achieved its goal. Property prices continued to rise and a new problem emerged – a shortage of affordable rental properties in the private sector. Within two years of its introduction, the restriction was withdrawn and, in calculating taxable rental income, a deduction is again available for landlords in respect of interest expenses incurred on loans to purchase rental properties.

The *Commission on Taxation* (2009, p10–12) highlighted the inequity that can arise as tax reliefs and exemptions (referred to as 'tax expenditures') have the potential to create differences between tax payers, to result in a lack of transparency and a lack of visibility in the allocation of public resources. The potential unequal distribution of public resources led the Commission to recommend that direct government expenditure should be used instead of tax expenditures. Where a tax incentive is proposed in the future, the Commission proposed that it be tested against the principles of equity, efficiency, stability and simplicity, alongside a cost/benefit evaluation of the proposal and consideration of an alternative direct expenditure approach.

6 However, finding the appropriate level of tax to apply to such products is a delicate balancing act. While such increases in tax may well have a direct benefit to the Exchequer, imposing too high a level of tax may well lead to costs incurred in policing illegal activities, that result from taxpayers refusing to pay the tax.

1.5 Classification of Taxes

Taxes can be classified in many different ways. The analysis here is concerned with the distinction between direct and indirect taxes, and with the classification of taxes by tax base. As highlighted in Section 1.4.2 above, taxes may also be classified by their rate structure, i.e., progressive, regressive or proportional.

1.5.1 Direct versus indirect

Direct taxes are those that are assessed directly on the individual or entity at whom or at which they are targeted. Examples include income tax, corporation tax, capital gains tax and capital acquisitions tax, all of which are levied directly on the taxpayer intended to bear the final tax burden. Indirect taxes, on the other hand, are taxes that are collected from persons other than those that are intended to bear the final burden of tax. VAT and customs and excise duties are examples of indirect taxes.

It is important to note that the final burden of taxation does not necessarily rest with the person that was intended to bear it. For example, in the case of VAT, the burden of taxation is targeted at the final consumer and collected from traders involved in the chain of supply. To the extent that the final price for the goods charged to the ultimate consumer is set by market forces and not by suppliers on a cost-plus-VAT basis, it may be necessary for suppliers to tolerate the VAT cost through reduced prices for customers.

1.5.2 Taxes on corporations

Taxes on corporations are generally levied on the corporate entity as direct taxes calculated as a percentage of taxable profits. Such taxes are often classified in accordance with the type of corporation tax system, i.e., in accordance with the treatment of shareholders with respect to underlying corporation tax paid by the company. Broadly speaking, there are two models – the classical system and the imputation system. However, many countries operate hybrids of these of systems, i.e., partial imputation systems.

Classical system

Under the classical system, no credit is given to shareholders for the underlying corporation tax paid on profits. Corporate profits are taxed in full without deduction for appropriations of profits by way of distributions. Distributions are taxed in the hands of individual shareholders and no credit is given for the corporation tax already paid by the company on the profits out of which such distributions are paid. Accordingly, there is double taxation of the same profits – the profits are taxed in the hands of the company and again as dividends in the hands of the shareholder. This is the system that has applied in Ireland since April 1999. While we have a system of dividend withholding tax in Ireland (see Chapter 11), this is simply a system for the advance payment of the shareholder's income tax liability. Credit is given to the shareholder for this advance payment of income tax, but no credit is given for the corporation tax paid on the corporate profits out of which dividends are paid.

Imputation system

Under an imputation system, corporation tax is "imputed" to the shareholders who receive dividends, and credit is given for this corporation tax in calculating the final income tax liability.

Assuming a company has taxable income of €100,000 and pays corporation tax at a rate of 12.5%, it will be in a position to pay a dividend of €87,500 to shareholders. Table 1.3 below compares the effective rate of tax applicable to this income under the classical and imputation system.

Table 1.3: Comparison of effective rates of tax under classical and imputation systems

	Classical	Imputation
	€	€
Company's taxable profits (A)	100,000	100,000
Corporation tax @ 12.5% (B)	12,500	12,500
Dividend to shareholder	87,500	(deemed) 100,000
Income tax @ 40%	35,000	40,000
Less: credit for corporation tax paid	-	(12,500)
Net income tax (C)	35,000	27,500
Total tax suffered	47,500	40,000
Effective rate of tax ((B + C)/A)	47.50%	40.00%

Under the classical system, assuming just one shareholder who pays tax at the marginal rate and (ignoring PRSI and the USC), the shareholder will be taxed under at 40% on the amount of the cash dividend received. Thus, additional tax of €35,000 will be payable at shareholder level and no credit is granted for the underlying corporation tax already suffered. Thus, the total tax suffered on the taxable profit of represents an effective rate of 47.50% (i.e., 12.5% + (87.5% × 40%)).

Under a system of full imputation, the shareholder is deemed to have received a gross dividend of €100,000 (albeit that a net cash amount of only €87,500 is received). The gross amount of €100,000 is taxed at the marginal rate of 40% and full credit is granted for the underlying corporation tax already suffered.

Thus, the total tax suffered on taxable profit represents a total effective rate of 40%.

In Ireland, prior to April 1999, credit was given to shareholders for a portion of the underlying corporation tax suffered by companies and, accordingly, Ireland operated a partial imputation system until 1999. This imputation system has been replaced with a classical system (see Chapter 28, section 28.2). See Chapter 19 (section 19.5) for the taxation treatment of distributions from an Irish resident company received by an Irish resident individual and Chapter 28 (section 28.2).

1.5.3 Classification by tax base

The tax base is some quantifiable collection of like items upon which tax is levied. The main tax bases upon which taxes are levied in Ireland are income and expenditure and, to a much lesser extent, wealth.

Income tax and corporation tax are both examples of taxes based on income. Value-added tax and excise duties are examples of taxes based on expenditure. Wealth taxes may be defined as taxes on the accumulated resources or wealth of an individual. Traditionally, they took the form of annual taxes on the taxpayer's net assets. Capital acquisitions tax is regularly referred to as a wealth tax. However, it can be argued that capital acquisitions tax is not a true tax on wealth but rather a form of income tax levied on movements in wealth or on capital transfers. On this basis, the only real forms of wealth tax that we have experience of in Ireland are the 1975 wealth tax (abolished within three years of its introduction) and a short-lived residential property tax, which was abolished in 1997. Similarly, many would argue that capital gains tax is, in effect, an income tax and, more specifically, a tax on realised capital income.

Choosing the most appropriate tax base is a controversial matter and, in practice, most administrations favour some balance of all three. A brief commentary on the problems associated with each of the alternative tax bases is worthwhile at this stage, in advance of considering the Irish tax base.

Income

Problems arise in defining income because the everyday meaning precludes certain factors that clearly constitute an increase in the value of economic resources. Arguments have been advanced in favour of a more comprehensive definition of income that would include capital gains, gifts and inheritances, lottery and gambling winnings, and various types of non-cash income. This is on the basis that capital appreciation is akin to interest or rent – i.e., it is a form of return for investors on certain types of capital asset. To preserve equity and neutrality, returns on non-income-bearing assets should be taxed on the same basis as income-bearing assets. This can be accomplished by widening the definition of income and applying the same tax system and rates to all forms of income. However, this is not the case in Ireland, where current income such as interest and dividends are taxed at rates of up to 40%, while capital income in the form of realised gains on assets is generally only taxed at a rate of 33%. Furthermore, unrealised capital gains are not taxed at all.

The other major problem with income as a basis for taxation is one of measurement. Even if we unanimously agree on a definition of income, measuring the factors to be included in that tax base can pose certain problems. How to account for inflation and adjusting nominal income such that taxpayers are taxable on their real purchasing power is one such problem. Indexing personal tax credits and rate bands in line with the consumer price index is one method by which the Government may give relief to taxpayers in times of high inflation.

Furthermore, even if we can accurately measure the real purchasing power of an individual's income, differing personal circumstances of taxpayers may create a drain on this income in varying degrees. The Irish system attempts to deal with this matter by providing for a system of tax credits granted to taxpayers on the basis of their personal circumstances (see Chapter 11).

In measuring income, the choice of unit of taxation is also very relevant. Moves towards "individualisation" of our tax system have caused considerable controversy in Ireland in recent times.[7]

Expenditure

Proponents of expenditure as the tax base argue that it eliminates the problems of a narrowing of the tax base on the basis of definitions. All expenditure would be taxed irrespective of whether the expenditure is out of salary, lottery winnings or capital transfers in the form of gifts or inheritances. Theoretically, expenditure should equate to income less savings. If we take the view that saving and investing constitute desirable social behaviour, expenditure tax is preferable to income tax on the basis that it encourages saving at the expense of spending. In addition, it would eliminate the need for wealth taxes, as all accumulated wealth would eventually be consumed.

On the downside, using expenditure as the tax base fails to take account of life-cycle patterns. Very often those who spend most are young people who have more active social lives and who are in the process of establishing homes. Such individuals are less likely to save and more likely to borrow than middle-aged individuals and senior citizens. Thus, there is a mismatch between income and expenditure, and the tax burden may be highest in years when surplus cash-flow is weakest.

In addition, the exclusion of savings from the tax base may mean that onerously high levels of taxation on consumption are necessary.

Wealth

Despite its potential as a tool for redistributing resources to the less well-off, wealth taxes have never proved popular in Ireland, due to problems associated with valuation of the tax base and difficulties associated with collection.

Is it fair to tax an individual with substantial low-return investments and little or no earnings potential more onerously than someone with few investments but with

7 See O'Halloran, M., *From Bóraimhe to Bit – The Art of Taxation* (Dublin: Irish Tax Institute 2005).

sought-after professional qualifications and substantial earnings potential? A comprehensive wealth tax would endeavour to establish the present value of earnings potential. Accordingly, measurement problems arise. Even more traditional tangible assets can be difficult to value. Very often a professional valuation is necessary to preserve objectivity. This can be very costly for a taxpayer.

The burden of collection of income taxes on items such as salary and interest can easily be transferred to employers and lending institutions. However, wealth taxes must be administered directly by the Government and, accordingly, can be expensive to collect.

Finally, wealth does not equate to cash-flow. It is feasible that a taxpayer may be forced to sell a capital asset in order to fund his wealth tax liability. This may be perceived as inequitable by the individual taxpayer and may not constitute desirable behaviour from the perspective of society as a whole.

1.6 The Tax Base in Ireland

In 1982, the Irish *Commission on Taxation* considered suitable alternative tax bases for the purposes of direct taxation in Ireland. It concluded that "the tax base should be defined on a comprehensive basis to include all real increases in the command over economic resources" (*Commission on Taxation*, 1982, p. 115). It argued in favour of a comprehensive definition of income, which would reflect the taxpayer's control over society's resources. Accordingly, the definition should include "capital gains, bequests and gifts received, lottery and casual gambling winnings, compensation payments for loss of office and non-money income" (*Commission on Taxation*, 1982, p. 117). Thus, all forms of increase in economic resources would be taxed in the same way, and this would preserve equity and eliminate behaviour targeted at channelling income to activities or items taxable on a more favourable basis. In addition, the inclusion of all types of receipt in the income tax base would eliminate the need for separate taxes on wealth, capital gains, and gifts and inheritance.

While it acknowledged the theoretical advantages of expenditure as the tax base, it argued that the complete replacement of income tax with a direct expenditure tax was not a feasible proposition for the foreseeable future. It did, however, suggest that a comprehensive income tax could be complemented by a progressive direct expenditure tax at higher rates. The application of a progressive system of rates to a comprehensive definition of income would lead to heavy taxation of windfall capital receipts that accrue irregularly over time and this could lead to certain inequities. To eliminate this problem, it proposed that a single rate of income tax should be applied to the comprehensive income tax base, and progressivity should be preserved by the introduction of a direct expenditure tax at higher progressive rates.

Despite the strong theoretical arguments put forward by the Commission in favour of a comprehensive definition of income, income tax in Ireland is currently applied to the more conventional narrow base, and separate taxes apply to realised capital gains and capital transfers in the form of gifts and inheritances. This system of direct taxation is supplemented by indirect taxes on expenditure in the form of VAT and duties. Thus, the proposals of the Commission have been largely ignored in this regard, and the result is that we currently have ten separate taxes applying in Ireland, each with its own unique set of rules and rates, etc. An analysis of the revenues from these different taxes in 2016 and 2017 is set out below in Table 1.4 and in the accompanying pie charts.

Table 1.4 Ireland – Total Annual Collected/Gross Receipts

	2016 **€m**	**2017** **€m**
Income Tax, Income Levy & USC	20,974	22,076
Value-Added Tax	16,558	17,903
Corporation Tax	8,206	9,347
Excise	5,842	6,070
Stamp Duties	1,215	1,220
Capital Gains Tax	839	842
Capital Acquisitions Tax	419	466
Local Property Tax	468	482
Customs	312	335
Collection on behalf of other Departments/ Agencies (PRSI, Health Insurance Levy etc)	10,758	12,216
Total	**65,591**	**70,957**

Source: Annual Report Revenue Commissioners 2017, www.revenue.ie

In his budget speech in 2009, the Minister for Finance acknowledged that the tax base was too narrow and announced his intension to broaden the Irish tax base in future years. This plan of action was in line with the recommendations of the second *Commission on Taxation* (2009, p. 2–5) and was implemented in 2012/13.

Figure 1.1: Ireland - Total Amount Collected/% Gross Receipts - 2016

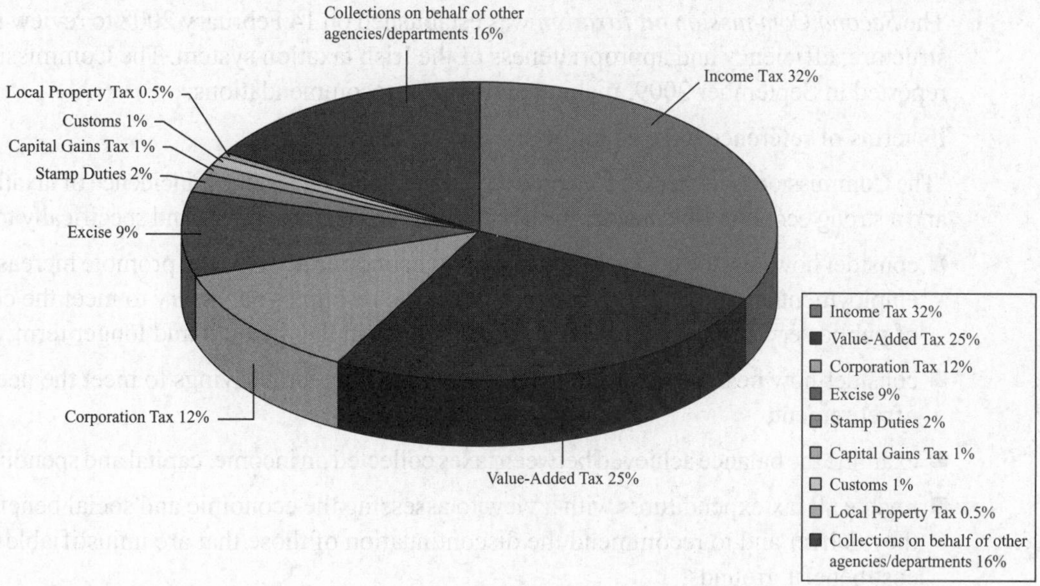

Collections on behalf of other agencies/departments 16%
Income Tax 32%
Local Property Tax 0.5%
Customs 1%
Capital Gains Tax 1%
Stamp Duties 2%
Excise 9%
Corporation Tax 12%
Value-Added Tax 25%

- Income Tax 32%
- Value-Added Tax 25%
- Corporation Tax 12%
- Excise 9%
- Stamp Duties 2%
- Capital Gains Tax 1%
- Customs 1%
- Local Property Tax 0.5%
- Collections on behalf of other agencies/departments 16%

Note: Any apparent discrepancies in totals are due to rounding.

Figure 1.2: Ireland - Total Amount Collected/%Gross Receipts - 2017

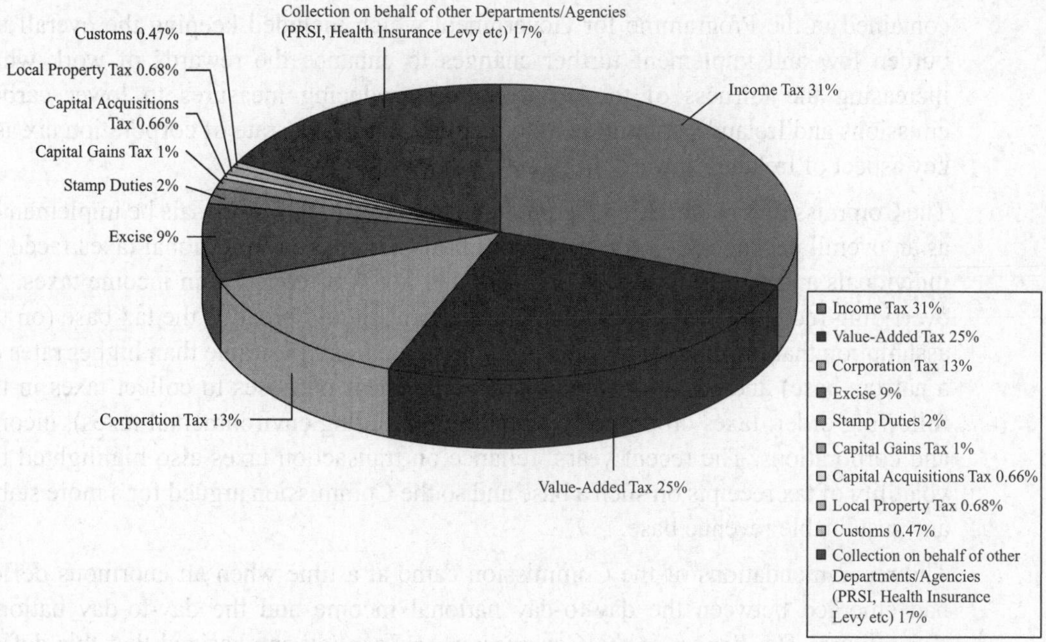

Collection on behalf of other Departments/Agencies (PRSI, Health Insurance Levy etc) 17%
Customs 0.47%
Local Property Tax 0.68%
Income Tax 31%
Capital Acquisitions Tax 0.66%
Capital Gains Tax 1%
Stamp Duties 2%
Excise 9%
Corporation Tax 13%
Value-Added Tax 25%

- Income Tax 31%
- Value-Added Tax 25%
- Corporation Tax 13%
- Excise 9%
- Stamp Duties 2%
- Capital Gains Tax 1%
- Capital Acquisitions Tax 0.66%
- Local Property Tax 0.68%
- Customs 0.47%
- Collection on behalf of other Departments/Agencies (PRSI, Health Insurance Levy etc) 17%

Note: Any apparent discrepancies in totals are due to rounding.

The Second Commission on Taxation

The *Second Commission on Taxation* was established on 14 February 2008 to review the structure, efficiency and appropriateness of the Irish taxation system. The Commission reported in September 2009, making almost 250 recommendations.

Its terms of reference were as follows:

'The Commission is invited, in the context of maintaining an equitable incidence of taxation and a strong economy, to consider the structure of the taxation system and specifically to

- consider how best the tax system can support economic activity and promote increased employment and prosperity while providing the resources necessary to meet the cost of public services and other Government outlays in the medium and longer term;
- consider how best the tax system can encourage long term savings to meet the needs of retirement;
- examine the balance achieved between taxes collected on income, capital and spending;
- review all tax expenditures with a view to assessing the economic and social benefits they deliver and to recommend the discontinuation of those that are unjustifiable on cost/benefit grounds;
- consider options for the future financing of local government, and
- investigate fiscal measures to protect and enhance the environment including the introduction of a carbon tax.'

The Commission was required to perform this review in the context of the commitments contained in the Programme for Government which included keeping the overall tax burden low and implement further changes to enhance the rewards of work while increasing the fairness of the tax system, introducing measures to lower carbon emissions and Ireland's commitment to retaining the 12.5% rate of corporation tax as a key aspect of Ireland's inward investment strategy.

The Commission's overarching recommendation was that its proposals be implemented as an overall package and on a tax neutral basis, i.e. that any additional taxes faced by individuals and families must be compensated for by a reduction in income taxes. An overriding recommendation was that Government should broaden the tax base (on the assumption that lower tax rates on a broad base are more desirable than higher rates on a narrow base) and for international competitiveness purposes to collect taxes in the following order: taxes on property, spending (including environmental taxes), income and corporations. The recent years' reliance on transaction taxes also highlighted the volatility of tax receipts on such a base and so the Commission argued for a more stable and sustainable revenue base.

The recommendations of the Commission came at a time when an enormous deficit had emerged between the day-to-day national income and the day-to-day national expenditure. *The Report of the Commission on Taxation* emphasized that this deficit cannot be bridged by taxation changes alone. Its recommendations can be analysed under the following headings, as reflected in the respective sections of the report:

- The macro economic framework and the balance of taxation,
- Structural issues with the tax system,
- Taxation on property,
- Supporting economic activity,
- A review of tax expenditures,
- Tax and a sustainable environment,
- Tax incentives for retirement savings,
- Future financing of local government.

National recovery

The downturn in the Irish economy resulted in the Government implementing some of the recommendations of the second Commission of Taxation relating to the widening of the tax base. The Government's National Recovery Plan (2010) emphasised the broadening of the tax base, stating that "the plan is concerned not just with the "quantity" of revenue to be raised but also with the "quality" of the measures adopted and their ability to deliver sustainable structural reforms" (p.90). However despite recommending the implementation of a property valuation tax, the focus was seen more on increasing the tax-paying population, stating that " An income tax system where more than 45% of tax units pay no income tax is not sustainable" (p.90).

These and other taxation measures were closely reflected in the conditions of the 2011 Joint EU/IMF Programme for Ireland (or the 'EU/IMF bailout' as it has come to be known).

Tax - An Ever-Changing Landscape

A review by Mr Seamus Coffey of Ireland's corporation tax code took place in 2016/2017. The terms of reference for the review included: tax transparency; avoiding preferential treatment; further implementing Ireland's international commitments; delivering tax certainty; maintaining competitiveness; and maintaining the 12.5% corporation tax rate.

The Review states that the increase in Ireland's corporation tax receipts can be expected to be sustainable up to 2020. It also acknowledges that Ireland has reached the highest standards with regard to tax transparency. This has been further confirmed by the recent awarding to Ireland by the OECD's Global Forum of the highest international rating on tax transparency and exchange of information.

The Review makes a number of recommendations to ensure that Ireland continues to meet the highest international standards, including:

- Scrutiny of proposed measures to meet OECD and EU standards on preferential treatment;
- Supporting the EU Directive on mandatory disclosure in line with OECD recommendations;

- The passage of the Taxation and Certain Other Matters (International Mutual Assistance) Bill through Dáil and Seanad Éireann should be facilitated;
- Updating and expanding the scope of Ireland's transfer pricing regime;
- Consideration of whether to change to a territorial tax system;
- Enhancement of the resources of the Revenue Commissioners to deal with international dispute resolution.
- The introduction of a cap on capital allowances claims with respect to intangible assets as a way of smoothing corporation tax revenues over time.

A number of the provisions of the Coffey report have been implemented in Finance Act 2017.

1.7 Stakeholders in Irish Taxation Policy and Administration

An understanding of the key "players" in Irish taxation policy and administration brings a sense of context to the study of any aspect of taxation. The key stakeholders in Irish taxation include Government, the Oireachtas, the Department of Finance, the Office of the Revenue Commissioners (Revenue), the Irish Tax Institute and the tax profession and, of course, the taxpayer community. The following is a summary of the structure and function of the Department of Finance, Revenue and the tax profession.

1.7.1 Department of Finance

The Department of Finance plays a key role in the economic, fiscal and financial management of Ireland's economy by advising and supporting the Minister for Finance and the members of the Houses of the Oireachtas. The Department also engages in the implementation of government policy, as laid down by each Programme for Government, and the management of the public sector. In carrying out its work the Department is guided by the following mission:

'The Department's mission is to manage Government finances and play a central role in the achievement of the Government's economic and social goals having regard to the Programme for a Partnership Government. In this way we will play a leadership role in the improvement of the standards of living of all Irish citizens.

In pursuing our mission, the Department is working for the period 2017 to 2020 towards achieving the following Strategic Goals:

- A sustainable macroeconomic environment and sound public finances.
- A balanced and equitable economy enabled by a vibrant, secure and well regulated financial sector.[8]'

8 Department of Finance Website, May 2018.

The work of the Department is divided into the following 4 divisions:

1. Fiscal Policy Division
2. Economic Division
3. Financial Services Division
4. EU and International Division

The Tax policy unit within the Fiscal Policy Division is *"responsible for the development of efficient and effective taxation policies which support and promote the Government's economic, social and environmental objectives through the publication of an annual Budget and Finance Act"*.[9]

The Budget and the Finance Bill

From a taxation perspective, one of the key functions of the Minister for Finance and his/her Department is to prepare the annual Budget for the Irish economy and to initiate the Finance Bills that will bring those changes from Budget to legislation[10]. The Finance Bill is unique in that it begins with the Budget, which is usually held in October[11]. The Constitution requires that each Government department prepare estimates of their receipts and expenditure for the coming financial year. Abridged versions of these estimates are usually published in advance of the Budget.

On Budget day, the Minister for Finance presents the following to the Dáil:

- Budget Measures – these are the changes to be introduced in the Budget and the cost to the exchequer of each of these measures
- Financial Resolutions – these allow for immediate budgetary changes to come into effect, for example, changes in excise duty on alcohol;
- Budget Statistics & Tables – these provide budgetary projections for the next three years
- White Paper on Receipts & Expenditure – this is the opening position for the Budget and is published the Saturday before the Budget.

At the end of the Budget debate, the Minister seeks permission to circulate the Finance Bill, and this is generally granted. The Finance Bill is then drafted by the Parliamentary Draftsmen, with the Attorney General reviewing if necessary. Once drafted, the Finance Bill progresses onto the first stage, accompanied by its Explanatory Memorandum.

The following graph demonstrates how the Finance Bill becomes the Finance Act.

9 Tax policy unit website, August 2012. http://taxpolicy.gov.ie

10 A bill is a draft statute. Bills are not drafted by the Oireachtas but by legislative drafters who are officials in the Office of the Parliamentary Council to the Government.

11 Historically, the Government presented its budget much later than October; however, the date of the delivery of the budget has been brought forward to satisfy European Union requirements.

Figure 1.3: How the Finance Bill becomes the Finance Act

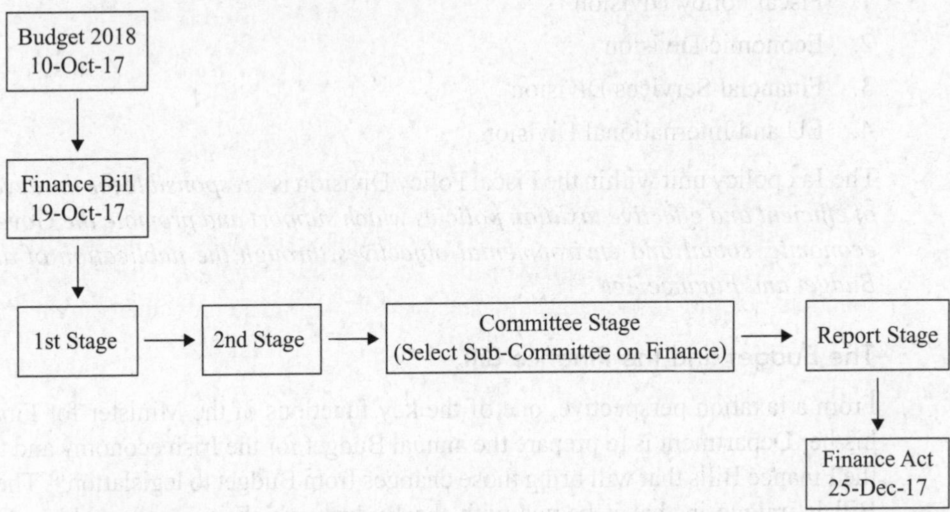

The OECD has previously criticised Ireland's budgetary approach as a disconnected series of annual set-piece events and its reform was a key focus of the Programme for a Partnership Government. A new budgetary committee (the Select Committee on Arrangements for Budgetary Scrutiny) was established in May 2016 to give all members of the Oireachtas input in determining budgetary policy. The other key elements of the new budgetary process include:

- The publication of the Government's Spring/Summer Economic Statement in June;
- Holding the National Economic Dialogue at the end of June;
- The publication of a Mid-Year Expenditure Report in July for the first time; and
- Circulation of the Tax Strategy Papers to the relevant Sectoral Oireachtas Committees in late July.

1.7.2 The Office of the Revenue Commissioners

The Office of the Revenue Commissioners was established by Government Order in 1923 and is responsible for the assessment, collection and management of taxes and duties. Its role also encompasses the implementation of proper import and export controls. Revenue is not responsible for determining taxation policy; setting taxation policy is the role of the Department of Finance. However, Revenue regularly provides policy advice on taxation issues to the Government and, to this end, has established four Revenue Legislation Services Divisions which have policy, legislation and interpretation functions for the various taxes. In fact, Revenue comprises 15 divisions as follows:

- Investigations and Prosecutions Division;
- Corporate Services Division;
- Revenue Solicitor's Office;
- Information, Communications Technology and Logistics Division;

- Collector General's Division;
- four Revenue Legislation Service Divisions (as described above);
- four Regional Divisions;
- Large Cases Division; and
- Planning Division.

The four Regional Divisions are concerned with customer service and are responsible for the compliance and audit functions in four geographically defined regions. The Large Cases Division is responsible for customer service, compliance and audit functions relating to the largest businesses and wealthiest individuals in the State.

Further information on the role, structure and powers of the Revenue Commissioners is provided in Chapter 7 of this book, within Section II on Value-Added Tax.

1.7.3 Tax Appeals Commission

Finance (Tax Appeals) Act 2015 established a new independent statutory body known as the Tax Appeals Commission (TAC), replacing the Office of the Appeal Commissioners. The main task of the TAC is the adjudication on, hearing, determining and disposing of appeals against decisions of the Revenue Commissioners. One of the most important measures to strengthen the independence of the TAC is the requirement for appeals to be submitted directly to the TAC rather than via Revenue. The TAC currently comprises of three Appeal Commissioners appointed by the Minister for Finance (two are permanent and the third was appointed on a two-year term in May 2017). This reform is being introduced to ensure an enhanced and cost-effective appeal mechanism for tax cases, providing transparency and increased certainty for taxpayers, and to ensure that the appeals forum meets the independence and impartiality requirements contained in Article 6 of the European Convention on Human Rights; in this regard, while there is no suggestion of actual partiality under the former system, it is important that the Appeal Commissioners be seen as fully independent and there must be no actual or perceived bias in the operation of the Appeals system. A number of administrative staff also support the Commissioners in their work. The TAC publishes reports of each of their determinations on their website at www.taxappeals.ie. As of 31 December 2017 the amount of all taxes and duties in dispute by way of tax appeal stood at almost €1.5bn.

1.7.4 The Tax Profession

Ireland has a very strong and highly skilled body of tax professionals. A properly trained cadre of tax professionals is essential to ensuring that Ireland is at the forefront of international tax professionalism; both in terms of the high standards set for professional qualification as a tax adviser and in continuing professional development.

The role of the tax adviser is to assist individual and corporate taxpayer clients in the efficient management of their tax obligations. Tax considerations are at the fore in any commercial or personal transaction. As a result the tax adviser works directly with the top-level decision makers in executing any deal. Broadly speaking, the work of a tax adviser can be split into two areas: tax compliance and tax consultancy.

Tax compliance involves ensuring that a taxpayer client meets their tax return and tax payment obligations on a periodic basis as well as for any once-off transactions that may take place. Tax consultancy is a core business advisory service and involves providing tax advice on transactions ranging from the incorporation of a small sole trader to advising a large multinational corporation on how to relocate their business headquarters to Ireland.

By fulfilling the above roles tax advisers assist in the more efficient running of the tax administration system. This is particularly relevant in terms of the self assessment system which operates in Ireland. A more onerous workload would be placed on the tax administration system in the absence of tax advisers.

The Irish Tax Institute - Leading through tax education

Founded in 1967, the Irish Tax Institute is the leading professional and educational body for Ireland's Chartered Tax Advisers (CTA) and is the only professional body exclusively dedicated to tax.

There are over 5,000 members who hold the Chartered Tax Adviser (CTA) qualification, the international mark of excellence in professional tax competency, in Ireland and over 30,000 worldwide. The Institute's members hold senior roles in professional services firms, global companies, Government, Revenue and state bodies. Delivered since 2003, the Tax Technician (TMITI) qualification is Ireland's only tax compliance qualification and there are now over 450 Tax Technician members of the Institute. There are also over 1,400 students pursuing the Institute's professional qualifications.

The Institute is part of a global network of Tax Institutes that includes the UK (Chartered Institute of Tax and the Association of Tax Technicians), Canada (the Canadian Tax Foundation) and Australia (Tax Institute of Australia). Members of this network collaborate on various projects including best international practice in tax education and assessment. The Institute is the Irish representative organisation at the EU collective organisation for tax institutes – CFE Tax Advisers Europe. The Institute is recognised as the competent authority for the tax profession in Ireland and the CTA qualification is recognised under EU Mutual Recognition Directive 2005/36.

The Irish Tax Institute's professional development programme ensures that members practise to the highest professional standards and that their tax expertise is underpinned by a comprehensive knowledge of the most up-to-date Irish and EU tax law.

The Institute works with members, Government and business to propose new policies and ideas on tax policy. Through its nationwide branch network and comprehensive committee structure, its members are actively involved in developing and advancing research on taxation, economic and social policy. Drawing on this expert team, the Irish Tax Institute produces a comprehensive suite of taxation publications covering the full range of tax topics and includes the leading tax journal in Ireland, *Irish Tax Review*.

CTAs and other professionals interact with the Revenue Commissioners on matters of tax administration via the Taxes Administration Liaison Committee (TALC). TALC was established in 1989 and is a liaison committee between the Revenue Commissioners, the Irish Tax Institute, the Consultative Committee of Accountancy Bodies of Ireland (CCABI) and the Law Society of Ireland.

TALC is a forum for the making of representations between Revenue and practitioners on the administration of tax in Ireland. It is not a forum for legislation or policy formation. TALC comprises Main TALC and six sub-committees as follows:

- TALC Direct Taxes Technical Sub-committee
- TALC Indirect Taxes Sub-committee
- TALC Sub-committee on Collection Issues
- TALC Simplification Sub-committee
- TALC Capital Taxes Sub-committee
- TALC Audit Sub-committee

The Irish Tax Institute is represented at all of the TALC committees by members and Institute executive staff.

When TALC was set up 1989, the terms of reference were set down as follows:

1. The function of the Committee is to review and make recommendations to achieve more effective and efficient administration of the direct taxes, stamp duties and value-added tax. These may relate to either administrative practices of the Office of the Revenue Commissioners or of tax practitioners.

2. In the formulation of any recommendations, the Committee shall have due regard to the views and responsibilities of the Office of the Revenue Commissioners and the interests of taxpayers and tax practitioners and its recommendations shall be consistent with the objective of achieving an efficiency and consistency of administration which has due regard to statute, minimises compliance costs, promotes the highest possible level of voluntary compliance by taxpayers and the expeditious treatment of taxpayers by the Office of the Revenue Commissioners.

3. The Committee shall not accept representations on behalf of, or consider matters relating to, individual cases.

4. Membership will be at senior level from the Office of the Revenue Commissioners and appropriate bodies representing tax practitioners. The Committee will itself keep under consideration its current membership and any requests for amendment or extension.

References and Recommended Further Reading

BARRET, A., J. LAWLOR, S. SCOTT (1997), *The Fiscal System and the Polluter Pays Principle: A Case Study of Ireland*, Ashgate Publishing.

BLACKWELL, J. and F. CONVERY (1991), 'The impact of the Urban Incentives in Ireland in *Proceedings of the Sixth Annual Conference of the Foundation of Fiscal Studies.*

CALLAN, T and B. NOLAN (1999), *Tax and Welfare Changes, Poverty and Work Incentives in Ireland 1987–1994,* Policy Research Series Paper No. 34, Dublin: The Economic and Social Research Institute.

CALLAN, T., B. NOLAN, J. WALSH, J., MCBRIDE, R. NESTOR (2000), "Basic Income in Ireland: A Study for the Working Group on Basic Income." *Final Report*, Department of the Taoiseach,
http://www.taoiseach.gov.ie

CALLAN, T., M. KEENEY, B. NOLAN, J. WALSH (2001), *Reforming Tax and Welfare*, Policy Research Series Paper No. 42, Dublin: The Economic and Social Research Institute.

CALLAN, T., R. LAYTE, A. VAN SOEST, J. WALSH, J. (2003) *Taxes Benefits and Labour Market Responses: New Evidence for Ireland*, Policy Research Series Paper No. 48, Dublin: The Economic and Social Research Institute.

COMMISSION ON TAXATION (1982), *First Report: Direct Taxation*, Dublin: The Stationery Office.

COMMISSION ON TAXATION (2009), www.commissionontaxation.ie.

DÁIL ÉIREANN, Dáil Debates, http://historical-debates.oireachtas.ie

DEEGAN, G., G. REDDIN, A. BOLSTER (Ed.) (2010), *Income Tax,* Irish Tax Institute.

DEPARTMENT OF FINANCE (2002), *Budget Speech 2003,*
http://www.finance.gov.ie

DEPARTMENT OF FINANCE (2004), *Budget Speech 2005,*
http://www.finance.gov.ie

DEPARTMENT OF FINANCE (2005), *Budget Speech 2006,*
http://www.finance.gov.ie

DEPARTMENT OF FINANCE (2006), *Budget Speech 2007,*
http://www.finance.gov.ie

DEPARTMENT OF FINANCE (2010), National Recovery Plan 2011–2014,
http://www.budget.gov.ie/RecoveryPlan.aspx

DEPARTMENT OF THE TAOISEACH (2002), *Basic Income – A Green Paper,* http://www.taoiseach.gov.ie

DOWLING, B. and O. KEEGAN (1992), 'Fiscal Policies and the Built Environment', *Environment and Development in Ireland*, Environmental Institute, UCD.

GOODBODY ECONOMIC CONSULTANTS (2005), *Review of Area-Based Tax Incentive Renewal Schemes,* Dublin: Department of Finance, http://finance.irlgov.ie

HEDERMAN O'BRIEN, M. (Ed.) (2002), *One Size Fits All? EU Taxation Policy,* The Institute of European Affairs and Irish Tax Institute.

HENEHAN, P.J. and A. WALSH (2003), "The Rule of Law or the Rule of Caprice", *Irish Tax Review*, 16(5): 447 - 456.

HERLIHY, J., P. MOORE, H. O'SULLIVAN, M. RYAN (Ed.) (2010), *Corporation Tax,* Irish Tax Institute.

HONOHAN, P. (2001), "European and International Constraints on Irish Fiscal Policy", in Budget Perspectives Proceedings of ESRI / FFS Conference, 09/10/2001.

INDECON (2005), *Review of Property-Based Tax Incentive Schemes,* Dublin: Department of Finance, http://finance.irlgov.ie

JAMES, S. and C. NOBES (2005), *The Economics of Taxation – Principles, Policy and Practice,* Prentice Hall.

KPMG (1996), *Study on the Urban Renewal Schemes,* Dublin: Department of the Environment.

KPMG (2009), *Taxing Times – Supplementary Budget 2009 and Current Tax Developments*.

LYMER, A., L. OATS, D. HANCOCK (2004), *Taxation – Policy and Practice*, AccountingEducation.com Publishing.

MADDEN, D. (2000), "Taxation, Debt and the Public Finances", in O'Hagan (ed.)*, The Economy of Ireland – Policy and Performance of a European Region*, eighth edition, Gill and McMillian.

MAGUIRE, T. (2018), *Direct Tax Acts,* Irish Tax Institute.

MARTYN, J., D. SHANAHAN, T. COONEY (Ed.) (2018), *Taxation Summary,* Irish Tax Institute.

OECD (2004), Analytical Databank,
http://www.oecd.org

OECD (2004), *Taxing Wages 2003/2004,*
http://www.oecd.org

OECD (2013), *Revenue Statistics 2013*,
http://www.oecd.org

O'HALLORAN, M. (2005), *From Bóraimhe to Bit – the Art of Taxation,* Irish Tax Institute.

O'HANLON, F., J. McCLEANE (Ed.) (2012), *The Taxation of Capital Gains*, Irish Tax Institute.

RÉAMONN, S. (1981), *History of the Revenue Commissioners*, Institute of Public Administration.

SMITH, A. (1776), *The Wealth of Nations Books IV–V*, London: Penguin (1999 reprint).

TOBIN, G., C. O'Brien (Eds) (2016) *Irish Tax Policy in Perspective*, Irish Tax Institute

REVENUE COMMISSIONERS (2002), *Effective Tax Rates for High Earning Individuals,* http://www.finance.gov.ie

REVENUE COMMISSIONERS (2004), *Effective Tax Rates of Top 400 Earners: Report for the Tax Year 2001,* http://www.finance.gov.ie

REVENUE COMMISSIONERS (2018), Annual Report – 2017, http://www.revenue.ie

2 INTRODUCTION TO THE EUROPEAN DIMENSION

Learning Outcomes

On completion of this chapter, you should be able to:

- ✓ Discuss the importance of Council Directive 2006/112/EC.
- ✓ Understand the primacy of EU legislation.
- ✓ Explain the concept of derogation.
- ✓ Understand the interplay between EU VAT legislation and domestic VAT legislation.
- ✓ Discuss the role of the various institutions of the EU in relation to VAT.
- ✓ Understand cross-border co-operation & mutual assistance in the field of VAT.
- ✓ Read and discuss an CJEU case.
- ✓ Have an overview of the development of VAT legislation within the EU
- ✓ Understand that BREXIT will have an impact on the VAT treatment of trade between the EU and the UK – the extent of such impact as yet unknown
- ✓ Complete Assignments and Questions in the corresponding chapter in *Irish Taxation: Law and Practice*, Volume 2.

2.1 Introduction

Any study of value-added tax (VAT) would not be complete without reference to the international dimension of VAT and, more importantly for Ireland, the European dimension. All developed countries (with the notable exception of the USA) and an increasing number of developing countries have value-added tax, or a variant, often referred to as general sales tax (GST).

The VAT system in operation throughout the European Union is currently provided for in Council Directive 2006/112/EC, which directive came into force on 1 January 2007. Prior to that date, the Sixth Directive (Council Directive 77/388/EEC) provided the basis for the VAT system throughout the EU from 1 January 1978 and prior to that again common VAT rules for the then EEC were laid out in the First and Second Directives.

Council Directive 2006/112/EC forms the basis for national VAT legislation in the 28 EU Member States[1]. Furthermore, many developing countries have modelled their VAT system on that of the EU and, hence, have modelled their national VAT legislation on the Sixth Directive.

It has always been a condition of entry for each applicant Member State to have in place, at the time of joining, a VAT system which accords with the VAT Directive in force at the time. Any derogation (see 2.4) sought and received by an applicant, i.e. prior to formal admission to the EU, will form part of its Treaty of Accession. Currently, the countries making application for admission to the EU include Turkey and a number of the former Yugoslav states. On 16 July 2009 Iceland applied to join the European Union [however the application was withdrawn in March 2015.]

A very important element of the European dimension to VAT, and one which is often overlooked, is the fact that each Member State contributes a proportion of its VAT yield to the European Commission in order to fund, in conjunction with customs duties and GNP resources, the Commission itself, the Common Agricultural Policy, and various structural, regional and cohesion funds. The contributions are collectively known as Community Own Resources (COR).

2.2 The Evolution of a Common System of VAT

VAT was not the first indirect tax the public was obliged to pay in Ireland. While VAT was introduced on 1 November 1972 as one of the prerequisites for Ireland to join the then European Economic Community (EEC) on 1 January 1973, it replaced two indirect taxes that operated in Ireland from the 1960s until our accession to the EEC, namely turnover tax at a rate of 2.5% (introduced in 1963) and wholesale tax at a rate of 5% (introduced in 1966).

Apart from replacing these taxes with VAT, the EEC prohibited, and continues to prohibit, the use by any Member State of a tax similar in nature to VAT. Hence the abolition of both wholesale and turnover taxes in Ireland and taxes in other Member States considered similar in nature to VAT.

In 1972, the then six Member States of the EEC Belgium, France, Germany, Italy, Luxembourg and the Netherlands had in place a broadly similar VAT system, which was based on the First Council Directive (67/227/EEC) and the Second Council Directive (67/228/EEC) of 11 April 1967.

While the First and Second Council Directives provided a very loose framework for the then six EEC Member States and the three new members Denmark, Ireland and the UK, it was felt that a more integrated framework was necessary to harmonise national VAT legislation. With this increased harmonisation and integration in mind, the European Commission drafted the Sixth Council Directive of 17 May 1977 (77/388/EEC).

1 Croatia acceded on 1 July 2013

In 1977 the Sixth Directive (Council Directive 77/388/EEC) was implemented and took effect from 1 January 1978. The Sixth Directive was a major step toward integrating and unifying the VAT systems throughout the expanded EU. At the time of its implementation the EU consisted of nine Member States with the then expectation of expansion to include 12 countries. The Sixth Directive consisted, eventually, of 61 Articles and 12 Annexes. For 18 of the current EU Member States who were not members at the time of its introduction in 1977 – Greece (joined in 1981), Spain and Portugal (1986), Sweden, Finland and Austria (1995) and Cyprus, Czech Republic, Estonia, Hungary, Latvia, Lithuania, Malta, Poland, Slovakia and Slovenia (May 2004), Bulgaria and Romania (2007) Croatia (July 2013) part of each State's negotiations contained an undertaking to have a VAT system conforming with the provisions of the Sixth Directive in operation on accession. Throughout its 29 year existence (1978–2007) the Sixth Directive was amended no less than 32 times.

A sign of just how complex VAT was becoming was the introduction of Council Regulation (EC) No 1777/2005, effective from 1 July 2006. The regulation gave legal effect to certain very specific guidelines (interpretations) in relation to a number of Articles of the Sixth Directive. These guidelines have been unanimously agreed by the VAT Committee (see 2.11 below). A recasting of this Regulation has taken place and Council Implementing Regulation 282/2011/EC came into force on 15 March 2011, replacing Regulation 1777/2005.

The Sixth Directive and certain provisions of the First Council Directive remained in force until their repeal by Council Directive 2006/112/EC of 28 November 2006. The repeal was effective from 1 January 2007. (The Second Council Directive was previously repealed by the Sixth Directive).

A full understanding of VAT would not be possible without reference to Council Directive 77/338/EEC, commonly called the Sixth Directive, which came into force on 1 January 1978 and continued in force for 29 years until it was replaced by the Council Directive 2006/112/EC on 1 January 2007.

2.3 Council Directive 2006/112/EC – The VAT Directive

2.3.1 Introduction

With effect from 1 January 2007 a new directive, Council Directive 2006/112/EC of 28 November 2006, came into force. As taxation is one of the areas where unanimous voting is required, the adoption of this directive was by unanimous vote of the Council of the European Union (the Council) (see 2.8).

From the First Directive, through the Second Directive and the Sixth Directive to Council Directive 2006/112/EC we can see the ever-increasing complexity of VAT and the ever-increasing pursuit of conformity to a common VAT system throughout the 28 Member States that currently form the European Union.

2.3.2 The VAT directive

Unlike its predecessor the Sixth Directive, Council Directive 2006/112/EC does not have a 'name'. Therefore throughout this book, from time to time, the current EU legislation in force governing the operation of VAT will be referred to as 'the VAT directive' or Council Directive 2006/112/EC.

The VAT directive was introduced on 1 January 2007 and replaced the Sixth Directive and that part of the Second Directive which was still in force at that time. At the time of its replacement the Sixth Directive had been amended several times and it was felt necessary to 'recast' it for reasons of clarity and rationalisation.

As with any Directive, the VAT directive has the dual purpose of securing the necessary uniformity of Community law and, at the same time, respecting the diversity of national traditions and structures. The aim of the VAT directive is the harmonisation of the law while, at the same time, respecting the principle of subsidiarity.

The VAT directive consists of a series of 'building blocks' through which the VAT system unfolds in a logical and rational manner. Thus Title I outlines the subject matter and scope of VAT, Title II defines the territorial scope of VAT, Title III defines an accountable person, i.e. a person who carries out transactions subject to VAT, Title IV defines taxable transactions, i.e. transactions which are subject to VAT, Title V defines the place where such transactions occur, and so on. It defines when VAT is chargeable, the amount on which VAT is chargeable, rates of VAT, exemptions from VAT, the right to deduct VAT and obligations. It also defines certain special schemes for traders and provides for derogation of its provisions.

2.3.3 Conformity and primacy

National VAT legislation, throughout the 28 EU Member States, must conform with Council Directive 2006/112/EC. Where national legislation does not accord with the VAT directive, it being Community-based legislation, then the VAT Directive takes primacy and the offending national legislation must be amended. Established case law of the European Court of Justice (ECJ) determines that an appellant may rely on the VAT directive in challenging national legislation. For further information on the primacy of the VAT directive, readers should consult the ECJ case of *Ursula Becker und Finanzamt Münster-Innenstadt* (Case 8/81).

The ECJ has, over time, established the principle of 'direct effect' in relation to the provisions of the VAT directive. Thus, a person aggrieved by certain provisions of national VAT legislation may rely upon the provisions of the VAT directive before their national tax authorities.

2.3.4 Amendments

An amendment to the VAT directive, Council Directive 2006/112/EC, may be made only by means of an amending Council Directive or by a Treaty of Accession regarding a new member state. The European Commission initiates all amendments, which may come about for a variety of reasons.

An amendment must have the unanimous approval of the Council. A varying period of time is always granted to Member States to transpose any change brought about through an amendment to the Directive into national VAT legislation.

2.4 Derogation from Council Directive 2006/112/EC

Derogation occurs where a Member State is allowed to either retain or introduce a measure to national VAT legislation that derogates from the "shall" provisions contained in the VAT directive[2]. It is very important to be aware of this concept as the VAT directive cannot be relied upon to challenge the particular derogation which, by its very nature, will not accord with the VAT directive. Derogation from the VAT directive is always given by means of a Council Decision addressed to the Member State(s) concerned. To obtain derogation from a particular provision, the applicant Member State must obtain the unanimous approval of the Council. A prime consideration in deciding whether or not to grant derogation is certainty that it will not lead to distortion of competition in the EU.

2.4.1 Irish derogations

In the case of Ireland, there are a number of derogations, some of which arose by way of retention of domestic legislation existing on commencement of the then Sixth Directive in 1978 and some of which were subsequently granted. Council Directive 2006/112/EC deals with derogation at Title XIII (Articles 370–396). Derogation is a complex matter. Some of the more important Irish derogations include those relating to property, catering and admission to sporting events. Many of the derogations held (either through retention or subsequent granting) have been rendered unnecessary through subsequent legislative changes or rulings of the Court of Justice of the European Union.

2.5 Community Legislation and Domestic Legislation – The Interaction

At the outset the interplay between legislation enacted at EU level (i.e. Directives, Regulations and Decisions) and domestic legislation (i.e. Acts, Regulations and Orders) may be difficult to understand. However, a basic understanding is necessary for a full appreciation of the operation of the VAT system.

EU Directives do not have 'direct application' in Member States. By this we mean that a directive itself is not considered to be legislation in force in any Member State. Therefore domestic legislation must be enacted to give effect to the provisions of an EU Directive.

2 All of the provisions in the VAT directive are prefaced by either the word "shall" or "may". Where the term "may" is used then implementation of the provision is at the discretion of the individual Member State. Where the term "shall" is used the Member State does not have any discretion and the measure must be implemented in domestic legislation, save where derogation is sought and granted.

However, EU Directives do have 'direct effect', i.e. a person is entitled to rely on a Directive if its provisions have not been given effect through the implementation (or interpretation) of obligatory domestic legislation giving effect to the provisions of the directive (see 2.3.3 above).

Under Article 288 of the Treaty on the Functioning of the European Union ("TFEU"), EU Regulations have 'direct application', i.e. EU Regulations do not require transposition into Irish law and are themselves considered to be legislation in force in each EU Member State.

EU decisions (Council Decision) addressed to particular Member States (e.g. in the case of derogation from the provisions of the VAT directive) have 'direct effect' and must be given force through the enactment of domestic legislation.

It is important to remember therefore that Community legislation will generally take priority over domestic legislation in so far as the operation of VAT is concerned.

2.6 Irish VAT Legislation: Value-Added Tax Consolidation Act, 2010

In the case of VAT, the provisions of Council Directive 2006/112/EC were - until some years ago - given effect in Ireland by way of the Value-Added Tax Acts, 1972. However, on 23 November 2010 the Value-Added Tax Consolidation Act, ("VATCA 2010") was signed into law by the President. This act marked the next stage in the evolution of VAT in Ireland.

VATCA 2010 is effective from 1 November 2010, the commencement of the taxable period in which it was enacted. VAT Act 1972 and all parts of subsequent acts which amended VAT Act 1972 (collectively referred to as Value-Added Tax Acts, 1972–2010) have been repealed. In addition, the Value-Added Tax Regulations, 2006 were replaced by Value-Added Tax Regulations, 2010 so as to ensure correct cross-referencing to VATCA 2010.

VATCA 2010 contains the laws which govern the operation of VAT in Ireland. The layout of VATCA 2010 to a large extent replicates the layout of the VAT Directive. This makes for reasonably straight forward cross-referencing and is a major improvement on the layout of previous Irish VAT legislation.

2.7 Role of the Court of Justice of the European Union

2.7.1 Introduction

Given the primacy of Community law and the development of legislation through the precedent of case law, the Court of Justice of the European Union (CJEU), formerly known as the European Court of Justice, plays a very important role as far as VAT is concerned.

The core mission of the CJEU is to strengthen the judicial protection of citizens of the EU and to ensure that EU law is interpreted uniformly throughout the EU.

To date, approximately 700 cases have been dealt with by the CJEU in relation to VAT. All judgments of the Court must be published in the *Official Journal of the European Communities* ("OJ").

Similar to our own Supreme Court, the CJEU is playing an increasing part in the interpretation of VAT legislation throughout the EU. Whilst the VAT directive lays out the groundwork it is increasingly left to the judiciary to interpret and therefore define rules relating to VAT.

2.7.2 Composition of the Court of Justice of the European Union

Since 1 July 2013, the CJEU has 28 judges, one from each Member State. Each judge is appointed for a term of six years. The judges come from a variety of legal backgrounds and few, if any, are judges in their own Member State. They are assisted by eight attorneys (Advocates-General).

While dealing with cases, the CJEU sits in chambers. The court is made up of eight chambers, each consisting of 5–7 judges. Each judge sits in two chambers. Finally, there is the Grand Chamber consisting of 13 judges. The Grand Chamber deals with the most serious problems, such as a challenge to Community law, the need to depart from earlier jurisprudence, etc.

Generally, five judges sit together in chamber to hear a VAT case.

2.7.3 Referrals for interpretation (preliminary rulings)

A VAT case may be referred, on a point of European law or its interpretation, to the CJEU for "preliminary ruling" by any of the courts in a Member State. Such a referral can be made by the Appeal Commissioners, by the District, Circuit, High or Supreme Courts in Ireland. Where interpretation of the European law is in doubt, the Supreme Court must refer the matter to the CJEU.

Generally, a referral is made to the CJEU to interpret a point of law or to interpret the meaning or intention of a particular part of the VAT directive. In such cases, the CJEU will issue a judgment in relation to the question(s) put to it – and only the question(s) put to it – and will then refer the matter back to the referring court in the Member State concerned to deal with the case. However, the referring national court dealing with the matter is bound by the interpretation of the CJEU and must accord with such interpretation in reaching its decision. Indeed, each and every decision/interpretation of the CJEU in relation to VAT must be given effect in the drafting and implementation of the national VAT legislation, in each Member State.

2.7.4 Infraction proceedings (failure to fulfil obligations)

Where the Commission is satisfied that a Member State has not transposed the VAT directive, or any amending Directive, into national VAT legislation, or where the

Member State is incorrectly interpreting or implementing Community law or has failed to implement a judgment of the CJEU, it may commence infraction proceedings against the Member State concerned at the CJEU.

Again, the decision of the CJEU is binding. It will also make a decision with regard to costs.

Prior to commencing infraction proceedings the Commission will issue a 'Reasoned Opinion' to the Member State concerned indicting its concern in relation to a particular matter. The Reasoned Opinion may seek an explanation of the matter, and will generally make a recommendation as to how the Commission wishes to see the matter resolved.

In the past, the Commission has successfully taken infraction proceedings against Ireland on the matter of the application of VAT to toll charges and, more recently, on the matter of how certain activities of local authorities are treated for VAT purposes. The CJEU held that toll charges were liable to VAT and were not VAT exempt, as had been the treatment in Ireland. As a result of that decision of the CJEU, Irish VAT legislation was changed so that commercially operated toll charges became liable to VAT at the standard rate (currently 23%) from 1 Sept 2001.
(Students are referred to the case study at the end of this chapter.)

On 16 July 2009 the CJEU issued a ruling in relation to certain supplies made by local authorities. The judgment stated that local authorities must be treated in the same way as normal businesses, when not to do so might lead to a distortion of competition. As a result, Ireland has been obliged to amend its legislation and bring local authorities and other 'public bodies' within the scope of VAT for certain activities. Domestic legislation giving effect to the judgment took effect from 1 July 2010. Ireland has been the subject of two recent cases at the CJEU. The first case involved the application of the reduced rate of 4.8% to the sale of horses. The court held, in its judgement of 14 March 2013, that the rate could not be applied to the sale of greyhounds and horses as the animals concerned were not bred specifically for human consumption (case C-108/11). In the second case (case C-85/11), involving VAT groups, the court, in its judgment of 9 April 2013, dismissed the infraction proceedings taken by the Commission against Ireland and held that it was permissible for non-taxable persons to become members of VAT groups – see 3.14 for more details on VAT groups.

2.7.5 The Advocate-General's opinion

As indicated above, eight Advocates-General assist the CJEU. The Advocate-General examines relevant past case law, the legislation and the case to hand. He/she will prepare an opinion in relation to the case, which is published on the official EU website. The opinion is not binding precedent.

The Court, in issuing a subsequent ruling, may agree with the opinion of the Advocate-General or may disagree.

In a very small number of cases the matter may proceed directly to judgement without an opinion of the Advocate-General.

2.7.6 Binding precedent

As indicated above, the interpretation of the CJEU in relation to the VAT directive or its decision in any referral, appeal or infraction proceeding is final and binding. There is no higher arbiter in relation to VAT.

The Court's findings set precedent, which must be adhered to and may not be overturned, save in the most exceptional of circumstances. Indeed, some few cases referred to the CJEU have not been heard, on the basis that the Court indicated it had already opined on the matter raised.

2.8 Role of the European Commission

2.8.1 Introduction

From a VAT perspective, the European Commission has a number of very important roles. Given that VAT is a Europe-wide tax as opposed to a national tax, the requirement of the Commission's input is central to the progression and operation of the VAT system.

The Commission has a specific Directorate-General, DG XXI, which deals with taxation, including customs, the harmonised excises and VAT.

2.8.2 Initiating and drafting legislation

The Commission has a fundamental role in both initiating and drafting amendments to the Sixth Directive.

Only the Commission may initiate an amendment to Council Directive 2006/112/EC. Where the Commission determines that a particular amendment is required, or one has been requested by the Council, it drafts a proposed amendment and presents it to the Council. The Council may accept the amendment in full or reject it. In the case of partial acceptance, the Commission will be requested to redraft, taking account of the views of the Council.

As there is a requirement for unanimous approval by the Council for acceptance of an amendment, drafting can sometimes be a very long process before consensus is reached.

In April 2016 the Commission Issued a communication (COM(2016) 148 final) to the Council, the European Parliament and the EESC entitled: "Towards a single EU VAT area - Time to decide". Among the topics it deals with are:

- Removing VAT obstacles to e-commerce in the single market
- VAT simplification package for SMEs
- Measures to tackle the VAT Gap*
- Definitive VAT regime for cross-border trade
- Greater freedom for member stares on VAT rate policy

* The VAT Gap is the difference between expected VAT revenue and VAT actually collected and is currently estimated by the Commission to be c.€170billion.

2.8.3 Monitoring transposition and implementation

Another key role of the Commission is monitoring the transposition of the VAT Directive and any subsequent amending Directives into national VAT legislation throughout the EU. The Commission continually monitors each Member State to ensure that each amending Directive has been transposed correctly into national legislation, as is obligatory.

In addition to transposition, the Commission will monitor implementation of the VAT Directive and amending Directives. It will ensure that both interpretation and administrative practice in relation to national VAT legislation is in accordance with the objectives of the VAT Directive.

2.8.4 Challenging divergence

The Commission will challenge any divergence from the objectives of the VAT Directive. Such divergence can occur as a result of incorrect transposition, incorrect interpretation or administrative practice in one or more Member States.

In the first instance, the Commission will write to the Member State(s) concerned advising it of their position, by way of a Reasoned Opinion (see 2.7.4 above), either asking for an explanation from or issue an instruction to the national tax authorities in relation to the issue. In the event of a failure to comply, the Commission will initiate a legal action at the ECJ, known as an infraction proceeding, against the Member State concerned (see 2.7.4 above).

It is worth noting that not all actions commenced by the Commission are successful. A binding decision will be made by the ECJ in all cases. The decision is binding on both the Commission and the Member State(s) concerned.

2.8.5 Lodging a complaint with the Commission

Any citizen of an EU Member State may lodge a complaint with the European Commission if they believe that a Directive, including the VAT directive, is not being implemented or if they believe national legislation is not compatible with EU legislation. The person does not have to be affected by the offending legislation or its non-implementation. There are set procedures for making a complaint. The Commission is obliged to keep the complainant fully informed in relation to the progress of the matter, the response of the Member State concerned and the actions being taken by the Commission.

Any action undertaken by the Commission will be published in official publications of the Commission indicating the issue of a Reasoned Opinion and/or the commencement of infraction proceedings.

An added incentive for the Commission is the fact that their own resources are funded from a percentage of the VAT yield in each Member State.

2.9 Role of the Council of the European Union

In adopting community laws the Council may be obliged to act by a simple majority of its members, by a qualified majority of its members or by a unanimous decision. In the policy area of taxation, the Council must act on the basis of a unanimous decision. The Council is the legislative body as far as VAT is concerned.

The Council is composed of different members (ministers from the governments of all 28 Member States) depending on the policy area being dealt with. In the case of VAT, the Council consists of the Ministers for Finance/Economics from each of the 28 Member States, sometimes referred to as ECOFIN.

2.10 Role of the European Parliament

The European Parliament has a very limited role in the policy area of taxation. When the Commission proposes a Directive, it must consult the Parliament. The Parliament may approve, reject or make amendments to the Commission's proposals. The Commission is not obliged to take any account of rejections or amendments recommended by the Parliament.

2.11 The VAT Committee

Article 398, Council Directive 2006/112/EC, established an advisory committee known as the VAT Committee. It consists of representatives of the Member States and the Commission. The VAT Committee prepares guidelines for the tax authorities of the Member States, particularly in areas that are open to interpretation. Such guidelines are not binding on the Member States.

In 1997, the Commission proposed a Directive that would make the VAT Committee's opinions binding by transforming the committee into a regulatory committee. The Council has not adopted the proposed Directive.

2.12 Mutual Assistance – Cross-Border Co-operation

Given that VAT is a Europe-wide tax, a necessary element is the ability of Member States to pursue liabilities in other Member States, i.e., cross-border. Thus, there needs to be a mechanism whereby, if an accountable person resident or established in one Member State incurs a VAT liability in another Member State and fails to discharge (pay) the amount due, the Member State owed the VAT can pursue the debt. The facility is used where an accountable person fails to pay an amount of VAT due.

A number of pieces of EU legislation deal with mutual assistance between Member States: Council Directive 2010/24/EU of 16 March 2010 & Council Regulation

904/2010 of 7 October 2010 being the most important. The scope of both pieces of legislation is quite wide and the Council Regulation automatically forms part of Irish VAT legislation without the need for transposition. The tax authorities in one Member State may seek the assistance of the tax authorities in another Member State in relation to a wide range of matters.

The tax authorities seeking information send details of the information required to the tax authorities where the accountable person with the records which can produce the information resides or is established. Increasingly, with the growth of trans-border multinationals, the tax authorities in Member States are actively seeking assistance from tax authorities in other Member States through the use of these mutual assistance provisions.

The assistance sought may range from the pursuit of an assessment against an individual to the request for information to '*... help them to effect a correct assessment of VAT*'. With the changes in relation to taxation of cross-border supplies of telecommunications, broadcasting and electronic services from 1 January 2015 it is anticipated that this mutual assistance legislation will become increasingly important.

2.13 Fiscalis Programme

This is an EU action programme set up to reinforce the functioning of the various indirect taxation systems (VAT, harmonised excises, customs, etc.) of the internal market. The programme aims to achieve a high common standard of understanding of Community law among the tax officials of the various EU Member States and to continually improve co-operation among officials of the Member States and the Commission.

The programme generally consists of the exchange of officials between Member States for periods not exceeding six months. It also consists of the provision of training courses by the Commission in the field of indirect taxation for officials of the Member States.

In addition to the 28 EU Member States, the programme is also open to officials from applicant countries.

2.14 Case Law Cross-Reference to Community Legislation

In reading case-law, i.e. cases referred to the CJEU, initiated prior to 31 December 2006 all reference to Community-based VAT legislation will be a reference to the relevant Article(s) in the Sixth Council Directive. With effect from 1 January 2007 all judgments on cases initiated thereafter will make reference to relevant Article(s) in Council Directive 2006/112/EC, the VAT directive or to articles in the Sixth Council Directive, depending on the tax periods before the Court.

Articles in the Sixth Council can be cross-referenced to Articles in Council Directive 2006/112/EC by referring to the Correlation Table, Annex XII, Council Directive 2006/112/EC.

2.15 Further Information

Further information on the institutes of the European Union may be found at: www.eur-lex.europa.eu

Further information on the decisions of the European Court of Justice may be found at: www.curia.europa.eu

Additional information on a wide range of publications about and by the various EU institutions may be accessed at www.bookshop.europa.eu

2.16 Brexit

Although there has been plenty of speculation over the past two years, little is known as to what the final outcome will be. What we can say is that where the UK ceases to be a member state of the European Union, irrespective of whether or not it remains in the Customs Union, there will be major change in how goods and services are traded between the remaining member states (including Ireland) and the UK.

The current obligation of the UK to accept the precedence of the VAT Directive will most likely cease (see 2.3 & 2.5 above). Additionally, the binding decisions of the CJEU may no longer apply to the interpretation of VAT legislation within the UK (see 2.7 above).

In any event major changes in relation to VAT will be on the way and you should be aware of this.

2.17 Summary

The following diagram summarises the European dimension of VAT.

VAT–The European Dimension

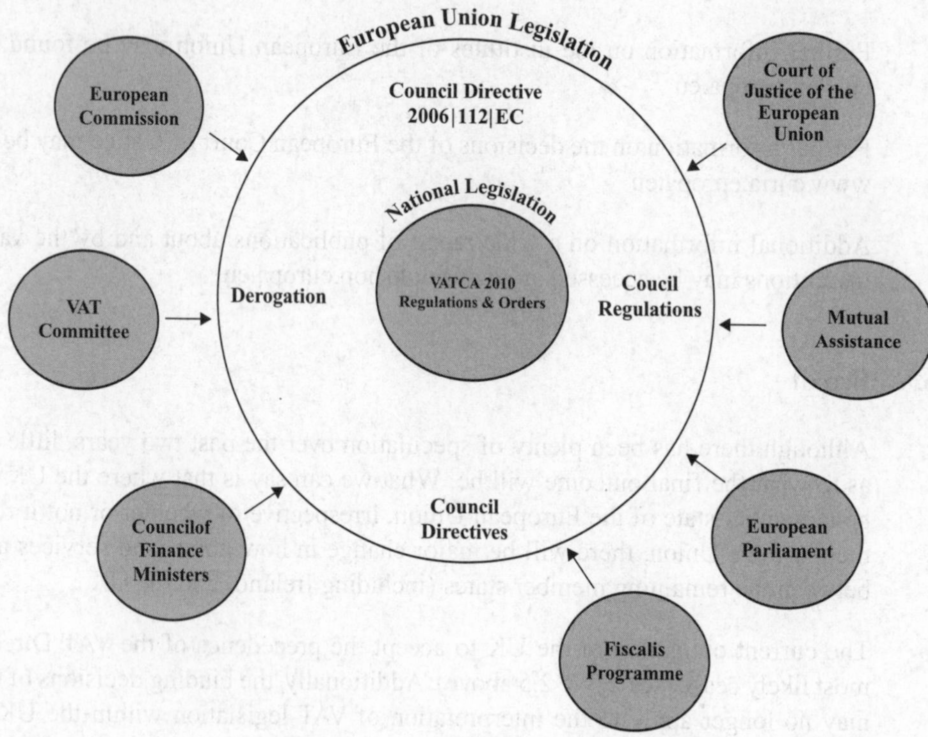

CASE STUDIES

Assignment 1

Commission of the European Communities v Ireland (Case C-358/97)

Your assignment is based on the judgment of the Court of Justice of the European Union in the case of the *Commission of the European Communities v Ireland* (Case C-358/97). The judgment was delivered on 12 September 2000.

Please read the judgment, which can be sourced at: www.europe.eu.int/cj/en/content/juris/index.htm.

It may take a second read to get used to the style of reporting used. The judgment is broken down into 79 numbered parts:

Part 1 outlines what the plaintiff, i.e., the European Commission, seeks.

Parts 2–9 outline the relevant Irish and European VAT legislation.

Parts 10–21 outline the procedure undertaken up to the commencement of litigation.

Part 22 outlines the substance of the case, i.e., the two areas where the Commission seeks a judgment.

Parts 23–58 deal with the first claim, i.e., the non-compliance with the Sixth Directive, being Ireland's failure to levy VAT on toll charges.

Parts 59–78 deal with the second claim, i.e., the failure by Ireland to pay to the Community's Own Resources (COR) the amount that should have been paid had VAT been levied on the toll charges.

Part 79 deals with the matter of costs. Finally, there is the decision of the Court.

Assignment 2

National Roads Authority v the Revenue Commissioners (Case C-344/15)

Your assignment is based on the judgment of the Court of Justice of the European Union (CJEU) in the case of the *National Roads Authority v the Revenue Commissioners* (Case C-344/15). The judgment was delivered on 19 January 2017.

Please read the judgment, which can be sourced at: http://curia.europa.eu.

It may take a second read to get used to the style of reporting used. The judgment is broken down into 51 numbered parts:

Part 1 outlines what the plaintiff, i.e., the European Commission, seeks.

Parts 3–15 outline the relevant Irish and European VAT legislation.

Part 16–28 outline the nature of the dispute procedure undertaken up to the commencement of litigation.

Parts 29 outlines the questions asked of the Court.

Part 30–34 sets out some observations of the Court.

Parts 35–51 set out how the Court deals with the questions asked of it and how it arrives at its decision.

Part 52 deals with the matter of costs. Finally, there is the decision of the Court.

3 THE GENERAL PRINCIPLES

Learning Outcomes

On completion of this chapter you will be able to:

- ✓ Explain when the charge to VAT arises.
- ✓ Describe the transactional nature of VAT.
- ✓ Describe what constitutes a supply of goods.
- ✓ Describe what constitutes a supply of services.
- ✓ Understand and distinguish between a multiple supply and a composite supply.
- ✓ Describe the VAT treatment of the appropriation of goods for private use or for the purposes of an exempt activity.
- ✓ Understand when a "self-supply" does/does not arise in the case of canteens.
- ✓ Appreciate the importance of the place of supply.
- ✓ Identify the rates of VAT that apply in Ireland and the goods and services to which they apply.
- ✓ Identify goods and services that are exempt from VAT.
- ✓ Discuss the distinction between "exempt" and "zero-rated".
- ✓ Explain the Two-Thirds Rule.
- ✓ Identify those persons who are obliged to register for VAT.
- ✓ Identify those persons who may register for VAT.
- ✓ Discuss the advantages and disadvantages of voluntarily registering for VAT, and describe the factors that should be considered in deciding whether or not to voluntarily register for VAT.
- ✓ Identify the circumstances where an application for group registration may be granted, and discuss the advantages and disadvantages of having a VAT group registration.
- ✓ Explain what constitutes the taxable amount.
- ✓ Explain what is meant by "deeming" in VAT legislation.
- ✓ Calculate a basic VAT liability for an accountable person.
- ✓ Complete Assignments and Questions in the corresponding chapter in *Irish Taxation: Law and Practice*, Volume 2.

3.1 General Principles

3.1.1 Introduction

Value-added tax (VAT) is a multi-stage, indirect tax on consumption.

VAT is only levied where there is consumption. By "consumption", we mean that services or goods supplied have been consumed. There are numerous examples from CJEU case law that deal with the concept of consumption.

By "multi-stage", we mean that VAT is applied at each stage in the production and distribution of goods and services.

VAT is classified as an indirect tax because (unlike direct taxes, such as income tax and corporation tax, which are paid directly to the Exchequer by the person to whom the tax is applied) it is collected and remitted to the Exchequer at various stages by accountable persons (VAT-registered traders). The VAT remitted at each stage is based on the value added by the trader, hence the name Value-Added Tax.

Although collected and remitted in stages, VAT is paid entirely by the final consumer. In most cases, the final consumer is the general public.

VAT is also charged on goods imported from outside the EU (see 4.2.1, Chapter 4) and on the intra-Community acquisition of goods (see 4.3.2, Chapter 4).

Net receipts from VAT for 2014 were €11.2 billion, an increase of 7.9% on the 2013 amount. VAT accounted for 27% of net Exchequer receipts in 2014, down from a high of c. 33% in 2007 indicating how heavily reliant the Exchequer is on the consumption of goods and services to generate public finance.

3.1.2 The transactional nature of VAT

VAT is a tax that is applied to a transaction. A transaction consists of a supply (of goods or services or both) for which there is consideration (generally a payment). In addition, there must be a direct link between the supply and the consideration.

Sometimes a transaction is "deemed" to occur to enable a charge of VAT to be applied. (See 3.17 for further discussion on the use of "deeming provisions" in VAT legislation.)

A transaction liable to VAT is generally referred to as a "taxable transaction". A transaction not liable to VAT is referred to as either an "exempt transaction" or as a "non-taxable transaction".

3.1.3 The scope of VAT

For VAT to apply to a particular transaction, the transaction must fall within the scope of VAT. Once a transaction is within the scope of VAT, it may be liable to VAT at one of five differing VAT rates, or it may be exempt from VAT (i.e., while the transaction is within the scope of VAT, it is specifically exempted from VAT).

This is an important concept and is central to understanding VAT. Most economic transactions are within the scope of VAT, if not within Ireland, then within the territory of another EU Member State.

An employee supplying his/her services to an employer is not within the scope of VAT. Furthermore, the issue of new stocks, new shares, new debentures or new securities made to raise capital, is also outside the scope of VAT.

3.1.4 National VAT legislation

The operation of VAT in Ireland is provided for through VATCA 2010, together with a number of regulations and orders. While VATCA 2010 is the primary source of VAT law, in Ireland many other pieces of legislation are made use of for the implementation and operation of VAT. For example, legislation concerning the operation of the appeals procedure and many other procedural and administrative matters in relation to VAT is provided for in the Taxes Consolidation Act 1997 (TCA97).

Each year, the VAT legislation is updated, generally by way of amendments contained in the Finance Act. They may also be amended by way of a European Communities Regulation, some of which provide for the immediate transposition of an updated provision of Council Directive 2006/112/EC (the VAT Directive).

In November 2006 a large number of the then existing VAT regulations (in the form of separate Statutory Instruments) were repealed and replaced by Value-Added Tax Regulation, 2006. This has now been replaced by Value-Added tax Regulations, 2010 [SI 639 of 2010]. These Regulations can be viewed at:

http://www.revenue.ie/en/practitioner/law/statutory/index.html#section2010

3.2 The Charge to VAT

Section 3 VATCA 2010 states:

s3
VATCA 2010

"Except as expressly otherwise provided in this Act, a tax called value-added tax is, subject to and in accordance with this Act and the Regulations, chargeable, leviable and payable on the following transactions:

(a) the supply for consideration of goods by a taxable person acting In that capacity when the place of supply Is the State;

(b) the import into the State;

(c) on the supply for consideration of services by a taxable person acting in that capacity when the place of supply is the State;

(d) on intra-Community acquisition for consideration by an accountable person of goods (other than new means of transport) when the acquisition is made within the State;

> *(e) the intra-Community acquisition for consideration of new means of transport when the acquisition is made within the State.*

This is referred to as the charging section and is the basis of the charge to VAT in Ireland. Analysing it, we see that, for VAT to apply, certain conditions must be met. These conditions define the scope of VAT in Ireland. The conditions are:

- there must be a supply of goods or services;
- the supply must be effected within the State (Ireland);
- the supply must be for consideration;
- the supply must be made by a taxable person, i.e., a person in business;
- the supply must be made in the course or furtherance of business, i.e. by *"a taxable person acting in that capacity."*

A further condition has been added through the interpretation of the CJEU (as exemplified in the case of Tolsma RJ (case C-16/93) among others): There must be a direct link between the supply and the consideration. Thus if there is a supply and there is a consideration but the direct link between both is missing then the supply is not within the scope of VAT.

In addition VAT is chargeable on imports into Ireland from non-EU countries at the appropriate VAT rate as applies to the sale of the goods within the State (see section 4.3.2).

VAT is also chargeable on the intra-Community acquisition of goods to Ireland by an accountable person and on the intra-Community acquisition of a new means of transport by any person.

3.3 VAT – A Worked Example of the Multi-Stage, Indirect Nature of the Tax

At this stage, a simple worked example will best illustrate the nature of VAT.

The term "input VAT" describes the VAT incurred by a VAT-registered person when he/she purchases goods or services from another VAT-registered trader (see section 3.11).

The term "output VAT" describes the VAT charged by a VAT-registered person when he/she sells goods or services to another person (including another VAT-registered trader).

As you can see in the example below, the output VAT charged by a supplier of goods or services equals the input VAT incurred by the person acquiring the goods or services.

Example 3.1

	Input VAT (23%)	Output VAT (23%)	VAT Remitted to Revenue
Manufacturer			
Produces goods	Nil		
Sale to wholesaler €10,000 + VAT.		€2,300	
Receives payment of €12,300			
Output VAT less Input VAT			€2,300
Wholesaler			
Acquires goods for €10,000 + VAT	€2,300		
Sale to distributor for €14,000 + VAT		€3,220	
Receives payment of €17,220			
Output VAT less Input VAT			€920
Distributor			
Acquires goods for €14,000 + VAT	€3,200		
Sale to distributor for €21,000 + VAT		€4,830	
Receives payment of €25,830			
Output VAT less Input VAT			€1,610
Retailer			
Acquires goods for €21,000 + VAT	€4,830		
Sale to customer for €30,000		€5,609	
Receives payment of €30,000 (inclusive of VAT of €5,609)[1]			
Output VAT less Input VAT			€779
Accumulated VAT remitted			**€5,609**

Ignoring the cost of the goods and looking only at the VAT amounts attached to the price, we see:[1]

- the manufacturer remits €2,300 VAT but collects it from the wholesaler;
- the wholesaler remits €920 VAT but collects €3,220 VAT (€2,300 + €920) from the distributor;
- the distributor remits €1,610 VAT but collects €4,830 VAT (€2,300 + €920 + €1,610) from the retailer;
- the retailer remits €779 VAT but collects €5,609 VAT (€2,300 + €920 + €1,610 + €779) from the customer.

1 A Ministerial Order implemented in 1973 prohibits retailers from advertising VAT-exclusive prices to the general public. This is why the price quoted to the general public is VAT-inclusive.

As you can see, the end customer ultimately pays the entire VAT of €5,609 that accumulates on the series of transactions.

Value-added

The value added by the wholesaler is the difference between sale price and cost price: €4,000 (€14,000 – €10,000). The VAT remitted is essentially based on the value added (€4,000 @ 23% = €920). In practice, this is calculated by deducting "input VAT" from "output VAT" (in this case, €3,220 – €2,300 = €920).

3.4 Supplies of Goods[2]

p3 ch1 VATCA 2010

The following constitute a supply of movable goods for VAT purposes:

- the transfer of ownership of goods by agreement;
- the sale of movable goods through an undisclosed agent;
- the handing over of goods that are subject to a hire-purchase agreement;
- the compulsory purchase or legal seizure of goods;
- the transfer of goods within a business by a business person from a taxable activity to an activity exempt from VAT;
- the appropriation of movable goods by a business person for private use.

While most supplies of goods are quite straightforward, more complex supplies cause problems. The latter two supplies identified above may be complex, particularly as the business person may not realise a supply has taken place. These issues are best explained in more detail.

3.4.1 Movable goods used for VAT-exempt purposes

If a business person applies movable goods previously used for making taxable supplies to an exempt use, then a supply for VAT purposes is "deemed" to have taken place (see 3.17 for further discussion of "deeming" in VAT legislation). For instance, if a bank which purchased a computer system for the purpose of its leasing business (taxable supplies) starts using the computer system for transacting its lending business (VAT-exempt supplies), then it is "deemed" to have made a taxable supply of the computer to itself. The "deemed" consideration (see 3.17) in respect of the supply is the cost to the bank of acquiring the goods. The bank must account for output VAT on the supply. The bank is said to have made a "self-supply".

2 Special provisions relate to the supply of immovable goods (land and buildings) – see Chapter 6.

3.4.2 Movable goods appropriated for non-business use

If a business person appropriates movable goods for private use, then a supply for VAT purposes is also "deemed" to have taken place. For instance, if a car-dealer who purchased a car for the purpose of his business (taxable supplies) decides to give the car to his daughter, then he is "deemed" to have made a taxable supply of the car to himself. The "deemed" consideration in respect of the supply is the cost to the car-dealer of acquiring the car. The car-dealer is said to have made a "self-supply" and he must account for output VAT on the supply.

3.5 Supply of Services

Section 25 VATCA 2010 states that:

> ***" ...'supply',*** *in relation to a service, means the performance or omission of any act or the toleration of any situation other than the supply of goods ..."*

The definition is a broad "catch-all" one. It basically states that a supply that is not a supply of goods, is a supply of services. Apart from the more obvious services, the following are also supplies of services for VAT purposes:

- the supply of food and drink fit for consumption without further preparation:
  - by a vending machine,
  - by a hotel, canteen, restaurant, etc;
- the operation of a canteen by a business – the business is said to have made a "self-supply";
- the supply of a service through an undisclosed agent;
- leasing and hiring of goods.

3.5.1 Self-supply of a service

As a result of a decision at the CJEU in the case of *Hotel Scandic Gasaback AB* (case C-412/03) both the legislation and administrative practice dealing with the "self-supply" of a service has been changed with effect from 1 May 2006.

According to section 27, VATCA 2010, a self-service is deemed to occur, subject to the presence of a VAT regulation, in any of the following circumstances:

(a) Where physical movable assets of the business, upon which input VAT has been claimed (see 3.11), are used for the private purposes of the business or employees or for any purpose other than the business (dealt with in section 3.4);

(b) Where a service is carried out free of charge by an accountable person for his/her own private use or that of employees or for any purposes other than those of such person's business;

(c) Where a business carries out a service for itself on the condition that if such a service was supplied by a third party, the input VAT incurred would not be deductible by the business.

However, before any of the above has effect in law, the specific circumstance must be provided for by way of VAT Regulations. To date, the only VAT Regulation made concerning the self-supply of a service is one which makes the supply of canteen services by a business, to its employees, a "self-supplied" service [Regulation 8, VAT Regulations 2010].

3.5.2 Company restaurants & canteens

Since 1 May 2006, the supply of services in a canteen provided by a business for its employees can be categorised as follows:

(a) where the canteen is operated by the business and a charge for meals is made, then VAT is accounted for on the actual receipts, or

(b) where the canteen is operated by a commercial caterer, acting as agent of the business and a charge for meals is made, then VAT is accounted for on the actual receipts by the business (which VAT is collected from the customer by the agent on behalf of the business), or

(c) where the canteen is operated by the business and no charge is made for meals, then VAT is accounted for on the cost of supplying the service (such cost may include caterer's charges, light, heat, catering equipment, canteen staff wages, fixed asset depreciation, canteen overheads, etc.), or

(d) where the canteen is operated by a commercial caterer acting as principal (i.e. not an agent of the business), then VAT is accounted for,

  (i) by the business on the cost of supplying the service (such cost may include caterer's charges, light, heat, catering equipment, canteen staff wages and canteen overheads), and,

  (ii) by the commercial caterer on the receipts from customers and charges which he makes to the business.

You will note that in the case of (c) and (d) above a "self-supply" of a service occurs, i.e., a supply is being made because the business uses it assets to provide a catering service and does not receive any payment from the customer in relation to such supply. [Note in the case of (c) above, no payment is made at all and in the case of (d) above, no payment is made to the business concerned.] In both cases, the business must account for VAT on a "deemed" consideration, i.e., the cost to it of supplying the catering service to its employees.

Example 3.2

A manufacturing company provides a free canteen service to its employees. The canteen occupies 15% of the factory space. The monthly light and heating bill is €10,000. The company pays €15,000 per month to an independent caterer. It also pays €3,000 wages per month to canteen staff and annual rates of €120,000. Even though it does not charge for the meals, it must pay VAT each month, at 9%, on the cost of supplying the service. The monthly VAT liability arising for the business in relation to the "self-supply" of a catering service amounts to €1,890 and is calculated as follows:

Cost (€)	*Apportionment*	*VAT (@9%)*	
10,000	*15%*	*135*	*[10,000 × 15% × 9%]*
15,000	*none*	*1,350*	*[15,000 × 9%]*
3,000	*none*	*270*	*[3,000 × 9%]*
120,000	*/12 × 15%*	*135*	*[120,000/12 × 15% × 9%]*
		€1,890	

3.5.3 Private use of a business property

Where property that formed part of the assets of a business at the time of its acquisition or development is used during the 20-year period immediately following such acquisition or development for:

- the private use of the person in business or his/her staff, or
- a purpose other than those of the business,

then a supply of services is deemed to take place, i.e., a "self-supply" has occurred (see Chapter 6).

3.6 Place of Supply

Place of supply rules are very important in determining if a particular supply of goods or services is within the charge of VAT in Ireland (see 3.2). Here we will look at the general rules that determine the place of supply of movable goods and services.

Remember that a supply will only be liable to Irish VAT when the place of supply is determined to be Ireland.

3.6.1 Place of supply of goods

In the case of goods being transported across a border, the place of supply is where transportation begins. In the case of goods not requiring transport, the place of supply is where the goods are when the supply is made.

However, the following important exceptions should be noted:

Where goods are assembled or installed by or on behalf of the supplier, the place of supply is where the goods are assembled or installed, e.g., an Irish manufacturer contracts with a French supplier to supply and install machinery on his premises in Ireland. As the machine is installed by or on behalf of the French supplier, the place of supply of the goods (the machine) is Ireland.

3.6.2 Council directives and regulations on place of supply of services

Council Directive 2008/08/EC of 12 February 2008, and Council Directive 2008/117/EC of 16 December 2008 amended the VAT Directive, substantially changing the rules in relation to the place of supply of services. The majority of the provisions came into force on 1 January 2010 (some of the provisions will come into force on various dates subsequent to 1 January 2010). The rules relating to cross-border services, in particular those relating to the place of supply are described at 3.6.3 below and in Chapter 4.

Where goods are supplied on board vessels, aircraft or trains where the destination is in a Member State other than the state of departure, then the place of supply is where the transport begins, e.g., goods supplied on a ferry travelling from Ireland to France are deemed to be supplied in Ireland and, as such, are liable to Irish VAT. Goods supplied on a ferry from France to Ireland are deemed to be supplied in France and are liable to French VAT.

Council Implementing Regulation 282/2011/EU, as amended by Council Regulation 967/2012/EU sets out in detail the rules relating to place of supply and provides guidance in the interpretation of the VAT Directive.

3.6.3 Place of supply of services

s33–35 VATCA 2010

In order to correctly determine the place of supply of a service, it is very important for the supplier to know if his supply is to another person in business (a B2B supply) or to a private person, a consumer (a 'B2C supply').

In the case of a B2B supply of a service, the general rule is that the place of supply is where the business customer has his/her establishment. If the business customer has more than one establishment, the place of supply is where the customer's establishment most concerned with the supply, is situated.

In the case of a B2C supply of a service, the general rule is that the place of supply is where the supplier has his/her establishment. If the supplier has more than one establishment, the place of supply is where the supplier's establishment most concerned with the supply, is situated. [However please see 4.10 for certain changes to the place of supply of certain services, effective from 1 January 2015].

However, there are some very important exceptions to these 'place of supply' rules. Among the most important exceptions to the place of supply rules are the following:

- Services connected with property (land and buildings) – the place of supply is where the property is located. Thus, where an architect based in Dublin designs a building in Spain, the place of supply of his/her services is Spain. The supply of the service is not liable to Irish VAT.
- Goods transport services and services ancillary to goods transport (excluding intra-Community transport services) provided to private persons (B2C) – the place (or places) the transport takes place.
- Passenger transport services – the place (or places) where the transport takes place.

Intra-Community goods transport services and services ancillary to goods transport provided to private persons (B2C) – the place where the transport of the goods commences.

The following services are deemed to be supplied where they are physically carried out:

- Cultural, artistic, entertainment, sporting, scientific and educational services;
- Admission charges and ancillary services relating to exhibitions, conferences and trade fairs;
- Work on and valuation of movable goods, contract work carried out for private persons (B2C).

Catering/restaurant services are subject to the following rules:

- The general rule is that the place of supply is where the service is carried out, i.e. where the restaurant is located;
- Where the catering service is carried out on board a ship/aircraft or train operating within the EU and where the first point of departure is the State – the place of supply is the State.

Where the supply consists of the short-term hire (30 days or less) of a means of transport (e.g. car hire) – the place of supply is where the goods are put at the disposal of the customer (both B2B and B2C).

Where certain services[3] are supplied to private persons (B2C) who are established/resident outside the EU – the place of supply is where the customer is established/resident.

Where services are supplied to private persons (B2C) by an intermediary acting in the name of and on behalf of another person – the place of supply is where the transaction underlying the supply is made (see section 4.9 for further discussion on this topic).

When certain services are supplied cross-border, both the place of supply and the person liable to charge and account for the VAT changes. (This issue is considered in further detail in Chapter 4 – Cross-Border Trade.)

3.7 Rates of VAT Applied to Taxable Goods and Services

Once it has been established that a particular supply of goods or services is within the scope (charge) of VAT in Ireland (see the conditions at 3.2 and 3.6), then either of the following applies:

3 This includes rights/copyrights, advertising services, legal and accounting services, financial and insurance transactions, hiring out of moveable goods (excluding means of transport) telecommunications, broadcasting and electronically supplied services.

The supply of the goods or services is liable to VAT (referred to generally as "taxable supplies", or alternatively, "taxable goods" or "taxable services" as appropriate) at one of the following rates:

■ 0%	"the zero rate";
■ 4.8%	applicable to the sale of live cattle, sheep, goats, pigs, deer, (and certain horses)
■ 5.4%	"the flat rate"
■ 9%	This reduced rate applies to certain supplies (typically related to the tourism sector); the sale of horses (non-foodstuff), greyhounds & the hire of horses.
■ 13.5%	the reduced rate;
■ 23%	the standard rate.

or

The supply of the goods or service is exempt from VAT (referred to as "exempt supplies").

3.7.1 The zero rate

Goods and services liable to VAT at the zero rate are listed in Schedule 2, VATCA 2010. The zero rate applies to the following:

- goods exported to destinations outside the EU;
- goods dispatched to VAT-registered customers in other EU Member States;
- goods purchased by travellers for destinations outside the EU;
- transport services associated with the export and import of goods (to/from destinations outside the EU);
- the supply, repair and hiring of sea-going vessels of 15 tonnes or more;
- the supply, repair and hiring of aircraft used by a transport undertaking operating chiefly for reward on international routes;
- goods and services supplied to VAT 13B authorised businesses (see 4.10, Chapter 4);
- most animal feeds (excluding pet foods);
- most fertilisers (excluding packs of less than 10 kg weight);
- food and drink (with some notable exceptions, including: alcohol, soft drinks, biscuits, chocolate, ice cream, crisps, etc., meals served in a hotel, restaurant, etc., and hot take-away food);
- oral medicines (for people and animals);
- seeds and plants used for food production;

- books and certain other printed matter;
- children's clothing and footwear;
- certain medical equipment;
- the supply of goods or services to "International Bodies", recognised as such by the public authorities in their host Member State.

The list is not exhaustive – for a complete list, VATCA 2010 should be consulted.

Section 71 Finance Act 2014 introduced amendments to VATCA 2010 that updated the services exempt from VAT, e.g. fostering, green fees, management of defined contribution pension schemes.

3.7.2 The reduced rate (9%)

Goods and services liable to VAT at the reduced rate (9%) are listed in Schedule 3, VATCA 2010 (paragraphs 3(1–3), 7, 8, 11, 12, 13(3), 13B(1–3). The rate applies to the following:

- the provision of food and drink
  - by a vending machine, or
  - in a hotel, restaurant, canteen, etc. (excluding alcohol and soft drinks);
- the provision of hot food, i.e., food heated to above ambient room temperature at a take-away outlet, supermarket, garage, etc;
- cinema admissions;
- fairground amusement admissions;
- admissions to museums, galleries, exhibitions, open farms, historic buildings, etc., including those operated by recognised cultural bodies;
- newspapers,
- hotel, guesthouse and caravan/campsite lettings;
- hairdressing.
- The sale & hire of horses (non-foodstuff)
- the sale of greyhounds

3.7.3 The reduced rate (13.5%)

Goods and services liable to VAT at the reduced rate (13.5%) are listed in Schedule 3, VATCA 2010. The reduced rate applies to the following:

- solid fuel, electricity, gas and oil used for domestic or industrial heating;
- biscuits (non-chocolate);

- commercial sports facility charges;
- golf clubs (membership and green fees; note that green fees are exempt from 1 March 2015);
- veterinary services;
- agricultural services;
- seeds and bulbs used for the agricultural production of bio-fuels;
- live poultry and live ostriches;
- shrubs and plants supplied by nursery and garden centres (non-food producing);
- magazines & certain printed matter; short-term car hire;
- works of art;
- certain antiques and manuscripts;
- repairs of goods (movable and immovable);
- personal services (health studio (excluding sunbeds), manicure, etc.);
- non-oral contraceptives;
- most photography and development services;
- car-driving instruction;
- property (land and buildings);
- building work (see Chapter 6);
- concrete and concrete blocks;
- waste disposal.
- insemination services

The list is not exhaustive – for a complete list, VATCA 2010 should be consulted.

3.7.4 The standard rate

Where the supply of goods and/or services is within the charge of VAT, but is not liable to VAT at either the zero or reduced rate and is not exempt from VAT (see 3.8), then the standard rate (23%) applies. Thus, most goods and services not listed at 3.7.1, 3.7.2, 3.7.3 and 3.8 are liable to VAT at the standard rate. Examples include the supply of adult clothing, cosmetics, jewellery, motor cars, computers, accountancy/legal services, etc.

3.8 VAT-Exempt Supplies

Supplies of certain goods and services are exempt from VAT. This means that VAT is not applied to transactions involving such goods and services, even though the supply is within the scope of VAT.

It is very important to distinguish between transactions that are exempt from VAT and transactions that are liable to VAT at the zero rate. At first, they may appear the same, i.e., no actual VAT arises. However, that is where the similarity ends. In the case of zero-rated goods, the trader is obliged to register for VAT, is obliged to retain records and, most importantly, can recover VAT charged to him by other VAT-registered traders and VAT charged on the importation of goods by him/her. In the case of exempt supplies, generally speaking, the trader cannot recover VAT charged to him/her by other VAT-registered traders or VAT charged on the importation of goods by him/her. He/she cannot register for VAT and is obliged, under VAT law, to retain only very limited records.

Goods and services that are exempt from VAT are listed in Schedule 1 of VATCA 2010. Exemption applies to the following:

- most financial services, including:
  - trading in shares;
  - banking services;
  - granting and managing credit,
  - management of certain investment undertakings;
- insurance services;
- insurance agency services;
- public postal services;
- national broadcasting services;
- the letting of property (land and buildings), including residential and student accommodation;
- educational services; [see note below]*
- professional medical services;
- dental services, dentures and dental prostheses;
- optical services;
- hospital services;

- care and welfare services;
- home care services supplied by persons recognised by the HSE under section 61A of the Health Act 1970;
- catering services to patients in a hospital/nursing home and to students in a school;
- promotion of and admission to circuses live musical and theatrical events (where no facilities for food or drink are available during the performance);
- passenger and accompanying baggage transport;
- travel agents and tour operators;
- betting and lotteries;
- lotteries;
- supply of investment gold (other than to the Central Bank of Ireland);
- funeral undertaking;
- supplies for the benefit of members by certain organisations (e.g., society/union membership, etc.);
- sporting facilities run by not-for-profit organisations;
- supply of movable goods where a right to deduct input VAT or acquisition did not arise;
- water supplied by Local Authorities and by Irish Water.

The list is not exhaustive and for a complete list, VATCA 2010 should be consulted.

* Educational services

In April 2017 the Revenue Commissioners updated their Tax & Duty Manual at Chapter 05–59. They have set out comprehensively what educational services qualify for exemption and those that do not. However where educational services are provided to an educational institution as opposed to the student then such service is not exempt from VAT with an exception in the case of such services being provided to an education body by another recognised education body. The chapter also sets out the criteria for exempting (and taxing) the various categories of vocational training.

FA2017 updated VATCA2010 as to what qualifies for exemption under educational services.

3.9 Multiple and Composite Supplies

s47 VATCA 2010

Where two or more supplies (of goods and/or services) are made together, it may be difficult to determine whether there is a supply of a service, or goods, or both. Consequently there may be difficulty in determining the rate of VAT to apply to the supply or to particular parts of the supply. This is a very complex area and has been the subject of a number of Appeal hearings in Ireland and judgements by the CJEU.

Since 1 May 2006, where more than one supply of goods and/or services are jointly supplied as part of a package for a single consideration, the supply is treated for VAT purposes as either a "composite supply" or as a "multiple supply". The legislation defines both but in order to fully understand each, three other types of supplies are defined, namely an individual supply, a principal supply and an ancillary supply.

3.9.1 Composite supply

A "composite supply" means a supply comprising two or more supplies of goods and/or services made in conjunction with each other, where one of the supplies is a principal supply and the other supplies are ancillary supplies.

A "principal supply" means the supply of goods or services which constitute the predominant part of a composite supply and to which any other supply made in conjunction with it is an ancillary supply.

An "ancillary supply" means a supply which is not physically and economically dissociable from a principal supply and can only be supplied as a means of better enjoying the principal supply.

In the case of composite supply, the VAT rate applicable to the entire composite supply will be the VAT rate applicable to the principal supply.

Example 3.3

A coal merchant supplies coal in bags at a single price per bagful. The supply of the bag is incidental to the supply of the coal. The supply of the bag of coal is liable to VAT at the reduced rate of 13.5%, notwithstanding that the rate of VAT applying to the coal bag is the standard rate, 23%.

3.9.2 Multiple supply

A "multiple supply" means two or more individual supplies made in conjunction with each other for a total consideration (price) covering all of the supplies and where the individual supplies do not constitute a "composite supply".

An "individual supply" is a supply of goods or services which forms part of a multiple supply but which is capable of being a supply of goods or a supply of a service in its own right.

In the case of a multiple supply (i.e. a supply consisting of more than one individual supply) the consideration will be apportioned between the various individual supplies and rates of VAT appropriate to each individual supply will be applied.

Example 3.4

A bookshop supplies a school book and an exercise book for a single consideration, neither of which is described as being supplied 'free'. Both are capable of being enjoyed independently and neither is designed to enhance the use/enjoyment of the other. The school book is liable to VAT at 0% and the exercise book is liable to VAT at the standard rate, 23%. The retailer will apportion the consideration received and will account for output VAT as appropriate.

3.9.3 Relevant case law

The matter of what constitutes a multiple or composite supply has been made further complicated by the recent determination of the CJEU in the case of Talacre (case C-251/05). In its judgement the Court held that the supply of a caravan/mobile-home with fittings was in fact a single supply, liable to VAT at two different rates, one for the caravan and one for the fitted furnishings (fridge, cooker, etc.). [Many would previously have considered the supply to be either a composite or multiple supplies.] In a more recent decision of the Court it has been held a single supply of a service may be subject to more than one rate of VAT [Commission v France case C-94/09] The Court stated "*... subject to compliance with the principle of fiscal neutrality inherent in the common system of VAT, Member States may apply a reduced rate of VAT to concrete and specific aspects of a category of supply covered by...*"

No doubt there will be further litigation in this area before the question of composite/multiple supplies is fully "bedded down".

3.10 The "Two-Thirds Rule"

s41 VATCA 2010 The "Two-Thirds Rule" applies where there is a contract for the supply of a service which involves the supply of goods (in order to apply, it is important that the contract be for the supply of a service and not for the supply of goods). An often-quoted example of where the two-thirds rule might apply is the repairing of a washing machine which requires the replacement of parts.

Where the VAT-exclusive cost of the goods in a contract for the supply of a service is less than two-thirds of the total contract price, the rate of VAT applicable to the entire supply is the rate applicable to the supply of the service provided as part of the contract.

Example 3.5

A property developer contracts with a plumber to supply and lay pipes for a number of houses which he is building. The plumber quotes a price of €225,000 plus VAT for the job.

The pipes and fittings cost the plumber €148,000 plus VAT. He prices his labour at €77,000.

As the cost of the materials to the builder does not exceed €150,000 (two-thirds of €225,000), the rate applicable to the service, 13.5%, is applied to the entire supply by the plumber. Thus, he will invoice the property developer for €225,000 plus €30,375 VAT.

Where the VAT-exclusive cost of the goods in a contract for the supply of a service exceeds two-thirds of the contract price, the rate of VAT applicable to the supply of the goods is applied to the entire contract. In general, this means that the standard rate (currently 23%) is applied to the entire contract, instead of the reduced rate (currently 13.5%).

Where the VAT-exclusive cost of goods exceeds two-thirds of the contract price, the supplier may still apply the reduced rate of VAT to the service element of the contract when he/she shows separate consideration for the goods and for the service. The goods will be liable at the rate of VAT applicable to the goods – generally, the standard rate.

Example 3.6

A bank contracts with a specialist supplier for the supply and installation of a safe at its premises. The specialist installer quotes a price of €500,000 for the supply and installation of the safe.

The cost of the safe to the installer is €400,000 and the installation charge amounts to €100,000.

As the cost of the safe to the installer exceeds two-thirds of €500,000, the rate applicable to the entire supply is 23%. However, as the recipient of the service is a bank, which is carrying on a VAT-exempt activity and as such cannot recover input VAT, the installer should consider showing separate consideration for the safe and for the installation, thus enabling him to apply 13.5% VAT to the installation cost.

3.11 Deduction of Input VAT

s59–64 VATCA 2010

Central to the operation of a value-added tax system is a right, on the part of the VAT-registered person, to deduct input VAT charged to him/her by suppliers of goods and services, and a right to deduct VAT charged at the point of entry on imports. VAT should not be a cost on the trader, but rather a cost for the final consumer.

Consider a retailer who purchases goods and then applies VAT on the sale. The retailer has paid VAT to his supplier when acquiring the goods for resale. In order to ensure that the charge of VAT is a cost only to the consumer, the retailer may, in computing his/her VAT liability, deduct the input VAT charged to him/her by suppliers. This right of deduction does not apply just to input VAT incurred on goods resold but extends to all input VAT incurred on purchases made to enable the VAT-registered trader carry on his/her business.

Thus, where a retailer incurs VAT on acquiring, he/she is entitled to reclaim from Revenue the VAT incurred on the acquisition. Similarly, where a haulier incurs input VAT on a truck or on diesel, he/she may reclaim the input VAT incurred.

In computing the amount of VAT he/she must pay over to the Revenue, the VAT-registered trader may claim a deduction for input VAT incurred. Where the output VAT payable on his/her supplies of goods and services exceeds the input VAT deductible on his/her purchases, an amount (the difference) is payable to Revenue. Where the input VAT deductible on his/her purchases exceeds the output VAT payable on his/her supplies of goods and services, the excess amount is reclaimed from Revenue.

Only a VAT-registered trader may deduct input VAT.

Sometimes a deduction of input VAT is referred to as a "recovery of input VAT" by the VAT-registered trader. You should be familiar and comfortable with the use of either deduction or recovery in relation to input VAT.

Deduction of input VAT is considered in further detail in Chapter 5 (Accounting for VAT: Invoicing, Deductions and Special Procedures/Categories).

3.12 Taxable Persons

A "taxable person" is any person who independently carries on any business in the State, elsewhere in the EU or anywhere in the world. Therefore, the concept of a taxable person covers persons who supply, in the course of business, goods and services which are liable to VAT and/or goods and services which are exempt from VAT.

A taxable person who supplies goods or services within the State, which are liable to VAT is also an "accountable person".

3.13 Accountable Persons

s5–18 VATCA 2010

The term "accountable person" is given to the person who is obliged to, or elects to, register for value-added tax, or to a person who waives exemption/opts to tax and registers for value-added tax. An accountable person is the only person who can legally charge VAT on a supply of goods or services within the State.

An accountable person charges VAT on his/her supplies (output VAT) and may recover VAT incurred on the purchase of goods and services (input VAT), with some notable exceptions (see section 5.3.2).

The Revenue Commissioners maintain a register of accountable persons. A VAT registration number is issued to each person who so registers. The VAT registration number consists of the letter IE followed by seven numeric characters and one alpha character, e.g., IE 9907112K. (The IE identifies the VAT registration as having being issued in Ireland.)

3.13.1 Persons obliged to register and account for VAT

The following persons are obliged to register for VAT:

- established traders supplying taxable goods only, with an annual turnover in excess of €75,000 in a continuous 12-month period;
- established traders supplying taxable services only, with an annual turnover in excess of €37,500 in a continuous 12-month period;
- established traders supplying both goods and services, where the turnover from the supply of taxable goods is at least 90% of the total turnover, must register for VAT if turnover exceeds or is likely to exceed €75,000 in a continuous 12-month period;
- established traders supplying both goods and services, where the turnover from the supply of taxable services exceeds 10% of total turnover, must register when total annual turnover exceeds €37,500 in a continuous 12-month period;
- non-established traders (foreign traders) supplying goods/services in Ireland, regardless of turnover;
- With effect from 1 September 2008 principal contractors who receive supplies of services consisting of construction operations from subcontractors;
- business persons who receive certain services from abroad (see section 4.4);

- business persons who acquire goods (value in excess of €41,000) from other EU Member States (see section 4.3.2);
- foreign traders who sell goods from abroad to persons in Ireland who are not registered for VAT (distance selling – see section 4.3.3) and whose annual turnover exceeds €35,000 in a calendar year.
- Government departments, government agencies and local authorities that receive certain services from abroad (see section 4.4) or that acquire goods (value in excess of €41,000) from other EU Member States (see section 4.3.2);

3.13.2 Persons who exercise a "landlord's option to tax"

In certain circumstances a landlord may opt to tax rental income in respect of the letting of property, which would otherwise be an exempt supply of a service. (see Chapter 6 for a fuller discussion on this.)

3.13.3 Persons who exercise a "joint option for taxation"

In certain circumstances the vendor and purchaser of property, the supply of which would otherwise be exempt from VAT, may jointly exercise an option in writing to have VAT chargeable on the supply of the property. (see Chapter 6 for a fuller discussion on this.)

3.13.4 Persons who "waive a right to exemption" in respect of a supply of investment gold

[see 3.15 below]

3.13.5 Electing to register for VAT

The following persons may voluntarily elect to register and account for VAT, although they are not obliged by law to do so:

- established traders whose turnover from the supply of taxable goods or services does not exceed the thresholds indicated above;
- farmers;
- sea fishermen who supply unprocessed fish to other accountable persons (e.g., to retailers, processors, etc.).

Some advantages of electing to register for VAT

VAT incurred on most business expenses, including set-up costs, may be recovered if a trader is registered for VAT. Often, input VAT on setup costs may be at the standard rate (currently 23%), while output VAT may be at the reduced (currently 13.5%) or zero rates. Thus, there may be a cash-flow advantage for the business in registering for VAT.

For example, a small café will charge VAT to its customers at a rate of 13.5% but may be in a position to reclaim VAT on the cost of furniture, fittings and equipment at a rate of 23%. Accordingly, in a start-up situation (at which time the business is least likely to exceed the relevant turnover threshold), voluntarily registering for VAT may lead to a VAT refund.

A person who supplies zero-rated children's clothes is likely to find him/herself in receipt of VAT refunds on a regular basis. VAT on outputs will be zero, while VAT on inputs (e.g., telephone expenses, electricity, etc.) will be at various rates of up to 23%.

Some disadvantages of electing to register for VAT

The main disadvantage of electing to register for VAT is the increased administrative burden:

- The business will be obliged to comply with the relevant VAT legislation and regulations, e.g., it will be obliged to issue VAT invoices, retain records that it otherwise would not have been obliged to retain and file returns on a regular basis. Such procedures can be expensive and time-consuming.
- The business will run the risk of being subjected to a VAT inspection and of being exposed to penalties and interest in respect of any additional amounts of VAT found to be due.
- The business may have to repay certain amounts of input VAT recovered upon cancellation of an election.

Given the very low thresholds for registration currently in force, the choice of electing to register for VAT will be available to only a very small minority of traders. More often than not, it will only be something that a trader who is employed and who sets up a small "after-hours" business will consider.

Where a trade is below the threshold for obligatory VAT registration, when deciding whether or not to elect to register for VAT consideration may be made of whether or not a trader is making supplies to other VAT-registered traders or private individuals.

Where supplies are being made to other VAT-registered traders, the additional charging of VAT will not increase the cost to the buyer. Where the customer is a private individual, adding VAT to the sales price may either make the supply too costly or may erode the profit for the traderI (in this regard, the rate of VAT applicable to the trader's goods or services is also relevant, i.e., whether it is 0%, 9%, 13.5% or 23%).

3.14 VAT Group Registration

s15 VATCA 2010

A number of accountable persons (including companies and individuals who make taxable or exempt supplies which are within the scope of VAT) and non-taxable persons may apply to the Revenue Commissioners for "group registration". The Revenue

Commissioners may grant group registration status to the applicants where they are satisfied that the applicants are closely bound by:

- financial,
- organisational, and
- economic links.

In general, the applicants must be under common control, i.e., one or other of the applicants must exercise control over the others through share-ownership or otherwise. All applicants must be established in the State and an applicant may only be a member of one VAT group.

Each group member will continue to issue and receive VAT invoices in their own name in respect of transactions with non-group members.

The effect of the VAT grouping is to treat all VAT group members as a single accountable person insofar as VAT is concerned.

Once the VAT group registration has been approved, one of the applicants, the nominated group remitter, will file VAT returns on behalf of the group. VAT returns for the other individual companies are no longer necessary. The other members are designated "non-remitters" and cannot file VAT returns. The "group remitter" completes form VAT 52 and the "non-remitter(s)" each complete form VAT 53 to apply to be treated as a VAT group.

VAT is generally not applied to transactions between group members[4]. Therefore, where one group member supplies goods or services to another group member, there is no requirement to issue a VAT invoice and VAT is not applied to the consideration.

While the VAT grouping provides administrative and possibly cash-flow benefits for the members, it should be noted that one of the effects of group membership is joint and several liability in relation to the VAT liability of any group member. For this reason, you generally do not find individuals or partnerships of individuals in VAT groups.

Where some of the VAT group members make VAT-exempt supplies (see section 3.8) the inclusion of such business in the group may dilute the input VAT recovery (see section 5.3.3) of the group as a whole. The input VAT recovery of the group must reflect the input VAT recovery of each member of the VAT group.

The Revenue Commissioners may compulsorily group-register companies that have financial, economic and organisational links where it would be in the interests of efficient administration of the tax, or collection of the tax, to do so.

4 It should be noted that property transactions between group members are excluded from the provisions of group membership, i.e., a supply of property from one group member to another may attract VAT.

In case C-85/11, involving VAT groups, the court, in its judgment of 9 April 2013, dismissed the infraction proceedings taken by the Commission against Ireland and held that it was permissible for non-taxable persons to become members of VAT groups.

3.15 Waiver of Exemption

A person who supplies investment gold may waive exemption from VAT, register for VAT and recover input VAT incurred on the purchase of gold while continuing to exempt the supply of investment gold (which he/she has converted the gold into).

A formal application must be made to Revenue (local tax office) to waive exemption. A waiver is not normally backdated prior to the taxable period in which the application is made.

3.16 The Taxable Amount (Consideration)

The amount on which tax is chargeable, sometimes referred to as the "consideration", must be ascertained in order to apply the charge of VAT.

In most instances, the amount is easily identifiable. For us, the general public, the price being displayed will be the taxable amount inclusive of the charge of VAT. For traders (e.g., buying from wholesalers/distributors), the price quoted is the taxable amount exclusive of VAT.

s36–45 VATCA 2010 The legislation defines the amount on which tax is chargeable as being

> *"...the total consideration which the person supplying goods or services becomes entitled to receive in respect of or in relation to such supply of goods or services, including all taxes, commissions, costs and charges whatsoever but not including value-added tax chargeable in respect of the supply."*

Where the consideration does not consist wholly of money, the amount on which tax is chargeable is an amount equal to the open-market price of the goods or services supplied.

s36 VATCA 2010 If, for any "non-business reason", the consideration is less than the open-market value, then the amount on which tax is chargeable is the open-market price.

This is a very important piece of legislation. Where Revenue believes that the amount on which the VAT charge has been calculated is below market value, anti-avoidance legislation enables it to impose market value and insist that the charge of VAT be calculated on the open-market price.

s38 VATCA 2010 Additional anti-avoidance legislation enables an officer of the Revenue Commissioners to determine the value on which VAT is chargeable on certain transactions between connected persons.

s10(4) VA 72 As outlined at 3.4 above, the use of goods for exempt purposes or the appropriation of goods for private use by an accountable person constitute taxable supplies, and the taxable amount for the purpose of charging VAT is the cost to the accountable person of acquiring the goods. Thus, where a car-dealer gives a new car from stock to his daughter, he must calculate the output VAT on the cost to him (exclusive of VAT) of acquiring the car.

3.17 "Deeming" Provisions in VAT Legislation

One of the less straightforward aspects of VAT is the use of "deeming provisions". Sometimes, a supply arises in circumstances where there is no consideration and/or where it is not in the "course or furtherance of business" – remember the conditions necessary for a charge of VAT.

Consider the case of the car-dealer who gifts a car to his daughter – there is no consideration and it is not in the course or furtherance of business. In order for a charge of VAT to arise, the supply is "deemed" to be for a consideration (the cost of acquiring the car) and it is "deemed" to be in the course or furtherance of business.

In the case of installed or assembled goods, the place of supply is "deemed" to be where the assembly or installation takes place. It could be where the supplier was located, it could be where the customer was located, but to define exactly where it is, VAT legislation uses the concept of "deeming".

In the case of a supply of food by a hotel, the legislation "deems" it to be a supply of a service and not a supply of goods.

In the case of an undisclosed agent, the VAT legislation "deems" that there is a simultaneous supply of a service to the agent and by the agent.

Where a local authority acquires goods from another EU Member State, the acquisition is "deemed" to have been made in the "course or furtherance of business" for the purpose of establishing a charge of VAT.

VATCA 2010 contains throughout the word "deemed", and it is a concept which you should understand, as it is necessary to ensure that certain transactions come within the charge (scope) to VAT. It may be small comfort, but a UK Appeal Court Judge once said of VAT and VAT practitioners:

> *"Beyond the everyday world, both Counsel have explained to us, lies the world of VAT, a kind of fiscal theme park in which factual and legal realities are suspended or inverted ... in this complex parallel universe relatively uncomplicated solutions are a snare and a diversion."*
>
> *– Lord Justice Sedley, Court of Appeal (E & W);*
> *Case: Royal and Sun Alliance Insurance Group plc. (co/3494/99).*

3.18 Self-accounting for VAT- [as applied to domestic transactions] - 'Reverse Charge'

s16 VATCA 2010

The concept of the 'reverse charge' is one which you need to familiarize yourself for a proper understanding of VAT. As the name implies, the term 'reverse charge' means that the obligation to charge VAT applies to the receiver of the service and not to the supplier of the service. Thus in situations where the 'reverse charge' applies it is the receiver of the service who must account for the VAT arising on the transaction and the supplier of the service must not charge, levy or account for the VAT arising.

The 'reverse charge' procedure is generally applied domestically in situations where VAT avoidance and evasion constitute a significant risk. Currently the 'reverse charge' procedure is applied, *inter alia*, to the following situations:

Construction Operations

s530(1) (a)–(f) TCA97

Where a construction service (see s530, TCA) is supplied to a principal (see s531(1), TCA97) then the principal is the accountable person in relation to that supply and the sub-contractor cannot charge VAT on his supply.

Finance Act 2012 introduced new obligations relating to accounting for VAT in certain supplies of construction services. Where a construction service is supplied by a person who is connected[5] with the recipient of the service then the recipient is the accountable person in relation to that supply and the supplier cannot charge VAT on his supply.

Scrap dealers (Finance Act 2011)

Finance Act 2011 extended the application of the 'reverse charge' procedure to persons engaged in the supply of scrap metal. Thus where any person in business supplies scrap metal to another person in business the recipient of the supply of the scrap must account for VAT arising on the value of the supply received. The person supplying the scrap metal cannot charge VAT on his supply.

Certain supplies to the National Asset Management Agency

Where the transfer of property to NAMA is effected by way of a 'vesting order' then NAMA must account for VAT arising on the supply received. The transferor of the property cannot charge VAT on his supply.

Who carries on business in the State must account for the VAT arising on the supply received. The vendor of the allowances cannot charge VAT on his supply.

5 Connected persons are defined at s97(3), VATCA 2010 and covers all manner of personal and corporate relationships.

Electricity, Gas & Certificates In Electricity/Gas

With effect from 1 Jan 2016 supplies of electricity/gas by a taxable person to a wholesaler (taxable dealer) of electricity/gas is subject to the reverse charge. The sale of electricity/gas certificates from one taxable person to anotherr will also be subject to VAT on the reverse charge basis, effective from 1 Jan 2016. The invoice issued by the supplier must indicate that the 'reverse charge' is applicable.

3.19 Summary

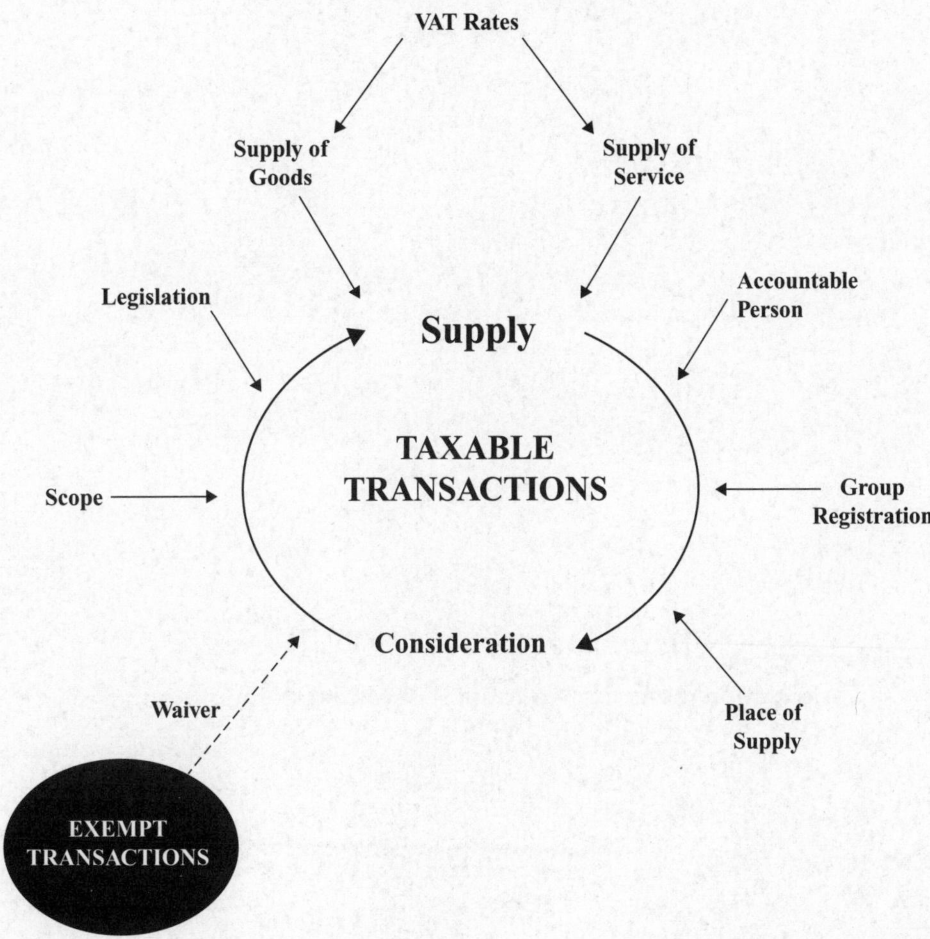

4 CROSS-BORDER TRADE

Learning Outcomes

On completion of this chapter you will be able to:

- ✓ Discuss the VAT implications of engaging in international trade with other EU Member States and with non-EU countries.
- ✓ Describe the distinction between the VAT treatment of goods and services supplied to and received from foreign traders.
- ✓ Explain the difference between exports/imports and dispatches/acquisitions, and describe the VAT treatment of each.
- ✓ List the circumstances in which VAT must be accounted for on intra-Community acquisitions.
- ✓ Explain the concept of "triangulation".
- ✓ Identify the place of supply of a variety of services supplied to or received from other countries.
- ✓ Explain the reverse charge principle.
- ✓ Identify the place of supply of intra-Community transport services.
- ✓ Describe the means of mitigating and/or recovering VAT on certain cross-border trade and the means for improving the cash-flow position of businesses involved in international trade.
- ✓ The place of supply of services provided by intermediaries.
- ✓ Describe the filing requirements in relation to cross-border trade in goods and services.
- ✓ Be aware of intermediary service rules.
- ✓ Be aware of the new rules relating to the supply of telecommnications, broadcasting and e-services to Consumers within the EU post 1 January 2015
- ✓ Complete Assignments and Questions in the corresponding chapter in *Irish Taxation: Law and Practice*, Volume 2.

4.1 Introduction

With Ireland's accession to the then EEC in January 1973, the creation of the Single Market in January 1993 and the growth during the 'Celtic Tiger' (and post-Celtic Tiger) years, trade with other EU Member States and third countries (those outside the EU) has expanded. Nowadays, almost every Irish business has some cross-border trading activity.

The Single Market refers to the economic marketplace, consisting of all 28 EU Member States. Historically, VAT presented one of the barriers to trade within the EU. With effect from 1 January 1993, measures were put in place, in so far as is possible and primarily in relation to goods, to ensure VAT does not act as a barrier to cross-border trade within the EU. Recently, further barriers to trade have been removed through the harmonisation of invoicing requirements (which is still ongoing) and the removal of the obligation for businesses in one Member State to appoint a fiscal representative in another Member State when trading there.

Further enhancements to the VAT system have been put in place via Council Directives 2008/8/EC, 2008/9/EC and 2008/117/EC which commenced in January 2010, and which should further reduce barriers to cross-border trade within the EU.

The most recent changes to the VAT treatment of cross-border services came into effect on 1 January 2015. These are very fundamental changes and once again have, as their aim, the removal of barriers to cross-border trade, while at the same time ensuring the integrity and security of the VAT system. [This chapter will discuss the VAT rules relating to cross-border trade as they currently operate].

Whether it be a multinational exporting computers to the USA, a fruit distributor acquiring oranges from Spain, a local authority buying a fire engine in the UK, or an Irish architect designing an office block in France, a transaction has occurred and thought must be given to applying the correct VAT treatment. From a that perspective, the following important distinctions must be made in order to apply the correct VAT treatment to cross-border trade:

- trade in goods or trade in services;
- goods and services supplied into Ireland and goods and services supplied out of Ireland;
- trade with other EU Member States and trade with third countries (non-EU countries); and
- trade with other businesses (B2B) and trade with consumers (B2C).

4.2 Goods Leaving Ireland

We will first look at cross-border trade in goods. Goods leaving Ireland may either be exported to third countries or dispatched to another EU Member State (B2B or B2C).

4.2.1 Goods exported to third countries (non-EU countries)

Place of supply

s32 VATCA 2010

As discussed previously (see 3.6, Chapter 3), the place of supply in relation to goods requiring transportation (as all goods to be exported require) is where transportation

Note that the terms "import" and "export" are not used in relation to trade with other EU Member States since the inception of the Single Market in January 1993. Instead, we refer to "intra-Community supplies" or "dispatches" (supplies to other EU Member States) and "intra-Community acquisitions" (supplies received from other EU Member States).

begins. Therefore, the place of supply is Ireland and a charge to VAT arises in Ireland. The goods must leave the country.

Rate of VAT

Sch2 VATCA 2010 The rate of VAT applicable to goods that are exported is 0% in all circumstances. The rate applicable to such goods if supplied within Ireland is ignored, and whether the purchaser is in business or is a private individual is irrelevant. The logic behind this zero-rating is to ensure that Irish products remain competitive in an international context. If domestic rates of VAT were applied to exports, traders based in jurisdictions with low VAT rates would have a competitive advantage over Irish traders. Furthermore, as VAT is a tax on consumption, we should recall that consumption in relation to exports will occur outside of Ireland.

Evidence of export

The legislation does not specify what constitutes evidence of export. However, an accountable person must retain sufficient evidence that the goods have been exported. Such evidence will include a cargo bill of lading, a cargo manifest, evidence of payment from abroad, contract for sale, etc.

In the absence of evidence, a Revenue official may contend that the goods have never left the country and apply the rate that would be appropriate if the goods were sold within the country.

Transportation and ancillary services

Transportation and ancillary transport services (loading, unloading, packing, etc.) supplied in Ireland in respect of the export of goods are liable to VAT at 0%. Therefore, the internal leg of the transport contract, e.g., from the factory in Athlone to the port in Cork, is also liable to VAT at 0%.

4.2.2 Goods dispatched to persons registered for VAT in other EU Member States ("Intra-Community dispatches", or "B2B supplies")

Where goods are dispatched from Ireland to VAT-registered traders in other EU Member States, the accountable person (in Ireland) must obtain and include his/her customer's VAT registration number on the invoice issued. He/she must also retain evidence that the goods have been dispatched. If the customer fails to supply a valid VAT registration number, then the provisions, outlined at 4.2.3 below, apply. The VAT-registered customer in the other EU Member State makes an intra-Community acquisition of the goods (see 4.3.2 below).

Place of supply

s29 VATCA 2010 As discussed previously (see 3.6.1, Chapter 3), the place of supply in relation to goods requiring transportation (as all goods to be dispatched require) is where transportation begins. Therefore, the place of supply is Ireland and a charge to VAT arises in Ireland.

Rate of VAT

Sch2 VATCA 2010 The rate of VAT applicable to goods that are dispatched to customers registered for VAT in other EU Member States is 0%. The goods must leave the country.

Evidence of dispatch

The legislation does not specify what constitutes evidence of dispatch. However, an accountable person must retain sufficient evidence that the goods have been dispatched. Such evidence will include the customer's VAT registration number, a cargo bill of lading, a cargo manifest, evidence of payment from abroad, contract for sale, etc. Because of the risk posed by "carousel fraud",[1] Revenue will be particularly vigilant.

4.2.3 Goods dispatched to persons not registered for VAT in other EU Member States ("distance selling", or "B2C supplies")

s30 VATCA 2010 Generally, distance selling applies to mail-order sales and goods advertised on the Internet but physically supplied cross-border B2C.

Place of supply

Where physical goods are dispatched by an accountable person established in Ireland, to persons not registered for VAT who reside in other EU Member States, the place of supply is Ireland, once a particular threshold in relation to such sales has not been breached.

However, once the threshold has been breached, the Irish-established trader must register for VAT in the country to which the goods have been dispatched and, accordingly, that country is the place of supply (alternatively, the Irish trader need not wait until the threshold is breached and may elect to register for VAT in the country to which the goods are dispatched from the outset). The trader is not required to have a presence in the country to register for VAT.

Registration threshold

The registration threshold for distance selling into Luxembourg, Austria, Germany, France and the Netherlands is €100,000 per calendar year. The registration threshold for distance selling into Ireland, Spain, Belgium, Finland, Greece and Portugal is €35,000 per calendar year. The registration threshold for distance selling into Italy is €27,889.

The registration thresholds for non-Euro countries are currently as follows:

- UK (including the Isle of Man): Stg£80,000 per calendar year;
- Sweden: SEK320,000 per calendar year;

1 "Carousel fraud" is the term given to a particular type of VAT fraud facilitated by the Single Market. It usually involves high-worth, low-volume goods (e.g., computer parts). The goods are invoiced from trader to trader across several EU Member States with a particular trader "dropping out" of the chain. This trader will supply the goods, most probably to a legitimate trader in the same Member State as himself/herself, and will not account for the VAT invoiced. The customer will deduct the VAT charged because he/she will have a valid VAT invoice. It is estimated that carousel fraud costs the UK exchequer c. Stg£1.5 billion per year.

- Denmark: DKK280,000 per calendar year;
- The more recent EU Member States have each set a distance-selling threshold in local currency equivalent approximately to €35,000.

Rate of VAT

Where goods are dispatched and the threshold is not reached, and the Irish trader does not elect to register in the other EU Member State(s), then Irish VAT at the appropriate rate is applied to the goods.

Once the Irish trader registers for VAT in the other EU Member State(s), then the place of supply is the country of destination and local VAT is applied to the goods.

4.3 Goods Coming into Ireland

Goods coming into Ireland are either imported from third countries or acquired from another EU Member State.

4.3.1 Goods imported from third countries

Place of supply

s3 VATCA 2010 Where goods are imported from third countries the place of supply is the point of importation.

Rate of VAT

VAT is applied to the total cost price (CIF), including any custom, excise, insurance and landing costs (transport costs) payable. The rate of VAT applicable is the same as that applicable to the supply of such goods within Ireland.

Thus, where a load of concrete blocks is imported from China, the rate of VAT applicable is 13.5%. Where a consignment of bananas is imported from Equador, the rate of VAT applicable is 0%. Where computer parts are imported from Japan, the rate of VAT applicable is 23%. The logic behind the application of VAT at the point of importation is again to ensure that Irish suppliers remain competitive relative to their foreign counterparts. If Irish VAT was not applied at the point of importation, then, all other things being equal, it would be cheaper for Irish customers to import products from abroad than it would be to purchase identical products from an Irish supplier.

However, where the importer has a VAT 13B authorisation, the rate of VAT applicable to the imported goods is 0% (see 4.10 below).

Transportation and ancillary services

The supply of domestic/intra-EU goods transport services in connection with the importation of goods, where the value of those services is already included in the declared value of the goods at importation, is zero-rated (see paragraph (2(2), Schedule 2, VAT 2010). The haulier supplying such services will be required to retain documentary evidence to support the zero rating. This may take the form of verification from the customs clearance agent or shipping company, etc.

4.3.2 Goods acquired from other EU Member States by persons registered (or required to register) for VAT in Ireland ("intra-Community acquisitions")

s3 VATCA 2010

Since 1 January 1993, a charge to Irish VAT arises on the acquisition of goods from other EU Member States. Sections 3(d) & (e), VATCA 2010 state:

> *"… a tax called value-added tax is, …, chargeable, leviable and payable on the following transactions;*
>
> *(d) the intra-Community acquisition for consideration by an accountable person of goods (other than new means of transport) when the place of supply Is the State;*
>
> *(e) the intra-Community acquisition for consideration of new means of transport when the acquisition is made within the State."*

This is a very important concept. We normally think of VAT applying to the supply of goods. However, in this case the legislation stipulates that the charge to VAT also applies to the acquisition of goods in certain circumstances.

s24 VATCA 2010

An intra-Community acquisition is deemed to occur where the dispatch or transportation of the goods ends in the Member State that issued the VAT registration number of the acquirer.

The procedure is a simple transposition of the procedure outlined in 4.2.2 (the dispatch of goods to a trader registered for VAT in another EU Member State). Accordingly, where an Irish-registered trader wishes to acquire goods from a French supplier, the Irish trader will furnish the French supplier with his/her Irish VAT number, the French trader will zero rate the goods in France and the Irish trader will account for Irish VAT on the acquisition in Ireland on his/her VAT return.

Where the Irish trader is not registered for VAT in Ireland, French VAT should be applied (see 4.3.3 below).

The procedure is discussed in further detail below and differs slightly where the subject matter of the intra-Community acquisition is a new means of transport.

Acquisition of goods by VAT-registered persons

s24 VATCA 2010

In the case of goods, other than new means of transport, only accountable persons (VAT-registered persons) must account ("self-account") for the charge of VAT on the value of the intra-Community acquisitions, i.e., acquisitions from other EU Member States. This principle is known as the "reverse charge". It is a very important principle.

Two important issues arise at this point, firstly, who must register and account for the VAT and, secondly, how do such registered persons self-account for the VAT in Ireland?

Who must self-account for VAT in Ireland in respect of intra-Community acquisitions?

s9 VATCA 2010

Anyone in business in Ireland who acquires goods (intra-Community acquisitions) totaling in excess of €41,000 in a continuous period of 12 months must register and account for VAT in respect of the acquisitions, if he/she is not already registered for VAT in Ireland in respect of VATable supplies.

By presenting his/her VAT registration number to the vendor in the other EU Member State, the person who acquires the goods will avoid the charge of foreign VAT.

The obligation to register and self-account for VAT in respect of intra-Community acquisitons extends to certain categories of persons who may not make accountable supplies in the normal course of their activities. Thus, anyone making VAT-exempt supplies – such as banks, insurance providers, hospitals, schools, charities, trades unions, unregistered farmers and fishermen, local authorities, Government departments, and statutory bodies, etc. is required to register for VAT in respect of intra-Community acquisitions. Such registration will only apply in respect of the intra-Community acquisition of the goods.

How is VAT accounted for on intra-Community acquisitions?

Once registered for VAT, the person accounts for VAT on the intra-Community acquisition by showing the VAT charged on the acquisition as output VAT on his/her VAT return.

In the case of accountable persons making taxable supplies in Ireland (i.e., persons registered for VAT in respect of taxable supplies of goods or services), a simultaneous input VAT credit for the same amount may be taken on the same return. This has the effect of rendering the intra-Community acquisition VAT neutral (i.e., output VAT = input VAT).

Thus, the outcome is similar to the accountable person buying the goods in Ireland. The Irish supplier will charge the trader VAT, but the trader will be in a position to recover the input VAT on his/her VAT return. Accordingly, the VAT will not be a cost.

Example 4.1

An Irish VAT-registered trader purchases a computer in France. He quotes his VAT registration and receives the goods without a charge of VAT. The acquisition of the goods creates an obligation on the Irish trader to account for VAT.

Thus, the trader will account for output VAT on the value of the goods received. However, as he/she uses the goods for the purposes of his/her taxable supplies, he/she may deduct a similar amount of input VAT. This renders the transaction VAT neutral.

In contrast, for persons not making taxable supplies (i.e., anyone making VAT-exempt supplies) who were obliged to register in respect of the intra-Community acquisition, an input VAT deduction may not be made. The output VAT (the charge of VAT arising on the acquisition) must be remitted by the VAT-registered person to the Collector-General.

Thus, the outcome is similar to the person buying the goods in Ireland. The Irish supplier will charge the insurance company VAT, but the insurance company will not be able to recover the input VAT, as it uses the computer for VAT-exempt supplies.

Example 4.2

An Irish insurance company purchases computers for €50,000 in France. As its supplies are VAT-exempt, it is not registered for VAT. As the value of its intra-Community acquisitions exceeds €41,000, it must register for VAT in Ireland. It quotes its VAT registration number to its cross-border supplier and receives the goods without a charge of VAT. The acquisition of the goods creates an obligation on the insurance company to account for VAT.

Thus, the insurance company will account for output VAT on the value of the goods received. However, as it uses the goods for the purposes of its VAT-exempt insurance supplies, it may not deduct input VAT (see below).

Acquisition of new means of transport

The legislation applies to everyone (whether or not an accountable person) in the case of new means of transport (which are defined in the legislation at section 1(1) and includes new cars, new pleasure crafts and new small aircraft). Thus, when anyone already registered for VAT in Ireland or someone not registered for VAT (e.g. a private individual), acquires a new means of transport from another EU Member State, he/she must account for VAT in respect of the acquisition. He/she must pay Irish VAT on the value of the means of transport. The vendor will not apply local VAT when he is satisfied that the new means of transport is dispatched from the Member State where purchased (see 4.2.2).

In the case of persons not already registered for VAT (private individuals), payment of the VAT is made at a local vehicle registration tax (VRT) office, operated by the Revenue Commissioners.

4.3.3 Goods acquired from other EU Member States by persons not registered (or required to register) for VAT in Ireland

Place of supply

Where physical goods are dispatched to Irish-resident persons not registered for VAT (usually, but not always, B2C trade) by an accountable person established in another EU Member State, the place of supply can be the Member State from which the goods are dispatched. However, once a certain threshold (€35,000 in the case of Ireland) is reached, the foreign-established trader must register for VAT in Ireland and, accordingly, the place of supply will be Ireland. Alternatively, they need not wait until the threshold is reached and may elect to register for VAT in Ireland from the outset.

VAT applicable

Where goods are dispatched and the threshold is not reached, and the foreign trader does not elect to register in Ireland, then the rate of VAT applicable in the country of dispatch is applied to the goods.

Once the foreign trader registers for VAT in Ireland, then the place of supply is Ireland and Irish VAT is applied to the goods. The trader is not required to have a presence in Ireland to register for VAT.

4.3.4 Goods installed or assembled

s29 VATCA 2010 Throughout the EU, where goods are installed or assembled by, or on behalf of, the supplier, the place of supply is the country where the goods are installed or assembled.

Thus, if a German engineering company supplies machinery to a business in Ireland and sends employees to Ireland to assemble and/or install the machine (or engages a third party in Ireland to instal/assemble the machine), the place of supply of the machine is Ireland.

Where goods are supplied cross-border under an installation/assembly contract the intra-Community dispatch/acquisition is disregarded. This is on the basis that the place of supply is where the installation assembly happens and is not the Member State of departure of the goods.

s10 VATCA 2010

Who must account for the VAT on the supply?

Once it has been established that the place of supply of the goods is Ireland, we must determine who is obliged to account for the VAT incurred.

Where the purchaser of the installed/assembled goods is a VAT-registered person or is making VAT-exempt supplies (including hospitals, schools, charities, etc.), or is an unregistered farmer or fisherman, a local authority, a Government department or a statutory body, then the purchaser must account for the output VAT arising on the supply. If not already registered for VAT, the installation/assembly will oblige the purchaser to register for VAT.

Where the goods have been purchased for the purpose of its business by a person making supplies of taxable goods or services, then a simultaneous input VAT credit may be deducted, thus rendering the transaction VAT neutral. In other cases (purchasers making VAT-exempt supplies, including hospitals, schools, charities, etc., or unregistered farmers and fishermen, local authorities, Government departments, and statutory bodies), the purchaser must self-account for and pay the output VAT arising on the goods and no input VAT deduction is available.

4.3.5 "Triangulation"

Triangulation is another product of the Single Market, introduced in 1993. It is an attempt to reduce the bureaucratic burden associated with cross-border trade in the EU.

Very often, goods are supplied to an accountable person in one EU Member State and are in turn supplied by that person to an accountable person in another EU Member State. However, it is common for the goods to be shipped from the country of the first supplier directly to the country of the final customer without entering the country of the intermediate supplier (see diagram below).

Triangulation

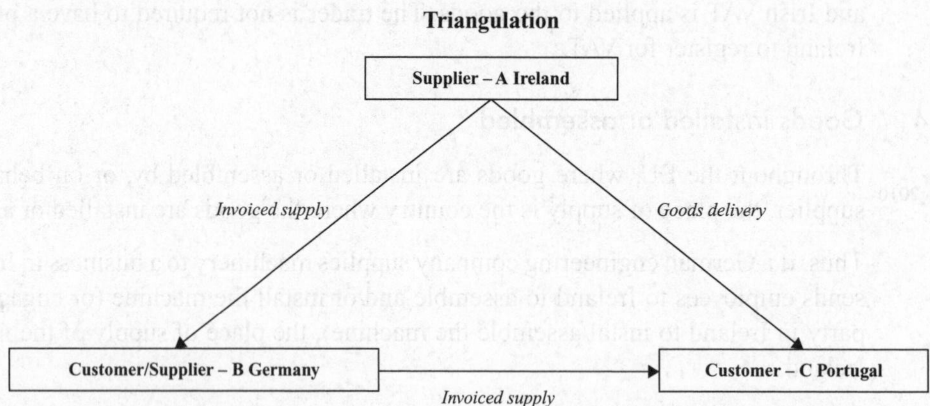

In the above scenario, Supplier A (established in Ireland) sells goods to Customer B (established in Germany) who in turn, as Supplier B, sells goods to Customer C (established in Portugal). Under the normal rules, Customer/Supplier B would be obliged to register for VAT in either Ireland (if he took ownership of the goods there), or in Portugal, as he has made an intra-Community acquisition of the goods there (if he doesn't take ownership in Ireland). This would have the effect of forcing many traders engaged in transactions throughout the EU to register for VAT in several (if not all) Member States.

The concept of "triangulation", which applies throughout the EU, provides that Customer/Supplier B is not obliged to register for VAT in Portugal in respect of its intra-Community acquisition there; however Company B reflects the intra-Community acquisition in its German records and Customer C is deemed to receive a domestic supply in Portugal from Company B and accounts for the Portuguese VAT on this supply on the 'reverse charge' basis.

The invoicing sequence in the case of "triangulation" is as follows:

- Supplier A quotes Customer B's VAT registration number on his/her invoice and zero-rates the supply.
- Supplier B quotes Customer C's VAT registration number on his/her invoice and does not apply VAT to the supply. Customer B makes the intra-Community Acquisition in his jurisdiction.
- Customer C self-accounts for VAT on the domestic supply to it of the goods.

4.4 Services Received from Abroad

Since 1 January 2010 the rules relating to the supply of services have fundamentally changed. Where a service is supplied cross-border then particular VAT rules apply, firstly, to determine the place where the supply takes place and, secondly, once the place of supply has been established, to determine who must account for the VAT in the jurisdiction where the supply has taken place.

4.4.1 The general rule

s34 VATCA 2010

The general rule in relation to the place of supply of a service supplied to a person in business (B2B) is where the business recipient of such supply is established. If the recipient has more than one place of business, then the place of supply is where the business most concerned with the supply is located. However, there are some exceptions to this rule in the case of a cross-border supply of services.

The general rule in relation to the place of supply of a service supplied to a person not in business (B2C) is where the business supplier of such supply is located. Again however, there are some notable exceptions to this rule in the case of a cross-border supply of services.

4.4.2 Accounting for VAT [as applied to cross-border services]

In the majority of cases, the Irish business person who receives the service becomes the person who must account for the VAT (output VAT). If not already registered, the person must register and self-account for VAT arising on the value of the service received.

Where the person in Ireland receives the service for the purpose of his/her taxable supplies, then he/she may claim a simultaneous input VAT credit, thus rendering the transaction VAT neutral.

In contrast to the intra-Community acquisition of goods by businesses, there is no threshold for registration in the case of receipt of such services.

s12 VATCA 2010

In some limited cases, the rule that the supplier of the service must register and account for VAT in Ireland is applied. In yet other cases, the place of supply is not Ireland, but rather where the supplier is established.

4.4.3 Services connected with immoveable goods (land and buildings) located in Ireland

Place of supply

s34(b) VATCA 2010

Throughout the EU, the place of supply of services connected with land and buildings is deemed to be where the property is located, irrespective of whether the service is supplied B2B or B2C.

Among the services covered by this provision are the services of builders, estate agents, surveyors, architects, engineers, etc. Furthermore, the services of insurance providers, consultants, solicitors, accountants, etc. are also deemed to be supplied where the property is located where their service is directly connected with property.

In addition, the provision of accommodation in hotels, guesthouses, campsites, holiday camps and places having a similar function are deemed to be services connected with land and buildings – confirming the place of supply to be where the premises is located.

Who must register and account for VAT in Ireland?

Where the services consist of construction operations and are supplied by a foreign sub-contractor to an Irish principal contractor and the property is located in Ireland, then the principal contractor is the accountable person and must account for VAT on the services received. The foreign sub-contractor is not an accountable person and does not register for VAT in Ireland.

In the case of a supply of services by foreign 'experts' or estate agents, the Irish business recipient must account for VAT on the service received.

In the case of 'the preparation and co-ordination of construction work'[2] by foreign suppliers, the Irish business recipient must account for VAT on the service received.

In all other cases, where foreign persons supply services connected with property located in Ireland, the foreign suppliers must register for and charge Irish VAT on their supplies, even though that foreign supplier has no establishment in Ireland.

4.4.4 Cultural, artistic, sporting, educational and entertainment services supplied in Ireland

Place of supply

The place of supply of admissions to such services (B2B and B2C), and any ancillary services, is where the service is physically performed (see 3.6.3, Chapter 3).

Who must register and account for VAT in Ireland?

Where such a service is supplied by a person not established in Ireland to a promoter or agent established in Ireland (B2B), then the Irish-established promoter or agent is deemed to have received the service and, as recipient, must account for VAT in Ireland (where the service is one which is not exempt from VAT).

Where such a service is supplied by a person not established in Ireland to a promoter or agent also not established in Ireland (B2B), then the promoter or agent is deemed to have received the service and, as recipient, must register and account for VAT in Ireland (where the service is one which is not exempt from VAT).

2 Such services include those supplied by architects and project managers

Where such a service is supplied by a person not established in Ireland, to private individuals, (B2C) then the supplier must register and account for VAT in Ireland (where the service is one which is not exempt from VAT).

4.4.5 Transport of goods services supplied to non-taxable persons (B2C)

Place of supply

In the case of transport to/from a destination outside the EU the place of supply is where the transport takes place.

In the case of transport to/from a destination within the EU the place of supply is the place of departure of the goods.

Who must register and account for VAT in Ireland?

In the case where the place of departure of the goods is Ireland and the destination of the transport service is within the EU, then the foreign transport supplier must register for VAT in Ireland and charge Irish VAT on the service supplied.

4.4.6 Short-term hire (30 days or less) of means of transport

Place of supply

The place of supply is where the means of transport is placed at the disposal of the customer.

Who must register and account for VAT in Ireland?

Where a foreign supplier physically places a means of transport at the disposal of a business customer (B2B) in Ireland, then the customer must account for the VAT.

Where a foreign supplier physically places a means of transport at the disposal of a private customer (B2C) in Ireland, then the foreign supplier must register and account for the VAT.

4.5 Services Supplied Abroad from Ireland

4.5.1 The general rule

s33–35 VATCA 2010 The general rule in relation to the place of supply of a service supplied to a person in business (B2B) is where the business recipient of such supply is established. If the recipient has more than one place of business, then the place of supply is where the business most concerned with the supply is located. However, there are some exceptions to this rule in the case of a cross-border supply of services.

The general rule in relation to the place of supply of a service supplied to a person not in business (B2C) is where the business supplier of such supply is located. Again however, there are some exceptions to this rule in the case of a cross-border supply of services.

Subject to any exceptions (see 4.4.3 – 4.4.6 above) and to "use and enjoyment" provisions (see 4.7) where an Irish supplier supplies services to business customers located outside of Ireland (B2B) he **will not** charge Irish VAT.

Subject to any exceptions (see 4.4.3 – 4.4.6 above) and to "use and enjoyment" provisions (see 4.7) where an Irish supplier supplies services to private persons located outside of Ireland (B2C) he **will** charge Irish VAT.

4.6 Intra-Community Transport of Goods

s34 VATCA 2010 The place of supply of intra-Community transport services, i.e., the cross-border transport of goods from one EU Member State to another, is no longer determined by specific rules, rather the new place of supply rules introduced on 1 January 2010 apply.

4.6.1 Goods transported from Ireland to another EU Member State

Where the customer is in business in another EU Member State the place of supply of the service (B2B) is where the customer is established. The customer will account for domestic VAT on the haulage service in the country in which he/she is registered for VAT.

The haulier should always obtain a copy of the customer's VAT registration number and include it on his/her invoice to the foreign customer.

Where the customer is established in Ireland, even where the goods are transported to another EU Member State, the place of supply is Ireland and the haulier charges Irish VAT.

Where the customer is a private individual in another EU Member State, the place of supply is Ireland (where transport begins) and the service (B2C) is liable to Irish VAT. The haulier must charge and account for Irish VAT.

4.6.2 Goods transported from another EU Member State to Ireland

Where the business customer is established in Ireland and where the haulier is established in another EU Member State the place of supply of the service is Ireland. The business will self-account for Irish VAT on the haulage service. The Irish business customer should advise the foreign haulier of his Irish VAT number.

Where the customer is a private individual in Ireland (B2C), the place of supply is in the other EU Member State (where transport begins) and the service is liable to domestic VAT in that country. Where the haulier is not established in that country (say, an Irish haulier goes over to collect the goods), he will have an obligation to register for VAT in that country and charge domestic VAT on the haulage service provided for that customer.

4.7 Cross-Border Services Use and Enjoyment Provisions

s35 VATCA 2010 In an attempt to eliminate certain "distortions of competition" that may arise due to the application or otherwise of VAT, "use and enjoyment" provisions, which are exceptions to the normal rules, are used. "Use and enjoyment" provisions usually create a charge of VAT or remove a charge of VAT which might otherwise arise under normal place of supply rules, with a view to eliminating distortions which might interfere with trade. Below is a list of the current use and enjoyment provisions. The place of use and enjoyment of the service is used to determine the applicability of VAT.

4.7.1 Services supplied to private individuals (B2C) located outside the EU

s34(m) VATCA 2010 Where an Irish service provider supplies any of the following services to a private individual (B2C) located outside the EU then the place of supply is where the customer is located and Irish VAT does not apply.

- transfers and assignments of copyright, patents, licences, trademarks and similar rights;
- hiring out of movable goods other than means of transport;
- advertising services;
- services of consultants, engineers, consultancy bureaux, lawyers, accountants and other similar services, data-processing and provision of information (but excluding services connected with immoveable goods);
- telecommunications services;
- radio and television broadcasting services;
- electronically supplied services; see 4.8
- the provision of access to, and of transportation or transmission through, natural gas and electricity distribution systems, and the provision of other directly linked services;
- acceptance of any obligation to refrain from pursuing or exercising, in whole or in part, any business activity or any such rights as are referred to in paragraph (i);
- banking, financial and insurance transactions;

s35(1) VATCA 2010 When a person established outside the EU hires out movable goods, and the goods are 'used and enjoyed' in Ireland then the place of supply is Ireland. For example, if a US company hires and uses computers in Ireland (B2B supply), the service is treated as taking place in Ireland and is chargeable to Irish VAT.

4.7.2 Hiring means of transport outside the EU

s35(2) VATCA 2010 Notwithstanding the provisions of s34 VATCA 2010, the place of supply of services, consisting of the hiring out of means of transport by a person established in the State, shall be deemed to be outside the Community where such means of transport are, or are to be, effectively used and enjoyed outside the Community.

4.7.3 Telecommunications & broadcasting services

s35(3) VATCA 2010 Where a telecommunications or broadcasting service provider, established outside the EU, a service (including a telephone access card) to a private person in Ireland, the place of supply is Ireland.

s35(4) VATCA 2010 Where a telecommunications provider, established in Ireland, supplies a service to a private individual (B2C) who is located outside the EU but who 'uses and enjoys' the service in Ireland, then the place of supply is Ireland.

The rules relating to telecommunications & broadcasting services supplies B2C are set to change with effect from 1 January 2015 (see 4.10).

4.7.4 Banking, financial and insurance services supplied to private individuals (B2C)

s35(5) VATCA 2010 Where a banking, financial or insurance service is supplied, in the course or furtherance of business, by a person established in the State to a private person not usually resident in the State, and where the service is used and enjoyed in the State, then the place of supply is the State. (However, most such services are exempt from VAT.)

4.7.5 Money transfer services

s34(6) VATCA 2010 Where money transfer services are supplied to a person in Ireland and are used and enjoyed in Ireland, then the place of supply of any intermediary service supplied to non-EU principals, which relates to such money transfer service, is Ireland.

4.8 Electronically Supplied Services

s1 VATCA 2010 Electronic services include the following:

(a) website supply, web-hosting, distance maintenance of programs and equipment;

(b) supply and updating of software;

(c) supply of images, text and information, and making databases available;

(d) supply of music, films and games, including games of chance and gambling, and of political, cultural, artistic, sporting, scientific and entertainment broadcasts and events; and

(e) supply of distance teaching.

Where electronic services are supplied by a non-EU-based trader to private individuals in the State (B2C), the place of supply is Ireland, the foreign supplier is obliged to register for Irish VAT irrespective of the value of his turnover.

This registration requirement may be avoided where the non-EU-based supplier avails of a special scheme (section 91, VATCA 2010 refers) that permits the supplier to register for VAT in any one EU Member State of his/her choice, in respect of all supplies of electronic services to private individuals throughout the EU. It is important to bear in mind that this regime applies only to electronically supplied services to private persons (B2C). The legislation ensures compliance with one of the primary OECD recommendations with regard to indirect taxation of e-commerce, i.e., that "consumption taxes should only apply in the jurisdiction of consumption".

4.9 Intermediary Services

An intermediary acting in his own name but for the account of a principal, is often referred to as an "undisclosed agent." Such a person is deemed to simultaneously buy in and supply on the service concerned.

An intermediary acting for his own account is often referred to as a "disclosed agent".

Where an intermediary, acting in the name of and on behalf of, a principal, supplies services it can sometimes be difficult to determine the place of supply of such services.

The place of supply of a service through such an intermediary to a non-taxable person is where the underlying transaction takes place.

Example 4.3

The Spanish private owner of a summer house in Donegal who wants to redesign the interior may ask an intermediary to find a company that will take care of the architectural aspects of the redesign. No matter where the intermediary is established, Irish VAT will be due on the commission fee because the place of supply of services connected with immovable property (i.e., the transaction underlying the supply of the intermediary's services) is where the property is located.

4.10 B2C Telecommunications, Broadcasting & e-Services - Rules on the Charge of VAT and Place of Supply

4.10.1 Introduction

With effect from 1 January 2015 new rules have come into force relating to the application of VAT on B2C transactions for the following services:

- Electronic services
- Telecommunications
- Broadcasting services

With effect from 1 January 2015 the place of supply of all B2C supplies of electronic, telecommunications and broadcasting services, supplied by a person established either within or outside the EU to Consumers located within the EU will be in the Member State where the Consumer is located.

This is one of the most far reaching VAT changes agreed upon within the last 20 years. It will involve significant changes in VAT accruing to Member States. From that date onwards significant VAT amounts will accrue to member states where the Consumer is located, which heretofore accrued to member states where the supplier was established.

Thus where a Consumer in Germany downloads a game, an application or music over the internet the VAT arising on the supply will be due in Germany. E-services suppliers, telecoms operators and broadcasters have all made significant changes to their VAT systems to be compliant by 1 January 2015.

4.10.2 Who is the supplier of the services?

There may, for instance be a games developer, a platform provider, a telecoms operator and a payments aggregator all involved in making a supply of e-services to a Consumer. Only one of the transactions can be the B2C supply, all of the others being B2B transactions leading to the final B2C supply.

Any taxable person 'taking part in a supply' of:

- e-services which are supplied through a telecommunications network, an interface or portal, or
- a telephone service provided through the internet (e.g. VoIP)

is presumed to have received and supplied those services in his or her own name (and is therefore liable to account for VAT on the supply) unless certain conditions are met.

The presumption above may be overridden where the actual service provider is explicitly indicated as the supplier and this is reflected in the contractual arrangements between the parties.

If you are taking part in the supply and –

a. you authorise the charge to the customer in respect of the supply,

b. you authorise the delivery of the supply to the customer, or

c. you set the terms and conditions of the supply

you have, or are presumed to have, received and supplied that service in your own name and you cannot explicitly indicate another person in the chain as the supplier. You are accountable for the VAT on the supply to your customer.

However, if you do not carry out any of the actions listed at (a), (b) and (c) above and both the service and the actual supplier of the service are explicitly indicated on each invoice issued in the supply chain and on the bill or receipt issued or made available to the final customer, the presumption that you have received and supplied the service in your own name can be overridden. Where that is the case, you will not be regarded as a principal and will, therefore not be obliged to account for the VAT in relation to the supply of that service. It is important to note that the economic reality of the transaction prevails and each transaction should be assessed individually to correctly identify the VAT treatment.

These are very important rules to establish who exactly is making the final B2C supply of the services concerned.

The VAT Implementing Regulation has indicated at Art 9a that Article 28 of the VAT Directive be interpreted as follows:

> *"...where electronically supplied services are supplied through a telecommunications network, an interface or a portal such as a marketplace for applications, a taxable person taking part in that supply shall be presumed to be acting in his own name but on behalf of the provider of those services unless that provider is explicitly indicated as the supplier by that taxable person and that is reflected in the contractual arrangements between the parties."*

4.10.3 The Union & non-Union Schemes

The non-Union scheme

For a number of years a scheme has enabled non-EU suppliers (and who do not have a fixed establishment in the EU) of electronic services register for VAT in one EU member state only. A quarterly VAT return is filed indicating the VAT payable in each EU member state. From 1 January 2015 this scheme has been extended to include B2C telecoms and broadcasting services supplied by persons not established in the EU. From 1 January 2015 this scheme is known as the 'non-Union scheme' (Art 57a, VAT Implementing Regs, 2011).

The Union scheme

An additional scheme, 'the Union scheme' was introduced on 1 January 2015 (Art 57a, VAT Implementing Regs, 2011). This scheme enables suppliers of e-services, telecommunications services and broadcasting services who are established in the EU (or if established outside the EU have a fixed establishment in the EU) to register for VAT in one EU member state and file VAT returns there in respect of B2C supplies made in other EU member states in which the person is not established.

In the case of a taxable person established in an EU member state that member state shall be the member state of identification for the person.

The scheme will not extend to services supplied by the taxable person in a member state where he is established.

4.10.4 Mini One Stop Shop ('MOSS')

The Mini-one-stop-shop is an optional scheme which allows businesses that supply telecommunications, broadcasting or e-services to Consumers in member states in which they do not have an establishment to account for the VAT due on those supplies via a web-portal in one Member States. Otherwise businesses making such supplies would be obliged to register for VAT, file returns and make payments in each member state in which they make these supplies. Both the Union & non-Union schemes are catered for within MOSS.

Example 4.4:

A company with a place of establishment in Ireland but with fixed establishments in the UK and Germany makes B2C supplies of electronic services in Ireland, UK, Germany, France, Italy, Hungary and Spain.

The supplies made in Ireland, UK and Germany will be declared on its periodic VAT returns in each jurisdiction. The supplies in France, Italy, Hungary and Spain can be included on a single VAT return (under the Union scheme) which will be filed as a separate VAT return in Ireland via the dedicated web-portal.

There are very strict rules outlining the circumstances when a person may be obliged to continue filing under the Mini-One-Stop-Shop and what acts of non-compliance will cause a person to leave the scheme[3].

Each member state was obliged to have the necessary web-portals in place by 1 October 2014 to enable suppliers of e-services, telecoms and broadcasting services to Consumers, register for the mini-One-Stop-Shop.

4.10.5 Relevant Legislation

Sections 91, 91A, 91B, 91C, 91D, 91E & 91F provide for the special schemes (Union & non-Union and MOSS – see 4.10.1 – 3 above).

In so far as EU legislation is concerned the relevant provisions contained in Council Implementing Regulation 282/2011/EU, have been inserted/amended by Council Implementing Regulation 1042/2013/EU of 7 October 2013 and are:

Articles 6a – 6b, 7, 9a, 13a, 18, 24, 24a – 24f, 31c, 57a – 57h, 58, 58a – 58c, 59, 59a, 60, 61, 61a, 61b, 62, 63, 63a – 63c & Annex I.

The relevant provisions of the VAT Directive which have been inserted/amended to give effect to the 2015 changes, are:

Articles 58, 59, 59a, 204, 358 – 369, 369a – 369k.

3 The alternative to the Mini-One-Stop-Shop is a VAT registration obligation in every member state where B2C supplies are made.

4.10.6 Some new Terms

A host of new terms have been introduced by the new legislation, including:

"Presumption for the Location of the Customer" - where the relevant services are provided by a supplier at a telephone box/kiosk, a wifi hotspot, an internet café, a restaurant/hotel and physical presence of the Consumer is required at such location then it is presumed the customer is established at that place and the services are used and enjoyed at that location. Where the relevant service is delivered via a fixed landline then it is presumed the customer is established at that place. Where the relevant service is delivered via a mobile network then it is presumed the customer is established in country identified by the mobile country code of the SIM card.

"Rebuttal of Presumptions" – A tax authority may 'rebut' any of the above presumptions where there are indications of 'misuse or abuse' by the supplier. A supplier may rebut any of the above presumptions on the basis of three items of non-contradictory evidence indicating that the cus-tomer is located elsewhere.

As you can imagine, the above definitions will take on added significance should two member states lay claim to the same revenues on the basis of the Consumer being located within their territory.

4.10.7 Conclusion

The above changes were far reaching and signified a major shift in the country of payment of VAT. The larger member states are seeing large inflows of VAT revenue which heretofore were paid in generally smaller member states which offered the attraction of low VAT rates on electronic services.

A Guide to the Mini-One-Stop-Shop has been published by the European Commission and is available at: http://ec.europa.eu/taxation_customs/resources/documents/taxation/vat/how_vat_works/telecom/one-stop-shop-guidelines_en.pdf

In addition the Revenue Commissioners have also published a MOSS guide (Revenue e-Brief No 123/15)

4.11 Zero-rating Scheme for Qualifying Businesses ("VAT 56 Authorisation")

s56 VATCA 2010

When 75% or more of the turnover of a person who is registered for VAT in Ireland derives from the following:

- exports, and/or
- dispatches to VAT-registered persons in other EU Member States, and/or
- contract work carried out on goods imported, which will subsequently be exported, and/or

- contract work, which is deemed to be supplied in another EU Member State, i.e. where the customer (the owner of the goods) is registered for VAT in another EU Member State,

then the VAT-registered person is a "qualifying person" and may apply to the Revenue Commissioners for a VAT 56 authorisation. The application is made by way of a VAT 56A form. Once granted, this authorisation will allow him/her to receive all imports at 0%, will allow him to receive and account for all intra-Community acquisitions at 0% and will enable all Irish VAT-registered persons to supply all goods and services to him/her at 0%. However, the purchase of cars, petrol, food, accommodation and entertainment services do not qualify for the 0% rate and the supplier must charge Irish VAT at the appropriate rate.

The authorisation is of enormous cash-flow benefit to the holder, is normally granted for a two-year period and is renewable. The holder is obliged to ensure that he/she continues to qualify for the authorisation, and he/she must advise Revenue and surrender the authorisation where his/her trade activity changes and he/she is no longer a qualifying person.

A copy of a VAT 56A application form can be found at Appendix I to this chapter[4].

4.12 Recovery of VAT incurred in Ireland by Foreign Traders

Where a foreign trader not established in Ireland incurs VAT on goods or services supplied to him in Ireland and he/she uses such goods and services for the purposes of his/her taxable supplies abroad, then he/she may reclaim the VAT incurred in Ireland.

A foreign trader can incur VAT in Ireland in many ways, e.g., he/she may have to purchase diesel in Ireland, he/she may have to pay Irish VAT on services supplied in Ireland, renting space at a trade fair, etc.

4.12.1 Foreign trader established in a Member State of the EU

The trader must file a claim electronically with the tax authority in the Member State in which he is registered for VAT. This claim will be processed locally and transmitted to the revenue Commissioners for further processing/verification.

The claim must be filed by 30th September of the year immediately following the year in which the VAT being reclaimed was incurred. Thus the deadline for reclaiming any VAT incurred in 2013 is 30th September 2014.

The foreign trader may make up to five applications for refunds of VAT within the time deadline stipulated.

Generally the VAT must be repaid within 4 months. However, if the tax authority has further queries this can be extended to 8 months. For instance the tax authority can request sight of invoices or importation documents.

4 This relief is provided for in section 56, VATCA 2010 but the forms are still referred to in terms of the sections applicable under the now revoked Value Added Tax Act 1972.

4.12.2 Foreign trader established in a country outside the EU

In the case of a foreign trader who is established outside the EU, but carries on an activity that would be liable to VAT if it were carried on in Ireland, a claim must be made under the provisions of the Thirteenth Council Directive. The name derives from the title of the European Council Directive implementing the right of recovery of VAT incurred in any EU Member State by a person not established in the EU.

Generally such VAT should only be repaid where reciprocal arrangements exist for Irish traders to recover input VAT incurred in the jurisdiction of the claimant.

The final date for filing the claim is 30th June of the year immediately following the year to which the claim relates. The claims must be filed directly with the Revenue Commissioners in Ireland, and must be supported by evidence of VAT registration/tax compliance in the country of establishment and by the original invoices issued by the Irish supplier of the taxable goods and services.

4.12.3 Trader established in Ireland seeking to recover VAT incurred in another Member State of the EU

Where a trader who is registered for VAT in Ireland incurs VAT in another Member State of the EU then he must file a claim electronically with the Revenue Commissioners. This claim will be forwarded to the relevant tax authority.

The claim must be filed by 30th September of the year immediately following the year in which the VAT being reclaimed was incurred. Thus the deadline for reclaiming any VAT incurred in 2013 is 30th September 2014.

The Irish trader may make up to either four five applications for refunds of VAT within the time deadline stipulated (depending on rules in the Member State concerned).

Generally the VAT must be repaid within four months; however if the foreign tax authority has further queries this can be extended to eight months. For instance the tax authority can request sight of invoices or importation documents.

4.12.4 Trader established in Ireland seeking to recover VAT incurred in other third countries

The rules will depend on the country concerned.

These are some of the many measures put in place to break down barriers to international trade and to eliminate distortion of competition, which may arise. It is not obligatory for any business to file a claim for the refund of VAT incurred in foreign countries.

Example 4.5: Cross-border refund claim by Irish trader

A trader who is VAT registered in Ireland hires a booth at a trade-show in October 2014 in Germany to display his goods. The trade-show organizer issues him with a German VAT invoice charging €2,500 VAT.

If the Irish trader wishes to recover the German VAT charged to him then he must file a claim, electronically, with the Revenue Commissioners not later than 30th September 2015. The claim will be processed and sent to the German tax authority who must repay within a period of four months from the date of receipt or eight months if they raise additional queries.

4.13 VAT 60A Procedure

As we have seen, the place of supply is one of the important factors in determining whether or not a supply is within the charge of VAT. If the place of supply of the goods or service is Ireland and all other necessary conditions are fulfilled, then the supply is liable to VAT in Ireland. Where the place of supply is Spain and all other necessary conditions are fulfilled, then the supply is liable to VAT in Spain, and so on.

Subsequent to 1 January 2010 most services supplied by Irish suppliers to business customers (B2C) located outside of Ireland will not be subject to Irish VAT as the place of supply will be where the business customer is located. However, where, exceptionally, Ireland is the place of supply, generally the standard rate (23%) will apply to services provided to foreign-established traders. As we have seen above, where the foreign trader uses the services for the purposes of making taxable supplies in his/her own country, he/she may reclaim the VAT charged via a cross-border VAT reclaim.

A procedure, known as the VAT 60A procedure, exists to enable the service provider to charge VAT at 0% on services supplied in Ireland to foreign traders. The authorisation, a VAT 60B is issued to the foreign trader by the Revenue Commissioners where a VAT 60A application has been filed and approved by the Revenue Commissioners. Once he/she presents the VAT 60B authorisation to the supplier of the services, the supplier is obliged to charge VAT at 0% on the particular service identified on the VAT 60B Comma authorisation. This facility is of cash-flow benefit to the foreign trader who now no longer has to make a cross-border VAT reclaim.

Among the conditions necessary to obtain a VAT 60B[5] authorisation are:

- the foreign trader must be carrying on an activity in his/her own country, which, if carried on in Ireland, would be a taxable supply;
- the foreign trader must have evidence of VAT registration and/or tax compliance in his/her own country;
- the foreign trader must not be making any taxable supplies in Ireland;
- the service being supplied to the foreign trader must be on a regular basis (it may not be a once-off supply of a service).

The VAT 60A procedure applies to the supply of services only and not to the supply of goods.

5 A copy of a VAT 60A form can be found at Appendix II to this chapter.

Example 4.6: VAT 60A procedure

A foreign haulier requires warehousing/storage facilities in Ireland. As such a service is connected to land and buildings the local supplier will charge Irish VAT at 23%. Where this is a regular occurrence, i.e. the facility is hired on an ongoing basis, the foreign haulier can apply for a VAT 60B.

Where the VAT 60B is approved then, upon presentation, the Irish premises owner will apply VAT at 0% to the provision of the warehousing/storage services.

4.14 Intrastat Filing

Since the abolition of fiscal controls on the movement of goods from one Member State to another within the EU on 1 January 1993, a mechanism had to be put in place to enable Member States to record statistical data in relation to the movement of such goods. The mechanism of recording such movement either into or out of Member States is by way of traders filing Intrastat returns.[6] The filing is only in respect of goods.

In the case of goods dispatched from Ireland to other EU Member States, the threshold for detailed filing is €635,000 annually. If the value of dispatched goods is less than this amount, then the value of the goods must only be included on the periodic VAT returns filed by the VAT-registered trader (simplified filing). Where the value of the goods exceeds the threshold, then a detailed monthly Intrastat return must be filed in addition to the simplified filing.

In the case of goods acquired in Ireland from other EU Member States, the threshold for detailed filing is €191,000 annually. If the value of acquired goods is less than this amount, then the value of the goods only must be included on the periodic VAT returns filed by the VAT-registered trader (simplified filing). Where the value of the goods exceeds the threshold, then the appropriate detailed Intrastat returns must be filed monthly in addition to the simplified filing.

As you can see, some traders may not have to file any Intrastat returns, some may have to file in respect of dispatches, some may have to file in respect of acquisitions and some may have to file in respect of both dispatches and acquisitions.

4.15 VAT Information Exchange System (VIES) Filing

s82–83 VATCA 2010

The VAT Information Exchange System (VIES) is a database of information available to the tax authorities containing information in relation to cross-border supplies of goods and services made by each accountable person registered for VAT (in all Member States) to person registered for VAT in other EU Member States. [It is often referred to as EC sales Listing in other Member States].

A 'VIES return' must be filed electronically, either monthly or quarterly, depending on whether goods or services and the value of the supplies by a VAT registered trader

6 A copy of an Intrastat return can be found at Appendix III to this chapter.

engaged in the B2B supply of goods/services to other EU member states. Once filed, the information is posted to a central database and is available to the VAT authorities in all EU Member States. Among other things, the database is used to combat fraud and to verify the veracity of VAT registration numbers supplied by traders in one Member State to traders in another Member State.

Prior to 1 January 2010 VIES filing was only obligatory in relation to goods. With effect from 1 January 2010 the filing obligation was extended to include services.

Any VAT-registered person who dispatches goods to a VAT-registered persons in another EU Member States or who supplies a service, the place of supply of which is the other Member State, is obliged to file a periodic VIES return.[7] Unlike the Intrastat return, there is no *de minimus* threshold.

The return will include the name and VAT registration number of the supplier, the VAT registration number of each customer and the value of sales to each customer compiled on a monthly/quarterly basis.

Any person may input any EU VAT registration to a specific European Commission website and receive confirmation as to whether the number is a valid registration or not.

Thus with effect from 1 January 2010 it is necessary for all Irish traders who supply goods or services to VAT registered customers located in other EU Member States to obtain the VAT ID of all such customers.

It is important not to confuse VIES filing obligations with place of supply rules. Thus where a service is supplied cross-border to a taxable person, i.e. to a person in business, then the place of supply is where that customer is established, irrespective of whether or not the supplier can obtain his/her VAT number. If it is not possible to obtain the VAT number then evidence as to the business status of the customer should be retained by the supplier.

Traders in Ireland are not obliged to file a VIES return in respect of cross-border services received.

7 A copy of a VIES return can be found at Appendix IV to this chapter.

4.16 Summary

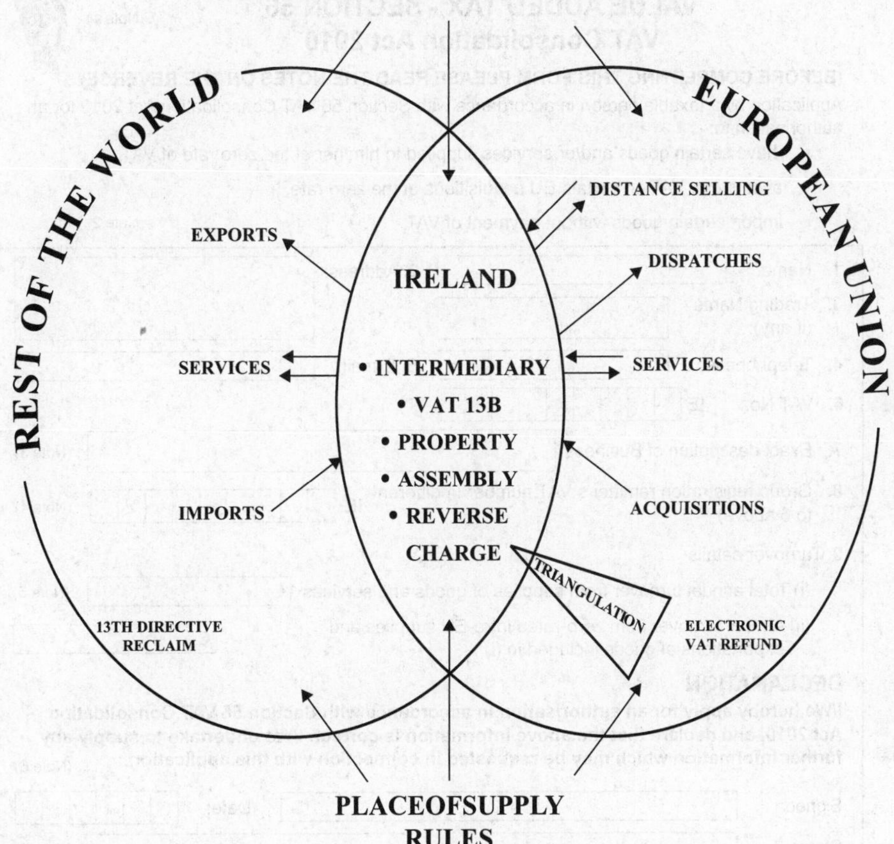
Cross-Border Trade
USE AND ENJOYMENT PROVISIONS
REST OF THE WORLD
EUROPEAN UNION
DISTANCE SELLING
EXPORTS
DISPATCHES
IRELAND
SERVICES
• INTERMEDIARY
SERVICES
• VAT 13B
• PROPERTY
• ASSEMBLY
IMPORTS
• REVERSE
CHARGE
ACQUISITIONS
TRIANGULATION
13TH DIRECTIVE
RECLAIM
ELECTRONIC
VAT REFUND
PLACEOFSUPPLY
RULES

Appendix I

Specimen of VAT 56A form

VALUE ADDED TAX - SECTION 56
VAT Consolidation Act 2010

(Note 1) 

(BEFORE COMPLETING THIS FORM PLEASE READ THE NOTES ON THE REVERSE)

Application by a taxable person in accordance with Section 56 VAT Consolidation Act 2010 for an authorisation to:

- have certain goods and/or services supplied to him/her at the zero rate of VAT,
- account for VAT on certain EU acquisitions at the zero rate,
- import certain goods without payment of VAT. (Note 2)

1. Name: 2. Address:
3. Trading Name (if any):
4. Telephone No.: 5. E-mail:
6. VAT No.: IE
7. Exact description of Business: (Note 3)
8. Group registration remitter's VAT number (if different to 6 above) IE (Note 4)
9. Turnover details:
   (i) Total annual turnover from supplies of goods and services € (Note 5)
   (ii) Annual turnover from zero-rated intra-EU supplies and exportations of goods included in (i) €

DECLARATION

I/We hereby apply for an authorisation in accordance with Section 56 VAT Consolidation Act 2010, and declare that the above information is correct. I/We undertake to supply any further information which may be requested in connection with this application. (Note 6)

Signed: Date:

Status: (Note 7)

***ACCOUNTANT'S CERTIFICATE**

(To be completed by the Accountant who normally prepares and/or audits the applicant's accounts)

I/We certify that the turnover for the year ended __________ in respect of the zero rated intra-Community supplies and exportations of goods amounted to € __________ and that this figure comprises at least 75% of the total annual turnover from supplies of goods and services for the same year.

Signed: Date:

Accountant's Name & Address:

(*Not applicable in the case of a new company (see Note 7))

This application should be submitted to the applicant's local Revenue office.
For addresses see the Contact Locator on www.revenue.ie

NOTES

Note 1

Information Leaflet January 2010, which explains the provisions of Section 56 VAT Consolidation Act 2010 in detail, is available on the Revenue website **www.revenue.ie** or from your local Revenue office.

Note 2

The provisions of Section 56 VAT Consolidation Act 2010 will apply in the case of all goods and services with the following exceptions:

(a) certain motor vehicles and petrol,
(b) services consisting of the provision of food and drink, the hire of certain motor vehicles, accommodation, entertainment, and other personal services.

Note 3

Please describe the exact nature of the business.

Note 4

A group registration (i.e. where a number of companies are treated as a single taxable person for VAT purposes) can only be authorised under Section 56 if at least 75% of the **group's** total annual turnover is derived from exportations of goods or intra-Community supplies. Individual members of the group registration cannot obtain authorisations unless the group as a whole is authorised.

Note 5

Total annual turnover includes exempt supplies but does not include goods which have been sold and subsequently leased back.

Note 6

If the application relates to a new business it should be supported by a statement from an appropriate State agency that it is estimated that the zero-rated intra-Community supplies and exportations of goods by the applicant will amount to at least 75% of the applicant's total turnover from supplies of goods and services in the first year of trading.

Note 7

The person who signs the application should be a person duly authorised to sign and be responsible for the accuracy of the information given, e.g. company secretary, owner or partner.

Appendix II

Specimen of VAT 60A form

VAT 60A

Application by a Foreign Trader who is not established in Ireland for relief from Value-Added Tax (VAT) on charges for Services supplied to it by Irish Supplier(s).

1. Details of Foreign Trader
Please complete this section in BLOCK LETTERS.
Please read notes on page 2.

Name: ____________________

Telephone Number: ____________________

Address: ____________________

Nature of Business: ____________________

Where are you established? ❑ **Within EU**
(*✓ Tick as appropriate*) ❑ **Outside EU**

Official Use Only
1. Customer ID:
2. C/TS or C/Reg required? ❑ Yes ❑ No
Received on:
3. Date of C/TS:
4. Letter sent:
Reply received:
5. Copy of lease required? ❑ Yes ❑ No
Received on:
6. Form 60B Issued on:
7. Period of validity of Approval to Zero-Rate
From: To:
Copy to IOT on

Tax Reference Number: ____________________
If you are established in the EU please quote your VAT Registration No. If you are established outside the EU please quote your tax reference number in the country in which you are established.

Is this your first application for relief? (*✓ Tick as appropriate*) ❑ **Yes** ❑ **No**

If no, please quote your Customer ID No. (*if available*): ____________________
You will have been allocated a Customer ID No. by us when you made your first application for relief

SPECIMEN

2. Details of Supplier of Services in Ireland
If there is more than one supplier, please provide the following details in respect of the other supplier(s) on a separate page.

Name: __________ **Telephone Number:** __________

Address:

VAT Registration No.: __________ **Local Tax Office :**

Nature of Service(s) to be supplied to Foreign Trader detailed in section 1: __________

Will that/those Service(s) be provided on a continuous basis?: (*✓ Tick as appropriate*) ❑ **Yes** ❑ **No**

Is the Irish supplier holding or will the Irish supplier hold stocks of goods in Ireland on behalf of the Foreign Trader detailed in section 1 [other than stocks of goods for onward consignment to regular customers, in accordance with Section 3(8) of the VAT Act, 1972 as amended]. (*✓ Tick as appropriate*)
❑ **Yes** ❑ **No**

Page 1 ***Please complete page***

3. Declaration

Anyone who knowingly makes a false statement for the purpose of obtaining relief from VAT is liable to penalties. Please delete text in bold, as appropriate, and then sign the declaration below if satisfied that it is accurate.

I/ ________________ **(if the foreign trader is a company, insert the company name here) wish(es)** to apply for relief from VAT on charges in respect of services supplied to **me/it** within Ireland.

I declare that—

(a) **I supply/** ______________ **(if the foreign trader is a company, insert the company name here) supplies** no goods or services in Ireland; *(The consigning of goods direct to Irish customers from outside Ireland does not constitute supply within Ireland.)*

(b) **I am/** ______________ **(if the foreign trader is a company, insert the company name here) is** not established in Ireland;

(c) **I am/** ______________ **(if the foreign trader is a company, insert the company name here) is** not registered nor **am I/is it** required to register for VAT in Ireland. *(If you need to check whether you are required to register for VAT in Ireland, please contact the Taxes Central Registration Office, Office of the Revenue Commissioners, 9/15 Upper O'Connell St., Dublin 1, Ireland. (Tel. 00 353 1 865 5000 or Fax 00 353 1 874 6078));*

(d) the services supplied to **me/** ______________ **(if the foreign trader is a company, insert the company name here)** by the Irish supplier detailed in section 2 will be used only in connection with the business detailed in section 1 above; and

(e) the particulars stated on this form are true and correct to the best of my knowledge and belief.

Signature: ______________ **Date:** ______________

Position in the Company (if applicable): ______________

If you are signing on behalf of a Company, you must be authorised to sign on behalf of the Company

IMPORTANT - ***Please read the following notes before you submit your application***

1. Before you submit this claim form please ensure that—
   - you have completed all sections including signing the declaration in section 3;
   - you have attached all supporting documentation i.e.
     - an in-date Certificate of Taxable Status if you are established ***within the EU***. This certificate is available from your own tax authorities , *or*
     - Certificate from the official authority of the country in which you are established if you are established ***outside the EU***. This certificate should contain the name, address and official stamp of the official authority, your name, address and business registration number and a statement as to the nature of the economic activity carried on by you, *and*
   - a certified true copy of the lease if the business in which you are engaged involves leasing.
2. A person is established in a Member State if that person has in that State:
   - the seat of his or her economic activity, *or*
   - a fixed establishment from which business transactions are effected, *or*
   - if no such seat or fixed establishment exists, his or her domicile or normal place of residence.
3. Claim form together with supporting documentation should be returned to:

   VAT (Unregistered) Repayments Section
   Office of the Revenue Commissioners
   Kilrush Road
   Ennis
   Co. Clare, Ireland.

   Tel: 00 353 65 684 1200. FAX : 00 353 65 684 9248. E-Mail : unregvat@revenue.ie
4. Further copies of this claim form may be obtained from the above address or downloaded from our website (www.revenue.ie/publications/curntfms/curfrms.htm).

Page 2 ***Issued: August 2000***

Appendix III

Specimen of Intrastat form

INTRASTAT

INTRA EU TRADE STATISTICS RETURN

FOR OFFICIAL USE

DECLARANT'S NAME AND ADDRESS

2 TRADER'S NAME AND ADDRESS

*** Please notify VIMA office of any change of address or trading circumstances ***

3 PERIOD OF DECLARATION Y Y M M	4 ARRIVALS (IMPORTS) INSERT A. DISPATCHES (EXPORTS) INSERT D.	5 NO. OF ITEMS	6 TRADER'S VAT REGISTRATION NO.	7 DECLARANT'S VAT REGISTRATION NO.

8 ITEM NO.	9 COMMODITY CODE (8 DIGITS)	10 EU COUNTRY OF CONSIGNMENT (IF ARRIVAL) CODE OR EU COUNTRY OF DESTINATION (IF DESPATCH) CODE	11 COUNTRY OF ORIGIN (CODE)	12 PRESUMED MODE OF TRANSPORT (CODE)	13 NATURE OF TRANSACTION (CODE)	14 INVOICE VALUE (ROUNDED TO NEAREST EURO)	15 DELIVERY TERMS (CODE)	16 STATISTICAL VALUE (ROUNDED TO NEAREST EURO) (SEE NOTE OVERLEAF)	17 NETT MASS IN Kgs (ROUNDED TO WHOLE NO.)	18 QUANTITY 2 SUPPLEMENTARY UNITS (ROUNDED TO WHOLE NO.)

***** FAILURE TO COMPLY BY THE DUE DATE COULD RESULT IN PROSECUTION *****

I DECLARE THAT THE INFORMATION GIVEN IN THIS RETURN IS TRUE.

RETURN TO:

OFFICE OF THE REVENUE COMMISSIONERS
VIMA OFFICE
P.O. BOX NO. 43, DUNDALK, CO. LOUTH.
PHONE: (042) 9353300 LoCALL: 1890 251010
FAX: (042) 9353388

NAME OF DECLARANT ______________ SIGNATURE OF DECLARANT ______________

DATE ______________ TELEPHONE NO. ______________ FAX NO. ______________

SEE NOTES OVERLEAF.

Brief Note on the completion of the INTRASTAT return. (Full explanatory notes are included in the current VIES & INTRASTAT Trader's Manual which is available from the return address shown overleaf.)

Box 4 Separate forms are used for ARRIVALS (imports) and for DISPATCHES (exports). In the case of ARRIVALS "A" must be inserted in this box and for DISPATCHES "D" must be used.

Box 5 The number of lines of data entered on each return must be inserted here. If a continuation sheet is used, then the box must show the total no. of lines including those on the continuation sheet(s).

Column 8 Each line of data must be numbered for each return, starting at 1 each time i.e. if an arrivals return and a dispatches return are being submitted for the same period each return must start at 1 and the total number of lines in each return entered in boxes 5 on each form respectively.

Column 9 For Commodity Code use the Combined Nomenclature or the first 8 digits of the appropriate Customs and Excise Tariff Code.

Column 10, 11, 12, 13, 15 See Tables below. (Ireland's Country Code IE should never appear in column 10)

Column 14 INVOICE VALUE is the invoice value of the goods rounded to the nearest EURO but does not include V.A.T.

Column 16 From 1/1/98, most traders are not required to complete this column - Contact VIMA office regarding thresholds.
For DISPATCHES (exports) the Statistical Value is the invoice value adjusted to an F.O.B. basis at point of exit from the State.
For ARRIVALS (imports) the STATISTICAL VALUE will be the invoice value adjusted to a C.I.F. basis at the point of entry to the State. (Value to be rounded to the nearest EURO)

Column 17 Weight of the goods (exclusive of packaging) in kgs. as required.

Column 18 For certain goods as well as the weight in kgs, the secondary quantities are required e.g. no. of units or square metres. The Combined Nomenclature or the Customs and Excise Tariff of Ireland should be consulted.

N.B. Where a Trader has no Intra-Community Trade in a particular return period, a "NIL" return should be submitted for that period.

CODES FOR USE IN COMPLETION OF INTRASTAT RETURN

BOX 10/11 - E.U. COUNTRIES CODE

	Code
AUSTRIA	AT
BELGIUM	BE
CYPRUS	CY
CZECH REPUBLIC	CZ
DENMARK	DK
ESTONIA	EE
FINLAND	FI
FRANCE	FR
GERMANY	DE
GREAT BRITAIN	GB
GREECE	GR
HUNGARY	HU
ITALY	IT
IRELAND	IE
LATVIA	LV
LITHUANIA	LT
LUXEMBOURG	LU
MALTA	MT
NETHERLANDS	NL
NORTHERN IRELAND	XI
POLAND	PL
PORTUGAL	PT
SLOVAKIA	SK
SLOVENIA	SI
SPAIN	ES
SWEDEN	SE

BOX 12 MODE OF TRANSPORT

	Code
AIR	4
FIXED Transport Installations	7
Own Propulsion	9
POST	5
RAIL	2
ROAD	3
SEA	1
Transport by Inland Waterway	8

BOX 13 NATURE OF TRANSACTION

	Code
Sales/Purchases etc	1
Returned goods or replacement goods	2
Aid Goods	3
Goods for processing	4
Goods after processing	5
Goods for/after repair	6
Joint defence or intergovernmental production programmes	7
Building materials for construction contracts etc	8
Other transactions including hire and operational leasing over 2 years	9

BOX 15 DELIVERY TERMS

	Code
Carriage Paid to	CPT
Carriage Insurance Paid to	CIP
Cost and Freight (C & F)	CFR
Cost, Insurance and Freight	CIF
Delivered at Frontier	DAF
Delivered Ex Quay	DEQ
Delivered Ex Ship	DES
Delivered Duty Unpaid	DDU
Delivered Duty Paid	DDP
Ex Works	EXW
Free Alongside Ship	FAS
Free on Board	FOB
Free Carrier	FCA
Other terms not listed above	XXX

INTRASTAT

INTRA EU TRADE STATISTICS RETURN

euro FORM

CONTINUATION SHEET NO.	3 PERIOD OF DECLARATION Y Y M M	4 ARRIVALS (IMPORTS) INSERT A. DISPATCHES (EXPORTS) INSERT D.	6 TRADER'S VAT REGISTRATION NO.	7 DECLARANT'S VAT REGISTRATION NO.

8 ITEM NO.	9 COMMODITY CODE (8 DIGITS)	10 COUNTRY OF DESTINATION (IF DESPATCH) CODE OR COUNTRY OF CONSIGNMENT (IF ARRIVAL) CODE	11 COUNTRY OF ORIGIN (CODE)	12 PRESUMED MODE OF TRANSPORT (CODE)	13 NATURE OF TRANSACTION (CODE)	14 INVOICE VALUE (ROUNDED TO NEAREST EURO)	15 DELIVERY TERMS (CODE)	16 STATISTICAL VALUE (ROUNDED TO NEAREST EURO)	17 NETT MASS IN Kgs (ROUNDED TO WHOLE NO.)	18 QUANTITY 2 SUPPLEMENTARY UNITS (ROUNDED TO WHOLE NO.)

INC 1(E)

Appendix IV

Specimen of VIES form

VIES STATEMENT

RETURN TO: OFFICE OF THE REVENUE COMMISSIONERS
VIMA OFFICE
P.O. BOX NO. 43 DUNDALK, CO. LOUTH
PHONE: (042) 9353300 FAX: (042) 9353388
LoCall: 1890-251010

FORM

FOR OFFICIAL USE

DECLARANT'S NAME AND ADDRESS

2 DECLARANT'S VAT REGISTRATION NO.

3 TRADER'S NAME AND ADDRESS

4 TRADER'S VAT REGISTRATION NO.

*** Please notify VIMA office of any change of address or trading circumstances ***

5 TYPE — M/Q/A1/A2

6 PERIOD — Y Y M M

7 TOTAL VALUE OF SUPPLIES OF GOODS (EXPORTS) IN EURO

8 NO. OF ITEMS

9 ITEM NO.	10 CUSTOMER VAT REGISTRATION NO. (See Table Overleaf)	11 VALUE OF SUPPLIES OF GOODS (EXPORTS) IN EURO	12 FLAG

13

I declare that the information given in this statement is true and complete.

Signature | Date

Full Name of Signatory | Area Code | Telephone No. | Area Code | Fax. No.

VS1(E) VIES11 [SEE NOTES OVERLEAF]

Brief notes on the completion of the VIES Statement. (Full details can be found in the current VIES and INTRASTAT Trader's Manual, which has been issued to each registered trader involved in Intra Community trade. Copies of the Manual are available from the return address overleaf.)

Box 7	This should be a total of all values entered in Column 11.
Box 8	The total number of lines of information should be entered here.
Column 9	Each line of data must be numbered in sequence starting with 1 for each return.
Column 10	You must quote your E.U. customer's VAT Registration No., not forgetting to include the national prefix. See table below. A Trader may contact VIMA to verify that a VAT Number quoted is valid.
Column 11	The total invoiced value of all goods supplied to the E.U. customer (whose no. you have shown in Column 10) is entered here, rounded to the nearest EURO.
Column 12	Insert "T" if the goods are involved in Triangulation (Contact VIMA for details).

Traders are advised that before inserting customers VAT Registration Number in Box 10, they should verify National Prefix and V.A.T. Number format with Table hereunder.

EU COUNTRY	NATIONAL PREFIX	V.A.T. NUMBER FORMAT	EXAMPLE
Austria	AT	One Letter and eight digits	AT U12345678
Belgium	BE	Nine digits	BE 123456789
Cyprus	CY	Eight digits and one letter	CY 12345678M
Czech Republic	CZ	Eight, nine or ten digits	CZ 12345678 CZ 123456789 CZ 1234567891
Denmark	DK	Eight digits	DK 12345678
Estonia	EE	Nine digits	EE 123456789
Finland	FI	Eight digits	FI 12345678
France	FR	Eleven digits	FR 12345678912
Germany	DE	Nine digits	DE 123456789
Greece	EL	Nine digits	EL 123456789
Hungary	HU	Eight digits	HU 12345678
Ireland	IE	Seven digits and one letter or six digits and two letters	IE 1234567A IE 1Z23456A
Italy	IT	Eleven digits	IT 12345678912
Latvia	LV	Eleven digits	LV 12345678912
Lithuania	LT	Nine or twelve digits	LT 123456789 LT 123456789123
Luxembourg	LU	Eight digits	LU 12345678
Malta	MT	Eight digits	MT 12345678
Netherlands	NL	Eleven digits and one letter	NL 123456789B12
Poland	PL	Ten digits	PL 1234567891
Portugal	PT	Nine digits	PT 123456789
Slovakia	SK	Ten digits	SK 1234567891
Slovenia	SI	Eight digits	SI 12345678
Spain	ES	Eight digits and one letter or seven digits and two letters	ES A12345678 or ES X1234567W
Sweden	SE	Twelve digits	SE 123456789012
United Kingdom	GB	Nine digits or twelve digits if the number represents a sub-company within a group	GB 123456789 or GB 123456789123

N.B. Where a Trader has no Intra-Community Supplies in a particular return period, a "NIL" Statement should be submitted for that period.

VIES STATEMENT CONTD.

4 TRADER'S VAT REGISTRATION NO.

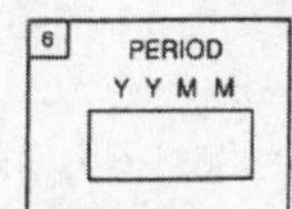
6 PERIOD
Y Y M M

9 ITEM NO.	10 CUSTOMER VAT REGISTRATION NO.	11 VALUE OF SUPPLIES OF GOODS (EXPORTS) IN EURO	12 FLAG	
B1	B2	B3	B4	E/L
B1	B2	B3	B4	E/L
B1	B2	B3	B4	E/L
B1	B2	B3	B4	E/L

B1	B2	B3	B4	E/L
B1	B2	B3	B4	E/L
B1	B2	B3	B4	E/L
B1	B2	B3	B4	E/L

B1	B2	B3	B4	E/L
B1	B2	B3	B4	E/L
B1	B2	B3	B4	E/L
B1	B2	B3	B4	E/L

B1	B2	B3	B4	E/L
B1	B2	B3	B4	E/L
B1	B2	B3	B4	E/L
B1	B2	B3	B4	E/L

B1	B2	B3	B4	E/L
B1	B2	B3	B4	E/L
B1	B2	B3	B4	E/L
B1	B2	B3	B4	E/L

VS1A(E)

5 ACCOUNTING FOR VAT: INVOICING, DEDUCTIONS AND SPECIAL PROCEDURES/CATEGORIES

Learning Outcomes

On completion of this chapter you will be able to:

- ✓ Identify who may issue a VAT invoice.
- ✓ Describe when an invoice should be issued and what it should contain.
- ✓ Describe the current and forthcoming procedures for electronic invoicing.
- ✓ Explain what deductions may be made by VAT-registered persons.
- ✓ List the qualifying activities in respect of which VAT deduction is allowed.
- ✓ List the items of expenditure in respect of which no input VAT deduction is allowable.
- ✓ Explain the concept of partial deduction.
- ✓ Understand the issues around VAT deduction by holding companies
- ✓ Identify who must account for VAT.
- ✓ Explain when VAT is due and payable.
- ✓ Explain when bad-debt relief and non-refundable deposit relief applies.
- ✓ Recognise when domestic VAT is subject to the reverse charge.
- ✓ Describe the cash receipts basis of accounting for VAT and the circumstances in which it may be used.
- ✓ Distinguish between a VAT period and an accounting period.
- ✓ Comment upon and understand the special schemes available for second-hand goods, travel agents and retailers.
- ✓ Discuss the potential application of the VAT system to local authorities.
- ✓ Explain the VAT treatment of VAT-registered farmers, flat-rate farmers, sea fishermen and agricultural contractors.
- ✓ Discuss the application of VAT to hire-purchase transactions.
- ✓ Complete Assignments and Questions in the corresponding chapter in *Irish Taxation: Law and Practice*, Volume 2.

5.1 Introduction

The main purpose of this chapter is to illustrate how a trader arrives at his/her VAT liability. Remember, it is the VAT-registered person (i.e. the accountable person) who must account for and pay the VAT which he/she has collected to the Collector-General.

This chapter will show how output VAT is arrived at, how deductions for input VAT incurred can be made and how a trader's VAT liability is computed. The chapter will also deal with certain categories of persons for whom accounting for VAT has its own peculiar rules.

5.2 VAT Invoices and Credit Notes

s66–73 VATCA 2010

VAT invoices are central to the operation of the VAT system, not only in Ireland but also throughout the EU. For the supplier of the goods and services, the VAT invoice forms the basis for identifying output VAT. For the customer, the VAT invoice forms the basis for identifying input VAT.

Similarly, VAT credit notes form the basis for reducing the output VAT of the supplier. For the customer, the VAT credit note forms the basis for reducing input VAT.

Certain rules relating to VAT invoices

5.2.1 Who may issue a VAT invoice/credit note?

Only a VAT-registered person may issue a VAT invoice or a VAT credit note. It is a serious offence for anyone other than a VAT-registered person to issue a VAT invoice.

5.2.2 In what circumstances must a VAT invoice be issued?

A VAT invoice must be issued by a VAT-registered person to another VAT-registered person in Ireland in respect of the taxable supply of goods or services. A VAT invoice must also be issued to a person registered for VAT in another EU Member State in respect of the taxable supply of goods or services. Furthermore, a VAT invoice must be issued to a person in another EU Member State in respect of distance selling. A VAT invoice must also be issued to State departments, local authorities, statutory bodies and persons carrying on exempt activities in respect of the supply of goods and/or services.

5.2.3 When must a VAT invoice/credit note be issued?

A VAT invoice must be issued, at the latest, by the fifteenth day of the month immediately following the supply of the goods or services, or following receipt of part-payment in respect of goods or services, the supply of which has not been completed.

A further VAT invoice must be issued, at the latest, by the fifteenth day immediately following agreement between the parties where an increased consideration is paid or is payable in respect of the supply previously invoiced.

A credit note must be issued, at the latest, by the fifteenth day of the month immediately following agreement between the parties where a reduced consideration is paid or is payable in respect of the supply previously invoiced.

5.2.4 What details must a VAT invoice contain?

A VAT invoice must contain the following information:

- the name, address and VAT registration number of the person supplying the goods or services to which the invoice relates;
- the name and address of the person to whom the supply of goods and services is made;
- a sequential number, which uniquely identifies the invoice;
- where appropriate, the VAT registration number of the person in the other EU Member State to whom the goods/services are supplied and an indication that the customer must self-account for the VAT;
- Where appropriate, in the case of a supply of goods, the VAT registration number of the person in the other EU Member State, and an indication that the invoice relates to an intra-EU supply of goods;
- the date of issue;
- the date of supply;
- a description of the goods or services supplied and, in the case of hiring, a description of the goods hired;
- the unit price exclusive of VAT and details of price reductions not included in the unit price;
- the consideration payable, exclusive of VAT;
- the rate(s) of VAT and the amount of VAT chargeable at each rate[1].
- Where the customer issues the invoice, the narrative "self-billing"
- Where the customer is liable for the payment of the VAT, the narrative "reverse-charge"

1 The amount of VAT indicated on the invoice issued by accountable persons must be specified in euro (€). The amount of the consideration may be expressed in any currency.

- Where the Travel Agent's margin scheme (see 5.5.2) is applied, the narrative "margin scheme – travel agents"
- Where one of the special schemes in used (see 5.5), one of the following narratives as is relevant "margin scheme – second hand goods" or "margin scheme – works of art", or "margin scheme – collector's items & antiques".

5.2.5 Electronic invoicing

s66–73 VATCA 2010

With effect from 1 January 2013 electronic and hardcopy invoices are treated similarly.

A hard copy invoice is no longer required to be issued. However, for the purpose of accountability and deductibility of VAT, an invoice (electronic or hardcopy) must exist. A supplier may now issue an invoice electronically to his customer.

The new rules are set out in Council Directive 2010/45/EU and apply from 1 January 2013.

Essentially electronic invoices are now on an equal footing with hardcopy invoices. The invoice issuer must be able to guarantee the authenticity, integrity and origin of electronic invoices. Special rules have also come into force with regards the storage of electronic invoices and access to same by the various tax authorities. The invoices must be retained in the same format as they have been issued.

With a paper invoice, it is very easy to establish whether the copy held by the supplier and that held by the customer are identical. This comparability must be capable of being carried out in the case of electronic invoicing.

The supplier is deemed to have issued the invoice and must retain a copy of it. The same details as are required on a physical invoice must also appear on an electronically issued invoice.

A specific regulation, Regulation 21, Value-Added Tax Regulations, 2010, lays down the conditions and system specifications governing the use and storage of electronic invoices. The changes which came into effect on 1 January 2013 have greatly simplified this area of VAT and through time, will result in greater usage of electronic invoices.

5.2.6 Self-billing (formerly known as Settlement vouchers)

A self-billing invoice is an invoice issued by the customer on behalf of a supplier. This mechanism is often used by large business customers (e.g., retail chains) who buy goods from a large number of smaller suppliers. The customers must be VAT-registered. The self-billing invoice becomes an invoice once accepted by the supplier. There must be a pre-existing agreement between both parties authorizing the customer to invoice on behalf of the supplier.

5.2.7 Debit notes

s59–62 VATCA 2010

A debit note is a credit note issued by a VAT-registered customer and becomes a credit note once accepted by the supplier.

5.3 Deductibility of Input VAT

s59–62 VATCA 2010

Section 59(2), VATCA 2010 states:

> *"In computing the amount of tax payable by an accountable person in respect of a taxable period, that person may, insofar as the goods and services are used by him for the purposes of his or her taxable supplies or of any of the qualifying activities, deduct ..."*

A VAT-registered person may deduct input VAT incurred by him/her with the exception of certain non-deductible VAT (see 5.3.2). Sometimes, the word "recover" is alternated with the word "deduct". In the context of input VAT, they have the same meaning.

Deduction of input VAT is an essential part of the VAT system. Deduction of input VAT ensures that only the end-user pays VAT. In order to deduct input VAT, the VAT-registered trader must be in possession of a valid VAT invoice, issued by his/her supplier, in respect of the VAT, that he/she proposes to deduct.

A deduction of input VAT can be made in relation to VAT incurred on goods and services acquired, which are being sold on, and in relation to VAT incurred on capital and expense items, which are used by the business for the purpose of its taxable supplies.

Among the items in respect of which an accountable person may make a deduction are:

- VAT charged by other accountable persons in the taxable period, where supported by invoices;
- VAT charged on goods bought under a hire-purchase agreement;
- VAT charged on the importation of goods (see Chapter 4, Cross-Border Trade);
- VAT applicable on the intra-Community acquisition of goods (equal to the output VAT accountable on the acquisition) (see Chapter 4, Cross-Border Trade);
- VAT charged on goods, which a business has used for a taxable activity and then applied for the purposes of an exempt activity, or which have been appropriated to private use (see Chapter 3, The General Principles);
- VAT applicable to the acquisition of developed property which is chargeable to VAT by virtue of a joint option for taxation (equal to the output VAT accountable on the supply) (see Chapter 6 Property Transactions and Building Services);
- VAT applicable to the surrender/assignment of a legacy lease (equal to the output VAT accountable on the supply – see Chapter 6, Property Transactions and Building Services);
- VAT applicable to the receipt of certain services received from abroad (see Chapter 4, Cross-Border Trade);

- the flat-rate addition (which is deemed to be VAT) paid by him/her to flat-rate farmers (see 5.7).

This list is not exhaustive but does include the main items in respect of which input VAT is deductible by an accountable person.

However a provision was introduced, effective from 1 January 2014, whereby if the amount of an invoice received by an accountable person has not been paid by six-months from the end of the taxable period in which the input VAT on the invoice has been claimed as a deduction, then the VAT deducted must be repaid to the Revenue by the accountable person. The only way this can be avoided is by way of prior agreement with the Revenue.

5.3.1 Qualifying activities

s59(2) VATCA 2010

A deduction may also be made for input VAT incurred on goods and services purchased where they are to be used by the taxable person in "qualifying activities". Among such qualifying activities are:

- the transport of passengers and their accompanying baggage outside Ireland;

  You will recall that passenger transport in Ireland is VAT-exempt, which precludes deduction of input VAT incurred, e.g., VAT on the cost of buying a bus, VAT on diesel, etc. However, input VAT may be recovered where the passengers are transported outside the State, e.g., by train to/from Belfast, by ferry to/from France, by plane to/from UK, USA, etc.

- the supply of goods in another EU Member State under the distance selling regime (see 4.2.3, Chapter 4);
- financial and insurance services and related intermediary services supplied to persons outside the EU;
- supplies of goods and services, the place of supply of which is outside Ireland and, which, if supplied in Ireland, would be liable to VAT;
- the issue of new stocks, new shares, new debentures or new securities.

For example, where an Irish architect who designs a building in London (place of supply is the UK) incurs Irish VAT (e.g., the rent of his office in Dublin, stationery, etc.), he may deduct input VAT incurred. This is on the basis that his services, which are liable to VAT in the UK, would be liable to VAT in Ireland were it the place of supply.

5.3.2 Non-deductible VAT

s60 VATCA 2010

A deduction of input VAT incurred on the purchase, importation or intra-Community acquisition of cars may not be made unless they are used as stock-in-trade (car-dealers), by a driving school for driving instruction, or by a car-hire firm.

A deduction of input VAT incurred on the purchase, importation or intra-Community acquisition of petrol may not be made unless it is used as stock-in-trade, i.e., it is for resale by petrol distributors, garages, etc.

A deduction of input VAT may not be made in relation to the purchase of accommodation, food and drink, entertainment, and personal services. deduction may be made in respect of VAT incurred on accommodation provided during attendance at a 'qualifying' conference by VAT registered persons.

Input VAT may not be deducted where the goods or services concerned are used exclusively for VAT-exempt or non-taxable supplies.

Example 5.1

A garage may deduct input VAT on a car because it is in the business of selling cars. However, a manufacturing company that buys a car for an employee cannot recover the input VAT incurred, as it is not in the business of buying and selling cars.

Example 5.2

A VAT-registered firm holds a Christmas party for its employees. It incurs input VAT on the hotel bill (drinks, hire of room, entertainment, meals, etc.). It cannot recover (deduct) the VAT incurred.

Example 5.3

An insurance company buys a computer. It cannot recover (deduct) the input VAT because the computer is used for a VAT-exempt activity.

5.3.3 Partial deduction of input VAT

s61 VATCA 2010

Where VAT has been incurred on goods and services that are used for both taxable and non-taxable supplies, referred to in legislation as "dual-use inputs", then special procedures must be put in place to ensure partial deduction (recovery) of input VAT incurred. Non-taxable supplies include exempt supplies and supplies outside the scope of VAT.

The cost should be directly attributed first, i.e., input VAT incurred on costs that can be directly attributed to taxable supplies may be fully deducted and input VAT incurred on costs that can be directly attributed to non-taxable supplies may not be deducted.

Where costs cannot be directly attributed, a partial deduction ratio must be computed. With effect from 1 January 2017 the deduction ratio must, in the first instance, be based on the ratio of taxable turnover to total tax exclusive turnover, where this ratio

> *"... correctly reflects the extent to which the dual-use inputs are used for the purposes of that person's deductible supplies or activities and has due regard to the rang e of that person's total supplies and activities".*

If however this apportionment method does not correctly reflect the extent to which the dual-use inputs are used then an alternative method which does so reflect must be used.

Example 5.4

A bank uses a computer for its exempt activities (bank account transactions, lending, etc.) and its taxable activities (car leasing, debt factoring, etc). It may recover (deduct) a portion of the input VAT incurred. Where the turnover from the exempt activities is €9m and the turnover from the taxable activities is €1m, then it may be possible to agree a recovery ratio of 10% with the Revenue Commissioners in relation to the VAT incurred on the computer.

Thus, where input VAT on the computer amounted to, say, €200,000, only €20,000 may be deducted.

However, where the computer processed, say, 150,000 transactions, of which 50,000 related to exempt transactions and 100,000 related to taxable transactions, it may be possible to seek a 66% recovery ratio in relation to the input VAT. Recovery ratios must be by way of agreement with the Revenue Commissioners.

5.3.4 Deduction of input VAT Motor Cars

A proportion of input VAT may be deducted on the purchase, hire, intra-EU acquisition or importation of certain motor vehicles, subject to the following conditions:

- The car (inc SUVs) must be first registered for VRT purposes on or after 1 January 2009
- It must have a level of CO_2 emissions of less than 156g/km (i.e. CO_2 emission bands A, B and C).
- It must be used primarily for business purposes. [Business purposes are defined as at least 60% business use].
- It must be used for business purposes for a period of two years or more.

If circumstances change within the two year period, i.e. the car is disposed of within two years, or it is used for less than 60% business purposes, and VAT credit has been claimed, then the accountable person is required to make an adjustment in the relevant taxable period, and repay a portion of the input VAT previously reclaimed.

If the car is disposed of or if 'business use' of the car by the accountable person drops below 60% then the claw-back of previously recovered VAT is calculated as follows:

Disposal or business use discontinues (or is used for less than 60% business use) within six months from date of purchase, acquisition or importation of the car	Clawback of all VAT deducted
Disposal or business use discontinues (or is used for less than 60% business use) in the period six to 12 months from date of purchase, acquisition or importation of the car	75% clawback of VAT deducted
Disposal or business use discontinues (or is used for less than 60% business use) in the period 12 to 18 months from date of purchase, acquisition or importation of the car	50% clawback of VAT deducted
Disposal or business use discontinues (or is used for less than 60% business use) in the period 18 to 24 months from date of purchase, acquisition or importation of the car	25% clawback of VAT deducted
Disposal or business use discontinues (or is used for less than 60% business use) after 24 months from date of purchase, acquisition or importation of the car	No clawback

Example 5.5

An accountable person purchases a new car for €30,000 in January 2009. He estimated that in excess of 60% of usage will be for business purposes. (comprising 80% taxable activities and 20% exempt activities). [Assume the VRT included in the price is €3,000.00]

The VAT included in the price is €5,048.78 (((30,000 – 3,000)/123) × 23) – note VRT is applied to the VAT-inclusive price of the car.

The VAT recoverable by the purchaser is €807.80 ((5,048.78 × 80%) × 20%).

5.3.5 Holding Company - Deduction of Input VAT

For VAT purposes holding companies can be classified into two categories, passive or active. Passive holding companies hold shares in subsidiaries and do not perform any transactions for economic gain. They simply hold the shares in their subsidiaries for investment purposes, In return they usually earn a dividend. These entities are not 'in business' and cannot register for VAT. As such they cannot deduct any domestic input VAT incurred. As they are not taxable persons they are not obliged to self-account for VAT on services received from abroad. However, any foreign VAT charged is not recoverable.

On the other hand, active holding companies, in addition to holding shares in subsidiaries, provide management services to such subsidiaries. There have been numerous cases at the CJEU concerning the VAT recovery position of such businesses. As these companies provide management services to subsidiaries they are 'in business' and as such entitled to recover input VAT.

Unfortunately, the extent to which such VAT is recoverable varies across the EU. In Ireland, the Revenue refuse to allow full deduction of input VAT, unlike the UK, and insist that the deductible VAT must be VAT arising on costs which are components of the management charge made to the subsidiaries. Where such a test cannot be satisfied the input VAT arising on costs cannot be deducted. At the time of writing, a number of cases are under appeal in relation to this matter.

5.3.6 Incomplete Invoices - Deduction of Input VAT

In deducting input VAT, it is usual that the person making the deduction is in possession of valid VAT invoices issued by, or on behalf of, the supplier of the goods/services. However, the CJEU has indicated that a deduction may still be made notwithstanding that the invoice may not have all of the necessary details. In Dankowski (C-438/09) the Court indicated that once the 'substantive' conditions relating to deduction were met then deduction of VAT was an entitlement, even if certain administrative conditions were not fulfilled. In the above-mentioned case the vendor was not registered for VAT but did issue an invoice showing VAT to his VAT registered customer. Where the service supplied is one which Is subject to VAT and where the VAT registered customer 'consumed' such service in making its taxable supplies then the 'substantive' conditions for deduction are met. The fact that the vendor was not registered for VAT could not be used by the tax authority to deny an input VAT deduction to the VAT registered customer. [Presumably the onus was on the tax authority to pursue the vendor and seek payment of the VAT charged by him].

5.4 Accounting for VAT

Part 9 ch3 VATCA 2010

Every accountable person is obliged to account for the VAT charged by him/her to others and to account for any VAT arising on intra-Community acquisitions made. An accountable person must also account for any VAT arising on the basis of a 'reverse charge' (see section 3.18) (e.g. certain construction services, receipt of services from abroad, etc.) and must also account for any VAT arising on the basis of a "self-supply" (e.g., the appropriation of goods from the business).

An accountable person accounts for VAT charged by completing a periodic VAT return and including on it the details of the output VAT arising on the transactions outlined above.

The general rule is that a person accounts for VAT on inputs and outputs on the invoice basis, i.e., by reference to invoices issued/received in a particular taxable period. However, certain persons may account for VAT on outputs on the basis of monies received (see 5.4.2).

5.4.1 When is VAT due?

In the case where a VAT invoice is required to be issued, VAT chargeable is due when the invoice in respect of the supply is issued, or, if an invoice does not issue in due time, the VAT is due within the period in which the invoice should have issued, i.e., on or before the fifteenth day of the month immediately following the month in which the goods or services were supplied.

Where there is no requirement to issue a VAT invoice, the VAT is due at the time the goods or services are supplied.

In the case of intra-Community acquisitions, the VAT is due on the fifteenth day of the month immediately following that during which the acquisition occurs.

Where a stage payment/advance payment is received prior to the supply/completion of the goods or services, the VAT is due when the part-payment is received.

In the case of the receipt of cross-border services, the VAT is due when payment is made for the services.

In cases where moveable goods are applied for the purposes of an exempt activity or where goods are appropriated for personal use, the tax is due when the exempt use or appropriation occurs.

5.4.2 VAT due on basis of cash receipts

Where more than 90% of an accountable person's turnover derives from supplies to persons who are not registered for VAT (B2C), or where an accountable person's total turnover does not exceed €2m in twelve continuous months, then such an accountable person may be authorised by the Revenue Commissioners to calculate the VAT due on the basis of payments received from customers.

Thus where a person who has been authorised to account for VAT on the basis of payments received is obliged to issue a VAT invoice (see 5.2.3) he is not obliged to account for VAT until payment for the supply has been received.

A person must apply to the Revenue Commissioner for this authorisation.

5.4.3 When is VAT payable?

It is very important to distinguish between VAT due and VAT payable. In the first instance, the VAT due and the VAT payable will rarely be the same amounts. This is due to the fact that the VAT due is the total output VAT as outlined above and the VAT payable is the VAT due less any input VAT that is deductible during the period.

In general, VAT payable must be paid to the Collector-General not later than the nineteenth day of the month immediately following a taxable period or an accounting period, whichever is appropriate.

In the case of a person who is obliged to account for VAT in respect of the intra-Community acquisition of a new means of transport, VAT is payable at the time of payment of vehicle registration tax (VRT) or, if VRT is not payable, at the time of registration of the vehicle.

5.4.4 Bad-debt relief

Bad-debt relief applies where an accountable person has accounted for VAT on a supply of goods or services in respect of which he/she has issued a VAT invoice and subsequently the debtor defaults, i.e. fails to pay the accountable person for the supply. There is no relief in the case of a debt relating to property.

Obviously, the relief will not apply to an accountable person who accounts for VAT on the cash receipts basis, as failure by a debtor to pay will not require adjustment to the VAT payable.

In the case of an accountable person accounting for VAT on the invoice basis, VAT is due in the period in which the invoice is issued. Where, subsequent to the issue of the invoice, the debtor defaults, then the supplier may reduce his/her VAT liability in the period in which the debt is being written off by the amount of the VAT on the bad debt.

Among the conditions which apply before the debt can be written off are:

- The accountable person must have taken all reasonable steps to collect the debt,
- The bad debt must be allowable as a deduction in arriving at tax-adjusted profits for income/corporation tax,
- The bad debt must be written off in the financial statements of the accountable person,
- The debtor may not be 'connected' to the accountable person writing off the debt.

As the purchaser will have deducted input VAT (remember, he/she has a valid VAT invoice), Revenue monitors the write-off of bad debts very closely, as the VAT amount involved is lost to the Exchequer.

Change of basis for accounting for output VAT

An accountable person may change from the monies-received basis to the invoice basis at any time. An accountable person may do this once he/she makes an application to the Revenue Commissioners and qualifies for the monies-received basis.

Adjustments are required in the event of a change of basis. Such adjustments are outlined in the Revenue Information Leaflet: "Moneys Received Basis of Accounting – October 2008".

5.4.5 What is a taxable period?

A taxable period consists of two calendar months, commencing on the first day of January, March, May, July, September and November.

5.4.6 An accounting period

For most VAT-registered persons, an accounting period is the same as a taxable period, i.e. two months.

The VAT return filed by the VAT-registered person in respect of a taxable period is known as a Form VAT 3. A sample form can be found at Appendix I to this chapter.

From time to time, the Collector-General may authorise accountable persons to make VAT returns and remit VAT payment for periods other than taxable periods.

Biannual VAT returns

Where a trader has an annual liability of less than €3,000 he may file two biannual returns each year.

Four monthly VAT returns

Where a trader has an annual liability of less than €14,000 but greater than €3,000 he may file three four-monthly returns each year.

Monthly VAT returns

Where an accountable person is in a permanent VAT repayment position, he/she may be authorised to make monthly VAT returns. This is of cash-flow benefit to the accountable person.

Annual VAT returns

The Collector-General may authorise accountable persons to file annual VAT returns, i.e., one VAT return per year.

In the case of certain authorised small traders, the VAT payable must be remitted not later than the nineteenth day of the month immediately following the annual accounting period.

In the case of all traders, an application may be made to the Collector-General to account for VAT payable on an annual basis. In order to avail of this treatment, the accountable person is obliged to set up a direct debit facility and make a monthly payment on account to the Collector-General.

Once the annual VAT return is filed, the balance of VAT payable, if any, must be paid by the nineteenth day of the month immediately following the annual accounting period. Where the balancing payment is in excess of 20% of the tax payable for the year, then an interest charge of circa 5.88% is applied to the balancing payment. This measure is to ensure that an accountable person does not postpone payment of what may be a very substantial VAT liability until the end of the accounting period.

5.4.7 Relief for non-refundable deposits

Where VAT has been accounted for on a deposit received in advance of a supply and where, due to a cancellation by the customer, the supply does not subsequently take place, then an adjustment may be made in the accounting period in which the cancellation occurs, reducing the amount of VAT due by the amount of VAT previously accounted for on the deposit, irrespective of whether or not the deposit is refunded to the customer. This is a new provision resulting from a recent decision of the ECJ. The reason for this relief is that as there has not been a supply (of goods or services) then there is not a transaction and therefore a charge to VAT cannot arise.

If a VAT invoice has been issued for the deposit received then a document, which the customer must treat as a credit note, must be issued by the supplier.

5.5 Margin & Special Schemes

VAT legislation provides for the use of 'Margin Schemes' and 'Special Schemes' in certain instances, by accountable persons in arriving at the amount of VAT which is payable by them. In general such schemes are used to prevent distortions which may arise in the VAT system and generally apply to the final link in the supply, i.e. the end supply of certain goods and services to consumers. In the case of margin schemes, as the name implies VAT is charged, levied and paid on the 'margin' applied by the vendor to his sale to the consumer. We will briefly look at some of the schemes currently available below.

5.5.1 General Margin Scheme

s87 VATCA 2010

The general margin scheme allows taxable dealers (an accountable person who purchased margin scheme goods) to apply VAT to the difference between the sale price and the purchase price of second-hand goods (including motor vehicles), works of art, antiques and collectors' items. The use of the scheme is at the discretion of the taxable dealer. If he chooses not to use the scheme for certain sales, then normal VAT rules apply.

Margin-scheme goods include the following:

- second-hand movable goods (including means of transport) but excluding new means of transport);
- certain works of art, collectors items and antiques;
- specified precious metals and precious stones (excluding, diamonds, rubies, sapphires, emeralds, gold, silver and platinum).

The Standard rate of VAT, currently 23%, applies to all supplies under the second-hand margin scheme.

The margin scheme applies to the supply, by taxable dealers, of second-hand goods acquired, from consumers, from taxable persons who were not entitled to recover VAT on their purchase of the goods and from other taxable dealers who applied the margin scheme to their sale of the goods (i.e. they did not mention VAT on their sales invoice issue in respect of their supply of the goods to another taxable dealer and instead indicated on the invoice that the margin scheme applied to the sale), but excluding new means of transport.
The scheme can also be extended to include the above indicated items where they have been imported from outside the EU.

In effect therefore the margin scheme applies to goods where the dealer was not charged VAT on his purchase of the goods. The dealer cannot deduct any input VAT included in the price of the goods purchased by him.

When the dealer sells any of the goods permissible under the margin scheme he cannot issue a VAT invoice in respect of such sale, irrespective of his customer.

The margin scheme operates by applying VAT, at the standard rate, to the margin between the purchase price and the sales price. The margin is inclusive of VAT and therefore the VAT arising on the margin is calculated by dividing the Margin amount by 123 and multiplying the result by 23.

A simplified arrangement is in place for individual items purchased and sold for less than €635. This provides that the taxable dealer accounts for VAT on his 'global margin' in the taxable period, i.e. he does not have to account for VAT on an item by item basis.

Example 5.6 – sale by a taxable dealer under margin scheme

Item purchased by a dealer for €600.00 from a consumer (no VAT charged). The item is subsequently sold for €1,500.00 under the margin scheme. The margin is €900.00 including VAT.

The VAT included in the sale price is €168.29 ((900/123) × 23)

In this example the 'profit' made by the dealer is €731.71 (900 – 168.29). Where second-hand goods are sold to a person who cannot recover VAT the margin-scheme is used as this minimises the amount of VAT payable by the dealer.

Example 5.7 – sale by dealer outside the margin scheme

Item purchased by a dealer for €600 from a consumer (no VAT charged). The item is subsequently sold for €1,500.00 + VAT outside the margin scheme.The VAT on the sale price is €345.00 (1,500 × 23%)

In this example the 'profit' made by the dealer is €900 (1,500 – 600). Generally where second-hand goods are sold to a person who can recover VAT then the margin-scheme is not used, e.g. selling antiques to a publican who wants to use them in his pub to create a certain ambiance as he can recover the VAT charged by the dealer.

Purchase and sale of second-hand motor vehicles under the margin scheme

As indicated above the margin scheme has been extended to include means of transport, which essentially means second-hand motor vehicles, small boats and small aircraft. Where a motor dealer purchases a second-hand motor vehicle from a person who was not entitled to reclaim VAT on his or her original purchase of the vehicle or accepts the trade-in of such a second hand motor vehicle, the dealer may apply the margin scheme to the resale of the vehicle. However, w.e.f. 21 December 2015 new means of transport (essentially cars less than 6 months old) are excluded from the scheme.

The following vehicles, *inter alia*, qualify for the scheme:

- Cars sold (or traded-in) to a taxable dealer by any person (in Ireland or another EU Member State) who was not entitled to deduct any VAT in relation to the original purchase of the vehicle, or
- Cars sold (or traded-in) by another taxable dealer within the margin scheme.

Example 5.8 – second-hand car accepted as part payment for a new car

A private individual trade-in a car against a new one. The taxable dealer allows a trade in value of €7,000 against the sale price of the new car, valued at €25,000 Including VAT). The dealer accounts for VAT on the €25,000 in the amount of €4,674.79.

Subsequently he sells the trade-in for €8,500. His margin on the sale of the trade in is €1,500, including VAT. The VAT which he must account for on the sale of the trade in is €280.48 ((8500 – 7000) /123 × 23).

Further information is available in Revenue Leaflet: "Margin Scheme - Second-hand Goods - December 2009".

5.5.2 Travel Agents Margin Scheme

s88 VATCA 2010

Until relatively recently, supplies of services by tour operators and travel agents in Ireland were treated as being VAT-exempt. However, at a relatively recent Appeal Commissioners hearing the services of tour operators were held to be liable to VAT. This prompted the introduction of a Travel Agents Margin Scheme (TAMS) in Ireland, with effect from 1 January 2010. This brings Ireland into line with the rest of the EU where TAMS (more often called TOMS, Travel Operators Margin Schemes), have operated for some time.

In effect VAT will be charged at the standard rate, 23%, on the supply of 'margin scheme services' by travel agents acting as principals (including tour operators). The margin is the difference between the selling price (which must include all costs, charges, taxes, etc) and the cost of 'bought-in' services, i.e. services which the travel agent purchases for the direct benefit of the customer, including, travel and accommodation services. Note that a travel agent is a person who acts as principal in the supply of 'margin scheme services' to travellers.

The travel agent (including tour operator) cannot deduct input VAT arising on the 'bought-in' services. However, travel agents can recover input VAT incurred on overheads which are not 'bought-in' services and which have been incurred by the travel agent in operating the business. Thus the travel agent (including tour operator) can recover input VAT arising on rent, light, heat, travel agents' commissions, etc., as any normal trader would.

This is an EU scheme that enables a travel agent to account for VAT in one Member State on all the travel services that he or she has supplied. Without such a scheme, a travel agent would be obliged to register and account for tax in each Member State where the services are supplied. The place of supply of margin scheme services is the place where the travel agent has established his or her business or has a fixed establishment from which he or she supplies those services. For travel agents established in Ireland the place of supply of their margin scheme services is Ireland, even though the travel itself may involve places outside Ireland.

The Irish scheme applies to travel agents (acting as principal) or undisclosed agents established in Ireland who supply travel packages to travellers. Other Irish businesses may come within the terms of the scheme when they add accommodation or passenger transport into a package, for example -

- organisers of sporting events, training courses, incentive travel or conference organisers;
- hotels buying in additional services for their guests and selling them on, such as transport etc.

However, any business, other than a travel agent's business, that supplies only incidental or once-off supplies of margin scheme services can account for the VAT on those supplies under the normal VAT rules and is not obliged to apply the margin scheme to them.

A travel agent acting as principal is a taxable person who buys and sells travel services in the course of his or her business activity, and includes in particular tour operators.

A travel agent acting in his or her own name but who is in fact acting on behalf of another supplier is a travel agent acting as an undisclosed agent. There is deemed to be a supply of the bought-in services to and from that undisclosed agent. Consequently the undisclosed agent is treated in the same way as a principal and is deemed to have bought-in the services for the benefit of the traveller. Such an undisclosed agent will come within the scope of the travel agent's margin scheme.

The scheme does not apply to supplies of travel services arranged by a travel agent acting as an intermediary or disclosed agent.

Example 5.9

A tour operator arranges a holiday in Ireland and sells the entire package for €1,100 to the traveller. In arranging the package the tour operator buys a hotel room for three nights for €450 + VAT and also breakfasts and evening meals to the value of €200 + VAT. In addition airport transfers and a tour to the value €200 are purchased.

The total cost of the bought-in services is:

Accommodation	*€510.75 (inc VAT at 9%)*
Meals	*€227.00 (inc VAT at 9%)*
Travel	*€200.00 (exempt from VAT)*
Cost	*€937.75*

The 'margin' is €162.25 (1,100 – 937.75)

The amount of VAT payable on the margin IS €30.33 ((162.25/123) × 23)

Thus we can see from the above example that of the €1,100 paid by the traveller, the yield to the Exchequer is €91.24 i.e., €30.33 paid over by the travel agent on his margin and €60.91 paid by the hotelier in respect of food and accommodation (which VAT cannot be reclaimed by the travel agent).

Further information is available in Revenue Leaflet: "Travel Agent's Margin Scheme - April 2010".

5.5.3 Retailers Special Schemes

Imagine a supermarket at the day's end. There is a cash register containing €15,000 upon which the retailer must account for VAT. During the course of the day, the retailer has sold goods at 0%, 9%, 13.5% and 23%. He/she must determine the proportion of his/ her turnover on which he/she must account for VAT at each of the three rates.

In the case of large outlets with EPOS (Electronic Point of Sales systems), the calculation is very simple. As each item is scanned, it is allocated one of the three VAT codes so that, at the end of the day, all the sales have been allocated to one of the three VAT rates. There is no need for any element of estimation.

However, in the case of smaller outlets, such pinpoint accuracy is not possible and the retailer must have some way of estimating what proportion of his/her sales are chargeable to VAT at each of the three rates. Such estimation must be fair and equitable to both the trader and the Exchequer. With this in mind, Revenue has approved three "Schemes for Retailers". In general, the schemes apportion the turnover on the basis of purchases. The most basic scheme (for traders whose annual turnover is less than €500,000) apportions turnover exactly on the basis of purchases, while the more developed schemes (for traders with a turnover between €500,000 and €1,500,000 and for traders with a turnover in excess of €1,500,000) allow the trader to apply margins to goods at each of the three VAT rates before apportionment.

There is also a special scheme available for chemists/pharmacists.

All of the above schemes, both margin and special, are explained fully on the Revenue web-site or in an Information Leaflet: "Retailers Special Schemes – January 2010".

5.6 The State and Local Authorities

Article 13 of the Council Directive 2006/112/EC states:

> *"States, regional and local government authorities and other bodies governed by public law shall not be considered taxable persons in respect of the activities or transactions in which they engage as public authorities ..."*

Until recently all Government departments, local authorities and non-commercial statutory bodies were considered to be outside the scope of VAT and in general could not register for VAT.

In 2009 the European Commission took Infraction Proceedings (see 2.7.4) against the Irish Government at the CJEU (case 554/07) in relation to the way in which State bodies are taxed in Ireland. The case was heard by the CJEU and on 16 July 2009 the decision went against Ireland.

As a result of this case there has, with effect from 1 July 2010, been a fundamental change in the way the State and local authorities are treated for VAT purposes. [Please note that the State includes hospitals, educational establishments, etc…]

Where the activities of such bodies are carried on by such bodies acting in their 'public body' capacity and where distortions of competition do not arise then their activities continue to be outside the scope of VAT.

However, where the activities carried out are 'commercial' in nature or where a distortion of competition could rise in other cases then the activities are subject to VAT and the body concerned is obliged to register for VAT.

Revenue has published limited guidance specifically directed to local authorities.

For the purposes of construction services the State and Local Authorities are considered to be principals and the reverse charge will apply [see 3.18 above].

From 1 January 2013 the registration threshold of €37,500 applies to turnover derived by public authorities from the provision of sporting and physical educational facilities (including pools). Once above this threshold public authorities will be obliged to account for VAT at the reduced rate, currently 13.5%, on income from such facilities.

In January 2017 the CJEU gave its Interpretation in relation to a dispute between the National Roads Authority (now TII) and the Revenue Commissioners [case C-344/15]. It determined in favour of the NRA. When the NRA commenced operating the Port Tunnel toll and the M50 toll the Revenue instructed the NRA to apply VAT to the toll charges. The CJEU ruled that the NRA, being a state organization, should not apply VAT to its toll charges as a necessary prerequisite would be that the non-application of VAT would result in 'distortion of competition' vis-à-vis commercial operators. The CJEU stated that no such distortion would arise, primarily because the commercial and state run tolls were not competing with each other. The Revenue was obliged to repay a large amount of VAT to the NRA. With effect from 1 April 2017 TII has ceased applying VAT to its tolls on the M50 and Port Tunnel. Needless to say, commercial operators of the other toll roads will continue to apply VAT (@ 23%) to their tolls.

5.7 Farmers

s6 VATCA 2010

From the outset, the VAT treatment of farmers can cause unnecessary confusion. Some basic information should ensure that this is not the case. One of the main reasons for the confusion that surrounds farmers and VAT is the use of the VAT system as an instrument of social policy. The current VAT Directive, as was the case with past VAT Directives enables Member States to implement special schemes to compensate groups such as farmers for VAT incurred.

For VAT purposes, a farmer is a person who engages in one or more of the activities listed in Part I, Schedule 4, VATCA 2010. Broadly speaking, the activities are crop production, cultivation, stock farming, forestry and fisheries.

Farmers are categorized into two groups, i.e., those who have elected, or are obliged, to register for VAT and those who are not so registered. Those farmers who are not registered for VAT are referred to as "flat-rate farmers". Flat-rate farmers constitute the majority of farmers in Ireland.

Very often, a farmer may engage in activities other than farming (as defined in Part II, Schedule 4). Where a farmer also carries out one of the activities listed below and the turnover from the activity or a combination of such activities does not reach the prescribed threshold, the farmer is not obliged to register and can continue to be a flat-rate farmer. Where the turnover exceeds the prescribed threshold, the farmer is obliged to register for VAT.

The relevant turnover thresholds are as follows:

- Where the farmer supplies agricultural services, the threshold is €37,500.
- Where the farmer is engaged in the supply of bovine semen, the threshold is €75,000.
- Where the farmer supplies nursery or garden-centre stock, the threshold is €75,000.
- Where the farmer is engaged in a combination of the above, the threshold is €37,500.

5.7.1 VAT-registered farmers

VAT-registered farmers have the same obligations and rights as any other accountable person. Their sales are liable to VAT at a variety of VAT rates, depending on the goods and services being supplied, e.g., wool (23%), live cattle, sheep, etc. (4.8%), milk, grass, barley, wheat, etc. (0%), and live poultry (13.5%). Many of the agricultural services which may be supplied by farmers are liable to VAT at the 0% or 13.5% rate, including ploughing, harrowing, rolling, supply and spread of fertilizers – all at the 0% rate. Sowing, planting, harvesting, reaping, mowing, baling, silage making, stock minding, land drainage and reclamation, pruning and hedge cutting – the reduced rate (13.5%). Transport, storage, management, product packaging and cleaning and the hire of machinery – the standard rate (23%).

5.7.2 Flat-rate farmers

Despite not being registered for VAT, a flat-rate farmer is nonetheless obliged to register for VAT in respect of intra-Community acquisitions (subject to the relevant threshold) and receipt of 'reverse charge' services (as any person in business is obliged to), but he/she is not registered in respect of his/her farming activities. Freshwater fishermen and fish farmers are regarded as flat-rate farmers; whilst sea fishermen are not (see 5.8).

A flat-rate farmer applies the "flat-rate addition" of 5.4% (increased from 5.2% to 5.4% from 1 Jan 2017) when he/she makes sales to VAT-registered persons. This amount is not VAT *per se*, but is nonetheless processed through the VAT system by the VAT registered buyer as though it were VAT. The flat-rate addition is paid to the farmer by the VAT-registered customer.

For example:

- Cattle are sold in the mart for €20,000. A flat-rate addition of €1,080 is paid to the farmer in addition to the €20,000.
- Milk is sold to the creamery for €3,000. A flat-rate addition of €162 is paid to the farmer in addition to the €3,000.
- Cabbage is sold to a retailer for €500. A flat-rate addition of €27 is paid to the farmer in addition to the €500.
- Wool is sold to a wool merchant for €15,000. A flat-rate addition of €810 is paid to the farmer in addition to the €15,000.

The VAT-registered buyer of the produce recoups the flat-rate addition by deducting the sum of the flat-rate additions paid to farmers in a taxable period from the amount of VAT due in arriving at the amount of VAT payable. The flat-rate addition is deemed to be VAT so as to enable the VAT-registered buyer to reclaim the amount on his/her VAT return (see 5.3).

Notwithstanding that the flat-rate addition is deemed to be VAT paid by a VAT-registered buyer, it is not deemed to be VAT in the hands of the farmer, and consequently the amount accrues for the benefit of the farmer. Accordingly, the purpose of the flat-rate addition is to compensate unregistered farmers for VAT incurred on farm expenses.

5.7.3 Disapplication of the flat-rate addition

Finance Act, 2016 introduced a provision to VAT legislation (section 86A) which enables the Minister, in certain circumstances, to remove the flat-rate addition from the sale of certain produce by 'flat-rate' farmers. This is an avoidance provision and will most likely only be invoked where abuse is detected.

5.7.4 Invoicing by flat-rate farmers

s86 VATCA 2010

A flat-rate farmer is obliged to issue an invoice to a VAT-registered buyer and show the consideration for the sale and, separately, the flat-rate addition. Legislation provides that the buyer may prepare the invoice and give a copy to the farmer. In this case, the farmer is deemed to have fulfilled his/her obligations. This is the most common method of invoicing, as the buyer is the person who will have to recoup the amount from Revenue and it gives him/her greater control and flexibility over issuing the invoice.

5.7.5 Direct VAT repayments to flat-rate farmers

In addition to the 5.4% flat-rate addition received from VAT registered buyers, a flat-rate farmer may apply directly to the Revenue Commissioners for repayment of input VAT incurred on the construction, extension and alteration of farm buildings and on land reclamation.

5.8 Sea Fishermen

s6 VATCA 2010

A sea fisherman whose sales consist of unprocessed fish to VAT-registered customers is not obliged to register for VAT but may elect to do so.

In addition, an unregistered fisherman is allowed to sell equipment used by him in his business and other goods (e.g., sales of fish to the general public) up to a value of €70,000 before he is obliged to register for VAT.

Where a sea fisherman elects, or is obliged to register for VAT, he/she has the same obligations and rights as any other VAT-registered person.

5.9 Agricultural Contractors

Sch 4 VATCA 2010

Agricultural contracting is the supply of a service which is liable to VAT, generally at zero or a reduced rate, currently 13.5%. Such services include fieldwork, reaping and mowing, threshing, baling, collecting, harvesting, sowing, planting, spraying, land drainage, hedge trimming and tree felling.

5.10 Horses & Greyhounds

Following a decision of the Court of Justice of the European Union in infraction proceedings taken against Ireland (Case C-108/11) in 2013, the VAT rates which apply to certain transactions involving horses and greyhounds have been changed from 1 January 2015.

The 9% VAT rate is to apply to the:

- supply of live horses, other than those normally intended for use as foodstuffs or for use in agricultural production,
- supply of greyhounds, and
- hire of horses.

The 4.8% livestock rate continues to apply to livestock in general, and to horses that are intended for use as foodstuffs or for use in agricultural production.

The 9% VAT rate will apply to insemination services for all animals, including livestock, horses and greyhounds, and also to the supply of livestock semen and horse semen.

5.11 Hire Purchase Transactions

Hire purchase transactions have a unique VAT treatment because they combine a taxable supply of goods and a VAT exempt supply of financial services, the finance/interest charge.

The supply of goods to a HP Company, such goods being hired by the HP Company to a customer by way of a hire purchase agreement, is a taxable supply on which the supplier is obliged to account for VAT. However the onward supply of the goods by the HP Company, at the end of the hire period, to the customer is not a supply for VAT. The finance/interest charge levied by the HP Company is exempt from VAT. The supplier will invoice the HP Company, who in turn will invoice the customer at the outset of the hire period.

However if the customer defaults and the HP Company is obliged to sell the repossessed goods then it will charge VAT on the supply and will also be entitled to deduct the VAT originally charged by the garage on the goods. This has the effect of giving bad-debt relief to the HP Company in the case of customer default.

A HP Company can avail of the margin scheme for second-hand vehicles (see 5.5.1).

[Note: HP transactions should not be confused with lease transactions, which for VAT purposes, is the supply of a service].

5.12 Vouchers

On 27 June 2016 the European Council adopted Council Directive (EU) 2016/1065, amending the VAT Directive in relation to the VAT treatment of vouchers. This is the first time that vouchers have been dealt with in the VAT directive, following more than 10 years of negotiations.

The rules will apply to vouchers issued after 31 December 2018.

A 'voucher' means an instrument where there is an obligation to accept it as consideration or part consideration for a supply of goods or services and where the goods or services to be supplied or the identities of their potential suppliers are either indicated on the instrument itself or in related documentation, including the terms and conditions of use of such instrument;

Single purpose vouchers, i.e. vouchers conferring rights to acquire goods or services where the place of supply and the VAT due on the goods/service is known at the time of issue of the voucher, will be subject to VAT at the time of issue of the voucher. Each transfer of the single purpose voucher will be treated as a supply of goods/services to which the voucher entitles a person to receive.

Multi-purpose vouchers, i.e. vouchers which are not single purpose vouchers, will not be subject to VAT at the time of issue. Rather the usual rules will apply whereby VAT will arise at the time of the supply of the goods/service.

Member states are obliged to amend domestic VAT legislation to give effect to this directive by 31 December 2018 at the latest.

[At the time of going to print legislation giving effect to the new rules relating to the taxation of vouchers has not been passed].

5.13 Summary

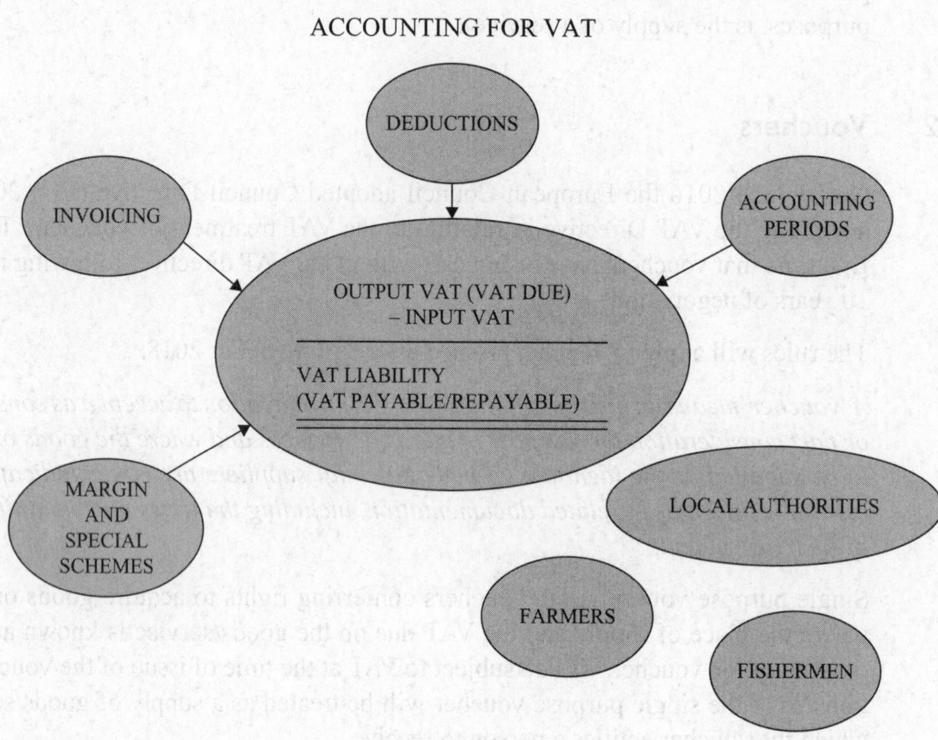
ACCOUNTING FOR VAT
DEDUCTIONS
INVOICING
ACCOUNTING PERIODS
OUTPUT VAT (VAT DUE)
– INPUT VAT
VAT LIABILITY
(VAT PAYABLE/REPAYABLE)
MARGIN AND SPECIAL SCHEMES
LOCAL AUTHORITIES
FARMERS
FISHERMEN

Appendix I

Specimen of VAT 3 form

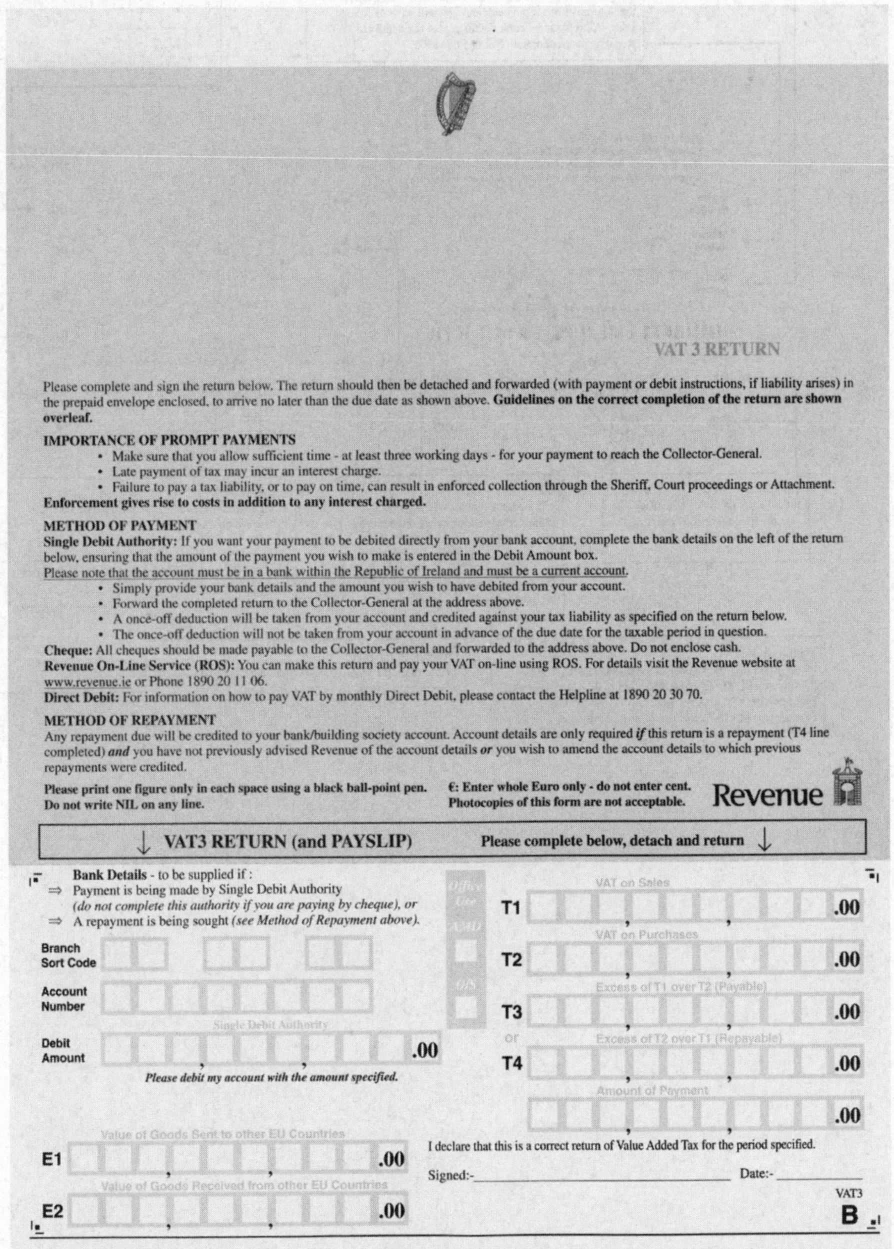

VAT 3 RETURN

Please complete and sign the return below. The return should then be detached and forwarded (with payment or debit instructions, if liability arises) in the prepaid envelope enclosed, to arrive no later than the due date as shown above. **Guidelines on the correct completion of the return are shown overleaf.**

IMPORTANCE OF PROMPT PAYMENTS

- Make sure that you allow sufficient time - at least three working days - for your payment to reach the Collector-General.
- Late payment of tax may incur an interest charge.
- Failure to pay a tax liability, or to pay on time, can result in enforced collection through the Sheriff, Court proceedings or Attachment.

Enforcement gives rise to costs in addition to any interest charged.

METHOD OF PAYMENT

Single Debit Authority: If you want your payment to be debited directly from your bank account, complete the bank details on the left of the return below, ensuring that the amount of the payment you wish to make is entered in the Debit Amount box.

Please note that the account must be in a bank within the Republic of Ireland and must be a current account.

- Simply provide your bank details and the amount you wish to have debited from your account.
- Forward the completed return to the Collector-General at the address above.
- A once-off deduction will be taken from your account and credited against your tax liability as specified on the return below.
- The once-off deduction will not be taken from your account in advance of the due date for the taxable period in question.

Cheque: All cheques should be made payable to the Collector-General and forwarded to the address above. Do not enclose cash.

Revenue On-Line Service (ROS): You can make this return and pay your VAT on-line using ROS. For details visit the Revenue website at www.revenue.ie or Phone 1890 20 11 06.

Direct Debit: For information on how to pay VAT by monthly Direct Debit, please contact the Helpline at 1890 20 30 70.

METHOD OF REPAYMENT

Any repayment due will be credited to your bank/building society account. Account details are only required ***if*** this return is a repayment (T4 line completed) ***and*** you have not previously advised Revenue of the account details ***or*** you wish to amend the account details to which previous repayments were credited.

Please print one figure only in each space using a black ball-point pen. Do not write NIL on any line.

€: Enter whole Euro only - do not enter cent. Photocopies of this form are not acceptable.

Revenue

↓ **VAT3 RETURN (and PAYSLIP)** **Please complete below, detach and return** ↓

Bank Details - to be supplied if :

⇒ Payment is being made by Single Debit Authority *(do not complete this authority if you are paying by cheque), or*

⇒ A repayment is being sought *(see Method of Repayment above).*

Branch Sort Code

Account Number

Single Debit Authority

Debit Amount .00

Please debit my account with the amount specified.

Office Use

AMD

O/S

VAT on Sales

T1 .00

VAT on Purchases

T2 .00

Excess of T1 over T2 (Payable)

T3 .00

or

Excess of T2 over T1 (Repayable)

T4 .00

Amount of Payment

.00

Value of Goods Sent to other EU Countries

E1 .00

Value of Goods Received from other EU Countries

E2 .00

I declare that this is a correct return of Value Added Tax for the period specified.

Signed:-__________ Date:-______

VAT3

B

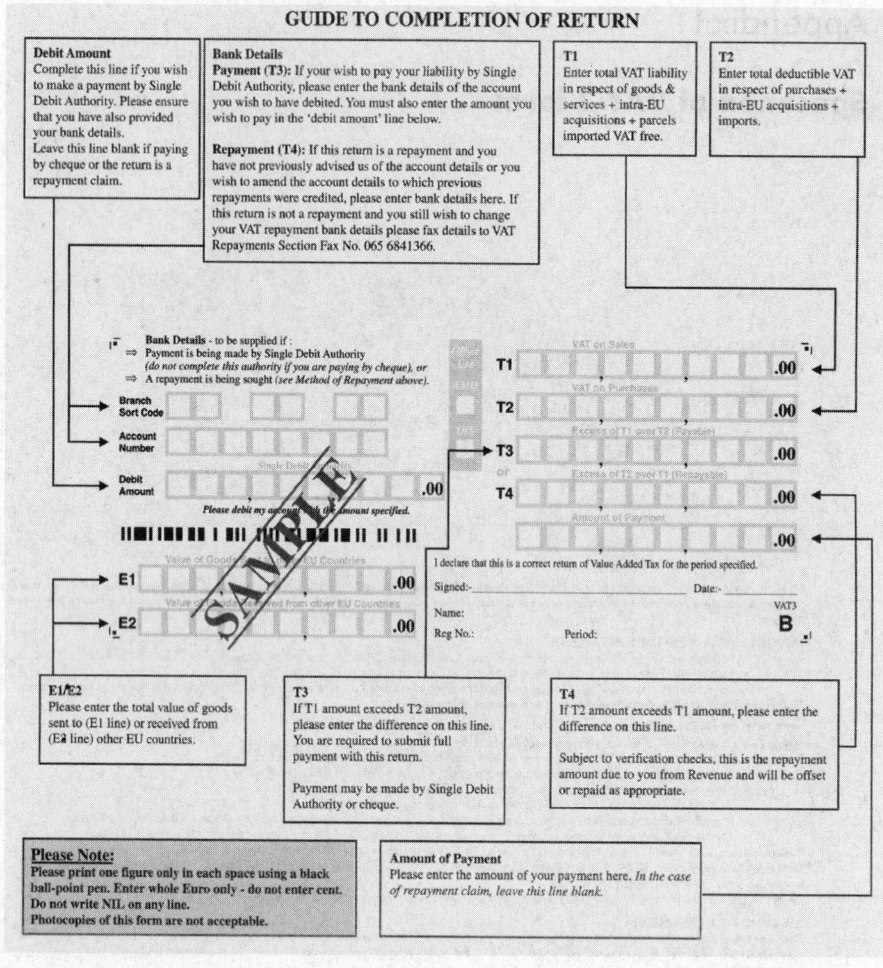

GUIDE TO COMPLETION OF RETURN

Debit Amount
Complete this line if you wish to make a payment by Single Debit Authority. Please ensure that you have also provided your bank details.
Leave this line blank if paying by cheque or the return is a repayment claim.

Bank Details
Payment (T3): If your wish to pay your liability by Single Debit Authority, please enter the bank details of the account you wish to have debited. You must also enter the amount you wish to pay in the 'debit amount' line below.

Repayment (T4): If this return is a repayment and you have not previously advised us of the account details or you wish to amend the account details to which previous repayments were credited, please enter bank details here. If this return is not a repayment and you still wish to change your VAT repayment bank details please fax details to VAT Repayments Section Fax No. 065 6841366.

T1
Enter total VAT liability in respect of goods & services + intra-EU acquisitions + parcels imported VAT free.

T2
Enter total deductible VAT in respect of purchases + intra-EU acquisitions + imports.

Bank Details - to be supplied if :
⇒ Payment is being made by Single Debit Authority *(do not complete this authority if you are paying by cheque), or*
⇒ A repayment is being sought *(see Method of Repayment above).*

Branch Sort Code

Account Number

Single Debit Authority

Debit Amount .00

Please debit my account with the amount specified.

SAMPLE

Value of Goods sent to other EU Countries

E1 .00

Value of Goods received from other EU Countries

E2 .00

VAT on Sales

T1 .00

VAT on Purchases

T2 .00

Excess of T1 over T2 (Payable)

T3 .00

or

Excess of T2 over T1 (Repayable)

T4 .00

Amount of Payment

.00

I declare that this is a correct return of Value Added Tax for the period specified.

Signed:- Date:-

Name:

Reg No.: Period:

VAT3

B

E1/E2
Please enter the total value of goods sent to (E1 line) or received from (E2 line) other EU countries.

T3
If T1 amount exceeds T2 amount, please enter the difference on this line. You are required to submit full payment with this return.

Payment may be made by Single Debit Authority or cheque.

T4
If T2 amount exceeds T1 amount, please enter the difference on this line.

Subject to verification checks, this is the repayment amount due to you from Revenue and will be offset or repaid as appropriate.

Please Note:
Please print one figure only in each space using a black ball-point pen. Enter whole Euro only - do not enter cent. Do not write NIL on any line. Photocopies of this form are not acceptable.

Amount of Payment
Please enter the amount of your payment here. *In the case of repayment claim, leave this line blank.*

6 PROPERTY TRANSACTIONS AND BUILDING SERVICES

Learning Outcomes

On completion of this chapter you will be able to:

- ✓ Broadly understand the new rules and new terms relating to VAT and property.
- ✓ Identify dealings in property that may constitute taxable supplies.
- ✓ Know what constitutes development in relation to property.
- ✓ Distinguish between supplies of goods and supplies of services in relation to property transactions.
- ✓ Distinguish between taxable and exempt property supplies and understand the importance of the joint option for taxation.
- ✓ Distinguish between taxable and exempt leases and short-term lettings and understand the importance of the landlords's option to tax a lease.
- ✓ Know who accounts for VAT on the taxable supply of property.
- ✓ Have an understanding of the transitional rules relating to the supply of developed property and the letting of property.
- ✓ Have a general understanding of the operation of the Capital Goods Scheme.
- ✓ Have a general understanding of the application of ToB to property sale.
- ✓ Describe the VAT treatment of building services.
- ✓ Explain the two-thirds rule and its application to the development of immoveable goods.
- ✓ Know who accounts for VAT on a building service.
- ✓ Understand the role and obligations of liquidator, receiver, mortgagee-in-possession or other person exercising a power in relation to the Capital Goods Scheme.
- ✓ Complete Assignments and Questions in the corresponding chapter in *Irish Taxation: Law and Practice*, Volume 2.

6.1 Introduction

The VAT legislation relating to various property transactions changed fundamentally with effect from 1 July 2008.

In 2005 the Revenue Commissioners commenced a review of the application of VAT to property transactions. What started off in 1972, at the introduction of VAT, as a relatively straightforward application of VAT law had become, by 2005, a very complex and specialised area within the VAT system; so much so that any property transaction of substance required the advice of a VAT specialist.

The current legislative provisions relating to VAT are an attempt to simplify the application of VAT to transactions concerning the sale and letting of commercial property.

While simplification was one of the driving forces in introducing the change, a key consideration was to protect the source of revenue for the State. Thus it should be borne in mind that, while simplification has been introduced, the new provisions ensure that the revenue accruing from VAT on property-related transactions is not reduced.

Additionally the new legislation brings our treatment of transactions relating to property broadly into line with the provisions of Council Directive 2006/112/EC, the recently recast VAT directive.

The application of VAT to property related transactions is dealt with in VATCA 2010 at Part 11, Chapters 93-98 and Part 8, Chapter 2, Sections 63-64.

Broadly speaking, and for ease of understanding, the new provisions can be broken into five categories, as follows:

- The supply of property – s93–95 VATCA 2010
- The letting of property – s96–97 VATCA 2010
- Transitional provisions relating to the each of the above categories – s95 VATCA 2010
- The Capital Goods Scheme – s63–64 VATCA 2010
- Building Services

The introduction to VAT as it relates to property transactions will, in this publication, be dealt with systematically under each of the above categories.

At this point it is important to recall that VAT is applicable only to transactions carried out in the course or furtherance of business. Therefore, for example, a person selling their place of residence will not fall within the scope of VAT as it is not carried out for a business purpose. The same cannot be said, however, where a private individual disposes of a rental property.

In general the purchaser of a property will issue a document called, “pre-contract VAT enquiries”, to the seller. This documents mirrors the VAT legislation on property transactions and enables the seller to inform the purchaser in relation to the proposed

VAT treatment of the sale. The document has been prepared by the Law Society of Ireland. Once both parties agree on the VAT treatment, the relevant VAT clause will be contained. In the document 'Conditions for Sale', the sale agreement which documents the transaction.

6.2 Some Definitions

Listed below are some terms and definitions with which you should be familiar and which we will refer to throughout this chapter:

- ***Capital Goods*** – this term refers to developed immovable goods, i.e., developed property. Thus the property must have been developed in order for it to be categorised as a "Capital Good".
- ***Developed/Development*** includes the construction, demolition, alteration, or reconstruction of any building on land or the carrying out of any engineering works in, on, over or under the lands which adapts it for a materially altered use. See 6.3.1.
- ***Minor Development*** – important in the context of whether or not a property is 'new' (see below). Two conditions are necessary before any development of property can be classified as "Minor":
  - The development must not adapt (or intend to adapt) the property for materially altered use, and
  - The cost of such development must not exceed 25% of the sale value of the property.
- ***Completed Property*** – means that development of the property has reached a stage whereby the property can be used for the purpose for which it has been designed. It should be noted that the development in relation to a "completed property" may vary depending on the property concerned. Thus, for example, in the case of a residential property, completion would entail developing the property to the point where a person could reasonably expect to move in and use it without any further development being necessary. However, in the case of a unit in a shopping centre, development to "shell and core" would constitute completion of the property. By "shell and core" we mean developed to a stage whereby the tenant can complete the development, by way of 'tenant fit-out', to his/her own requirement. It is ususal for tenants to "fit out" units to their own specifications/requirements.

New Property – Important with regards to the charge to VAT on the supply of property. Following completion, a property is considered to be a 'new' for a period of five years following such completion.

However, where the property is disposed of within the first five years following completion to an unconnected person, the property only remains a "new" for a period of 24 months following first occupation.

It may be possible for a property which is no longer considered 'new' to re-acquire its 'new' status, thus potentially bringing any future supply of the property within the charge to VAT (see 6.3.1).

- ***Joint Option for Taxation*** – This term refers to the joint exercise of an option by the vendor and purchaser to have VAT charged on the supply of a property which would otherwise be exempt from VAT.
- ***Landlords Option to Taxation*** – this term refers to an option exercised solely by the landlord to charge VAT (at 23%) on the letting of a certain property which would otherwise be exempt from VAT.

s97(3), VATCA 2010

- ***Connected Person*** – in relation to the letting of property, the question of whether or not the lessor and the lessee are connected persons is relevant (see 6.5). In addition, in relation to determining the period during which a property remains 'new', a disposal to a connected person is relevant. A 'connected person' as defined is quite complex and covers a variety of relationships between the lessor/lessee and vendor/purchaser.

Individuals are connected with:

- Their spouse;
- Their relatives or relatives of their spouses;
- Individuals (or spouses of individuals) with whom they are in partnership;
- The beneficiary of a trust where the individual is a trustee.

Companies (including bodies of persons) are connected with:

- Persons who control that company;
- Other companies that act in pursuit of a common purpose with that company;
- A person(s) with a reasonable commonality of interests who have the power to determine the activities of two or more companies.

- ***Capital Goods Owner*** – For the purposes of the Capital Goods Scheme a Capital Goods Owner is any person who while acting in the course or furtherance of business, incurs expenditure on the acquisition or development of a Capital Good. In the case of a flat-rate farmer (see 5.7) the acquisition or development of a building or structure designed for use in, and used in, a farming enterprise is excluded.
- ***Capital Goods Scheme*** – is a mechanism for regulating VAT deductibility over the "VAT life" of a Capital Good. (See 6.7).

6.3 The Supply of Developed Property

6.3.1 The Supply of property

The supply includes the supply of a freehold or the supply of a "freehold equivalent" i.e., an interest in property which amounts, in substance, to a freehold interest, e.g., a very long lease.

A supply of property involves the transfer of ownership or the transfer in substance of the right to dispose of the property as owner or otherwise. It is not necessary that legal title be transferred.

6.3.2 The charge of VAT

Two conditions must be fulfilled for the supply of developed property to come within the charge of VAT:

(1) The property must have been developed (note minor development – see 6.2 – does not constitute development), and
(2) The supply must be for consideration in the course or furtherance of business.

Thus, any property supplied prior to completion, which fulfills both of the above conditions, is liable to VAT at 13.5%.

In the case of a completed property (see 6.2), a third condition must be fulfilled, namely the property must be 'new' (see 6.2). This condition does not apply in the case of the sale of residential property by the developer of the property or a person connected with the developer – such supplies will always be liable to VAT at 13.5%.

6.3.3 What Constitutes "Developed"/"Development"?

It is important to understand what constitutes "development" for VAT purposes. "Development" is defined as follows:

s2(1) VATCA 2010

"development" *in relation to any land, means—*

(a) The construction, demolition, extension, alteration or reconstruction of any building on the land, or

(b) the carrying out of any engineering or other operation in, on, over or under the land to adapt it for a materially altered use,

The definition is very broad and it may be more appropriate at this stage to say what does not constitute development. it is only essential repairs and maintenance (e.g., painting, cleaning, repairing structural defects, etc.) that will not constitute development for VAT purposes.

Development and 'new' property

Development, subject to certain conditions, can make a property 'new' for VAT purposes. Therefore if a property is not already 'new' and development work is carried out which is not considered to be a 'minor development', then the property will be considered 'new' and the supply of the property (within the specified timeframe – see 6.2) will be liable to VAT.

In contrast, minor development will not impact on the VAT status of a property. Thus, if a property is not already 'new' and development work is carried out that is considered to be a 'minor development', the property will not be considered 'new' and the supply of the property will continue to be exempt from VAT.

6.3.4 The exempt supply of property

When a completed property is no longer a 'new' then its supply exempt from VAT.

Thus, the first or subsequent sale of a completed property after a period of five years from completion is exempt from VAT.

The subsequent sale of a property within the five-year period, but following two years of occupation, is also exempt from VAT.

With effect from January 2010 when ownership of a property is transferred by way of a vesting order made by the Courts to the National Asset Management Agency (NAMA), and where the supply would be exempt from VAT, NAMA may, on its own, exercise a joint option for taxation, which will render the supply liable to VAT.

A Capital Goods Scheme adjustment will have to be made by the Capital Goods Owner in respect of a VAT exempt supply affected within the "VAT life" of the completed property (see Capital Goods Scheme – section 6.7).

6.3.5 Making an exempt supply of property liable to VAT

Both parties to the sale of property which is not new may exercise a joint option, in writing, to tax the (otherwise exempt) transaction. This will render the sale liable to VAT at 13.5%.

6.3.6 Supply of property in connection with a contract to develop the property

This anti-avoidance provision renders the supply of property in connection with an agreement to develop the property as always liable to VAT regardless of whether or not the property is developed or whether the transaction is carried out in the course or furtherance of business.

6.3.7 Who accounts for the VAT on the taxable supply of property?

In almost all cases it is the vendor who must account for any VAT charged on the supply of property. However, the notable exception is in the case where a joint option to tax an otherwise exempt supply of property has been exercised. In such cases it is the purchaser who is obliged to account for the VAT charged on the supply, on a 'reverse charge' basis (see Chapter 3, section 3.18).

In addition, with effect from January 2010, when ownership of a property is transferred by way of a vesting order made by the Courts to the National Asset Management Agency (NAMA), the recipient of the property, NAMA, accounts for VAT on the supply on the reverse-charge basis.

6.3.8 The application of the Capital Goods Scheme

Where the supply of property is exempt from VAT, it will be important for the vendor to determine whether or not an adjustment under the Capital Goods Scheme ('CGS') is required (see 6.7).

The "VAT life" of a completed property is the period in which a Capital Goods Scheme adjustment must be made, should such adjustment be required, upon the supply of such completed property. In the VAT legislation it is referred to as the 'adjustment period' (see 6.7).

In the case of a freehold or freehold equivalent, the "VAT life" is a period of 20 years from the date such interest in the property was acquired. If the property was developed subsequent to such acquisition (but prior to 1 July 2008) then the "VAT life" is for a period of 20 years from such development.

In the case of works on a previously completed property the "VAT life" is normally 10 years from date of completion of the works. [see 6.7.3. below].

6.3.9 Option to acquire property

Often an option can be granted to purchase property at some future date. Where the option is over exempt property (either undeveloped or completed) then the option is exempt from VAT. Where the option is over property which is taxable (e.g. new or developed) the option is liable to VAT at the reduced rate of 13.5%.

6.4 Transitional Provisions Relating to the Supply of Developed Property

6.4.1 Why the need for transitional provisions?

Completed Properties which are held (by the 'holder') under freehold, freehold equivalent or long lease (i.e., a lease of 10 years or more and referred to as a 'legacy lease' in this chapter) prior to 1 July 2008 (i.e., acquired or developed under the 'old'

VAT rules applying to property), are referred to as "transitional properties" and the rules outlined below apply to the supply, on or after 1 July 2008, of such properties. Such supplies are always treated as supplies of goods.

6.4.2 The "VAT life" of transitional property

The "VAT life" of a completed property is the period in which a Capital Goods Scheme adjustment must be made, should such adjustment be required, upon the supply of such completed property. In the VAT legislation it is referred to as the 'adjustment period' (see 6.7).

In the case of a freehold or freehold equivalent, the "VAT life" is a period of 20 years from the date such interest in the property was acquired. If the property was developed subsequent to such acquisition (but prior to 1 July 2008) then the "VAT life" is for a period of 20 years from such development.

In the case of a "legacy lease" (i.e., a lease of 10 years or more) which was created and held by a person in business prior to 1 July 2008, the "VAT life" is a period of 20 years from the creation of the lease or the number of years in the term of the lease, whichever is the shorter.

In the case of a "legacy lease" i.e., a lease of 10 years or more obtained by way of assignment or surrender prior to 1 July 2008 and the current assignor is a person in business; the "VAT life" is the period remaining in the lease (unexpired part of the term) from the date of the then assignment or 20 years, whichever is the shorter.

6.4.3 VAT treatment of freeholds and freehold equivalents where the holder was entitled to deduct any part of the input VAT incurred on the acquisition or development of the property

The same rules apply as are outlined at 6.3 in respect of the supply of the completed property on or after 1 July 2008.

6.4.4 VAT treatment of freeholds and freehold equivalents where the holder was not entitled to deduct any part of the input VAT incurred on the acquisition and/or development of the property

The supply of the completed property, on or after 1 July 2008, is exempt from VAT. However, where both the seller and buyer are accountable persons, i.e., in business, then they may exercise a joint option for taxation (see 6.2 for definition).

Such a joint option for taxation will release, under a Capital Goods Scheme adjustment, (see 6.7), a portion of the input VAT previously denied to the vendor.

6.4.5 VAT treatment of legacy leases where the holder was entitled to deduct any part of the input VAT incurred on the acquisition of the lease or development subsequent to acquiring the lease

The assignment or surrender of a legacy lease, on or after 1 July 2008, is taxable as a supply of goods, where it occurs within the "VAT life" of the lease (see 6.4.2).

The same rules apply to any subsequent assignment or surrender of an assigned legacy lease.

6.4.6 VAT treatment of legacy leases where the holder was not entitled to deduct any part of the input VAT incurred on the acquisition of the lease

The assignment or surrender is an exempt supply of goods.

However, as in the case of transitional freeholds/freehold equivalents, where, in the case of an assignment, both the assignor and assignee are accountable persons, i.e., in business, then they may exercise a joint option for taxation (see 6.2) of the supply of goods. Where, in the case of a surrender, both the person making the surrender and the landlord are accountable persons, they may exercise a joint option for taxation of the supply of goods.

6.4.7 The application of the Capital Goods Scheme

Where the supply of a transitional property is exempt from VAT, then it is important that the vendor establish whether or not an adjustment under the capital goods scheme is necessary (see 6.7).

If on or after 23 February 2010 a transitional property is used for the first time or there is a change in use of the property, what is referred to as the 'big swing' test is applied (see 6.7.6 below).

There are a number of other limited situations where a Capital Goods Scheme adjustment applies in the case of the disposal of a transitional property.

6.4.8 Who accounts for VAT on the supply of a transitional property?

In the case of the sale of a freehold or freehold equivalent transitional property which is liable to VAT, it is the vendor who must account for any VAT charged on the supply of property.

In the case of the sale of a freehold or freehold equivalent transitional property which would normally be exempt from VAT, but where a joint option for taxation has been exercised, then the purchaser is obliged to account for the VAT charged on the supply on the 'reverse charge' basis.

In the case of the assignment or surrender of a legacy lease it is the assignee (in the case of an assignment) or the landlord (in the case of a surrender) who must account for any VAT charged on the supply of property, where such person is an accountable person, i.e., is in business or is a Department of State or a Local Authority. Otherwise it is for the assignor or surrenderor to account for any VAT charged.

6.4.9 What is the amount liable to VAT on the supply of a transitional property?

In the case of the supply of a freehold or a freehold equivalent, the consideration passing from the purchaser to the vendor is the amount which is liable to VAT (at 13.5%).

In the case of an assignment or a surrender of a legacy lease a formula is used to determine the amount of VAT chargeable. The equation is as follows;

$$\text{VAT due} = \frac{T \times N}{Y}$$

Where:–

T = the total amount of VAT incurred on the acquisition of the legacy lease or on the development of the property

N = the number of full years plus 1, that remained in the VAT life of the property when the legacy lease is being assigned or surrendered

Y = the total number of years in the VAT life of the property or 20, whichever is the lesser

Example 6.1

Company A grants Company B a 30-year lease on 1 July 2002. VAT of €2m was charged on the then capitalised value of the long lease. Company B deducted this VAT as it used the property to make taxable supplies of goods/services.

Company B assigns the lease to Company C on 1 July 2013.

This is a "legacy lease" as the interest was held by Company B on 1 July 2008. The "VAT life" or adjustment period of the legacy lease is 20 years from 1 July 2001. The assignment is taxable, on the reverse charge basis, as it occurs within the VAT life of the legacy lease.

Using the above formula, T = €2m, N = 10 (year 2022 – year 2013 + 1), Y = 20

Therefore the VAT due and payable on the lease by Company C (under reverse charge) is €1,000,000 and that taxable amount, or consideration for VAT purposes is €7,407,407.41 (1,000,000/13.5 × 100). The input VAT deductible by Company C will depend on its use of the property.

6.4.10 Obligatory documentation upon assignment/surrender of legacy lease

The assignor or surrenderor of a legacy lease must compute the amount of VAT chargeable on the assignment/surrender and make this information available to the acquirer, together with confirmation of the number of intervals remaining in the adjustment period (VAT life – see 6.7.3) at the time of assignment/surrender.

6.4.11 Sale of a 'legacy lease' reversion

Each 'legacy lease' will have a reversion, i.e., the interest in the property held by the person (the landlord) who created the lease. Where the landlord sells a reversionary interest (which will generally consist of the property and the right to collect rent on the legacy lease) on or after 1 July 2008, then such sale will be exempt from VAT where no development work has been carried out on the property subsequent to the creation of the legacy lease either by or for the benefit of the landlord.

If the completed property was developed by or on behalf of the landlord subsequent to the creation of the legacy lease, then if the property is a 'new property' (see 6.2 for definition) at the time of sale, the supply will be liable to VAT.

6.4.12 Sale of a reversion following surrender of the legacy lease

Where the completed property is sold by the landlord following the surrender of a legacy lease then, until such time as the surrendered lease would have expired, the rules as set out at 6.3.2–6.3.4 will apply to the sale.

6.4.13 Post-letting expenses & legacy lease

Prior to 1 July 2008 when a landlord charged VAT on the creation of a long lease (now referred to as a 'legacy lease') he was allowed to recover input VAT on certain costs subsequent to him having created the long lease. The practice continues as regards legacy leases. Thus in the case of legacy leases the landlord (or successor to the landlord where the landlord has sold the reversion) input VAT may be recovered by the landlord on the following expenses:

- Carrying out services under the terms of the lease which hare reflected in rent payable,
- Rent collection and review,
- Expenses relating to options to extend/end the lease,
- Electricity/gas/power/heat/refrigeration supplied by the landlord,
- Routine overheads including audit fees and office expenses.

In the case of legacy leases the Revenue practice in relation to 'shared services' is to continue for the present. Thus where a landlord, under the terms of a lease, agrees to receive services on behalf of a number of tenants on the basis of reimbursement he can pass on the VAT incurred on such services to the individual tenants. The tenants, in turn, can recover this VAT, in so far as it relates to their taxable activity.

6.5 The Letting of Property

6.5.1 Introduction

The letting of property is a supply of a service for VAT purposes. In the first instance the letting of all property is exempt from VAT. [However, a very long lease which is considered to be freehold equivalent is a supply of goods and this sub-section does not apply to such lease (see 6.3.1)].

6.5.2 Option to tax

A landlord may exercise an option to tax rents. Once the option is exercised then the rents are no longer exempt from VAT but liable to VAT at 23%. The landlord charges the VAT and issues a VAT invoice in accordance with legislation.

The option to tax rents is specific to each letting. Thus it must be exercised individually for each letting. A landlord may therefore have a mix of taxable and exempt lettings.

The landlords's option to tax a letting is exercised in the following ways:

- By claiming a deduction for input VAT incurred on the development or acquisition of property which is intended to be used for letting,
- By agreeing with the tenant in writing (before the 15th day of the month following commencement of the letting) that the letting will be taxable,
- By issuing a document to the tenant indicating that the letting will be taxable.

6.5.3 Amount on which VAT is chargeable upon opting to tax

All of the consideration attributable to the service of letting the property is liable to VAT. Obviously the rents are liable to VAT at 23%. The table below indicates the VAT treatment of other payments associated with a letting.

Table 6.1

Nature of payment	*Landlord opts to tax rents*	*Rents exempt from VAT*
Premium payable by tenant to landlord for grant of lease	Liable to VAT at 23%	Exempt from VAT
Premium payable by landlord to tenant as inducement to enter lease	Not a supply – therefore no VAT applicable	Not a supply – therefore no VAT applicable
Premium payable by landlord to tenant other than as inducement to enter lease	Liable to VAT at 23%	Liable to VAT at 23%
Premium payable by tenant to landlord upon surrender	Liable to VAT at 23%	Exempt from VAT
Premium payable by existing tenant upon assignment to another person	Liable to VAT at 23%	Liable to VAT at 23%
Premium received by existing tenant upon assignment to another person	Liable to VAT at 23%	Liable to VAT at 23%

6.5.4 Prohibition on option to tax

In certain circumstances a landlord cannot opt to tax a letting, including the following:

- Where the property is let for residential purposes,
- Where the letting is between connected persons and the tenant is not entitled to deduct more than 90% input VAT,
- Where the property is occupied by the landlord or a person connected to the landlord (though the letting may be to an unconnected party).

6.5.5 Terminating an option to tax

An option to tax must be terminated in the following circumstances:

- Where the landlord and the tenant become connected persons and where the tenant has a VAT recovery ratio of less than 90% (see Chapters 5.3.1 – 5.3.3),
- Where the property becomes occupied by a person connected to the landlord and where that connected person has a recovery ratio of less than 90%,
- Where the property is used for residential purposes,

An option to tax may be terminated at any stage by the landlord notifying the tenant in writing. However, the cancellation of the option to tax cannot be earlier that the date the tenant is so notified.

Where an option to tax is terminated during the VAT life[1] of the property concerned then an adjustment under the Capital Goods Scheme ('CGS') must be made by the landlord (see 6.7).

6.5.6 Short-term letting of property (less than 56 days)

Where a property (house, apartment, or similar) is let for a period of less than 56 days then the rate of VAT is 9% (in accordance with paragraph 11, Schedule 3, VATCA2010).

The provision of holiday accommodation is also subject to VAT at 9%.

1 The "VAT life" of a capital good is the period during which a Capital Goods Scheme adjustment must be made, should such adjustment be required In VAT legislation it is referred to as the 'adjustment period' (see 6.7).

6.6 Transitional Provisions Relating to the Letting of Property

6.6.1 Waiver of exemption

Where prior to 1 July 2008, the landlord had in place a 'waiver of exemption',[2] then certain transitional measures apply to such lettings.

Thus you will appreciate there are many lettings currently in place where the landlord, prior to 1 July 2008, waived exemption in relation to such lettings.

From 1 July 2008 a new waiver of exemption cannot be put in place.

An existing waiver of exemption does not extend to any property acquired or developed after 1 July 2008. However a waiver of exemption can be extended to a letting created after 1 July 2008, where the development of the property had commenced on 18 February 2008 and the waiver was in place prior to 18 February 2008.

A waiver of exemption in respect of a property let to a connected person (see 6.2, for definition), must, subject to certain exceptions[3], be cancelled on 1 July 2008. Upon cancellation, the landlord must pay to the Revenue the excess, if any, of the VAT deducted upon the acquisition and/or development of the property concerned, over the VAT charged on rental of the property concerned, during the operation of the waiver (called the cancellation amount). [Where there are properties let to unconnected tenants then the waiver will continue in force for such properties].

A waiver of exemption in respect of property let to unconnected persons or to connected persons in the circumstances outlined in footnote 2 may be cancelled at any time by the landlord, upon the payment of the cancellation amount, if such sum is due, i.e., if the input VAT on acquisition/development exceeds the output VAT on rents.

The Capital Goods Scheme ('CGS') does not apply to the properties which are within the waiver of exemption. This is because VAT incurred on acquisition and/or development of the properties concerned is taken into account in calculating the cancellation amount payable, if and when the waiver is cancelled. Thus a CGS adjustment is not required when a property, which was subject to a waiver which has been cancelled, is sold.

---

2 Prior to 1 July 2008 where a letting was for a period of less than 10 years it was considered to be a supply of a service and as such it was exempt from VAT. However the landlord was able to waive such exemption and thereafter apply VAT at 23% (the standard rate of VAT at the time) to the rents received. The waiver by the landlord extended to all rents in respect of all letting of less than 10 years which he made. [By waiving the exemption the landlord was able to deduct input VAT on the acquisition/development of the property].

3 Where the VAT on the rents charged to a connected person exceeds a certain amount, as determined by a formula in VAT legislation, then the landlord is not obliged to cancel his waiver in respect of a letting to a connected person. The cancellation of a waiver is not obligatory where the waiver relates to a letting of a property held by a landlord under a legacy lease acquired between 18 February and 30 June 2008 from an unconnected landlord.

6.7 The Capital Goods Scheme – Implications for the Ongoing Use of a Capital Good

6.7.1 Introduction

The Capital Goods Scheme ('CGS') is a mechanism for regulating VAT deductibility in relation to a Capital Good over the "VAT life" (see 6.7.3 for definition) of the developed property. The VAT life and consequently the application of the CGS is unique to each property.

Not every accountable person will have to make a VAT deductibility adjustment under the CGS. In fact, only those accountable persons, who make an exempt use or exempt supply of the property, will be obliged to make an adjustment. Additionally, persons not previously registered for VAT who exercise a joint option for taxation in respect of the supply of property may be able to obtain a refund of VAT, by way of a deductibility adjustment, under the CGS.

6.7.2 Who does the scheme apply to?

The CGS applies to the following categories of persons:

- Any person in business (an accountable person) who was charged VAT on the acquisition or development of immovable goods.
- Any person in business (an accountable person) who, on 1 July 2008, held a legacy lease and who, subsequent to that date, assigned or surrendered such legacy lease.
- Any person in business (an accountable person) who, subsequent to 1 July 2008, was charged VAT on the assignment or surrender of a legacy lease.

Any of the above categories of persons is known as a Capital Goods Owner.

The CGS does not apply to a person who acquired property in a private capacity (i.e., other than in the course or furtherance of business). Also the scheme does not apply to persons who acquired property upon which VAT was not charged. However, the CGS does apply to property acquired by way of a transfer of a business, upon which VAT was not chargeable.

6.7.3 The VAT life of a property

In general the VAT life, the 'adjustment period', of a property, for each owner, is as follows:

- 10 intervals, i.e., 10 years in the case of redevelopment (refurbishment) of a previously completed property
- 20 intervals, i.e., 20 years in the case of developed capital goods
- 20 or less intervals in the case of a legacy lease (see 6.4.2)

The intervals in the adjustment period are as follows:

- The initial interval is for a period of one year from the completion of the property by the owner or, in the case of a purchaser, one year from the date of purchase
- The second interval begins on the day the initial interval ends and ends at the end of the capital goods owner's accounting year end during which the initial interval ends. This shorter interval is to align the subsequent intervals with the initial interval.
- A number of subsequent intervals, each for a period of one year commencing at the end of the previous interval, until the end of the adjustment period.

In the case of a property developer the initial interval commences on the date the property is completed (see 6.2 for definition).

In the case of a purchaser of developed property the initial interval begins on the date the property is purchased.

6.7.4 Obligation for the owner at the end of the initial interval

At the end of the initial interval, the owner must review his/her use of the property in that period. He/she must divide the usage as between exempt and taxable use. For example a bank might have both taxable and exempt supplies. In another situation, the owner may be letting the property and may have opted to tax some of the leases and opted not to tax others. Again there is both taxable and exempt use.

Where the proportion of taxable use in this interval was equal to the proportion of input VAT recovered on the acquisition/development of the property, then an adjustment is not required.

Where the proportion of taxable use in this interval was less than the proportion of input VAT recovered on the acquisition/development of the property, then an adjustment is required. An amount of VAT will be payable by the owner.

Any adjustment made is made to the total amount of tax incurred, i.e., the tax charged on the acquisition/development of the property.

Example 6.2

VAT of €2,500,000 was charged by a vendor on the sale of a completed property to Colco, a trading company. Colco recovered all the VAT on the acquisition of a property (as it intended to make fully taxable supplies). At the end of the initial interval, it calculated that 80% of its supplies were taxable or qualifying activities; the other 20% were exempt supplies. Therefore there was both taxable and exempt use of the property in the initial interval.

Initial Interval adjustment

The total tax incurred = €2.5m

The amount of total tax deducted = €2.5m.

The initial interval proportion of deductible use = 80%

The total reviewed deductible amount = the total tax incurred × the initial interval proportion of deductible use = €2.5 × 80% = €2m

An adjustment using the formula A – B must be made, where

A = the amount of total tax deducted = €2.5m

B = the total reviewed deductible amount = €2m

Adjustment = A – B = €2.5m – €2m = €500,000

Colco must pay, as output VAT, the excess of A over B, i.e., €500,000.

Where the proportion of taxable use in this interval was greater than the proportion of input VAT recovered on the acquisition/development of the property, then an adjustment is also required. An amount of VAT will be repayable by Revenue to the owner.

Example 6.3

VAT of €2,500,000 was charged by a vendor on the sale of a completed property to Dolco, a trading company. Dolco recovered 80% of the VAT on the acquisition of a property (as it intended that 80% of its supplies would be taxable or qualifying activities, while the other 20% would be exempt supplies). At the end of the initial interval, it calculated that 90% of its supplies were taxable or qualifying activities; the other 10% were exempt supplies.

Initial interval adjustment

The total tax incurred = €2.5m

The amount of total tax deducted = €2.5m × 80% = €2m.

The initial interval proportion of deductible use = 90%

The total reviewed deductible amount = the total tax incurred × the initial interval proportion of deductible use = €2.5 × 90% = €2.25m

An adjustment using the formula A – B must be made, where

A = the amount of total tax deducted = €2m

B = the total reviewed deductible amount = €2.25m

Adjustment = A – B = €2m – €2.25m = €250.000

Dolco will be entitled to a VAT refund of €250,000.

In the case of a property developer who builds residential units and who in the first interval lets them (exempt), then there is no obligation on him to carry out an adjustment at the end of the initial interval.

6.7.5 Obligation for the owner at the end of the second and subsequent intervals

The owner must carry out the same review as between taxable and exempt usage for each interval. A comparison should then be made with the proportion of taxable usage in the initial interval.

Where the proportion differs an adjustment must be carried out.

Any adjustment made is the difference between the base tax amount and the reference deduction amount. As the computations under the CGS are complex perhaps this is best illustrated by way of example. Let us use the details in Example 6.3 and extend it to the next two intervals.

Example 6.4

VAT of €2,500,000 was charged by a vendor on the sale of a completed property to Dolco, a trading company. Dolco recovered 80% of the VAT on the acquisition of a property (as it intended that 80% of its supplies would be taxable or qualifying activities, while the other 20% would be exempt supplies).

At the end of the initial interval, it calculated that 90% of its supplies were taxable or qualifying activities; the other 10% were exempt supplies.

[See above example for initial interval deduction for Dolco].

At the end of the second interval Colco calculated that, for that period, 95% of its supplies were taxable or qualifying activities; the other 5% were exempt supplies.

At the end of the third (subsequent) interval it calculated that 60% of its supplies were taxable or qualifying activities; the other 40% were exempt supplies.

The number of intervals in the adjustment period is 20.

Initial Interval adjustment

[See previous example 6.3 for initial interval deduction for Dolco].

Second Interval adjustment

The total tax incurred = €2.5m

The amount of total tax deducted = €2.5m × 80% = €2m.

The initial interval proportion of deductible use = 90%

The total reviewed deductible amount the total tax incurred × the initial interval proportion of deductible use = €2.5 × 90% = €2.25m

The base tax amount = amount of total tax incurred/no of intervals = €2.5m/20 = €125,000.

The reference deduction amount = total reviewed deductible amount/no of intervals = €2.25m/20 = €112,500

Proportion of deductible use = 95% (taxable use/total use for the interval)

The interval deductible amount = base tax amount × proportion of deductible use = €125,000 × 95% = €118,750

An adjustment using the formula C − D must be made, where

C = the reference deduction amount, and

D = the interval deductible amount

C − D = − €6,250 (112,500 − 118,750)

As D > C, VAT credit of €6,250 is due to Dolco in the VAT period immediately following the interval.

Third Interval adjustment

The total tax incurred = €2.5m.

The amount of total tax deducted = €2.5m × 80% = €2m.

The initial interval proportion of deductible use = 90%.

The total reviewed deductible amount = the total tax incurred × the initial interval proportion of deductible use = €2.5 × 90% = €2.25m

The base tax amount = amount of total tax incurred/no of intervals= €2.5m/20 = €125,000.

The reference deduction amount = total reviewed deductible amount/no of intervals = €2.25m/20 = €112,500.

Proportion of deductible use = 60% (taxable use/total use for the interval).

The interval deductible amount = base tax amount × proportion of deductible use = 125,000 × 60% = €75,000.

The adjustment using the formula C – D must be made, where C = the reference deduction amount, and

D = the interval deductible amount

C – D = €37,500 (112,500 – 75,000)

As C > D, VAT of €37,500 is due by Dolco in the VAT period immediately following the interval.

6.7.6 CGS obligation for the owner with 'big swings' in taxable use

Where taxable use in any interval varies from the taxable use in the initial interval by greater than 50% then a full adjustment, based on the full amount of VAT incurred on acquisition/development, must be made.

This type of adjustment would occur where for instance a property was let with an option to tax the rents and where in the case of a new tenant the landlord cancelled the option to tax within the VAT life of the property. It may also occur where the taxable activities of the owner change upwards/downwards by a factor of more than 50%.

Example 6.5

A Limited provides training courses (exempt educational supply) representing 80% of turnover and designs software (taxable supply) representing 20% of turnover. In the initial interval it incurred VAT of €405,000. Thus in the 1st interval input VAT is restricted to 20% and the company reclaims €81,000 (405,000 × 20%).

The base tax amount is €20,250 (405,000 / 20 years)

The total reviewed deductible amount is €81,000 (405,000 × 20%)

The reference deductible amount is €4,500 (81,000 / 20 years)

During year 5 (the 5th interval) the company wins a large software contract whereby turnover from software supplies in year 5 amounts to 90%. As the proportion of deductible use in year 5 differs by more than 50 percentage points from the initial interval proportion of deductible use (90% – 20%) a 'big-swing adjustment is triggered.

The interval deductible amount is €18,225 (base tax amount × 90%)

The 'big swing' adjustment is calculated by the formula:

Adjustment = (C – D) × N

C = reference deductible amount

D = interval deductible amount

N = number of full intervals remaining + 1

Adjustment = (4,500 – 18,225) × 16 (15+1years) = – €219,600

The company can claim an input VAT deduction of €219,600 in the VAT period immediately following the end of the 5th interval.

6.7.7 Development by the tenant

Where the tenant has a leasehold interest in a completed property (see 6.2 for definition) and carries out development (not minor development) then the tenant creates a Capital Good in respect of that development, of which he is the Capital Good Owner. This development is refurbishment and the adjustment period consists of 10 intervals.

The same obligations as outlined above also rest with the tenant in respect of any necessary adjustments at the end of each interval.

6.7.8 The Capital Goods Record

Every Capital Good Owner is obliged to create and maintain a "capital goods record" in respect of each property owned. Among the details which must be maintained are:

- The amount of VAT charged to the owner upon acquisition/development
- The amount of VAT deducted initially
- The commencement date of the adjustment period
- The number of intervals in the adjustment period
- The details to appear in a capital goods record can be found at Regulation 27(v), VAT Regulations, 2010.
- The initial interval proportion of deductible use (see Example 6.2)
- The total reviewed deductible amount (see Example 6.3)
- The proportion of deductible use for each interval (see Example 6.3 and 6.4)
- Details of any adjustments under the scheme
- Details of any sale of the property.

A property may have several capital goods records. Thus, if a refurbishment is carried out by the owner a CGR in respect of this refurbishment must be maintained in addition to the record relating to the acquisition of the property. Also, if for instance the tenant carries out works to the same property a CGR in respect of these works will have to be maintained by the tenant.

6.8 The Capital Goods Scheme – Implications for Disposal of a Capital Good

6.8.1 Introduction

VATCA 2010 Part 8 ch2 s63–64

When a capital good (a developed property) is disposed of (sold, or in the case of a legacy lease, assigned or surrendered) during the VAT life of the property (the adjustment period) then account must be taken of the effects of the Capital Goods Scheme.

It is important to remember that the VAT life of the property will have been determined prior to the time of the sale (generally it will be 10 or 20 years) and where the property is sold, it is highly likely that the VAT life will not have expired.

Broadly speaking, the disposal of the capital goods will fit into one of the following categories:

- If the sale of the property is taxable, either because it comes within the charge to VAT (see 6.3.2) or because the joint option for taxation is invoked (see 6.2) then for the remaining periods in the VAT life of the property (the remaining intervals), the property is treated as having been used for fully taxable purposes by the vendor.
- If the sale of the property is exempt from VAT, either because it is outside the charge to VAT (see 6.3.2) or because the joint option for taxation is not invoked (see 6.2) then for the remaining periods in the VAT life of the property (the remaining intervals) the property is treated as having been used for exempt purposes by the vendor.

It is important to understand that the "VAT life" of the property is for the duration in which the property is owned by a person. Where the property is sold within its current "VAT life" to another person and the sale is liable to VAT, then a new "VAT life" for the property begins upon acquisition of the property by the new owner.

6.8.2 Taxable sale of a Capital Good during its VAT life

Where the sale of the property is liable to VAT, then one of four possible events under the CGS will occur:

- If the vendor had been entitled to deduct all of the input VAT on his/her acquisition of the property (or the assignor in the case of a legacy lease on the property) and used the property for fully taxable activities in the initial interval, then no adjustment under the CGS is required.

Example 6.6

Chargemore & Son, an accountancy firm, has a purpose built office completed in October 2009 at a cost of €2.5m with VAT charged of €337,500. As it used the property for taxable supplies it deducted all of the input VAT and did not need to make any adjustments under the CGS during the course of its ownership of the building. It merges with another firm in May 2016 and sells the property for €8m.

As the property is no longer 'new' (i.e., it is over 5 years old) the sale is exempt from VAT. Therefore the options are to sell the property without VAT or for the vendor and purchaser to exercise the joint option for taxation and apply VAT at 13½% to the sale. We will assume the joint option for taxation has been exercised and a taxable sale of the property ensues.

As a joint option for taxation has been exercised, the purchaser must self-account for the VAT arising on the sale. As VAT is being charged on the sale and as the property was used for fully taxable purposes during the six intervals prior to the sale, no adjustment under the capital goods scheme is required.

Thus VAT of €1,080,000 will apply to the sale (€8m @ 13.5%). The purchaser must account for this VAT and the amount of it which may be deducted as input VAT by the purchaser will depend on the use to which the purchaser puts the property.

In the event that a joint option for taxation is not exercised by both parties to the sale, and the sale is therefore exempt from VAT, Chargemore & Sons will have to pay €236,250 (i.e., €337,500 × (13 + 1)/20) to the Revenue as output VAT upon the sale of the premises. (13 is the number of full intervals remaining in the 20-year 'VAT life' of the property).

If the vendor had not been entitled to deduct any of the input VAT on his/her acquisition of the property (or the assignor in the case of a legacy lease on the property) then an adjustment under the CGS is required. The transfer will result in a payment to him of some of the input VAT incurred at the outset, based on the following formula:

$$\frac{E \times N}{T}$$

Where E = the non-deductible VAT

N = the number of intervals remaining in the adjustment period, plus 1

T = total number of intervals in the adjustment period. (20)

See Example 6.11.

If the vendor had deducted some of the input VAT (partial deduction) on his/her acquisition of the property (or the assignor in the case of a legacy lease on the property) then an adjustment under the CGS is required. The transfer will result in a payment to him of some of the input VAT incurred at the outset, using the above formula.

If the vendor had deducted all of the input VAT on his/her acquisition of the property (or the assignor in the case of a legacy lease on the property) and had not used the property for fully taxable activities in the initial interval, then an adjustment under the CGS is required.

6.8.3 VAT exempt sale of a Capital Good during its VAT life

Where the sale of the property is exempt from VAT, then one of two possible events under the CGS will occur:

(1) Where the vendor (or the assignor in the case of a legacy lease on the property) was not entitled to deduct any of the input VAT incurred on acquisition of the property, then no adjustment is required.

(2) Where the vendor (or the assignor in the case of a legacy lease on the property) was entitled to deduct some or all of the input VAT on acquisition then an adjustment, based on the VAT use by the vendor and the number of intervals remaining, must be carried out under the CGS.

Example 6.7

The same facts as in Example 6.7; however, we will now assume that the joint option for taxation has not been exercised, and so the sale will continue to be exempt from VAT.

In this case there will be a claw-back of a portion of the input VAT initially recovered by ***Chargemore & Sons*** *to reflect the fact that the property was used for taxable purposes for only six full years (2009–2016) of the VAT life (adjustment period).*

The adjustment is computed by using the formula $\frac{B \times N}{T}$

Where B = the total reviewed deductible amount = €337,500

N = number of full intervals remaining + 1 = 15

T = total number of intervals in the adjustment period (VAT life) = 20

Adjustment = €337,500 × 15/20 = €253,125

Thus Chargemore will have to pay €253,125 to the Revenue as output upon sale of the premises. It will not charge VAT to the purchaser.

6.8.4 Taxable v Exempt sale of the property – Commercial Considerations

Consider the above two Examples 6.6 and 6.7.

In Example 6.6 VAT in the amount of €1,080,000 will apply to the sale of the property. In addition the vendor will be able to recover all input VAT incurred on Costs associated with the sale. Given that the joint option for taxation was exercised by both parties a new 'VAT life', this time for the purchaser, commences in 2016 and will extend for a 20-year period, or until such time as the purchaser sells the property, if within this 20-year period.

In Example 6.7 a CGS adjustment in the amount of €253,125 must be made by Chargemore & Son. Additionally it cannot recover input VAT on costs associated with the sale. The sale of the property will be exempt from VAT and there will not be a new 'VAT life' for the property in the hands of the purchaser.

Exercise 6.1

Imagine you are the Chartered Tax Adviser to **Chargemore & Son**. **Chargemore & Son** tells you it has an offer from another accountancy firm for the office and also an offer from an insurance provider.

What VAT advice might you give to **Chargemore** in relation to the sale of the property? [Hint: one purchaser is a fully taxable supplier and the other is a fully VAT-exempt supplier].

6.8.5 Tenant development – CGS Implications

It is a very common occurrence now for a tenant to carry out certain works to an already completed building in order to prepare it for opening. Such works may involve putting in a mezzanine floor, individualised wall claddings, displays, lighting, etc. As we saw in 6.7.7, under the new rules such work constitutes refurbishment and in itself creates a "VAT life" for a 10-year period for the tenant who carried out the refurbishment.

The property in question could therefore have two parallel "VAT lives"; a 20-year VAT life for the owner who is letting the property to the tenant in relation to the property itself, and a 10-year VAT life for the tenant in respect of the refurbishment carried out by the tenant.

The general rule is that where the tenant vacates the property during the VAT life of the refurbishments, then a claw-back of a proportion of the VAT incurred on the refurbishment will occur. However there are two ways in which this claw-back can be avoided:

- Where the tenant uses the property for fully taxable use in the initial interval and enters a written agreement with the person to whom the lease is assigned/surrendered that such person will "take over" his obligations under the CGS. The tenant must issue a copy of the 'capital goods record' (see 6.7.8 for definition) and such information is used to enable the person who acquired the fit-out to operate the CGS. In these circumstances an adjustment by the tenant under the CGS is not required.
- Where the refurbishment carried out is removed prior to assignment/surrender then an adjustment by the tenant under the CGS is not required.

6.8.6 Exercising and terminating the Landlords' option to tax – Implications for the CGS

As you will be aware the letting of immovable goods is, in the first instance, exempt from VAT. Where a landlord exercised an option to tax then the use of the property in his hands, i.e., the letting, is liable to VAT at 23%. You can therefore understand that by exercising the option to tax and thereafter terminating the option during the course of the VAT life of the property, you will create the necessity for a VAT adjustment under the CGS in the period(s) in which the option is exercised (if previously there was an exempt letting) or cancelled (where previously there was a taxable letting).

A landlord might decide to exercise or terminate an option to tax the lease any number of times during the course of the VAT life for a variety of reasons. Perhaps the most likely cause for a change would be a change in tenancy whereby a tenant with full VAT recovery is replaced by a tenant with no/limited VAT recovery, or vice versa.

A tenant will full VAT recovery will be VAT neutral, i.e., he/she would be entitled to deduct in full the VAT charged by the landlord. In contrast VAT on rents for a tenant with no/limited VAT recovery would represent a real cost, as such VAT would not be deductible.

Example 6.8

Rentco Ltd buys an office building in 2008 for €3m upon which VAT of €405,000 has been charged and fully recovered by Rentco Ltd (on the basis that it will make fully taxable supplies). It rents the office to Haulco in 2008 and having opted to tax the rents charges VAT at 23% on the annual rent of €500,000. Haulco, a haulage company, is able to recover this VAT in full.

In 2012 Haulco surrenders its lease and Rentco Ltd looks for a new tenant. In February 2013, Busco Limited, a company which operates a fleet of buses, rents the premises. It will not be in a position to recover the €115,000 VAT (500,000 × 23%) which will be the charge each year on the rents (as its supplies are VAT exempt) and asks Rentco Ltd to consider not applying VAT to the rents.

If Rentco Ltd decides not to apply VAT to the rents (as may well be necessary to attract Busco Limited to take up the lease) it must carry out an adjustment under the CGS.

We will assume that no adjustments were made by Rentco Ltd in the previous periods as the property was used fully for taxable use, i.e., rented with an option to tax exercised by Rentco Ltd.

The adjustment will be made using the formula C − D

Where C = the reference deduction amount = total reviewed deductible amount/no of intervals

= €405,000/20 = €20,250

And D = the interval deduction amount = base tax amount × proportion of deductible use

= €405,000/20 × 0% = 0

C − D = €20,250 − 0 = €20,250

Thus at the end of the interval in which the exempt letting is made, Rentco Ltd will have to make an adjustment of €20,250 and pay this as output VAT. It will thereafter have to make the same adjustment every year.

Exercise 6.2

As the Chartered Tax Adviser (CTA) to Rentco Ltd what would you advise in relation to the request by Busco Ltd to exempt the rental charge? Are there any tax implications for Rentco Ltd, other than VAT?

6.8.7 Letting of residential property by a developer prior to sale – Implications for the CGS

Where a property developer sets out to build residential accommodation for supply, he is entitled to deduct all input VAT as his intention at the time that it is incurred (generally the construction phase) is to make a VATable supply of property.

For whatever reason the developer may not be able to realise sales and, as a temporary Measure, may be forced to let the property on a short-term basis for a period of time. The letting of residential property is exempt from VAT and, as we have seen earlier, it is not possible for a landlord to opt to tax lettings of residential property (see 6.5.4).

In the case of the letting of residential property, the landlord does not have to carry out the initial interval adjustment but must carry out the subsequent interval adjustments over the period of letting of the property prior to sale.

Note if he sets out to develop property for rental only and not for sale then he would not be entitled to register for and recover input VAT from the outset.

Example 6.9

Devco Ltd builds 70 houses over a period of time. In January 2010, 20 houses are completed and remain unsold. In order to defray costs, Devco lets them to tenants on a renewable yearly lease until such time as they can be sold. All of the VAT incurred on construction was recovered by Devco. The VAT incurred on construction of the 20 houses remaining was €600,000.

For the initial interval Devco is not obliged to make an adjustment under the Capital Goods Scheme.

For the second and each subsequent interval for which the houses are let Devco must make an adjustment under the CGS.

The adjustment in the second and subsequent intervals is as follows (assuming all 20 houses remain let):

Total tax incurred = €600,000

Initial interval of deductible use	*= 100% (as the houses are built with the intention to sell and the initial interval exempt use is disregarded)*
Total Reviewed Deductible amount	*= Total tax incurred × initial interval of deductible use*
	= €600,000 × 100% = €600,000
Reference deductible amount (C)	*= Total Reviewed Deductible amount/20 intervals = €30,000*
Base tax amount	*= €30,000 (600,000/20 intervals)*
Proportion of deductible use each subsequent interval)	*= 0% (as the property is used for fully exempt lettings in*
Interval deductible amount (D)	*= Base tax amount × Proportion of deductible use = 0*
Adjustment	*= C − D = 30,000 − 0 = €30,000*

Therefore in the second and each subsequent interval Devco will be obliged to repay €30,000 under the CGS in respect of the exempt use of the property.

6.8.8 The transfer of a business [ToB] as a going concern – implications for the CGS

As we noted earlier, a ToB is not considered to be a supply for VAT purposes. Thus the price received for the transfer, which will most likely include both tangible and intangible assets, will not carry the charge of VAT. This will have implications for the CGS.

Guidance issued by the Revenue Commissioners in November 2015 give a very broad interpretation of ToB in relation to the transfer of property. Thus ToB can arise in the following situations:

- Where properties are let at the time of sale
- Where a let property is being sold to the tenant
- Where a portfolio of properties, some of which are let, some vacant and some partially complete are sold to a single purchaser

- The sale of a vacant property which was let in the past
- The sale of a vacant property which was used to make taxable supplies in the past.

Where a property is included in the transfer of the business, the CGS implications will depend on whether or not the transfer occurred when the completed property was 'new' or 'not new for VAT purposes.

[At the time of going to print the Revenue Commissioners are in the process of redrafting guidelines in relation to Transfer of Business and its application to property transfers].

Transfer when a completed property is 'new' for VAT purposes

In these circumstances the vendor is considered to have made a taxable supply of the property (even though VAT is not charged) and his 'adjustment period' for the property is ended.

The purchaser is deemed to have been charged VAT (on the value of the property) and is deemed to have recovered this to the extent that he will use the property for taxable supplies. A 20-year adjustment period for the purchaser begins upon his acquisition of the business. If the purchaser does not have full deductibility in relation to the property then an adjustment must be carried out upon acquisition.

Example 6.10

Transco Ltd built a new warehouse and office which were completed in October 2009. It used by the company fully for its taxable transport and warehousing activities. In January 2013, the business was taken over by Haulco Ltd for €25m of which €12m referred to the premises. VAT was not charged on the sale price as this was the transfer of a business. The property, being less than five-years old, is 'new' for VAT purposes.

For Transco Ltd its adjustment period ended upon sale of the premises. It has already deducted all of the input VAT on the property and makes no further adjustment.

For Haulco Ltd its adjustment period is for 20 years from January 2013 (when it acquired the property). VAT in the amount of €1.62m (12m × 13.5%) is deemed to have been charged on the property; as Haulco uses the property fully for its taxable activity, it would be entitled to recover this VAT in full.

Therefore using the formula $F - G$ to calculate any VAT payable by Haulco on the acquisition where $F =$ the deemed VAT chargeable , i.e., €1.62m and $G =$ the deemed VAT deductible, i.e., also €1.62m we see that no VAT is payable on the property by Haulco Ltd on acquisition of the business.

Example 6.11

Lylo Ltd, a firm of undertakers purchased new premises in January 2009. It paid €5m for the premises and incurred VAT of €675,000 which was irrecoverable because Lylo's activity undertaking is exempt from VAT. In March 2012, it sold the business to a competitor Morelo Ltd for €15m of which €8m referred to the premises. VAT was not charged on the sale price as this was the transfer of a business. The property, being less than five-years old, is 'new' for VAT purposes.

There is a CGS adjustment for both parties upon transfer because if the transfer of business rules did not apply the sale of the property would be liable to VAT.

For Lylo Ltd the CGS adjustment is as follows:

$$\frac{E \times N}{T}$$

Where E = the non-deductible VAT (€675,000)

N = the number of intervals remaining for Lylo + 1 (17 + 1 = 18)

T = total number of intervals in the adjustment period. (20)

Using the formula VAT in the amount of €607,500 can be claimed by Lylo Ltd in the VAT period in which it sold the business.

For Morelo Ltd the CGS adjustment is as follows:

$$F - G$$

Where F = the amount of VAT that would have been charged were the supply liable to VAT (€1.08m, being €8m × 13.5%)

G = the amount of VAT that would have been deductible by Morelo (€0, as the premises are used for an exempt activity by Morelo)

Using the formula the amount of VAT payable by Morelo on its acquisition of the property is €1.08m (1.08 − 0).

Transfer when a completed property is not 'new' for VAT purposes

In these circumstances a joint option for taxation between the vendor and the purchaser cannot be put in place, as the transfer of the business is not liable to VAT. Accordingly, where the transfer of the property occurs within the adjustment period, the purchaser essentially "steps into the shoes" of the vendor and must comply with all of the vendors obligations for the remainder of the adjustment period applicable to the property. In essence, the purchaser is treated as having owned the property from the date it was acquired by the vendor. The vendor must hand over his Capital Goods Record to the purchaser at the time of the transfer. The subsequent use to which the property is put by the purchaser will determine if he has to make any ongoing annual adjustments under the CGS.

Example 6.12

A Ltd acquired a new completed property in January 2010. A Ltd used it for the purpose of a taxable activity until he sold his business in April 2017 to B Ltd for €10m. As the property is seven-years old on transfer, it would be exempt from VAT if it was not the transfer of a business.

VAT is not deemed on the transfer. A Ltd is obliged to hand over its Capital Goods Record to B Ltd.

The adjustment period for A Ltd was from January 2010 to April 2017 and for B Ltd is from April 2017 to January 2030, i.e., 20 years in total from January 2010.

6.9 Building Services

6.9.1 Introduction

Work consisting of the development of immovable goods (land and buildings), including the installation of fixtures, is considered to be the supply of a service and not the supply of goods. Thus, where a builder supplies concrete blocks and builds a wall with the blocks, he has made a supply of a service for VAT purposes. The rate of VAT applicable will be the rate determined by section 46 VATCA and the appropriate schedule to the Act.

In the case of a supply of labour only (no materials included), the appropriate rate of VAT is 13.5%.

In the case of a supply of labour and materials, the appropriate rate of VAT is determined by the "Two-Thirds Rule". (See Chapter 3, section 3.10.)

6.9.2 The "Two-Thirds Rule" and the development of immovable goods

s41 VATCA 2010 The "Two-Thirds Rule" can also apply in respect of the development of immovable goods. Where the value (cost) of movable goods (materials) used in the supply of a service consisting of the development of immovable goods (land and buildings) exceeds two-thirds of the total amount on which VAT is chargeable in respect of the supply, then the rate of VAT applicable to the supply is 23%.[4]

Where the value (cost) of movable goods (materials) used in the supply of a service consisting of the development of immovable goods (land and buildings) does not exceed two-thirds of the total amount on which VAT is chargeable in respect of the supply, then the rate of VAT applicable to the supply is 13.5%.

6.9.3 Place of supply

As discussed in detail at in Chapter 3 (Section 3.6.3), the place of supply of services connected with property is where the property is located. This includes all building services.

Where an Irish VAT-registered builder supplies services for a building being built in Germany, the place of supply is Germany.

Where a French VAT-registered builder supplies services for a building being built in Denmark, the place of supply is Denmark.

6.9.4 Person who must account for VAT

The accountable person in respect of building services may be either: (i) the supplier of the services or (ii) the recipient of the services. Which person accounts for the VAT depends on certain rules, as outlined below.

Where the relationship between the building service provider and the person who receives the building service is a contractor/sub-contractor relationship, i.e., Relevant

4 In the case where the "Two-thirds Rule" is broken, i.e., where the cost of materials exceed two-thirds of the charge for the service, the service provider can split his/her charge and invoice the labour amount at 13.5% and the materials amount at 23%.

Contracts Tax legislation applies, the recipient of the service (the principal contractor) is the accountable person for VAT. The service provider (the sub-contractor) does not charge VAT on the supply of his services, rather the recipient of the building service must self-account for VAT on the building service received. The service supplier must nonetheless issue a document (in lieu of an invoice) to the principal contractor, which, in addition to the usual items which appear on a VAT invoice, must include the narrative "*VAT ON THIS SUPPLY TO BE ACCOUNTED FOR BY THE PRINCIPAL CONTRACTOR*".

Finance Act 2012 introduced a further set of circumstances where the recipient of a building service must account for the VAT on the supply. Where the supplier and recipient of the service are connected (see 3.18) then the recipient must account for the VAT on the supply and the supplier does not charge VAT.

Where the relationship between the building service provider and the person who receives the building service is

- not that of a contractor/sub-contractor nature, i.e., Relevant Contracts Tax legislation does not apply, or
- not one in which the supplier and recipient of the building service are treated as connected,

then the supplier is the accountable person for VAT. The service provider charges VAT on the supply of his services, and issues the usual VAT invoice (see 3.18 above for further information).

6.9.5 Liquidators & Receivers – Property

Finance Act 2013 & Finance (No. 2) Act 2013 both have introduced new provisions in relation to the role and obligations of liquidators, receivers, mortgagee-in-possession and other persons exercising a power. The purpose of these new provisions is to clarify the VAT treatment of supplies of goods and services made by these categories of persons.

Thus in the course of winding up a business a liquidator, receiver, mortgagee-in-possession or other person exercising a power is liable for VAT on any service supplied and can also opt to charge VAT on rents, etc. The receiver must remit VAT charged on services supplied by the person in receivership, including any VAT on rents collected.

The new provisions also oblige the liquidator, receiver or other person exercising a power to make the necessary 'deductibility adjustments' arising under the Capital Goods Scheme together with any other adjustments necessary under the transitional rules for property.

Furthermore the obligations of the Capital Goods Owner now devolve to the liquidator, receiver, mortgagee-in-possession or other person exercising a power for the duration of their activity. Where a CGS adjustment results in an increased deductibility then such benefit will go to the liquidator, receiver, mortgagee-in-possession or other person exercising a power. A Capital Goods Record must be prepared and handed over by the liquidator, receiver, mortgagee-in-possession or other person exercising a power for the duration of their activity.

Where a Capital Good reverts to the owner following a receivership or period of possession then the CGS obligations will also revert to that owner.

7 RIGHTS AND OBLIGATIONS OF ACCOUNTABLE PERSONS AND THE ROLE OF REVENUE

Learning Outcomes

On completion of this chapter you will be able to:

- ✓ General understanding of certain rights and obligations that pertain to VAT-registered persons.
- ✓ Describe the role and structure of the Revenue Commissioners in relation to VAT.
- ✓ Describe the powers and sanctions available to Revenue in managing and policing the VAT system, and in dealing with VAT-registered persons.
- ✓ Be aware of mandatory disclosure obligations.

7.1 Introduction

The VAT system is completely dependent on the goodwill and participation of accountable persons, i.e., the VAT-registered traders who operate the VAT system and collect the tax on behalf of the Collector-General, as is their obligation under domestic VAT legislation.

So far in the chapters on VAT, we have discussed the European context, the charge of VAT and how VAT is applied to transactions. We have also examined the legislation and how VAT-registered traders arrive at their VAT liability.

To ensure the smooth operation of the VAT system, many rights and obligations are enshrined in legislation. In this chapter, we will discuss some such rights and obligations. The chapter is also concerned with Revenue powers and the role of the Revenue Commissioners with regard to the operation of the VAT system.

The Revenue Commissioners, sometime ago, published a Charter of Rights for taxpayers (see Appendix IV to this chapter).

With effect from 24 December 2008 fundamental changes to the 'penalty regime' applicable in the case of non-compliance with VAT legislation have taken effect. (See 7.4.8 Penalties).

7.2 Rights and Obligations

7.2.1 Keeping records

s84–85
VATCA
2010

"Every accountable person shall, in accordance with regulations, keep full and true records of all transactions which affect or may affect his liability to tax".

A VAT-registered person is obliged to retain records for six years. However, the Revenue Commissioners may authorise a person to destroy records within this period. This authorisation may be granted on foot of a request from the VAT-registered person and will generally be preceded by an inspection of the records concerned.

The records which must be retained are specified in Regulations 27, Value-Added Tax Regulations, 2010 [SI No 548 of 2006]. (An extract is included at Appendix I, to this chapter).

In the case of a person who acquires or develops taxable property or a person who has, prior to 1 July 2008 waived exemption in relation to short leases, there is a further obligation to retain records for a six-year period following disposal of the property or cancellation of the waiver.

7.2.2 Responsible officer

s107
VATCA 2010

In the case of a body of persons (e.g., a company), the responsible person for the body is the secretary or the person acting as secretary. Any notification served on the secretary is deemed to be served on the company. Any obligation of the company with regard to VAT is also an obligation of the secretary.

The secretary may retain from the company an amount of money necessary for the payment of VAT should the matter arise, and the secretary is indemnified in respect of such retention.

7.2.3 Foreign trader's/promoter's declaration

s17
VATCA 2010

Where a foreign (non-established) trader (referred to as a "mobile trader") proposes to sell goods in the State, there is an obligation on the owner or controller of the premises (the premises provider), from which the goods will be sold, to notify Revenue in advance. Additionally, when a foreign (non-established) promoter of cultural, musical or entertainment services supplies services in the State, there is an obligation on the owner or controller of the premises, from which the service will be supplied, to notify Revenue in advance.

The details which must be supplied in relation to such mobile traders and promoters are:

- the name and address of the mobile trader/promoter;
- the date on which the goods and services will be supplied;

- the venue where the goods or services will be supplied; and
- the address of the premises from which such supplies will be made.

Failure to notify Revenue in advance may have very serious consequences for the premises provider:

> *"... the Revenue Commissioners may, where it appears necessary to them to do so for the protection of the revenue, make such premises provider jointly and severally liable with a mobile trader or promoter, as the case may be, for the tax chargeable in respect of supplies made by that mobile trader or promoter on the premises provider's land ..."*

7.2.4 Letter of expression of doubt

s81 VATCA 2010 Where a VAT-registered person has a doubt as to the correct VAT treatment applicable to a particular transaction, which may have a bearing on his/her liability to VAT, then he or she may file an expression of doubt with the Revenue Commissioners at the same time as he/she files their periodic VAT return.

The letter, which must be in written form, should be accompanied by any necessary documentation in support of it. Where Revenue issues a notification to the person concerned in response to an expression of doubt, which results in a greater liability to VAT in respect of the particular transaction concerned, and where the person pays such an amount in the same VAT period in which the notification is received, interest will not be applied to such additional amount.

Revenue may refuse to accept a letter of expression of doubt where they believe the VAT treatment is straightforward. A VAT-registered person may appeal such a refusal.

7.2.5 VAT registration

s65 VATCA 2010 A person who is obliged to register for VAT is obliged to furnish the details required by regulation to the Revenue Commissioners, to enable them to register the person for VAT.

Liquidators and receivers are obliged to register for VAT when they dispose of the assets of a company. There is no registration threshold.

In the case of small traders, Form STR1 must be completed and filed.

In the case of sole traders/partnerships/joint ventures, Form TR1 must be completed and filed.

In the case of limited/unlimited companies, Form TR2 must be completed and filed.

A copy of Form TR1 and Form TR2 are included at Appendix II, to this chapter.

7.2.6 Interest payable on VAT due

s114 VATCA 2010 Where an amount of tax is payable and the accountable person has not paid the amount, simple interest at 0.0274% per day is applied to the amount until such time as payment is made. This roughly equates to 10% per year.

In the case of a person who is authorised to make an annual return for VAT and who, at the end of the year, owes in excess of 20% of the VAT payable for the year, then interest at the rate of 0.0274% × 183 (5%) is applied to the outstanding balance.

As interest is statutory (i.e., determined by law to be payable), it is not negotiable.

In the case of a detection of underpaid VAT going back for a number of years, the interest charge can be very high. For instance, if an underpayment of VAT of €10,000 for the year 2003 is detected, the interest charge (at *c.* 10% × seven years) amounts to approximately €7,000.

7.2.7 Refund of VAT

s99 VATCA 2010 Where an accountable person's input VAT exceeds the output VAT, the excess is repaid to the person by Revenue. This payment by Revenue is commonly referred to as a "VAT repayment". Additionally, where an accountable person overpaid VAT, Revenue may repay the overpaid amount.

For tax periods commencing on or after 1 May 2003, the prior period for which a refund may be claimed is four years. Thus, if an accountable person realises that he/she has overpaid VAT for some reason or other, the claim for repayment must be lodged within four years of the end of the tax period concerned.

7.2.8 Unjust enrichment

s100 VATCA 2010 This is a somewhat controversial area and the subject of litigation. Unjust enrichment may arise where a claimant seeks a refund of VAT which, due to a mistaken assumption on his part, he has paid to the Revenue as VAT. Any such claims must be submitted in writing setting out the full details of the claim. Before repaying the amount the Revenue Commissioners may determine whether or not the claimant would be 'unjustly enriched' by such refund and in this regard they may have regard to the following:

- The extent to which the cost of the overpaid amount was passed on by the claimant to others in the price charged for the goods/services
- Any loss of profit borne by the claimant due to the mistaken assumption made in relation to the operation of the tax
- Any other factors which the claimant may bring to their attention.

Where Revenue believes that by refunding an amount of VAT to an accountable person, such person will be unjustly enriched, it can refuse to make the refund.

Consider a mechanic who charged VAT at 23% on car repairs for a period of time and calculated the VAT payable on this basis. Some years later his registered tax consultant spots the mistake and advises him that the appropriate rate of VAT was 13.5%. He prepares a claim and lodges it with Revenue for the difference of 7.5%. Where there is no evidence that he will reimburse the customers he overcharged, Revenue may refuse to repay the overpayment, as the person will have been "unjustly enriched".

The matter is highly complex and has not as yet been fully explored. After all, the mechanic may argue that he is simply increasing profits, on which he may have to pay additional income tax.

7.2.9 Interest on refunds of VAT

s105 VATCA 2010

The Revenue Commissioners are obliged to pay interest at 0.011% per day (4% per year) on VAT repayments due to taxpayers who have not been repaid. This follows a specific period. This obligation was brought about by a high-profile High Court case in which Revenue was compelled to pay substantial interest in a case where it was obliged to repay large sums of VAT following an earlier, successful Supreme Court challenge by a VAT-registered person.

Interest is payable by Revenue:

> *... "Where a mistaken assumption in the operation of the tax is made by the Revenue Commissioners and, as a result, a refundable amount is payable to a claimant ..."*

In any case involving undue delay, other than a "mistaken assumption" on the part of Revenue, in making a VAT repayment, interest is also payable following the expiry of a six-month period immediately following the tax period in which the repayment was due.

7.2.10 Appeals

s119 VATCA 2010

By far the most important right available to accountable persons is the right of appeal. The right of appeal acts as a check on the power of the Revenue Commissioners, and their use of that power. It also serves to link the tax system and the Courts. A right of appeal exists in relation to the following:

- an assessment raised by Revenue in relation to overstating an amount of VAT on an invoice;
- an assessment raised by Revenue in relation to a person not registered for VAT issuing a VAT invoice;
- the compulsory VAT group registration of a number of companies;
- the assessing of a premises provider in respect of VAT payable by the mobile trader/ promoter;

- a refusal to make a VAT repayment;
- the compulsory registration of a person for VAT by the Revenue Commissioners.
- a determination by the Revenue Commissioners in relation to the value, upon which VAT is chargeable, of certain transactions between connected persons.

Time limits are set down for appeals, and the procedures applying to income and corporation tax appeals are applicable in the case of VAT appeals.

The Tax Appeals Commission

The Finance (Tax Appeals) Act, 2015 ("the 2015 Act") makes a number of changes to the legislation governing the hearing and determination of tax appeals, primarily in the Taxes Consolidation Act, 1997. The 2015 Act envisages that the Appeal Commissioners may draw up rules of procedure with respect to any of their functions. The Appeal Commissioners hear cases where there is a dispute between an appellant and Revenue Commissioners.

The Tax Appeals Commission, as the office in now known, has drawn up rules and procedures relating to the hearing of Appeals. Among the areas in which new rules and procedures apply, are:

- Acceptance of Appeals
- Statement of Case
- Case Management Conferences
- Giving of Directions
- Adjudication without Hearing
- Hearings
- Determinations
- Late Appeals
- Transitional Arrangements

Previously there were only two Appeal Commissioners, who are appointed by the Minister for Finance and the office was supported by the Office of the Revenue Commissioners.

An Appeal Commissioner may refer a case to the European Court of Justice for clarification in relation to interpretation or implementation of Community provisions (Council Directive 2006/112/EC– see Chapter 2). The Appeal Commissioners in Ireland have only very recently availed of this avenue. In the UK, by contrast, the equivalent of the Appeal Commissioner, the VAT Tribunal, sends cases to the CJEU on a regular basis.

Either the Appellant or the Revenue Commissioners being dissatisfied with a determination of the Commissioners as being erroneous on a point of law may by notice in writing require the Commissioners to state and sign a Case Stated for the Opinion of the High Court.

7.3 The Role and Structure of the Revenue Commissioners

A VAT system would not be complete without a monitoring and policing function. Such a function is carried out by the Revenue Commissioners, who are entrusted with the "care and management" of VAT. Their duties extend to drafting legislation, making determinations, auditing taxpayers, dealing with appeals, maintaining a register of taxpayers and managing the system generally. We will now examine the divisions of the Revenue Commissioners which deal with VAT matters in a variety of ways.

With effect from 1 January 2003 the separate division in the Revenue Commissioners known as the Office of the Chief Inspector of Taxes has been integrated with the General Civil Service.

The Board of the Revenue Commissioners is composed of three Commissioners who are appointed by the Minister for Finance.

A number of divisions within the Office of the Revenue Commissioners deal with the day-to-day monitoring and policing of the VAT system. Certain divisions retain files on accountable persons. They also carry out VAT audits, verify VAT repayments and give assistance to accountable persons in dealing with their VAT affairs. There are five divisions dealing with the day-to-day policing and monitoring of the VAT system: the "Large Cases" division and four geographically arranged divisions.

A separate division, known as the "Indirect Taxes" division, co-ordinates policy, legislation and international functions for all indirect taxes (including VAT).

The Collector-General's division collects VAT and any interest charges, and makes VAT repayments.

The "Customs and Excise" division applies and collects VAT on imports and on the intra-Community acquisition of private means of transport (private cars, pleasure boats and small planes).

In 2015 the Revenue issued a document, "Statement of Strategy 2015–2017" In it they have set out their mission, culture, ethos & values, strategies and strategic drivers.

7.4 The Powers of the Revenue

The Revenue Commissioners have very wide-ranging powers in relation to both accountable persons and records of transactions (supplies). We have outlined below the more common powers; there are additional powers, which are not discussed here.

7.4.1 Inspection of records

s108 VATCA 2010

Authorised officers of the Revenue Commissioners have extensive and wide-ranging powers with regard to the inspection of records. VAT-registered persons have certain obligations when it comes to presenting records and assisting Revenue:

- A VAT-registered person or his/her employees or associates are required to produce records of the business requested by an authorised officer.
- A VAT-registered person or his/her employees or associates are required to provide all reasonable assistance to an authorised officer.
- A VAT-registered person or his/her employees or associates may not *"obstruct or delay"* an authorised officer in the course of his/her duties.
- A person is not obliged to disclose any professional advice rendered to a VAT-registered client.

The authorised officer is obliged to produce his/her authorisation on request. Generally speaking, advance notice will be given to the accountable person in respect of a proposed audit/inspection. Once notification has been received, the accountable person has the opportunity to present a written notification to Revenue of any underpayments of VAT of which he/she is aware. Where such disclosure is complete, Revenue will mitigate penalties, which they will apply in the event of additional VAT being payable.

7.4.2 Removal of records

An authorised officer of the Revenue Commissioners may search, without a warrant, any premises where he has reason to believe a business is being carried on and may remove any records from the premises for the purpose of examination.

7.4.3 Search of the person

An authorised officer of the Revenue Commissioners may search any person for any records that he believes are on the person and which he believes may be used in criminal proceedings.

7.4.4 Raising assessments/estimates

Revenue may raise assessments where it believes there has been an under-declaration of VAT liability.

Section 110 estimates

s110 VATCA 2010 Where an accountable person fails to lodge a VAT return for a taxable period, Revenue may estimate the amount of VAT payable and raise an estimate for that amount. Also where a person fails to register for VAT then the Revenue may register such person and raise a s110 estimate where they form the opinion that he/she is an accountable person.

An accountable person may appeal a s110 estimate where he/she claims not to be a accountable person only within a 14-day period of being notified of the estimate.

Where a VAT return is not lodged, the amount of the s110 estimate may be pursued by Revenue. Where a VAT return is subsequently filed for the period and where the liability is paid, the s110 assessment is discharged.

Section 111 assessments

s111 VATCA 2010 Where Revenue believes that the VAT paid in a taxable period(s) is less than the VAT it considers payable, or where the VAT refunded exceeds the VAT it considers refundable, it may raise an assessment for the amount it considers payable.

The accountable person may appeal such an assessment to the Appeal Commissioners, in the first instance, within a 21-day period of being notified of the assessment.

7.4.5 Determinations by Revenue

s17(2) VATCA 2010 The provision of facilities for taking part in sporting and physical education activities, and services closely related thereto, by non-profit-making organisations or local authorities is exempt from VAT.

However, where Revenue is satisfied that such exemption results in a distortion of competition, Revenue may determine that such bodies are accountable persons and their supplies of services are liable to VAT.

Where requested by an accountable person, Revenue may determine whether a particular supply of goods or services is exempt from VAT or liable to VAT.

Where requested by an accountable person, Revenue may determine the rate of VAT applicable to a supply of goods or services.

7.4.6 The making of VAT regulations

Revenue is empowered to make regulations

> *"... as seem to them to be necessary for the purpose of giving effect to this Act [VAT Act] and of enabling them to discharge their functions thereunder ..."*

7.4.7 Mandatory disclosure relating to the promotion of tax related transactions

SI no 7 of 2011 introduced an obligation on the part of taxable persons, their advisers and consultants to disclose to the Revenue Commissioners details in relation to promoting tax related transactions. This is a very complex area of legislation.

The mandatory disclosure rules apply to transactions that have as a primary benefit, the obtaining of a tax advantage. A tax advantage includes a tax reduction, a tax deferral, tax relief, tax avoidance or a tax refund. Disclosure is mandatory immediately after the tax related transaction is marketed or made available for use.

An obligation to disclose arises where any one of the following factors is present:

- There is a confidentiality clause concerning the tax related transaction,
- A payment of a fee to the promoter on a contingency basis for the tax related transaction arises, or
- There is present documentation/implementation concerning the tax related transaction.

7.4.8 Penalties

s115–118 VATCA 2010

Penalties, for failure to comply with certain obligations are broadly broken down into two categories insofar as VAT is concerned.

In the first instance, there are the specific penalties consisting of a fixed amount of €4,000 for certain defined offences. Thus failure to register for VAT, failure to retain specific records, failure to issue a proper invoice (by an accountable person or by a flat-rate farmer) or failure to file a VAT/VIES return by the due date can each result in a fine of €4,000 for each offence. Likewise, failure to produce records, failure to assist an authorised officer, charging VAT while not registered, obstructing a person whom Revenue has required to value a premises, etc are liable to a fine of €4,000 upon conviction.

Such penalties can be pursued by way of summary proceedings (summons), and Revenue may institute proceedings for a period of up to three years after the date of the offence.

Section 116, VATCA provides for Penalties in the case of 'deliberately' or 'carelessly' making incorrect VAT returns. Prior to 2009, the penalty regime dealt with the concepts of negligence or fraud and the new legislation would appear to replace the concept of negligence with the act of doing something carelessly and the concept of fraud, with the act of doing something deliberately.

A scale of penalties, which is set out in the Revenue publication *Code of Practice for Revenue Audits and other Compliance Interventions* is incorporated into VAT legislation at section 116. Broadly speaking an accountable person may make an 'unprompted voluntary disclosure' or a 'prompted voluntary disclosure' prior to the actual commencement of a revenue audit. The former category applies where the

Revenue have not notified the taxpayer of the commencement of a revenue audit, the latter category applies from the time of notification until the actual commencement of the audit. In each case a window of opportunity is afforded to an accountable person to make a disclosure to the Revenue Commissioners in relation to any incorrect VAT return which has been made either deliberately or carelessly. Mitigated penalties range from 3% to 75% of the undeclared amount of output VAT (or the overclaimed amount of input VAT) as the case may be. [In the case of persistent infringement the penalty, set at 100% of the tax, will not be mitigated].

In addition, where a person 'carelessly' makes use of any VAT record, a penalty of €3,000 may be imposed. Where a person 'deliberately' makes use of any VAT record a penalty of €5,000 may be imposed.

The penalty regime also provides that an authorised officer of the Revenue Commissioners or a member of the Garda Síochána may, where they have reason to believe that a criminal tax offence has been committed, arrest a person who is not established in the State, or arrest a person who is likely to flee the State.

7.4.9 Time limits

In general, there is a four-year cap to the raising of assessments (see 7.4.4 above). However, in the case of negligence or fraud this cap is not applicable and assessments may be raised retrospectively prior to this period.

Additionally, where a taxable person discovers an under-declaration or over-claim in relation to VAT and fails to correct this without undue delay the four year cap on assessments is also removed as the person is deemed to have filed the incorrect return 'deliberately' (s116(9) TCA97).

7.4.10 Technical issues

Where Revenue determines that additional VAT is payable in relation to a certain transaction or series of transactions (either supplies received or supplies made), and it can be established that what was at issue was of a technical nature and therefore subject to the possibility of differing interpretation, then a penalty should not be applied as the commission/omission was neither deliberately nor carelessly made. It may be necessary to draw the Revenue official's attention to such circumstances at the conclusion of an audit/inspection.

7.4.11 Code of Practice for Revenue Audit

The Revenue Commissioners have over the years published various guides dealing with penalties and Revenue audits. The most recent publication is the "Code of Practice for Revenue Audits and other Compliance Interventions", published in November 2015.

7.4.12 Publication of defaulters

Section 1086, TCA97 imposes certain obligations on the Revenue Commissioners to publish details about certain taxpayers who pay tax, interest & a penalty.

Where a 'qualifying disclosure' is made and has been accepted by the Revenue then publication will not take place. Publication will also not occur where the tax, interest and penalty combined does not exceed €33k or where the penalty does not exceed 15% of the tax due.

References and Recommended Further Reading

CASSIDY, B. & M. READE (Eds.) (2018), *Law of Value-Added Tax,* Irish Tax Institute

BRODIE, S., G. DILLON, D. KENNEDY and F. MITCHELL (Ed.) (2017), *Value-Added Tax and VAT on Property,* Irish Tax Institute

MARTYN, J., D. SHANAHAN, and T. COONEY (Ed.) (2018), *Taxation Summary,* Irish Tax Institute

Appendix I

Value-Added Tax Regulations 2010
Regulation 27

Accounts

27. (1) The full and true records of all transactions that affect or may affect the accountable person's liability to tax and entitlement to deductibility, which every accountable person is required to keep in accordance with Chapter 7 of Part 9 and section 124(7) of the Act, shall be entered up to date and include—

(a) in relation to consideration receivable from registered persons—

(i) the amount receivable from each such person in respect of each transaction for which an invoice or other document is required to be issued under Chapter 2 of Part 9 of the Act, and

(ii) a cross-reference to the copy of the relevant invoice or other document,

(b) in relation to consideration receivable from unregistered persons—

(i) a daily total of the consideration receivable from all such persons,

(ii) a cross-reference from that daily total to the relevant books or other documents which are in use for the purposes of the business, and

(iii) where the accountable person uses an electronic cash register or point of sale system, the complete record of each entry on that register or system, uniquely identified by sequential number, date and time of such entry,

(c) in relation to consideration receivable from persons registered for value-added tax in another Member State—

(i) the amount receivable from each such person in respect of each transaction for which an invoice is required to be issued under Chapter 2 of Part 9 of the Act, and

(ii) a cross-reference to the copy of the relevant invoice,

(d) in relation to intra-Community acquisitions of goods, in respect of which the accountable person is liable to pay the tax chargeable—

(i) the amount of the consideration relating to those acquisitions, and

(ii) a cross-reference to the relevant invoice,

(e) in relation to importations of goods, a description of those goods together with—

(i) particulars of their value as determined in accordance with section 53(1) of the Act,

(ii) the amount of the consideration relating to the purchase of the goods if purchased in connection with the importation,

(iii) the amount of tax, if any, paid on importation, and

(iv) a cross-reference to the invoices and customs documents used in connection with the importation,

(f) in relation to goods supplied in accordance with section 19(1)(f) of the Act, being goods developed, constructed, assembled, manufactured, produced, extracted, purchased, imported or otherwise acquired by the accountable person or by another person on his or her behalf, and applied by the accountable person (otherwise than by way of disposal to another person) for the purposes of any business carried on by him or her—

(i) a description of the goods in question, and

(ii) the cost, excluding tax, to the accountable person of acquiring or producing those goods, except where tax chargeable in relation to the application of the goods would, if it were charged, be wholly deductible under Chapter 1 of Part 8 of the Act,

(*g*) in relation to goods supplied in accordance with section 19(1)(g) of the Act, being goods appropriated by an accountable person for any purpose other than the purpose of his or her business or disposed of free of charge, where tax chargeable in relation to the goods—

(i) on their purchase, intra-Community acquisition or importation by the accountable person, or on their development, construction, assembly, manufacture, production, extraction, or application in accordance with section 19(1)(f) of the Act, as the case may be, was wholly or partly deductible under Chapter 1 of Part 8 of the Act, or

(ii) where the ownership of those goods was transferred to the accountable person in the course of a transfer of a totality of assets, or part thereof, of a business and that transfer of ownership was deemed not to be a supply of goods in accordance with section 20(2) of the Act,

a description of the goods in question and the cost, excluding tax, to the taxable person, of acquiring or producing them,

(h) in relation to services deemed to be supplied by a person in the course or furtherance of business in accordance with section 27(1) of the Act—

(i) a description of the services in question, and

(ii) particulars of the cost, excluding tax, to the accountable person of supplying the services and of the consideration, if any, receivable by him or her in respect of the supply,

(i) in the case of the supply of services in circumstances that, by virtue of any of the provisions of Chapter 3 of Part 4 or section 104(2) of the Act, are deemed to be supplied outside the State—

(i) the full name and address of the person to whom the services are supplied,

(ii) the nature of the services,

(iii) the amount of the consideration receivable in respect of the supply, and

(iv) a cross-reference to the copy of the relevant invoice or other document,

(j) in the case of the receipt of goods and services in the State in respect of which the recipient of those goods and services is liable to pay the tax chargeable—

(i) a description of the goods and services in question, and

(ii) a cross-reference to the relevant invoice,

(k) in relation to discounts allowed, or price reductions made, to a registered person subsequent to the issue of an invoice to such person—

(i) the amount credited to such person, and

(ii) except in a case in which section 67(5)(a) of the Act applies, a cross-reference to the corresponding credit note,

(l) in relation to discounts allowed, or price reductions made, to unregistered persons—

(i) a daily total of the amount so allowed, and

(ii) a cross-reference to the goods returned book, cash book or other record used in connection with the matter,

(m) in relation to bad debts written off—

(i) particulars of the name and address of the debtor,

(ii) the nature of the goods or services to which the debt relates,

(iii) the date or dates on which the debt was incurred, and

(iv) the date or dates on which the debt was written off,

(n) in relation to goods and services supplied to the accountable person by another accountable person—

(i) the amount of the consideration payable,

(ii) the corresponding tax invoiced by the other accountable person, and

(iii) a cross-reference to the corresponding invoice,

(o) in relation to goods and services supplied to the accountable person by unregistered persons, and goods and services in respect of which flat-rate farmers are required in accordance with section 86 of the Act to issue invoices—

(i) a daily total of the consideration payable to such persons, and

(ii) a cross-reference to the purchases book, cash book, purchases dockets or other records which are in use in connection with the business,

(p) in relation to goods and services supplied to the accountable person by flat-rate farmers who are required, in accordance with section 86 of the Act, to issue invoices—

(i) the amount of the consideration payable (exclusive of the flat-rate addition) and the amount of the flat-rate addition invoiced by each such farmer, and

(ii) a cross-reference to the corresponding invoice,

(q) in relation to discounts or price reductions received from registered persons, subsequent to the receipt of invoices from such persons, except in a case in which section 67(5)(a) of the Act applies—

(i) the amount of the discount or price reduction, and the corresponding tax received from each such person, and

(ii) a cross-reference to the corresponding credit note,

(r) in relation to discounts or price reductions in relation to goods and services supplied to the accountable person by flat-rate farmers who are required, in accordance with section 86 of the Act, to issue invoices—

(i) the amount of the discount or price reduction (exclusive of the flat-rate addition) and the amount of the corresponding flat-rate addition, and

(ii) a cross-reference to the invoice issued in connection with the goods and services in question,

(s) in relation to discounts or price reductions received other than those referred to in subparagraphs (q) and (r)—

(i) a daily total of the amounts so received, and

(ii) a cross-reference to the cash book or other record used in connection with such matters,

(v) in relation to each capital good in respect of which a capital goods owner is required to create and maintain a capital good record in accordance with section 64(12) of the Act—

(i) the total tax incurred,

(ii) the amount of the total tax incurred which is deductible in accordance with Chapter 1 of Part 8 of the Act,

(iii) the date on which the adjustment period begins,

(iv) the number of intervals in the adjustment period,

(v) the initial interval proportion of deductible use,

(vi) the total reviewed deductible amount,

(vii) the proportion of deductible use for each interval,

(viii) details of any adjustments required to be made in accordance with Chapter 2 of Part 8 of the Act, and

(ix) details of any sale or transfer of the capital good or details of any assignment or surrender of a lease where section 64(7)(b) of the Act applies in relation to that capital good,

and

(w) in respect of supplies of goods specified in paragraphs 1(1) to (3), 3(1) and (3) and 7(1) to (4) of Schedule 2 to the Act—

(i) the name and address of the person to whom the goods are supplied,

(ii) a description of the goods supplied,

(iii) the amount of the consideration,

(iv) a cross-reference to the copy of the relevant invoice, and

(v) a cross-reference to the relevant customs and transport documents

(2) The accounts kept in accordance with paragraph (1) are required to set out, separately, the consideration, discounts, price reductions, bad debts and values at importation under separate headings in relation to—

(a) exempted activities, and

(b) goods and services chargeable at each rate of tax including the zero rate.

(3) In relation to a person authorised in accordance with section 80(1) of the Act to determine the amount of tax which becomes due by such person by reference to the amount of moneys which he or she receives, references in this Regulation to consideration in respect of the supply of goods or services are to be construed as references to such moneys received in respect of such supply.

Appendix II

Specimen of Form TR1

TAX REGISTRATION **TR1**

This form can be used to register 'Persons', i.e., Individuals, Partnerships, Trusts or Unincorporated Bodies for Income Tax, VAT, and as an Employer for PAYE/PRSI.

Companies (including foreign companies) requiring to register for Corporation Tax, VAT and PAYE/PRSI (as an employer) should complete **Form TR2**.

PAYE employees taking up their first employment should complete **Form 12A.**

Please complete ALL parts of this form as required IN BLOCK CAPITALS, sign the declaration below and return it to your Revenue District Office. Without accurate information the registration(s) will be delayed and/or you may experience delays in receipt of Returns and other forms.

Part A. *General Details*

1. **State the full name of the person,** *(including a trust, partnership, club or society)*, **who is to be registered**
2. **If trading under a business name, state** Trading as
3. **Legal Format** (please tick the appropriate box)
   Sole Trader ☐ Partnership ☐ Other (specify) ☐
4. **If you,** *(or the trust, partnership, club or society)*, **were registered for any tax in this country previously, what reference numbers did you hold?**
   PPS Number | Employer (PAYE/PRSI) | Value Added Tax (VAT)
5. ***(Individuals only)* State**
   If married, your pre-marriage name, where different | Your date of birth DD / MM / YYYY | Your mother's maiden name
6. **Marital Status**
   Tick ☑ the relevant box — Single ☐ Married ☐ Widowed ☐ Married but living apart ☐ Divorced ☐
7. **If you are married, give the following information**
   Spouse's forename | Spouse's surname | Spouse's PPS number | Date of Marriage DD / MM / YYYY
8. **Business Address** | **Private Address** *(if different)*
   Phone: Area Code | Number
   Fax: Area Code | Number
   Mobile Phone Number
9. **If you want your tax affairs to be dealt with in Irish, tick ☑ the box** ☐

Declaration ***This must be made in every case before you can be registered for any tax***

I declare that the particulars supplied by me in this application are true in every respect

NAME *(in BLOCK LETTERS)* **SIGNATURE**

CAPACITY *(individual, secretary, partner, trustee etc.)* **DATE** DD / MM / YYYY

Page 1

Part A. continued | **General Details**

10. Type of business

(a) is the business ☐ mainly retail ☐ mainly wholesale ☐ mainly manufacturing

☐ building & construction ☐ service and other

(b) Describe the business conducted in as much detail as possible. Give a precise description such as 'newsagent', 'clothing manufacturer', 'property letting', 'dairy farmer', 'investment income', etc. **Do not** use general terms such as 'shopkeeper', 'manufacturer', 'computers', 'consultant', etc.

If the application is a property related activity you may also need to complete Panel 27.

11. When did the business or activity commence? DD / MM / YYYY

12. To what date will annual accounts be made up? DD / MM / YYYY

13. Adviser Details

Give the following details of your accountant or tax adviser, if any, who will prepare the accounts and tax returns of the business.

Name

Address

Phone: Area Code **Number** **Mobile Phone Number**

Fax: Area Code **Number** **Tax Adviser Identification Number (TAIN)**

Client's Reference

If correspondence relating to VAT (ie VAT 3's) is being dealt with by the acountant or tax adviser tick ☑ the box

14. Partnership, Trust or Other Body

Give the following information in respect of all partners, trustees or other officers. Under 'Capacity', state whether precedent acting partner, partner, trustee, treasurer, etc. If necessary please continue on a separate sheet.

Name	Private Address	Capacity	PPS number (Partners only)
(i)			
(ii)			
(iii)			
(iv)			

15. If you rent your business premises, state

The name and address of the landlord (not an estate agent or rent collector)

The amount of rent paid per week ☐, month ☐ or year ☐ (Tick ☑ frequency) €

The date on which you started paying the rent DD / MM / YYYY

The length of the agreed rental/lease period.

16. If you acquired the business from a previous owner, state

The name and current address of the person from whom you acquired it

The VAT / registered number of that person.

Part B. Registration for Income Tax (non-PAYE)

17. Are you registering for Income Tax? (Tick ☑) **Yes** ☐ **No** ☐

Part C. Registration as an Employer for PAYE / PRSI

18. Are you registering as an employer for PAYE/PRSI? (Tick ☑) **Yes** ☐ **No** ☐

If your answer is 'No', there is no need to answer questions 19, 20 or 21. Continue to PART D.

19. Persons Engaged

(i) How many **employees** are: **Full time -** usually working 30 hours or more per week? ☐

Part time - usually working less than 30 hours per week? ☐

(ii) State the date your first employee commenced or will commence in your employment DD / MM / YYYY

20. What payroll and PAYE/PRSI record system will you use? (Tick ☑ the relevant box)

Tax Deduction Cards (Revenue Supplied) ☐ **Other Manual System** ☐ **Computer System** ☐ **Disk** ☐

21. Correspondence on PAYE/PRSI

If correspondence relating to PAYE/PRSI is being dealt with by an agent, tick ☑ this box ☐ and give the following details if different from 13 above.

Name
Address

Phone: Area Code **Number** **Mobile Phone Number**

Fax: Area Code **Number** **Tax Adviser Identification Number (TAIN)**

Client's Reference

Part D. Registration for VAT

22. Are you registering for VAT? (Tick ☑) **Yes** ☐ **No** ☐

If your answer is 'No', there is no need to answer questions 23 to 28.

23. Registration

(i) State the **date** from which you require to register DD / MM / YYYY

(ii) Is registration being sought only in respect of **European Union (EU) acquisitions?** (This applies only to farmers and non-taxable entities) (Tick ☑) **Yes** ☐ **No** ☐

(iii) Are you registering

(a) because your **turnover exceeds** or is likely to exceed the **limits** prescribed by law for registration? (a) ☐

or

(b) because you wish to **elect to be a taxable person**, (although not obliged by law to be registered)? (b) ☐ (Tick either (a), (b) or (c) as appropriate)

or

(c) because you are in receipt of **Fourth Schedule Services?** (c) ☐

(iv) State your expected turnover for the next 12 months €

Part D. continued — Registration for VAT

24. Are you applying for the moneys received basis of accounting for goods and services? (Tick ☑) Yes ☐ No ☐

If your answer is 'Yes', is this because

(a) expected annual turnover will be less than €635,000 (a) ☐

or (Tick either (a) or (b) as appropriate)

(b) at least 90% of your expected annual turnover will come from supplying goods and services to persons who are not registered e.g. hospitals, schools or the general public. (b) ☐

25. If your business is a foreign business registering in this State
State the expected annual turnover from supplies of taxable goods or services within the State €

26. State your bank or building society account to which VAT refunds can be made (compulsory)

Bank/Building Society

Branch Address

Sorting Code

Account Number

27. Property Details for VAT purposes

(a) Address of the property

(b) Date purchased or when development commenced DD / MM / YYYY

(c) Planning permission reference number, if applicable

(d) A signed statement from your client confirming that the property in question will be purchased and/or developed and will be disposed of or used in a manner which will give rise to a VAT liability i.e.

- by outright sale of the property or
- by creation of a long term lease i.e. lease more than ten years or
- by waiver of exemption in respect of short term lettings i.e. less than 10 years.

28. Exemption Waiver (in respect of the letting of property only)

(Such services are normally exempt from VAT).

Do you wish to waive exemption from VAT in respect of property letting? (Tick ☑) **Yes** ☐ **No** ☐

Note the waiver of exemption applies to all rents receivable from short-term lettings including those from properties other than that mentioned above. An option to 'Waiver of Exemption' cannot be backdated.

Additional Information

The following leaflets will provide additional information on the taxation aspects of running your own business. They are available from your local revenue office or from Revenue's Form's and Leaflets service at **LoCall 1890 30 67 06** or at **www.revenue.ie**

IT48 Starting in Business – A Revenue Guide
IT50 PAYE/PRSI for Small Employers
Employers Guide to operating PAYE and PRSI for certain benefits

If you have further information queries or concerns contact your Revenue District Office or Employer PAYE Enquiries at **LoCall 1890 23 63 36**.

If you wish to receive an employer pack tick ☑ here. ☐

If you want information on payment options, including **Direct Debit,** contact the **Collector General** at **LoCall 1890 20 30 70.**

Revenue On-Line Service (ROS) Save time – File On-Line
Once registered, you can access your tax details and file returns on-line using Revenue On-Line Service (ROS). ROS is available 24 hours a day, 365 days a year. It is easy, instant and secure.

For further details on ROS, visit our website at **www.revenue.ie** or call the ROS Information Desk at **LoCall 1890 20 11 06**.

Page 4

Specimen of Form TR2

TAX REGISTRATION TR2

This form can be used to register a limited company for Corporation Tax, for PAYE/PRSI (as an employer), and/or for VAT.

***Persons**, other than companies requiring to register, should complete **Form TR1** or **PAYE employees** taking up their first employment should complete **Form 12A**.*

Please complete all parts of this form as required IN BLOCK CAPITALS, sign the declaration below and return it to your Revenue District. Without accurate information the registration(s) will be delayed and/or you may experience delays in receipt of Returns and other forms.

Part A. General Details

1. **State the full name of the company as it is registered under the Companies' Acts**
2. **If trading under a business name, state** Trading as
3. **Business Address**

   Phone: Area Code **Number** **Fax: Area Code** **Number** **Mobile No.**
4. **Registered Office Address**

   Phone: Area Code **Number** **Fax: Area Code** **Number**
5. **Legal Format** (please tick ☑ appropriate box)

   Co-operative Society | **Private Unlimited Company** | **Statutory Body**

   Public Limited Company | **Private Limited Company** | **Branch of Foreign Company**

   Other (specify)
6. **Date company was registered** *(Irish registered companies)* DD / MM / YYYY
7. **Companies registration office (CRO) number** *(Irish registered companies)*
8. **When did the business or activity commence?** DD / MM / YYYY
9. **To what date will annual accounts be made up?** DD / MM / YYYY
10. **Foreign registered company**
    (i) Address in this State of fixed place of business

    Phone Area Code **Number** **Fax: Area Code** **Number**

    (ii) Is trading stock held at this address?(Tick ☑) **Yes** **No**

    (iii) Address in this State where the company's books and records will be produced for inspection by Revenue Officials

    Phone Area Code **Number** **Fax: Area Code** **Number**

10. **If you want your tax affairs to be dealt with in Irish, tick ☑ the box**

Declaration

This must be made in every case before the company can be registered for any tax.

I declare that the particulars supplied by me in this application are true in every respect

NAME *(IN BLOCK LETTERS)*

SIGNATURE **DATE** DD / MM / YYYY

(To be signed by the company secretary or other officer authorised)

Page 1

Part A. continued — General Details

12. If the company was registered for any tax in this country previously what reference numbers did it hold?

Corporation Tax
Employer (PAYE/PRSI)
Value Added Tax

13. Type of Business

(a) is the business ☐ mainly retail ☐ mainly wholesale ☐ mainly manufacturing ☐ building & construction ☐ service and other

(b) Describe the business conducted in as much detail as possible. Give a precise description such as 'newsagent', 'dairy farmer', 'textile manufacturer', 'property letting', 'investment income' etc. **Do not** use general terms such as 'shopkeeper', 'manufacturer', 'computers', 'consultant' etc.

If the application is a property related activity you may also need to complete Panel 30.

14. Directors Give the following information in relation to each director. If necessary, continue on a separate sheet.

Name	Private Address	Shareholding	PPS No.
(i)		%	
(ii)		%	
(iii)		%	

15. Company Secretary If this is one of the directors above the name will suffice.

Name	Private Address	PPS No.

16. Shareholders Give the details of any shareholder (other than a director whose details are shown above) who has 50% or more beneficial interest in the issued capital.

Name	Private Address	Shareholding	PPS No.
		%	

17. Adviser Details

Give the following details of the company's accountant or tax adviser, if any, who will prepare the accounts and tax returns of the company.

Name
Address

Phone: Area Code **Number** **Mobile Phone Number**
Fax: Area Code **Number** **Tax Adviser Identification Number (TAIN)**
Client's Reference

If correspondence relating to VAT (ie VAT 3's) is being dealt with by the acountant or tax adviser tick ☑ the box

18. If the business premises is rented, state

(i) The name and address of the landlord (not an estate agent or rent collector)

(ii) The amount of rent paid per week ☐, month ☐ or year ☐ (Tick ☑ frequency) €

(iii) The date on which the company started paying the rent DD/MM/YYYY

(iv) The length of the agreed rental/lease period

19. If the business was acquired from a previous owner state

(i) The name and current address of the person from whom it was acquired

(ii) The VAT/ registered number of that person

Part B. Registration for Corporation Tax

20. Are you registering for Corporation Tax (Tick ☑ the relevant box) Yes ☐ No ☐

Part C. Registration as an Employer for PAYE/PRSI

21. Are you registering as an employer for PAYE/PRSI (Tick ☑ the relevant box) Yes ☐ No ☐
If the answer is 'No', there is no need to answer questions 22, 23 or 24. Continue to Part D.

22. Persons Engaged

(i) How many **employees** are: **Full time** - usually working 30 hours or more per week? ☐

Part time - usually working less than 30 hours per week? ☐

(ii) State the date your first employee commenced or will commence in your employment DD / MM / YYYY

23. What payroll and PAYE/PRSI record system will be used (Tick ☑ the relevant box)
Tax deduction card system (Revenue Supplied) ☐ Other manual system ☐ Computer system ☐ Disk ☐

24. Correspondence on PAYE/PRSI
If correspondence relating to PAYE/PRSI is being dealt with by an agent, tick ☑ this box ☐ and give the following details, if different from 17 above.

Name **Address**			
Phone: Area Code	Number	Mobile Phone Number	
Fax: Area Code	Number	Tax Adviser Identification Number (TAIN)	
Client's Reference			

Part D. Registration for VAT

25. Are you registering for VAT? (Tick ☑ the relevant box) Yes ☐ No ☐
If your answer is 'No', there is no need to answer questions 26 to 31.

26. Registration

(i) State the **date** from which you require to register the company DD / MM / YYYY

(ii) Is registration being sought only in respect of **European Union (EU) acquisitions**? (This applies only to farmers and non-taxable entities) (Tick ☑ the relevant box) Yes ☐ No ☐

(iii) Are you registering the company
(a) because **turnover exceeds** or is likely to exceed the **limits** prescribed by law for registration? (a) ☐
or (b) because you wish to **elect it to be a taxable person** (although not obliged by law to be registered)? (b) ☐
or (c) because it is in receipt of **Fourth Schedule services** (c) ☐
Tick ☑ either (a), (b) or (c) as appropriate

(iv) State the expected turnover for the next 12 months €

27. Are you applying for the moneys received basis of accounting for goods and services? (Tick ☑ the relevant box) Yes ☐ No ☐
If your answer is 'Yes', is this because

(a) expected annual turnover will be less than €635,000 (a) ☐
or
(b) at least 90% of your expected annual turnover will come from supplying goods and services to persons who are not registered, e.g. hospitals, schools or the general public (b) ☐
Tick ☑ either (a) or (b) as appropriate

Part D. continued — Registration for VAT

28. If your business is a foreign business registering in this State
State the expected annual turnover from supplies of taxable goods or services within the State. €

29. State the bank or building society account to which VAT refunds can be made (Compulsory)

Bank/Building Society

Branch Address

Sorting Code

Account Number

30. Property Details for VAT purposes

(a) Address of the property

(b) Date purchased or when development commenced DD / MM / YYYY

(c) Planning permission reference number, if applicable

(d) A copy of the minutes* of the meeting/meeting of the partners, where it was resolved that the property in question would be purchased and/or developed and would be disposed of or used in a manner which would give rise to a VAT liability i.e.
- by outright sale of the property, or
- by creation of a long term lease i.e. lease more than ten years, or
- by waiver of exemption in respect of short term lettings i.e. less than 10 years.

31. Exemption Waiver (in respect of the letting of property only)
(Such services are normally exempt from VAT).

Do you wish to waive exemption from VAT in respect of property letting? Tick ☑ **Yes** **No**

(**Note:** the waiver of exemption applies to all rents receivable from short-term lettings including those from properties other than that mentioned above. An option to 'Waiver of Exemption' cannot be backdated.)

*The minutes should show the date of the meeting, the names of all those present at the meeting and should be signed by the company secretary or precedent acting partner in the case of a partnership.

Additional Information

The following leaflets will provide additional information on the taxation aspects of running a business. They are available from your local revenue office or from Revenue's Form's and Leaflets service at **LoCall 1890 30 67 06** or at **www.revenue.ie**

IT48	Starting in Business – A Revenue Guide
IT50	PAYE/PRSI for Small Employers
Employers Guide to operating PAYE and PRSI for certain benefits	

If you have further information queries or concerns contact your Revenue District Office or Employer PAYE Enquiries at **LoCall 1890 23 63 36**.

If you want information on payment options, including **Direct Debit**, contact the **Collector General** at **LoCall 1890 20 30 70**.

Revenue On-Line Service (ROS) Save time – File On-Line

Once registered, you can access your tax details and file returns on-line using Revenue On-Line Service (ROS). ROS is available 24 hours a day, 365 days a year. It is easy, instant and secure.

For further details on ROS, visit our website at **www.revenue.ie** or call the ROS Information Desk at **LoCall 1890 20 11 06**.

Page 4

Appendix III

Extract from the Revenue publication Code of Practice for Revenue Audit and other Compliance Interventions

The following table sets out the net penalty after mitigation appropriate to each category of tax default:

TAX-GEARED PENALTIES[1]			
		Mitigated penalty	
Default category	***Base Penalty***	***first prompted qualifying disclosure***	***unprompted qualifying disclosure***
Deliberate behaviour	100% of under declaration	50%	10%
Careless behaviour with significant consequences	40% of under declaration	20%	5%
Careless behaviour without significant consequences	20% of under declaration	10%	3%

[1]Note that second and third disclosures (i.e. under declaration/over claim of VAT) incur significantly increased penalties.

Appendix IV

Revenue's Customer Service Charter

Revenue 

Revenue collects taxes and duties which fund the provision of public services for the benefit of all citizens.

Revenue protects society through its Customs Service working on frontier control.

The effective and fair administration of tax and customs law requires Revenue and citizens to recognise certain basic rights and responsibilities.

This Customer Charter sets out mutual expectations in this context.

Consistency, Equity and Confidentiality

- Revenue will administer the law fairly, reasonably and consistently and will seek to collect no more than the correct amount of tax or duty
- Revenue will treat the information you give us in confidence and ensure that it will not be used or disclosed except as provided for by law

Revenue

	You can expect	We expect you
Courtesy and Consideration	■ to be treated courteously, with consideration and in a non- discriminatory way in your dealings with Revenue.	■ to treat Revenue officials with courtesy and to give them all reasonable co-operation
Information and Assistance	■ to be given the necessary information and all reasonable assistance to enable you to clearly understand and meet your tax and customs obligations and to claim your entitlements and credits	■ to provide true and correct information in all your contacts with Revenue and to advise Revenue in a timely manner of developments (such as change of address, commencement or cessation of business) that are relevant to your tax and customs affairs
Presumption of Honesty	■ to be treated as honest in your dealings with Revenue unless there is clear reason to believe otherwise and subject to Revenue's responsibility for ensuring compliance with tax and customs law	■ to deal in an honest way with Revenue by returning the tax and duty which you are due to pay and seeking only those entitlements and credits to which you are due
Compliance Costs	■ that Revenue will administer the tax and duty regimes in a way that will minimise, as far as possible, compliance costs	■ to maintain proper records and accounts and to ensure that your Returns and Declarations are completed fully, accurately and in a timely manner

Complaints, Review and Appeal

There are comprehensive complaints and appeal procedures open to all customers of Revenue and we encourage you to avail of these if you are in any way dissatisfied with the service you receive from us.

You can expect

- That if you make a complaint, Revenue will deal with it promptly, impartially and in confidence.
- That availing of Revenue's own complaints procedures will never prejudice your rights to raise issues with the Ombudsman or lodge, within the statutory time limits, a formal appeal to the Office of the Appeal Commissioners against an assessment raised by Revenue or against certain determinations made by Revenue officials.

Full details, including contact points, are contained in Leaflet CS4 which is available in any Revenue public office, from our Forms and Leaflets LoCall number 1890 30 67 06 and on our website, www.revenue.ie.

8 OVERVIEW OF THE IRISH INCOME TAX SYSTEM

Learning Outcomes

On completion of this chapter you will be able to:

- ✓ Explain the legislative framework of income tax.
- ✓ Identify the two main methods of collecting income tax in Ireland.
- ✓ Explain how companies and other bodies may be obliged to account for income tax payments to Revenue.
- ✓ Classify various sources of income in accordance with the correct Case or Schedule.
- ✓ Explain the terms "gross income", "total income" and "taxable income".
- ✓ Identify sources of income that are exempt from income tax.
- ✓ Compute the restriction of certain reliefs for "high income earners."
- ✓ Draft a *pro forma* tax computation.

8.1 Introduction

Income tax is the cornerstone of the Irish system of taxation. The gross receipts from income tax for 2016, as reported in the Revenue Commissioners' 2017 Annual Report, amounted to €22,076 million[1] (see Chapter 1, section 1.6). Accordingly, income tax accounted for 31% of total net tax receipts for 2017 – more than the combined take from all other direct taxation measures, namely corporation tax, stamp duties, capital acquisitions tax and capital gains tax. Thus, though criticised for not being sufficiently comprehensive,[2] income tax has the broadest base of all direct taxes applicable in Ireland and, consequently, a significant part of the tax legislation is concerned with income tax measures. In addition, it is important to bear in mind that many of the

The Irish Tax Institute would like to acknowledge the use of some material from *Income Tax* by Gearóid Deegan and George Reddin, edited by Anne Bolster and published by the Irish Tax Institute in 2010. Such material has been adapted specifically for students with the addition of focused commentary and examples.

1 Published figures are inclusive of USC and withholding taxes.

2 In 1982, the Irish Commission on Taxation argued in favour of a more comprehensive definition of income that would include capital sums received. Under the Irish system, such sums are distinguished from other sources of income and may be separately subject to capital gains tax and/or capital acquisitions tax. Readers are referred to the commentary in 1.6.

definitions and provisions found in the income tax code also extend to other tax heads. This is particularly obvious in the context of corporation tax.

This chapter broadly considers the key income tax principles. It is concerned with distinguishing between the different sources of income that are liable to income tax and with how such sources of income are taxed. The chapter sets out a comprehensive *pro forma* income tax computation, which provides a framework for consolidating the many component computations of an individual's overall income tax liability. The remainder of Section III is concerned with the detailed rules relating to many of these component computations.

8.2 Income Tax Framework

The British Prime Minister, W.E. Gladstone first introduced a system of income tax to Ireland in 1853. The Income Tax Act 1967 was, in effect, a consolidation of the original measures introduced by Gladstone, together with subsequent adaptations necessitated by the establishment of the Free State, the Constitution of 1937 and Finance Acts from 1923 onwards. Readers are referred to the commentary at 1.1.2.

The 1967 Act is now consolidated with subsequent Finance Acts from 1968 to 1997 into the Taxes Consolidation Act 1997 (TCA97). The 1967 Income Tax Act had been amended by almost every annual Finance Act since 1967 and therefore, consolidation was required. In fact, TCA97 brings together three areas of tax law, these being Income Tax, Corporation Tax and Capital Gains Tax. It is important to note that TCA97 in no way changed the existing tax law that was in force prior to the consolidation process. The aim of the consolidation was to combine all the legislation relevant to a particular area of tax law into one section of an Act as opposed to having to refer to the original Act and subsequent Finance Acts to find the particular applicable provisions. Amendments to TCA97 are included in subsequent Finance Acts.

In addition to the income tax legislation, readers should also be aware of decided case law which assists in the interpretation of the legislation. Documented details of Revenue practice in specific areas are also helpful.

8.3 Introduction to Income Tax Principles

Income tax is a tax on the income of an individual for a year of assessment. Up until 5 April 2001, the tax year ran from 6 April to the following 5 April, e.g., the 2000/01 year of assessment ran from 6 April 2000 to 5 April 2001. With effect from 1 January 2002, the tax year is now aligned to the calendar year[3].

3 Thus, the year 2001 was a "short" transitional tax year, which ran from 6 April 2001 to 31 December 2001.

Income tax is payable by all individuals (save for some exceptions). Broadly speaking, there are two methods of paying income tax:

- through the "pay as you earn" (PAYE) system, i.e., by deduction at source from salary/wages (considered in detail in Chapter 23); and/or
- through the self-assessment system, i.e., for "non-PAYE" individuals who make direct payments of tax to the Revenue Commissioners to cover their liability for a year of assessment (considered in detail in Chapter 10).

It is important to also bear in mind that companies and other statutory bodies may have an obligation to account for income tax to the Revenue Commissioners. Such entities are required to withhold income tax from certain payments and to pay amounts withheld to the Collector-General.

8.4 Withholding Taxes

In certain circumstances, a payment in discharge of a liability for services rendered or annual payments must be paid under the deduction of income tax at source. Examples of such withholding taxes are as follows:

- **PAYE (payroll taxes)** – An employer or payer of an occupational pension must deduct income tax, PRSI (not applicable for pensions) and the universal social charge (previously the health contribution levy and the income levy), where appropriate, from the salaries/wages or pension payments to employees. Readers are referred to Chapter 23.

- **Professional services withholding tax (PSWT)** – Tax at the standard rate is deducted from payments made for professional services by Government Departments, State bodies, local authorities, health boards, etc. Examples of professional services include medical, dental, pharmaceutical, optical, architectural, auditing and legal services.

- **Relevant contract tax (RCT)** – Payments made by a principal contractor to a sub-contractor in respect of payments on foot of contracts in the construction, forestry and meat-processing industries may be subject to withholding tax. Where the principal contractor receives appropriate authorisation, RCT need not be deducted from the gross payment. In the absence of a "0%" authorisation, the principal contractor may deduct:

  - 20% RCT if instructed by Revenue (standard rate), or

  - 35% RCT which is the default rate where no authorisation is received for the 0% or 20% rate

From 2015 onwards, where principal contractors do not apply the authorised RCT rates, a tax geared penalty regime is imposed. The penalty rates vary from 35% to 3%.

- **Standard rate income tax** – The payer of certain annual payments must deduct tax at the standard rate of income tax from such payments. Examples of annual payments subject to this withholding tax are deeds of covenant and patent royalties (see Chapter 12).

Where tax is deducted under any of the above headings, the recipient may claim credit for such tax in calculating the tax liability that arises on receipt of the payment. The withholding tax may be allowed as a credit against:

  - Corporation tax – where the recipient is a corporate entity;
  - Income tax – where the recipient is a sole trader or a partner in a partnership.

8.5 Income Categorisation

Income is classified into different Schedules for tax purposes. Originally there were six such Schedules – Schedules A to F inclusive.

Schedule A was concerned with the taxation of imputed rent from property owned irrespective of whether or not such property was actually let. Similarly, Schedule B was concerned with measuring income from farming as the imputed rental value of the land. Both of these Schedules were abolished in 1969. The existing legislation ensures that rents only actually received are subject to tax and also that income from farming is calculated on a more objective basis.

Schedule C is concerned with tax at source levied on banks and other agents that collect and cash foreign dividends and that pay government interest and dividends from public revenue. These provisions are outside the scope of the analysis in this text and, accordingly, readers should concern themselves only with Schedules D, E and F.

Schedule D is the most comprehensive of the Schedules and is consequently further classified into five Cases – Cases I to V.

Correct categorisation of income is essential to ensure that the appropriate rules are applied in determining:

- how much income is taxed in a year of assessment;
- how the income is taxed; and
- how the losses, if any, arising from such income may be utilised.

A summary of the various income classifications, all of which are considered in detail in the chapters to follow, is set out below:

Schedule D	Case I	■ Trading income of self-employed sole traders and partners
	Case II	■ Professional and vocational income of self-employed sole practitioners and partners
	Case III	■ Investment income (not subject to deduction of tax at source) ■ Income from foreign employments and foreign investments (not subject to deduction of tax at source)
	Case IV	■ Irish deposit interest (subject to deduction of tax at source) ■ Foreign investment income (subject to deduction of Irish tax at source) ■ Covenant income ■ Miscellaneous sources of income not specifically taxable under any other Case or Schedule
	Case V	■ Rents from Irish property
Schedule E		■ Income from Irish employments and directorships ■ Irish pensions
Schedule F		■ Dividends from Irish resident companies

8.6 Exempt Sources of Income

A number of income sources are exempt from income tax in accordance with specific statutory measures. These are summarised as follows:

s195 TCA97 **Artists**

Certain earnings of individuals, which in the opinion of the Revenue Commissioners are derived from a work or works adjudged to have cultural or artistic merit, are exempted from tax up to a ceiling of €50,000 (€40,000 up to 2014). "A Work" is defined as an original and creative work, whether written, composed or executed as the case may be, which falls into one of the following categories:

- a book or other writing;
- a play;
- a musical composition;
- a painting or other like picture;
- a sculpture

The individual must be resident or ordinarily resident or domiciled in Ireland or in an EU/EEA member state and not resident elsewhere (i.e. outside the EU/EEA). A formal claim for exemption must be made to Revenue and the exemption only applies from the tax year in which the claim is made.

Even though the above income (subject to the earnings ceiling) is exempt from tax, nevertheless, such income must be included in the individual's annual tax return.

s232 TCA97 **Forests/Woodlands**

Profits or gains arising from the occupation of woodlands managed on a commercial basis and with a view to the realisation of profits are exempt from tax. Dividends paid out of such tax-free income are also exempt from tax.

Again, even though the above income is exempt from tax, such income must be included in the individual's annual tax return.

s189 TCA97 **Payment in respect of personal injuries to permanently incapacitated individuals**

Any payments made to, or in respect of, an individual by a Court order or under "out of court" settlements in respect of damages received for personal injury, where the individual is permanently and totally incapacitated by reason of mental or physical infirmity from maintaining themselves as a result of such injury, are exempt from income tax. Likewise, any income, including rental income arising from the investment of such awards, is exempt from tax. However, the amount of any such income must be included in the individual's annual tax return.

s189A TCA97 **Trusts for permanently incapacitated individuals**

Income arising to the trustees of a trust, which has been set up for the benefit of a permanently incapacitated individual and which has been funded by subscriptions from the general public, is exempt from tax. The income paid by the trustees to the incapacitated individual is also exempt from tax. Section 10 FA 2014 provides that on the death of the incapacitated individual, the undistributed fund of the trust may pass to the deceased estate. This only applies where the deceased is survived by a spouse/civil partner or child.

Even though the above income is exempt from tax, such income must be included in the individual's annual tax return.

s190 TCA97 **Payments made by the Haemophilia HIV Trust**

Income payments made by the Haemophilia HIV Trust to beneficiaries under the Trust are exempt from tax.

s191 TCA97 **Hepatitis C compensation**

Compensation payments made by the "Hepatitis C Tribunal" or received through the courts are exempt from tax. Any investment income arising from the compensation payments is also exempt from income tax, provided that the income is the individual's sole or main income and that the person is permanently and totally incapacitated. "Sole or main income" means that the total of such "compensation" income must be in excess of 50% of the aggregate of the individual's total income from all sources for the year concerned.

Even though the above income is exempt from tax, such income must be included in the individual's annual tax return.

s192 TCA97 **Payments in respect of Thalidomide children**

Compensation payments made to Thalidomide children, and the income derived from the investment of such payments, are exempt from tax.

s192A TCA97 **Compensation payments under employment law**

Compensation awards paid following a formal hearing by a relevant authority under employment law in respect of the infringement of employees' rights and entitlements under that law are exempt from income tax.

s192B TCA97 **Payments to foster parents**

Payments made by the Health Service Executive to foster parents in respect of the care of foster children are exempt from income tax. Also exempt are certain discretionary payments by the Health Service Executive to carers relating to the care of former foster children (those aged 18 or over) who suffer from a disability, or until such children reach 21 years or complete their full-time education course.

s216B TCA97 **Payments under Scéim na bhFoghlaimeoirí Gaeilge**

Income received for the provision of student accommodation by persons in Gaeltacht areas under the Irish language student scheme known as Scéim na bhFoghlaimeori Gaeilge is exempt from tax.

s205A TCA97 **Magdalen Laundry Payments**

Section 77 Finance (No. 2) Act 2013 exempts from income tax receipt of payments from the Minister for Justice, Equality and Defence by women who were previously admitted to the Magdalen Laundries. The ex gratia payments are payable following the findings in the Magdalen Commission Report. The list of laundries are set out in Schedule 3A TCA97.

s216 TCA97 **Profits from lotteries**

Profits from a lottery to which a license under the Gaming and Lotteries Act 1956 applies are exempt from tax.

s865 TCA97 **Interest paid on tax overpaid**

Interest paid by the Revenue Commissioners on tax overpaid is exempt from tax.

s42 TCA97 **Savings certificates**

Interest payable on savings certificates issued by the Minister for Finance is not liable to tax, provided the amount invested does not exceed the amount which the recipient is authorised to hold. At the time of going to print, up to €120,000 worth of each issue of savings certificates may be held by an individual (€240,000 per joint holding).

s197 TCA97 An Post savings schemes

Any bonus or interest payable to an individual under An Post savings schemes (i.e., Index-Linked Savings Bond and Index-Linked National Installment Savings) is not liable to tax provided the amount invested does not exceed the amount which the recipient is authorised to hold. At the time of going to print, the maximum subscription is €120,000 per individual (€240,000 per joint holding) for Savings Bonds and €1,000 per individual per month for Installment Savings.

s200 TCA97 Foreign pensions

Certain foreign pensions are exempt from tax provided:

- it is a pension awarded for past services in a foreign employment, or is payable under the law of the foreign country in which it arises, and this law corresponds to the provisions of Chapters 12, 16 or 17 of Part II of or Chapters 4 or 6 of Part III of the Social Welfare (Consolidation) Act 1993, or any subsequent Act together with which that Act may be cited, apply, and
- it would have been exempt from tax in the foreign country, had it been received by a person resident in that foreign country.

s204/205 TCA97 Military and other pensions, gratuities and allowances

The following are exempt from tax:

- all pensions and gratuities awarded in respect of wounds and disabilities granted under the Army Pensions Act, 1923 to 1980 and any related Acts. The relief is restricted only to the amount of the pension solely attributable to the disability and is certified by the Minister for Defence;
- military gratuities and demobilisation pay granted to officers of the National Forces or the Defence Forces of Ireland on demobilisation;
- deferred pay within the meaning of the Defence Act 1954;
- gratuities granted in respect of service with the Defence Forces;
- military service pensions payable to Veterans of the War of Independence, their widows and dependents.

s204A TCA97 Garda Reserve Payments

Section 10 Finance (No. 2) Act 2013 exempts from tax receipt of the annual allowance payable to reserve members of an Garda Siochana.

s204B TCA97 Compensation for certain living donors

Section 6 FA 2014 introduced an exemption from income tax for compensation payments to kidney donors. The exemption applies from 1 January 2015 onwards.

8.7 Restriction of Certain Reliefs for High Income Earners

Section 17 Finance Act 2006 introduced a restriction on the amount of reliefs available to "high income earners" effective from 1 January 2007. The objective of Section 17 was to ensure that "high earners" could not reduce their tax liability to nil or a negligible amount by the use of tax shelters. The restricted reliefs are as follows:

- capital allowances on specified plant and machinery claimed by passive partners in a manufacturing trade;
- capital allowances and losses from property incentive schemes;
- patent royalty income (pre-November 2010) and patent distributions;
- exempt artists income;
- interest on money to buy shares in certain companies and partnerships;
- exempt distributions and exempt income from certain mining profits; and
- donations to sports bodies.
- For the years 2007, 2008 and 2009 the maximum amount of reliefs an individual could use in a year was limited to the greater of €250,000 (the threshold amount) and 50% of "adjusted income". Adjusted income means taxable income after adding back the restricted reliefs. Any relief denied is carried forward to the following year(s).

Section 23 of the Finance Act 2010, lowered the threshold amount from €250,000 to €80,000 and the 50% of adjusted income to 20% of adjusted income. Using the same facts as those in Example 8.1 above, the impact of Section 23 Finance Act 2010 is as follows:

Example 8.1

	€	
Case I	*255,000*	
Case V	*500,000*	
	755,000	
Less		
"Section 23" relief	*(500,000)*	
Trade Capital Allowances	*(5,000)*	*Note 1*
Taxable Income	*250,000*	
Add back restricted relief	*500,000*	
Adjusted Income	*750,000*	
Less "Section 23" relief	*(150,000)*	*Note 2*
Taxable Income	*600,000*	

Note 1: Ordinary Trade Capital Allowances are not subject to the restriction.

Note 2: Relief restricted to greater of 20% of adjusted income (€750,000) and €80,000.

If an individual's adjusted income is less than the "income threshold amount" of €125,000 or the amount of the specified reliefs is less than the "relief threshold amount" of €80,000, the restrictions will not apply.

Example 8.2

	€	€	€	€
Income	*55,000*	*85,000*	*95,000*	*124,500*
Tax Shelter	*325,000*	*325,000*	*325,000*	*325,000*

Even though the tax shelter amounts exceed the "relief threshold amount" of €80,000, the restriction does not apply since the income levels are below the "income threshold amount" of €125,000.

Example 8.3

	€	€	€	€	€
Case V Income	*250,000*	*350,000*	*400,000*	*500,000*	*600,000*
"Section 23" relief	*250,000*	*250,000*	*250,000*	*250,000*	*250,000*
Adjusted income	*250,000*	*350,000*	*400,000*	*500,000*	*600,000*
Restricted relief	*80,000*	*80,000*	*80,000*	*100,000*	*120,000*
Taxable Income	*170,000*	*270,000*	*320,000*	*400,000*	*480,000*
Restriction calculation:					
Higher of 20% × adjusted income	*50,000*	*70,000*	*80,000*	*100,000*	*120,000*
and €80,000	*80,000*	*80,000*	*80,000*	*80,000*	*80,000*

Example 8.4

	€	€	€	€	€
Case1 Income	*250,000*	*350,000*	*400,000*	*500,000*	*600,000*
Tax Shelter	*250,000*	*250,000*	*250,000*	*250,000*	*250,000*
Pension Contribution	*20,000*	*20,000*	*20,000*	*20,000*	*20,000*
Adjusted income	*230,000*	*330,000*	*380,000*	*480,000*	*580,000*
Restricted relief	*80,000*	*80,000*	*80,000*	*96,000*	*116,000*
Taxable Income	*150,000*	*250,000*	*300,000*	*384,000*	*464,000*
Restriction calculation:					
Higher of 20% × adjusted income	*46,000*	*66,000*	*76,000*	*96,000*	*116,000*
and €80,000	*80,000*	*80,000*	*80,000*	*80,000*	*80,000*

8.8 Calculation of Income Tax Liability

An income tax liability for an individual should be presented in accordance with the prescribed *pro forma* computation set out in Appendix I to this chapter. Calculating a liability involves firstly calculating the taxable amount of income from various sources and then classifying these amounts in accordance with the correct Case or Schedule. Broadly speaking, tax is applied to the sum total of income from all sources, subject to deductions for certain reliefs and payments. The following terms are relevant:

- **Gross income** is the sum of the individual amounts of income from all sources less deductions or losses that can specifically be set off against that income.
- **Total income** is gross income after the deduction of certain "charges". Relief for charges paid is considered in detail in Chapter 12.
- **Taxable income** is total income, as defined above, less personal allowances and reliefs allowable at the marginal rate of tax. Readers are referred to Chapter 11 for a discussion of the reliefs available at the marginal rate of tax.

In general, income tax is applied to taxable income as defined above at rates of 20% and 40%. The 20% rate only applies to a certain amount of an individual's income, known as the "standard rate band" of income (the amount of this band varies depending on the marital status of the taxpayer and, in the case of married couples/civil partners, depending on whether or not both spouses/civil partners earn income). The balance of taxable income (if any) is taxed at the higher rate of 40%.

Tax credits are then deducted from the income tax figure. In general, non-refundable tax credits are granted on the basis of the personal circumstances of the taxpayer and, in respect of certain payments made by the taxpayer. The maximum benefit available from non-refundable credits is to reduce an individual's tax liability to nil; where they exceed the liability, the excess is not refunded. In contrast, refundable tax credits represent taxes already deducted at source from income received by the tax payer during the tax year, e.g., PAYE, RCT, PSWT, etc. Where such credits exceed a taxpayer's income tax liability, the excess if fully refundable.

Effective from 1 January 2009 a new levy was introduced known as an income levy. The levy is applied to income before capital allowances and pensions deductions. Effective from 1 January 2011, the income levy and health contribution levy were replaced by the universal social charge (USC). Readers are referred to Chapter 11 for further analysis of the USC and applicable rates.

8.9 Summary of Chapters to Follow

The foregoing is, as the name of the chapter suggests, an **overview** of the income tax system. In the chapters to follow, more detailed analysis is provided:

- Chapter 9 is concerned with the territorial scope of income tax.
- Chapter 10 deals with the administration of the self-assessment system. Much of the analysis has application for taxpayers assessed to corporation tax as well as for individuals and partners assessed to income tax.
- Chapters 11, 12 and 13 deal with the basis of taxation of single, widowed and married individuals/civil partners, and examine the allowances, reliefs and tax credits to which they may be entitled.
- Chapters 14 to 17 deal with the tax treatment of business profits and losses, whether derived from a trade or profession.
- Chapter 18 deals with partnerships.
- Chapter 19 deals with the taxation of investment or "passive" income and foreign-earned income.
- Chapters 20 to 23 deal with the taxation of employment income and provide an analysis of how the PAYE system operates.

Appendix I

Pro Forma Income Tax Computation

Income Tax Computation for the year 2018

Schedule D		**€**	**€**
Case I (Self-Employed Traders)			
Adjusted Case I profit in basis period		X	
Less:	Case I losses carried forward	(X)	
	Case I capital allowances	(X)	
	Allowable retirement annuity premium	(X)	X
Case II (Self-Employed Professionals)		X	
Adjusted Case II profit in basis period		X	
Less:	Case II losses carried forward	(X)	
	Case II capital allowances	(X)	
	Allowable retirement annuity premiums	(X)	X
Case III			
e.g., Government security interest, income from abroad		X	X
Case IV			
e.g., Irish building society and commercial bank interest		X	
income received under deduction of tax at source		X	
miscellaneous income		X	X
Case V			
Rents from property situated in the Republic of Ireland, i.e., Case V profit after allowable expenses		X	
Less: Case V losses carried forward		(X)	X
Schedule E: Income from Employments/Offices:			
Salary/wages/directors' fees/pensions		X	
Bonus/commission		X	
Benefits-in-kind		X	
Taxable lump sums		X	
Less:	Employee's contributions to a Revenue-approved scheme	(X)	
Less:	Allowable retirement annuity premiums (in respect of non-pensionable employment)	(X)	X

	Schedule F		
	Distributions/dividends from companies resident in the Republic of Ireland		X
	Gross Income		**X**
	Less: Case I/II losses arising in 2018 (s381 TCA97)	(X)	(X)
	Deduct: Relief for charges paid during 2018		
	Qualifying covenants/annuities paid in 2018	(X)	
	Patent royalties paid in 2018	(X)	(X)
	TOTAL INCOME		**X**
	Deduct: Personal allowances/reliefs *(available at marginal rate),*	(X)	(X)
	e.g., permanent health insurance		
	e.g. maintenance or treatment in nursing home		
	TAXABLE INCOME		**X**
	Taxed as follows (assume married and two incomes):		
	Standard Rate Band 69,100 @ 20%		X
	Interest subject to DIRT @ 37%		X
	Balance @ 40%		X
	Total tax		X
Deduct:	**Non-refundable tax credits**		
	e.g., Married persons' tax credit	(X)	
	Employee's tax credit (PAYE credit)		
	Deposit interest retention tax (DIRT)	(X)	
Add	Income tax deducted from payments *made*, e.g., tax deducted from covenants/annuities	X	(X)
Add	PRSI	X	
Add	USC	X	
Deduct:	**Refundable tax credits**		
	e.g., tax withheld on covenant/annuities received under deduction of income tax	(X)	
	PAYE paid	(X)	
	Dividend withholding tax	(X)	
	Net Income Tax Due		**X**

9 THE SCOPE OF INCOME TAX

Learning Outcomes

On completion of this chapter, you should be able to:

- ✓ Define important concepts such as residence and ordinary residence.
- ✓ Discuss the criteria used to determine the domicile of an individual.
- ✓ Explain what impact residence, ordinary residence and domicile have on the charge to Irish taxation.
- ✓ Describe the reliefs from Irish taxation which are available for foreign employment income and calculate the amount of any such reliefs.
- ✓ Explain the concept of the Domicile Levy and how it impacts on citizens of Ireland who are Irish domiciled.

9.1 Introduction

The purpose of this chapter is to establish how residence and domicile impact on the Irish income tax system. The extent of an individual's liability to Irish income tax depends on whether the individual is:

- resident in Ireland;
- ordinarily resident in Ireland; and/or
- domiciled in Ireland.

All the concepts mentioned above, i.e., resident, ordinarily resident and domiciled, have a very precise meaning. The former two are defined in tax legislation; the latter, not having a statutory meaning, is based on precedents and case law.

This chapter details the issues of relevance in determining an individual's residence status for Irish tax purposes and examines the implications of residence and domicile on Irish tax liabilities. The chapter also expands on further concepts, such as:

- Domicile of origin
- Domicile of choice
- Domicile of dependence
- Remittance basis of taxation
- Reliefs available for foreign employment income

9.2 Residence

9.2.1 Background

s819 TCA97 Prior to 6 April 1994, the residence and ordinary residence position of an individual was based largely on tests and practices that evolved from UK court decisions over the course of a number of years. The 1994 Finance Act effectively abolished the use of these tests and practices and replaced them with statutory rules. These "new" residence rules took effect from 6 April 1994.

9.2.2 Position with effect from 6 April 1994

An individual is regarded as resident in Ireland for a tax year if he/she is present in the State:

- at any one time or several times in the year of assessment for a period which in total amounts to 183 days or more; or
- at any one time or several times in the year of assessment and the preceding year for a period which in total amounts to 280 days or more. However, he/she will not be regarded as resident for any tax year in which he/she spends a period in the whole amounting to 30 days or less in the State, and no account shall be taken of such a period for the purpose of the 280-day test.

In determining the number of days an individual was present in Ireland, an individual was deemed to be present if he/she was in the country at the end of the day, i.e., at midnight. However, Finance (No. 2) Act 2008 amended the definition to include any part of a day[1].

Alternatively, where the above rules are not satisfied an individual may elect to be Irish-resident in any tax year in which he/she is present in the State with the intention and in such circumstances that he/she will be resident in the State in the following tax year. The main advantage of electing to be Irish-resident in these circumstances is that the individual will have full entitlement to Irish personal allowances, reliefs and tax credits (see Chapter 11).

There is no facility to elect for non-residence; where the 183-day and 280-day tests outlined above are satisfied, residence status cannot be avoided.

Example 9.1

Eric Bertrand was seconded to Ireland on 15 July 2017 on a 12-month contract. During that period he did not return to his home in France or visit any other country. He left Ireland on 1 August 2018.

---

1 This can lead to practical difficulties, e.g., an individual who flies into Ireland on a stopover would be treated under the new legislation as being present in Ireland for that day. Revenue have catered for this and other circumstances in their leaflet, RES 1.

Residence position:

2017

From 15 July to 31 December 2017 he spent 170 days in Ireland. He is not resident in Ireland in 2017 since he did not spend 183 days or more in Ireland during 2017, nor did he spend 280 days in Ireland during the current and the preceding tax years, i.e., during the years ended 31 December 2016 and 2017. However, he may elect to be Irish-resident if he is in a position to demonstrate that he came to Ireland in 2017 with the intention and in circumstances such that he would be resident in Ireland in 2018.

2018

From 1 January 2018 to 31 July 2018, he spent 212 days in Ireland. He is resident in Ireland for 2018 since he spent more than 183 days in the State in 2018. There is no facility to elect for non-residence albeit that he intended returning to France at the end of the 12-month contract.

Example 9.2

Assume the same facts as Example 1 except that Eric had to return to France permanently on 1 May 2018 due to ill health.

Residence position:

2017

As above – no change.

2018

From 1 January 2018 to 1 May 2018, he spent 121 days in Ireland. This is less than 183 days. However, he is resident in Ireland in 2018 by virtue of the 280-day rule, i.e., since he spent more than 280 days in Ireland on combining the current and previous years' days of presence in the State (170 + 121 = 291).

Example 9.3

Mariola de la Fuente was seconded to Ireland from Spain on a 12-month contract with effect from 1 February 2017. She left Ireland and returned to Spain on 28 January 2018.

Residence position:

2017

She is resident in Ireland in 2017 under the 183-day rule since she spent 334 days in the State in that year.

2018

She is not resident in Ireland in 2018 under the 183-day rule since she only spent 28 days in the State in that year. She has spent 361 days in the State in the current and preceding tax years and would appear to satisfy the 280-day test. However, as she cannot be regarded as resident for any tax year in which she spends a period in the whole amounting to 30 days or less in the State, she is not Irish resident in 2018.

9.2.3 Ordinary residence

s820 TCA97 An individual is ordinarily resident in Ireland for a tax year if he/she has been resident for each of the three tax years preceding that year.

An individual will not cease to be ordinarily resident for a tax year until such time as the individual has three consecutive tax years of non-residence. Thus, an ordinarily resident individual will become non-ordinarily resident for a tax year when he/she has been non-resident for each of the three tax years preceding that tax year. In effect, it is necessary to have been non-resident in each of the three tax years following the year of departure from Ireland.

Example 9.4

Michael Reilly has lived and worked in Ireland all his life. He moved to Australia permanently on 1 August 2017. Thus, he will be regarded as Irish-resident in 2017, but non-Irish-resident thereafter. He will remain ordinarily resident in Ireland for the years of assessment 2018, 2019 and 2020 and will become non-ordinarily resident in 2021, i.e., in the tax year of assessment following three consecutive tax years of non-residence.

Example 9.5

Miguel Tito was seconded to Ireland on 16 July 2017 on a five-year contract. He had previously been resident in Spain where he had worked and lived all his life. On the assumption that he does not elect to be Irish-resident in 2017, he will be regarded as non-Irish resident in 2017. He will remain non-ordinarily resident for the years 2018, 2019 and 2020. He will become ordinarily resident in Ireland in 2021 on the basis that he will be Irish-resident in the years 2018, 2019 and 2020.

9.2.4 Domicile

Domicile is not defined in the Income Tax Acts. It is a complex legal concept, upon which there is a considerable volume of case law. Generally, a person is domiciled in the country of which he/she is a national and in which he/she spends his/her life. However, it is not always possible to equate domicile to home, as in certain circumstances an individual may be domiciled in a country which is not and has never been his home. A person may have two homes but he can only have one domicile.

There are three general principles in relation to domicile:

(i) No person can be without a domicile.

(ii) No person can have more than one domicile at the same time, at any rate for the same purpose.

(iii) An existing domicile is presumed to continue until it has been proved that a new domicile has been acquired.

Domicile of origin

An individual is born with a domicile known as a domicile of origin. Normally, this is the domicile of his/her father. However, where the parents have not married, or if the father dies before his birth, the child's domicile will be the same as that of his/her mother. If, before he/she has reached the age of majority (normally 18 years of age), the parent from whom he/she has taken his/her domicile changes his/her domicile, the minor's domicile will also change.

Domicile of choice

Once an individual has reached the age of majority, he/she can reject his/her domicile of origin and acquire a new domicile, known as a domicile of choice. In order to abandon his/her domicile of origin, the individual must prove conclusively that he/she has severed all links with the country in which his/her domicile of origin lies. A domicile cannot be lost by a mere abandonment. It can only be lost by the positive acquisition of a domicile of choice.

A domicile of choice is the domicile that any independent person can acquire for himself/herself by a combination of residence and intention. To acquire a domicile of choice, an individual must establish a physical presence in the new jurisdiction and have an intention to reside there indefinitely.

A domicile of choice can in turn be abandoned. This will involve either the acquisition of a new domicile of choice or the revival of the domicile of origin. Here, again, the two factors of residence and intention will be required. In this regard, decisions from a number of cases are relevant.

Case law

In *Revenue Commissioners v Shaw & Anor H.C.* [1982 ILR] ILR, McWilliam J. stated:

> *"In order to acquire another domicile, a person must have the intention of doing so together with actual residence in the country of his choice. The intention must be an intention to reside in that country for an unlimited time. A domicile of origin persists until it has been shown to have been abandoned and another acquired and the onus of proving a change of domicile is on the person alleging it."*

In the case of *Claire Proes v Revenue*, it was held in a judgment delivered in the High Court in June 1997 that, having previously acquired a domicile of choice in the UK, the appellant, Mrs Proes, while having resided in Ireland for a period of 10 years, did not revive her domicile of origin. This was on the basis that Mrs Proes never ceased to have an intention to return to reside permanently in the UK.

It should be noted that any question as to whether or not an individual who was Irish-domiciled has acquired a foreign domicile of choice is to be determined by reference to Irish law and not by reference to the law of the "foreign" country.

9.3 Implications of Residence, Ordinary Residence and Domicile

Residence status (together with ordinary residence status and domicile) determines the territorial scope of Irish taxation, i.e., the extent to which an individual's various sources of income are subject to Irish tax. In addition, an individual's residence status determines his entitlement to the personal allowances, reliefs and tax credits discussed in Chapter 11. In general, an Irish-resident individual will have full entitlement to the basic tax reliefs available in calculating his/her Irish tax liability, while a non-resident individual will not. There are some exceptions to this rule in the case of Irish citizens, individuals who move abroad for health reasons and individuals resident in certain countries with which Ireland has a double taxation agreement.

Having examined the meaning of the terms residence, ordinary residence and domicile, the effect which they have upon the scope of an individual's income tax liability is now considered.

9.3.1 Individual resident and domiciled

In general, an individual who is resident and domiciled in Ireland is liable to Irish income tax on all his/her worldwide income as it arises (historically there was an exception to this rule in the case of non-ordinarily resident citizens - see 9.3.2 below).

Example 9.6

Tom Jones, who is married and is the sole earner, has the following sources of income in the tax year 2018:

	€	
Salary paid by Irish company	*20,000*	
UK dividends	*5,000*	
USA rents	*6,000*	*(retained in USA bank account)*
Total	*31,000*	

Tom Jones is resident and domiciled in Ireland. He is therefore liable to income tax on his worldwide income of €31,000 for 2018, regardless of the fact that the USA rents are not remitted to Ireland.

9.3.2 Individual resident but not domiciled/not ordinarily resident

s71 TCA97 An individual who is resident but not domiciled in Ireland (e.g., a citizen of the United States working in Ireland for a temporary period of two years, who is regarded as tax-resident in Ireland) is liable to Irish income tax in full on:

- income arising in Ireland, and
- foreign income only to the extent that it is remitted to Ireland (this is known as 'the remittance basis' and is considered in 9.3.6 in greater detail).

The remittance basis of taxation only applies to non-Irish domiciled individuals.

Example 9.7

Alex Smith, who is married, has the following sources of income in 2018:

	€
Salary paid by Irish company	*25,000*
UK dividends	*10,000*
USA rents	*15,000*
Total	*50,000*

Alex Smith is resident but not domiciled in Ireland. He remits €5,000 of his USA rental income to Ireland but none of his UK income.

He is liable to Irish tax on income arising in Ireland and remittances out of foreign income.

Assessable Income 2018:	€
Schedule E	*25,000*
Schedule D Case III:	
USA rents	*5,000*
Total	*30,000*

9.3.3 Individual not resident but ordinarily resident

s821 TCA97 An individual who is not resident but is ordinarily resident and domiciled is taxable on the same basis as a resident and domiciled individual (i.e., on worldwide income) with the exception of income from:

- a trade or profession, no part of which is carried on in Ireland
- an office or employment all the duties of which are performed outside Ireland (apart from "incidental duties" – see below)
- other sources (i.e., other foreign income) the total of which do not exceed €3,810 (once the other income exceeds €3,810, the full amount of that other income is taxable and not just the excess).

An individual who is not resident and not domiciled, but who is ordinarily resident, is taxable on the same basis as a resident, non-domiciled individual (i.e., on Irish income as it arises and on other foreign income remitted to Ireland), with the exception of income from any of the three sources listed above.

When determining what fulfils the condition of an office or employment "all the duties of which are performed outside the State", the Revenue Commissioners concessionally accept that no charge to Irish tax will arise where the Irish duties of an employment are merely incidental. This will normally be the case where the time in a tax year during which the duties of an office or employment are performed in Ireland does not exceed 30 days.

While the Irish Revenue Commissioners have stated their willingness to "normally" look at the number of days in quantifying incidental duties, in the UK case of *Robson v Dixon* 48 TC 527, it was held that duties were not merely incidental if they formed an essential or critical element of the duties of the employee (even if only of brief duration).

Example 9.8

An Irish engineer goes to work in Saudi Arabia on a long-term contract. While abroad and still ordinarily resident in Ireland, he receives foreign rental income of €3,000 per annum and other foreign investment income of €600 per annum. He has no other sources of investment income. As he does not carry out his profession in the State and as his foreign income falls below the €3,810 threshold, he does not have a tax liability in Ireland in respect of the foreign income.

On the other hand, if the other foreign investment income was more than €3,810, then he would have an exposure to Irish tax in respect of all his foreign rental and investment income while he remains ordinarily resident. This is because other foreign income would have exceeded the limit of €3,810.

9.3.4 Individual not resident and not ordinarily resident

s18(3) TCA97

An individual who is neither resident nor ordinarily resident, irrespective of domicile, is liable to Irish income tax only on income arising in Ireland, i.e., income from property located in the State and income from employments, trades and professions the duties of which are exercised in Ireland.

9.3.5 Summary table of tax implications of residence, ordinary residence and domicile

Residence, ordinary residence and domicile status	***Extent of liability to Irish tax***
Resident, ordinarily resident and Irish-domiciled	Taxable on all Irish and worldwide income.
Not resident, but ordinarily resident in Ireland and Irish-domiciled	Taxable on all Irish and foreign-sourced income in full. However, income from the following sources is exempt from tax: (a) income from a trade, profession, office or employment all the duties of which are exercised outside Ireland; and (b) other foreign income, provided that it does not exceed €3,810.
Not resident, but ordinarily resident in Ireland and not Irish-domiciled	Taxable on Irish source income in full and other foreign income only to the extent that it is remitted to Ireland.

	Income from the following sources is exempt from tax: (a) income from a trade, profession, office or employment all the duties of which are exercised outside Ireland; and (b) other foreign income, provided that it does not exceed €3,810.
Resident and ordinarily resident in Ireland but not Irish-domiciled	Taxable on Irish source income in full and foreign income only to the extent that it is remitted to Ireland.
Resident but not ordinarily resident and Irish-domiciled	Taxable on all Irish and worldwide income.
Not resident, not ordinarily resident, irrespective of domicile	Taxable on Irish-sourced income in full and taxable on income from a trade, profession or employment exercised in Ireland.

9.3.6 Remittances/SARP

s71(3) TCA97 As mentioned above, certain individuals are liable to Irish income tax on remittances to Ireland out of "foreign income". Such remittances are assessed to tax under Case III of Schedule D. Only remittances out of income are liable to income tax.

Special Assignee Relief Programme (SARP)

Background:

The Finance Act 2006 abolished the remittance basis of taxation on employment income where the duties of a foreign contract were exercised in Ireland. Industries responded negatively to the change on the grounds that it was a disincentive for attracting high-caliber executives to work in Ireland and hence would negatively impact on inward investment to Ireland. In response to this, the Finance (No. 2) Act 2008 introduced a form of "assignment relief" effective from 1 January 2009. The relief applied to certain employees who were assigned from abroad to work in Ireland. However the conditions were very stringent and later Finance Acts modified the requirements for entitlement to the relief. Below is an analysis of the position effective from 2014. Readers are referred to earlier editions of this publication for the tax treatment pre-2014.

S825C TCA97 The relief applies to a "relevant employee" in receipt of "relevant income" employed by a "relevant employer" or "associated company".

A "relevant employee" (who can be Irish domiciled) is one who:

- was a full-time employee of a relevant employer for the 6 months immediately prior to arrival in Ireland and had previously exercised the duties of that employment outside Ireland

- arrived in Ireland between 2015 and 2020 to perform the duties of the his/her employment for the relevant employer or an associated company
- performed the duties of that employment in Ireland for a minimum period of 12 months from the date of first performing those duties in Ireland
- was not resident in Ireland for the five years immediately prior to arriving in Ireland to take up the duties of his/her employment.

A "relevant employer" refers to a company incorporated and resident in a Tax Treaty country and includes companies resident in countries with which Ireland has a Tax Information Exchange Agreement. An "associated company" is one which controls or is under the control of the relevant company (i.e. the employer company).

The definition of "relevant income" includes income from the relevant employer which is not less than €75,000. In calculating relevant income, bonuses, benefits in kind (see Chapter 21), termination payments, pay in lieu of restrictive covenants and share-based remuneration are excluded. Therefore the employee's basic pay must be at least €75,000. The relief operates by applying a deduction of a "specified amount" from the income of the employment. The "specified amount" is 30% of the income over €75,000.

There is a certification requirement on the part of the employer to confirm that within 30 days of arrival; that the 6 month period is met, the individual is moving to Ireland at the request of the relevant employer to perform the duties of the employment, and that the duties will be performed for a minimum period of 12 consecutive months. The employer must file a return of information by 23 February in the following year setting out the names of each relevant employee and include details of their employment, nationality etc.

Example 9.9

Jeff Armstrong has been employed for many years by a US multinational company. On 1 January 2018 he was transferred to the Irish subsidiary. It is expected that he will live and work in Ireland for at least 2 years. His salary will be €650,000 p.a. with payroll tax deductions of €290,000.

The relief is:

(€650,000 − €75,000) × 30% = €172,500. Applying Jeff's marginal tax rate of 40% this results in a tax refund due to him of €69,000 (i.e., €172,500 × 40%).

The relief may be claimed for a maximum period of 5 consecutive years commencing with the year of first entitlement. In addition, employees who qualify for the relief may also receive, free of tax, certain expenses of travel and certain costs associated with the education of their children in Ireland.

It should be noted that the relief applies to income tax only, it does not apply to PRSI or USC. Where SARP is claimed, the employee may not claim other reliefs in the same years such as; Cross Border Workers relief, Remittance Basis on employment income relief, Foreign Earnings Deduction (considered at 9.4.3 below) and surrender of R&D credit relief for key employees (considered at 9.4.4 below).

> **Tax Facts**
>
> Following the introduction of the application of PAYE to foreign employees working in Ireland (who were paid from abroad), some foreign employers encountered staffing and operational difficulties. The introduction of SARP was seen as an attempt to counteract these difficulties. To further improve Ireland's chances of attracting further international businesses to Ireland, a new form of SARP which has wider application was introduced in Finance Act 2012.

9.4 Employment Income Reliefs

Generally, being tax-resident in Ireland means that most sources of income are assessable to Irish tax. However, there are some reliefs which are available to reduce the Irish tax payable on employment income earned outside Ireland. These reliefs are considered below.

9.4.1 Cross-border relief

s825A TCA97

This is sometimes known as "Trans-Border Relief". The relief is typically aimed at employees who are resident in Ireland but carry out the duties of their employment in another country. In these circumstances, in the absence of any special relief, the employee is taxable in both countries. For example, an employee living in Dundalk and working in Newry would be taxable in both the UK and Ireland.

Subject to certain conditions being met, cross-border relief extends to duties carried out in the UK. While the relief applies to the UK, it is not confined exclusively to the UK. The main conditions to qualify for the relief are as follows:

- The employee must be present in the State for at least one day in each week.
- The office or employment must be a "qualifying employment".
- The duties of the qualifying employment must be performed wholly outside the State in a country with which Ireland has a double taxation agreement. The full amount of the income from the qualifying employment must be subject to tax in the foreign country and must not be exempt or relieved from tax in that country.
- The foreign tax due on the income from the qualifying employment must have been paid, and the individual must not have any right to any repayment of that foreign tax.
- The income from the qualifying employment must not qualify for any of the following reliefs:
  - remittance basis of taxation
  - split-year treatment (see 9.4.2 below).

"Qualifying employment" is defined as an office or employment held outside the State in a country with which Ireland has a double taxation treaty, but only if, for the tax year for which the relief is claimed, the office or employment is held for a continuous period of not less than 13 weeks. The relief does not apply to employees of the State or semi-State bodies.

While qualification for the relief is dependent on the duties of the office or employment being performed outside the State, duties carried out within the State, that are incidental to the performance of the duties outside the State are nevertheless ignored. In addition, the individual must return to the State and be physically present there at least one day in every relevant week in a tax year (a relevant week is one in which the individual is absent from the State for one or more days for the purposes of performing duties of the employment; therefore there is no requirement for the individual to be back in the State for a day in a week in which the employee is on holidays outside the State).

Until 31 December 2009 the requirement was that the individual be physically present in the state "at the end of" at least one day. The Finance Act 2010 amended the relief in relation to the definition of a day to bring it in line with the definition of a day for residence purposes. It is now only necessary for the individual to be physically present for any part of a day.

Relief is granted using the following formula:

$$\frac{A \times B}{C}$$

where:

A = the individual's liability to Irish income tax before deduction of credit for foreign tax paid,

B = the individual's total income excluding the income from the qualifying employment, and

C = the individual's total income including the income from the qualifying employment.

Example 9.10

Jack Daly is married and resident in the State. His wife works in the home looking after their two children, aged five and nine. He earned a salary of €60,000 in 2018 from a qualifying employment in Northern Ireland. He travelled home for at least one day every weekend. He took up this foreign employment during the year and, before he did so, had income from an employment in the State of €10,000. During 2018, he received Irish rental income of €4,200.

Jack Daly is liable to tax in the UK on the salary of €60,000 and paid the tax due in full in the sum of €10,000. He satisfied the other conditions for relief under s825A for 2018.

	€	€
Income from qualifying employment (before foreign tax)		*60,000*
Other employment income		*10,000*
Case V		*4,200*
*Gross income **(C)***		*74,200*

	€	€
Tax payable:		
€43,550 @ 20%	*8,710*	
€30,650 @ 40%	*12,260*	*20,970*
€74,200		
Less:		
Non-refundable tax credits		
Married person's credit	*(3,300)*	
Home-carer's credit	*(1,200)*	
PAYE allowance credit	*(1,650)*	*(6,150)*
*Income tax liability **(A)***		*14,820*

Having calculated the income tax chargeable, the other elements in the formula for the "specified amount" are:

	€
*Total income for year **(C)***	*74,200*
*Total income for year excluding income from qualifying foreign employment **(B)**, i.e., €74,200 – €60,000*	*14,200*
*Income tax liability **(A)***	*14,820*

The "specified amount" is: $€14,820 \times \frac{€14,200}{€74,200} = €2,836$

Section 825A grants the relief by reducing Jack Daly's tax payable (A) so that it equals the specified amount, i.e., in effect, the relief restricts the Irish tax liability to €2,836, which is the portion of the tax charge referable to the non-qualifying employment income.

9.4.2 Split-year residence

s822 TCA97 This section sets out the specific rules relating to the Irish income tax treatment of an individual, both in the year of departure from Ireland and in the year of arrival in Ireland. These specific rules only apply to income from an employment.

Year of Arrival

For the purposes of calculating Irish income tax an individual's employment income, the individual who takes up residence in Ireland during a tax year is treated as not being resident for that part of the tax year prior to the date of arrival. This treatment is applied only to employment income from an office or employment exercised outside the State prior to the date of arrival. In effect, this means that the individual's foreign employment income earned prior to the date of arrival will not be subject to Irish income tax.

In order to qualify for split-year residence treatment, the Revenue Commissioners must be satisfied that the individual took up residence in Ireland with the intention that he/she would be resident in Ireland for the following tax year. The individual must also not have been resident in Ireland for the tax year prior to that in which he/she takes up residence.

Example 9.11

John (an Irish domiciled individual) returns to Ireland on 1 July 2018 to commence a three-year contract with Multinational plc. He worked in the USA for the previous five years. In the period 1 January 2018 to 30 June 2018, John earned €50,000 from his foreign employment. He also earned foreign rental income in the amount of €2,000 in the same period. From 1 July 2018 to 31 December 2018, his Irish employment earnings were €40,000.

John is Irish resident, not ordinarily resident and Irish domiciled in 2018; he is therefore liable to Irish income tax on all his income with the exception of the foreign employment income of €50,000 earned between 1 January 2018 and 30 June 2018, due to split-year residence relief.

Year of Departure

For the purposes of calculating Irish income tax an individual's employment income, in the tax year in which he/she ceases to be resident in Ireland, he/she will be treated as not being resident in Ireland after the date of departure. In effect, this means that the individual will not be liable to Irish income tax in respect of any foreign employment income arising after the date of departure. This applies provided he was tax-resident in Ireland prior to departure. To qualify for the relief, the individual must not be resident in Ireland in the following tax year.

Example 9.12

Mary, who is Irish-domiciled, has been resident in Ireland for more than five years. She leaves Ireland on 1 July 2018 to take up permanent residence in Spain. In the period 1 January 2018 to 30 June 2018, she received €30,000 employment income and €10,000 rental income from an Irish property. Following her departure, she earned €20,000 employment income in Spain and €500 deposit interest from her savings, which she invested in Spain. Mary is Irish resident, ordinarily resident and domiciled in 2018; she is therefore liable to Irish income tax on her worldwide income. However, provided Mary can demonstrate that she will not be tax-resident in Ireland in 2019 she will not be liable to Irish tax on the employment income of €20,000 earned from 1 July 2018 to 31 December 2018.

9.4.3 Foreign Earnings Deduction (FED)

s823A TCA97

Sections 12 and 13 of FA 2012 reintroduced a tax deduction for overseas assignees. The FED relief operates by reducing an individual's taxable employment income, based on the amount of qualifying days spent working abroad. The relief was only available for 2012, 2013 and 2014, however section 16 FA 2014 extended the relief to 2017 and section 11 FA 2016 extended the relief to 2020.

The FED relief applies to individuals on assignment in certain countries. For 2012 these countries were; Brazil, Russian, India, China and South Africa (known as the "BRICS" countries). FA 2013 extended the list to include: Egypt, Algeria, Senegal, Tanzania, Kenya, Nigeria, Ghana and Congo. FA 2014 extended the list to include; Japan, Singapore, South Korea, Saudi Arabia, UAE, Qatar, Bahrain, Indonesia, Vietnam, Thailand, Chile, Oman, Kuwait, Mexico, and Malaysia. FA 2016 extended the list to include; the Republic of Columbia and the Islamic Republic of Pakistan.

Relief is available where an individual spends periods of at least 3 consecutive days working in any of the listed countries and these periods amount to at least 30 qualifying days in total in the year. During these 3 (or more) consecutive days, the employee must have been carrying out the duties of their employment. In calculating the 30 qualifying days, weekends and public holidays may be included.

In the employment income to be reduced by FED relief, benefits in kind, termination payments, pay in lieu of restrictive covenants and pension contributions are excluded. However unlike SARP, share based remuneration may be included. Relief is capped at €35,000 (the specified amount); this means that the maximum tax refundable is €14,350 (i.e. €35,000 × 40%). The relief applies to tax only; it does not apply to PRSI or USC.

The formula for calculating the relief is:

$$D \times \frac{E}{F}$$

where:

D = number of qualifying days

E = qualifying employment income

F = aggregate number of days in the year that the employee was employed

Where FED is claimed, the employee may not claim other reliefs in the same years such as Split Year Residence relief, Cross Border Workers relief, Remittance Basis on employment income relief, SARP and surrender of R&D credit relief for key employees.

Example 9.13

John Grimes is the marketing executive for an Irish resident trading company. John has to oversee marketing activities in Russia and India and he regularly works in these countries. During 2018 he spent 65 qualifying days between the two countries. His basic salary is €258,000, his BIK is €20,000 and he pays €8,000 annual pension contributions. His FED calculation is:

D = 65

E = €250,000 (€258K − €8K)

F = 365

€250,000 × 65/365 = €44,520; however, the relief is restricted to the maximum specified amount of €35,000.

John is therefore due a refund of €14,000 (i.e., €35,000 × 40%).

9.4.4 Surrender of R&D credit for Key Employees

s472D TCA97 Companies which incur expenditure on qualifying research and developments (R&D) activities may claim special tax credits by reference to the amount of the R&D spend (see Chapter 29).

Finance Act 2012 introduced s472D TCA97 which grants the company the ability to transfer a portion of the R&D credits due to it to its key employees, following the making of a qualifying R&D claim. The employee claims relief for the credits by means of tax refunds on making a claim to their own tax office.

The main conditions to claim the relief are as follows:

The employee must be a "key employee" of the company. Key employees are:

1. Employees who were never directors of the company, or connected to any directors.
2. Hold less than 5% of the company shares and are not connected with any other individual or associated company who hold 5% or more of the company.
3. In the year of the company's claim spent 50% of their time on R&D activities which gives rise to new knowledge plus 50%[2] of their emoluments must qualify as R&D expenditure.

The credit can only be surrendered where the company is liable to corporation tax (thus excluding loss-making companies) and cannot exceed the company's corporation tax liability in the year of the claim.

The employee is charged to PAYE (see Chapter 23) as normal in the year that the company makes the R&D claim and then submits a tax return after that year-end seeking a tax refund, based on the tax credit surrendered to him by the company. The refund is only processed if the total income tax payable on the employee's (and his spouse/civil partner, where jointly assessed – see Chapter 13) total income is at a rate of at least 23%. Any unutilised relief can be carried forward to the next tax year, provided the individual remains an employee of the company. The employee does not have to be a key employee in the year following the R&D claim. Section 13 F(No. 2)A 2013 now provides that the claimant is a chargeable person (see Chapter 10), and so must submit a tax return.

Example 9.14

Science Limited had qualifying R&D credits for the year ended 30 September 2018 of €500,000 and a corporation tax liability of €225,000. The company decided to surrender €25,000 of its credits to a qualifying key employee, Patrick Rogan. Patrick is single and his only source of income is from Science Limited. His salary, income tax and R&D claims for the three years following Science Limited's claim are as follows:

Tax Year	*Salary*	*PAYE*	*Refund Claim*	*Net Income Tax*	*Effective Tax Rate*
2018	*€100,000*	*€30,000*	*€7,000*	*€23,000*	*23%*
2019	*€50,000*	*€10,000*	*€0*	*€10,000*	*20% (no claim)*
2020	*€110,000*	*€35,000*	*€9,700*	*€25,300*	*23%*

2 Introduced by F(No. 2)A 2013.

As long as Patrick remains an employee of Science Limited he can obtain tax refunds to the value of €25,000. He will carry the remaining refund due of €8,300 (€25,000 – €7,000 – €9,700) into tax year 2021 and further if required.

9.5 Domicile Levy

Section 150 Finance Act 2010 introduced a new "tax" known as a "Domicile Levy". It inserted a new Part 18B into the TCA97.

The Domicile Levy of €200,000 is assessable annually on "relevant individuals". For the levy to apply the relevant individual must:

(i) be domiciled[3] in Ireland; **and**

(ii) have yearly worldwide income of greater than €1 million; **and**

(iii) have an Irish tax liability of less than €200,000; **and**

(iv) own property in Ireland, the market value of which on 31 December in the tax year in question exceeds €5 million.

Worldwide income is calculated (regardless of the individual's residence position) in accordance with TCA97, but does not take account of allowable deductions which would normally be deductible in arriving at total income (s70 FA2017 confirmed that capital allowances and losses are also not deductible). In addition, income which would otherwise be exempt from tax (e.g. artists income less than €50,000) is included in determining the €1 million limit. Any foreign taxes which have already been applied to the income are ignored, however Irish tax is deductible. In determining the market value of property, no account is taken of any loans/mortgages due.

Example 9.15

Neil Murphy is Irish domiciled and is a citizen of Ireland. He emigrated to Canada in 1980 and has lived there since then. Over the years he amassed great wealth and bought a number of investment properties in Ireland, the current market of value of which exceed €5 million. As he is non-resident/non ordinarily resident in Ireland his only Irish tax liability is on the Irish rents. However with falling rental values and an inability to find tenants for some of the properties, the tax liability is now €150,000 (therefore under the threshold of €200,000). His worldwide income is in excess of €1 million per annum.

Neil Murphy is liable to the domicile levy. The actual levy payable is €50,000, i.e., €200,000 less the Irish tax liability of €150,000.

Section 85 FA 2014 provides for imposition of tax geared penalties where an individual deliberately or carelessly makes an incorrect return. (Readers are referred to Chapter 10 on audit settlement).

3 Up to 2011 there was a requirement that the individual also be a citizen of Ireland, this requirement was abolished in Finance Act 2012.

9.6 Double Tax Agreements

As demonstrated in this chapter, a charge to income tax can arise either because of residence/ordinary residence in Ireland or if not resident/not ordinary resident by virtue of income arising in Ireland. For the latter, the recipient may be resident in another country and under the domestic laws of that country; the Irish income is taxable in that country also. Effectively the one source of income is taxed twice. For the avoidance of this double taxation, Ireland has entered into a number of double taxation agreements (also known as 'treaties') with many countries. Depending on the terms of the treaty, a source of income may be exempted in the say the country where it is earned and then taxed in the country of residence of the recipient. On the other hand it may be taxed in both countries but with one country allowing credit for the tax is paid in other country. A detailed analysis of the double tax treaties is outside the scope of this publication, however a list of all the countries with which Ireland has entered into double taxation agreements is included at Appendix 1.

Appendix 1

Albania	Korea (Rep. of)	Turkey
Armenia	Kuwait	UAE
Australia	Latvia	Ukraine
Austria	Lithuania	United Kingdom
Bahrain	Luxembourg	USA
Belarus	Macedonia	Uzbekistan
Belgium	Malaysia	Vietnam
Bosnia Herzegovina	Malta	Zambia
Botswana	Mexico	
Bulgaria	Moldova	
Canada	Montenegro	
Chile	Morocco	
China	Netherlands	
Croatia	New Zealand	
Cyprus	Norway	
Czech Republic	Pakistan	
Denmark	Panama	
Egypt	Poland	
Estonia	Portugal	
Ethiopia	Qatar	
Finland	Romania	
France	Russia	
Georgia	Saudi Arabia	
Germany	Serbia	
Greece	Singapore	
Hong Kong	Slovak Rep.	
Hungary	Slovenia	
Iceland	South Africa	
India	Spain	
Israel	Sweden	
Italy	Switzerland	
Japan	Thailand	

10 THE SELF-ASSESSMENT SYSTEM

Learning Outcomes

On completion of this chapter, you should be able to:

- ✓ Discuss the criteria used to determine if an individual is a chargeable person.
- ✓ Explain what impact "pay and file" obligations have for a chargeable person.
- ✓ Describe the two types of Revenue audit and their implications for a chargeable person.
- ✓ Discuss the mechanics of appeal procedures.

10.1 Introduction

The purpose of this chapter is to identify which categories of taxpayer come within the self-assessment system, the implications of this and what rights, if any, a taxpayer has under the self-assessment system.

Broadly speaking, two alternative collection/assessment systems apply in Ireland:

- self-assessment; and
- PAYE ("pay as you earn") (considered in Chapter 23).

With the latter, the responsibility for the collection of the tax and payment of the tax to the Revenue Commissioners lies with the employer. Therefore, an employee who has no income other than wages/salaries has no tax return filing obligations or tax payment obligations, since the tax deducted via PAYE satisfies the responsibility for both (see 10.1.1 below). FA 2012 and FA 2013 also introduced some changes to the self-assessment system. A number of the changes are of an administrative nature and hence outside the scope of this publication.

10.1.1 Chargeable Persons

Income tax is paid under the self-assessment system by "chargeable persons". Generally speaking, a chargeable person can be described as one whose income tax liability is not collected in full through the PAYE system. However, a "proprietary" director is regarded as a chargeable person even where the director's only income is a salary subject to PAYE. The term "proprietary director" means a director of a company who is the beneficial owner of, or is able, either directly or indirectly, to control more than 15% of the ordinary share capital of the company.

Key employees who file claims for R&D tax credits (see Chapter 11) are chargeable persons following the introduction of this obligation in s13 F(No. 2)A 2013.

Chargeable persons, unlike their PAYE counterparts, must pay their respective tax and file their tax returns on or before a specified date. Failure to do so will result in:

- interest on the late payment of tax;
- interest on the inadequate payment of tax; and
- a penalty for the late filing of a tax return (known as a surcharge). These concepts are considered in the following paragraphs.

10.2 The Pay and File System

Section 78 Finance Act 2001 introduced a common date for tax-return filing and payment of income tax, which is known as the "Pay and File" system. The changes were introduced to simplify the income tax system and make it work more effectively.

The Pay and File system provides for a single date, 31 October, for the:

- payment of preliminary income tax due for the current tax year;
- payment of the balance of income tax due for the previous tax year;
- filing of a tax return for the previous year.[1]
- filing calculation of tax liability.

Example 10.1

31 October 2018 is the specified date for the:

- *payment of preliminary income tax for the year of assessment 2018;*
- *payment of the balance of income tax for the year of assessment 2017;*
- *filing of a tax return for the year of assessment 2017.*

10.3 Payment of Tax and Penalties for Late Payment

Income from which tax is not deducted at source must be accounted for on a self-assessment basis. Examples of such sources of income are trading income, investment income, rental income, etc. A feature of the self-assessment system is the requirement that liabilities to the USC and PRSI for the self-employed are fully integrated into the income tax system. Therefore, in arriving at the amount of income tax to be paid, the liability for these items must be included.

1 31 October is also the relevant date for filing the capital gains tax return. The self-assessment system as it applies to capital gains tax is covered in detail in Chapter 24.

10.3.1 Preliminary tax

s959AO TCA97 Preliminary tax is due for payment on 31 October in the tax year in question. It is effectively a payment on account of the ultimate income tax liability for that tax year. Thus, preliminary tax due on 31 October 2018 is a provision against the ultimate income tax liability for the tax year 2018. As mentioned earlier, in arriving at the amount of preliminary tax to be paid, the liability for the USC and PRSI for the self-employed must be included.

The payment could be better described as an "up-front payment" since the tax is being paid before the tax year in question has expired. As a result, there can be uncertainty in calculating the amount of tax due. To address this uncertainty, the legislation allows the taxpayer to use one of the following options in estimating the tax payable:

(a) 90% of the ultimate tax liability for the relevant tax year; or

(b) 100% of the tax liability for the preceding tax year; or

(c) 105% of the tax liability for the pre-preceding year (but only if paying the tax by direct debit)[2].

In order to avoid interest charges arising, the preliminary tax payment must be:

- at least equal to an amount using the lowest of the above three options; and
- paid by 31 October in the relevant tax year (except in the case of option (c), where tax may be paid by direct debit over 12 months ending on 31 December).

Example 10.2

Preliminary tax due on 31 October 2018 may be calculated using the lower of the following options:

(a) 90% of the ultimate tax liability for the year of assessment 2018; or

(b) 100% of the tax liability for the year of assessment 2017; or

(c) 105% of the tax liability for the year of assessment 2016 (but only if paying the tax by direct debit).

10.3.2 The charge to interest on late payment of tax

Preliminary tax is due on or before 31 October in the tax year in question, and the amount paid must be in accordance with one of the three options outlined at 10.3.1 above. Payment of the balance of income tax must be paid by 31 October in the following year. Failure to do so will result in interest being charged from 31 October in the year that the tax fell due to the date of eventual payment. The rate of interest chargeable on tax underpaid is 0.0219%.

2 If a taxpayer is using either of options (b) or (c) above, i.e., 100% of the previous year's liability or 105% of the pre-preceding year's liability, EIIS relief must be excluded in calculating the tax due.

10.4 Tax Returns and Penalties for Late Filing

All chargeable persons are required to submit a tax return and self-assessment tax calculations to the Collector-General not later than 31 October following the end of the tax. This applies whether requested to do so by the Revenue Commissioners. Thus, 31 October 2018 is the specified date for the filing of tax returns for the year of assessment 2017.

> **Tax Facts**
>
> As an incentive for taxpayers to file and pay tax electronically, Revenue have extended the pay and file deadline date of 31 October 2018 to 14 November 2018.

The Revenue Commissioners up to 2012 were obliged to issue an income tax assessment following receipt of a tax return. The particulars to be stated on an assessment had to include the amounts of income assessed under each of the different Schedules D, E and F; details of reliefs and tax credits, tax deducted and resultant net tax due. The vast majority of chargeable persons must pay & file under the mandatory "e-filing" system. One of the changes to the self assessment system is that Revenue Commissioners will no longer issue an assessment to the "e-filers"; instead those individuals must submit their own calculation of the self-assessed tax (in a format similar to that on the Revenue issued assessments). For the individuals who are not obliged to e-file, provided they file their tax return by 31 August (instead of the later date of 31 October) they will not be required submit their own calculation of the self-assessed tax. Instead Revenue will issue an assessment in the traditional way.

10.4.1 Surcharge for late filing of tax returns

If a tax return is not submitted by the specified date, a surcharge on the liability arising for the year (after credit for PAYE already paid, but before credit for tax paid directly) is applied regardless of the fact that the tax liability may have been paid in full and on time.

s1084 TCA97

Tax returns, if not submitted on time, will be liable to a surcharge calculated as follows:

- 5% of the tax liability for the year of assessment to which the tax return relates, subject to a maximum of €12,695. This applies where the tax return is delivered within two months of the filing date (e.g., for the tax year 2017, this means any date between 1 November 2018 and 31 December 2018 inclusive).

- 10% of the tax liability for the year of assessment to which the tax return relates, up to a maximum of €63,485. This applies where the tax return is not delivered within two months of the filing date (e.g., for the tax year 2017, a tax return filed after 31 December 2018 is liable to a surcharge of 10%).

10.5 Interest on Tax Overpaid

s865 TCA97

Interest on tax overpaid only applies where there is a "valid claim" for repayment. A valid claim will only be deemed to be made where all necessary information, which the Revenue Commissioners reasonably require to certify the claim, has been submitted by the individual. Where Revenue forms the view that a valid claim has not been made, it is up to the individual to submit whatever information the Revenue Commissioners feel they reasonably require before a valid claim is deemed to have been made.

The rate of interest is calculated on a daily basis at the rate of 0.011%.[3] The period from which interest runs depends on whether the overpayment is as a result of a mistake by the individual or by Revenue. Where the overpayment arises because of a mistaken application of the law by the Revenue Commissioners, and the claim for repayment is made within the requisite time limit, interest shall commence to run from the day after the end of the chargeable period in which the overpayment arises, or if later, the date of payment.

Where the overpayment cannot be ascribed to a mistaken application of the law by the Revenue Commissioners, the overpayment will carry interest from a day which is 93 days after the day on which a "valid claim" for the repayment had been filed with the Revenue Commissioners. Interest will not be paid where the overall amount due is less than €10.

Interest paid to a taxpayer on the overpayment of tax is not subject to withholding tax and is exempt from income tax.

10.6 Expressions of Doubt

s959P TCA97

Where a taxpayer is in doubt as regards an item to be included in a return of income, he is regarded as having made a full disclosure if he draws the attention of the Inspector of Taxes the doubtful item. A doubt may arise in relation to the tax treatment of a number of issues, e.g., as to whether:

- a particular source of income is taxable; or
- a particular expense deductible for Schedule D Case I/II purposes; or
- expenditure which qualifies for relief as a tax credit/tax allowance.

However, this provision will not apply where the Inspector of Taxes or the Appeal Commissioner is of the opinion that the doubt was not genuine and that the taxpayer was acting to avoid or evade tax.

3 The Minister for Finance may change the rate of interest on overpayment of tax from time to time by Ministerial Order.

10.7 Maintenance of Records

s886 TCA97 Every taxpayer who carries on a trade, profession or other activity, the profits or gains of which are chargeable under Schedule D, or who is chargeable to tax under Schedule D or Schedule F in respect of any other sources of income, or has chargeable gains is obliged to retain records which will enable true returns to be made of such profits or gains. Linking documents (i.e., documents drawn up in the making up of accounts and which show details of the calculations linking the records to the accounts) must also be retained.

Records include accounts, books of account, documents and any other data maintained manually or by any electronic, photographic or other process relating to:

- all sums of money received and expended in the course of the trade, profession or other activity and the matters in respect of which the receipt and expenditure take place
- all sales and purchases of goods and services
- the assets and liabilities of the trade, profession or other activity.

Records must be kept in written form in an official language of the State and may, with the consent of the Revenue Commissioners (in accordance with s887 TCA97), be kept by means of any electronic, photographic or other process.

Records and linking documents must be retained for a period of six years after the completion of the transactions to which they relate.

s887(5) TCA97 A person who fails to comply with the above will be liable to a penalty of €1,520. A person who preserves records by electronic, photographic or other methods must furnish details relating to the process to the Revenue Commissioners if so requested. The penalty for failure to do so is €1,265.

10.8 Revenue Audits

s951 TCA97 Under s951 TCA97, all chargeable persons are required to make a tax return to the Revenue Commissioners for each year of assessment that they are so chargeable. The information sought in the tax return is at the discretion of the Revenue Commissioners but must:

- show all sources of income and any deductions/tax credits claimed for the year of assessment; and
- be signed by the taxpayer.

Following receipt of the tax return, the Inspector of Taxes may examine the tax return. The purpose of the examination of the tax return by the Inspector of Taxes is to establish whether or not the entries are accurate. If he is not satisfied that the entries are accurate, the tax return is selected for a Revenue audit. The Inspector of Taxes is entitled to take whatever actions within his powers are deemed necessary to meet this objective.

Unless the Inspector of Taxes suspects that the tax return has been filed on a negligent or fraudulent basis, he is subject to a time limit within which to begin an examination of the tax return. The relevant time limit is four years from the end of the tax year within which the return was filed.

Example 10.3

A taxpayer files his tax return for the year of assessment 2017 on 15 October 2018. The Inspector of Taxes has until the end of 2022 (four years from the end of the tax year in which the tax return was filed) to examine this tax return. If the Inspector of Taxes suspects that the tax return was filed on a fraudulent or negligent basis, he is not subject to any time limit.

10.8.1 Types of Revenue audit

There are basically two types of audit:

- desk audit
- field audit

Desk Audit

This type of audit applies where verification of specific claims for expenses, allowances or reliefs is required. The procedure generally applies to straightforward issues. The audit is conducted by letter or telephone enquiries.

Field Audit

A field audit is conducted at the business premises of the taxpayer. Advance notice must be given in writing to the taxpayer.

10.8.2 Inspection of documents and records

s905 TCA97 Section 905 TCA97 is the most widely used power by an Inspector of Taxes to test the accuracy of tax returns; it is the section that permits him/her to inspect supporting records on the taxpayer's premises.

The Inspector of Taxes may:

- examine all records that the taxpayer is obliged to retain for tax purposes which relate to any trade, profession, other source of profits, any tax liability or any repayments of tax, or any property (defined as "any asset relating to a tax liability");
- require any person present on the business premises, other than a customer, to produce any records or property;
- search for any records or property if he/she believes that they have not been produced;
- examine and take copies or extracts from any records;
- remove any records and retain them for a reasonable time for the purposes of inspection;

- request information from a third party (e.g., a financial institution, a supplier, or a customer). Where a request for such information is not forthcoming, he/she may apply to the High Court for an order to secure such information.

10.8.3 Where additional tax is due

If an Inspector of Taxes, having examined the books and records of the taxpayer, establishes that there is additional tax payable, he will advise the taxpayer of such tax. Where a taxpayer is dissatisfied with the findings of the Inspector of Taxes, he/she has the right to seek a review. This review may be undertaken by:

- another Revenue official at a local level, i.e., either by the appropriate District Inspector or by the Regional Director; or
- where a taxpayer does not wish the review to be undertaken locally, he or she can request that the review be undertaken either by the Director of Customer Services alone, or jointly by the Director of Customer Services and an external reviewer.

If the taxpayer is still dissatisfied following a review, he may ask the Inspector of Taxes to issue an assessment. On receipt of the assessment, he may appeal against the assessment. Lodging an appeal gives the taxpayer the right to have the case heard before the Appeal Commissioners. Appeal procedures are considered at 10.9 below.

10.8.4 Audit settlement

If, having examined the books and records of the taxpayer, additional tax becomes payable, interest and possibly penalties are added to the additional tax.

Interest

Statutory interest is payable and is charged at a daily rate of 0.0219%.

Recovery of Penalties.

The Inspector of Taxes and the taxpayer may reach agreement on a cash settlement, which includes a sum in lieu of Revenue instigating penalty proceedings through the courts.

Finance (No. 2) Act 2008 provides that where the Revenue Commissioners and the taxpayer cannot agree on the level of penalty (or the taxpayer fails to pay an agreed penalty) the Revenue Commissioners may apply to the courts (District, Circuit or High court depending on the level of penalty) for a determination as to whether a penalty arises.

The rate of the penalty ultimately payable by the taxpayer depends on the category of the tax default. Penalties range from 10% to 100% of the tax payable.

> **Tax Facts**
>
> Following the Finance (No. 2) Act 2008, where cases are referred to the courts for determination on the amount of penalty payable, such cases will no longer be held *in camera* (i.e., in private).

10.9 Appeal Procedures

s933(1)(a) TCA97

Section 933(1)(a) TCA97 entitles a taxpayer to appeal against any assessment to income tax made by an Inspector of Taxes if the taxpayer does not agree that the assessment is correct. Such an appeal must be made by giving notice in writing to the Inspector of Taxes, and the notice must specify the grounds of the appeal. Lodging an appeal does not preclude the taxpayer and the Inspector of Taxes from reaching agreement on the content of the assessment subsequently. Where no such mutual agreement arises, the Appeal Commissioner is responsible for appointing the time and place of the appeal hearing. This information is conveyed to the Inspector of Taxes who in turn advises the taxpayer. An appeal must be lodged against an assessment within 30 days of the date of issue of the assessment. The time limit may be extended to 12 months where the taxpayer was prevented by absence, sickness or other reasonable cause from making the appeal on time.

Appeal Commissioners are appointed by the Minister for Finance to act as arbiters between the Inspector of Taxes and the taxpayer in cases of dispute. Where an estimated assessment is made in the absence of a tax return, an appeal will be allowed only after:

- the tax return has been submitted; and
- the tax due on the basis of the tax return has been paid.

Where a taxpayer feels that there is a delay by the Inspector of Taxes in listing an appeal, he will be able to apply to the Appeal Commissioners for an early listing. The Appeal Commissioners may dismiss an appeal where there is evidence of non-co-operation by the taxpayer for requests for information by the Appeal Commissioners.

Where appeals against assessments to income tax are heard by the Appeal Commissioners and neither party to the hearing pursue the matter further in the higher courts (see below), the determination of the Commissioners is final and conclusive.

A taxpayer aggrieved by a decision of the Appeal Commissioners may apply for a rehearing before a Circuit Court judge. The taxpayer or the Inspector of Taxes may also appeal against the Appeal Commissioners' decision to a higher court, e.g., the High Court or Supreme Court, but may only do so on a point of law.

11 TAX CREDITS, TAX BANDS, UNIVERSAL SOCIAL CHARGE AND PRSI

Learning Outcomes

On completion of this chapter, you should be able to:

- ✓ Explain the difference between refundable and non-refundable tax credits.
- ✓ List the various tax credits and allowances for the 2018 income tax year and describe the criteria for determining entitlement to relief for allowances/ reliefs/tax credits.
- ✓ Explain how tax bands are applied in different circumstances.
- ✓ Calculate marginal relief where total exemption from income tax is not due.
- ✓ Calculate a net tax liability/refund using the above.
- ✓ Explain how the Universal Social charge operates.
- ✓ Understand the difference between definition of income for Income Tax purposes and that for Universal Social charge purposes.

11.1 Introduction

The purpose of this chapter is to establish what entitlements a taxpayer has in terms of allowances, reliefs, rate bands and tax rates. It is important to understand the different key concepts and how they impact on a taxpayer's tax liability.

Personal tax credits – non-refundable

These are non-refundable credits (see 8.8) which are available based on personal circumstances – for example, the married person's/civil partner's tax credit and the single parent tax credit.

Non-personal tax credits – non-refundable

These are credits based on certain payments by the taxpayer. Unlike personal tax credits these can arise only where a taxpayer has actually made a payment towards something specific – for example, health expenses or permanent health insurance. Like personal tax credits, these are also non-refundable.

Refundable tax credits

These credits arise in relation to specific tax amounts already paid to Revenue in respect of specific sources of income, such as payroll taxes or PAYE ("pay as you earn"), dividend withholding tax and professional fees withholding tax. These credits are refundable where they exceed the actual liability of the taxpayer.

Reliefs available as deductions

Such reliefs are allowable at the taxpayer's marginal rate of tax, i.e. they reduce the amount of income potentially taxable at the higher marginal rate. For example, relief as a deduction is available for certain qualifying health expenses.

Tax rates and tax bands

There are two tax rates currently in operation, the standard rate of 20% and the higher rate of 40%. A tax band is the amount of income taxable at a specified rate. Thus the standard rate band is the amount of income taxable at the standard rate of 20%. The tax bands that currently apply depend on the taxpayer's personal circumstances (e.g., single, widowed, married or in a civil partnership) and, in the case of married couples/ civil partners, on whether or not both parties are working.

Low income exemption and marginal relief

Taxpayers aged 65 years of age or older who are in receipt of low income, where this income is below a "specified amount", may be exempt from income tax. Where the income exceeds a specified amount, full exemption from income tax is not available; however, marginal relief may apply. The specified amount is determined by reference to the taxpayer's personal circumstances, including whether they are single, married/civil partnered, with or without dependent children.

11.1.1 *Pro forma* income tax computation

Below is a *pro forma* computation, which shows where both refundable and non-refundable tax credits are included in the computation of tax liability. Before addressing the detail of the computation, it is worth revisiting three important concepts discussed in paragraph 8.8, These are:

- gross income;
- total income; and
- taxable income.

Gross income

This is the aggregate of the various sources of income which have been computed in accordance with the Taxes Acts.

Total income

This is gross income less charges. Charges will be covered in more detail in Chapter 12.

Taxable income

This is total income less allowances/reliefs allowable at the individual's marginal rate of tax.

Income tax computation of Mr X for 2018			**€**
Income	Schedule D	– Case I	X
		– Case III	X
	Schedule E		X
Gross income			X
Less: Charges (covered in Chapter 12)			(X)
Total income			X
Less: Deductible reliefs			(X)
Taxable income			X
Tax thereon			X
Less: Non-refundable tax credits			(X)
			X
Less: Refundable tax credits			(X)
Net income tax due/(refundable)			X

The various components of the above, i.e., credits and reliefs, are discussed in more detail throughout the remainder of this chapter.

11.2 Personal Tax Credits – Non-Refundable

Personal tax credits are determined by reference to the individual's personal tax circumstances. Personal tax credits are non-refundable. Details of the main personal tax credits for 2018 are set out in the reference material in Appendix I to this chapter.

Example 11.1

Pat is single and an Irish resident. In 2018 he will receive interest from government stock of €5,000 (tax not deducted at source). He has no other income. His tax assessment will be as follows:

	€
Tax on €5,000 20% =	*1,000*
Less:	
Single Person Tax Credit	*(1,650)*
Excess credit	*(650)*

The excess credit of €650 is non-refundable.

11.2.1 Basic Personal Tax Credits

There are three categories of personal tax credits:

(i) single

(ii) married/civil partners

(iii) widowed/surviving civil partners

11.2.2 Single Person's Tax Credit: €1,650

s461 TCA97 The Single Person's Tax Credit is available to an individual who is:

- single;
- s1023 TCA97 married/civil partner but has elected under s1023 TCA97 for separate assessment (see Chapter 13 on taxation of married couples/civil partners);
- s1018(4) TCA97 married/civil partner but has elected under s1018(4) for single assessment;
- separated without a legally binding document (see Chapter 13 on taxation of married couples/civil partners).

11.2.3 Married/civil partner's Tax Credit: €3,300

s461 TCA97 The Married/civil partner's Tax Credit is available to an individual who is:

- married/in a civil partnership, living with his/her spouse/civil partner and assessed to tax under joint assessment;
- widowed/surviving civil partner in the tax year, where the deceased spouse was the assessable spouse/civil partner;
- s1026 TCA97 separated or divorced/civil partnership dissolved but has elected under s1026 TCA97 to remain jointly assessed.

11.2.4 Widowed/surviving civil partner's Tax Credit: €2,190

s461A TCA97 The Widowed/surviving civil partner's Tax Credit is available to an individual who is a widow or widowed/surviving civil partner and who has no dependent children. The credit is granted in the tax year following the year of bereavement. (See 11.2.6 below for the Widowed/surviving civil partner's Parent Tax Credit that applies in the five years following the year of bereavement.)

11.2.5 Single Person Child Carer Credit (formerly One-Parent Family Credit): €3,300

s462B TCA97 An increase in an individual's personal credit is available where the individual is not entitled to the married/civil partner's credit but maintains a "qualifying child" during the tax year. The amount of credit depends on whether the individual is:

- single (or separated/divorced and not qualifying for the Married/Civil Partner's Credit); or
- widowed/surviving civil partner's.

A "qualifying child" is a child who:

- is under the age of 18 years; or
- if over 18 years, is receiving full-time education at any university, college, school or other educational establishment; or
- is permanently incapacitated by reasons of mental or physical infirmity from maintaining himself/herself and, where the child has reached 21 years of age, was incapacitated before reaching that age; and
- is in the custody of and is maintained by the claimant at his/her own expense for the whole or part of the tax year.

Prior to 2014 it was possible for both parents to claim the former One Parent Family Credit. Effective from 1 January 2014, Section 7 F(No. 2)A 2013 restricts the claim to only one parent; being the 'primary claimant'. The primary claimant is the parent with whom the child/children reside for the greater part of the year. The primary claimant may agree not to claim the credit but instead allow the other parent of the child/children claim the credit as the 'secondary claimant'.

Any income that the qualifying child may have is disregarded for the purposes of entitlement to the credit. The inclusion of the Single Person Child Carer Credit has the effect of increasing the total credit of the single/widowed parent to bring it in line with the Married Persons'/civil partner's Credit:

	Single €	Widowed €
Basic personal tax credit with no qualifying child	1,650	2,190
Above with Single Person Child Carer Credit	3,300	3,300

There is no entitlement to the credit in the case of a husband or a wife where the wife is living with her husband or the parties to a civil partnership are living together. Also there is no entitlement to the credit or for unmarried couples/couples not in a civil partnership but living together "as man and wife".

11.2.6 Widowed/Surviving Civil Partner (SCP) Parent Tax Credit

s463 TCA97 A widow who maintains a qualifying child (as described above) receives the Widowed/SCP Parent Tax Credit for the five years immediately following the year of bereavement. The additional credit is as follows:

- Year one following bereavement – €3,600
- Year two following bereavement – €3,150
- Year three following bereavement – €2,700
- Year four following bereavement – €2,250
- Year five following bereavement – €1,800

The individual is entitled to claim the tax credit for each of the five years after the year of bereavement provided that, in relation to each year for which the credit is claimed, the following conditions are met:

a) the individual has at least one qualifying child residing with him/her for the whole or part of the year;
b) the individual has not remarried/entered into a civil partnership before the commencement of the year; and
c) the individual has not been living as "man and wife" with another person in the year.

A qualifying child for the purposes of the condition at a) above is as defined for the purposes of the One-Parent Family Credit at 11.2.5 above.

Example 11.2

A widow (bereaved in 2016) has one dependent child who is in full-time education. She has not remarried and lives alone with her child.

Her entitlements for the tax year 2018 are as follows:

	€	
Single Person's Tax Credit + Single Person's Child Carer Credit	*3,300*	
Widowed Parent additional credit	*3,150*	*(Year two following bereavement)*
Total	*6,450*	

Example 11.3

Assume the same facts as above, except that the widow during 2018 co-habits with a partner "as man and wife". She will be entitled to neither the Widowed Parent Tax Credit nor the Single Person's Child Carer Tax Credit. She is entitled to only €2,190 (that being the Widowed Parent Tax Credit without a dependent child).

11.2.7 Home Carer's Tax Credit: €1,200

s466A TCA97 The Home Carer's Tax Credit is available to a spouse/civil partner who "works at home" to care for children, the aged or incapacitated persons. The amount of the credit is €1,200. The conditions which must be met to qualify are as follows:

- The married couple/civil partner must be jointly assessed to tax.
- The home carer must care for one or more dependent persons. A dependent person is:
  - a child for whom social welfare child benefit is payable, i.e., children under 16 years, or children over 16 but under 19, who are in full-time education, or
  - a person aged 65 years or over, or
  - a person who is permanently incapacitated by reason of physical or mental infirmity.

The dependent(s) must normally reside with the married couple for the tax year.

A relative may, however, reside in a neighbouring residence on the same property or within two kilometres of the claimant where there is a direct system of communication between the home carer's residence and the residence of the dependent.

If the home carer has income of €7,200 or less, the full €1,200 credit is available. Where the income is equal to or more than €9,600, there is no credit available. For income between €7,200 and €9,600, the credit is restricted by half of the excess of the home carer's income over the limit of €7,200. The following table illustrates some examples of the amount of the restriction for given levels of income:

Income of Home Carer		***Tax Credit Due***	***Restriction of Tax Credit***
1.	*€7,200*	*€1,200*	*Nil*
2.	*€7,450*	*€1,075*	*€7,450 – €7,200 = €250 ÷ 2 = €125*
3.	*€7,950*	*€825*	*€7,950 – €7,200 = €750 ÷ 2 = €375*
4.	*€8,200*	*€700*	*€8,200 – €7,200 = €1,000 ÷ 2 = €500*
5.	*€8,450*	*€575*	*€8,450 – €7,200 = €1,250 ÷ 2 = €625*
6.	*€8,700*	*€450*	*€8,700 – €7,200 = €1,500 ÷ 2 = €750*
7.	*€8,950*	*€325*	*€8,950 – €7,200 = €1,750 ÷ 2 = €875*
8.	*€9,050*	*€275*	*€9,050 – €7,200 = €1,850 ÷ 2 = €925*
9.	*€9,200*	*€200*	*€9,200 – €7,200 = €2,000 ÷ 2 = €1,000*
10.	*€9,400*	*€100*	*€9,400 – €7,200 = €2,200 ÷ 2 = €1,100*
11.	*€9,600*	*€0*	*€9,600 – €7,200 = €2,400 ÷ 2 = €1,200*

For example in 3 above, 'Income of the Home Carer', let us assume that the home carer is in receipt of interest on government stock to the amount of €7,950 each year.

The restriction is calculated as half of the excess of the home carer's income of €7,950 over €7,200, i.e., (€7,950 – €7,200) = €750/2 = €375.

Thus, the tax credit due is €1,200 – €375 = €825.

The Home Carer Credit and the increased rate band (see 13.2.1) may not be claimed together. The claimant may choose whichever of the two is more beneficial. Readers are referred to Chapter 13, Example 13.1 for an illustration of this point.

11.2.8 Incapacitated Child Tax Credit: €3,300

s465 TCA97 A tax credit of €3,300 is granted to an individual for each incapacitated child of the individual. "Child" includes any child who is in the custody of the claimant and who is maintained by the claimant. The credit is granted if, in the tax year, the child:

- is under 18 years of age and is permanently incapacitated by reason of mental or physical infirmity; or
- if over the age of 18, is permanently incapacitated by reason of mental or physical infirmity from maintaining himself/herself and has become so before he or she reached the age of 21 years. Alternatively, if the child became permanently incapacitated after the age of 21 years, he or she must have been in full-time education at the time.

The income of the child is not taken into account in determining entitlement to the credit.

11.2.9 Age Tax Credit: €245/€490

s464 TCA97 A tax credit is available to an individual if the individual or their spouse/civil partner is 65 years of age or over in the tax year. In the case of a married individual/civil partner, the tax credit is €490 regardless of whether one or both are over 65 years. For single individuals, the tax credit is €245.

11.2.10 Blind Person's Tax Credit: €1,650

s468 TCA97 A credit of €1,650 is available to an individual if that individual or his/her spouse is blind during the whole or part of the tax year. Where both parties are blind, the credit is €3,300.

A blind person who is a registered owner with the Irish Guide Dog Association may claim €825 for the maintenance of a guide dog. This allowance is granted at the claimant's marginal rate of tax.

11.2.11 Employee Tax Credit: €1,650 (maximum)

s472 TCA97 The Employee Tax Credit is sometimes known as the PAYE Tax Credit. It is granted to an individual who is in receipt of "emoluments" subject to PAYE deductions. Emoluments are salary, fees, bonus, holiday pay, overtime, etc. Emoluments paid by a body corporate to a proprietary director of the body corporate and emoluments paid by the same body corporate to the spouse or child of such proprietary director are not entitled to the PAYE credit.

A proprietary director is a director who owns more than 15% of the ordinary share capital of the company.

In addition, emoluments paid by self-employed individuals (or by a partnership in which the individual is a partner) to his/her spouse or child will not qualify the recipient for relief.

A child of a proprietary director/self-employed individual is entitled to the relief where:

- the child works full-time throughout the tax year; and
- the child's income for the tax year from this employment is at least €4,572.

The employee tax credit is also available to recipients of certain pensions and benefits payable by the Department of Employment Affairs and Social Protection and to certain individuals who are liable to Irish tax on foreign employment income. If the individual suffers withholding tax similar to PAYE in his/her home country, the credit is granted as if the emoluments were subject to Irish PAYE.

A maximum credit of €1,650 is available for 2018. If tax at the standard rate on the qualifying emoluments for the tax year is less than this amount, the credit is restricted to that lower amount. For example, if emoluments for 2018 amount to only €5,000, then the employee tax credit is calculated as €1,000 (€5,000 × 20%).

11.2.12 Earned Income Credit: €1,150 (maximum)

s472AB TCA97 As stated at 11.2.11 above, the Employee Tax Credit is not granted to a proprietary director or a self-employed individual. Section 3 FA 2016 introduced an Earned Income Credit for such individuals in receipt of qualifying earned income. The credit is only available where the recipient in receipt of income taxed under Schedule E or Schedule D (Cases I and II). The maximum credit allowed is €1,150. If the individual is already entitled to Employee Tax Credit then the maximum amount allowed overall is €1,650.

11.2.13 Dependent Relative Tax Credit: €70

s466 TCA97 A credit of €70 is available to an individual who proves that he/she maintains at his/her own expense any person who is:

- a relative or a spouse's relative who is incapacitated by old age or infirmity from maintaining himself/herself; or
- a widowed/SCP parent or the widowed/SCP parent of a spouse whether incapacitated or not; or
- a son or daughter who resides with the claimant and whose services the claimant is compelled to depend on by reason of old age or infirmity.

The credit will not be due if the income of the person for whom the claim is made exceeds the maximum rate of the old age contributory pension for a person aged over 80 years living alone. For 2018, the income limit was €14,753.

If two or more people jointly support the relative, the tax credit is apportioned according to the amount expended by each individual on the maintenance of the relative.

11.3 Other Tax Credits – Non-Refundable

At 11.2 above, personal tax credits, which are automatically available depending on an individual's circumstances, were covered in detail. Other tax credits exist where the individual makes payments for certain types of expenditure. Again, as with personal tax credits, these credits are non-refundable. They are considered in detail in the following paragraphs.

11.3.1 Tax credit for rents paid by certain tenants

s473 TCA97 A tax credit was available to an individual for rent paid (subject to certain conditions and maximum limits) on private rented accommodation which formed his/her only or main residence. Sec 14 FA 2011 abolished the rent credit for new tenants (not new tenancies) on/after 8 December 2010. For tenants who were paying rent under a tenancy on 7 December 2010, the rent credit was phased out and 2017 was the last year that the credit could be claimed. The text below demonstrates how the credit applied for 2017.

The maximum limits for 2017 were:

	Under 55 years of age	Over 55 years of age
	€	€
Married/CP/widowed/SCP	400	800
Single	200	400

Rent" for the purposes of the tax credit does not include:

- any amount relating to the cost of maintenance or repairs which, in the absence of an agreement to the contrary, would normally be the responsibility of the tenant;
- any amount relating to the provision of goods or services;
- any amount which relates to a right or benefit other than the right to use the premises;
- any amount subject to a right of reimbursement or a subsidy from any source enjoyed by the person making the payment, unless such reimbursement or subsidy cannot be claimed.

Example 11.4

A single individual aged 40 who has been renting a property since 2009 pays rent of €3,000 in the year ended 31 December 2017. The relief granted by way of a tax credit will be €200 @ 20% = €40.

(Note: The tax credit is confined to 20% of the maximum limit.)

Example 11.5

A widowed individual aged 60 who has been renting a property since 2009 pays rent of €700 in the year ended 31 December 2017. The relief granted by way of tax credit will be €700 × 20% = €140.
(Note: The tax credit is confined to 20% of the amount of rent actually paid.)

Example 11.6

A single individual aged 70 who entered into his first tenancy on 1 January 2017 pays rent of 4,000 in the year ended 31 December 2017. No credit is available as the rent is in respect of new tenancy entered into after 7 December 2010.

11.3.2 Relief for fees paid for third-level education

s474 TCA97 Relief is available in respect of "qualifying fees" paid by an individual on his/her own behalf or on behalf of other persons in respect of an "approved course" for the academic year when that course commences in the tax year in question. The relief is by way of a tax credit calculated as the fees paid at the standard rate of tax.

"Qualifying fees" in relation to an approved course and an academic year means the amount of fees chargeable in respect of tuition to be provided in relation to that course in that year which, with the consent of the Minister for Finance, the Minister for Education and Science approves for the purposes of this section. Relief will not be available in respect of any amount of the fees recoverable, directly or indirectly, by the individual or by other persons, from any source.

An "approved course" means:

- a full-time or part-time undergraduate course of study in an approved college which:
  - is of at least two academic years' duration, and
  - which has been approved by the Minister for Education and Science, having regard to the code of standards laid down in relation to the quality of education to be offered on approved courses;

or:

- a postgraduate course of study in an approved college which must be at least one academic year but not more than four academic years in duration and must lead to a postgraduate award based on either a thesis or an examination.

An "approved college" for the purposes of this section means a college or institution of higher education in the State, or a college, university or similar institution outside the State where certain additional conditions are fulfilled.

For the purposes of the relief, the Minister for Education and Science will approve the colleges, courses and the level of fees in respect of each course that will qualify for the relief. The Minister must provide this information to the Revenue Commissioners by 1 July in each year.

Where the Minister is satisfied that an approved college or an approved course in that college no longer meets the appropriate code of standards laid down, the Minister may, by notice given in writing to the approved college, withdraw the approval of that college or course. Notice of withdrawal must be published in *Iris Oifigiúil* and will only have effect from the following tax year.

Any claim for relief under this section must be accompanied by a statement in writing from the college stating the following:

- that the college is an approved college for the purposes of this section;
- the details of the course undertaken by the individual or other persons;
- the duration of the course; and
- the amount of fees paid in respect of the course.

For 2018 the relief is determined as follows:

- for full time courses, the first €3,000 is ignored, and
- for part time courses, the first €1,500 is ignored.

The maximum amount allowable for qualifying fees is €7,000 per course, per student. Relief is only due where the fees paid are not refundable by the college[1].

Example 11.7

Aoife paid €4,000 in qualifying fees in 2018 in respect of a part-time approved course. She is entitled to a tax credit of €500, i.e. (€4,000 – €1,500) × 20%.

11.3.3 Medical and dental insurance

Medical

s470 TCA97 Relief is available only for payments made to an authorised insurer (e.g., VHI, Laya Healthcare, Aviva Healthcare).

The contract of insurance must provide for the reimbursement of medical, surgical or nursing expenses resulting from sickness or accident to the individual, his/her spouse, children or other dependents.

Tax relief at source (TRS)

Tax relief for medical insurance is granted at source (TRS). With a standard rate of income tax of 20% for the 2018 tax year, the policy-holder pays a reduced premium (80% of the gross amount) to the medical insurer.[2] Revenue will give a credit for the remaining 20% to the medical insurer.

1 Inserted by s14 F(No. 2)A 2013.

2 Section 8 F(No. 2)A 2013 capped the relief at €1,000 per adult and €500 per child.

The effect of the TRS is that an individual who might not otherwise be in a position to claim tax relief on medical insurance premiums (e.g., an individual exempt from tax), can obtain tax relief at source by paying a reduced premium.

Example 11.8

Audrey is single with no dependents and has been a member of VHI for many years. She pays tax at the top rate of 40%. She receives her VHI subscription renewal for €1,500 on 1 July 2018.

	€	
Amount paid by Audrey to VHI	*1,300*	*(Net of TRS)*
Amount recovered by VHI from Revenue	*200*	*(€1,000 × 20%)*
Total	*1,500*	

Audrey does not have to make any further claim to Revenue. The fact that she pays tax at 40% is irrelevant. She has received the only tax relief due to her at the standard rate of tax under TRS and which is capped at €200 (i.e. €1,000 × 20% = €200).

Example 11.9

Julie is exempt from income tax. She receives her Laya Healthcare subscription renewal for €1,000 on 1 July 2018.

	€	
Amount paid by Julie to Laya Healthcare	*800*	*(Net of TRS)*
Amount recovered by Laya Healthcare from Revenue	*200*	*(€1,000 × 20%)*
Total	*1,000*	

Despite the fact that Julie pays no tax, she is still entitled to pay her Laya Healthcare subscription net of the standard rate relief.

Dental

Finance Act 2004 introduced tax relief for premiums paid for non-routine dental cover on policies, providing dental insurance only. The tax relief is calculated in the same way as that for medical insurance.

11.3.4 Medical expenses

s469 TCA97 Relief is available for health expenses incurred on the provision of healthcare in respect of an individual, his/her spouse and other persons. Relief is not available for medical expenses which have been (or will be) reimbursed under a contract of insurance (e.g., VHI, Laya Healthcare), from any public or local authority by way of compensation, or from other sources.

"Health expenses" include expenses incurred on:

- services of a practitioner
- diagnostic procedures carried out on the advice of a practitioner
- maintenance or treatment in a hospital or approved nursing home
- drugs or medicine supplied on the prescription of a practitioner
- physiotherapy prescribed by a practitioner

- orthopedic treatment prescribed by a practitioner
- transport by ambulance
- supply or repair of medical, surgical or dental appliances used on the advice of a practitioner
- maternity care
- educational psychological assessments and speech and language therapy services for children

The legislation specifically excludes expenses relating to:

- routine ophthalmic treatment (sight-testing, advice on use of spectacles/contact lenses, and the provision and repairing of spectacles/contact lenses); and
- routine dental treatment (extraction, scaling and filling of teeth, and the provision and repairing of artificial teeth/dentures).

The relief is normally granted in the tax year in which the expenses are paid. However, if the individual so wishes, he/she may apply to have the relief granted in the year of assessment in which the expenses were incurred.

Note that expenses relating to maintenance in a qualifying nursing home, are granted at the marginal rate of tax. All other qualifying medical expenses are granted as a credit at the standard rate of tax.

Example 11.10

Michael, who is single, incurs expenditure in 2018 as follows:

	€	
Pharmacy	*300*	*(prescribed drugs €200, non-prescribed medication €100)*
Dentist	*250*	*(€50 for check-up and polishing, €200 being balance due for orthodontic treatment)*
GP bills	*190*	
Hospital bill	*1,050*	*(€1,000 for operation/maintenance, €50 for telephone calls and laundry)*
Nursing home fees	*15,000*	*In respect of his mother.*

Michael' qualifying health expenses are as follows:

	€	
Pharmacy	*200*	*(only prescribed drugs are allowed)*
Dentist	*200*	*(routine treatment not allowed)*
GP	*190*	
Hospital bill	*1,000*	*(non-medical expenditure not allowed)*
	1,590	

Michael will be entitled to a deduction of €15,000 at the marginal rate of tax. He will receive a tax credit of €318 (€1,590 × 20%) in respect of the remaining qualifying health expenses.

11.3.5 Fisher Credit

s472BA TCA97

Section 6 FA 2016 introduced a Fisher tax credit of €1,270 for 2018 and following years. The credit can be claimed by an individual who spends a total of eight hours per day for at least 80 days a year fishing at sea in a registered fishing vessel. There is no tax credit due for a fish farmer or if the Seafarer's allowance was claimed in the same year.

11.4 Tax Credits – Refundable

s470A TCA97

Refundable tax credits arise in respect of specific tax payments. They represent tax actually paid and are therefore refundable where they exceed the net tax liability after the deduction of non-refundable credits. Examples of refundable tax credits are as follows:

PAYE

These are payroll taxes which an employer is obliged to deduct under the "pay as you earn" system.

Dividend withholding tax

Dividends payable to Irish-resident shareholders suffer dividend withholding tax (DWT) at source. Tax is deducted at the standard rate and the net dividend is paid to the shareholder.

Professional services withholding tax

Tax at the standard rate is deducted from payments made for professional services by Government Departments, State bodies, local authorities, health boards, etc. Examples of professional services are medical, dental, architectural, engineering, accountancy services, etc.

Example 11.11

Dr. Purcell is a medical doctor. He completes medical examinations on behalf of the Gardaí. The amount of fee income relating to this work in his accounts year ended 31 December 2018 was 10,000. The withholding tax deducted at source was 2,000. The gross income of 10,000 will be incorporated into his fee income for the year and a credit will be given for the retention tax withheld.

Consequently Dr. Purcell will receive a net cheque of 8,000 from the Gardaí. Assuming Dr. Purcell pays income tax at a marginal rate of 40%, his tax position will be as follows (ignoring PRSI and USC):

	€
Income	*10,000*
Taxed at 40%	*4,100*
Less Credit for withholding tax deducted	*(2,000)*
Net Liability	*2,100*

Relevant contracts tax (RCT)

Principal contractors must deduct tax at a rate of 35% from certain payments to sub-contractors. This tax must be deducted where the payee has a history of tax non-compliance. From 2011, a lower withholding rate of 20% applies where the payee has substantially complied with their tax compliance obligations. There is no need to deduct tax where the sub-contractor is tax compliant. Revenue will advise the principal contractor of the appropriate rate of tax in advance of payment being made to the sub-contractor. Examples of the types of payments subject to this tax are payments in respect of building contracts, forestry operations and meat-processing operations.

Tax on annual payments

There is an obligation on the payer of annual payments to deduct tax at the standard rate of tax. A Deed of Covenant is an example of an annual payment (see Chapter 12).

Deposit interest retention tax (DIRT)

DIRT is deducted from deposit interest at source by the financial institution or deposit-taker. Up to 31 December 2008 the DIRT rate was 20% and it has increased most years since then. From 1 January 2014 to 31 December 2016 the rate was 41%, however for 2017 the rate was lowered to 39%. The rate will decrease by 2% each year until the rate reduces to 33% by 2020. For 2018 the rate is 37%.

DIRT is only refundable in the case of individuals who are either aged 65 years or older, or incapacitated. For individuals under 65 years of age, DIRT is available as a non-refundable credit.

Examples of tax computations where there is a combination of refundable and non-refundable tax credits are set out below.

Example 11.12

Pat is single and is 60 years old. In the year of assessment 2018 he received interest on government stock in the amount of €3,000 and an annuity of €2,000 from which tax was deducted at source at the standard rate of 20%, i.e., €400.

His tax assessment is as follows:

	€
Tax on €5,000 at 20%	*1,000*
Less:	
Non-refundable tax credit –	
Single Person's Tax Credit	*(1,650)*
Tax liability	*Nil*
Tax deducted at source	*(400)*
Refund due	*400*

The excess credit of €650 is non-refundable. Only the actual tax deducted at source of €400 is refundable.

Example 11.13

Mary is single and is 60 years old. In the year of assessment 2018 she received interest on government stock in the amount of €3,000 and deposit interest of €2,000 from which DIRT of €740 was deducted at source.

Her tax assessment is as follows:

	€
Tax on €3,000 × 20%	*600*
Tax on €2,000 × 37%	*740*
	1,340
Less:	
Non refundable credits -	
Single person's tax credit	*(1,650)*
DIRT deducted	*(740)*
	(2,390)
Tax liability	*nil*
Excess non-refundable credits	*1,050*

Example 11.14

Jane is single and is 66 years old. In the year of assessment 2018 she received interest on government stock in the amount of €3,000 and deposit interest of €2,000 from which DIRT of €740 was deducted at source.

Her tax assessment is as follows:

	€
Tax on €3,000 × 20%	*600*
Tax on €2,000 × 37%	*740*
	1,340
Less:	
Non refundable credits -	
Single person's tax credit	*(1,650)*
Tax liability	*nil*
DIRT deducted	*(740)*
Refund due	*740*

11.5 Allowances and Reliefs Deductible at Marginal Rate

Allowances, which are not deductible as tax credits are allowed as deductions from total income and accordingly are relieved at the individual's higher rate of tax, i.e., the marginal rate of tax.

Examples of such reliefs include expenditure on an Employment and Investment Incentive Scheme (EIIS) and Employed person taking care of an incapacitated individual.

The allowances deductible at the marginal rate are described below, together with the criteria for qualifying for the tax deduction.

11.5.1 Employed person taking care of an incapacitated individual: €75,000

s467 TCA97 This is sometimes known as a "housekeeper" allowance. The allowance is available when the claimant employs a person (including a person whose services are provided by or through an agency) to take care of an incapacitated individual. The allowance is available if the claimant or a relative of the claimant is totally incapacitated owing to physical or mental infirmity. In the case of a married person/civil partner who is jointly assessed, the relief also applies if either the spouse/civil partner or a relative of the spouse/civil partner is incapacitated.

s465, 466 TCA97 If an allowance is claimed under this section, a tax credit may not be claimed under s465 TCA97 (Incapacitated Child Tax Credit) or s466 TCA97 (Dependent Relative Tax Credit) in respect of the employed person.

The amount of the allowance is the lower of the expense actually borne by the claimant or €75,000 (up to 2014, the max amount was €50,000).

Where two or more individuals are entitled to the allowance in respect of the same incapacitated individual:

- the aggregate of the deductions may not exceed €75,000; and
- the allowance granted is apportioned between them in proportion to the amount borne by each of them in employing the employed person.

11.5.2 Home Renovation Incentive (HRI) Scheme

Section 5 F(No. 2)A 2013 introduced a new section; 477B TCA97. This section provides for tax relief for homeowners by way of an income tax credit of 13.5% in respect of qualifying expenditure on repair, renovation or improvement works carried out on the homeowner's main home by 'qualifying contractors'. Section 8 FA 2016 extended the scheme to tenants of properties owned by a housing authority provided they have received permission from the housing authority to carry out such works. The qualifying period is from 25 October 2013 to 31 December 2018. While there is no upper limit on expenditure on qualifying works, the tax credit will only be given in relation to a maximum of €30,000 (before VAT at 13.5%), the tax credit is therefore capped at €4,050. The minimum spend on which a tax credit is given is €5,000 (before VAT at 13.5%), in this case the minimum tax credit is therefore €675.

A 'qualifying contractor' is one who is tax compliant, is registered for VAT and has a RCT rate determination of 0% or 20%. Prior to the commencement of any works, the contractor must advise Revenue online of the work about to be undertaken. The contractor must also advise on the name, address and the LPT unique number for the property on which the work will be undertaken.

For a homeowner to qualify for the tax credit; they must occupy their main home*, pay income tax under PAYE or self- assessment and their LPT and Household Charge obligations must be up to date (not applicable for tenants of a housing authority). The homeowner must be on Revenue's Local Property Tax Register as an owner or joint owner of the main home. The tax credit is only available against income tax paid and not USC or PRSI liabilities. Therefore if a homeowner is exempt from income tax, the HRI tax credit is not available. The properties that don't qualify for the tax credit are:

- Rental properties or holiday homes
- New builds
- A complete reconstruction of an uninhabitable house.

The type of work that qualifies for the HRI tax credit includes:

- Painting and decorating
- Rewiring
- Tiling
- Supply and fitting of kitchens
- Extensions
- Garages
- Landscaping
- Supply and fitting of solar panels
- Conservatories
- Plastering
- Plumbing
- Bathroom upgrades
- Supply and fitting of windows
- Attic conversions
- Driveways
- Septic tank repair or replacement
- Central heating system repair or upgrade
- Supply and fitting of built- in wardrobes

* Section 13 FA 2014 extended the relief to landlords who comply with the requirements laid down by the Private Residential Tenancies Board (PRTB). Only expenditure in the period from 15 October 2014 to 31 December 2016 will qualify.

The type of work that does not qualify for the HRI tax credit include; carpets, furniture, white goods (such as fridges, dishwashers) and services (such as architect's fees) which are liable to a VAT rate of 23%.

The credit is payable over the two years following the year in which the work is carried out and paid for. Qualifying work which is carried out between 1 January 2015 and 31 December 2015; the tax credit is payable in 2016 and 2017. For chargeable persons, the HRI will be added to their existing personal tax credits and will therefore reduce their self- assessment tax liability. For PAYE taxpayers, the credit will be included in their certificate of tax credits and the benefit of the tax credit will be spread evenly over the two tax years.

Tax Facts

The introduction of the HRI scheme is seen as a measure to encourage homeowners to engage only tax compliant contractors. The payment of the HRI tax credit is effectively a refund of the VAT paid on the home improvements (subject to a maximum payable).

11.5.3 Help to Buy Scheme

s477C TCA97

Section 9 of Finance Act 2016 introduced a scheme to assist first-time buyers to obtain a deposit to purchase or build their first home known as 'Help to Buy' (HTB). The scheme is in fact a repayment of income tax (including DIRT) paid by the claimant(s) over the four tax years prior to making the application. The claimant has the option of selecting all or any of the previous four tax years. HTB does not include properties acquired for investment purposes.

The HTB payment is calculated at the lower of:

- €20,000 (of income tax and DIRT paid over the four tax years prior to making an application) and
- 5% of the purchase value.

There is a maximum purchase value of €600,000 which applies where, in the period from 19 July 2016 to 31 December 2016, a contract for the purchase of a new house/ apartment was entered into, or in the case of a self-build; the first instalment of the loan was drawn down. After that period the maximum purchase value is €500,000.

HTB will only apply where:

- a mortgage is taken out to purchase or build the home and where the loan to value ratio is a minimum of 70%, i.e. the loan must be at least 70% of the purchase value of the property
- The claimant must have signed a contract to purchase the home on or after 19 July 2016 and on or before 31 December 2019. In the case of a self-build, the first-time buyer must have drawn down the first instalment of the mortgage loan on or after 19 July 2016 and on or before 31 December 2019

- The property must be occupied by the first-time buyer claimant, or at least one of the first-time buyers in the case of more than one buyer, for a period of 5 years from the date of occupation. Otherwise there is a clawback of the refund
- The claimant must be tax compliant in respect of all relevant periods.
- The building contractor(s) must be VAT registered and tax compliant to become a qualifying contractor for the purposes of HTB. In the case of a self-build property, a solicitor is required to submit evidence of the drawdown of the first instalment of the loan.

The HTB payment is provided at deposit stage following the signing of a contract to purchase or, in the case of a self-build, following the drawdown of the first instalment of the relevant mortgage.

11.5.4 Permanent health benefit schemes

s471 TCA97 Relief is available in respect of premiums paid under a permanent health benefit scheme approved by the Revenue Commissioners which provides for periodic payments to an individual in the event of loss or diminution of income resulting from ill health.

The amount of the premium allowable is limited to 10% of the individual's "total income". "Total income" is gross income from all sources less specific deductions and allowances (e.g., losses, capital allowances) and charges on income (e.g., annual payments such as payments under Deeds of Covenant).

Example 11.15

Mary earned €30,000 salary in 2018. She has no other income. She paid €3,500 in permanent health premiums.

She may claim only €3,000 due to the restriction of 10% of income.

Any benefit receivable by the employee under a permanent health scheme which has been approved by the Revenue Commissioners is normally taxable as emoluments under Schedule E. The person paying the benefit is required to deduct income tax from the benefit under the PAYE system. If the individual paying the premiums is assessed to tax under Schedule D, Revenue may agree to tax the benefits as part of the income of the trade or profession.

Tax relief is granted at source on contributions to Revenue-approved permanent health benefit schemes where the contributions are deducted from an individual's pay. The employer may deduct the premiums from gross pay for tax and PRSI purposes. If the contributions are not paid through the payroll, tax relief may be claimed as described above.

11.5.5 Tax relief for donations to eligible charities and other approved bodies

s848A TCA97 Tax relief was granted for donations to "eligible charities" and other "approved bodies" up to 2012. Finance Act 2013 abolished the relief for individual donors (but not for companies).

11.5.6 Relief for gifts of money to the State

s483 TCA97 When a person makes a gift of money to the Minister for Finance for use for any purpose for, or towards the cost of which, public monies are provided, tax relief is available to the donor. The relief is based on the full amount gifted in the relevant tax year and accepted by the Minister. The donor claims a deduction equal to the amount of the gift in computing total income for the year.

The donor does not, however, retain power to stipulate how any funds donated must be used. How public monies are used is entirely at the discretion of the Minister.

11.5.7 Donations to certain sports bodies[3]

s847A TCA97 Tax relief is available for donations to approved sports bodies for the funding of capital projects. In order to qualify for this relief, the following conditions must be met:

- The body must be approved by the Minister for Arts, Sport and Tourism.
- The estimated aggregate cost of the project must not be greater than €40 million.
- The sports body must hold a certificate from the Revenue Commissioners stating that the body is, in the opinion of Revenue, a body of persons to which s235 TCA97 applies, i.e., its income is exempt from tax because it is a body established for and existing for the sole purpose of promoting athletic or amateur games or sports, and such income is applied solely for those purposes.
- The body must also hold a valid tax clearance certificate.

The minimum qualifying donation in any year to any sports body will be €250 and will be available at the individual's marginal rate of tax.

Relief

The method of granting tax relief on donations will depend on whether the donor is:

- a PAYE individual; or
- an individual taxed under the self-assessment system.

PAYE individual

The relief will be given on a "grossed-up" basis to the approved body, rather than by way of a tax credit to the donor. This in effect means that the approved body will be treated as having received a donation net of income tax.

3 Readers are referred to Chapter 8 (Section 8.7) for restriction on reliefs for high income earners.

Example 11.16

An individual donates €500 to an approved sports body.

(a) If the individual is on the standard rate of income tax, i.e., 20%, the value of the donation to the sports body will be €625. The sports body receives €500 from the individual and can claim a repayment of €125 from Revenue at the end of the tax year. Thus, the individual has effectively given the sports body an amount of €625 before tax relief at a rate of 20%.

(b) If the individual pays tax at the higher rate of 40%, the value to the sports body will be €833. The sports body receives €500 from the individual and can claim a repayment of €333 from Revenue at the end of the tax year. Thus, the individual has effectively given the sports body an amount of €833 before tax relief at a rate of 40%.

Thus, if a higher-rate taxpayer on the PAYE system wants to donate €1,000 to a sports body, he/she can accomplish this by simply paying an amount of €600 to the sports body. The tax relief is, in effect, given at source as a deduction from the amount of the donation.

The PAYE individual must complete an "Appropriate Certificate" and forward it to the approved body so that it can claim the amount of tax on the grossed-up donation.

Self-assessment

The individual claims the relief for the amount paid. There is no grossing-up and therefore no tax repayment due to the charity, i.e., the donation is treated as paid gross to the charity.

Example 11.17

A donation of €500 is paid by an individual liable to tax at 20%. The value to the approved sports body is €500. The individual has a tax saving of €100 (€500 × 20%); the donation costs the individual only €400. If the individual paid tax at the higher rate of 40%, he/she would have a tax saving of €200 (€500 × 40%), and the donation would cost the individual only €300.

The approved sports body has already received €500 and no further amount is due to the approved sports body.

11.5.8 Seafarer Allowance

s472B TCA97 A seafarer may claim an allowance of €6,350 which can be set against income from a qualifying employment i.e. a seafaring employment. The €6,350 allowance is granted as a deduction in arriving at taxable income. The deduction cannot be set against other income of the individual, or against the income of his/her spouse /civil partner. To qualify for the allowance:

- the seafarer must be at sea for at least 161 days in the tax year.
- the seafarer's employment must be performed wholly on board a sea going ship in the course of an international voyage. A seagoing ship means a ship other than a

fishing vessel that is registered in the shipping register of a European Member State and is used solely for the purposes of carrying passengers or cargo for reward. The voyage must begin or end in a port outside the State.

- The seafarer must not be a Public Sector employee.

11.5.9 Relief for investment in corporate trades

s488–508 TCA97 For many years, two schemes of relief commonly known as the Business Expansion Scheme Relief (BES) and a Seed Capital Investment (SCI) incentive were available to investor individuals. Finance Act 2011 proposed to end the BES relief and replace it with a new relief known as the Employment and Investment Incentive Scheme (EIIS). However the new relief had to be given approval by the EU before it could be implemented. This approval was granted on 25 November 2011. Until this date BES continued to be available. Readers are referred to earlier editions of this publication for an analysis of the BES relief.

Employment and Investment Incentive Scheme (EIIS)

Relief is given as a deduction from total income and the maximum amount which qualifies for relief in any one tax year is €150,000 (minimum investment must be €250). The relief is available to each spouse/civil partner, subject to availability of income in his/her own right. The relief is available to "qualifying individuals" who subscribe for "qualifying shares" in a "qualifying company" only. The expiry date for the relief is 31 December 2020. The conditions which must be satisfied to qualify for the relief are quite extensive, and some of the important concepts are explained at Appendix II. Relief is initially available to an individual at the fraction 30/40. A further 10/40ths tax relief will be available where it has been proven that employment levels have increased at the EIIS company at the end of the holding period of four years or where evidence is provided that the company used the capital raised for expenditure on research and development. An investor who cannot obtain relief on all his/her investment in a year of assessment, either because his/her investment exceeds the maximum of €150,000 or his/her income in that year is insufficient to absorb all of it, can carry forward the unrelieved amount to following year 2019, subject to the normal limit of €150,000 on the amount of investment that can be relieved in any one year.

Example 11.18

Lisa Wiley who is single and age 60, made an investment of €70,000 in a qualifying EIIS company on 30 December 2018. Her salary for 2018 was €140,000 with tax deducted of €39,012 and she had no other income in 2018. She paid €20,000 pension contribution since she is not a member of an occupational pension scheme.

The calculation of the relief due is as follows (ignoring USC):

	€	€
Schedule E		*140,000*
Less pension contribution		*(20,000)*
*Less EIIS relief**		*(52,500)*
Taxable Income		*67,500*
34,550 × 20%		*6,910*
32,950 × 40%		*13,180*
		20,090
	€	**€**
Less non refundable credits		
Single	*1,650*	
PAYE	*1,650*	
		(3,300)
		790
Less refundable credits		–
PAYE paid		*39,012*
Refund due		*22,222*

** Only 30/40ths of relief is available now, i.e. €70,000 × 30/40 = €52,500.*

11.5.10 Start up Refunds for Entrepreneurs

s493 TCA97 Start up Refunds for Entrepreneurs (SURE) (previously known as Seed Capital investment) was introduced to encourage individuals to set up their own business. The relief is deductible from total income and may be claimed for any of the six years immediately prior to the tax year in which the investment takes place. The individual must subscribe for shares in a new company. The new company must be carrying on trading operations of an EIIS nature. The maximum relief in any one tax year is €100,000 (subject to overall limit of €700,000). The expiry date for the relief is 31 December 2020.

To qualify for the relief, the individual must:

- be a full-time employee or a full-time director with the new company at any time up to six months after the end of the tax year in which the business is established;
- derive not less than 75% of his/her total income from Schedule E sources, income from other sources not being more than €50,000 in each of the three years of assessment preceding the year of assessment immediately prior to the year of assessment in which the employment commences;
- not have possessed or have been entitled to acquire more than 15% of the ordinary share capital, loan capital or voting power of a company other than a seed capital

company except where the individual owns more than 15% of only one other company, provided:

- the company's turnover in each of the three accounting periods (prior to the accounting period in which the investment is made in the seed capital company) did not exceed €127,000, and
- the company is a trading company other than a company trading in land or financial services;

- acquire at least 15% of the issued ordinary share capital of the seed capital company and retain that 15% for one year (previously two years) from the date of the investment or from the date on which the company commences to trade, whichever is later.

Example 11.19

John Granger who is single was made redundant on 1 May 2018. He received a lump sum payment on termination of €160,000. He set up a manufacturing company and invested €100,000 in the company by buying 100,000 €1 shares.

His income and tax paid in previous years are as follows:

	2017	***2016***	***2015***	***2014***	***2013***	***2012***
	€	**€**	**€**	**€**	**€**	**€**
Salary	*75,000*	*73,000*	*69,000*	*65,000*	*35,000*	*30,000*
Other Income	*2,000*	*1,800*	*1,500*	*1,000*	*500*	*300*
Tax Paid	*21,340*	*21,256*	*20,292*	*19,800*	*6,340*	*4,386*

The relief is calculated as follows:

	2017	***2016***	***2015***	***Total***
	€	**€**	**€**	**€**
Salary	*75,000*	*73,000*	*69,000*	
Other Income	*2,000*	*1,800*	*1,500*	
Total	*77,000*	*74,800*	*70,500*	
Less SURE	*77,000*	*23,000*	*0*	
Taxable Income	*0*	*51,800*	*70,500*	
Tax due (A)	*0*	*10,660*	*20,292*	
Tax paid (B)	*21,340*	*21,256*	*20,292*	
Refund due (B–A)	*21,340*	*10,596*	*0*	***31,936***

11.5.11 Investment in films

s481 TCA97 Tax relief at the marginal rate of tax was available for some years for individuals who made an investment in a company to produce a film with the maximum amount of relief set at €50,000. Finance Act 2013 removed the tax relief from the individual investor and instead grant a tax credit to the film production company.

11.5.12 Retirement relief for sportspersons

s480A TCA97 A tax relief is available to certain retiring sportspersons who are resident in the State, an EEA State or and EFTA State[4]. The relief is given by way of a repayment of tax in the year in which the sportsperson ceases permanently to be engaged in that sport.

The relief is granted by allowing a deduction from earnings equal to 40% of those earnings derived directly from actual participation in the sport concerned for up to ten years of assessment for which the sports person was resident in the State. The deduction is calculated by reference to 40% of gross receipts (i.e., before deducting expenses) and may be claimed for any 10 years after the year of assessment 1990/91.

The relief has a number of conditions attaching to it:

- The individual must be resident in the State or an EEA or an EFTA State in the year of retirement.
- The relief is applied by allowing a deduction of 40% of the gross earnings (before deducting expenses) from the income from that sport.
- The claim for the deduction may be made up to 4 years after the end of the year of retirement. The claim can be for the 14 years up to year of retirement subject to a maximum of 10 years.
- The relief is given in respect of earnings derived directly from the participation in the sport, such as prize money and performance fees.
- Other earnings, such as sponsorship fees, advertisement income, newspaper or magazine articles, etc., are excluded.
- If the sportsperson recommences to engage in that sport, the relief will be clawed back.
- The repayment will not carry interest.
- The relief cannot create or augment a loss.
- The relief will not affect the calculation of "net relevant earnings" for the purpose of ascertaining maximum pension contributions.

4 Inserted by s15 F(No. 2)A 2013, up to 2013,the sportsperson had to be resident in Ireland and not elsewhere. 'EFTA State' means a State other than an EEA State which is a member of the European Free Trade Association.

Tax Facts

Finance (No. 2) Act 2013 Amendments

The inclusion of residence in an EEA/EFTA State is to comply with EU law. The option to pick 10 years out of the previous 14 years up to year of retirement optimises the relief due.

11.6 Tax Rates and Rate Bands 2018

The following table illustrates the rates and bands which apply for the 2018 year of assessment. Note that references to "married" include civil partners and references to "widow/er" include surviving civil partners:

	Rate Band €	Rate of Tax	Description of Rate
Single/Widow(er): no dependent children			
First	34,550	20%	Standard
Balance		40%	Higher
Single/Widow(er): with dependent children			
First	38,550	20%	Standard
Balance		40%	Higher
Married couple: one income			
First	43,550	20%	Standard
Balance		40%	Higher
Married couple: two incomes	€		
First	69,100*	20%	Standard
Balance		40%	Higher

* Note: The maximum standard rate tax band for a married couple with one spouse earning is €43,550. However, where both spouses are assessed to income tax in the year of assessment, the standard rate tax band may be increased up to a maximum of €69,100, provided the spouse with the lower income has assessable income of at least €25,550. If that spouse's assessable income is less than €25,550 for the year of assessment, then the increase in the standard rate band above €43,550 is restricted to the amount of that spouse's income.

In determining the income of a spouse for the purposes of increasing the standard rate tax band, capital allowances, trading losses and pension contributions applicable to that income must be deducted first.

Income from deposit interest, which is subject to deposit interest retention tax (DIRT) of the spouse, is also deducted from the spouse's income in determining the increase in the standard rate band.

The following examples will best demonstrate the above:

Example 11.20

A married couple, with one spouse working and earning €80,000, is jointly assessed. The couple's income tax liability will be as follows:

		€	€
Taxable income			80,000
Tax thereon	*€43,550 × 20%* ***Note 1***	8,710	
	€36,450 × 40%	14,580	
			23,290

Note 1: *The rate band is restricted to €43,550 since this is the maximum rate band for a single income couple.*

Example 11.21

A married couple is jointly assessed, with one spouse earning €50,000 and the other spouse earning €30,000. The couple's income tax liability will be as follows:

		€	€
Taxable income	*(€50,000 + €30,000)*		80,000
Tax thereon	*€69,100 × 20% (€43,550 + €25,550)* ***Note 2***	13,820	
	€10,900 × 40%	4,360	
			18,180

Note 2: *The maximum rate band of income of €69,100 is utilised as the spouse with the lower income has assessable income of at least €25,550.*

Both Examples 11.21 and 11.22 below show total income of €80,000. However, the tax liability in Example 11.21 is €3,110 less than the liability in Example 11.22 (i.e., €21,290 – €18,180). This tax saving is achieved due to the couple in Example 11.21 having an additional €15,550 of taxable income charged at the standard rate instead of the higher rate of 40%. The tax saving is therefore €15,550 × (40 – 20)% = €3,110.

Example 11.22

A married couple is jointly assessed, with one spouse earning €70,000 and the other spouse earning €10,000. The couple's income tax liability will be as follows:

		€	€
Taxable income	*(€70,000 + €10,000)*		80,000
Tax thereon	*€53,550 × 20% (€43,550 + €10,000)* ***Note 3***	10,710	
	€26,450 × 40%	10,580	
			21,290

Note 3: *The maximum rate band of €69,100 is not utilised, as the assessable income of the spouse with the lower income is less than €25,550. The rate band of €43,550 can be increased only by the actual income, in this case €10,000.*

Example 11.23

John and Jamie are jointly assessed. John has Schedule E employment income of €50,000. Jamie is self-employed. Her assessable profit for 2018 is €32,900. Her capital allowances for 2018 are €12,900. She pays allowable pension contributions in the amount of €3,000.

John and Jamie's assessable income and rate bands for 2018 are as follows:

		Jamie €	John €
Schedule E employment income (net)		–	50,000
Schedule D Case I income-tax adjusted profit		32,900	–
***Less:** Capital allowances*		(12,900)	
		20,000	
***Less:** Pension contributions*		(3,000)	
			–
		17,000	50,000
Total joint assessable income			67,000
Tax thereon	*€60,550 (€43,550 + €17,000) × 20%* ***Note 4***	12,110	
	€6,450 × 40%	2,580	
			14,690

***Note 4:** The married couple band of €43,550 can be increased only by the actual income, in this case €17,000.*

11.7 Low Income Exemption and Marginal Relief

Exemptions from income tax are available to individuals with small incomes. The exemption limits are increased for individuals aged 65 years or over. Marginal relief applies where the income does not greatly exceed the relevant exemption limit.

11.7.1 Low Income - Age exemption

s188 TCA97 There is total exemption from income tax for an individual aged 65 years or over if gross income does not exceed the following limits:

€18,000 – single person/widow(er)/surviving civil partner
€36,000 – married couple/civil partners (jointly assessed)

The appropriate age limits are satisfied if either the individual (or his/her spouse) attains the relevant age at any time during the tax year.

The above exemption limits are increased by €575 for each of the first two dependent children maintained by the individual/married couple/civil partners and by €830 for each dependent child in excess of two.

Example 11.24

A married couple, both aged 65 have three dependent children. The exemption limit is increased by €1,980 ((€575 × 2) + €830) to €37,980.

The definition of dependent child is the same as that used for the purposes of the single person child carer credit.

11.7.2 Marginal relief

s188 TCA97 Marginal relief will apply where the total income (i.e., gross income less charges of the individual) exceeds the specified income limit, but is not greater than twice the specified income limit. In such cases, the maximum income tax liability for the year may not exceed 40% of the difference between his/her total income and the specified income limit.

Example 11.25

Tom is married, aged 66 and has two dependent children. His gross income for 2018 is €45,100 and he pays qualifying charges of €1,000 and permanent health insurance premiums of €100.

	€
Income tax computation (ignoring marginal relief)	
Income	*45,100*
Less: Charges	*(1,000)*
Total income	*44,100*
Less: Deductible reliefs	*(100)*
Taxable income	*44,000*
	€
€43,550 at 20%	*8,710*
€450 at 40%	*180*
	8,890
Less:	
Married tax credit	*(3,300)*
Tax due	*5,590*
Less marginal relief (see below)	*(2,810)*
Net tax due	*2,780*
Marginal relief computation	
Income	*45,100*
Less: Charges (as above)	*(1,000)*
Total income (for exemption purposes only)	*44,100*
Less: Specified limit (married, over 65, with two dependent children)	*(37,150)*
	6,950
Maximum final tax liability restricted to €6,950 × 40%	*2,780*

> **Tax Facts**
>
> An Irish-resident, non-domiciled individual is not taxable on foreign income unless remitted to the State. For marginal relief purposes, "total income" is deemed to include all foreign income, even if it is not remitted to the State and is not taxable. This also applies to a non-resident individual who is liable to Irish income tax arising on income in Ireland.

Marginal relief is further complicated if the individual is in receipt of deposit interest, which is subject to deposit interest retention tax (DIRT). Marginal relief is available if the taxpayer's total income does not exceed twice the appropriate specified income limit plus the gross interest received. If marginal relief is available, then it is calculated in the normal way. The maximum tax payable is the lower of the tax calculated per the income tax computation after deducting the DIRT paid or the 40% tax using the marginal relief calculation.

11.8 Relief for Pension Contributions

Tax relief is available at the marginal rate for pension contributions paid by individuals. There are different types of pension schemes, which can be loosely divided into two categories:

- pensions schemes for employed individuals;
- pensions schemes for self-employed individuals.

The maximum amount of pension contributions for which an individual may receive tax relief (under either category) varies with age and is as follows:

Age	**% of earnings**
Up to 29	15%
30 to 39	20%
40 to 49	25%
50 to 54	30%
55 to 60	35%
Over 60	40%

In addition to the above limits, there is an overall earnings cap of €115,000 for 2018.

Example 11.26

Mary Kate, aged 31, paid €60,000 pension contributions in 2018. Her assessable income as a barrister in 2018 was €295,000.

	€
Case II Income	*295,000*
Subject to earnings cap	*115,000*

Maximum percentage allowed for age range 30 to 39	*20%*
Maximum allowed	*23,000*
Amount paid	*60,000*
Balance	*37,000*

The unutilised balance of €37,000 may be carried forward and claimed in the following year(s).

11.8.1 Contributions by self-employed individuals

This category also extends to individuals employed in a non-pensionable employment, i.e., an employment where there is no pension scheme in place for the employees. The maximum allowable contributions and earnings cap referred to above are applied to "net relevant earnings". Net relevant earnings are earnings from trades, professions and non-pensionable employment after deducting capital allowances, losses and charges (to the extent that they exceed non-trade income).

Example 11.27

Eddie Fox, aged 55, is single and self-employed. He pays €8,000 (gross) per year under a deed of covenant to his aunt who is permanently incapacitated. His Case I profit for 2018 is €120,000, capital allowances are €4,000 and he also pays €6,000 pension contributions.

		€	€
Case I income			*120,000*
Less:			
Capital allowances		*(4,000)*	
Payment under deed of covenant (see Chapter 12)		*(8,000)*	*(12,000)*
"Net relevant earnings"			*108,000*
Less pension contributions			*(6,000)*
			102,000
Taxed as follows:			
€34,550 × 20%		*6,910*	
€67,450 × 40%		*26,980*	
		33,890	
Add: tax due on deed of covenant			
€8,000 × 20%		*1,600*	
		35,490	
Less: non-refundable credits			
Single credit	*1,650*		
Earned Income Credit	*1,150*	*(2,800)*	
Tax liability		***32,690***	

A further example illustrating the methodology for calculating net relevant earnings and the allowable pension contribution is included at Appendix III to this chapter.

11.8.2 Pensionable employment

Pensionable employment is one where the employer has put a pension scheme in place for the benefit of his/her employees. This is known as an "occupational pension scheme". Such schemes are generally Revenue-approved.

For the pension schemes which do not have Revenue approval, contributions made by the employer on behalf of the employee are treated as a taxable benefit in the hands of the employee. Furthermore any contributions made by the employee are not tax deductible. Conversely, for Revenue-approved schemes, any contributions made by the employer are not treated as a taxable benefit in the hands of the employee and the contributions made by the employee are tax-deductible for PAYE[5] purposes. The contribution limits and earnings cap referred to above at 11.8 also apply to contributions to an occupational pension scheme.

Example 11.28

Mary Jane earns €3,000 per month from her employment with Zed Co Ltd. Zed Co Ltd has a Revenue-approved pension scheme in place into which Mary Jane pays 3% of her salary:

	€
Gross salary	*3,000*
*Less pension contribution****	*(90)*
Net pay	*2,910*

For PAYE purposes, Mary Jane's "pay" is €2,910 and not €3,000. Her pension contributions are therefore effective for tax purposes. However, for PRSI & USC purposes "Pay" is €3000.

Employees generally pay a fixed percentage to a pension scheme, e.g., 3% of pensionable salary. For some employees this contribution may not be sufficient, and such employees have the option of making an additional pension contribution. These top-up contributions are known as "Additional Voluntary Contributions" (AVCs). In determining the maximum contributions allowable, AVCs are added to the regular pension contribution.

11.9 Universal Social Charge (USC) and Income Levy

11.9.1 Background to Income Levy

The income levy was introduced with effect from 1 January 2009 through the Finance (No. 2) Act 2008. The section introduced a new Part 18A to TCA97 and sixteen sections of legislation – Section 531A to 531N.

5 Up to 2010 such contributions were effective for tax and PRSI purposes, however from 2011 onwards there is no relief for PRSI purposes.

The income levy remained in force up to 2010. It was payable in addition to tax, PRSI and health levy. Readers are referred to the 8th edition of this publication for further analysis of the income levy.

Universal Social Charge

The USC was introduced by Finance Act 2011 and is effective from 1 January 2011. It replaced both the income levy and health levy. The USC mirrors the income levy in a number of ways; however the main difference is the wide scope of its application. Previously a number of categories of individuals were exempt from both the income levy and health levy, for example because they were holders of a medical card, no such blanket exemption exists for the USC. The main features of the USC are set out below.

The USC is applied to "relevant emoluments" and "relevant income".

"Relevant emoluments" means emoluments to which PAYE is applied but excludes social welfare payments and payments similar in character to social welfare payments. Details of such payments are included at Appendix IV.

"Relevant income" is income from all sources apart from exempt income (referred to at 11.9.2 below) and relevant emoluments. An interesting feature of the USC is that certain income which is exempt or otherwise relieved from income tax is not exempt from the USC, for example:

- Dividends from companies' exempt income from woodlands occupation, and certain mining operations.
- Profits or gains from exempt income from woodlands occupation, and certain mining operation.
- Exempt income from farmland leasing.
- Income qualifying for Artist's exemption.

Also the USC is applied to income before deducting certain losses, non-trade capital allowances and pension contributions. This contrasts with income tax rules where income, after deducting losses, capital allowances and pensions, is liable to income tax. The only losses allowable are trade losses carried forward (i.e. under s382 TCA97) and the only capital allowances allowable are those specific to the trade and on which "normal" wear & tear is claimed, i.e. accelerated capital allowances are not allowable. Maintenance and covenant payments which are deductible for tax purposes are also deductible for USC purposes. The reason for this is due to the fact that the recipients of such payments are liable to pay USC on this income.

The USC is collected in the same way as income tax, i.e. through the PAYE system for employees/recipients of occupational pensions and the self assessment system.

11.9.2 Exempt Income

The following income is exempt from the USC:

- All social welfare payments including social welfare payments from abroad.
- Payments in lieu of social welfare payment, e.g. Community Employment Schemes etc. (as included at Appendix IV).
- Income subject to DIRT (deposit interest retention tax).
- Income which does not exceed the exempt annual amount (referred to at 11.9.3 below).
- Miscellaneous income as included at Appendix V.

11.9.3 Exempt Individuals

Where the individual's income does not exceed the exempt amount of €13,000 they are exempt from the USC. Note that if the income exceeds the exempt amount of €13,000 (regardless of how small the excess is), USC is payable on all the income in accordance with the table below.

11.9.4 Rates and Income Thresholds

The rates and income thresholds for 2018 are as follows:

Category 1 - Under 70 Years - No Medical Card	
first €12,012	0.5%
the next €7,360	2%
the next €50,672	4.75%
Over €70,044	8%
Category 2 - Over 70 Years - or Under 70 Years with Medical Card where relevant income does not exceed €60,000	
first €12,012	0.5%
Over €12,012	2%
Category 3 – Under or over 70 Years – with/without a Medical Card in receipt of "Relevant Income" > €100K	
first €12,012	0.5%
the next €7,360	2.5%
the next €50,672	4.75%
the next €29,956	8%
Over €100K**	11%

**3% surcharge for self-assessed individuals whose 'relevant income' exceeds €100,000 in a year regardless of age.

FA 2012 introduced a further 5% "surcharge" on the amount of reliefs claimed under the property based incentive reliefs and accelerated capital allowances. Coverage of such reliefs is outside the scope of this publication.

Example 11.29

	€	€
Income from self-employment:		*120,000*
Income from PAYE employment:		*60,000*
		180,000
USC liability:		
€12,012 @ 0.5% =	*60.06*	
€7,360 @ 2% =	*147.2*	
€50,672 @ 4.75% =	*2406.92*	
€89,956 @ 8% =	*7,196.48*	
€20,000 @ 11% =	*2,200.00*	
	12,010.66	

Example 11.30

Following on from example 11.27, Eddie Fox's PRSI and USC is calculated as follows:

PRSI		
116,000 × 4%		*4,640*
USC		
12,012 × 0.5%	*60.06*	
7,360 × 2%	*147.2*	
50,672 × 4.75%	*2406.92*	
29,956 × 8%	*2396.48*	
8,000 × 11%	*880*	
108,000		*5,890.66*

- *The PRSI is calculated by allowing only the capital allowances of €4,000, the pension and covenant payments are ignored*

- *The USC is calculated by allowing the capital allowances of €4,000 and covenant payment of €8,000, the pension payment is ignored.*

Further examples of the application of USC and PRSI are included on a selected basis in the chapters that follow. Individuals with income from employments will suffer USC and PRSI at source and hence are not included in such examples.

11.10 Operation of PRSI

11.10.1 Overview

The principal act for pay-related social insurance (PRSI) is the Social Welfare (Consolidation) Act 2005. Most of the content of the Act is devoted to the benefits and entitlements of the insured individual. The material dealing with PRSI contributions and insurability of employment is concentrated in ss9-16 of the Act and Regulations made thereunder.

In the case of the vast majority of contributors (i.e., individuals who pay PRSI contributions), contributions are collected by the Revenue Commissioners through the PAYE system, and are then passed on to the Department of Employment Affairs and Social Protection for inclusion in the Social Insurance Fund. The PAYE system is also used for the collection and maintenance of information on the duration of the employee's insurable employment, on which his/her eligibility for virtually all the PRSI benefits depends.

The PRSI system applies to all individuals employed in the State under a contract of service. A fixed percentage of the worker's reckonable earnings is payable by both the employee and the employer. The precise percentage payable depends on the PRSI class under which the individual is insured.

In addition to deducting PAYE & USC, employers are also obliged to deduct PRSI.

The social insurance (i.e. PRSI) contribution varies depending on the level of earnings of the employee and the benefits for which the individual is insured.

11.10.2 Universal Social charge

Readers will be aware from Chapter 11 that the health contribution was abolished and is now replaced by the USC effective from 1 January 2011. Employers and pension providers must deduct USC as appropriate from each payment to the employee/ pensioner.

11.10.3 Insurable employment

The First Schedule to the Social Welfare (Consolidation) Act 2005 defines insurable employment as:

> *"Employment in the State under any contract of service or apprenticeship, written or oral, whether expressed or implied, and whether the employed person is paid by the employer or other person, and whether under one or more employers".*

11.10.4 PRSI classes

There are different levels of PRSI contributions, each of which is given a particular letter code and called a contribution class. The particular type of contribution determines entitlement to the various social welfare benefits, e.g., civil servants who are insured at the "modified rates", i.e., lower rates, are not entitled to personal social welfare pensions or to unemployment benefits. The different classes are considered below:

Class A

This is the standard PRSI class, and includes more than 65% of the insured employee population. It comprises employees in commercial, service and agricultural employments. PRSI under class A provides cover for all social welfare benefits.

Classes B, C, D and H

These classes apply to permanent and pensionable public sector employees, such as civil servants, registered doctors and dentists employed in the Civil Service, gardaí, teachers, nurses, local authority staff, members of the Defence Forces, etc. Insured persons in these classes pay reduced rates of contribution since they are only covered for a reduced range of benefits, specifically widow's and orphan's pensions and deserted wife's benefit.

Class J

Class J contributions comprise an employee's contribution in respect of the levies, plus a small employer's contribution in respect of occupational injuries. This class applies to:

- Employed persons over 66 years of age;
- Persons employed under the Community Employment Scheme where such employment commenced prior to 6 April 1996;
- Persons in employment of a subsidiary nature – the term "subsidiary employment" is defined in the regulations as being an employment exercised by persons who are concurrently insurable at the modified rates (such persons are not permitted to pay full rate (Class A) contributions, any such employment is insured at Class J);
- Persons employed under a contract of service whose gross earnings per week are less than €38, i.e., the employment is deemed to be of inconsiderable extent (€38 limit applies to total earnings where an individual has a number of employments).

Class K

This class is used as a method for deducting the levies at source from the PAYE income of persons who are not insurably employed and therefore not liable to PRSI. Examples include:

- Persons in receipt of an occupational pension who are not insurably employed;
- Persons employed by a spouse.

Class S

This class is used for certain directors and self-employed contributors.

11.11 PRSI Rates

Broadly speaking, private sector employees are liable for PRSI at a rate of 4%. Employer's PRSI is levied at a rate of 10.85%, with a lower rate for income of €376 per week or less. The rate of PRSI for the self-employed is 4%.

Readers are referred to Appendix III for a summary of the PRSI rates applicable for class A.

11.12 Employer Duties

Monthly remittance

Employers must remit the tax and PRSI deducted by them under the PAYE system on a form P30 to the Collector-General (collection arm of the Revenue Commissioners) within 14 days of the end of each income tax month. Thus, tax and PRSI deducted from January 2018 salary must be remitted by 14 February 2018.

Where an employer is using ROS (i.e. Revenue's electronic filing system), the due date is the 23rd of the month and not the 14th where both the P30 and the liability are transmitted using ROS. The vast majority of employers are obliged to file and pay on line but some employers in exceptional circumstances may paper file.

s991 TCA97 Under s991 TCA97 interest accrues at a daily rate of 0.0274% (where the payment not made on time.

End-of-year returns

P35

After the end of each tax year, an employer must submit an end-of-year tax return (known as a P35) showing in relation to each employee:

- Name of the employee;
- PPS number of the employee (if known);
- Date of commencement/leaving the employment, if same occurred during the tax year;

- Total amount deducted in respect of:
  - pay (after pension deductions),
  - tax,
  - employee PRSI,
  - employer PRSI;
- Total number of insurable weeks.

The latest date for filing form P35 is 46 days after the end of the year of assessment, e.g., form P35 for 2017 had to be filed by 15 February 2018. For "e-filers" this date is extended to 23 February. Failure to do so may result in a penalty imposition of €2,535.

P60

Each employee is entitled to receive a form P60 after the end of the year of assessment. The information on the form P60 mirrors that contained on form P35.

Employee leaving

Where an employee leaves an employment, the employer must provide the employee with a cessation certificate known as a form P45. Form P45 must contain the following information:

- Name of the employee;
- PPS number of the employee (if known);
- Date of leaving the employment;
- Amount of weekly/monthly tax credits;
- Amount of weekly/monthly SRCOP;
- Total pay (after pension deductions), tax, employee and employer PRSI deductions from the previous 1 January to date of leaving (or from date of commencement of employment if later than 1 January);
- Total number of insurable weeks.

Form P45 must indicate that emergency tax was applied, if relevant.

11.13 False Claims

Section 21 FA 2011 introduced a penalty of €3,000 for incorrectly claiming tax credits/allowances/reliefs etc. The section is aimed at "employees" who would not otherwise be chargeable persons. The penalty also applies to agents who knowingly or carelessly assist incorrect claims. The same section also introduced a payment date of 30 September for tax due by employees or other persons not within the self-assessment system. A new section (s960Q TCA97) was included to recover tax overpaid from the person to whom a refund was paid.

Appendix I

Main Personal Tax Credits

	Tax Year 2012	Tax Year 2013	Tax Year 2014	Tax Year 2015	Tax Year 2016	Tax Year 2017	Tax Year 2018
	€	€	€	€	€	€	€
Single Person	1,650	1,650	1,650	1,650	1,650	1,650	1,650
Married Couple/CP	3,300	3,300	3,300	3,300	3,300	3,300	3,300
Widowed/ SCP							
– in year of bereavement	3,330	3,330	3,330	3,330	3,330	3,330	3,330
– without dependent children	2,190	2,190	2,190	2,190	2,190	2,190	2,190
– with dependent children	1,650	1,650	1,650	1,650	1,650	1,650	1,650
Widowed/ SCP							
– first year after bereavement	3,600	3,600	3,600	3,600	3,600	3,600	3,600
– second year after bereavement	3,150	3,150	3,150	3,150	3,150	3,150	3,150
– third year after bereavement	2,700	2,700	2,700	2,700	2,700	2,700	2,700
– fourth year after bereavement	2,250	2,250	2,250	2,250	2,250	2,250	2,250
– fifth year after bereavement	1,800	1,800	1,800	1,800	1,800	1,800	1,800
One-Parent Family							
– widowed/ SCP person	1,650	1,650	1,650	1,650	1,650	1,650	1,650
– other person	1,650	1,650	1,650	1,650	1,650	1,650	1,650
Incapacitated Child Max.	3,300	3,300	3,300	3,300	3,300	3,300	3,330

	Tax Year 2012	Tax Year 2013	Tax Year 2014	Tax Year 2015	Tax Year 2016	Tax Year 2017	Tax Year 2018
	€	€	€	€	€	€	€
Dependent Relative Max. Income Limit	70 13,837	70 13,837	70 13,837	70 13,837	70 14,060	70 14,504	70 14,753
Blind Person Both Spouses Blind	1,650 3,300	1,650 3,300	1,650 3,300	1,650 3,300	1,650 3,300	1,650 3,300	1,650 3,330
Age Credit: Single Married/CP	 245 490	 245 490	 245 490	 245 490	 245 490	 245 490	 245 490
PAYE Max Earned Income Credit.	1,650	1,650	1,650	1,650	1,650 550	1,650 950	1,650 1,150
Home-carer Max.	810	810	810	810	1,000	1,100	1,200
Employment of Carer for Incapacitated Person Max.	50,000 @ Marginal Rate	50,000 @ Marginal Rate	50,000 @ Marginal Rate	75,000 @ Marginal Rate	75,000 @ Marginal Rate	75,000 @ Marginal Rate	75,000 @ Marginal Rate

Appendix II

Conditions for EIIS Relief

Qualifying Individual

A qualifying investor is an individual who:

- is resident in Ireland for the tax year in respect of which he/she makes the claim;
- subscribes on his/her own behalf for eligible shares in a qualifying company; and
- is not connected with the company, i.e.
  - he/she, or an associate of his/hers, is a partner of the company;
  - he/she possesses, or is entitled to acquire, in the event of the company being wound up, more than 30% of (a) the issued ordinary share capital of the company or (b) the loan capital and issued share capital of the company, or (c) the voting power in the company.
  - he/she controls the company
  - he/she is investing in the company as part of a deal whereby a person connected with the company in turn invests in a separate company with which the individual is connected

Prior to 2017 Finance Act, the shareholdings of relatives were not aggregated for the purposes of the 30% test. With effect from 2 November 2017 such holdings are aggregated.

Investors must purchase new ordinary share capital in the company. Shares must carry no preferential rights. The maximum investment is €150,000 and the minimum investment by an individual in any one company which qualifies is €250. The initial relief is 30% of the qualifying investment and was subject to the high income restriction[6]. The additional 10% relief will be available, where it has been proven that employment levels have increased at the EIIS company at the end of the holding period of 4 years or where evidence is provided that the company used the capital raised for expenditure on research and development. Where the additional 10% relief available, it will not be subject to the high income restriction. There must be no condition which would eliminate the risk to the investor. The individual must continue to be a "qualifying investor" for a period of four years (prior to 13 October 2015 the holding period was three years) after the shares have been issued.

6 Section 16 F(No. 2)A 2013 removed the relief from the high income restriction for investments after 15 October 2013.

Qualifying Companies

In order for the individual to obtain tax relief, the investment must be made in a qualifying company.

A qualifying company is one which:

- is a Micro, Small or Medium Sized Enterprise within the European Commission
- is incorporated in Ireland or another European Economic Area (EEA) State;
- is resident in Ireland or is resident in another EEA State and carries on business in the State through a branch or agency;
- is not regarded as a firm in difficulty for the purposes of the Community Guidelines on State Aid for rescuing and restructuring firms in difficulty;
- throughout the 3 year holding period:.
- carries on relevant trading activities from a fixed place of business in Ireland, or
- consists wholly of the holding of shares or securities of, or the making of loans to one or more qualifying subsidiaries of the company, or
- both the holding of such shares or securities, or the making of such loans and the carrying on of relevant trading activities from a fixed place of business Ireland.
- is an unquoted company
- has its issued share capital fully paid up.

A company will not cease to be regarded as a qualifying company if it is wound up or dissolved during the three year relevant period, provided it can be shown that the winding up or dissolution is for bona fide commercial reasons, and not part of a scheme or arrangement the main purpose of which (or one of the main purposes of which) is the avoidance of tax.

Qualifying Companies and Subsidiaries

A qualifying company can have subsidiaries provided generally that:

(a) the subsidiaries are at least 51% owned by the qualifying company; and

(b) the subsidiaries are themselves qualifying companies, or carry out certain services for, or functions on behalf of, the qualifying company or its subsidiaries.

The maximum investment by all investors in any one company or group of companies is €15,000,000 subject to a maximum of €5,000,000 in any one twelve month period.

Qualifying Trade

If the company is not trading at the time the shares are issued, relief cannot be claimed until the company commences trading. It must however commence trading within two years of the share issue, or spend at least 30% of the funds raised under the scheme on R&D activities which are connected with and undertaken with a view to carrying on relevant trading activities.

The following trading activities are not eligible for the EIIS:

- Adventures or concerns in the nature of trade
- Dealing in commodities or futures in shares/ securities
- Financing activities
- Professional service companies
- Dealing in or developing land
- Forestry
- Operations carried on in the coal industry or in the steel and shipbuilding
- Film production

Appendix III

Methodology for calculating tax deductible self-employed pension contribution

Income Tax Computation of Belinda age 40 for 2018

Schedule D	€
Case I	*95,000*
Less capital allowances	*(3,000)*
Less losses	*(4,500)*
Relevant earnings	*87,500*
Deduct pension contribution	*(21,375)*
	66,125
Case III	*8,000*
Gross Income	*74,125*
Less charges	*(10,000)*
TOTAL (NET STATUTORY) INCOME	*64,125*

Step 1

"Net relevant earnings" is calculated as "relevant earnings" less charges to the extent that they may not be relieved against other non-trading sources of income.

Non-trading income (Case III income) of €8,000 absorbs €8,000 of charges. Therefore, additional charges of €2,000 (€10,000 – €8,000) are offset against relevant earnings of €87,500, giving "net relevant earnings" of €85,500.

Step 2

Age 40, % applied is 25%

Step 3

She can subtract the lower of:

Amount paid

OR

% net relevant earnings

25% of €85,500 = €21,375

Appendix IV

List of Social-Welfare-Like Payments

- Department of Employment Affairs and Social Protection and FÁS
- Rural Social Scheme
- Farm/Fish Assist
- Community Employment Scheme
- Tús (community work placement initiative)
- Job Bridge (internship scheme)
- Job Initiative Scheme
- FÁS (non apprentice payments)
- Jobseeker's Allowance and Jobseeker's Benefit
- One-Parent Family Payment
- Widow(er)'s Pension
- Disability Allowance
- Adult Dependent of a recipient of the non-contributory State Pension
- Domiciliary Care Allowance
- Health Service Executive (HSE)
- Blind Welfare Supplementary Allowance
- Mobility Allowance
- Department of Education and Skills
- Vocational Training Opportunities Scheme (VTOS)
- Youthreach Training Allowances
- Senior Traveller Training Allowances
- Back to Education Initiative (BTEI) Training Allowances paid to Youthreach, STTC or VTOS eligible participants on a pro-rata basis.
- Vocational Education Committees' Scholarship Scheme

- Fund for Students with Disabilities
- Student Assistance Fund
- Millennium Partnership Fund for Disadvantage

Department of Agriculture, Food and the Marine

- Farm Retirement Pensions
- Farm Retirement Workers Pensions

Foreign Government

- Social welfare-type payments received from another country.

Appendix V

Legislative references for exemptions, deductions and credits (contained in TCA97).

Section	Title
42	Interest on savings certificates
188	Exemption from BIK - Travel Pass, new bicycle scheme, share options
189	Payments in respect of personal injuries
189A	Special trust for permanently incapacitated
190	Hemophilia Trust
191	Hepatitis C
192	Thalidomide
192A	Exemption in respect of certain payment under employment law
192B	Foster Care Payment
193	Income from Scholarships
194	Child benefit
194A	Early Childcare Supplement
195A	Exemption in respect of certain expense payments
196	Expenses of members of Judiciary
196A	State Employees: Foreign Service Allowance
196B	Employee of certain agencies: foreign service allowances
197	Bonus or interest paid under installment savings schemes
198	Certain interest not to be chargeable
199	Interest on certain securities
200	Certain foreign pensions
201	Exemptions and reliefs in respect of tax under section 123 (including SCSB)
202	Relief for agreed pay restructuring
203	Payments in respect of Redundancy
204	Military & other pensions, gratuities and allowances
205	Veterans of war of independence
216A	Rent a Room relief
216B	Scéim na bhFoghlaimeoiri Gaeilge
216C	Childcare service relief

Appendix VI

PRSI Rates 2018

Employee Class A1

	PRSI	
	Employer	**Employee**
	10.85%	4%

Self Employed

4% (minimum €500)

Notes:

(a) Employee

2018 No PRSI on income of €352 p.w. or less

No USC on income of less than €250.00 p.w.

(b) Employer (ER)

2018 ER PRSI is 8.60% on earnings of €376 p.w. or less

(c) Self Employed There is no liability to PRSI where reckonable income is below €5,000. This test is applied separately to the income of husband and wife and civil partners.

12 RELIEF FOR CHARGES AND INTEREST

Learning Outcomes

On completion of this chapter, you should be able to:

- ✓ Explain the meaning of the word "charge" and describe how tax relief is granted for charges.
- ✓ Discuss the criteria required to qualify for tax relief on borrowings to invest in a company or partnership.
- ✓ Describe the circumstances in which tax relief may be granted under the TRS system and identify interest payments outside the scope of TRS.

12.1 Introduction

The term "charges" is given primarily to annual sums which a person is under a legal obligation to pay and from which income tax is deductible at source. Examples of such charges are patent royalties and payments under Deeds of Covenant (considered at 12.2 below). Income tax at the standard rate is deducted from these payments and is remitted to the Revenue Commissioners.

The term "charges" is also applied to certain sums which a person is under a legal obligation to pay, but which may be paid gross, i.e., without the deduction of tax at source. This chapter considers the various charges, differentiating between those requiring payment to be made:

- under the deduction of income tax; and
- without the deduction of income tax.

The basic principle is that "charges on income" are deducted in arriving at the individual's total or statutory income. In the case of charges paid under deduction of tax, the payer of the charges is accountable for the tax deducted.

This chapter also considers the tax treatment of certain interest payments. Section 12.3.1 below deals with relief as a charge for interest paid on certain loans to invest in companies or partnerships. Such interest payments constitute sums that may be paid without deduction of tax. 12.3.2 below deals with "mortgage interest relief", i.e., relief for interest on borrowings to fund the borrower's principal private residence. This relief, previously granted as a tax credit, is now available at source as a reduction in the amount of the periodic mortgage repayment.

12.2 Deeds of Covenant and Patent Royalties

Payments in respect of Deeds of Covenant and patent royalties are made under deduction of tax at the standard rate.

12.2.1 Deeds of covenant

A Deed of Covenant is a legal instrument by which a person binds himself/herself (the covenantor) to make periodic payments of income to another person (the covenantee).

The advantage to be derived from such a deed is that it enables the covenantor to divest part of his/her statutory income by transferring it to the covenantee. Any amount may be paid under a Deed of Covenant; however, only covenants in favour of certain individuals qualify for tax relief.

The covenantor's total income is reduced by the gross amount that he/she covenants to pay. Tax relief is therefore obtained at the marginal rate. However, he/she must account for the tax which he is obliged to deduct at source. The covenantee is taxed under Schedule D Case IV at their higher rate (20% or 40%, depending on their total income) on income from covenants. The covenantee may obtain the benefit of personal reliefs and tax credits (to the extent that these are not covered by other income) against the income received under the covenant, and, depending upon the amount of the gross payment, may receive a repayment of the tax deducted at source.

Example 12.1

Edward Cox (covenantor) is single, age 55 and is self-employed. He pays €8,000 (gross) per year under Deed of Covenant to his aunt (covenantee) who is permanently incapacitated and is over 66 years. She has no other income.

Edward (Covenantor)'s income tax computation	**€**	**€**
Case II income		*120,000*
Less payment under Deed of Covenant		*(8,000)*
Taxable income		*112,000*
Taxed at:		
€34,550 × 20%	*6,910*	
€77,450 × 40%	*30,980*	
	37,890	
Less non-refundable credit		
Single credit	*(1,650)*	
	36,240	
Add tax due on Deed of Covenant		
€8,000 × 20%	*1,600*	
Tax liability	*37,840*	
PRSI		
120,000 × 4%		*4,800*

USC		
12,012 × 0.5%	*60.06*	
7,360 × 2%	*147.2*	
50,672 × 4.75%	*2406.92*	
29,956 × 8%	*2396.48*	
12,000 × 11%	*1320*	
112,000		*6331*

Edward's Aunt (Covenantee)'s income tax computation	**€**	**€**
(Assume single, incapacitated with no other income)		
Income under Deed of Covenant		*8,000*
Taxed as follows:		
€8,000 × 20%	*1,600*	
Less non-refundable credit:		
Single Person's Credit	*(1,650)*	
Tax liability	*Nil*	
*Less refundable credit:**		
Tax deducted on Deed of Covenant	*(1,600)*	
Tax overpaid	***(1,600)***	

The covenantee may claim a tax refund of €1,600.

Edward's Aunt Is not liable to PRSI since she is over 66 years and not liable to USC since her income is under €13,000.

** Ignoring age credit.*

12.2.2 Covenants qualifying for relief as a charge

Minor Children

s795(1) TCA97 Covenants in favour of the covenantor's own minor children are ineffective for tax purposes. A minor child for this purpose is an unmarried individual under 18 years. Section 795(1) TCA97 treats the income from the covenant as being that of the covenantor, i.e., the parent. However, unrestricted tax relief may be claimed on covenants in favour of permanently incapacitated minors, other than from parents to their own minor incapacitated children.

Adults

s792 TCA97 Section 792 TCA97 provides for tax relief as follows:

- unrestricted tax relief may be claimed on covenants in favour of permanently incapacitated adults;
- tax relief may be claimed on covenants in favour of adults aged 65 or over 65, but the relief is restricted to 5% of the covenantor's total income, i.e., gross income less certain deductions, such as expenses, capital allowances, etc.

All covenants must be capable of lasting more than six years. In practice, for a covenant to be tax effective it should be drawn up to cover a minimum period of seven years. Also, it should not contain a provision for revocation of the covenant within the seven-year period.

12.2.3 Patent royalties

The payment of royalties and other sums for the use of a patent are generally made under deduction of standard rate tax. The gross royalty is allowed as a deduction in arriving at the statutory income of the taxpayer, but the taxpayer is accountable for the tax deducted.

It should be noted that annuities, annual payments and patent royalties are not allowable deductions in arriving at the trade or professional profits under the rules of Cases I and II Schedule D (dealt with in Chapter 15), but are treated as charges to be deducted in arriving at statutory income. The tax treatment is similar to that of covenants.

Example 12.2

John Rogers is single. His only source of income is from a trade and amounts to €120,000. He paid patent royalties of €10,000 in 2018.

His tax, PRSI and USC calculations for 2018 are as follows:

	€	€	€
Case I income			*120,000*
Less patent royalty payment			*(10,000)*
Taxable income			*110,000*
Taxed as follows:			
€34,550 × 20%	*6,910*		
€75,450 × 40%	*30,180*		
		37,090	
Less non-refundable credits:			
Single Person's Credit		*(1,650)*	
		35,440	
Add tax due on patent royalty:			
€10,000 × 20%		*2,000*	
Tax liability			*37,440*
PRSI			
120,000 × 4%			*4,800*
USC			
12,012 × 0.5%	*60.06*		
7,360 × 2%	*147.2*		

50,672 × 4.75%	*2406.92*	
29,956 × 8%	*2,396.48*	
20,000 × 11%	*2,200*	
120,000		*7,210*

Note that the patent royalty payment is not deductible for USC purposes.

12.3 Interest

Tax relief is granted in different ways for different types of interest. Broadly speaking, the following interest payments will qualify for some form of income tax relief:

- Certain interest expenses will be deductible as trading or professional expenses in arriving at taxable Case I or Case II income (see Chapter 15).
- Interest incurred on loans used to purchase both residential and commercial rental properties will generally be available as a deduction in calculating taxable Case V income (see Chapter 19).
- Interest paid on money to invest in certain companies and partnerships is deductible as a charge. This issue is considered in detail at 12.3.1 below.
- Interest paid on money to fund the borrower's principal private residence is granted at the standard rate of tax either as a tax credit or under the "tax relief at source" system. This is considered in 12.3.2 below.

12.3.1 Interest on loans to acquire shares in a company or partnership

The following types of interest was eligible for relief as charges on income:

s248 TCA97
- Section 248 TCA97 provided for relief on interest incurred in years up to and including the 2013 tax year on loans taken out prior to 8 December 2010 to acquire shares in companies.

s253 TCA97
- Section 253 TCA97 provided for relief on interest incurred in years up to and including the 2016 tax year on loans taken out prior to 15 October 2013 to acquire a share in a partnership.

Payment of such interest was not subject to the deduction of tax at source.

Relief for individuals on interest on loans applied in acquiring interests in companies

s248 TCA97

Tax relief was granted as a charge to individuals for interest paid on loans taken out prior to 8 December 2010 to acquire ordinary shares in or to lend money to certain "qualifying companies". Interest relief was not given on loans to acquire shares in quoted companies. A quoted company is a company whose shares are listed on the Irish Stock Exchange or any other stock exchange, or are quoted on an unlisted securities market of any stock exchange.

s253 TCA97 Sec 11 FA 2011 abolished the relief for loans taken out after 7 December 2010. For qualifying loans taken out taken out prior to 8 December 2010, relief was phased out as follows:

Year %	allowed:
2011	75%
2012	50%
2013	25%
2014 & onwards	0%

Readers are referred to earlier editions of *Irish Taxation: Law and Practice* for analysis of the operation of the relief for prior years.

Relief to individuals on loans applied in acquiring an interest in a partnership

s253 TCA97 Tax relief was available to an individual who obtains a loan taken out prior to 15 October 2013 to purchase a share in a partnership or to advance money to a partnership. The money advanced had to be used wholly and exclusively for the purposes of the trade or profession carried on by the partnership. Any interest paid on the loan was available for relief if, throughout the period from the application of the proceeds of the loan until the interest was paid:

- the individual personally acted in the conduct of the trade or profession carried on by the partnership; and
- the individual did not recover any capital from the partnership.

If the individual recovered any amount of capital from the partnership without using that amount to pay off the loan, he/she was be treated as if he/she had repaid that amount out of the loan, and accordingly, the interest on the amount of capital so recovered no longer qualified for relief.

The individual was treated as having recovered an amount of capital from the partnership if:

- he/she received a consideration of that amount for the sale of any part of his/her interest in the partnership;
- the partnership returned any amount advanced by him/her; or
- he/she received a consideration of that amount for assigning any debt due to him/her from the partnership.

Section 3 F(No. 2)A 2013 abolished the relief for loans taken out on or after 15 October 2013. For qualifying loans taken out prior to 15 October 2013 (or loans taken out after 15 October 2013 to replace qualifying loans taken out prior to that date), relief was phased out as follows:

Year %	allowed:
2014	75%
2015	50%
2016	25%
2017 & onwards	0%

12.3.2 Home loan interest relief

s244 TCA97

Relief is available in respect of interest paid on a "qualifying loan". The interest eligible for relief on a "qualifying loan" is confined to:

- yearly interest charged to tax under Schedule D; or
- interest (whether short or annual) paid to banks, building societies, stockbrokers or discount houses,
- in respect of a loan taken out for the purchase, repair, development or improvement of a residential premises situated in the State, Northern Ireland or Great Britain which is the sole or main residence of:
  - the claimant,
  - a former or separated spouse/civil partner,
  - a dependent relative.

A borrower may take out a mortgage (i.e. a loan secured on a property) or an unsecured loan to fund a property purchase. The conditions for entitlement to tax relief on the interest are the same for both "mortgage interest" and "loan interest". However the method of granting the tax relief is different:

Mortgage interest: tax relief is granted at source and is known as "TRS". It takes the form of reduced mortgage repayments to the loan provider. TRS is discussed below.

Loan interest: tax relief is granted in the traditional way i.e. by applying for the tax relief directly to Revenue.

Hereafter for ease of illustration, references to interest allowable under s244 TCA97 will only be referred to as "mortgage interest".

Mortgage interest restrictions

Relief is subject to an upper limit based on whether the claimant is single or married/civil partner or widowed/surviving civil partner. The maximum relief allowable is higher in the case of first-time buyers, i.e. those in their first seven years of entitlement to mortgage interest relief.

For 2018, qualifying interest is restricted to €2,250 for a single person and €4,500 in the case of a married person/civil partner and widowed person/surviving civil partner.

For "first time buyers", the aforementioned limits are increased to €7,500 and €15,000 respectively.

For some years up to and including 2008, mortgage interest relief was granted at a rate of 20% regardless of whether the borrower was a first-time buyer or not. The only difference for a first-time buyer was the increased annual limits. Each year since 2008 there have been changes to the amount of interest which qualifies for relief with proposals to phase out the relief. In general interest paid on qualifying home loans taken out between 1 January 2004 and 31 December 2012* will (subject to aforementioned restrictions) qualify for relief up to 31 December 2020. The tables below best illustrate the position for 2018. Readers are referred to earlier editions of this publication for an analysis of the operation of the relief for prior years.

Section 7 FA 2014 provided that the premises may be located in an EEA state.

First Time Buyers – Maximum interest allowable

Tax Year 1st PPR purchased	Max Allowable Interest M/S €	2017 % Allowable	Max Allowable Interest 2018 €	2018 % Allowable
2012	20K/10K	20%	15,000/7,500	20%
2011	20K/10K	20%	4,500/2,250	15%
2010	20K/10K	15%	4,500/2,250	15%
2009	20K/10K	15%	4,500/2,250	15%
2008	20K/10K	30%	4,500/2,250	30%
2007	6K/3K	30%	4,500/2,250	30%
2006	6K/3K	30%	4,500/2,250	30%
2005	6K/3K	30%	4,500/2,250	30%
2004	6K/3K	30%	4,500/2,250	30%

Non - First Time Buyers – Maximum interest allowable

Tax Year 1st PPR purchased	Max Allowable Interest M/S €	2017 % Allowable	Max Allowable Interest M/S €	2018 % Allowable
2012	6K/3K	15%	4,500/2,250	15%
2011	6K/3K	15%	4,500/2,250	15%
2010	6K/3K	15%	4,500/2,250	15%
2009	6K/3K	15%	4,500/2,250	15%
2008	6K/3K	15%	4,500/2,250	15%
2007	6K/3K	15%	4,500/2,250	15%
2006	6K/3K	15%	4,500/2,250	15%
2005	6K/3K	15%	4,500/2,250	15%
2004	6K/3K	15%	4,500/2,250	15%

*FA 2013 introduced transitional arrangements for loans taken out in 2013 where:

i. Interest is paid on a loan taken out in 2013 to construct a home on a site, where that site was bought by way of a loan taken out in 2012, or

ii. Interest is paid on a loan to repair, develop or improve a home where loan approval was in place in 2012 and part of the loan was used in 2012 and the balance used in 2013 on such repair, development or improvement.

Tax relief at source (TRS)

Mortgage interest relief is not given through the tax system but is, instead, granted "at source". As a result, the tax relief is given when the borrower makes a mortgage payment to the mortgage lender. The qualifying interest element of the repayment is reduced by a percentage depending on whether the tax payer is a first time buyer or not and depending on the year the mortgage was taken out (see table below) (thereby giving the tax relief to the borrower) while the mortgage lender will be repaid an equivalent amount by the Revenue Commissioners.

Tax relief at source (TRS) arrangements do not change the basic qualifying conditions for mortgage interest relief. The same upper limits to the relief (which depend on the marital status of the claimant and on whether or not the claimant is a first-time buyer) apply under TRS. However, under the TRS scheme, the residence must be situated in the State. Relief for qualifying interest on a sole or main residence in Northern Ireland or Great Britain continues to be given, but outside of TRS.

Example 12.3

Mary Costello, who is single, bought her first home in Dublin in 2012. Her mortgage provider, Ace Mortgages Ltd., calculates that her monthly gross repayments for 2018 will be €900, of which €850 represents interest. Her estimated interest for 2018 is €850 × 12, i.e., €10,200.

This is the sixth year of Mary's mortgage. As a single first-time buyer, Mary Costello may claim maximum interest relief of €1,500 in 2018 (20% × €7,500). Relief under TRS will be granted as follows:

	€
Gross repayment per month	*900*
Less TRS (€1,500/ 12 months)	*(125)*
Net repayment to Ace Mortgages Ltd.	*775*

The Revenue Commissioners will refund Ace Mortgages Ltd. the TRS amount of €125.

All banks and building societies operating in the State, as well as local authorities, are within the TRS system, as are mortgage lenders in other EU Member States which lend on the security of properties based in the State.

The net effect of the TRS scheme means that the tax relief is granted in an efficient manner. The borrower obtains the tax relief in the form of reduced mortgage repayments when the repayments are made. It is not necessary to claim the relief on an annual tax return. Adjustments to the tax relief (for example, as a result of changes in interest rates) are made automatically by the mortgage lender. The TRS system results in an extension of the relief to persons who have qualifying loans but would not otherwise get any relief because their taxable income is insufficient to avail of the tax relief. Under the TRS arrangements, a person who pays no tax is entitled to the same reduced interest payments as someone who has a liability to income tax.

13 TAXATION OF MARRIED COUPLES

Learning Outcomes

On completion of this chapter, you should be able to:

- ✓ Describe the different assessment options available to married couples.
- ✓ Calculate the tax relief available to couples in the year of marriage.
- ✓ Discuss the tax impact which the death of a spouse has on the surviving spouse.
- ✓ Explain how a separated couple might qualify for joint assessment.
- ✓ Describe how divorced couples are taxed and what options for assessment are available to them.

13.1 Introduction

The purpose of this chapter is to explain the basis of assessment for married couples. and couples of a civil partnership. Following the passing of the Civil Partnership and Certain Rights and Obligations of Cohabitants Act 2010, tax legislation had to be introduced to reflect the tax status of couples who entered into a Civil Partnership. This legislation is contained in Finance (No. 3) Act 2011. Generally speaking civil partners are treated the same as married couples and cohabitants are treated as single persons. For ease of reading, (for this chapter only) references to "married couples" include parties to a Civil Partnership, "widows/widowers/widowed" include surviving civil partners and "separated/divorced" include civil partners who have separated or have had their Civil Partnership dissolved.

Complexities arise where couples separate or divorce, or where one spouse dies. Often, one party is left with custody of dependent children. This chapter addresses the tax treatment of these categories of "spouses". The specific areas covered in this analysis are therefore as follows:

- methods of assessment
- year of marriage
- year of death separated/divorced spouses
- year of separation.

For ease of illustration, all examples in this chapter ignore for income levy, PRSI and the USC.

13.2 Basis of Assessment

It is important to be aware that for a couple to be taxed as a married couple, it is not sufficient to be just legally married. Irish tax law states that the couple must be "living together as man and wife". Therefore, a married couple who by choice decide to live apart may not be taxed as a married couple.

Married couples have three options as to how they wish to be assessed to income tax:

(i) Joint assessment

(ii) Separate assessment

(iii) Single assessment.

13.2.1 Joint assessment

s1017, s1018 TCA97

Under s1017 TCA97, a husband and wife may be assessed to income tax on the combined incomes of both. Technically, an election for such treatment is required. However, the Revenue Commissioners will deem an election to have been made for joint assessment where there is no specific evidence to support the election.

Married couples who are assessed to tax on the basis of joint assessment may elect to have either spouse regarded as the assessable spouse. This election must be made to the Inspector of Taxes in writing before 1 April in the tax year in question. The assessable spouse assumes responsibility for the joint tax liability of both spouses. The assessable spouse:

- is assessed on the combined total income;
- receives the combined tax credits; and
- files a joint tax return, which includes full details of the couple's joint income.

The assessable spouse is deemed to be the spouse with the greater total income.

Under joint assessment, a married couple is entitled to:

- a personal tax credit which is double the Single Person's Tax Credit;
- the Home Carer's Tax Credit (subject to certain conditions);
- double the maximum mortgage interest relief available to a single person; and
- an increased standard rate band.

With the introduction of "individualisation", the standard rate band has been restricted somewhat in recent years in the case of married couples. As previously discussed in 11.6, the standard rate band available to married couples is now as follows:

- where only one spouse has income in his/her own right, the standard rate band is €43,550;

- where each spouse has income in his/her own right, the maximum standard rate band is €69,100 (i.e., €43,550 + €25,550). The increase above the standard rate band of €43,550 is the lower of:

  (a) €25,550; or

  (b) the specified income of the lower-earning spouse.

The increased standard rate band is available as an alternative to the Home Carer's Tax Credit (see 11.2.7). A married couple may claim whichever of the two is more beneficial to them. The specific circumstances of each couple must be considered independently in determining this.

Example 13.1

Option 1 – not claiming Home Carer Tax Credit

		€	€
Income – husband			*90,000*
Income – wife			*3,000*
			93,000
Taxed as follows:			
€46,550 at 20%		*9,310*	
€46,450 at 40%		*18,580*	
			27,890
Less non-refundable tax credits:			
Married Person's Credit		*(3,300)*	
PAYE Credits – husband		*(1,650)*	
– wife	*(Note 1)*	*(600)*	
			(5,550)
Tax liability			***22,340***

Note 1: The PAYE Credit cannot exceed the amount of PAYE income taxed at the standard rate – in this instance, €3,000 @ 20%, i.e., €600.

Option 2 – claiming Home Carer Tax Credit

	€	€
Income – husband		*90,000*
Income – wife		*3,000*
		93,000
Taxed as follows:		
€43,550 at 20%	*8,710*	
€49,450 at 40%	*19,780*	
		28,490
Less non-refundable tax credits:		
Married Persons' Credit	*(3,300)*	

PAYE Credits (€1,650 + €600)	*(2,250)*	
Home Carer's Credit	*(1,200)*	
		(6,750)
Tax liability		***21,740***

Difference is (€22,340 – €21,740), i.e., €600.

Therefore, Option 2, i.e., availing of the Home Carer's Tax Credit, is more beneficial in this case.

13.2.2 Separate assessment

Separate assessment is available to couples who have opted or who are deemed to have opted for joint assessment. Under separate assessment, income tax is assessed, charged and recovered separately from each spouse.

Where either a husband or wife elects for separate assessment, they can retain the tax saving, if any, of joint assessment and at the same time have their income tax assessments and returns of income dealt with separately. The personal credits and reliefs available to both husband and wife are the same as in the case of joint assessment and the total tax payable cannot be greater than the amount payable if an application for separate assessment had not been made.

s1023 TCA97 An election for separate assessment must be made not later than 1 April in the tax year in question. An election applies for the year of claim and subsequent years and may be withdrawn only by the spouse who made the application.

Where separate assessment for income tax is claimed, the personal tax credit, Incapacitated Child Tax Credit (where applicable), Age Tax Credit and Blind Person's Tax Credit are divided equally between the spouses. Other tax credits and reliefs are generally granted to the spouse who actually bears the cost. Any unused balances of tax credits and reliefs of one spouse are set against the income of the other. Also, any unused standard rate band of one spouse may be transferred to the other.

Readers are referred to Example 13.2 below, which illustrates that the combined liability under separate assessment is the same as the joint assessment liability.

13.2.3 Single assessment

s1016, s1018 TCA97 Single assessment is also known as separate treatment. This form of assessment treats each spouse as a single person, i.e., as if they had not married. In view of the fact that it is normally beneficial for married couples to be jointly assessed for income tax, s1018 TCA97 deems an election to have been made for joint assessment. For single assessment to apply, either spouse must, before the end of the tax year, give notice in writing to the Inspector of Taxes that they wish to be assessed as single persons. Where such a notice is given to the Inspector of Taxes, both spouses are assessed as single persons until such time as the election is withdrawn by the spouse who made it.

Since both spouses are effectively treated as single persons, there are no provisions whereby one spouse may transfer any balance of unused standard band or tax credits to the other spouse. The benefit of any unused tax credits is therefore lost and for this reason, single assessment is generally less advantageous than joint assessment or separate assessment.

Example 13.2

A married man has a salary of €90,000 and his wife has a salary of €6,000. They have no children. If an election for single assessment was sought under s1016 TCA97, their income tax liabilities for the tax year 2018 would be as follows:

Single Assessment

Husband			***Wife***		
	€	**€**		**€**	**€**
Income		*90,000*	*Income*		*6,000*
Taxed as follows:			*Taxed as follows:*		
€34,550 @ 20%	*6,910*		*€6,000 @ 20%*	*1,200*	
€55,450 @ 40%	*22,180*				
		29,090			*1,200*
Less non-refundable credits:			*Less non-refundable credits:*		
Single Person's Credit	*(1,650)*		*Single Person's Credit*	*(1,650)*	
PAYE Credit	*(1,650)*		*PAYE Credit*	*(1,200)*	*(Note 1)*
		(3,300)			*(2,850)*
Tax liability		***25,790***	*Tax liability*		***Nil***

Note 1: The PAYE credit is limited to the PAYE income @ 20%.

Contrast the above with the following where, using the same facts, the married couple did not elect to be singly assessed:

Joint Assessment

	€	**€**
Income – husband		*90,000*
Income – wife		*6,000*
		96,000
	€	**€**
Taxed as follows:		
€49,550 @ 20%	*9,910*	
€46,450 @ 40%	*18,580*	
		28,490
Less non-refundable credits:		
Married Person's Credit	*(3,300)*	
PAYE Credits	*(2,850)*	
		(6,150)
Tax liability		***22,340***

The difference between the two calculations is €3,450, which may be explained as follows:

	€
■ *Wife has unabsorbed tax credits of (€2,850 – €1,200)*	*1,650*
■ *The standard rate band for a married couple is €43,550 + value of other spouse's income (subject to max. €25,550). Under joint assessment, the Husband has therefore decreased his 40% rate band by €9,000 @ 20% [(40–20)%]*	*1,800*
Total tax saving	***3,450***

Separate Assessment

Husband			***Wife***		
	€	**€**		**€**	**€**
Income		*90,000*	*Income*		*6,000*
Taxed as follows:			*Taxed as follows:*		
€34,550 @ 20%	*6,910*		*€6,000 @ 20%*	*1,200*	
€9,000 @ 20%*	*1,800*				
€46,450 @ 40%	*18,580*				
		27,290			*1,200*
Less non-refundable credits:			*Less non-refundable credits:*		
Single Person's Credit	*(1,650)*		*Single Person's Credit*	*(1,650)*	
PAYE Credit	*(1,650)*		*PAYE Credit*	*(1,200)*	
Surplus credits of spouse	*(1,650)*				
		(4,950)			*(2,850)*
Tax liability		***22,340***	*Tax liability*		***Nil***

** Surplus 20% band of spouse: €43,550*

Readers will observe from the above workings that the combined liability under separate assessment (€22,340 + Nil) is the same as for joint assessment (€22,340).

13.2.4 Year of marriage

s1020 TCA97

Married couples are taxed as single persons in the year of assessment in which the marriage takes place. If the total of the tax payable as single persons exceeds the amount which would have been payable if they were married and jointly assessed for the whole year, they are entitled, on making a joint claim, to additional tax relief. The relief is calculated by the formula:

$$\frac{A \times B}{12}$$

where:

A = the additional tax payable when comparing the combined single person's assessments with the joint assessment for the year in which the marriage takes place, and

B = the number of income tax months from the date of marriage to the end of the tax year (part of a month being treated as a month).

A claim for relief must be made jointly and in writing after the end of the tax year in which the marriage took place.

Example 13.3

Assume date of marriage is 1 October 2018.

	Husband	*Wife*	*Total*
	€	€	€
Tax payable under single basis	*10,000*	*1,000*	*11,000*
Tax payable under joint basis			*(9,900)*
Excess tax liability			*1,100*

Therefore, the year of marriage relief is calculated as follows:

$$€1{,}100 \times \frac{3}{12} = €275$$

The tax liability of €11,000 is therefore reduced by €275 to €10,725.

13.3 Year of Death

Where a party to a marriage dies, the taxation treatment of his/her income for that year depends on the method of tax assessment in force and also on which party to the marriage dies.

s1018 TCA97 If a married couple is taxed under the single assessment provisions, the death of one spouse does not affect the taxation of the other spouse in that year. The surviving spouse continues to be taxed as a single person on his/her own income. However, the surviving spouse may elect under s1018 TCA97 before the end of that tax year for joint assessment for the year of death.

Where a couple is jointly assessed, the tax treatment in the year of death will vary depending on whether or not the deceased spouse was the assessable party. The position where the assessable spouse dies is considered at 13.3.1 below, while 13.3.2 below deals with the provisions that apply on the death of a non-assessable spouse.

Death results in a cessation for tax purposes of all the sources of income of the deceased spouse, and assessments are made for the period to the date of death. Earlier years may be revised according to the cessation rules of each Case and Schedule (readers are referred to Chapter 14 for commentary on the cessation rules that apply to Case I/Case II).

Where there is a cessation of the assessable spouse's sources of income on his/her death. If the deceased spouse possessed a source of income which was assessable under Schedule D Case I/II, and the source of income passes in its entirety to the surviving spouse, the Revenue Commissioners will as a concession, allow the income source to be treated as a continuing source, provided the surviving spouse did not previously possess any such sources of income and provided it is more beneficial to the couple.

Example 13.4

John Joe and Mary Farrelly are jointly assessed. They have no children. John Joe dies on 1 July 2018. He was self-employed as a shop-owner and prepared accounts to 30 September. Mary opts to continue with the trade. The couple's income for the year of death and the preceding year is as follows:

2018		**€**	
John Joe:	*Case I*	*90,000*	*(based on accounts to year ended 30/09/2018)*
Mary:	*Salary*	*60,000*	
	UK dividends	*1,000*	
2017			
John Joe:	*Case I*	*78,000*	*(based on accounts to year ended 30/09/2017)*
Mary:	*Salary*	*20,500*	
	UK dividends	*600*	

The income tax liabilities for 2018, assuming the concessional basis is applied, are as follows:

Period 1 January 2018 to 1 July 2018:

Assessment for John Joe

	€	**€**	**€**
Case I (Note 1) – Self			*45,000*
Salary – Spouse			*30,000*
UK dividends – Spouse			*500*
			75,500
Taxed as follows:			
€69,100 @ 20%		*13,820*	
€6,400 @ 40%		*2,560*	
		16,380	
Less tax credits:			
Personal tax credit	*(3,300)*		
Earned Income credit	*(1,150)*		
PAYE Tax Credit	*(1,650)*		
		(6,100)	
Tax due		*10,280*	

Period 1 July 2018 to 31 December 2018:

Assessment for Mary

	€	**€**	**€**
Case I (Note 1)			*45,000*
Salary			*30,000*
UK dividends			*500*
			75,500

Taxed as follows:		
€34,550 @ 20% (Note 2)		*6,910*
€40,950 @ 40%		*16,380*
		23,290
Less: tax credits:		
Personal tax credit	*(3,300)*	
PAYE Tax Credit	*(1,650)* **(Note 3)**	
		(4,950)
Tax due		*18,340*

Note 1: Since the Case I income is to be treated as a continuing source, John Joe is assessable on six months of the income of the accounting period which forms the basis period for 2018, i.e., year ended 30 September 2018. The remaining six months are assessed on Mary.

Had the cessation of trade provisions been applied, the Case I assessable figure for 2017 would have been increased by €3,000 (€81,000 – €78,000) on revision to actual basis for the year. This would have resulted in an additional liability of €1,230. Readers are again referred to Chapter 14 for relevant commentary on the cessation provisions.*
** Calculated as (€90,000 * 3/12) + €78,000 * 9/12).*

Note 2: Since the couple has no dependent children, the standard rate band is €34,550. If John Joe and Mary had dependent children, the standard rate band of €38,550 would apply.

Note 3: Mary is entitled to the full year's PAYE Tax Credit post-death.

13.3.1 Death of an assessable spouse

On the death of an assessable spouse:

- An assessment is made on the income of both spouses from the beginning of the relevant tax year to the date of death with the full Married Person's Tax Credits and rate bands applying.
- The surviving non-assessable spouse is assessed on his/her income from the date of death to the end of the year of assessment and is granted the full Married Person's Tax Credits but the single standard rate band.

Example 13.5

John and Martina, a married couple, are taxed under joint assessment. John, the assessable spouse, dies on 1 October 2018. The following is the couple's income for 2018:

		€
John (from 01/01/2018 to 01/10/2018):		
	Salary	*155,000*
	UK interest	*4,000*
	Irish dividends (gross)	*1,000*
Martina (for full year)		
	Salary	*120,000*
	UK dividends	*6,000*

The calculation of the tax liability is therefore as follows (ignoring PRSI, USC and tax deducted at source):

Joint Assessment

John	€	€
Salary – self		*155,000*
UK interest – self		*4,000*
Irish dividends – self		*1,000*
Salary – spouse		*90,000*
UK dividends – spouse		*4,500*
		254,500
Taxed as follows:		
€69,100 × 20%	*13,820*	
€185,400 × 40%	*74,160*	
		87,980
Less non-refundable credits:		
Married Person's Credit	*(3,300)*	
PAYE Credit	*(3,300)*	
		(6,600)
Tax liability (before deduction of refundable tax credits)		***81,380***
Martina		
Salary (¼)		*30,000*
UK dividends (¼)		*1,500*
		31,500
Taxed as follows:		
€31,500 × 20%		*6,300*
Less non-refundable credits:		
Married Person's Credit	*(3,300)*	
PAYE Credit	*(1,650)*	
		(4,950)
Tax liability		***1,350***

*The combined liability for 2018 is **€82,730**.*

13.3.2 Death of a non-assessable spouse

On the death of a non-assessable spouse:

- The surviving spouse is assessed for the full tax year on his/her own income for the full year and on the non-assessable spouse's income for the period to the date of death.
- The assessable spouse is granted the Married Person's Tax Credit and standard rate band.

Example 13.6

Assume the same facts as in Example 13.5 except that Martina was the assessable spouse prior to John's death.

The calculations of the tax liabilities are therefore as follows (again ignoring PRSI, USC, and tax deducted at source):

Joint Assessment

Martina		**€**
Salary – spouse		*155,000*
UK interest – spouse		*4,000*
Irish dividends – spouse		*1,000*
Salary – self		*120,000*
UK dividends – self		*6,000*
		286,000
Taxed as follows:		
€69,100 × 20%	*13,820*	
€216,900 × 40%	*88,760*	
		100,580
Less non-refundable credits:		
Married Person's Credit	*(3,300)*	
PAYE Credits	*(3,300)*	
		(6,600)
Tax liability		***93,980***

Example 13.6 shows an uplift in the tax liability of €11,250 (i.e., €93,980 – €82,730), notwithstanding that the same level of income has been assessed in both examples.

13.4 Effects of Separation and Divorce

The provisions relating to the taxation of married couples apply to a situation where a husband and wife are "living together". A husband and wife are treated, for income tax purposes, as living together unless:

- they are separated or divorced; or
- they are separated in such circumstances that the separation is likely to be permanent.

Tax is not deducted at source from maintenance payments following a separation or divorce.

13.4.1 Separation - maintenance payments

A separation is treated as "likely to be permanent" where the husband and wife are living apart by mutual consent or by force of circumstances, and their separation has continued for a considerable period of time – usually taken as a minimum of one year. If a husband and wife are not treated as living together, then they are treated as separated spouses and are taxed as single persons. However, there are options that they may consider as to how they wish to be assessed for tax purposes.

Maintenance payments from one spouse to the other where the payments are made under maintenance arrangements drawn up on or after 8 June 1983 (which are legally enforceable) may be treated as:

Income of the payee

s1025 TCA97 Such payments are allowed as a deduction from the income of the payer for tax purposes and chargeable to income tax under Case IV of Schedule D in the hands of the recipient. In these circumstances, both parties are taxed as single individuals.

Income of the payer

s1026 TCA97 An election may be made to be jointly assessed. In such instances the maintenance payments are regarded as income of the payer and are therefore ignored for tax purposes. The couple is effectively taxed as if the separation had not taken place.

Example 13.7

Chris and Carla separated in 2005. During the year of assessment 2018, Chris earned €90,000 from his employment. He paid €15,000 in maintenance payments to Carla (now his ex-wife) who has no other source of income. The calculation below determines which of the two taxation options is more beneficial:

Option (a)

Single Assessment – Chris			***Single Assessment – Carla***		
	€	€		€	€
Income – Chris		*90,000*	*Income – Carla*		*15,000*
Income – ex-wife		*–*			
		90,000			
Less maintenance payment		*(15,000)*			
		75,000			
Taxed as follows:			*Taxed as follows:*		
€34,550 @ 20%	*6,910*		*€15,000 @ 20%*		*3,000*
€40,450 @ 40%	*16,180*				
		23,090			
Less non-refundable credits:			*Less non-refundable credits:*		
Single Person's Credit	*(1,650)*		*Single Person's Credit*	*(1,650)*	
PAYE Credit	*(1,650)*	*(3,300)*	*PAYE Credit*	*–*	*(1,650)*
Tax liability		*19,790*	*Tax liability*		*1,350*
Combined liability:	***21,140***				

Option (b)

Joint Assessment		
	€	€
Income – Chris		*90,000*
Income – Carla		*–*
		90,000
Taxed as follows:		
€43,550 @ 20%	*8,710*	
€46,450 @ 40%	*18,580*	
		27,290

Less non-refundable credits:		
Married Person's Credit	*(3,300)*	
PAYE Credit	*(1,650)*	
		(4,950)
Tax liability		*22,340*
Difference		***1,200***

Based on the figures above is more beneficial to opt for single assessment with Chris claiming a deduction for the maintenance payments.

If an individual wholly or mainly maintains a former spouse, but does not qualify for a tax deduction for the maintenance (e.g., not paid pursuant to a legal agreement), the Married Person's Tax Credit may still be claimed but without the additional standard rate band.

Maintenance payments for the benefit of children

Maintenance payments for the benefit of children of the marriage are always ignored.

13.4.2 Year of separation

In Example 13.7 above, we observed that where a taxpayer claims a deduction for maintenance payments, the Married Person's Tax Credit is unavailable. However, in the year of separation, an individual who had been entitled to the Married Person's Credit is entitled to claim a deduction for legally enforceable maintenance payments in addition to the Married Person's Tax Credit. This is because the entitlement to the Married Person's Credit preceded the maintenance payments.

The provisions relating to the taxation of separated spouses come into immediate effect on the date of separation. Except in the case of an election for joint assessment under s1026 TCA97, each spouse is taxed as a single person from the date of separation. Where a couple was jointly assessed prior to the date of separation, special rules apply for the year of separation. The rules are somewhat similar to those applying for the year of death (see 13.3 above), except that there is no cessation of any sources of income merely by virtue of the separation.

An assessment is made on the assessable spouse for the full year to include the income of both spouses to the date of separation and his/her own income for the period from the date of separation to the following 31 December. Since the assessable spouse is assessable on the income of the other spouse for part of the year, he/she is granted the Married Person's Tax Credit and the married person's standard rate tax band for the full year.

The other spouse is assessed as a single person on his/her income from the date of separation to the following 31 December. The Single Person's Tax Credit and the single rate band are granted against the income for that period.

Example 13.8

Michael and Margaret Brennan are formally separated by a Deed of Separation dated 1 October 2018. They have no children. They were jointly assessed for all years prior to separation. They had the following income in 2018:

	€
Michael	
Salary	*55,000*
UK interest	*4,000*
Irish dividends (gross)	*1,000*
Margaret:	
Salary	*45,000*
UK dividends	*6,000*

The income tax liabilities for 2018 are as follows (ignoring PRSI, USC and tax deductions at source):

Joint Assessment

Michael (full year)		
	€	**€**
Salary – self		*55,000*
UK interest – self		*4,000*
Irish-taxed dividends – self		*1,000*
Salary – spouse (¾)		*33,750*
UK dividends – spouse (¾)		*4,500*
		98,250
Taxed as follows:		
€69,100 @ 20%	*13,820*	
€29,150 @ 40%	*11,660*	
		25,480
Less non-refundable credits:		
Married Person's Credit	*(3,300)*	
PAYE Credit	*(3,300)*	
		(6,600)
Tax liability		***18,880***
Margaret (from 1/10/2018 to 31/12/2018)		
Salary (¼)		*11,250*
UK dividends (¼)		*1,500*
		12,750
Taxed as follows:		
€12,750 @ 20%		*2,550*
Less non-refundable credits:		
Single Person's Credit	*(1,650)*	
PAYE Credit	*(1,650)*	
		(3,300)
Tax liability		***Nil***

13.4.3 Divorce

The Fifteenth Amendment to the Irish Constitution repealed the constitutional ban on divorce, enabling the Oireachtas to legislate so as to give individuals whose marriage had irretrievably broken down the right to divorce and remarry. The Family Law (Divorce) Act 1996 provides the necessary statutory framework to give effect to the constitutional amendment. The Act makes a number of specific provisions in relation to taxation.

s1026 TCA97 The joint assessment provisions (under s1026 TCA97) are extended to couples whose marriage has been dissolved under either s5 of the Family Law (Divorce) Act 1996 or under the law of another country, recognised as valid in Ireland. Both spouses must be resident in the State and not have remarried.

If the election for assessment is made under s1026, the couple is assessed to income tax without regard to maintenance payments and is granted the Married Person's Tax Credit. If the spouses each have income in their own right, apart from the maintenance payments, the income tax applicable to their respective incomes is calculated by the separate assessment procedure but treats the payer's income as undiminished by the maintenance payments (i.e., maintenance payments are ignored). These provisions apply to payments made under maintenance arrangements made after 7 June 1983. In the case of maintenance arrangements made before that date, these provisions will not apply unless:

- the maintenance is varied or a new arrangement is entered into; or
- both parties jointly elect in writing.

14 INCOME FROM TRADES AND PROFESSIONS

Learning Outcomes

On completion of this chapter you will be able to:

- ✓ Describe the six 'Badges of Trade' and discuss the associated case law.
- ✓ Explain the basis of assessment for Case I/II in an ongoing business.
- ✓ Calculate assessable Case I/II for the first three years after commencement.
- ✓ Calculate assessable Case I/II for the final year of cessation and for the penultimate year.
- ✓ Calculate assessable Case I/II where a business changes its accounting date.
- ✓ Describe the advantages/disadvantages of a sole trader versus incorporation.

14.1 Introduction

Income from a trade is assessed to tax under Schedule D Case I. Examples of traders include electrical contractors, plumbers, carpenters, etc.

Income from a profession is assessed to tax under Schedule D Case II. Examples of professionals include tax consultants, accountants, solicitors, etc.

The rules for determining taxable income for Cases I and II are identical and are considered in detail in Chapter 15. This chapter is concerned with identifying those activities that constitute trading. It also deals with the basis of assessment rules for Case I and Case II.

14.2 Trade

Tax is charged under Schedule D Cases I and II on "the full amount of the profits or gains" of trades and professions respectively. Section 3 TCA97 defines trade as follows:

> *"'trade' includes every trade, manufacture, adventure or concern in the nature of trade."*

This definition does not provide much assistance in deciding whether or not a particular activity constitutes a trade. It is important to determine if a particular activity constitutes a trade because, if a trade does not exist, the profit from that activity may not be within the charge to income tax, but instead could be within the charge to capital gains tax.

In deciding if an activity constitutes a trade, we are guided by:

- a large body of case law on this subject
- the Badges of Trade, set down by a Royal Commission (UK) established in 1954.

It is sometimes difficult to decide whether a particular activity constitutes trading (and is therefore liable to income tax) or constitutes a transaction liable to capital gains tax. Given the fact that trading income is liable to income tax at marginal rates as high as 60% (including PRSI, USC and additional 5% USC if claiming certain "property" reliefs), while capital gains tax is payable at 33%, the distinction is very important. In addition, there are certain exemptions available under the capital gains tax legislation, which have no parallel in the income tax code. For example, gains on disposals of wasting assets, i.e., assets with an expected life of less than 50 years are exempt from capital gains tax but would be subject to income tax where they accrue to an individual who trades in such assets.

In 1954, a Royal Commission was set up in the UK to consider the practical factors that should be taken into account in deciding whether trading is being carried on. The factors recommended by the Royal Commission to be taken into account are commonly known as the "Badges of Trade".

They are stated in the report of the Royal Commission as follows:

1. The subject matter

While almost any form of property can be acquired to be dealt in, those forms of property such as commodities or manufactured articles, which are normally the subject of trading, are only very exceptionally the subject of investment.

Again, property that does not yield to its owner an income or personal enjoyment merely by virtue of its ownership is more likely to have been acquired with the object of a deal than property that does.

2. The length of period of ownership

Generally speaking, property meant to be dealt in is realised within a short time after acquisition. But there are many exceptions to this as a universal rule.[1]

3. The frequency or number of transactions by the same person

If realisations of the same sort of property occur in succession over a period of years, or there are several such realisations at about the same date, a presumption arises that there has been dealing in respect of each.

1 For example, a distillery that distils whiskey may require a number of years of ownership before the product is sold.

4. Supplementary work on, or in connection with, the property realised

If the property is worked on in any way during the ownership so as to bring it into a more marketable condition, or if any special exertions are made to find or attract purchasers, such as the opening of an office or large-scale advertising, there is some evidence of dealing. For when there is an organised effort to obtain profit, there is a source of taxable income. But if nothing at all is done, the suggestion tends the other way.

5. Circumstances of sale

There may be some explanation (such as a sudden emergency or opportunity calling for ready money) that negates the idea that any plan of dealing prompted the original purchase.

6. Motive

There are cases in which the purpose of the transaction or the sale is clearly discernible. Motive is never irrelevant in any of these cases. What is desirable is that it should be clearly realised that the purpose of the transaction could be inferred from surrounding circumstances in the absence of the seller's intentions and even, if necessary, in the face of his/her own evidence.

A number of the important tax cases on this question are now considered.

In *Erichsen v Last* 4 TC 422, Lord Justice Cotton gave the following definition of trading:

> *"... where a person habitually does and contracts to do a thing capable of producing a profit, and for the purpose of producing a profit, he carries on a trade or business".*

In the case of *Martin v Lowry* 11 TC 297, an agricultural machinery merchant who had never had any connection with the linen trade, purchased from the UK government the whole of its surplus stock of aeroplane linen (44 million yards worth!).

Failing in his original endeavour to sell the linen in one lot, the merchant engaged in an advertising campaign, rented offices and employed staff to sell the linen to the public. The House of Lords held that the profit arising from the sale of the linen arose from a trade. The judges referred repeatedly to the mantle of trading which the merchant had donned as a result of the elaborate selling organisation employed by him.

In the case of *Wisdom v Chamberlain* 45 TC 93, the taxpayer purchased silver bullion as a hedge against devaluation. It was held by the Court of Appeal that the transaction in question constituted an adventure in the nature of trade. Harman LJ stated:

> *"In the first place it seems to me that supposing it was a hedge against devaluation, it was nevertheless a transaction entered into on a short-term basis for the purpose of making a profit out of the purchase and sale of a commodity, and if that is not an adventure in the nature of a trade I do not really know what is. The whole object of the transaction was to make a profit."*

The profit objective is not an infallible test in deciding whether or not a particular transaction is an adventure in the nature of a trade, as can be seen from the following statement by Donovan LJ in the case of *Jenkinson v Freedland* 39 TC 636:

> *"It cannot be right, therefore, to assert, as the Crown did before us, that whenever something is bought to resell at a profit an adventure or concern in the nature of trade necessarily results, and any finding of the Commissioners to the contrary must be perverse. Otherwise there would hardly be any need to introduce capital gains tax. It would virtually be here already. The true position in my opinion, is that all the facts in each case must be considered, not merely the motive of acquisition, and a conclusion arrived at from such a comprehensive review."*

In the case of *Rutledge v The Commissioners of the Inland Revenue* 14 TC 490, the taxpayer was a moneylender who purchased a large quantity of toilet paper while in Berlin on a totally separate matter. Lord Sands, in considering the matter, stated in relation to the appellant:

> *"He made a large purchase and brought the toilet paper to this country and effected a sale at a profit. The nature and quantity of the subject dealt with exclude the suggestion that it could have been disposed otherwise than as a trade transaction. Neither the purchaser nor any purchaser from him was likely to require such a quantity for his private use. Accordingly, it appears to me a quite reasonable view for the Commissioners to have taken that this transaction was in the nature of trade. From beginning to end the intention was simply to buy and resell. Your Lordship in the Chair has indicated that there may be cases of purchase and resale at a profit where the transaction cannot be said to be in the nature of trade. In particular, this may be the case where there is no definite intention of reselling when the purchase is made. But I do not think we can regard what was done here as other than 'an adventure … in the nature of trade' within the meaning of the Act."*

No single test is decisive in establishing trading, and in the case of *Marson v Morton* (1986) 59 TC 381, the judge reviewed and broadened the Badges to some degree by identifying the following key questions:

- Has the taxpayer undertaken a similar transaction?
- Is the transaction related to the trade the taxpayer otherwise carries on?

- How is the transaction financed?
- Was the item normally the subject of trading?
- Was the transaction typical of the trade in an item of that nature?
- Was work carried out on the item for the purposes of resale?
- Was the item sold as it was bought, or broken down into saleable lots?
- Did the item provide enjoyment, pride of possession or produce an income?
- What was the taxpayer's intention when the item was purchased?

The judge summed up the issue as follows:

> *"Was the taxpayer investing money or was he doing a deal?"*

14.3 When Does a Trade Commence?

The date on which the trade or profession commences is a question of fact. There are no specific rules for determining when a trade commences. However, there is a distinction between commencing to trade and preparing to commence trading. The leading case concerning this issue is *Birmingham & District Cattle By-Products v CIR* [1919].

In this case, a company carried on the business of processing and marketing butchers' by-products. From June to October 1913, its directors were engaged in securing premises and plant and arranging for the supply of by-products. A works manager was taken on in August. Actual processing commenced in October. It was held that the company had commenced to trade in October. Trade was held to commence when the company first received raw materials for manufacture.

14.4 When Does a Trade Cease?

In general, it can be said that a trade ceases when all of its trading stock has been disposed of or when it ceases to manufacture. The fact that a person ceases to purchase more stock does not of itself constitute a cessation. This point was highlighted in *Gordon and Blair Ltd. v IRC* [1962].

In that case, a brewing company ceased brewing but continued to sell beer, which was supplied by another company. It was held that the company had ceased the trade of brewing beer and had commenced the trade of selling beer.

14.5 Illegal Trades

Profits or gains arising from an unlawful activity are within the charge to income tax under Case IV. This applies not only to trading income but to all income.

14.6 Basis of Assessment

The rules for determining the basis of assessment for Case I and Case II are identical, and no distinction between the two applies in the commentary that follows.

A trader will usually prepare accounts for a 12-month period. In order to correctly work out the income tax arising on trading income, it is necessary to consider which accounts and profits are taken into account ("assessed") in particular tax years. In examining the basis of assessment rules, a number of different scenarios need to be examined:

- ongoing business
- commencing business
- ceasing business
- business changing its accounting period

14.6.1 Ongoing business

Ongoing businesses are subject to a "current year" basis of assessment (also known as "Normal Basis"). This means that the profits of the 12-month accounting period ending in the tax year in question are taxable in that year.

Example 14.1: Ongoing Business

Romeo has traded for many years. His tax-adjusted profits are:

	€
Year ended 30 June 2016	*120,000*
Year ended 30 June 2017	*130,000*
Year ended 30 June 2018	*150,000*

Assessable:

2016 tax year – year ended 30 June 2016	*120,000*
2017 tax year – year ended 30 June 2017	*130,000*
2018 tax year – year ended 30 June 2018	*150,000*

14.6.2 Commencing business

There are special rules in the legislation to deal with traders who are commencing in business. When a business commences trading, the taxable profits assessable for the first three tax years of trading are as follows:

First Tax Year

Profits are assessable on an actual basis, i.e., the profits assessable are those from the date of commencement until the end of the tax year.

Second Tax Year

Profits to be assessed in the second tax year are as follows:

- If there is only one set of accounts made up to date within that year and these accounts are for a full 12 months, the full amount of the profits of the 12 months ending on that date should be included.

- If there is only one set of accounts made up to a date within that year and these accounts are for less than 12 months, the full amount of the profits of the 12 months ending on that date are assessed (this assumes that the business has been trading for at least 12 months at that stage, and it is possible to work back 12 months to calculate the assessable income).

- If there is more than one set of accounts made up to a date or dates within that tax year, the full amount of the profits of the 12 months ending on the later or latest of those dates should be included.

- In any other case, the actual profits for the tax year must be accounted for.

Third and subsequent years

The assessment for these years is on a current year basis. However, if the actual profits of the second year (i.e., the profits attributable to the tax year, which runs from 1 January to 31 December) are lower than those assessable in accordance with the rules for year two (as set out above), the taxpayer may elect to offset that difference against the profits of the third year of assessment.

When the profits of the third year of assessment are insufficient to absorb the full amount of the difference arising from the second year review, any balance can be carried forward as a loss available to be offset against profits of subsequent years of assessment.

These rules are best illustrated by the following examples:

Example 14.2: Commencing to Trade

Don commenced to trade on 1 September 2016. He prepared his first accounts to 31 August 2017 and his second set of accounts to 31 August 2018.

Tax-adjusted Case I profits for both of these periods are as follows:

Year ended 31 August 2017	*€100,000*
Year ended 31 August 2018	*€150,000*

Assessable:

2016

Profits from 1 September 2016 to 31 December 2016, i.e., tax-adjusted accounting profit for the year to 31 August 2017 × 4/12 = €100,000 × 4/12 = €33,333.

2017

*As there is only one set of accounts made up to a date within the year and it is for a full 12 months, the profits assessable are those for the 12 months to 31 August 2017, i.e., €100,000.**

2018

Tax-adjusted accounting profit for the year to 31 August 2018, i.e., €150,000.

**2017 – Actual*

($\frac{8}{12}$ × €100,000) +($\frac{4}{12}$ × €150,000)

€66,667 + €50,000 = €116,667

As the actual profits for year two are greater than the assessed profits, no adjustment is required to year three.

Example 14.3

John commenced to trade on 1 April 2016.

His profits for the first two years of trading are as follows:

	€
Tax-adjusted Case I for year to 31 March 2017	*60,000*
Tax-adjusted Case I for year to 31 March 2018	*40,000*

John's assessments for the three years are as follows:

Basis of assessment		€
Year 1 – 2016	*Actual ($\frac{9}{12}$ × €60,000)*	*45,000*
Year 2 – 2017	*Profits to 31 March 2017*	*60,000*
Year 3 – 2018	*Current year basis*	*40,000*
	*Deduct: Third year option relief **	*(15,000)**
		25,000

** Third year option:*	€
– Assessed – Year 2	*60,000*
– Actual – Year 2 ($\frac{3}{12}$ × €60,000) + ($\frac{9}{12}$ × €40,000)	*45,000*
Excess	*15,000*

14.6.3 Ceasing a business

Section 67 TCA97 provides for the following basis of assessment in the final years of a business up to cessation.

Year of cessation:	– actual profits from 1 January to date of cessation
Penultimate year:	– revised under self assessment to "actual" profits if these exceed the profits previously assessed on a current year basis

Example 14.4: Ceasing Business

Brooklyn will cease to trade on 31 August 2018. Results will be as follows:

	€
Year ended 30 April 2017	*80,000*
Year ended 30 April 2018	*50,000*
Period ended 31 August 2018	*20,000*
Assessable:	
2018 (year of cessation) – actual	
1 May 2018 to 31 August 2018 €20,000 × 4/4	*20,000*
1 Jan 2018 to 30 April 2018 €50,000 × 4/12	*16,667*
	36,667
2017 (penultimate year)	
Original Assessment	
Year ended 30 April 2017	*80,000*
Actual basis:	
1 January 2017 to 31 August 2017 €50,000 × 8/12	*33,333*
1 September 2017 to 31 December 2017 €80,000 × 4/12	*26,667*
	60,000

As the profits assessed on a normal (current year) basis are greater than the profits that arise on an actual basis, there will be no revision of the penultimate year in this case.

Example 14.5

Michael ceased to trade as a sole trader on 30 June 2018.

His tax-adjusted Case I profits for recent years are as follows:

	€
Year to 30 June 2018	*100,000*
Year to 30 June 2017	*80,000*
Year to 30 June 2016	*50,000*

His assessments for the three years up to the date of cessation are as follows:

Year	*Basis of Assessment*	€	
2018	*Actual (€100,000 × 6/12)*		*50,000*
2017	*Original – current year basis*	*80,000*	
	Actual (6/12 × €100,000) + (6/12 × €80,000)	*90,000*	
	As the actual assessment is higher, Michael will be taxed on the actual basis.		
	Final assessment		*90,000*
2016	*Current year basis*		*50,000*

14.6.3.1 Post-cessation receipts

Where a trade has ceased, accounts will be prepared to the date of cessation as determined using the principles set out above. However, it can happen that after the business has ceased, income is received. This income is known as post-cessation receipts and the following rules apply:

- Post-cessation receipts are assessed under Case IV and the receipt of such income does not affect the cessation rules.
- A deduction may be made against the post-cessation receipts for any expenses incurred which would have been allowed if the trade had not ceased. (Readers are referred to Chapter 15 for commentary on the deductibility of certain expenses.)
- Unused capital allowances at the date of cessation may be set against the post-cessation receipts. (Readers are referred to Chapter 16 for commentary on the calculation of capital allowances.)

14.6.4 Short Lived Business

Where a trade or profession commences and ceases within three tax years, it is possible that the basis of assessment rules could result in the assessed profits exceeding the actual profits earned during the lifetime of the trade/profession. In such cases a claim can be made under s68 TCA97 to have the profits of year 2 assessed on an actual basis.

For the relief to apply, the commencement and cessation must take place within three tax years. The relief would not apply where, for example, a business commenced on 1/11/2015 and ceased on 30/6/2018. In this case, even though the life of the business is less than three years, the commencement and cessation take place within four tax years i.e. years 2015 to 2018 inclusive.

14.6.5 Business changing its accounting period

A business, for a variety of reasons, may change its accounting period. For the purposes of basis of assessment, three situations can arise where there is a change in accounting date:

i) There may be more than one accounting period ending in any given tax year.

ii) The accounting period ending in the tax year may be shorter/longer than 12 months in duration.

iii) There may be no accounting period ending in the tax year.

Where any of the above occurs, the following rules apply:

- The profits assessable in the tax year in which the change occurs are the profits of the 12 months to the latest accounting year-end. If there is no accounting period ending in the tax year, the assessable profits are the actual profits for the income tax year, i.e., the profits attributable to the period from 1 January to 31 December.
- The profits of the preceding tax year will be revised on the basis of the new accounting year-end of the tax year in which the change occurs, if those profits are higher than the profits originally assessed.

Example 14.6: Change of Accounting Period

1. More than one accounting period ending in the year of assessment

Results are as follows:	**€**	**€**
12 months ended 30 September 2017	*35,000*	
12 months ended 30 September 2018	*23,400*	
2 months ended 30 November 2018	*36,000*	
Assessable:		
2018 – 2 accounting periods		
Profits assessed are those for the 12 months to the later accounting date.		
2/2 × €36,000	*36,000*	
10/12 × €23,400	*19,500*	*55,500*
2017 – Original assessment	*35,000*	
Corresponding period:		
2/12 × €23,400	*3,900*	
10/12 × €35,000	*29,167*	*33,067*

As the profits originally assessed in 2017 are higher, no revision is required.

2. Short/Long accounting period

Results are as follows:	**€**	**€**
Year to 30 September 2016	*100,000*	
Year to 30 September 2017	*255,500*	
8 months to 31 May 2018	*120,000*	
Assessable:		
2018 8/8 × €120,000	*120,000*	
4/12 × €255,500	*85,167*	*205,167*
2017 – Original assessment	*255,500*	
Revision to corresponding accounting period (i.e., year ended 31 May 2017):		
4/12 × €100,000	*33,333*	
8/12 × €255,500	*170,333*	
		203,666

As the profits originally assessed in 2017 are higher, no revision is required.

3. No accounting period ending in year of assessment

Results are as follows:	**€**
12 months ended 31 October 2016	*120,000*
24 months ended 31 October 2018	*275,000*
Assessable:	
2017 – No accounting period	
Assessment based on actual profits to 31 December 2017:	
12/24 × €275,000	*137,500*

2016 – Original assessment		*120,000*
Revise to actual basis:		
10/12 × €120,000	*€100,000*	
2/24 × €275,000	*€22,917*	*122,917*

As the revised figures on an actual basis are higher than the original figures, a revision to the actual basis is required.

14.7 The Decision to Operate as a Sole Trader or to Incorporate the Business

An individual who is trading successfully may consider incorporating the business. The trader may be considering expanding the business and needing capital to do so. Raising capital may be more easily achieved through a corporate entity. For example, a trader cannot raise capital through the EIIS. However certain companies (subject to conditions being satisfied) can look to outside investors as a means of raising capital. The outside investors obtain tax relief for investing in a "EIIS company" making it an attractive option for the investors. Likewise Seed Capital Investment relief can only be availed of by a company.

The decision to incorporate must be done having considered all tax and legal implications. There are advantages and disadvantages for operating as a sole trader or through a company by incorporating the business. Only the tax implications are considered here.

14.7.1 Sole Trader – advantages and disadvantages

Advantages:

- Current year losses may be offset against other income.
- Business assets and profits remain in the ownership of the trader.
- Only one annual tax return for filing purposes.
- Since profits of the year are taxed in full, drawings are therefore not taxable. The trader has the flexibility to take the drawings as and when needed without attracting a further tax liability.

Disadvantages:

- Profits are liable to marginal rate taxes (including PRSI and USC). This can be up to 55% (60% if including 5% USC on certain "property" reliefs claimed).
- A trader cannot raise capital through EIIS.
- A trader cannot avail of Seed Capital Investment Relief.

14.7.2 Incorporation – advantages and disadvantages

Advantages:

- Corporation tax is payable on trading profits at a rate of 12.5%.
- Ability to raise capital through EIIS (where conditions are satisfied).
- Ability to avail of Seed Capital Investment Relief (where conditions are satisfied).

Disadvantages:

- A company is a separate legal entity, therefore all business assets are in the ownership of the company. The director/shareholder has no access to such assets unless by way of a sale to the director/shareholder, which has CGT implications for the company.
- Close company implications (e.g. income tax withholding obligations on loans to director, surcharge on undistributed after tax investment income).
- More onerous filing obligations for a company.
- Cash extraction by the director/shareholder has tax implications (up to 55%/60% income tax, PRSI and USC).

14.7.3 The tax implications of cessation of a trade and incorporation

Should the trader decide to incorporate, there is a deemed cessation of the trade (albeit the business is continued though an incorporated entity). As outlined at 14.6.3 above, where the accounting year end is other than 31 December and the profits are increasing up to the date of cessation, the penultimate year will be revised to an actual basis. Any uplift in profits when compared with those of the basis period will be taxable.

14.7.4 The tax implications for a proprietary director post incorporation

A proprietary director is a chargeable person for self-assessment purposes (as discussed in Chapter 10). This means that the director has the same payment and filing obligations as those of a sole trader. Should the director have no income other than a salary (which is subject to PAYE/PRSI at source) there is therefore only a tax return filing requirement with no obligation to pay preliminary tax. However if the director has investment income or any other income, the liability of which is not covered by at source deductions, preliminary tax is payable on that income.

14.7.5 Start Up relief for long-term unemployed

s472AA TCA97

Section 6 F(No. 2) A 2013 introduced a relief from income tax for long term unemployed individuals who start a new business. The relief applies from 25 October 2013 to 31 December 2018.

The relief provides an exemption from income tax on profits up to a maximum of €40,000 per annum for a period of two years to individuals who set up a qualifying business (relief does not extend to USC and PRSI). The individual must have been immediately prior to commencement of the business:

- unemployed for twelve months or more, and
- during that period have been in receipt of any of the following:
  - ☐ crediting contributions
  - ☐ jobseeker's allowance
  - ☐ jobseeker's benefit
  - ☐ the one-parent family payment
  - ☐ partial capacity payment

Periods of time spent on certain government training courses and schemes will be treated as part of a period of unemployment. Examples of training courses and schemes are FÁS training courses, Community Employment Schemes, Job Initiative and Back to Education Schemes.

The business must be set up between 25 October 2014 and 31 December 2018 and must be a new unincorporated business and not a business that is bought, inherited or otherwise acquired.

The amount of relief in year 1 depends on when the new business started. If the new business started in January, the cap is the maximum of €40,000 since the basis period for year 1 commencement is for 12 months. If the start date is later in the year, the cap is reduced proportionately according to the month of commencement. For example if the start date is 1 March the cap is €33,333 (i.e. €40,000 × 10/12). The relief therefore operates as follows:

- Year 1 - Profits are relieved from income tax once that they are less than the cap (as adjusted if required)
- Year 2 - Profits are relieved from income tax once they are less than the €40,000 cap
- Year 3 - Profits for any part of this year which fall within the first 24 months of business are relieved if they are less than the cap.

Where a business starts on 1 January, then the two years (24 months) relief is utilised in year 1 and year 2 and there is no relief available for year 3. Where a business starts later in the year then there is still some relief available for year 3.

Example 14.7

John Daly starts a new business on 1 March 2018 and prepares accounts the adjusted profits of which are:

- *for the 10 months up to 31 December 2018 = €40,000*
- *for the year to 31 December 2019 = €45,000*
- *for the year to 31 December 2020 = €45,000.*

Year 1 Relief

The business started on 1 March, therefore relief is €40,000 × 10/12 = €33,333, leaving €6,667 taxable.

Year 2 Relief

The first €40,000 is relieved leaving €5,000 taxable.

Year 3 Relief

Since there are two months left within the first 24 months then the cap for those two months which can be relieved is €40,000 × 2/12 = €6,667. This leaves €38,333 taxable.

The total amount relived from income tax is therefore:

- *2018 - €33,333*
- *2019 - €40,000*
- *2020 - €6,667*
- *Total - €80,000*

Tax Facts

In 2009, a Start Up Exemption was introduced for companies (considered at Chapter 29, 29.10) commencing a new business, however there was no equivalent exemption for unincorporated businesses. Section 6 F(No. 2)A 2013 has now bridged that gap.

15 ADJUSTED INCOME TAX COMPUTATION

Learning Outcomes

On completion of this chapter you will be able to:

- ✓ Describe the method used in practice to calculate the profits of a trade or profession.
- ✓ Calculate the tax-adjusted Case I/II income for a sole trader/professional.
- ✓ Describe the treatment of various items included in the profit and loss account.
- ✓ Explain how movements in provisions are treated for tax purposes.
- ✓ Discuss the meaning of the term "wholly and exclusively".
- ✓ Distinguish between capital items and items that are revenue in nature.

15.1 Introduction

This chapter examines the calculation of profits assessable to tax for a sole trader or a professional. It looks at the general process involved in arriving at a taxable figure by examining the tax principles involved. The specific legislative provisions are discussed in detail.

In theory, one of two approaches could be used to calculate the assessable profits of a sole trader:

(i) Using the source information of the business, it is possible to recreate all the income of that type earned in the year and work out all the tax-deductible expenses for that type of income

(ii) Alternatively, one could use a "shortcut" and work from the figures that will already have been prepared for the business accounts adjusting these to arrive at the total taxable profits.

Method (ii) is the easiest and quickest method. It is the method that is used in practice and the recommended approach for examination questions.

The remainder of this chapter is concerned with using the financial statements of a business as a starting point and with the various adjustments necessary to arrive at taxable profits.

The skill is in identifying all of the tax adjustments required. This requires a familiarity with:

- the vast body of specific legislative provisions which operate to prohibit certain expense deductions, or otherwise adjust the treatment for tax purposes from the accounting treatment;
- various court decisions in Ireland, the UK and the EU. While UK legislation is not binding in Ireland it may be persuasive, particularly where the legislation in the UK is similar to that in Ireland and particularly where there is no equivalent Irish interpretation;
- established Revenue practice, such as Statements of Practice, Information Leaflets and Guidance Notes issued by Revenue, together with Revenue precedents.

15.2 Using the Financial Statements to Calculate Taxable Income

This approach involves effectively taking the "profit before tax" figure in the profit and loss account or income statement and adjusting it to arrive at taxable Case I income. The "profit before tax" figure is the total accounting income booked to the profit and loss account or income statement net of the total expenses booked in accordance with accounting rules and generally accepted accounting practice (GAAP).

In the vast majority of cases, the accounts will not show the final Case I figure to be taxed for the period. This is because the "profit before tax" figure is made up of not only the business' trading/professional income, but also income from other sources (e.g. deposit interest, dividends etc.) and profits/losses on the disposal of assets.

In addition, while the Revenue Commissioners require GAAP to be used in the computation of taxable Case I income, a number of established tax principles (which derive from both case law and specific legislative provisions) give rise to differences between the accounting profit and taxable Case I income. The main reasons for these differences are specifically disallowed items (e.g., business entertainment – see 15.3.4 below) and adjustments necessary to counter the lack of consistency and objectivity in the accounting treatment of many items, such as depreciation and general provisions.

To overcome these differences, the accounting profits are adjusted so that non-Case I items and non-deductible expenses are stripped out. Thus, an adjustment to the profit-before-tax figure will be made because:

(a) there are expenses in the profit and loss account or income statement which are not deductible in arriving at Case I income and which must therefore be added back for tax purposes;

(b) there is income or gains/losses in the profit and loss account or income statement which is not taxable as Case I income and which must therefore be deducted in arriving at taxable Case I; or

(c) there are costs which are not deductible in the profit and loss account or income statement but which are allowable in calculating Case I income.

To establish the adjustments required for parts (a) and (b) above, a review of all the income and expense items that are included in the detailed profit and loss account or income statement should be undertaken. In light of the criteria at 15.3 below, it is then a question of determining whether each of the items is taxable as Case I income or is an allowable Case I deduction, as appropriate.

The adjustments required for the items listed at (c) are potentially more difficult to establish as these expense items are not already in the profit and loss account but nevertheless are Case I adjustments, e.g., double rent allowance in a designated area.

15.3 Adjusting Items

For the purposes of this analysis, all references are to the profit and loss account albeit that some sole trade businesses may choose to adopt the terminology and accounting practices of international accounting.

There are four very important considerations to bear in mind when examining the items included in the profit and loss account or income statement:

1. It is necessary to consider whether the item is capital in nature or income/revenue related. In general, an adjustment is required for capital items. A number of Irish and UK decisions help to clarify the distinction between "capital" and "revenue". It is important to bear in mind that some capital expenses, which are disallowed for the purposes of calculating Case I, may be deductible in calculating chargeable gains.
2. The item must be "trade" related. In general, items that do not relate to the trade are adjusted for in arriving at taxable Case I. The legislation specifically requires that for amounts to be deductible under Case I, the expenditure must be incurred "wholly and exclusively" for the purposes of carrying on the trade. This concept of "wholly and exclusively" is a complex area and has been the subject of much case law in Ireland and the UK over many years. It is explained in more detail below, and one of the main cases is outlined.
3. In general, items of expenditure must have been incurred in the period. An adjustment will be required if an item relates to a movement on a general provision. Movements in provisions are only allowable where they relate to specific items, the amount of which can be determined with exactitude. Rough estimates of future expenditure are not allowable.
4. Certain specific items of expenditure are disallowed by statute notwithstanding that they are revenue in nature and may have been incurred wholly and exclusively for the purposes of the trade. The main provisions disallowing specific types of expenditure are addressed at 15.3.4 below.

The commentary that follows is concerned with elaborating on these considerations and with presenting examples of matters which may be addressed under the four headings as described. It is important to bear in mind that many of the issues addressed in this context are more relevant for companies. This is particularly true in the case of adjustments arising as a consequence of the application of accounting standards. Readers are referred to Chapter 29 for detailed commentary on the subtle differences between the adjusted profits computations of sole traders and those of companies.

The application of the four considerations in determining the deductibility of an expense item in the profit and loss account can be summarised diagrammatically as follows:

ELIGIBILITY TEST TO CLAIM A TAX-DEDUCTIBLE EXPENSE

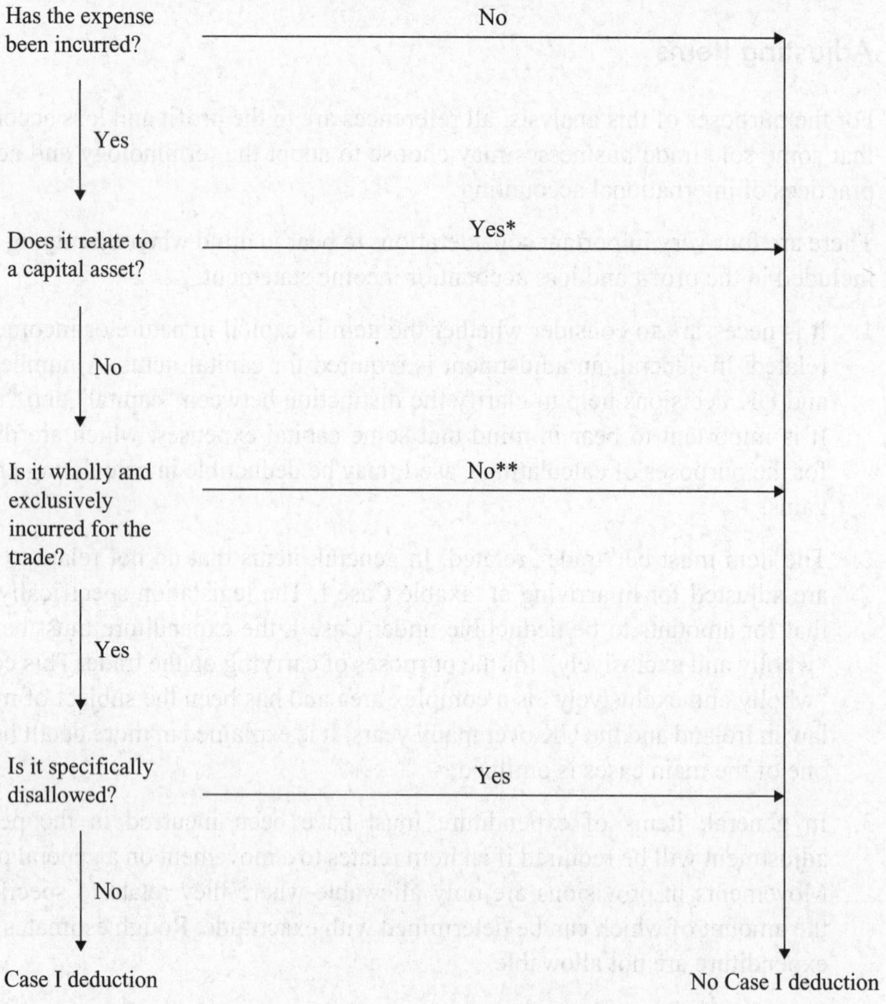

* Consider capital allowances

** Deductible under another Case, or for CGT purposes? Allowable in some other form?

15.3.1 Income or capital

Income tax is not assessed on capital profits; it is only assessed on income profits. Therefore, the only expenses which will be allowed in its calculation are income expenses. This is supported by the fact that, under ordinary accounting principles, capital expenditure is not ordinarily charged to the profit and loss account in arriving at net profit. However, in certain incidences, businesses will charge capital expenditure to the profit and loss account, either because the amount is small and immaterial from an accounting perspective or because the distinction between capital and revenue is not always clear. It is therefore necessary to establish whether particular items in the profit and loss account are capital or revenue in nature. There are some factors that should be considered when deciding whether an expense item is capital or revenue in nature. These factors are:

- the treatment of the expenditure in the accounts
- the reason for the expenditure and a common-sense approach
- the lasting quality of the asset/item on which expenditure has been incurred
- the form in which the transaction is carried out.

Capital expenditure is generally taken to be expenditure incurred by a business on an item which is used in the trade (rather than consumed by the trade) and which is expected to have a certain useful life. The key requirement derived from case law is that there must be "an enduring benefit for the trade". Obvious examples of this would be the purchase of new machinery, buildings, etc.

In most situations, the legislation grants capital allowances at 12.5% or 4% for capital expenditure incurred (in this regard, readers are referred to Chapter 16) However, a full tax deduction for this type of expenditure could take a minimum of eight years (12.5% per annum over 8 years = 100%). Therefore, businesses naturally seek to write off certain purchases as trade deductions. Readers should always bear in mind that capital items are commonly included in repair charges and that these should be properly reclassified as capital for the purposes of the tax computation.

A number of common items that need to be adjusted for on the basis that they are capital as opposed to revenue in nature are now discussed in turn.

Repairs and renewals versus improvements

It is important to distinguish between repairs and improvements, as improvements will generally be regarded as capital in nature while repairs will be allowed as a revenue expense.

s81(2)(g) TCA97 Section 81(2)(g) TCA97 specifically disallows a deduction for "any capital employed in improvements of premises occupied for the purposes of the trade or profession".

In addition, the replacement of an asset in its entirety will generally be regarded as capital expenditure, while the replacement of a component part will be classified as tax-deductible repairs.

Due to the nature of claims by taxpayers and disagreements with tax inspectors over the distinction between repairs and improvements, numerous cases have been referred to the courts over the years. In the case of *JT Hodgins v Plunder & Pollak* (Supreme Court 19 January 1955, ITR Vol. 2 p. 267), a large building covering a weighbridge on the grounds of a factory was destroyed in a storm. The company built a much smaller building as a replacement and sought a tax deduction, which the Inspector disallowed. The Supreme Court decided that no improvement had occurred as the new building was considerably smaller than the previous one and was only a small part of the factory as a whole. Therefore, the expenditure was allowable.

Depreciation/Write-off of goodwill

Depreciation represents a notional write-off against profits for accounting purposes of the cost of the capital asset over its useful economic life. Depreciation rates for accounting purposes can be quite arbitrary, and policies can vary between businesses. Accordingly, accounting depreciation must be added back for tax purposes. A system of capital allowances or tax depreciation calculated on a more objective basis in accordance with clearly defined rules compensates for the add-back in relation to accounting depreciation. Readers are referred to Chapter 16 for further commentary on capital allowance claims.

Goodwill is generally taken to be the difference between the overall purchase price paid for a trade and the sum of the assets actually bought. Thus, it may be perceived as the price of purchasing the trade "name". Purchased goodwill is an intangible asset, which is capitalised in the balance sheet and usually written off over a period of 20 years or less. Like depreciation, the write-off represents a notional expense in relation to a capital item and, accordingly, is not allowable for tax purposes and must be added back in arriving at tax-adjusted Case I.

Amortisation of government grants

Capital grants are treated as deferred revenue for accounts purposes and are amortised or credited to the profit and loss account over the useful life of the asset purchased with the grant. Thus, their treatment is a mirror image of the treatment of depreciation. As the deferred revenue credited to the profit and loss account is a notional amount based on the perceived useful economic life of the asset, the amount amortised is not taxable and, accordingly, is deducted from the accounting profit figure for the purposes of arriving at tax-adjusted Case I. The benefit of the grant is effectively taxed through the capital allowance system, as the capital allowance claim on the asset is generally calculated on a net-of-government-grant basis.

Disposal of fixed assets

Profits or losses that arise on the sale of fixed assets arise as a result of a capital transaction. Consequently, under the general principles outlined in s81 TCA97, such profits/losses would not qualify as a Case I receipt/deduction and must be deducted/added back in the computation. Instead, relief may be given for any inherent loss on disposal through the capital allowances system in the form of a balancing allowance.

Where the sales proceeds exceed the written down value of the asset for capital allowance purposes, capital allowances claimed to date may be clawed back. In addition, it is possible that the transaction in question gives rise to a chargeable gain/loss, and this must always be borne in mind from a capital gains tax perspective. For example, a loss recorded in the accounts on the sale of a building indicates that a chargeable transaction has taken place, and the chargeable gain or loss will need to be calculated in accordance with the capital gains tax principles outlined in Section IV of this book.

Expenses relating to the acquisition/disposal of capital assets

Expenses relating to capital transactions, e.g., legal fees, professional fees, estate agents, fees, etc., are not allowable Case I deductions and, accordingly, must be added back. However, these costs may be relieved under the capital gains tax system when the assets to which they relate are ultimately sold. It is important to bear in mind that professional fees, legal expenses, etc., of a revenue or trading nature are tax-deductible, e.g., debt-collection costs or preparation of legal contracts with suppliers or customers.

By concession, Revenue allows a deduction for interest on funds used to finance capital expenditure for the purposes of a trade.

15.3.2 "Wholly and exclusively"

s81 TCA97

In order to be allowed as a deduction, expenditure must be "wholly and exclusively" incurred for the purposes of carrying on the trade. This is legislated for in s81 TCA97 under the heading "General rule as to deductions".

It provides that:

> *"(1) The tax under Cases I and II of Schedule D shall be charged without any deduction other than is allowed by the Tax Acts.*
>
> *(2) Subject to the Tax Acts, in computing the amount of the profit or gains to be charged to tax under Case I or II of Schedule D, no sum shall be deducted in respect of –*
>
> *(a) any disbursements or expenses, not being money wholly and exclusively laid out or expended for the purpose of the trade or profession …"*

The word "wholly" refers to the amount of money expended. If only part of the money was spent for the purposes of the trade, then in principle it is not deductible. However, in practice, if it is possible to distinguish between the business and private expenses, Revenue will permit the business element to be deductible. Typically this apportionment is carried out on motor expenses, telephone and light and heat. The word "exclusively" refers to the motivation behind incurring the expense. The expense must be incurred solely for the purpose of the trade and there must be no other purpose or requirement involved.

It is important to note that where a business-owner incurs expenses which relate to the personal or private lives of employees of the business, such expenses are fully deductible on the basis that they are costs of rewarding employees and as such are a business expense. Thus, only the private elements of expenses relating to the owner of a business are disallowed. Such expenses, and indeed the owner's salary, are simply appropriations of the trading profit. Allowing a tax deduction for these amounts on the basis that they constitute salary or remuneration of some sort would involve incorrectly classifying the profits of the sole trade operation as Schedule E income.

Example 15.1

John's profit and loss account for the year ended 31 December 2018 is as follows:

	€	€
Sales		*300,000*
Cost of sales		*(100,000)*
Gross Profit		*200,000*
Less Expenses:		
Depreciation	*20,000*	
*Salaries and wages**	*65,000*	
Light and heat	*1,000*	
Telephone	*1,500*	
Motor expenses	*3,000*	
Miscellaneous	*4,000*	*(94,500)*
Profit before tax		*105,500*

**The salaries and wages include a salary of €25,000 paid to John.*

John operates from a room in his own home. The light and heat expense relates to the expense for the house as a whole for the year. John has agreed with his Inspector of Taxes that one-fifth of this amount is business related.

The telephone expense relates to a separate line, which John has put in place exclusively for business purposes.

The motor expenses comprise an amount of €1,000 in respect of John's own car, which is used 50% for business purposes (as agreed with the Inspector of Taxes), and €2,000 in respect of a salesman's car which is used 60% for business purposes.

The miscellaneous expenses are all allowable.

John's Case I computation is as follows:

	€	
Profit before tax	*105,500*	
Add back:		
Depreciation	*20,000*	
Drawings	*25,000*	
Light and heat	*800*	*(⁴⁄₅ private)*
Motor expenses	*500*	*(private element of owner's motor expenses)*
Tax-adjusted Case I	*151,800*	

Note: The owner cannot pay himself a salary and the amount paid is in effect drawings or an appropriation of the profits of the business. He is not taxed under Schedule E on this amount or on any other benefits accruing from his involvement in the business.

The private element of the salesman's motor expenses are allowable on the basis that they are a cost of rewarding an employee. The benefit accruing to the salesman would be taxable in his hands under Schedule E as a benefit-in-kind. In this regard, readers are referred to Chapter 21.

The meaning of the term "wholly and exclusively" has been considered frequently in both Irish and UK case law. The case of *Mallalieu v Drummond* ([1981] STC 391) illustrates the rigid application of the principle by the courts. In this case, a barrister was seeking a deduction for the cost of the black clothing that she wore in court. Her main argument was that as she would not ordinarily wear such clothing, she was using it "wholly and exclusively" for her trade. Therefore, the expenditure on the clothing should be deductible. The case was ultimately referred to the House of Lords where it was held that as decent human beings must wear clothing, the expenditure was not incurred "wholly and exclusively" for the trade, even though she would not normally wear this type of clothing.

It is important to bear in mind that expenses which are not wholly and exclusively for the purpose of the trade may be deductible against another specific category of income or gain. For example, a rates charge on a property rented out by the sole trader will be disallowed against Case I but may be allowed against Case V income. Alternatively, the expense may be deductible against total income as a charge. For example, a deed of covenant payment by a sole trader to his 70-year-old widowed mother will not be an allowable Case I deduction. Accordingly, if booked to the business profit and loss account, the amount will have to be added back for the purposes of arriving at taxable Case I. However, the amount will be deductible from total income as a charge. In this regard, readers are referred to Chapter 12.

A useful approach in dealing with the issues considered thus far may be to look at adjustments to the profit before tax figure (i.e., add-backs and deductions) from the point of view of income or capital and then further apply the wholly and exclusively test in each case. The following diagram illustrates the suggested approach.

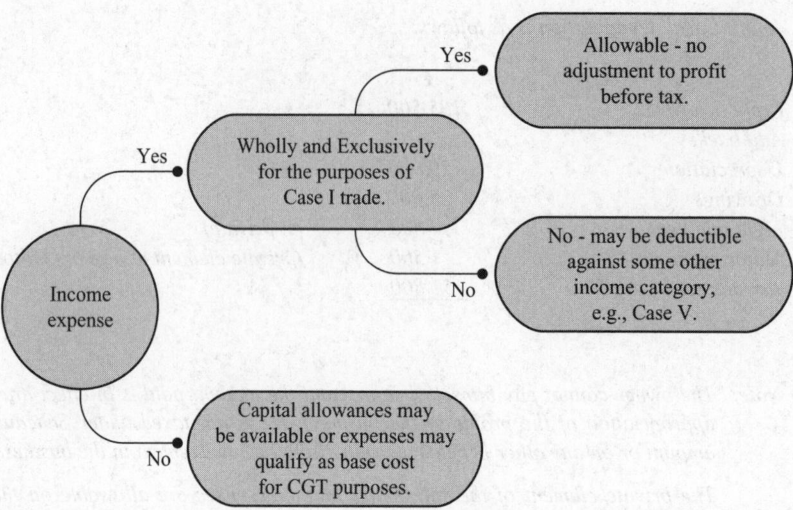

Further adjustments must be looked at in the light of the treatment of movements on provisions and specific legislative principles.

15.3.3 Movements in general provisions and accruals

Any general provisions that do not relate to specific transactions or events will not be allowed as a deduction and should be added back in the tax computation. An example of a general provision is a provision for bad debts calculated as a percentage of debtors. Only bad debts written off in the accounts as irrecoverable and provisions for bad debts, which can be reliably estimated and which relate to specific identifiable debtor balances, will be allowed as a deduction.

This logic also applies to other provisions. For example, a general stock obsolescence provision calculated as a percentage of closing stock would not be allowable, but a provision relating to some specific items of damaged or non-saleable stock would be allowed in full. However, standard examination questions generally tend to focus on movements in bad debt provisions as such provisions are commonly encountered in practice. An understanding of the underlying effect of movements on provisions on the final profit figure is imperative to an understanding of the tax adjustments necessary. Thus, readers are advised to study the commentary in Appendix 1 in relation to the accounting and tax treatment of bad debts and bad debt provisions before considering the following examples.

Example 15.2

The bad debts charge in the profit and loss account of Mr Andrews is €120,000 and can be broken down as follows:

	€	€
Trade debts written off as irrecoverable		*60,000*
Debts previously written off now recovered		*(15,000)*

Movement in Specific Bad Debt Provision		
– Opening provision	*25,000*	
– Closing provision	*40,000*	*15,000*
	€	**€**
Movement in General Bad Debt Provision		
– Opening provision	*30,000*	
– Closing provision	*90,000*	*60,000*
		120,000

Tax Implications

1. The bad debts written off are allowed as a Case I deduction in full, while the bad debts recovered are taxed as trading income.
2. The increase in the Specific Bad Debt Provision of €15,000 is allowed in full as a Case I deduction.
3. The increase in the General Bad Debt Provision of €60,000 is disallowed in full and must be added back in the Case I tax-adjusted profit computation.

Example 15.3

Included in the profit and loss account of Ms Simpson is a bad debts charge of €90,000. This charge can be broken down as follows:

		€	€
Bad debts written off			*55,000*
Bad debts recovered			*(10,000)*
Specific Bad Debt Provision	*– Opening*	*20,000*	
Closing	*–*	*90,000*	*70,000*
General Bad Debt Provision	*– Opening*	*65,000*	
Closing	*–*	*40,000*	*(25,000)*
			90,000

Assess the components of the above expense for tax purposes.

The tax consequences of the above bad debt charge of €90,000 are as follows:

- Bad debts written off as a fully allowable expense against Case I (no add-back);
- Bad debts recovered is taxed as trading income (no deduction);
- An increase in Specific Bad Debt Provision of €70,000 is allowed in full as a Case I deduction (no add-back);
- A decrease in General Bad Debt Provision of €25,000 is not taxable, as a corresponding increase in a general provision is not an allowable expense. Therefore, the amount of the decrease should be deducted from the accounting profit to arrive at the amount of tax-adjusted Case I income.

Readers should bear in mind that general bad debt provisions are unlikely to feature in company accounts prepared under IFRS in the future. Readers are referred to the commentary in Chapter 29 for further commentary on the treatment of bad debt provisions under IFRS.

Accounting treatment of provisions

Where businesses adopt the accounting treatment of provisions recommended by either Financial Reporting Standard (FRS) 12 or International Accounting Standard (IAS) 37, concerns over adjustments of profits in respect of provisions are to some extent eliminated. However, in general the provisions of accounting standards only apply to companies. Prior to the introduction of FRS 12 in 1999, it was common practice for companies to include general provisions in their accounts based on "roughly" estimated future liabilities.

FRS 12 deals with the accounting treatment of provisions and contingent liabilities in company accounts. It deals only with provisions for expected liabilities and not with provisions for impairment of assets, such as provisions for depreciation and bad debts. The standard only allows a provision to be charged to the profit and loss account when the following conditions are met:

(a) there is a present obligation;

(b) arising as a result of a past event;

(c) it is probable that expenditure will be required;

(d) the expenditure can be reliably estimated.

Recent case law has strengthened the links between accounting standards and accounts for taxation purposes. In *Herbert Smith v Honour* ([1999], STC 173), the UK tax authorities sought to disallow a provision for future rents of a building, which the company was no longer occupying. This provision was allowable under FRS 12 as it met all four conditions noted above. In his decision allowing the provision as a tax deduction, the judge stated "if a particular statute provision applies to the situation, commercial accounting must give way". Therefore, as there was no specific legislation dealing with the company's provision, it was deemed to be an allowable expense. The Irish Revenue Commissioners issued a statement in September 2000 stating that provisions for losses in accordance with FRS 12 are now allowable, whereas they may previously have sought to disallow them. It is anticipated that this guidance will also apply to provisions in accordance with IAS 37.

Thus, if a company intends repairing a roof in the next 12 months at an expected cost of €7,000 and has signed a contract for this work, the creation of a provision for such repairs this year is fully allowable for tax purposes.

The reader should bear in mind that even if GAAP are followed in creating provisions, the deduction must still pass the "wholly and exclusively" test of s81 to ensure that relief is granted. In addition, provisions in accounts for capital expenditure would not be allowed whereas a provision for an item, which is revenue in nature (e.g., a provision for redundancies), may be allowable.

15.3.4 Specific adjustments

Notwithstanding what has already been said regarding provisions, the income/capital distinction and the "wholly and exclusively" test, there are certain items, that although revenue in nature and incurred for the purposes of carrying on the trade, are disallowed for tax purposes. Further, adjustments must be looked at in the light of specific legislative principles. Some of the common "statutory" adjustments are considered below. The analysis below also looks at certain adjusting items, which may fall within one of the categories already addressed at 15.3.1 and 15.3.2 above, but which nonetheless merit separate discussion because of the frequency with which they are found in the profit and loss account.

Entertainment expenses

s840 TCA97 The legislation prohibits a tax deduction in respect of business entertainment.

Business entertainment is defined in the legislation as:

"... entertainment (including the provision of accommodation, food and drink and any other form of hospitality in any circumstances whatsoever) provided directly or indirectly – in connection with a trade".

This disallowance will operate where the entertainment is provided by a person carrying on the trade, or by a member of staff or any other person performing services for the proprietor. Thus, amounts expended on the entertainment of customers, suppliers, professional advisors, etc., must be added back for tax purposes.

The term "business entertainment" does not extend to the provision of facilities for members of staff unless the provision to them of these facilities is incidental to the entertainment of clients. Hence, expenses such as the provision of a canteen primarily for the staff is allowable, as is specific entertainment of staff, e.g., a staff Christmas party. However, the expense of providing entertainment for staff members, which is merely incidental to the provision of entertainment for clients or customers, is disallowed.

Example 15.4

Tom incurred the following costs relating to the launch of a new product:

	€
Staff dinner after final testing of product	*1,000*
Hotel room hire for launch	*2,000*
Food and drink for clients at launch	*1,500*
Dinner for staff and selected clients	*3,000*
	7,500

The costs relating to client entertainment are not allowed and are added back, being the amounts of €1,500 and €3,000.

The distinction between business entertainment and business development is an important one and while it may be considered that attracting potential customers is business development, careful consideration needs to be given to each item of expenditure. The following types of expenditure will generally be allowed as business development:

- promotion of events;
- sponsorship of competitions;
- associations with business seminars, including hiring of facilities.

Gifts to customers

s840(5) TCA97 The disallowance of business entertainment also extends to gifts. This would appear to extend to the cost of making gifts to customers at Christmas. This disallowance operates even though the making of such gifts may be considered important in maintaining the goodwill of the business. However, a distinction may however be drawn between entertainment and promotion and Revenue will not normally seek to disallow the handing out of free samples of products to customers or potential customers.

Interest on under-/over- and late payment of taxes

In general, interest is charged at a daily rate of 0.0219% (0.0273% prior to 1 July 2009) on the late payment of taxes. Such interest is not an allowable deduction for tax purposes. Correspondingly, any interest received as a result of a tax overpayment is refunded at a daily rate of 0.011% and is exempt from tax. This interest income should be deducted from the accounting profits in arriving at tax-adjusted Case I.

Patent royalties

s243 TCA97 Patent royalties are treated as charges for tax purposes (see Chapter 12). As such they are not allowed as a trade expense and must be added back in calculating tax-adjusted figures.

Political subscriptions and donations

Political subscriptions and non-trade contributions are not allowable as they would not be "wholly and exclusively" for the trade under s81. Thus, they must be added back. Trade subscriptions are allowable.

Relief is available for certain charitable donations (companies only) and donations to sporting bodies where certain conditions are met. These conditions have already been discussed in Chapter 11 and are reproduced here in Appendix II.

Taxes and penalties

Any taxes or penalties charged to the profit and loss account, such as stamp duty, parking fines, etc., are not allowed and must therefore be added back.

Motor leasing expenses restriction

Pre 1 July 2008

s377 & 380M Historically motor lease repayments were restricted where the retail price of the car exceeded a certain ceiling. The ceiling has changed over the years but has remained at €24,000 since 2007 (a full list of the historical limits is given in Chapter 16). In essence the restriction was intended to limit the allowable leasing charges for "expensive cars" only (i.e. those costing over the prescribed ceiling) without regard to engine size or the level of carbon emissions. Readers are referred to earlier editions of this publication for the tax treatment of leased cars pre 1 July 2008.

Post 1 July 2008

For cars registered on/after 1 July 2008 the method of restricting the leasing charges is now linked primarily to the level of carbon emissions with the ceiling of 24,000 still preserved but its application has changed somewhat. As a result, there is a distinct tax advantage for cars with a list price of less than 24,000 and with low carbon emission levels. The examples below demonstrate the changes. For leasing charges on cars registered prior to 1 July 2008 the old regime for restriction still applies (as described above).

Categories of cars:

- Up to 155g/km (A, B & C)
- Between 156 and 190g/km (D & E)
- Above 190g/km (F & G)

Categories A, B & C

- The limit of €24,000 is applied even where the actual retail price is less than €24,000.

Example 15.5

John White leases a business car with carbon emissions level of 120g/km (Category A). The list price of the car is €12,000 and the annual leasing charges are €5,000. The allowable leasing charges are:

$$€5{,}000 \times \frac{€24{,}000}{€12{,}000} = €10{,}000$$

The allowable leasing charges are therefore doubled i.e. amount allowable is €10,000.

Categories D & E

- Limit is 50% of the lower of cost and €24,000.

It is important to note that it is the retail price of the car when it was manufactured that is included in the formula and not the cost to the company of acquiring the car in the case of second-hand cars.

Example 15.6

John White leases a business car with carbon emissions level of 160g/km (Category D). The list price of the car is €36,000 and annual leasing charges of €5,000. The allowable leasing charges are:

$$€5{,}000 \times \frac{€24{,}000 \times 50\%}{€36{,}000} = €1{,}667$$

Categories F & G

- No allowances are available.

Example 15.7

John White leases a business car with carbon emissions level of 220g/km (Category F). The list price of the car is €66,000 and the annual leasing charges are €15,000. There is no tax allowable lease charge.

Finance lease payments

A business is entitled to a full deduction for finance lease payments including both capital and interest elements (this is adjusted by adding back the lease interest and allowing the lease payment/rental in full, or by simply allowing a deduction for the capital element of the payment).

For a detailed commentary on the accounting treatment of finance leases and a worked example of the necessary adjustments for tax purposes, readers are referred to Appendix III.

Operating leases

The total lease rentals are charged to the profit and loss account over the period of the lease. As with a finance lease, the lessee is entitled to tax relief for the total rentals arising, but in this case no adjustment is required to the computation as the full rentals have already been deducted in arriving at profit before tax. There is no capital element in the lease rentals.

Pension fund contributions

s774 TCA97

Contributions to a Revenue-approved Pension Scheme are allowed on a paid basis. This differs from the accountancy treatment under FRS 17 which ensures that the charge to the profit and loss is the annual contribution whether paid in the period or not. Any contribution not actually paid in the period is disallowed for tax purposes. The contribution will only be allowed in the period in which it is actually paid. Additionally, where an employer makes abnormally high "special" contributions, Revenue will determine a period over which the deduction will be allowed depending on the circumstances. The "spread" is usually calculated by dividing the special contribution by the normal annual contribution.

Example 15.8

Assume that the normal annual contribution of a business is €50,000, the full amount of which is allowed as a Case I deduction, During the year, the business made an additional special lump sum contribution of €150,000 to the Approved Scheme. The special contribution will be allowable over a three-year period. Therefore €100,000 will be added back and €50,000 (in addition to normal annual contribution of €50,000) may be claimed in the current year and each of the next two years.

Insurance expenses

The main focus in considering insurance expenses should be to ensure that all insurance premiums have been incurred for the purposes of the trade and do not contain any elements of private expenditure, e.g., private house insurance being included on a business policy.

Certain insurance expenditure incurred on capital items will be allowable, e.g., building and contents insurance for the premises from which the business trades. Thus, there are certain cases where although an item is capital in nature, or the underlying asset is capital, the expense will be allowed. The same holds true for the interest expense incurred in acquiring a trading premises. Such deductions are allowed due to a Revenue concession as opposed to strict legislative interpretation.

For example, Keyperson insurance has insurance on the lives of key individuals in the business – for example, an employee who is central to the management and control of the business and who may be responsible for a large element of the goodwill of the business. It may be considered that the death, sickness or disability of such an individual could give rise to a substantial loss of profits or trade of the business. Notwithstanding that, the taxpayer is really insuring against loss of profits, the triggering event would be the death of the key individual. Keyperson insurance is allowed as a deduction for the purposes of the tax computation where certain conditions are met. However, it should be noted that any benefit paid under such a policy will be treated as a trading receipt for the period in which it is paid. If the payment does not qualify for a deduction, then any receipt/payment from the proceeds of the policy will not be taxable.

Embezzlement

As a broad rule, losses arising as a result of embezzlement or misappropriation by an employee are likely to be allowed, but not those arising from the misdeeds of a proprietor.

Illegal payment

A new s83A TCA97 effective from 1 January 2008 disallows expenditure (e.g., bribes), the making of which constitutes a criminal offence. The disallowance of the expenditure extends to payments both inside and outside the State.

Pre-trading expenditure

s82 TCA97 Section 82 TCA97, provides that Revenue expenditure incurred within three years prior to the commencement of trading is deductible where the following conditions are met:

- The expense must be of a type which would otherwise be allowable as a trading expense.

- The expense and charges can only be offset against income from the trade or profession and not against any other income.

- The relief is only available for new businesses.

The expenditure falling within the provisions will be deemed to have been incurred at the time when the trade or profession is commenced.

Trademark registration

s86 TCA97 A specific deduction is provided by s86 TCA97 for the cost of the registration of trademarks. The accounting treatment may have been to capitalise this amount and write it off over a period. This can be reversed and a deduction taken in the year to which the expenditure relates.

Employee expenses

The following items are discussed in turn:

(i) wages and salaries;

(ii) long-term unemployed relief;

(iii) redundancy payments;

(iv) travel and subsistence.

(i) Wages and salaries

Wages and salaries of employees are normally allowed in full on the basis that they are wholly and exclusively incurred for the purposes of carrying on the trade. However, where payments are deemed to be "excessive", the full payment may be disallowed on the basis that it is not necessary for the carrying on of the trade.

In the case of *Copeman (HM Inspector of Taxes) v William Flood & Sons Ltd,* 24 TC 53, it was held that remuneration paid to directors of a company was not wholly, exclusively and necessarily incurred for the purposes of the trade.

As already illustrated in 15.3.2 above, any withdrawals taken by the trader (even though they might refer to this as "wages") are not allowable and must be added back in the computation. One of the important things to note is that a sole trader is assessed to income tax on profit; the drawings are irrelevant to the trader's tax position. If wages are paid to the trader's spouse or family, they are allowable provided they are "wholly and exclusively" for the purpose of the trade.

(ii) Long-term unemployed

s88A Section 88A TCA97 had for many years provided a double deduction for employee salaries and employer's PRSI contributions where long-term unemployed individuals were employed under the former Revenue Job Assist Scheme. The double deduction was removed in 2014. Section 7 Finance Act 2014 proposed changes to s88A which saw the introduction of a new employment incentive scheme, known as JobsPlus. Under the JobsPlus scheme employers receive certain payments where they employ staff who have been unemployed for more than 2 years. These payments are exempt from income tax.

(iii) Redundancy payments

s203 TCA97 Where an employer pays a lump sum under s46 Redundancy Payments Act 1967 to an employee, that sum is an allowable deduction in computing taxable profits. The deduction is available in computing profits under Case I. Where the Minister makes the payment in the first instance but is reimbursed by the employer, it is regarded as being paid by the employer.

Where the payment is made after the discontinuance of the trade or profession it is regarded as made on the last day of the trade or profession.

(iv) Travel and subsistence

Payments for travel and subsistence may be made on the basis of vouched receipts or under Revenue-approved rates. Payments in excess of Revenue-approved amounts should be cleared in advance. Travel between home and the office is not treated as an allowable business expense.

A businessman who pays for his own lunch does not spend his money exclusively for the purposes of his business – *Caillebotte (HM Inspector of Taxes) v Quinn,* 50 TC 222.

15.4 Income not Taxable under Case I/II

While the commentaries on the distinction between revenue and capital, the principle of "wholly and exclusively", movements on provisions and statutory adjustments are relevant to both income and expense items, the analysis thus far has focused on expense items. The purpose of this section is to focus attention on certain receipts and items of income, which regularly appear in the profit and loss account.

All items of income, which do not relate to Case I trading activities must be deducted and instead categorised under the appropriate case, or alternatively, classified as a capital receipt for capital gains tax purposes, or alternatively classified as tax-exempt income. It is important to note that the figure deducted is that which is credited to the profit and loss account. This may be different from the figure to be included under the relevant case heading.

- Deposit interest is taxable under Case III if no DIRT was deducted at source and under Case IV if tax was deducted at source.
- Irish source rental income is taxable under Case V.
- Irish dividends or distributions received are taxable under Schedule F and accordingly, must be deducted from the "profit before tax" figure in arriving at tax-adjusted Case I/II.
- s44 TCA97 Interest on Government Securities (s44 TCA97): interest received on securities issued by the Minister of Finance is exempt. Other interest received on Government Securities is paid without deduction of tax at source and is therefore taxable under Schedule D Case III.
- Revenue Grants

s223, 224, 226 TCA97 Revenue grants are taxable apart from the following, which are specifically exempt from tax (s226 TCA97): the JobsPlus Scheme[1], the Market Development Fund, the Employment Subsidy Scheme, EU Programme for Peace and Reconciliation in Northern Ireland and Border Counties (s226 TCA97), initiatives of the International Fund for Ireland (s226 TCA97), Údarás na Gaeltachta Employment Grants (s223 TCA97 and s224 TCA97).

- s225 TCA97 Employment grants given under s3 or s4 of Shannon Free Airport Development Limited (Amendment) Act 1970, s25 of the Industrial Development Act 1986 or under s12 of the Industrial Development Act 1993 are not taxable.
- There may be other exempt receipts included in a trader's accounts that should be excluded for the purposes of income tax. These include:
- profits or gains arising from the occupation of woodlands managed commercially with a view to profits (s232 TCA97),
- Insurance proceeds of a revenue nature are fully taxable, whereas if they relate to capital items, i.e., buildings or machinery, they must be adjusted for (i.e., deducted from the "profit before tax" figure). In these circumstances, they may give rise to a chargeable gain.
- Compensation and damages will very often be classified as capital in nature and accordingly, should be deducted in arriving at tax-adjusted Case I. However, where receipts are in respect of revenue items, e.g., loss of earnings, they are taxable in full and no adjustment is necessary.

1 Effective from 1 July 2014 (s226(k)).

Appendix I

Bad and Doubtful Trade Debts

The accounting treatment of "Bad Debts" can be categorised as follows:

(a) Bad debts, i.e., amounts due that are considered irrecoverable, are written off against accounting profit as a trade expense.

(b) Bad debts subsequently recovered are credited to the profit and loss account as a trade receipt.

(c) An increase in the Specific Bad Debt Provision is treated as a trade expense against the accounting profit, as is an increase in the General Bad Debt Provision.

(d) A decrease in the Specific Bad Debt Provision is treated as a trade receipt, as is a decrease in the General Bad Debt Provision. Thus, such amounts are credited to the profit and loss account (i.e., they increase accounting profit).

The tax implications of each element of the overall charge can be identified as follows:

(1) Bad debts written off are allowable in full as a Case I deduction, e.g., if the debtor has gone into liquidation without paying the debt, it is written off as irrecoverable.

(2) Bad debts recovered are treated as taxable Case I income. For example, if a liquidator of a debtor company recovers monies from the sale of assets and distributes this to the creditors, the debt which was written off, but which has been recovered, or is known to be recoverable, is now taxable.

(3) An increase in the Specific Bad Debt Provision is an allowable Case I deduction, e.g., an amount provided for specifically, debt by debt against those debts which are genuinely considered doubtful.

For example:	€
Opening Specific Bad Debt Provision 1/1/2018	10,000
Closing Specific Bad Debt Provision 31/12/2018	25,000
Increase in Specific Bad Debt Provision (expense)	15,000

This expense charged to profit and loss account is fully allowable as a Case I deduction.

(4) A decrease in the Specific Bad Debt Provision is treated as taxable Case I income, i.e., the amount credited to profit and loss account is treated as a fully taxable trade receipt.

(5) An increase in the General Bad Debt Provision is not an allowable Case I deduction and must therefore be added back. This provision is an amount of the total debtors at the period end (usually a percentage of the total debtors) which the trader feels will be "bad" based on previous experience.

	€
Opening General Bad Debt Provision 1/1/2018	(9,000)
Closing General Bad Debt Provision 31/12/2018	16,000
Increase in General Bad Debt Provision	7,000

This expense charged to profit and loss account is not allowable as a Case I deduction.

(6) A decrease in the General Bad Debt Provision is not treated as taxable income and is therefore deducted from the accounting profit.

Appendix II

Donations

Approved Bodies

s848A TCA97 Up to 2001 various reliefs existed for donations to different bodies. The Finance Act 2001 introduced a new s848A and Sch. 26A into the TCA97, which effectively consolidated all of the legislation relating to donations, to provide for relief in a uniform manner for donations to "approved bodies". These include bodies already eligible to receive tax-deductible donations (e.g., bodies providing education in the arts, certain bodies approved for research, etc., and educational bodies authorised by the Revenue Commissioners as meeting certain conditions). Readers are referred to Chapter 11, Section 11.5.4 for 2014 changes for individual donors.

Qualifying Donation

A donation must also satisfy the following conditions:

- minimum donation of €250, no maximum* figure except where associated with the charity and a 10% cap on income applies;
- it must not be subject to any condition of repayment;
- neither the donor nor any person connected with him/her can receive a benefit in consequence of making the donation directly or indirectly;
- it is not conditional on, nor associated with or part of an arrangement involving the acquisition of property by the approved body otherwise than by way of gift from the donor or person connected with him;
- the donation is not otherwise deductible for tax.

**Readers are referred to Chapter 8, Section 8.7 for restriction on reliefs for high income earners.*

Approved Bodies

The following are the types of "approved bodies" that qualify for tax relief:

- eligible charities (who have been tax-exempt for at least two years);
- educational institutions or bodies including primary, second-level or third-level, if they meet certain conditions (e.g., their programmes are approved by the Minister for Education and Science or the institution provides courses which are validated by the Higher Education Training and Awards Council);
- the Scientific and Technological Education (Investment) Fund;

- a body approved for Education in the Arts by the Minister for Finance;
- First Step Limited;
- certain other named bodies, including the following:
  - The Equine Foundation,
  - The Institute of Ophthalmology,
  - The Mater College for Research and Postgraduate Education,
  - St. Luke's Institute of Cancer Research.

A body to which s209 of the Taxes Consolidation Act 1997 applies, i.e., a body for the promotion of the observance of the Universal Declaration of Human Rights or the implementation of the European Convention for the protection of Human Rights and Fundamental Freedoms or both,

- The Foundation for Investing in Communities Limited or any of its 90% subsidiaries as may be approved by the Minister for Finance.
- US-Alliance Limited.

Donations to Certain Sports Bodies

s847A TCA97

Section 41 Finance Act 2002 introduced a new section, s847A, to the TCA97, which operates in a similar manner to s848A as outlined above.

Section 847A provides for relief for qualifying donations to approved sports bodies, to enable the sports body to construct facilities, purchase significant equipment or to repay a loan to carry out any of these transactions.

Approved Body

An approved body is one which is established to promote athletic or amateur games or sports. In order to qualify as an approved sports body, the organisation must hold a valid tax clearance certificate, and also a valid certificate from Revenue stating that the organisation qualifies for the exemption from income tax/corporation tax set out in s235 TCA97 (i.e., bodies established to promote athletic or amateur games or sports).

The Relief

For a donation to qualify for relief it must be at least €250 in the year of assessment; there is no upper limit on the qualifying donation. The donation does not reduce the individual's income for the purposes of determining his or her net relevant earnings.

Approved Project

To qualify for relief the donation must be used to fund a project, which has been approved by the Minister for Tourism, Sports and Recreation, and for which the sports body holds a valid certificate. The Minister will not certify projects costing in excess of €40 million. To be approved the project must fall into one of the following categories:

- purchase of land or buildings (or the construction or refurbishment of a building or part of a building) to be used for sporting activities by the approved sports body;
- purchase of permanently based equipment to be used for sporting activities by the approved sports body;
- the improvement of playing pitches, surfaces or facilities by the approved sports body;
- the payment of loan interest on funds borrowed by the approved sports body for any of the above activities.

Appendix III

Finance Lease Repayments

Under GAAP, a finance lease is a contract between a lessor and a lessee for the hire of a specific asset whereby substantially all of the **risks and rewards** of ownership of that asset are transferred to the lessee. It usually involves payment by the lessee to a lessor of the **full** cost of the capital asset together with a return on the finance provided by the lessor. The accounting treatment of such a finance lease is as follows:

1. The capital cost of the fixed asset is capitalised with a corresponding liability created for the "capital element" of the finance lease.
2. Each lease repayment to the lessor includes a "capital" and "finance charge" element. The capital element is used to reduce the lease liability while the finance charge element is debited to the Profit and Loss Account as a trading expense.

For tax purposes, because assets held under finance leases will generally not qualify for capital allowances, the full amount of the finance lease repayment, i.e., both the capital and the interest element, will be deductible in arriving at taxable Case I. Thus, the appropriate treatment is as follows:

1. The amount of finance lease charges which have been debited to the profit and loss account as a trading expense are added back in the Case I computation.
2. The company is allowed a deduction against Case I income for the total of the finance lease repayments (capital and interest element) made during the accounting period.

This figure is derived as follows:

		€
	Opening leasing liabilities per balance sheet due within one year and after more than one year	X
Plus:	Capital cost of fixed asset additions acquired under finance leases during the period	X
Plus:	Finance lease charges to the profit and loss account	X
Less:	Closing leasing liabilities per balance sheet due within one year and after more than one year	(X)
■	Finance lease repayments made in period	X

It is this final figure, which is allowed as a deduction against Case I profits.

Example Appendix III.1:

B Limited:

The following information is relevant for the accounting period ended 31 March 2018:

			€
1.	*1 April 2017: Opening Lease Liabilities*	*< 1 year*	*6,000*
		> 1 year	*12,000*
2.	*A machine was acquired under a finance lease in October 2017. The capitalised cost of this fixed asset is €14,000.*		
3.	*Total finance lease charges included in the profit and loss account for the year is €7,700.*		
4.	*31 March 2018: Closing Lease Liabilities*	*< 1 year*	*10,000*
		> 1 year	*16,000*

Tax consequences

1. The figure of €7,700 for the finance lease charges is added back to the accounting profit in the tax-adjusted profits computation.

2. The company is allowed a deduction for the total finance lease repayments, calculated as follows:

		€
1/4/2017	Opening Lease Liabilities	18,000
Plus:	Machine acquired under finance lease	14,000
Plus:	Finance lease charges expensed	7,700
Less:	Closing Lease Liabilities at 31/3/2018	(26,000)
	Total finance lease repayments	13,700

Assets acquired under a hire-purchase agreement qualify for capital allowances on the cost of the asset with no allowance for the lease payments made.

16 CAPITAL ALLOWANCES

Learning Outcomes

On completion of this chapter you will be able to:

- ✓ Explain the terms "plant" and "industrial buildings".
- ✓ Calculate the capital allowances available for expenditure on plant and machinery, motor vehicles and industrial buildings.
- ✓ Identify the income tax year in which assets are acquired and disposed of with particular reference to the rules that apply on commencement, cessation and change of accounting date.
- ✓ Calculate balancing allowances and charges on disposals of plant and motor vehicles.
- ✓ Explain the income tax implications of disposals of industrial buildings.

16.1 Introduction

In computing taxable profits, generally no deduction is allowable for capital expenditure or the depreciation of capital assets. To compensate for this statutory disallowance, capital allowances are available in respect of certain capital expenditure on plant and machinery, motor cars and industrial buildings.

In addition, capital allowances have been offered as a 'carrot' to encourage investment in certain types of capital expenditure projects, e.g., hotels, private nursing homes, urban renewal buildings, private convalescent homes, buildings used for certain childcare facilities, buildings used for third-level educational purposes and buildings used as private hospitals. Readers are referred to *Income Tax* by Deegan, Reddin and Bolster for commentary on the specific regimes applicable to these incentive measures. The analysis here is concerned with the more general rules, which apply to the broad categories of expenditure, namely, plant and machinery, motor vehicles and industrial buildings. Each category of asset is considered separately as capital allowances are calculated in different ways for different types of asset.

As set out in Appendix I to Chapter 8, capital allowances reduce the amount of assessable Case I/II income, and in some instances may even result in the creation (or increase) of a Case I/II loss (this is discussed further in Chapter 17).

16.2 Plant and Machinery

16.2.1 Case law

There is no definition of plant and machinery in the Income Tax Acts. In theory, the term should therefore be given its ordinary meaning. However, over the years, the term "plant" has acquired an artificial and largely judge-made meaning. One of the earliest definitions of plant was given by Lindley L.J. in the case of *Yarmouth v France* (19 QBD647) when he stated:

> *"In its ordinary sense, it includes whatever apparatus is used by a businessman for carrying on his business, not his stock in trade which he buys or makes for sale; but all goods and chattels, fixed or movable, live or dead, which he keeps for permanent employment in his business."*

Lindley's definition contains three important elements:

(i) The item must be an "apparatus".

(ii) It must be used for the carrying on of a business.

(iii) It must be kept for permanent use in the business.

This test was further refined in the case of *J Lyons & Co Ltd v Attorney-General* (1944 1 All ER 477) by Uthwatt J. who posed the question as to whether the lamps which were the subject matter of that case were "properly to be regarded as part of the setting in which the business is carried on, or as part of the apparatus used for carrying on the business?"

In the case of *Jarrold v John Good & Sons Ltd* (40 TC 681), it was recognised that "setting" and "plant" are not mutually exclusive concepts. That case decided that the fundamental test as to whether an apparatus constitutes "plant" is whether it fulfils the function of plant, in that it is the means by which a trading operation is carried out. Applying the test in that case, it was found that special partitioning used by the taxpayer to subdivide floor space to accommodate fluctuating office accommodation requirements was plant.

The "functional" test set out in *Jarrold v Good* has been applied in many subsequent tax cases. The cases fall into two broad categories. The first category consists of cases where the point at issue is whether or not a whole structure constitutes plant. In the case of *Schofield v R & H Hall Ltd* (40 TC 538) the company had built silos on the dockside. Grain could be delivered from ships to the silos from which, in turn, it could be dispensed to customers easily. It was decided that the silos were plant for the purposes of capital allowances. In the case of *IRC v Barclay Curle & Co Ltd* (45 TC 221), the taxpayer had constructed a dry dock, a process requiring the excavation of the site and the construction of a concrete lining. The Revenue agreed that such expenditure as that incurred on the dock gate, the operating gear and the electrical and pumping installations related to plant, but argued that the expenses of excavation and concreting did not.

However, the expenditure on the concrete lining was held to be in respect of plant because it could not be regarded as the mere setting in which the trade was carried on but was an integral part of the means required for the trading operation. Hence, a structure, which fulfils the function of plant, is *prima facie*, plant.

The second category of cases concerns the application of the functional test so as to distinguish between setting and plant. The operation of the functional test in these circumstances is well illustrated by three important UK tax cases:

- *Benson v Yard Arm Club Ltd* ([1979] STC 266);
- *IRC v Scottish & Newcastle Breweries Ltd* ([1982] STC 296); and
- *Wimpy International Ltd v Warland* ([1988] STC 149).

In the case of *Benson v Yard Arm Club Ltd*, the taxpayer acquired a ship and incurred expenditure for the purpose of converting it into a floating restaurant. The taxpayer claimed that the expenditure was on plant and claimed capital allowances on it. It was held that the ship was not plant as it played no part in the carrying on of the business activities but was merely the place in which they were carried on. The ship failed therefore to be regarded as plant on the functional test in that it was not part of the apparatus employed in the commercial activities of the business. Templeman L.J. stated:

> *"There are borderline cases in which a structure forming part of business premises has been held to be plant because it does not merely consist of premises providing accommodation for the businesses but also performs a function in the actual carrying on of the business. Premises or structures forming part of premises, which have the characteristics and perform the function of plant, merit the claim for capital allowances. In my judgment it follows that if a chattel such as a ship or a hulk only provides accommodation for a business and has the characteristics and only performs the function of premises that chattel does not qualify as plant for the purposes of capital allowances."*

This case can be contrasted with that of *IRC v Scottish and Newcastle Breweries Ltd.* In this case the taxpayer incurred expenditure on electric light fittings, decor and "murals" for its hotels and public houses. The decor consisted of pictures, plaques, tapestries and other items which were either hung on or screwed to the wall and were movable. The "murals" were panels, which were screwed to the wall and were removable. It was held that as hotel-keepers, the taxpayer provided an "atmosphere" conducive to the comfort and well-being of its customers and any items intended to create or enhance that atmosphere fulfilled a function in the carrying on of the business.

Lord Lowry went on to explain that not everything which provided atmosphere in a hotel trade was necessarily plant. Contrasting the position of wallpaper and murals painted on a wall with the detachable "murals" in the case under appeal, he said:

> *"... the mural paintings and the wallpaper when executed or applied, are part of the walls and not plant, whereas the 'murals', being apparatus, are plant. The fact that two things perform the same function or role is not the point. One thing functions as part of the premises, the other as part of the plant."*

In *Wimpy International Ltd v Warland*, the taxpayer company operated a chain of restaurants providing "fast food". The company was losing money and following a takeover, the new management decided to make major changes to the premises and incurred expenditure on the installation of, *inter alia*, shop fronts, light fittings and wiring, raised floors, floor and wall tiles, suspended ceilings, balustrade and stairs. The company claimed that the items installed were "plant". Fox L.J. stated:

> *"There is a well established distinction, in general terms, between the premises in which the business is carried on and the plant with which the business is carried on. The premises are not plant."*

He went on to explain the "functional" test as follows:

> *"It is proper to consider the function of the item in dispute. But the question is what does it function as? If it functions as part of the premises it is not plant. The fact that the building in which a business is carried on is, by its construction, particularly well suited to the business, or indeed was specially built for that business, does not make it plant. Its suitability is simply the reason why the business is carried on there. But it remains the place in which the business is carried on and is not something with which the business is carried on ..."*

The Court upheld the Special Commissioners' decision that the disputed items were not plant.

The distinction between buildings and apparatus remains difficult. In the UK it has been held that the following items were not plant since they performed no function in the particular trade:

(i) a prefabricated building at a school used to accommodate a chemical laboratory *St John's School v Ward* [1974] STC 69;

(ii) a false ceiling in a restaurant *Hampton v Forte's Autogrill Ltd* [1980] STC 80; and

(iii) an inflatable cover over a tennis court *Thomas v Reynolds* [1987] STC 135.

On the other hand, it has been held that a swimming pool at a caravan site was plant since it was part of the apparatus of the business, *Cooke v Beach Station Caravans Ltd* [1974] STC 402. Decorative screens placed in the window of a building society's offices were held to be plant because the screens were not the structure within which the business was carried on, *Leeds Permanent Building Society v Proctor* [1982] STC 821.

Furthermore, it is interesting to note that the Irish Courts could well take a different view from their UK counterparts. For instance, in the UK case of *Dixon v Fitch's Garage Limited* [1975] STC 480 it was held that a canopy over a petrol station was not plant. However, in the Irish case of *S O Cullacháin v McMullan Bros* (HC 1991), it was held by the Supreme Court that such a canopy was plant.

There are a number of items which are incorporated into buildings and which are normally regarded as plant for the purposes of capital allowances. The principal items are:

- lifts;
- electrical installations and fittings;
- heating and ventilation systems;
- special housing for machinery and equipment;
- sprinkler systems;
- special foundations or reinforced flooring for machinery and equipment;
- boilers;
- movable partitioning.

Whether an item qualifies as plant must be determined by reference to the facts of the particular case. An item, which may qualify as plant in one situation, may not qualify in another.

Machinery and plant are not confined to things used physically but extend to the intellectual apparatus of the trade or profession. Thus it was held in the Irish case of *Breathnach v McCann* (4 ITC 121) that a barrister's law books were plant.

16.2.2 Amount of capital allowances on plant and machinery

An annual 'wear & tear' allowance of 12.5% which is given on a straight-line basis for eight years for plant, machinery motor vehicles.

A simple example illustrating a *pro forma* allowance computation is as follows:

Example 16.1

Andrew is a printer who operates as a sole trader and makes up his accounts to 31 December each year. He acquired three printing machines at a cost of €500,000 on 10/1/2015.

	12.5% Machine
	€
Addition 2015	*500,000*
Wear & Tear 2015*	*(62,500)*
*TWDV** 31/12/2015*	*437,500*
Wear & Tear 2016	*(62,500)*
TWDV 31/12/2016	*375,000*
Wear & Tear 2017	*(62,500)*
TWDV 31/12/2017	*312,500*
Wear & Tear 2018	*(62,500)*
TWDV 31/12/2018	*250,000*

* *Annual capital allowance for plant and machinery*
** *Tax Written Down Value*

16.2.3 Qualifying conditions for wear & tear allowance

s284 TCA97 To qualify for a wear & tear allowance:

- a person must carry on a trade, profession, employment or office;
- a person must have incurred capital expenditure on the provision of plant or machinery for the purposes of the trade, profession, or employment; and
- the plant or machinery must be in use for the purposes of the trade, etc., at the end of the person's basis period, in order to qualify for the wear & tear allowance for a year of assessment.

It is worth elaborating on this last point. It is not necessary for the asset to be used for the full duration of the accounting period in order to qualify for a wear & tear allowance; it only needs to be in use for the purposes of the trade at the end of the basis period.

Example 16.2

Jenny is a baker with an accounting year end of 30 September. She sold some kitchen appliances on 29 September 2018, replacing them on the same day with more energy-efficient appliances.

Despite the fact that the old appliances had been used for 364 days of the accounting year, Jenny will not be entitled to claim wear & tear on them, as they were not in use at the end of the accounting period. Conversely, although the new appliances have only been in use for 1 day of the accounting period, Jenny will be entitled to a full year's wear & tear as the appliances were in use at the end of the accounting period.

16.2.4 Part private use

Section 284(1) TCA97 provides that in order to qualify for a wear & tear allowance, the machinery or plant, while used for the purpose of the trade, must be wholly and exclusively so used. This section does not prevent the making of an allowance where an item of plant is used partly for business purposes and partly for other purposes. Where an item of plant is used partly for business purposes and partly for private use, only the part of the wear & tear allowance relating to the business use is allowable for capital allowances purposes.

Example 16.3

A trader acquired a Volkswagen van for €19,000 on 1 June 2015. He travels a total mileage of 20,000 miles and estimated private mileage of 5,000 miles (three-quarters of total mileage is business). He makes up accounts to 31 December each year.

	€	Allowance ¾ €
Cost	*19,000*	
Wear & tear 2015 @ 12.5%	*(2,375)*	*1,781*
TWDV 31/12/2015	*16,625*	
Wear & tear 2016	*(2,375)*	*1,781*
TWDV 31/12/2016	*14,250*	
Wear & tear 2017	*(2,375)*	*1,781*
TWDV 31/12/2017	*11,875*	
Wear & tear 2018	*(2,375)*	*1,781*
TWDV 31/12/2018	*9,500*	-

16.2.5 Qualifying expenditure

Section 316(1) TCA97 provides that capital expenditure does not include any expenditure allowable as a deduction in computing the profits or gains of the person incurring the expenditure.

The total allowances claimed over the life of the asset cannot exceed the actual cost of the plant or machinery purchased. In addition, only expenditure net of any grants received in respect of the plant/machinery is taken into account for the purposes of capital allowances.

Example 16.4

A trader acquired a machine in June 2018 for €700,000 and obtained a government grant of €100,000 in respect of it. His capital allowances will be based on €600,000 (i.e., €700,000 – €100,000) and the capital allowances available in 2018 will be €75,000 (i.e., €600,000 × 12.5%).

16.2.6 Basis of assessment

It is important to note that capital allowances are given for tax years. The capital allowances for a particular tax year of assessment are calculated by reference to the plant or machinery in use at the end of the basis period for the tax year. For example, the expenditure incurred on assets which are in use in a business at the end of the accounts year ended (say) 31 October 2018 would qualify for capital allowances in the 2018 tax year.

It is important to note that the amount on which wear & tear allowances are claimed for a particular tax year would not only include plant/machinery purchased in the current period, but also plant/machinery purchased in preceding periods (where there is a balance of wear & tear capable of being claimed).

Example 16.5

A butcher has a year-end of 30 June. He had the following purchases of assets in 2017 and 2018:

		€
1 August 2017	*Refrigerator*	*10,000*
1 September 2017	*Meat-cutter*	*4,000*
1 January 2018	*New sign*	*2,000*
1 February 2018	*Freezer (defective - sold on 1 March 2018)*	*900*
15 August 2018	*New cash register*	*3,000*
20 December 2018	*Desk for office*	*500*

The Capital Allowances for 2018 would be as follows:

	€
Cost	*16,000*
Wear & tear 2018	*(2,000)*
TWDV 31/12/2018	*14,000*

Even though the refrigerator and the meat-cutter were purchased in the 2017 income tax year, they will only qualify for capital allowances for the first time in 2018. This is on the basis that they were purchased in (and in use at the end of) the accounting period to 30 June 2018, which forms the basis period for the 2018 income tax year.

Even though the freezer was acquired in the accounting year ended 30 June 2018 (basis period for the 2018 tax year), the butcher will not be entitled to any wear & tear allowance for 2018, as the freezer was not in use for the purposes of the trade at the end of the basis period.

Even though the cash register and desk for the office were acquired in the tax year 2018, they form part of the assets acquired for the accounting year ended 30 June 2019 (basis period for the 2019 tax year). Consequently, no wear & tear will be obtained in the 2018 tax year for these assets.

Unusual situations may arise however, where one accounting period forms the basis of assessment for more than one tax year (commencement situations) and where an accounting period forms the basis of assessment of no year of assessment (cessation situations or change of accounting date). The legislation contained in s306 TCA97 provides for such situations as follows:

"(a) Where two basis periods overlap, the period common to both shall be deemed to fall in the first basis period only;

(b) Where there is an interval between the end of the basis period for one year of assessment and the basis period for the next year of assessment then, unless the second mentioned year of assessment is the year of the permanent

discontinuance of the trade, the interval shall be deemed to be part of the second basis period;

(c) Where there is an interval between the end of the basis period for the year of assessment preceding that in which the trade is permanently discontinued and the basis period for the year in which it is permanently discontinued, the interval shall be deemed to form part of the first basis period."

Basis period less than 12 months

In addition, it is important to bear in mind that where the basis period is less than 12 months in duration (e.g. on commencement/cessation), the annual wear & tear allowance is proportionately reduced. These aspects are best illustrated by the following series of examples.

Example 16.6: Commencement

A trader commences business on 1 December 2017 and prepares accounts annually to 30 November. He incurs expenditure of €12,000 on an item of plant in December 2017.

The first accounts to 30 November 2018 will form the basis of assessment for 2017 (1 December 2017 to 31 December 2017) and 2018 (1 December 2017 to 30 November 2018). There is an overlap for the 2017 and 2018 tax years in respect of the period 1 December 2017 to 31 December 2017. Therefore the expenditure in that period first qualifies for allowances in 2017.

In addition, as the basis period for 2017 is from 1 December to 31 December, then the wear & tear allowable for 2017 must be restricted to one-twelfth. Accordingly, the wear & tear allowance for 2017 is €12,000 × 1/12 = €1,000.

Example 16.7

Jane commenced trading on 1 October 2016 and makes up accounts to 30 September each year. In the year ended 30 September 2017, she purchased the following assets which were put to use immediately:

		€
1 October 2016	*Desk and chairs*	*2,000*
1 October 2016	*Computers and printers*	*5,000*
10 January 2017	*Telephone system*	*6,000*
30 June 2017	*Projector and screen for presentations*	*2,000*

There were no additions during the year ended 30 September 2018. The adjusted Case I profits were as follows:

	€
30 September 2017	*100,000*
30 September 2018	*150,000*

What are the assessable profits and capital allowances for the first three tax years?

Jane's first tax year of assessment will be 2016 and the basis period will be 1 October 2016 to 31 December 2016. The assessable profits will be €100,000 × 3/12 = €25,000.

The first accounts to 30 September 2017 will form the basis of assessment for 2016 (1 October 2016 to 31 December 2016) and 2017 (1 October 2016 to 30 September 2017). There is an overlap for the 2016 and 2017 tax years in respect of the period 1 October 2016 to 31 December 2016. Therefore the expenditure in that period first qualifies for allowances in 2016.

It is necessary to identify for capital allowance purposes the assets in use at the end of the 2016 basis period, i.e., 31 December 2016. The assets acquired were the desk and chairs, €2,000, and computers and printers, €5,000, on 1 October 2016. The length of the basis period is three months and therefore the capital allowances will have to be reduced proportionately as the basis period is less than one year.

Wear & tear Computation 2016

	€
Additions	*7,000*
Wear & tear (€7,000 × 12.5% × 3/12)	*(219)*
TWDV at 31/12/2016	*€6,781*

Jane's second tax year of assessment will be 2017 and the basis period will be the 12 months ending 30 September 2017. The profits assessable in 2017 will be the profits of the first 12 months to 30 September 2017, i.e., €100,000.

Again, it is necessary to identify the assets in use at the end of the basis period. The desk and chairs, €2,000, computers and printers, €5,000, telephone system, €6,000, and projector and screen, €2,000, were all in use.

As the basis period is of 12 months' duration, there is no reduction necessary in the capital allowances. Consequently, a full year's wear & tear will be granted.

Wear & tear Computation 2017

	2016 Additions	***2017 Additions***	Total
	€	€	€
TWDV at 1/1/2017	*6,781*	0	
Additions		*8,000*	
Wear & tear @ 12.5%	*(875)**	*(1,000)*	*1,875*
TWDV at 31/12/2017	*5,906*	*7,000*	

**€7,000 × 12.5%*

Jane's third tax year of assessment will be 2018, and the basis period will be the 12-month accounting period ending in the year of assessment, i.e., year ended 30 September 2018. The assessable profit will be the tax-adjusted accounting profits for the year ended 30 September 2018, i.e., €150,000.

There were no additions for this period. As a result the wear & tear for 2018 is as follows:

Wear & tear Computation 2018

	2016 Additions	***2017 Additions***	Total
	€	€	€
TWDV 1/1/2018	*5,906*	*7,000*	
Wear & tear	*(875)*	*(1,000)*	*1,875*
TWDV 31/12/2018	*5,031*	*6,000*	

SUMMARY:

	Case I	Capital Allowances
	€	€
2016	*25,000*	*219*
2017	*100,000*	*1,875*
2018	*150,000*	*1,875*

Example 16.8: Cessation

A trader ceases business on 31 December 2018. He makes up his accounts as follows:

Year ended 30 September 2015

Year ended 30 September 2016

Year ended 30 September 2017

15 months to 31 December 2018

Assuming no revision to actual for 2017, the period from 1 October 2017 to 31 December 2017 will not be used as the basis for any tax year. Expenditure in that period will first qualify for an allowance claim for 2017.

Example 16.9: Cessation

Mary has been trading for many years but due to ill-health has decided to cease to trade on 31 May 2018. Mary makes up accounts to 30 September each year.

Her adjusted trading profits were as follows:

	€
Year ended to 30/9/2016	*100,000*
Year ended to 30/9/2017	*120,000*
Period to 31/5/2018	*10,000*

Details of Mary's capital allowance computations are as follows:

Cost and TWDV 31 December 2016	Cost	TWDV
	€	€
Machine A put into use in 2015	*10,667*	*8,000*
Machine B put into use in 2015	*24,000*	*18,000*

Mary also acquired Machine C on 1/10/2017 for €10,000.

Given that Mary had falling profits, there is no revision to "actual" of the assessable profits for the penultimate year. Thus, the basis period for 2017 is the 12 months to 30 September 2017 and the basis period for 2018 is the period from 1 January 2018 to 31 May 2018. Accordingly, the profits of the period 1 October 2017 to 31 December 2017 are not assessed to tax. For capital allowances, this period is treated as part of the 2017 penultimate year and the machine purchased on 1 October 2017 is treated as an addition in the capital allowance computation for 2017.

2017 Wear &Tear

	2015 Additions		2017 Additions
	Machine A	Machine B	Machine C
	€	€	€
TWDV 1/1/2017	*8,000*	*18,000*	–
Additions			*10,000*
	8,000	*18,000*	*10,000*
Wear & tear	*(1,333)*	*(3,000)*	*(1,250)*
TWDV 31/12/2017	*6,667*	*15,000*	*8,750*

Note: A permanent discontinuance of the trade by Mary requires consideration as to whether a balancing allowance/charge arises in 2018. This is discussed in greater detail in 16.2.7.

Example 16.10

David decided to change his accounting date from 30 April to 30 September in 2017. His profits were as follows:

Year ended 30 April 2016	*€50,000*
Year ended 30 April 2017	*€80,000*
5 Months ending 30 September 2017	*€15,000*
Year ended 30 September 2018	*€45,000*

The 2017 assessment will be based on the 12-month period to 30 September 2017 (the later of the two accounting dates ending in the year).

2016 will be based on the 12 months to 30 September 2016, if greater than the profits for the 12 months to 30 April 2016.

2016

Originally based on 30 April 2016 – €50,000

Year ended 30 September 2016:

(7/12 × €50,000) + (5/12 × €80,000)

€29,167 + €33,333 = €62,500

Basis period 1/10/2015 to 30/9/2016

2017

Basis period 1/10/2016 to 30/9/2017

(7/12 × €80,000) + €15,000

€46,667 + €15,000 = €61,667

2018

Basis period 1/10/2017 to 30/9/2018

€45,000

The details of David's capital allowances are as follows:

	Cost	*TWDV 1/1/2016*
	€	*€*
Machine A (put into use in 2011)	*16,000*	*6,000*
Machine B (put into use in 2011)	*32,000*	*12,000*
Machine C acquired 1/6/2016	*50,000*	

As Machine "C" was acquired in the revised basis period for 2016, it therefore first qualifies for capital allowances in 2016.

Wear &Tear 2016, 2017 and 2018	2011 Additions		2016 Additions
	Machine A	Machine B	Machine C
	€	€	€
TWDV 1/1/2016	*6,000*	*12,000*	–
Additions	–	–	*50,000*
	6,000	*12,000*	*50,000*
Wear & tear 2016	*(2,000)*	*(4,000)*	*(6,250)*
TWDV 31/12/2016	*4,000*	*8,000*	*43,750*
TWDV 1/1/2017	*4,000*	*8,000*	*43,750*
Wear & tear 2017	*(2,000)*	*(4,000)*	*(6,250)*
TWDV 31/12/2017	*2,000*	*4,000*	*37,500*
Wear & tear 2018	*(2,000)*	*(4,000)*	*(6,250)*
TWDV 31/12/2018	–	–	*31,250*

16.2.7 Balancing charges/allowances

The purpose of capital allowances is to give the trader a tax deduction for his/her net capital outlay on the plant used in his/her business. The net outlay of a trader, who spends €100 on a piece of plant and who receives €30 on the sale of the plant a few years later, is €70 (€100 – €30). Capital allowances are given on the original cost (i.e., €100) and these are adjusted to the net capital outlay of the trader when the plant is sold and the proceeds of the sale become known.

If the net capital outlay is more than the capital allowances given, additional capital allowances are given by way of a balancing allowance. If the net capital outlay is less than the capital allowances granted, the excess capital allowances are restricted by way of a balancing charge.

A balancing charge or allowance is calculated by comparing the tax written down value of the asset disposed of with the proceeds. If the tax written down value is higher than the proceeds, a balancing allowance arises. If the tax written down value is less than the proceeds a balancing charge arises.

A balancing charge or allowance for a year of assessment is made by reference to events occurring in the basis period for the tax year in question (where basis periods overlap or there is an interval between basis periods, the rules as outlined previously apply).

Any of the following events gives rise to a balancing charge or balancing allowance:

- the machinery or plant ceases to belong to the trader;
- the machinery or plant permanently ceases to be used for the purposes of the trade;
- the permanent discontinuance of the trade (money received on the sale of plant or machinery after the cessation of a trade may be taken into account when computing balancing allowances or charges).

It is important to note that a balancing allowance/charge will only arise if a wear & tear allowance has been claimed in respect of the plant/machinery in question.

Balancing charges and allowances are to be computed as if machinery or plant had been sold at open market price, where:

- a trade ceases and the trader does not sell the plant or machinery;
- machinery is sold at less than market price or given away;
- machinery is transferred from business to private use.

Example 16.11

John makes up his accounts to 30 June each year. In the year to 30 June 2018 he sold a machine for €50,000. The TWDV of the asset was €30,000. The asset originally cost €80,000.

	€
Proceeds	*50,000*
TWDV	*(30,000)*
Balancing charge	*20,000*

If the sales proceeds were €25,000, a balancing allowance of €5,000 would occur.

A balancing charge in effect claws back the excess of capital allowances given over the net capital outlay by the trader. The balancing charge can therefore never exceed the capital allowances granted.

Example 16.12

A machine cost €6,000. The trader sold the asset for €10,000. The TWDV of the asset was €2,250. The calculation is as follows:

	€
Sales proceeds	*10,000*
TWDV	*(2,250)*
Apparent balancing charge	*7,750*

The balancing charge of €7,750 is greater than the actual allowances claimed, and is restricted to the amount claimed, €3,750 (i.e., cost €6,000 – TWDV €2,250).

A balancing charge will not arise in respect of disposals of plant and machinery occurring on or after 1 January 2002, where the disposal proceeds are less than €2,000.

Example 16.13

The sales proceeds of a machine on 1 June 2018 was €1,500. The TWDV was €1,200. Technically a balancing charge of €300 would occur but as the sales proceeds are less than €2,000, no balancing charge will arise.

Where plant or machinery disposed of is replaced by the owner, he/she may elect for the cost of the replacement plant or machinery to be reduced by the amount of the balancing charge rather than being assessed immediately on the balancing charge.

This reduction in the cost of the replacement plant will be treated as if an initial allowance of that amount was given.

Example 16.14

Jenny prepares accounts to 30 June each year. During the year to 30 June 2018, she disposed of an asset and replaced it with a similar asset. The details were as follows:

	€
Original cost of asset	*10,000*
TWDV at 31/12/2017	*7,500*
Sale proceeds	*9,000*
Cost of replacement asset	*15,000*

The calculation is as follows:

Proceeds	*9,000*
Less	
TWDV	*(7,500)*
Balancing charge	*1,500*

If the replacement option is claimed, the balancing charge of €1,500 will not be taken into account in 2018 and capital allowances will be claimed on the replacement asset as follows:

Capital allowances 2018	*€*
Additions	*15,000*
Less	
Balancing charge on original asset	*(1,500)*
Qualifying cost of replacement asset	*13,500*
Wear & tear 2018	*(1,688)*
TWDV 31/12/2018	*11,812*

16.2.8 Leasing

Capital allowances are available to persons who incur expenditure on plant and use the plant for trading purposes. However, it is not unusual for traders to lease plant rather than purchase it. The lessee cannot claim capital allowances in this situation but would instead claim deductions for the payments as noted in Appendix III of Chapter 15.

Persons who purchase plant and lease it to traders are entitled to claim the capital allowances on the cost of the plant, if the plant is leased on such terms that the burden of wear & tear falls directly on the lessor.

16.2.9 Motor vehicles

General

Motor vehicles are defined as vehicles used for the conveyance by road of persons or goods or the haulage by road of other vehicles. The rate of wear & tear for expenditure incurred on motor vehicles on or after 4 December 2002 is 12.5%, calculated on a straight-line basis. The rate however is 40% for taxis and for cars used for short-term hire to the public (see below) on a reducing balance basis.

Restriction for "expensive" cars

s373 TCA97 Readers will be aware from Chapter 15 that there are restrictions on allowable motor leasing charges where the carbon emission levels exceed 155g/km and the list price of the car exceeds a specified ceiling (€24,000 since 2007). The restrictions on capital allowances for motor vehicles follow very similar rules (readers are referred to earlier editions of this publication for the treatment of motor vehicles acquired pre 1 July 2008).

Position for motor vehicles post 1 July 2008

With effect from 1 July 2008, a new regime for calculating capital allowances on business cars was introduced by reference to the carbon emissions level of the car.

Categories of cars:

- Up to 155 g/km (A, B & C)
- Between 156 and 190 g/km (D & E)
- Above 190 g/km (F & G)

The specified limit remains at €24,000 and applies as follows:

Categories A, B & C

- The limit of €24,000 is applied even where the actual cost is less than €24,000.

Categories D & E

- Limit is 50% of the lower of cost and €24,000.

Categories F & G

- No allowances are available.

Any proceeds arising on the disposal of such cars will be similarly restricted when calculating balancing allowances or balancing charges. This restriction does not apply to cars which are used in the ordinary course of trade for hiring to the general public.

Where a car is used partly for business purposes and partly for private use by an individual, only the part of the capital allowance relative to the business use is allowable as a set-off against the individual's trading income.

Example 16.15

Seamus Smith purchases a business car on 1 September 2018 with a carbon emissions level of 150 g/km (a category C car). The cost price is €36,000, however, the amount on which allowances are available is restricted to €24,000 (the specified amount).

The car is disposed of for €21,000 a few years later. The calculation of the balancing allowance/charge on the disposal will be calculated by comparing the TWDV with the proceeds as adjusted i.e., €21,000 × €24,000/36,000 = adjusted proceeds of €14,000.

Example 16.16

John O'Carroll purchases a business car on 1 November 2018 with a carbon emissions level of 130 g/km (a category B car). The cost price is €12,000. However, the amount on which allowances are available is increased to €24,000 (the specified amount).

The car is disposed of for €6,000 a few years later. The calculation of the balancing allowance/charge on the disposal will be calculated by comparing the TWDV with the proceeds as adjusted i.e., €6,000 × 24,000/12,000 = adjusted proceeds of €12,000.

Example 16.17

Aiden Finlay purchases a business car on 1 December 2018 with a carbon emissions level of 160 g/km (a category D car). The cost price is €36,000, however, the amount on which capital allowances are available is restricted to €12,000 (50% of the lower of the cost and specified amount of €24,000).

The car is subsequently disposed of for €18,000 a few years later. The calculation of the balancing allowance/charge on the disposal will be calculated by comparing the TWDV with the proceeds as adjusted i.e., €18,000 × 12,000/36,000 = adjusted proceeds of €6,000.

Example 16.18

Mike Brady purchases a business car on 1 December 2018 with a carbon emissions level of 250 g/km (a category G car). The cost price is €70,000, capital allowances are not claimable.

The car is subsequently disposed of for €40,000 a few years later – no balancing allowance/ charge will arise.

Taxis and short-term hires

s286 TCA97 The rate of wear & tear allowance is 40% for cars used for qualifying purposes, which are defined as cars in use as taxis or for short-term hire to members of the public.

16.3 Industrial Buildings

Allowances are available on expenditure incurred on industrial buildings. The allowances are quite different from those available for expenditure on plant and machinery.

16.3.1 Definition of industrial building

Overview

An "industrial building or structure" is defined in s268 TCA97 as a building or structure in use:

- for the purpose of a trade carried on in a mill, factory or other similar premises;
- for the purpose of a trade which consists of the operation or management of an airport and which is an airport runway or airport apron used solely or mainly by aircraft carrying passengers or cargo for hire or reward;
- for the purpose of a trade which consists of the operation or management of an airport (other than airport runways and aprons);
- for the purpose of a dock undertaking;
- for the purpose of growing fruit, vegetables or other produce in the course of a trade of market gardening;
- for the intensive production of cattle, sheep, pigs, poultry or eggs in the course of a trade other than the trade of farming;
- for the purpose of the trade of hotel-keeping;
- for the purpose of a trade consisting of the operation or management of a private registered nursing home within the meaning of s2 of the Health (Nursing Homes) Act 1990. Finance Act 2009 has provided for the phasing out of capital allowances for such expenditure;
- for the purpose of a trade consisting of the operation or management of a convalescent home providing treatment for acutely ill patients;

- for the purpose of a trade which consists of the operation or management of a qualifying hospital. Finance Act 2009 has provided for the phasing out of capital allowances for such expenditure;
- for the purpose of a trade which consists of the operation or management of a qualifying sports injury clinic; or
- for the purpose of a trade which consists of the operation or management of a qualifying mental health centre. Finance Act 2009 has provided for the phasing out of capital allowances for such expenditure;
- for purpose of a trade where consists of the operation of specialist palliative care.
- caravan sites and camping sites kept under the control of the Tourist Traffic Acts 1939 to 2003.

Specific exclusions

The definition of an industrial building specifically excludes any building or structure in use:

- as a dwelling house (other than a holiday cottage or residential unit);
- as a retail shop;
- as a showroom or office;
- for a purpose ancillary to any of the above.

s268(8) TCA97

Where part of a building or structure is, and part is not, an industrial building or structure, and the capital expenditure on the non-industrial section does not exceed 10% of the total capital expenditure incurred on the whole building, then the whole building will be treated as an industrial building. Where the cost of the office or shop, etc., exceeds 10% of the total expenditure, the full cost of the office or shop is disallowed and not just the excess over the 10%.

Example 16.19

	€
Site cost	*100,000*
Cost of factory	*410,000*
Cost of offices	*40,000*
	550,000

Cost of offices / *Total cost (excluding site cost)* = *€40,000* / *€450,000* = *8.89%*

Therefore the offices will qualify for capital allowances.

If the position were as follows:

	€
Site cost	*100,000*
Cost of factory	*410,000*
Cost of offices	*50,000*
	560,000

$$\frac{\textit{Cost of offices}}{\textit{Total cost (excluding site cost)}} = \frac{\textit{€50,000}}{\textit{€460,000}} = \textit{10.87\%}$$

As the fraction exceeds 10%, no part of the expenditure on the office qualifies for capital allowances.

"Office" is not defined. In the case of *Inland Revenue Commissioners v Lambhill Ironworks Limited* (31 TC 393), it was held that the drawing office of a firm of structural steel engineers was an "industrial building or structure" being on the industrial side of the concern rather than on the managerial side. The Lord President commented in this case that a drawing office of a certain type was no more an "office" within the meaning of the Income Tax Act than a machine shop was a shop.

In looking at s268(8) TCA97, the first thing to be determined is what exactly constitutes "the whole of a building or structure".

In the case of *Abbott Laboratories Limited v Carmody* (44 TC 569), a factory had been built on a large site. The factory was built in four main blocks: a chemical block: a pharmaceutical block, a maintenance block and an administration block. The blocks were connected to each other by pipes and roadways and all shared a common boilerhouse. The administration block was connected to the pharmaceutical block by means of a covered passageway. The company claimed an industrial building allowance in respect of the cost of construction of the entire factory. The Revenue resisted an allowance on the cost of the administration block. On appeal to the Special Commissioners, the company contended that all of the buildings constituted an industrial building for the purposes of the industrial building allowance. The Special Commissioners held that the definition of industrial building or structure was "not apt to apply to an extensive factory site so that it falls to be treated as one unit for the purpose of an industrial building allowance". The matter went to the High Court but was ultimately decided in favour of the Revenue.

16.3.2 Qualifying expenditure

Qualifying expenditure is capital expenditure incurred on the construction of an industrial building or structure. The expression "capital expenditure on the construction of an industrial building or structure" includes expenditure on part of a building or structure. The expenditure need not be on the construction of a building or structure, which is complete in itself. The expression includes capital expenditure on items such as the following:

- preparing, tunnelling and levelling land for foundations;
- strengthening the structure of an existing building, for example, to make it safe to increase the load put upon a floor;
- the erection of additional interior walls in an industrial building; and
- additions to, and improvements of, entrances, stairways, ramps, access roads and main supplies of water gas and electricity.

It should be noted that the expenditure must be of a capital nature, and that it must be incurred on the construction of the building or structure.

The following expenditure is specifically excluded:

- acquisition cost of land;
- expenditure on the provision of machinery or plant or any asset which is treated as machinery or plant;
- any expenditure, which qualifies for an allowance as being capital expenditure on scientific research or mining development allowance.

Expenditure is incurred on the day on which the relevant sum becomes payable.

Although the legislation is silent on the meaning of the date when the sum becomes payable, it may be interpreted as the agreed date for payment as specified in the agreement between the buyer and seller. If the date of payment is not specified in the agreement, then it may be acceptable to assume that the payment is due one month from the date of the invoice. In practice, the date of issue of the invoice is frequently taken as the date the sum becomes payable.

16.3.3 Industrial buildings annual allowance

This analysis is primarily concerned with the calculation of an Industrial Buildings writing down allowance (usually referred to as Industrial Buildings annual allowance or IBAA). Initial allowances and free depreciation may be claimed in certain incidences in respect of urban renewal properties. In this regard, readers are referred to the commentary in *Income Tax* by McAteer, Reddin and Deegan.

An IBAA may be claimed each year, on expenditure incurred on an industrial building until the cost of the building is fully allowed. This allowance is calculated on a straight-line basis. It is calculated on the expenditure net of any grants received, but before deducting any industrial building initial allowance which may have been claimed. An IBAA may be claimed by the person who is entitled to the relevant interest, i.e., the person who has incurred the expenditure, provided the building is an industrial building as already defined and is in use for that purpose. Generally, expenditure on industrial buildings is written off on a straight-line basis over a 25 year period, so that a trader may claim an IBAA of 4% of the qualifying cost each year. Where an individual incurs expenditure on certain items, such as nursing homes, crèches etc., the write off is 15% per annum for six years and 10% in year seven.

16.3.4 Purchasers of certain buildings

The allowance is made primarily to the person who incurs expenditure on the construction of an industrial building. However, s279 TCA97 however extended the allowance to persons who buy an industrial building before it has been used or within one year after it commences to be used, provided the allowance has not been claimed by any other person.

The purchaser of such a building is deemed to incur expenditure at the time when the purchase price becomes payable and not when the actual construction expenditure was incurred.

The amount on which the allowance is granted depends on whether the expenditure on the construction of the building was incurred by a builder or non-builder.

Construction incurred by a builder

If the sale by the builder is the only sale of the relevant interest, before the building is used or within one year after it commences to be used, the allowance is granted on the "net price paid" to the builder. Where there is more than one such sale, before the building is used or within one year after it commences to be used, the allowance is granted by reference to the "net price paid" on the first sale by the builder (unless the last purchaser pays a lower price).

In other words, the "net price paid" to the builder remains the figure by reference to which allowances are given unless the last purchaser pays a lower price.

The cost of land is excluded from the "net price paid" by the operation of the following formula:

$$\text{Amount paid} \times \frac{\text{Actual Construction Costs}}{\text{Actual Construction Costs} + \text{Cost of Land}}$$

Construction expenditure incurred by a non-builder

The purchaser is deemed to incur expenditure, on the date when the purchase price becomes payable, equal to the lower of the actual construction costs incurred by the non-builder or the "net price paid" by the purchaser of the building.

Where there is more than one sale, before the building is used or within one year after it commences to be used, the allowance is based on the lower of the actual construction costs incurred by the non-builder or the "net price paid" by the last purchaser.

The cost of land is excluded from the "net price paid" by the operation of the following formula:

$$\text{Amount paid} \times \frac{\text{Actual Construction Costs}}{\text{Actual Construction Costs} + \text{Cost of Land}}$$

16.3.5 Balancing allowances and balancing charges

A balancing charge or allowance may arise:

(a) where the relevant interest in an industrial building is sold; or

(b) where the building is demolished or destroyed or ceases altogether to be used; or

(c) where the relevant interest is a leasehold one and comes to an end except by the person entitled to that interest acquiring the reversionary interest.

No balancing charge or allowance can arise when any of the above events occurs after the tax life of the building has expired. In the case of industrial buildings where the qualifying expenditure was incurred after 16 January 1975, the tax life is generally 25 years. Thus, where such buildings are disposed of within that 25 year period, a balancing allowance or charge may arise[1].

As in the case of plant and machinery, balancing charges and allowances are calculated by comparing the tax written down value of the building with the proceeds of sale. A balancing charge cannot exceed the allowances already granted.

Example 16.20

An industrial building, with a qualifying cost €500,000 in 2008 is sold in 2018 for €700,000. The tax written down value is €300,000.

The position would be as follows:

	€
Sales proceeds	*700,000*
TWDV	*(300,000)*
Balancing charge	*400,000*
Restricted to allowances granted	*200,000*

If the building was sold in 2033, no balancing charge would arise.

Second-hand industrial buildings

Where a purchaser buys an industrial building on which capital allowances have already been claimed by the vendor, then the purchaser may be entitled to an annual allowance, depending on how long the building has been in use prior to his/her purchase of it. In the case of industrial buildings with a tax life of 25 years, a sale by a vendor after 25 years does not attract a balancing charge or allowance and the purchaser is not entitled to any allowances on the expenditure incurred by him/her. If such a building has been in use for less than twenty-five years, he/she will be entitled to industrial buildings annual allowance on the cost to the original purchaser or on his/her own cost, whichever is the lower. The annual allowance is calculated as follows:

- Calculate the residue after sale by the vendor:

  Where a balancing charge arises, the residue after sale is equal to the written down value of the building plus the balancing charge.

  Where a balancing allowance arises the residue after sale is equal to the written down value after deducting the balancing allowance.

- Calculate the number of unexpired years for which an industrial buildings annual allowance could have been claimed by the vendor.

- The annual allowance available to the purchaser is the residue divided by the number of unexpired years.

1 Where capital allowances are claimed in respect of the refurbishment of a building, the tax life of the building runs from the time the expenditure is incurred and not from the time the building is first used.

Thus in example 16.20 above, the second-hand purchaser may claim allowances on the residue, in this case €500,000, over a remaining unexpired tax life of 15 years. Thus, his industrial buildings annual allowance will be €33,333 each year for a period of 15 years.

16.3.6 Temporary disuse of industrial building or structure

A building is not deemed to cease to be an industrial building if it merely falls temporarily out of use. When a building or structure is an industrial building or structure immediately before any period of temporary disuse, it is deemed to continue to be an industrial building or structure during the period of temporary disuse. An annual allowance will continue to be granted during that period.

There is no statutory definition of the term "temporarily out of use". Thus, whether or not a building is temporarily out of use in particular circumstances is a question of fact to be decided in each case.

16.3.7 Lessors

A lessor of a building is entitled to claim the allowances if he/she lets the building to a lessee who uses it as an industrial building. Where a lessor incurs expenditure on a building and does not lease it to a lessee who uses it as an industrial building, capital allowances may still be claimed by the lessor provided the building is leased to:

- the IDA; or
- SFADCo; or
- Údarás na Gaeltachta,

and provided that they in turn lease it to a person who uses it as an industrial building.

Appendix I

Motor Car Restrictions

TCA s373 Under s373 TCA expenditure on cars is restricted for the purposes of capital allowances. The limit has been increased on a number of occasions. For convenience, the limits and the periods to which they apply are summarised in the following table:

Period during which expenditure incurred	*Limit* €
(1) Before 16 May 1973	None
(2) 17 May 1973 to 28 January 1976	3,174.35
(3) 29 January 1976 to 5 April 1986	4,444.08
(4) 6 April 1986 to 27 January 1988	5,078.95
(5) 28 January 1988 to 25 January 1989	7,618.43
(6) 26 January 1989 to 29 January 1992	8,888.17
(7) 30 January 1992 to 26 January 1994	12,697.38
(8) 27 January 1994 to 8 February 1995	16,506.60
(9) 9 February 1995 to 22 January 1997	17,776.33
(10) 23 January 1997 to 2 December 1997	19,046.07
(11) 3 December 1997 to 1 December 1998	19,680.94
(12) 2 December 1998 to 30 November 1999	20,315.18
(13) From 1 December 1999 to 31 December 1999	20,950.68
(14) From 1 January 2001 to 31 December 2001	21,585.55
(15) From 1 January 2002 to 31 December 2005	22,000.00
(16) From 1 January 2006	23,000.00
(17) From 1 January 2007	24,000.00

17 LOSSES

Learning Outcomes

On completion of this chapter you will be able to:

- ✓ Calculate the final income tax liability of an individual after claiming all possible loss relief.
- ✓ Describe how a loss relief claim under s381 can displace certain other personal reliefs and tax credits.
- ✓ Identify the due date for making a claim under s381.
- ✓ Describe the form of relief under s382 and identify the circumstances in which loss relief under s382 will be unavailable.
- ✓ Explain how a taxpayer may not benefit from double relief for aggregated losses.
- ✓ Calculate loss relief on commencement.
- ✓ Explain how Case I or Case II capital allowances may be used to create or augment a Case I or Case II loss.
- ✓ Describe the nature of relief for losses arising under other miscellaneous Cases and Schedules.

17.1 Introduction

This chapter deals with the treatment of a loss sustained by an individual in carrying on a trade, profession or employment. Trading or professional losses may generally be relieved in one of two ways:

s381 TCA97
- ■ against other sources of income in the year in which the loss arises under s381 TCA97;

s382 TCA97
- ■ against future Case I or Case II income from the same trade or profession under s382 TCA97.

In addition, terminal loss relief may be available in certain circumstances on the cessation of a trade or profession.

17.2 Relief for Losses under s381 TCA97

Relief is granted to a person who, in carrying on a trade, profession, vocation or employment, sustains a loss during a year of assessment. A loss for an accounting period is computed in the same manner as a profit would be computed under Cases I and II of Schedule D.

Strictly, relief for a loss under s381 should be calculated for the actual tax year i.e., for the tax year 1 January to 31 December. In practice, a loss for a twelve-month accounting period, ending in the year of assessment, is normally taken as the loss for that year. The Revenue Commissioners will, however, insist upon the strict statutory basis (i.e., loss for the year to 31 December):

- for the first three years of assessment on commencement of a trade or profession;
- for any year of assessment following a year in which a claim has been made on the strict statutory basis;
- for the year of cessation, i.e., the loss from 1 January to the date of cessation.

The taxpayer can always insist on obtaining relief for a loss on the strict statutory basis. Relief under s381 is obtained by reducing the taxpayer's gross statutory income (i.e., gross income before charges on income and reliefs) for the tax year in question by the amount of the loss. Losses incurred in the tax year may be set-off against the other income of that tax year under this section.

Example 17.1

Mr Jones, who has traded for many years, incurred a trading loss (as adjusted for tax purposes) of €20,000 in the year ended 31 July 2018. The other assessable income in the 2018 tax year was Irish rental income of €15,000 and UK dividends of €10,000.

2018	€
Case 1	*Nil*
Schedule D Case III – UK dividends	*10,000*
Schedule D Case V – rental income	*15,000*
	25,000
Less s381 loss 2018	*(20,000)*
Income before deduction of charges on income and reliefs	*5,000*

A s381 TCA97 loss is deemed first to reduce the earned income of the individual, then his/her unearned income (see 19.1), next the earned income of his wife/her husband, and finally the unearned income of his wife/her husband. This is relevant in calculating the maximum allowable for tax relief on pension contributions.

Section 11 FA 2014 introduced a provision to limit loss relief for individuals engaged in a "non-active capacity". This section limits the loss relief to €31,750 (or the actual loss if lower). An individual is regarded as being in a non-active capacity where:

- He/she does not work for the greater part of his/her time on the day-to-day management of the trade/profession
- He/she spends an average of less than 10 hours per week personally engaged in the activities of the trade/profession
- The activities are not carried on a commercial basis

Where the basis period is less than 12 months, the limit of €31,750 is reduced proportionately. Section 11 FA 2014 introduced a new s381B TCA97 and students should note that this restriction has application for partnerships (considered in Chapter 18).

17.2.1 Claim

It is important to note that the taxpayer must make a claim to obtain the relief under s381. The claim must be made within two years of the end of the tax year to which the claim relates. In the above example, the claim for relief under s381 must be made on or before 31 December 2019. When a loss is utilised under s381 relief for the loss cannot be obtained under any other section.

It should be noted that the full amount of the loss must be claimed under s381 to the extent that it can be absorbed by the taxpayer's gross income. It is not possible to use only part of a loss under s381 so as to leave sufficient income to be covered by reliefs/charges. This can be important where it is not possible to carry forward unused reliefs/charges to future tax years.

Example 17.2

Mr Mitchell sustained a loss as adjusted for tax purposes of €20,000 in the year ended 30 June 2018. The trader's other assessable income for 2018 consisted of UK rental income of €12,000 and he had reliefs of €5,000.

Relief for the trading loss is due as follows:

2018	**€**
UK rental Income – Schedule D Case III	*12,000*
Less s381(1) loss available	*(20,000)*
Assessable income	*Nil*
Available for relief under s382 for 2018	*8,000*

It is not possible to claim only €7,000 of the loss under s381(1) in 2018, leaving the balance of income to be covered by the 2018 reliefs of €5,000.

17.3 Creating or Augmenting a Loss with Capital Allowances

s392 TCA97 Under s392 TCA97, it is possible to create or augment a Case I/II loss by having capital allowances deducted in computing the loss.

The capital allowances taken into account are the allowances due for the tax year in which the loss arises, but only to the extent that they are not required to offset any balancing charges due for that year.

Example 17.3

Mr Ryan, who has traded for many years, has the following profits and capital allowances:

	€	€
Profit – year ended 30/9/2018		*4,000*
Capital allowances 2018		*17,000*
Balancing charge 2018		*3,000*

The s381 loss for 2018 is as follows:		€
Profit – year ended 30/9/2018		*4,000*
Less Capital allowances 2018	*(17,000)*	
Balancing charge 2018	*3,000*	*(14,000)*
s381 loss 2018		*(10,000)*

17.3.1 Capital allowances brought forward

Capital allowances brought forward cannot be used to create or augment a s381 loss. However, they can be used to reduce profits and offset balancing charges for the year. As a result, it is important to ensure that the order in which current year capital allowances and capital allowances brought forward is correct, so as to maximise their benefit.

Example 17.4

Mr Curran, who has been trading for many years, makes up his accounts annually to 30 September. His accounts for the year to 30 September 2018 show a profit for tax purposes of €10,000. He has capital allowances for 2018 as follows:

	€	€
Wear & tear		*15,000*
Balancing charge		*(1,000)*

The capital allowances forward are €5,000.

The s381 loss for 2018 is		€
Capital allowances forward		*(5,000)*
Profit chargeable 2018		*10,000*
		5,000
Capital allowances 2018	*(15,000)*	
Less: balancing charge	*1,000*	*(14,000)*
s381 loss 2018		*(9,000)*

17.3.2 Extent to which capital allowances are to be taken into account

Where, in a commencement situation, the capital allowances taken into account for creating or augmenting a s381 loss are allowances for the year of claim, they will be restricted to the excess over the profit of the basis period.

Example 17.5

Mr Purcell commenced trading on 1 June 2016. Recent results for tax purposes are as follows:

	€
Year ended 31/5/2017	*4,000*
Year ended 31/5/2018	*3,000*
Capital allowances (as adjusted) were as follows:	
2017	*4,800*
2018	*2,000*

Mr Purcell claimed relief under s381 for 2017.
As this is a commencement, the Revenue will insist on the actual loss being computed for s381 purposes.

		€
i.e.,	*(€4,000 × $^5/_{12}$) + (€3,000 × $^7/_{12}$)*	*3,417*
Less capital allowances		*(4,800)*
Loss		*(1,383)*

This loss will be restricted to the amount by which the capital allowances exceed the assessable profits for 2017 i.e.,

2017 Assessment	€
Assessable 2017	*4,000*
Less capital allowances	*(4,800)*
Loss available for relief	*(800)*

17.4 Carry Forward of Losses under s382 TCA97

Where a person carrying on a trade or profession sustains a loss in respect of which relief has not been wholly given under s381 or under any other provision of the Income Tax Acts, he/she may claim that any portion of the loss for which relief has not been given may be carried forward against subsequent assessments of profits of the same trade.

Relief under s382 is to be given as far as possible against the first subsequent year of assessment. For this purpose, the taxable profits for the next year available to cover the loss forward are the taxable profits for that year after deducting the relevant capital allowances. Any unrelieved balance of that loss is carried forward again to the next year of assessment and so on indefinitely so long as the trade or profession continues until the loss carried forward is fully used up.

Example 17.6

Mr McGrath has been in business for many years and makes up accounts to 31 December. Recent results are as follows:

	Profit/(Loss)
Year ended	€
31 December 2016	*(20,000)*

	€
31 December 2017	5,000
31 December 2018	6,000

A claim was made for relief under s381 for 2016. Mr McGrath also had rental income in 2016 of €10,000.

Assessments are as follows:

		€	€
2016	Rental income	10,000	
	Less s381 loss	(20,000)	Nil
2017	Case I	5,000	
	Less s382 loss	(5,000)	Nil
2018	Case I	6,000	
	Less s382 loss (balance)	(5,000)	1,000

The loss for the year ended 31 December 2016 has been utilised as follows:

		€
s381	2016	10,000
s382	2017	5,000
s382	2018	5,000
		20,000

A loss can be carried forward only to the extent that it has not been effectively allowed under s381 or in apportioning and aggregating profits and losses in computing an assessment.

Example 17.7

Mr Moran commenced business on 1 May 2016. His results for the first years were as follows:

	Profit/(loss) €
Seven months to 30 November 2016	(40,000)
Period to 31 October 2017	5,000
Period to 31 December 2018	45,000

Assessable profits for first three tax years:

			Assessment
2016	01/05/2016 – 31/12/2016	€	€
	(€40,000) + (1/11 × €5,000)	(39,545)	Nil
2017	12 months to 31/10/2017		
		€	€
	€5,000 + (1/7 × (€40,000))	(714)	Nil
2018	Period ended 31 December 2018		

		€	€
Profits €45,000 × 12/14		*38,571*	
Less loss forward (see Note):		*(34,545)*	*4,026*
Note:		*Total loss*	*(40,000)*
Less utilised:			
2016		*455*	
2017		*5,000*	*5,455*
			(34,545)

17.4.1 Third year of assessment - second-year 'look-back' relief

As discussed in 14.6.2, the profits assessable in the third year of assessment are based on the basis period of 12 months ending during the year of assessment, but this figure can be reduced by the excess of the profits of the 12 month period ending during the second year of assessment over the actual profits for the year. Where this deduction is greater than the amount of the original profits assessable for the third year, then the excess is treated as if it were a loss forward under s382.

Example 17.8

Mr Kearney commenced to trade on 1 October 2016. His results for the first years were as follows:

	Profit
	€
Period 1 October 2016 to 30 September 2017	*10,000*
Year ended 30 September 2018	*500*
Year ended 30 September 2019	*5,000*

Computation of assessable profits:			Assessable
2016	*01/10/2016 – 31/12/2016*		€
	€10,000 × 3/12		*2,500*
2017	*01/10/2016 – 30/09/2017*		
	€10,000		*10,000*
2018	*Year ended 30 September 2018*	*(Note)*	*Nil*

Note:	€
Amount assessable for second year 2017	*10,000*
Less actual profits 2017:	
((9/12 × €10,000) + (3/12 × €500))	*(7,625)*
Excess	*2,375*

Final 2018 assessment: (€500 – €2,375) = (€1,875), i.e., Nil.

The excess of €1,875 is carried forward under s382 against trading profits for 2019.

17.4.2 Same trade

In order to ensure that losses can be carried forward under s382, the same trade has to be continued without interruption. Losses forward cannot be set against the profits of a new trade and if trading has permanently ceased, then pre-cessation losses cannot be carried over to a later year when the trade is reactivated.

Whether a trade currently being carried on is the same trade as that in which the losses were incurred is a question of fact, as indeed is the question of whether or not a trade has permanently ceased and recommenced or has merely been suspended. When a trade has merely been suspended, losses can be carried forward and relieved under s382.

s382 TCA97

It is interesting to note the UK tax case of *Gordon & Blair Limited v IRC* (40 TC 358). The appellant company carried on a business as brewers. In October 1953, it ceased brewing but continued to bottle and sell beer supplied to its specification by another brewery. The company claimed that it carried on the same trade before and after October 1953, so that losses sustained prior to that date could be set-off against subsequent profits. It was held that the company had ceased trading as brewers and commenced a fresh trade of selling beer. The losses prior to October 1953 could not be carried forward under the UK equivalent of s382 TCA97.

s69 TCA97

If a trade or profession ceases to be carried on by one person and is then carried on by another person or persons, s69 TCA97 provides that the trade is to be treated as permanently discontinued at that time and a new trade has been set up. Accordingly, trading or professional losses at the date of deemed cessation cannot be carried forward.

By concession, the provisions of s69 do not apply where a person dies and the trade or profession is carried on by the surviving spouse (see 13.3).

17.5 Terminal Loss

Where a trade or profession is permanently discontinued and in the 12 months to the date of discontinuance a loss has been sustained (referred to as a "terminal loss"), the loss may be set-off against the trading profits for the three years of assessment prior to the year of cessation provided that relief is not claimed for the loss under any other section. For further commentary on the nature and calculation of this relief, readers are referred to the analysis in *Income Tax*, Finance Act 2010 by Deegan, Reddin and Bolster (Ed).

17.6 Schedule D Case III

s382 TCA97

There is no statutory relief for Case III losses. By concession, Case III losses incurred in a foreign trade may be carried forward for offset against future profits of the same trade (assessed under Case III) in the same way as trading losses, etc., under s382 TCA97.

17.7 Schedule D Case IV

A loss incurred in any activity, the income from which would be chargeable under Case IV, may be set-off against other Case IV assessments for the same year and any unused balance may be carried forward against Case IV assessments in future years.

17.8 Schedule D Case V

A Case V loss incurred in any year may be set-off against Case V profits assessed for the same year and any unused balance carried forward against subsequent Case V assessments.

Example 17.9

Mr Brown had the following net rents (after deduction of all allowable expenses) in respect of let properties situated in Ireland. The properties had been let for many years.

			Profit/(Loss)
		€	**€**
Period ended 31 December 2016			*(5,000)*
Year ended 31 December 2017			*2,000*
Year ended 31 December 2018			*8,000*
Assessments are as follows:			
2016	*Period ended 31 December 2016*		*Nil*
2017	*Year ended 31 December 2017*	*2,000*	
	Less loss carried forward	*(5,000)*	*Nil*
2018	*Year ended 31 December 2018*	*8,000*	
	Less loss (balance)	*(3,000)*	*5,000*

17.9 Schedule E

A loss from an employment might arise in exceptional circumstances, for instance, where a manager remunerated on a share of profits has to suffer a share in a loss, or where a commercial traveller has guaranteed debts incurred and suffers a loss in one year because of a large bad debt.

It is important to note that relief for Schedule E losses can be claimed only under s381. There is no provision to claim relief under any of the other loss sections.

18 TAXATION OF PARTNERSHIPS

Learning Outcomes

On completion of this chapter you will be able to:

- ✓ Identify the existence of a partnership.
- ✓ Explain how partners are assessed for income tax.
- ✓ Calculate the amount assessable on each partner, including where there is a change in the profit-sharing ratio.
- ✓ Calculate the capital allowances and charges due to each partner, including where there is a charge in the profit-sharing ratio.
- ✓ Explain the treatment of losses.
- ✓ Calculate the amount assessable on each partner where there is interest on capital and/or salaries paid to partner(s).
- ✓ Explain the rules that apply where a partner joins or leaves the partnership.

18.1 Definition

Fundamental to understanding partnerships and taxation is the Partnership Act 1890 and the definition therein of exactly what is a partnership.

Section 1(1) sets out the definition as follows:

> *"Partnership is the relation which subsists between persons carrying on a business in common with a view of profit."*

18.2 Existence of Partnership

The leading case in respect of this is *Inspector of Taxes v Cafolla & Co*[1]. In this case, Joseph Cafolla converted his sole trader business in Dublin into a partnership with his sons. Under the terms of the partnership agreement, Mr Cafolla reserved to himself very extensive and far-reaching powers over the direction and control of the firm. In particular, he had the power to put an end to the partnership at any time, to reclaim the premises, the stock and the goodwill and to resume the carrying on of the business as a sole trader.

---

1 1949 IR210.

Nevertheless it was held by the Special Commissioner of the Revenue, and it was subsequently challenged in the High Court and the Supreme Court, that a partnership existed in this case. Indeed in the High Court, McGuire, J indicated that there was abundant evidence for such a finding. It was argued that Mr Cafolla was entitled at any time to obtain the beneficial entitlement of the income of the firm and therefore the income of the firm should be deemed to be Mr Cafolla's sole income under section 20(1) of the Finance Act 1922.

However, the Supreme Court held by 3:2 majority that the income of the firm arose from the carrying on of the firm's business under the terms of the partnership agreement and under this agreement the sons undertook to devote the whole of their time to the business of the firm. Thus, although under the terms of the partnership agreement, Mr Cafolla was able to resume the restaurant business as a sole trader at any time, by doing so he would not be receiving the income of "the firm". Thus, the firm's income was not something of which he could have beneficial enjoyment at any time for the purpose of section 20(1) of the Finance Act 1922 and therefore it was incorrect to deem it be his income for income tax purposes. In this way, the Supreme Court maintained the strict distinction between the sole trader's business and that of the subsequent partnership.

The other leading case was *Macken v Revenue Commissioners*[2] which concerned an oral agreement between Mr Macken, his daughter and his son, whereby Mr Macken agreed to admit his daughter and son as partners into his painting business which, up to then, he had operated as a sole trader. The question for the High Court was whether after the date of the oral agreement, the business continued to be carried on as a sole trade operation or whether the parties were carrying on the "business in common".

The Revenue Commissioners claimed that no partnership existed at the date of the oral agreement, but that the transfer of the father's business to his children took place on the date of the execution of the partnership agreement, a number of months later, and the estate duty was to be assessed on this basis.

The profits of the business were in fact shared between the three partners for the period between the oral agreement and the written agreement, and the Revenue Commissioners in assessing income tax treated the three parties as partners. Nonetheless, Teevan, J held that the oral agreement was simply an agreement to enter partnership at a future date and that the partnership did not commence at the date of the oral agreement. The parties were not carrying on a business in common since there was no perceptible change in the manner in which the business was carried on after the oral agreement. In addition, the parties had not reached agreement at that time on one of the vital terms of the agreement, namely a determination of which assets were to be brought into the partnership. The other factors considered by Teevan, J can be framed as questions, which may provide assistance in determining whether a business is being carried on in common after a pre existing business purportedly admits a partner. These are as follows:

2 1962 IR302.

1. Has the business name of the firm been changed?
2. Are the bank accounts in the name of the purported partners?
3. Have notices been issued to those parties who have been contracting with the pre-existing business to advise them of a change in structure?
4. Has the transfer of debts from the pre-existing business to the new business taken place?
5. If the pre-existing business was a partnership, has a registration in the Register of Business Names been effected?
6. How was the relationship between the parties treated by the Revenue Commissioners for tax purposes?

18.3 Relevant Legislation

The taxation of partnerships is covered in s1007 to 1012 of the Taxes Consolidation Act 1997[3].

Important aspects of partnerships covered in the legislation are as follows:

Section 1007 – Interpretation

Section 1008 – Separate assessment

Section 1009 – Partnership involving companies

Section 1010 – Capital allowances

Section 1011 – Provision as to charges under s757

Section 1012 – Modifications of provisions as to appeals.

Section 1007, 1008, 1010 and 1012 are the subject matter of this analysis and explanations of these sections, followed by practical examples are set out below.

18.4 How are Partners Assessed?

A partnership is not a legal entity *per se*. For taxation purposes all partners in a partnership are assessed on their share of the profits in the partnership, as if all are sole traders. Partners are individually liable for their respective taxation liabilities in connection with their share of the firm's profits.

3 Section 1013 deals with limited partnerships, which are outside the scope of this chapter.

18.4.1 Relevant period

The definition of a 'relevant period' is of fundamental importance for the taxation of partnerships. It broadly means a continuing period during which a trade is carried on by two or more persons in partnership and during which a complete change of proprietorship did not occur at any time.

A relevant period in relation to a given partnership trade begins:

(a) when the trade is set up or commenced by two or more persons in a partnership, at the time when the trade is commenced, e.g., John & Bernard commenced business in partnership on 1 July 2018;

(b) where the trade having previously been carried on by a sole trader becomes carried on by a partnership (including the partnership of which the former sole trader is a member), at the time of succession, e.g., John and Bernard are sole practitioner solicitors who decide to cease as sole practitioners on 30 June 2018 and commence partnership on 1 July 2018 together;

(c) where the trade having previously been carried on by a partnership becomes carried on by another partnership, none of whose members was a member of the previous partnership at the time of succession, e.g., John and Bernard are carrying on a partnership and Shay and Ray are admitted to the partnership on 30 June 2018 and John and Bernard retire on that date.

A relevant period in relation to a partnership trade ends on the happening of whichever of the following events first occurs:

(a) The trade is in fact discontinued, e.g., John and Bernard are in partnership and decide to cease business on the 30 June 2018.

(b) The partnership is succeeded by a sole trader (including a sole trader who has been a member of the partnership), e.g., John and Bernard are in partnership and Bernard retires on 30 June 2018, with John continuing as a sole trader in business.

(c) The partnership is succeeded by a new partnership and no member of the old partnership becomes a member of the new one, e.g., John and Bernard are in partnership and Shay and Ray are admitted to partnership on 1 July 2018 and John and Bernard retire on 30 June 2018.

For a relevant period, the partnership is regarded as an entity having a continued existence despite any changes in its constitution, e.g., if John and Bernard are in partnership and Shay is admitted as a partner on July 2018, the partnership continues.

Example 18.1

John was a sole practitioner solicitor for many years. In 2013, he decided with Bernard to create a partnership to include both himself and Bernard.

In 2014, Shay is admitted into the partnership. John retires in 2015 and Ray is admitted to the partnership as a partner.

In 2016, Bernard dies and ceases to be a partner.

In 2017, Shay and Ray are unable to continue and they decide to go their separate ways.

In this example, the relevant period starts in 2013.

Shay's admission in 2014 and the retirement of John in 2015 have no effect. Nor does the death of Bernard in 2016.

The partnership ceases in 2017 and the relevant period ends.

18.5 Apportionment of Profits (losses)

s1008 TCA97

In the case of a trade (or profession) carried on by a partnership, profits arising to a partner in the trade (or losses sustained by a partner in the trade) are taxable (or relieved) as if they were, respectively, profits (or losses) of a separate trade carried on by him/her on his/her own account. The amount of any profits (or losses) attributable to a partner is determined in accordance with the partnership agreement in force for the accounting period. The tax-adjusted accounting profits of the partnership are calculated in the normal way (using the Case I/II rules addressed in Chapter 15). However, there are some additional features, which are unique to partnerships, and these are addressed in further detail at 18.8 below.

Where the profit sharing ratio is constant for the duration of the basis period in any given income tax year, then the tax adjusted accounting profits are split in that ratio for that basis period.

Example 18.2

John, Joan and Bernard have been in partnership for several years preparing accounts to 30 September each year and sharing profits and losses equally. On 1 October 2018, they changed the profit sharing ratio to 3:2:2 respectively (John: Joan: Bernard). Tax adjusted accounting profits for the year ended 30 September 2018 amounted to €420,000.

Assessable Case I/II for 2018 is as follows:

	€
John	*140,000*
Joan	*140,000*
Bernard	*140,000*

Albeit that the profit sharing ratio changed during the income tax year, the profits are split in the profit sharing ratio that applies for the basis period, i.e., the accounting year ended 30 September 2018.

Where the profit-sharing ratio changes during the basis period, it is necessary to time-apportion the tax-adjusted accounting profits and to apply the relevant profit-sharing ratios to each component amount.

Example 18.3

Facts as per example 18.2 above, except in this instance, the profit sharing ratio changes to 3:2:2 on 1 April 2018.

Assessable Case I/II for 2018 are as follows:

	Total	*John*	*Joan*	*Bernard*
	€	€	€	€
Tax-adjusted profits from 1/10/2017–31/3/2018	*210,000*	*70,000*	*70,000*	*70,000*
Tax-adjusted profits from 1/4/2018–30/9/2018	*210,000*	*90,000*	*60,000*	*60,000*
Total assessable Case I/II for 2018	*420,000*	*160,000*	*130,000*	*130,000*

18.5.1 Partnership profits not allocated to partners

s1008 TCA97 Section 1008 TCA97 provided that undistributed profits of a partnership were assessed on the precedent acting partner (see 18.10) under Schedule D Case IV at 20%. Section 30 Finance Act 2007 amended this, effective from 1 January 2007, whereby the undistributed profits are allocated for tax purposes to each partner and taxed at the appropriate marginal rate.

18.6 Charges and Capital Allowances

Capital allowances are calculated for the partnership in the normal way, i.e., in accordance with the rules addressed in Chapter 16. The total capital allowance claim is split between the partners on the basis of the profit-sharing ratio that applies in the actual income tax year.

Similarly, charges paid during the year are allocated between the partners in their profit-sharing ratio for the income tax year. Thus, where the profit sharing ratio changes during the income tax year, it is necessary to time apportion the total claim.

This differs from the treatment of tax-adjusted accounting profits, which are split by reference to the ratio that applies during the basis period.

Example 18.4

Facts as per Example 18.2 above except in this instance, a capital allowance claim has been calculated for the partnership in the amount of €84,000.

The profit-sharing ratio changes to 3:2:2 on 1 October 2018.

The capital allowance claim for 2018 must be time apportioned and allocated as follows:

	Total	*John*	*Joan*	*Bernard*
	€	€	€	€
Capital allowance claim 1/1/2018–30/9/2018 (9/12ths)	*63,000*	*21,000*	*21,000*	*21,000*
Capital allowance claim 1/10/2018–31/12/2018 (3/12ths)	*21,000*	*9,000*	*6,000*	*6,000*
Total capital allowance claim 2018	*84,000*	*30,000*	*27,000*	*27,000*

Example 18.5

As above, except in this instance, the profit-sharing ratio changes to 3:2:2 on 1 April 2018.

The capital allowance claim for 2018 must be time-apportioned and allocated as follows:

	Total	John	Joan	Bernard
	€	€	€	€
Capital allowance claim 1/1/2018–31/3/2018	21,000	7,000	7,000	7,000
Capital allowance claim 1/4/2018–31/12/2018	63,000	27,000	18,000	18,000
	84,000	34,000	25,000	25,000

18.7 Losses

Losses are apportioned in a similar manner to profits, i.e., in the profit-sharing ratio that applies for the basis period.

Example 18.6

John and Bernard are in partnership sharing profits/losses 2:1.

The partnership results for the year ended 31/12/2018 show a loss of (€90,000)

Apportioned	€
John – Loss	*(60,000)*
Bernard – Loss	*(30,000)*

Losses may also be created or augmented by current capital allowances either to convert a small profit to a loss or to increase the loss incurred for the particular period.

Example 18.7

Bernard and John are in partnership sharing profits/losses 2:1.

The partnership results for the year ended 31/12/2018 are as follows:

Profit	*€3,000*
Capital allowances	*€6,000*

Apportioned	Profit	Capital allowances	Net loss
	€	€	€
John	2,000	(4,000)	(2,000)
Bernard	1,000	(2,000)	(1,000)

Example 18.8

John and Bernard are in partnership sharing profits/losses 2:1.

The partnership results for the year ended 31/12/2018 are as follows:

Loss	*(€9,000)*
Capital allowances	*€6,000*

Apportioned	***Loss***	***Capital allowances***	***Increased loss***
	€	**€**	**€**
John	*(6,000)*	*(4,000)*	*(10,000)*
Bernard	*(3,000)*	*(2,000)*	*(5,000)*

Each partner has discretion as to how he may utilise his losses in a particular period. The options available are:

1. The loss may be offset against other income in the year of assessment (s381), or
2. The loss may be carried forward and set off against profits arising from the partner's several trade in future years (s382).

How losses are utilised will depend on the additional income and credits available in the year of assessment in which the loss was incurred and the tax bands at which the partners may be taxed.

Example 18.9

John and Bernard are in partnership sharing profits/losses 2:1.

The partnership results for the year ended 31/12/2018 are as follows.

Schedule D, Case I Loss	*(€90,000)*

Apportioned	**€**
John	*(60,000)*
Bernard	*(30,000)*

John also has Schedule E income for the year ended 31/12/2018 of €90,000. He therefore has the option to:

1. Offset the partnership loss against Schedule E income under section 381;

or

2. Carry the loss forward against Schedule D, Case I/II profits in future years under section 382.

Scenario 1 (John's tax credits amount to €5,000)

	€
Schedule E – Income	*90,000*
Loss relief – Section 381	*(60,000)*
Assessable income	*€30,000*
Taxable × 20% =	*6,000*
Credits/reliefs	*(5,000)*
Net tax payable	*1,000*

Scenario 2 (John's tax credits amount to €8,000)

	€
Schedule E – Income	*90,000*
Loss relief – Section 381	*(60,000)*
Assessable income	*30,000*
Taxable × 20% =	*6,000*
Credits	*(8,000)*
Net tax payable	*Nil*
Loss of credits	*(2,000)*

In this option the excess of credits cannot be utilised and are therefore lost for the year of assessment.

It would therefore be appropriate to carry forward the Schedule D loss to be offset against Schedule D profits in the future years.

18.7.1 Unutilised capital allowances

It should be borne in mind that, while capital allowances augment a loss for s381 purposes, unutilised capital allowances may not be carried forward by a partner who has insufficient income to absorb his share of the capital allowances. In these circumstances, the unutilised capital allowances revert to the partnership and are added to the capital allowance claim of the subsequent period and are subdivided again in that period in accordance with the profit-sharing ratio for that subsequent period.

Example 18.10

Ann and Mary share profits of a partnership equally. Ann has no other sources of income, but Mary has sufficient other income to utilise partnership losses and capital allowances in full. Partnership results for 2017 and 2018 are as follows:

		€
2017:	*Tax adjusted loss*	*(40,000)*
	Capital allowances	*6,000*
2018:	*Tax adjusted profit*	*15,000*
	Capital allowances	*8,000*

In 2017, Ann is allocated a loss of €20,000 and capital allowances of €3,000. She is unable to utilise either of these amounts under s381. She may carry forward the unutilised loss of €20,000 against her Case I/II income for 2018 of €7,500 (50% of €15,000). However, her capital allowance claim for 2017 of €3,000 reverts to the partnership and is added to the claim for 2018. Thus, the total capital allowance claim for 2018 available for allocation is €11,000. (€8,000 from 2018 + €3,000 from 2017). This is split in the profit-sharing ratio for 2018, i.e., equally between both partners. Accordingly, Ann loses 50% of her 2017 allocation. In these circumstances, Revenue may give relief to Ann by making a new apportionment, provided that all partners agree to such a re-apportionment in writing.

18.8 Adjustments Unique to Partnerships

There are two further areas to be examined in relation to partnership taxation:

1. Interest on capital.
2. Partners' salaries.

Both of these items constitute adjustments to accounting profits and have implications for the total amount of income attributable to individual partners.

18.8.1 Interest on capital

Partnership agreements can have a clause which states that the partners are entitled to interest on capital invested by them in the partnership. As such, interest on capital is simply an appropriation of profits. It is not an allowable deduction for Case I/II purposes.

This interest is charged against the profits of the partnership before apportionment of the profits and is added back to the individual partner's share of profits for the purposes of determining the total amount assessable on that partner.

Example 18.11

John and Bernard invested €300,000 and €100,000 respectively in the partnership and they agreed to pay 5% of the capital by way of interest before apportioning profits/losses, which are agreed at 2:1.

			€	€
Profits for year ended 31/12/2018				*80,000*
Interest on capital	*– John*		*15,000*	
	– Bernard		*5,000*	
				(20,000)
Profit per accounts				
				€60,000
Apportionment:		*John*	*40,000*	
		Bernard	*20,000*	

Adjusted profit computation: 31/12/2018		
Profit per accounts		*60,000*
Add: Interest on capital		*20,000*
Adjusted profit		*80,000*
Apportionment:	***John***	***Bernard***
Interest on capital	*15,000*	*5,000*
Share of profits 2:1	*40,000*	*20,000*
Assessable income	*€55,000*	*€25,000*

18.8.2 Partners' salaries

Again, partnership agreements will usually contain a clause that partners will receive a salary prior to the apportionment of profits/losses. This is particularly the case where there may be a dormant (or sleeping) partner in the firm who has only invested capital in the partnership and who does not take any active part in the trade of the partnership.

Example 18.12

John, Bernard and Aisling are in partnership. John does not take any active part in the business of the firm. It was agreed that Bernard would receive a salary of €30,000 per annum and Aisling a salary of €50,000.

Profits/losses were shared equally.

Net profit after charging salaries for year ended 31/12/2018 amounted to €210,000.

Tax Computation:	***€***
Profit per accounts	*210,000*
Add: Partners' salaries	*80,000*
Adjusted profit	*€290,000*

Apportionment:	***John***	***Bernard***	***Aisling***	***Total***
	€	*€*	*€*	*€*
Partners salaries	*–*	*30,000*	*50,000*	*80,000*
Profits 1:1:1	*70,000*	*70,000*	*70,000*	*210,000*
Assessable	*€70,000*	*€100,000*	*€120,000*	*€290,000*

18.9 Joining and Leaving an Existing Partnership

Where a new partner joins an existing partnership, the new partner will be commencing to trade and accordingly, the commencement rules (addressed in Chapter 14) will apply to the new partner in respect of the assessment of his share of partnership profits. The commencement rules will not apply to the other partners who will be subject to the normal current year basis of assessment applicable for individuals continuing in business. Where a partner leaves a partnership which continues in business after his leaving, then the cessation provisions will apply to that partner, but not to the other partners who are continuing to trade. Obviously, in both of these cases, there may be a change in the profit-sharing ratio, which would require that profits and capital allowances be time-apportioned as in the case of Examples 18.3, 18.4 and 18.5 above.

18.10 Administration

The precedent partner is responsible for the preparation for the firm's annual return (Form 1 – firms) for filing with the Revenue by the due date (31 October each year). This form can be downloaded from the Revenue website (www.revenue.ie.) and a copy is included at Appendix I.

In effect this return includes all the sources of income of the partnership. It also shows full details of any capital gains tax assessable and any capital assets acquired by the partnership.

The precedent partner is the partner who, being resident in the State, is the first named in the partnership agreement.

If there is no agreement, the precedent partner is the partner named singly or with precedence over the other partners in the usual name of the firm. For example, in the case of Murphy, Smith & Jones, Murphy is the precedent partner.

If the person named with precedence is not an acting partner, then the precedent acting partner is the precedent partner.

Any reference to a precedent partner shall, in a case where no parties are resident in the State, be construed as a reference to the agent, manager or factor of the firm resident in the State.

18.11 Modification of Provision as to Appeals

Where the Inspector of Taxes has made a determination, he/she may give notice of it to the precedent partner.

If the determination is not appealed against or if any appeal against it has been settled, it is to be binding on all the partners and no question as to its correctness can be raised by any partner on an appeal against an assessment made on him/her.

Where the Inspector of Taxes' apportionment of partnership profit/joint allowances is not accepted by one or more of the partners, all the partners and not only the one who appeals, have the right to be informed of, and to be present at, the hearing of the matter by the Appeal Commissioners.

Appendix I

2017155

Form 1(Firms)
Partnership Tax Return 2017

TAIN

GCD

Tax Reference Number
Remember to quote this number in all correspondence or when calling at your Revenue office

This Tax Return is for use by partnerships

The Return should be made by the partner

- who is the first named in the agreement of partnership, or
- who is named singly or with precedence in the usual name of the firm if there is no agreement, or
- if the partner named with precedence is not an acting partner then by the precedent acting partner

If no partner is resident in the State the Return should be made by the firm's agent, manager or factor resident in the State

Return Address

Office of the Revenue Commissioners
Collector-General's Division
PO Box 354
Limerick

RETURN OF INCOME AND CAPITAL GAINS OF THE PARTNERSHIP IN THE YEAR ENDED 31 DECEMBER 2017
RETURN OF CHARGEABLE ASSETS ACQUIRED BY THE PARTNERSHIP IN THE YEAR ENDED 31 DECEMBER 2017

The **Precedent partner** is required by Section 959I of the Taxes Consolidation Act 1997, as amended, to prepare and deliver a return of partnership income and gains for 2017 on or before 31 October 2018

Each partner is required to make a separate personal return on Form 11, in addition to this Return

Revenue On-Line Service (ROS) allows you to file this form electronically. Access ROS at **www.revenue.ie**

Expression of Doubt: If you have a genuine doubt about the correct application of tax law to any item in the return, provide details of the point at issue in the entry fields provided on page 11

Note: Each partner affected by this tax treatment should also indicate an Expression of Doubt on his/her own personal tax return

When completing this Return, remember

- Write clearly and accurately within boxes
- Any panel(s) or section(s) that do not require an entry should be left blank
- In date boxes enter the format of Day/Month/Year, e.g. 31/10/2017
- Use BLUE ink when completing this form
- If there is not enough space in any of the panels provided on the form, attach a separate schedule set out in the same format as the relevant panel(s)
- If submitting this return use any envelope and write "Freepost" above the Return Address. You do not need to attach a stamp
- Legislative references relate to Sections of the Taxes Consolidation Act 1997, unless otherwise stated

YOU MUST SIGN THIS DECLARATION

I DECLARE that, to the best of my knowledge and belief, this form contains a correct statement for the purposes of assessment to tax for the year 2017 and a correct statement of capital gains which accrued and of chargeable assets acquired in the year 2017

Signature   Date DD/MM/YYYY

Capacity of Signatory

Full Name of Partnership/Firm (if different from above)

Contact Details (in case of query about this return)

Agent's TAIN   Contact Name

Client's Ref.   Telephone or E-Mail

2017155 **Tax Reference Number**

ANY PANEL(S) OR SECTION(S) THAT DO NOT REQUIRE AN ENTRY SHOULD BE LEFT BLANK.

A - PARTNERSHIP DETAILS [1 - 3]

Panel A is set out on pages 2 and 3; entries should be made on both pages where relevant

1. If there are **any changes** under the following headings, not already notified to Revenue, enter the **new details** here

(a) **Nature of Primary Trade / Profession**

(c) **Business Address of Primary Trade / Profession**

Particulars of the Several Partners during Accounting Period(s) covered in Panel B on pages 4 - 6

2. Partners **resident** in Ireland

Complete columns **(i)** to **(v)** below on behalf of all partners

	PPS No. of Partner (i)	Partners share of Case I/II (ii)	Partners share of other income (iii)	Insert ☒ in box if salary received (iv)	Insert ☒ in box if interest on capital received (v)
(a)		·00	·00		
(b)		·00	·00		
(c)		·00	·00		
(d)		·00	·00		
(e)		·00	·00		
(f)		·00	·00		

3. Partners **not resident** in Ireland

Complete columns **(i)** to **(v)** below on behalf of all partners

	PPS No. of Partner or Name & Address of Partner (i)	Partners share of Case I/II (ii)	Partners share of other income (iii)	Insert ☒ in box if salary received (iv)	Insert ☒ in box if interest on capital received (v)
(a)		·00	·00		
(b)		·00	·00		

2017155 **Tax Reference Number** [ ]

ANY PANEL(S) OR SECTION(S) THAT DO NOT REQUIRE AN ENTRY SHOULD BE LEFT BLANK.

Panel A is set out on pages 2 and 3; entries should be made on both pages where relevant

1. (b) **Name and Address of Precedent Acting Partner**

Particulars of the Several Partners during Accounting Period(s) covered in Panel B on pages 4 - 6

2. Partners **resident** in Ireland

Complete columns **(vi)** to **(xi)** below if there were changes in the Partnership or in the Basis of Distribution of Profits in this Accounting Period

	Basis of distribution of profits* at start of period (%)	Insert ☒ in box if partner commenced	Insert ☒ in box if partner ceased	Insert ☒ in box if there was a change in the distribution of profits	Date of Event	Basis of distribution of profits* at end of period (%)
	(vi)	(vii)	(viii)	(ix)	(x)	(xi)
(a)					DD/MM/YYYY	
(b)					DD/MM/YYYY	
(c)					DD/MM/YYYY	
(d)					DD/MM/YYYY	
(e)					DD/MM/YYYY	
(f)					DD/MM/YYYY	

*after salary and interest on capital

*after salary and interest on capital

3. Partners **not resident** in Ireland

Complete columns **(vi)** to **(xi)** below if there were changes in the Partnership or in the Basis of Distribution of Profits in this Accounting Period

	Basis of distribution of profits* at start of period (%)	Insert ☒ in box if partner commenced	Insert ☒ in box if partner ceased	Insert ☒ in box if there was a change in the distribution of profits	Date of Event	Basis of distribution of profits* at end of period (%)
	(vi)	(vii)	(viii)	(ix)	(x)	(xi)
(a)					DD/MM/YYYY	
(b)					DD/MM/YYYY	

*after salary and interest on capital

*after salary and interest on capital

2017155 **Tax Reference Number**

ANY PANEL(S) OR SECTION(S) THAT DO NOT REQUIRE AN ENTRY SHOULD BE LEFT BLANK.

B - PROFITS FROM TRADES, PROFESSIONS OR VOCATIONS [101 - 146]

	Primary Trade	Subsidiary Trade
101. Description of Trade, Profession or Vocation *(You must clearly describe the trade)*		

Do not submit accounts with this Return. Instead you must give an extract of information from the accounts in Extracts From Accounts, Lines 110 - 146

	Primary Trade	Subsidiary Trade
102. If this source of income ceased during 2017 state the date of cessation	DD/MM/YYYY	DD/MM/YYYY
103. Amount of adjusted net profit for accounting period	·00	·00
104. Amount of adjusted net loss for accounting period	·00	·00
105. Income assessable under S. 98A(4), (Reverse Premiums in trading situations) if not already included above	·00	·00
106. Balancing Charges	·00	·00

Capital Allowances for 2017 [107 - 109]

	Primary Trade	Subsidiary Trade
107. Machinery and Plant	·00	·00
108. Industrial Buildings and/or Farm Buildings Allowance	·00	·00
109. Other Capital Allowances	·00	·00

EXTRACTS FROM ACCOUNTS [110 - 146]

Accounts Information Period (must be completed)

	Primary Trade	Subsidiary Trade
110. From	DD/MM/YYYY	DD/MM/YYYY
111. To	DD/MM/YYYY	DD/MM/YYYY

Extracts From Accounts must be completed in all cases where the business being carried on in partnership includes the carrying on of a trade or profession, except where Line 112 below applies

	Primary Trade	Subsidiary Trade
112. If the partnership has previously submitted accounts information relating to this return state the Form 1(Firms) return with which accounts were submitted	YYYY	YYYY

113. Insert ☒ in the box if the partnership is a Registered Farm Partnership as defined by S. 667C ☐

Income

	Primary Trade	Subsidiary Trade
114. Sales/Receipts/Turnover	·00	·00
115. Receipts from Government Agencies (GMS, etc.)	·00	·00
116. Other Income including tax exempt income	·00	·00

2017155 **Tax Reference Number**

ANY PANEL(S) OR SECTION(S) THAT DO NOT REQUIRE AN ENTRY SHOULD BE LEFT BLANK.

	Primary Trade	Subsidiary Trade
Trading Account Items		
117. Purchases	.00	.00
118. Gross Trading Profits	.00	.00
Expenses and Deductions		
119. Salaries/Wages, Staff costs	.00	.00
120. Sub-Contractors	.00	.00
121. Consultancy, Professional fees	.00	.00
122. Motor, Travel and Subsistence	.00	.00
123. Repairs/Renewals	.00	.00
124. Depreciation, Goodwill/Capital write-off	.00	.00
125. (a) Provisions including bad debts - positive	.00	.00
(b) If negative, state amount here	.00	.00
126. Other Expenses (Total)	.00	.00
Capital Account and Balance Sheet Items		
127. Cash/Capital introduced	.00	.00
128. Drawings (Net of Tax and Pension contributions)	.00	.00
129. (a) Closing Capital Balance - positive	.00	.00
(b) If negative, state amount here	.00	.00
130. Stock, Work in progress, Finished goods	.00	.00
131. Debtors and Prepayments	.00	.00
132. Cash/Bank (Debit)	.00	.00
133. Bank/Loans/Overdraft (Credit)	.00	.00
134. Client Account Balances (Debit)	.00	.00
135. Client Account Balances (Credit)	.00	.00
136. Creditors and Accruals	.00	.00
137. Tax Creditors	.00	.00
138. (a) Net Assets - positive	.00	.00
(b) If negative, state amount here	.00	.00

2017155 **Tax Reference Number**

ANY PANEL(S) OR SECTION(S) THAT DO NOT REQUIRE AN ENTRY SHOULD BE LEFT BLANK.

Extracts from Adjusted Net Profit/Loss Computation

Profit/Loss per Accounts	**Primary Trade**	**Subsidiary Trade**
139. Net Profit per Accounts	·00	·00
140. Net Loss per Accounts	·00	·00
Adjustments made to Profit/Loss per Accounts		
141. Motor Expenses	·00	·00
142. Donations (Political and Charitable)/Entertainment	·00	·00
143. Light, Heat and Phone	·00	·00
144. Net gain on sale of fixed/chargeable assets	·00	·00
145. Net loss on sale of fixed/chargeable assets	·00	·00
146. (a) Stock relief claimed under S. 666	·00	·00
(b) Stock relief claimed under S. 667B	·00	·00
(c) Stock relief claimed under S. 667C	·00	·00

C - EXEMPT INCOME

Income from Sources Exempt from Tax

201. (a) Profit, gains or distributions from **Woodlands** ·00

(b) If a loss, enter the amount of the loss ·00

D - IRISH RENTAL INCOME [301 - 313]

Residential Property

301. Where the registration requirements of Part 7 of the Residential Tenancies Act 2004 have been complied with in respect of all tenancies which existed in relation to residential premises in the year 2017, insert ☒ in box ☐

302. Number of properties let

303. Gross Rent Receivable ·00

304. **Expenses**

(a) Repairs ·00

(b) Allowable interest ·00

(c) "Section 23" type relief where 2017 is the **first** year of claim ·00

(d) Pre-letting expenditure on vacant properties allowed by S. 97A ·00

(e) Other ·00

305. Amount of chargeable profit / allowable loss after expenses **but** before Capital Allowances

(a) Net profit on residential property ·00

(b) Net loss on residential property ·00

Commercial property, land and all other sources of Irish rental income

306. Number of properties let

307. Number in hectares, if applicable

308. Gross Rent Receivable ·00

309. **Expenses**

(a) Repairs ·00

(b) Allowable interest ·00

(c) Other ·00

2017155 **Tax Reference Number**

ANY PANEL(S) OR SECTION(S) THAT DO NOT REQUIRE AN ENTRY SHOULD BE LEFT BLANK.

310. Amount of chargeable profit / allowable loss after expenses **but** before Capital Allowances
(a) Net profit on commercial property .00
(b) Net loss on commercial property .00

311. Amount of chargeable profit from all sources, after expenses **but** before Capital Allowances (Total of Line 305 and Line 310 - if a loss show **0.00**) .00

312. Total Capital Allowances available for 2017 .00

313. Amount of losses in this year .00

E - OTHER IRISH INCOME [314 - 319]

Income from which Irish income tax was not deducted

314. Income (interest on Government or other loans, deposit accounts, etc. and discounts, payable without deduction of Irish income tax) .00

Income from which Irish income tax was deducted

315. Interest paid or credited on deposits with the Commercial Banks, Building Societies, ACC Loan Management Ltd., An Post (other than interest on Special Savings Accounts), etc. (show the **gross** amount paid or credited **before** the application of retention tax) .00

316. Gross Distributions (i.e. distributions **plus** dividend withholding tax) .00

317. **Patent royalty income where tax was deducted at source**
(a) Gross amount of Irish Patent Royalty income previously exempted under S. 234 .00
(b) Gross amount of other Irish Patent Royalty income .00

318. Other income received in 2017 .00

319. **Investment Undertakings (S. 739G(2A))**
(a) Gain on deemed disposal (S. 739E(1)(b)(ii)) .00
(b) Gain on deemed disposal (S. 739E(1)(ba)) .00
(c) Name & Address of the Investment Undertaking (S. 739E(2A)(b)), include Eircode (if known)

F - FOREIGN INCOME [401 - 417] (Enter amounts in €)

Securities and Possessions outside the State

401. Income from securities and possessions outside the State .00
Foreign rental losses may be offset **only** against foreign rental profits

Foreign Bank Accounts (S. 895)

Give the following details for each foreign bank account opened in 2017 of which the partnership was the beneficial owner of the deposits held

402. Name and address of deposit holder (bank, etc.)

403. Date account was opened DD/MM/YYYY

404. Amount of money deposited on opening the account .00

405. Name and address of intermediary through whom account was opened, include Eircode (if known)
(Include details of interest received from these accounts at Line 401)

Foreign Life Policies (S. 730H, 730I, 730J, 730K)

Give the following details in respect of policies issued in 2017 from ANY Member State of the EU or EEA, or from a Member State of the OECD with which Ireland has a Double Taxation Agreement

406. Name and address of person who commenced the Foreign Life Policy, include Eircode (if known)

2017155 **Tax Reference Number** **ANY PANEL(S) OR SECTION(S) THAT DO NOT REQUIRE AN ENTRY SHOULD BE LEFT BLANK.**

407. Terms of the policy

408. Annual premiums payable .00

409. Name and address of the person through whom the Foreign Life Policy was acquired, include Eircode (if known)

(Include details of income received from these accounts at Line 401)

Offshore Funds

Give the following details in respect of each material interest in 'regulated offshore fund(s)' (those coming within S. 747B(2A)) acquired in 2017 in the EU or EEA, or in a Member State of the OECD with which Ireland has a Double Taxation Agreement

410. Name and address of Offshore Fund(s)

411. Date material interest was acquired DD/MM/YYYY

412. Amount of capital invested in acquiring the material interest .00

413. Name and address of intermediary (if any) through whom the material interest was acquired, include Eircode (if known)

(Include details of income received from these accounts at Line 401)

Other Offshore Products

Give the following details for each material interest acquired in 2017 in (i) other offshore products (including foreign life assurance policies) OUTSIDE the EU or EEA, or outside a Member State of the OECD with which Ireland has a Double Taxation Agreement and in (ii) 'unregulated funds' (those not coming within S. 747B(2A)) within the EU or EEA, or within any Member State of the OECD with which Ireland has a Double Taxation Agreement

414. Name and address of Offshore Products

415. Date material interest was acquired DD/MM/YYYY

416. Amount of payment made in acquiring the material interest .00

417. Name and address of intermediary (if any) through whom the material interest was acquired, include Eircode (if known)

(Include details of income received from these accounts at Line 401)

G - INCOME/PROFIT FROM SOURCES NOT SHOWN ELSEWHERE

(Include sums received after discontinuance of trade or profession and sums deemed to be income of the partnership under S. 806)

501. (a) Gross amount of income/profit from sources not shown elsewhere .00

(b) Detail(s) of income/profit source(s)

2017155 **Tax Reference Number** | | | | | | | | **ANY PANEL(S) OR SECTION(S) THAT DO NOT REQUIRE AN ENTRY SHOULD BE LEFT BLANK.**

H - ANNUAL PAYMENTS, CHARGES, INTEREST PAID AND DONATIONS [601 - 605]

601. Gross amount of **Rents, etc. payable to Non-Residents** in 2017 — .00

602. **Clawback of Employers' Tax Relief at Source (TRS)**
If you are an employer and have paid medical insurance premiums to an authorised insurer on behalf of your employees, **enter the amount of tax relief at source** granted to you in respect of these premiums — .00
Note: do not enter the amount of the insurance premiums paid

603. Gross amount of payment of **Charges/Annuities, incl. Patent Royalties** where tax was deducted — .00

604. Interest on mortgage or loan (including bank overdraft interest) — .00

605. **Approved Sports Bodies** - Amount of Donations made in 2017 — .00

I - PARTNERSHIP PROFITS: BALANCE OF PROFITS APPORTIONED UNDER S. 1008(2)(a)(ii) [701-703]

701. Amount of profits apportioned under S. 1008(2)(a)(ii) — .00

702. Apportionment required

703. State why the aggregate of profits arising to partners before S. 1008(2)(a)(ii) is less than the full amount of the partnership profits

J - CHARGEABLE ASSETS ACQUIRED IN 2017 [801 - 808]

Enter the number of assets acquired and the consideration given

Description of Assets	Number of Assets	Consideration
801. Shares (quoted & unquoted)		.00
802. Residential Premises		.00
803. Commercial Premises		.00
804. Agricultural Land		.00
805. Development Land		.00
806. Business Assets		.00
807. Antiques/Works of Art		.00
808. Other		.00

PAGE 9

2017155 **Tax Reference Number**

ANY PANEL(S) OR SECTION(S) THAT DO NOT REQUIRE AN ENTRY SHOULD BE LEFT BLANK.

K - CAPITAL GAINS ACCRUED IN 2017 [901 - 916]

Description of Assets	No. of Disposals	Disposals between connected persons Insert ☒ in box	Aggregate Area in Hectares	Aggregate Consideration (Substitute market value where disposal not made at arm's length)
901. Shares/Securities - Quoted		☐		.00
902. Shares/Securities - Unquoted		☐		.00
903. Agricultural Land/Buildings		☐		.00
904. Development Land		☐		.00
905. Commercial Premises		☐		.00
906. Residential Premises		☐		.00
907. Venture Fund Gains (Sec. 541C(2)(a))		☐		.00
908. Other Assets		☐		.00

909. **Total Consideration** .00

910. Incidental cost(s) of disposal(s) .00

911. Aggregate net consideration (after incidental costs of disposals) .00

912. (a) Cost of acquisition (if assets acquired prior to 6/4/1974 or acquired otherwise not at arm's length substitute market value for cost) - indexed where appropriate .00

(b) Insert ☒ in box if not at arm's length ☐

913. Amount of enhancement expenditure claimed (indexed where appropriate) .00

914. Amount of Chargeable Gain(s) .00

Particulars of Distribution between Partners of Capital Gains Accrued in 2017

915. Partners **resident** in Ireland

PPS No. of Partner	Basis of Distribution (%)	Amount of Chargeable Gain
	.	.00
	.	.00
	.	.00
	.	.00
	.	.00

916. Partners **not resident** in Ireland

Name, address and PPS No. (if any) of Partner	Basis of Distribution (%)
	.
	.

2017155 **Tax Reference Number** ☐☐☐☐☐☐☐☐☐ **ANY PANEL(S) OR SECTION(S) THAT DO NOT REQUIRE AN ENTRY SHOULD BE LEFT BLANK.**

Expression of Doubt

If you have a genuine doubt about the correct application of tax law to any item in the return, insert ☒ in the box and provide details of the point at issue in the entry fields provided below ☐

(This section is only for genuine Expressions of Doubt as provided for by S. 959P. It should not be used for general notes or comments)

(a) Provide full details of the facts and circumstances of the matter to which the Expression of Doubt relates

(b) Specify the doubt, the basis for the doubt and the tax law giving rise to the doubt

(c) Identify the amount of tax in doubt in respect of the chargeable period to which the Expression of Doubt relates ☐☐,☐☐☐,☐☐☐ .00

(d) List the supporting documents that are being submitted in relation to the matter involved. These documents should accompany this return

(e) Identify any published Revenue guidelines that you have consulted concerning the application of the law in similar circumstances

The Revenue Commissioners collect taxes and duties and implement customs controls. Revenue requires customers to provide certain personal data for these purposes and certain other statutory functions as assigned by the Oireachtas. Your personal data may be exchanged with other Government Departments and agencies in certain circumstances where this is provided for by law. Full details of Revenue's data protection policy setting out how we will use your personal data as well as information regarding your rights as a data subject are available on our **Privacy** page on **www.revenue.ie**. Details of this policy are also available in hard copy upon request.

19 TAXATION OF INTEREST, DIVIDENDS AND RENTAL INCOME

Learning Outcomes

On completion of this chapter you will be able to:

- ✓ Describe the different sources of income assessable to tax under Schedule D Cases III, IV and V and Schedule F.
- ✓ Explain the basis of assessment for the different sources of income assessable to tax under Schedule D Cases III, IV and V and Schedule F.
- ✓ Explain how a taxpayer might claim credit for tax deducted at source from income assessable under Schedule D Case IV and Schedule F.
- ✓ In relation to Schedule D Cases III, IV and V and Schedule F, explain:
- ✓ what sources of income are exempt;
- ✓ how losses are treated;
- ✓ what deductions (if any) may be claimed.
- ✓ Describe the tax relief associated with 'special savings investment accounts' (SSIAs).
- ✓ Describe the tax treatment of shares issued in lieu of dividends.
- ✓ Calculate the tax liability of an individual in receipt of various sources of "passive" income.

19.1 Introduction

Income may be divided into two categories:

- "earned", and
- "unearned".

"Earned" income is essentially derived from two sources, namely employment and self-employment. The tax treatment of these sources is dealt with elsewhere in this publication.

This chapter addresses the tax treatment of "unearned" income, e.g., interest, dividends, rental and investment income and foreign sourced "earned" income. The same rates of income tax apply to both earned and unearned income[1].

---

1 This is to be contrasted with the corporation tax position, whereby the rate of corporation tax applicable to passive or unearned income is generally twice that applicable to earned or trading income (see Chapter 28).

The chapter is divided as follows:

- Paragraph 19.2 deals with Schedule D Case III. This includes interest received without deduction of tax and foreign-sourced income.
- Paragraph 19.3 deals with Schedule D Case IV. This includes investment income subject to tax at source and miscellaneous other sources of income not taxable under any other Case or Schedule.
- Paragraph 19.4 is concerned with Schedule D Case V, i.e., the tax treatment of rental income from property in the State.
- Paragraph 19.5 deals with Schedule F, i.e., the tax treatment of dividends and distributions received from Irish resident companies.

19.2 Schedule D Case III

The following are the main categories of income assessable under Schedule D Case III:

- interest, annuities and other annual payments not liable to Irish tax at source;
- all "discounts" – a profit on a discount transaction may be realised either by holding a bill (e.g., a bill of exchange, a promissory note, etc.) until its maturity, or by selling it earlier at a price in excess of that paid for it;
- interest on any securities issued under the authority of the Minister for Finance where such interest is paid without deduction of tax – examples include National Loan Stock or securities issued by such bodies as Bord na Móna and the ESB;
- dividends paid on ordinary credit union share accounts only up to the 2014 tax year[2] (dividends/interest paid on credit union special share accounts are liable to DIRT);
- income arising from foreign securities and possessions to the extent that it has not suffered Irish tax at source – examples include rents from property situated abroad, dividends and interest from UK companies, income from foreign employments or businesses and interest from foreign securities. Readers are referred to 19.3.5.1 for the tax treatment of interest from EU Countries effective from 1 January 2005;
- shares issued in lieu of dividends receivable from a non-resident company. The cash dividend foregone is liable to tax under Case III without any tax credit.

19.2.1 Basis of assessment

s70 TCA97 Case III income is assessed to tax on the income arising in the year of assessment. Income arises for Case III purposes when it is received, unlike Cases I, II and V, where income arises when it is earned (and not necessarily received). For the purposes of determining

2 Section 23 F(No. 2)A 2013 introduced a new section 267AA TCA97 whereby dividends paid by credit unions are all subject to DIRT from 1 January 2014.

when an individual first becomes taxable under Case III, it is the date on which income first arises from the Case III source that is relevant and not the date on which the Case III source is acquired. The cessation of a Case III source is the date on which the source is disposed of and not the date on which the income ceases. If a source continues to exist but does not produce income in any particular year, there is no cessation. Death constitutes a cessation of a Case III source. Where a husband and wife both have Case III income, they are regarded as having two separate sources of Case III income.

19.2.2 United Kingdom dividends and interest

UK dividends

The assessment is based on the cash amount received exclusive of any tax credit in respect of the dividends received.

Example 19.1

An Irish-resident individual receives a dividend payment from a UK plc. The information on the voucher (i.e., dividend counterfoil) reads:

Net dividend	*stg£99*
Tax credit	*stg£10*

The individual is assessed to tax under Schedule D Case III on the euro equivalent of stg£99. The tax credit is ignored and may not be refunded.

UK interest

Interest from UK securities is assessable under Schedule D Case III. Under the terms of the Ireland/United Kingdom Double Taxation Agreement (Article 12), the interest is liable only to Irish tax where the recipient is a resident of Ireland. Any UK tax deducted at source may be recovered in full on foot of an appropriate claim to the UK tax authorities.

Example 19.2

An Irish-resident individual receives an interest payment from UK debenture stock. The information on the voucher (i.e., interest counterfoil) reads:

Gross interest	*stg£100*
Tax deducted	*stg£20*
Net interest	*stg£80*

The individual is assessed to tax under Case III on the euro equivalent of stg£100. The UK tax deducted of stg£20 may be recovered in full on foot of an appropriate claim to the UK tax authorities.

19.2.3 Allowable deductions

The allowable deductions which may be set against Case III income for tax purposes are limited – the main one being a deduction for foreign tax borne on foreign income to the extent that it is not allowed as a credit under a double taxation agreement. However, in the case of foreign rents, deductions are normally allowed for interest, rates, repairs, insurance, management and collection expenses. Similarly, in the case of foreign trades, deductions are normally allowed for trading expenses. For commentary on allowable trading expenses, readers are referred to Chapter 15.

19.3 Schedule D Case IV

Tax is charged under Schedule D Case IV on any annual profits or gains not falling under any other Case of Schedule D and not falling under any other Schedule. In addition to certain specific sources directed by the legislation to be charged under Case IV, the Case embraces all profits and gains not otherwise chargeable under another Schedule.

19.3.1 Basis of assessment

s74 TCA97 The basis of assessment for Case IV is normally the actual profits arising in the year of assessment. The amount assessable under Case IV is "the full amount of the profits or gains arising". There is no specific direction as to how these profits or gains are to be determined.

19.3.2 Losses

s383 TCA97 Where in any year of assessment a person sustains a loss on a transaction (being a transaction which, had a profit arisen would have been assessable under Schedule D Case IV), then such loss may be set off against other profits assessable under Case IV for that year of assessment. Any portion of the loss for which relief is not so given may be carried forward and relieved against subsequent profits assessed under Case IV.

19.3.3 Statutory sources of Case IV income

The following are the main categories of income specifically assessable under Case IV on the basis of the legislation:

(a) income subject to tax at source;

(b) sale of patent rights for a capital sum;

(c) partnership profits not allocated to partners; (readers are referred to (c) overleaf for F.A. 2007 changes)

(d) income subject to deposit interest retention tax (DIRT);

(e) certain dividend payments by credit unions;

(f) post-cessation receipts;

(g) shares in lieu of dividends;

(h) profits from unlawful activities.

Income received by an individual under deduction of income tax is charged to tax under Schedule D Case IV. Section 59 TCA97 provides that credit is given for the tax deducted, against the tax payable by the individual. The assessment is on the gross amount of the income. An example of income chargeable under this case is a payment received under a Deed of Covenant. The payer deducts tax at the standard rate from the payment due to the payee and the payee claims credit for it against his/her own tax liability.

Example 19.3

Malachy Jones pays €8,000 (gross) per year under a Deed of Covenant to his aunt who is over 66 years. He must deduct standard rate tax in the amount of €1,600 from the gross payment. Thus, his aunt receives a net amount of €6,400 on an annual basis. In 2018, his aunt is assessed to tax under Schedule D Case IV as follows:

	€	€
Income under Deed of Covenant		*8,000*
Taxed as follows:		
€8,000 × 20%		*1,600*
Less non-refundable credits:		
Single person's credit		*(1,650)*
Tax liability		*Nil*
Less		
Tax deducted on Deed of Covenant		*(1,600)*
Tax overpaid		*(1,600)*

Malachy Jones' aunt may claim a refund of €1,600.
She is not liable to PRSI since she is over 66 years and not liable to USC since her income is under €13,000.

(b) Sale of patent rights for a capital sum

s757 TCA97 Section 757 TCA97 provides that where a person resident in Ireland sells any patent rights and the net proceeds of the sale consist wholly or partly of a capital sum, he/she is assessable to tax under Schedule D Case IV. The amount receivable is spread over six years, i.e., one-sixth of the lump sum is assessed in each year. The taxpayer may elect to have the total amount receivable charged to tax in the year in which it is received.

A person not resident in Ireland who sells Irish patent rights is also liable to tax under Schedule D Case IV on the amount receivable, provided the proceeds of the sale consist wholly or partly of a capital sum. However, the purchaser of the patent rights is obliged to deduct income tax at the standard rate on the amount payable to the non-resident. The non-resident may elect to have the sum receivable spread over six years for the purposes of being assessed to tax.

(c) Partnership profits not allocated to partners

s1008 TCA97 As discussed in Chapter 18, effective from 1 January 2007, the undistributed profits are allocated for tax purposes to each partner and taxed at the marginal rate.

(d) Income subject to Deposit Interest Retention Tax (DIRT)

s256 TCA97 Section 256 TCA97 provides that interest paid on deposits held in banks, building societies and other similar institutions is, in most cases, subject to DIRT. This means that the interest is paid under deduction of tax and, as such, is assessable in the hands of the recipient under Case IV. (DIRT is considered in more detail at 19.3.5.)

(e) Post-cessation receipts

s95 TCA97 Section 95 TCA97 provides that sums received after the cessation of a trade or profession, which could not be brought into account while the business or profession was being carried on, are taxed under Schedule D Case IV. The charge is extended to consideration received for the transfer of the right to receive post-cessation receipts.

(f) Shares in lieu of dividends

It is common for companies when declaring dividends to give their shareholders the option of receiving additional share capital in the company rather than the cash dividend. Readers will recall that where such shares are received from non-resident companies, the receipt is taxable under Case III. Section 816 TCA97 provides that where the paying company is an Irish-resident company, which is not a quoted company, the individual is taxed on an amount equal to the cash distribution (net of any tax credit) that he/she would have received had the option not been exercised to take the additional share capital. There is no entitlement to a tax credit against the tax on income assessable. For the tax treatment of shares in lieu of dividends from quoted resident companies, readers are referred to the analysis at 19.5.5 below.

(g) Profits from unlawful activities

Profits or gains may be charged to tax notwithstanding that:

- the source from which the profits or gains arose is not known to the Revenue Commissioners;
- the profits or gains are not known to have arisen wholly or partly from a lawful source of activity.

Such profits or gains are charged as miscellaneous income under Schedule D Case IV. This provision effectively nullifies the decision of the Supreme Court in the case of *Hayes v Duggan* (1 ITC 269). These provisions were further extended by DCITPA 1996 Disclosure of Certain Information for Taxation and Other Purposes Act 1996 in relation to income or gains, which derive, or are suspected to derive, from criminal activity.

19.3.4 Non-statutory instances of Case IV

The following are examples of sources of income liable to tax under Schedule D Case IV. The legislation does not specifically state that these sources of income are liable to tax under Case IV, but case law has held that they are so assessable:

- casual profits, i.e., profits of a casual nature not chargeable to tax under Schedule E or Schedule D Cases I or II;
- profits from the hire of movable assets where a similar trade is not carried on;
- fees, etc., not arising from land, e.g., shipping dues;
- lettings of premises in such circumstances that the relationship of landlord and tenant does not exist between the owner and the lessee, e.g., lettings of halls for dances, meetings, etc.;
- casual literary activities that do not constitute the exercise of a profession;
- fees from sporting or fishing rights;
- green fees from non-members received by a golf club, if not amounting to a trade assessable under Schedule D Case I;
- copyright royalties.

19.3.5 Deposit interest retention tax (DIRT)

s257 TCA97 Deposit interest retention tax is charged on the payment of certain interest by specified institutions. Section 257 TCA97 provides for the deduction of "appropriate tax" (DIRT) on the payment of deposit interest by a "relevant deposit-taker".

The following are "relevant deposit-takers" for the purposes of the DIRT provisions:

(a) a bank which has been granted a license under s9 Central Bank Act 1971 or under a similar law of another EC Member State;

(b) a building society (within the meaning of the Building Society Act 1989 or established under a similar law of another EC Member State);

(c) a credit union (from 1/1/2002);

(d) Trustee Savings Bank;

(e) the Post Office Savings Bank.

Rates of DIRT

Prior to 1 January 2009, where interest was paid at intervals which did not exceed 12 months, the rate of DIRT was 20% (where interest payments were at intervals which exceeded 12 months, the rate was 20% + 3%). The rate for 2018 is 37% regardless of when the interest interval is (i.e. whether the interest paid is paid at intervals of less than or more than 12 months).

Treatment in hands of recipient

s261 TCA97

Under the provisions of s261 TCA97, DIRT paid on a relevant deposit account is deemed to be in full settlement of the income tax liability on that income, even if the individual is liable to tax at the higher rate. However, the gross interest is liable for PRSI where appropriate, but not for the USC.

Refunds of DIRT

A relevant deposit-taker must deduct DIRT unless instructed otherwise by the Revenue Commissioners. Certain categories of deposit-holders, although subject to the deduction of DIRT at source, may be entitled to a refund if the DIRT exceeds their overall tax liability. Examples of such categories are considered below.

s267 TCA97

(a) **Charities** (as recognised for tax purposes) are entitled to a refund of DIRT by virtue of s267(2) TCA97. However they may avoid the need to reclaim DIRT deducted on interest received by arranging with the Revenue Commissioners to have interest paid gross.

s263 TCA97

(b) **Individuals who are not resident in Ireland** may elect to have Irish deposit interest paid to them free of DIRT by making an appropriate written declaration of non-residency to the deposit-holder (s263 TCA97). In the past, false declarations of non-residency were commonplace in Ireland with many taxpayers using bogus non-resident accounts to evade liability to DIRT.

s189A(2) TCA97

(c) **Special trusts for permanently incapacitated individuals** are entitled to refunds of DIRT where interest income is exempt from income tax under s189A(2) TCA97.

s267(1)(a) TCA97

(d) **An individual who was**, or whose spouse was, at some time during the relevant tax year, **aged 65 or older** (s267(1)(a) TCA97) may be entitled to a refund of DIRT. Section 34 Finance Act 2007 provides that the deposit taker may pay the interest gross, i.e., without the deduction of DIRT, where:

- at any time in a year of assessment, the individual beneficially entitled to the interest or his or her spouse is 65 years of age or over and their total income does not exceed the relevant income exemption limit; and
- such individual makes a declaration to that effect to the relevant deposit taker.

s267(1)(b) TCA97

(e) A refund of DIRT is also granted to an individual who was, or whose spouse was, throughout the relevant tax year, or from some time during the tax year, permanently incapacitated by reason of mental or physical infirmity, from maintaining himself/herself (s267(1)(b) TCA97). Section 34 Finance Act 2007 also provides that the deposit taker may pay the interest gross i.e. without the deduction of DIRT, where:

- the individual beneficially entitled to the interest or his or her spouse is permanently incapacitated or where the persons entitled to the interest are trustees of a special trust are permanently incapacitated individuals who are exempt from tax under Section 189A (2); and

- the deposit taker receives the appropriate notification from the Revenue Commissioners.

s266A TCA97

(f) **First time buyers** of a principal private residence may obtain a refund of DIRT. Section 22 FA 2014 introduced a provision whereby first-time buyers can claim a refund of DIRT on their savings in respect of a 'relevant purchase'. A relevant purchase is the conveyance of a dwelling on or after 14 October 2014 but before 31 December 2017 into the name of a first purchaser(s) for use as his or her (or their) place of residence. The refund is limited to the DIRT on savings of a maximum of:

- 20% of the purchase price of the property, or
- in the case of self-builds, 20% of the completion value of the property

in the 48 month period prior to the relevant purchase or relevant completion date, as appropriate.

An individual not within any of the above categories (e.g., an individual under 65 years and not permanently incapacitated by reason of mental or physical infirmity, from maintaining himself/herself or a 'first time buyer') is not entitled to a refund of DIRT even if he/she is in a repayment situation for the tax year or is otherwise completely exempt from income tax.

Example 19.4

Ethel Jones is 64 years old and has been a widow for many years. Her only source of income is derived from deposit interest. The gross interest paid to her in March 2018 is €18,000. Her assessment to tax for 2018 is as follows:

	€	€
Schedule D Case IV		18,000
Taxed as follows:		
€18,000 × 37%	6,660	
Less non-refundable credits:		
Widowed person's tax credit	(2,190)	
DIRT	(6,660)	
		(8,850)
Excess tax credits (non-refundable)		(2,190)
Tax liability		Nil

Ethel Jones may not claim a refund/use as offset of the excess tax credit of €2,190. However, if she was permanently incapacitated by reason of mental or physical infirmity from maintaining herself, she would be entitled to the refund/offset against other liabilities. She is liable to PRSI as follows:

PRSI

18,000 × 4% 720

The excess tax credit of €2,190 may not be claimed as an offset against the PRSI. Ethel Jones has no USC liability since deposit interest is exempt from USC.

Example 19.5

Assume the same facts, as above in Example 19.4 except that Ethel Jones is 67 years of age and DIRT is deducted at source. Her assessment for 2018 is as follows:

Income Tax

- *No liability - covered by low income exemption. She is entitled to a refund of DIRT (€6,660)*

PRSI

- *No liability - exempt since she is over 66 years)*

USC

- *No liability - deposit interest is exempt from USC*

Ethel Jones may also arrange to have such interest paid without the deduction of DIRT, subject to making the appropriate declaration to the deposit taker.

Foreign deposit Interest

Section 20 Finance Act 2005 introduced changes to the tax treatment of interest paid by EU Banks, Building Societies etc. Previously such interest was liable to tax (under Schedule D Case III) at the depositor's marginal rate. From 1 January 2005 the interest is liable to tax at the "DIRT" rate of tax, provided any tax (if due) is paid by the tax return filing date for the year concerned. Up to 2013, this tax treatment was beneficial to the account holder when DIRT rates were less than the marginal rate of tax. With the increase of the DIRT rate to 41% from 2014 to 2016, the treatment conferred no benefit to the account holder who otherwise paid tax at 40%. As stated previously the DIRT for 2018 has been lowered to 37%.

19.3.6 Special term accounts

s261A TCA97

Section 57 of the Finance Act 2001 introduced two deposit-based accounts, which attracted favourable tax treatment. Section 23 F(No. 2)A 2013 abolished the opening of these accounts on/after 16 October 2014.

Position up to 15 October 2014

There are two types of account to choose from:

- a medium-term account; and
- a long-term account.

A medium-term account is for a term of at least three years' duration and a long-term account is for a term of at least five years' duration.

s256 TCA97

These accounts are deposit-based and the legislation specifically prohibits returns that are linked in any way to stocks, shares, debentures and listed or unlisted securities. The list of relevant is set out in s256 TCA97 and includes credit unions.

There are a number of conditions relating to Special Term Accounts:

- the account holder must be aged over 16;
- the account must be in the name of the beneficial owner;
- the maximum monthly contribution is €635. However, a once-off contribution of €7,620 may be added to the fund;
- the individual may only hold one account. However, married individuals may hold two joint accounts simultaneously;
- withdrawals from the account may not be made within the three-year or five-year period, except:
  - (a) an individual whose account commenced before his/her sixtieth birthday may make a single withdrawal without penalty on or after his/her sixtieth birthday.
  - (b) withdrawals may be made without penalty on the death of the account-holder.
- the deposit interest rate may not be guaranteed for a period of more than 12 months;
- interest may accumulate within the account. The deposit-holder may elect to withdraw the interest provided that he/she does so within 12 months of it being credited to the account.

Taxation of special term accounts

Medium-term account[3]

A charge to tax arises on a medium term account if the interest realised on the account exceeds €480 per annum. Interest up to €480 is not taken into account in computing total income. Interest realised in excess of this amount is charged to DIRT.

Long-term account[4]

A charge to tax arises on a long-term account if the interest realised on the account exceeds €635 per annum. Interest up to €635 is not taken into account in computing total income. Interest realised in excess of this amount is charged to DIRT.

3 Section 23 F(No. 2)A 2013 – account will no longer be classified as special term account on the 3rd anniversary of its opening.

4 Section 23 F(No. 2)A 2013 – account will no longer be classified as a special term account on the 5th anniversary of its opening.

If the conditions regarding the accounts are breached within the three- or five-year terms, the legislation makes provisions for the taxation of the amounts, which were previously exempt on the basis of being below the €480 or €635 thresholds.

19.4 Schedule D Case V

This section details the taxation implications on the receipt of income from property and easements, which are chargeable to income tax under Schedule D Case V.

19.4.1 Income assessable

s18 TCA97 Section 18 TCA97 charges to tax rent arising from Irish property and receipts from easements. The term "easement" includes any right, privilege or benefit in, over or derived from premises - e.g., a right-of-way. Foreign rents are assessable under Case III of Schedule D.

19.4.2 Basis of assessment

s75(3) TCA97 The basis of assessment for Case V is the income arising in the year of assessment. For example, the rental income receivable during the year ended 31 December 2014 is assessable in the tax year 2014. Unlike Schedule D Cases I and II, there are no special rules for calculating Case V in the years of commencement and cessation.

It is the date on which income first arises from the Case V source, and not when the Case V source is acquired, that creates a commencement. Income arises when the person chargeable becomes entitled to it, even though the income may not necessarily be received.

Example 19.6

Brendan Smith who owns an apartment enters into a lease agreement with a tenant. The lease is effective from 1 February 2018 at an agreed rent of €1,500 per month. The rent due for February and March is paid on time. However, the rent for April to December inclusive remains unpaid at 31 December 2018. The arrears of €13,500 are eventually paid in February 2019.

Brendan Smith is assessable on Case V income of €16,500 for 2018 (i.e., €1,500 × 11 months).

The date of cessation of a Case V source is the date on which the source is disposed of, not the date on which the income ceases. If a source continues to exist, but does not produce income in any particular year, there is no cessation.

Death constitutes a cessation of a Case V source.

19.4.3 Deductions

s97(2) TCA97 Section 97(2) TCA97 sets out the types of deduction which may be made from the gross rents received. In computing the net rents assessable under Case V, the following expenses may be deducted:

- "rent" payable in respect of the property (e.g., ground rent);
- rates payable on the property;
- cost of goods provided, or services rendered, in connection with the letting;
- cost of maintenance, repairs, insurance and management of the property;
- interest on monies borrowed for the purchase, improvement or repair of the property (see below for restrictions);
- mortgage protection policy premia.

A deduction is not allowed in computing net rents for any capital expenditure (with the exception of the capital expenditure referred to in paragraph 19.4.5).

Pre-letting expenses are also not allowed apart from the exception included in Finance Act 2017. The deductible expenses are those incurred on residential premises which have been vacant for at least 12 months and which are then let as residential premises between 25th December 2017 and 31 December 2021. The expenditure must have been incurred in the 12 months prior to the premises being let as residential premises.

The deduction is subject to a cap and to a claw-back in certain circumstances. The deduction allowed is capped at €5,000 per vacant premises. If the landlord ceases to let the property as residential premises within 4 years of the first letting; the deduction will be clawed-back in the year in which the property ceases to be let as residential premises. This cessation can arise either because of a sale of the property or change of use from rented residential property.

While not provided for in the legislation, the Revenue Commissioners allow accountancy fees on a concession basis, fees incurred for the purposes of preparing a rent account are an allowable deduction in computing Case V income for income tax purposes.

Only the expenses relating directly to that portion of a property which is let are allowable deductions for Case V purposes. If only part of a property is let, expenses incurred on the property as a whole are apportioned. An example of a Case V computation illustrating the apportionment of deductions from the rental income of a property, which is partially let, and partially occupied, is set out below.

Example 19.7

A landlord has owned a property for some time. Half of the property is let and the landlord occupies the other half. In 2018 the rents receivable were €6,000, the expenses on the house as a whole were as follows:

	€
Insurance	*500*
Rates	*700*
Cleaning	*300*
Repairs	*2,000*

The landlord is not claiming rent-a-room relief (see 19.4.6 below)

The following is the Case V computation for 2018:

	€	€
Gross rents		*6,000*
**Allowable expenditure*		
Insurance	*250*	
Rates	*350*	
Cleaning	*150*	
Repairs	*1,000*	
		(1,750)
Case V		*4,250*

**As half the property is let, only half of the relevant expenditure is allowed as a deduction.*

Interest on borrowed monies

Interest paid on monies borrowed for the purchase, improvement or repair of the let property is allowed as a deduction. However, there are some restrictions. Section 16 Finance Act 2003 was introduced to counter contrived arrangements between spouses. Where one spouse buys out the interest of the other spouse in the family home, then moves to another property and lets the original family home, the interest on the borrowed monies (to buy out the other spouse's interest) is not allowed as a deduction against the rental income from the original family home. This restriction only applies to residential lettings.

Section 11 Finance Act 2006 introduced a provision whereby relief for interest paid is conditional on the borrower registering with the Private Residential Tenancies Board (PRTB). This condition is effective from 1 January 2006.

Finance Act 2009 provided that interest on monies borrowed to purchase, improve or repair a residential premises be restricted to 75% of qualifying expenditure with effect from 7 April 2009. The restriction applied regardless of whether the loan was taken out before or after 7 April 2009. Section 16 Finance Act 2016 introduced a phased return of the 100% deduction. For 2018, the restriction is 85% and by 2021 there will be full restoration of the 100% deduction. For certain residential properties, the restriction was already modified in the 2015 Finance Act. Section 15 provided that from 1 January 2016, a 100% interest deduction is allowable in respect of residential property which is let for a period of 3 years to a tenant or tenants in receipt of certain social housing supports. The PRTB must be informed of the tenancy.

Pre-letting expenses and expenses between lettings

In computing the net rents assessable, no deduction is allowed for pre-letting expenses incurred prior to first occupancy (with the exception for residential premises provided for in Finance Act 2017 discussed above). Thus, no deduction is available for any rent payable or interest paid on monies borrowed for the purchase, improvement or repair of any property to the extent that such expenses are incurred prior to the date on which the premises are first occupied by a lessee. However, it should be borne in mind that expenses incurred by the lessor in negotiating a lease for the property are allowable deductions in computing the assessable rental income. This is in accordance with the ruling in the Irish case of *Stephen Court Ltd v J A Brown* (H.C. 1982 No. 293 S.S.).

In this case a letting agent was appointed by the lessor to negotiate a lease for the property and to prepare the necessary documents. The letting agent was not entitled to any fee until a letting had been agreed. It was held by McWilliam J. in the High Court that the expenses of negotiating the lease and preparing the necessary documents were incurred during the currency of the lease and not for the purpose of setting up the lease. It was also held that such expenses were not expenses of a capital nature but were expenses of management.

Expenses incurred in the period between the termination of one lease and the granting of a new lease of the same premises are allowed provided the following two conditions are met:

(i) the person who was the lessor of the premises immediately before the termination of the lease did not occupy the premises during the post-termination period but was entitled to possession of the premises; and

(ii) the premises became subject to another lease granted by the same lessor at end of that period.

19.4.4 Losses

A loss or deficiency arises when the total allowable deductions exceed the gross rental income receivable for the year of assessment. A deficiency arising on a Case V computation in any year of assessment is carried forward and set-off against Case V profits in subsequent year(s) of assessment.

Note that capital allowances arising in a year must be deducted in priority to losses carried forward from previous years.

Uneconomic lettings arise where the rent received under a lease is not sufficient, taking one year with another, to cover the landlord's outgoings. In this context, outgoings cover maintenance costs, repairs, insurance and premises management costs. In these circumstances, a loss arising from such uneconomic lettings may not be offset against other rental profits and may not be carried forward.

In the case of a loss arising from lettings outside the State (and therefore assessable under Schedule D of Case III), it is understood that in practice, the Revenue Commissioners concessionally allow such a loss to be carried forward and set against future profits from the same property. To ensure that there is no scope to offset a Case III loss from lettings outside the State against other Case III income (i.e. income other than that from foreign rents), Section 16 FA 2014 introduced a provision to prevent this.

19.4.5 Capital allowances

s284(7) TCA97

In the case of furnished lettings, capital allowances may be claimed on expenditure incurred on fixtures and fittings, e.g., furniture, fitted kitchens, carpets, curtains, etc. For expenditure incurred post-4 December 2002, the rate is 12.5% per annum, also on a straight-line basis. These capital allowances may only be offset against Case V income and must be deducted in priority to losses carried forward from a previous year.

Example 19.8

A landlord spent €1,000 on fixtures and fittings on 1 February 2018 for use in a rented residential property, which has been let continuously since 2013. He may claim capital allowances as follows:

2018

€1,000 × 12.5% = €125.00

For each year thereafter he may claim €125 until the full expenditure of €1,000 is written off.

19.4.6 "Rent a room" relief

s216A TCA97

Section 32 Finance Act 2001 inserted a new section, s216A TCA97, which exempts from income tax, "relevant sums" derived from the renting out of a room in a "qualifying residence", which do not exceed a prescribed limit of €14,000 (the limit was €10,000 from 2008 to 2014 and 12,000 from 2015 to 2016).

"Relevant sums" are defined as all sums received for the use of the accommodation, and include sums arising in respect of goods and services, for example, meals, cleaning, laundry, etc.

A "qualifying residence" is defined as a private residence situated in the State which is occupied by the owner as his/her principal private residence during the tax year.

Profits or gains or any losses in respect of relevant sums are ignored for the purpose of the Income Tax Acts. Relevant sums are calculated without any deduction for expenses.

It is important to note that should the relevant sums exceed the €14,000 limit, all of the income is taxable and not just the excess. Despite the relevant sums not being taxable, an individual is nonetheless obliged to disclose them when filing his/her tax return for the year in question.

In addition, an individual who qualifies for rent a room relief has the choice of electing not to claim this relief each tax year (this might be an option where, for example the individual expected to make a rental loss and had other rental income against which the loss could be offset). Wear & tear allowances are deemed to be granted unless an election to not claim this relief has been made. If an individual elects not to claim this relief, the election must be made to the Inspector of Taxes, in writing, on or before the return-filing deadline for the year.

The receipt of relevant sums does not affect an individual's entitlement to mortgage interest relief (see Chapter 12) and capital gains tax relief on the disposal of a principal private residence (see Chapter 27). Section 14 of the Finance Act 2007 removed the exemption for children residing with their parents who pay "rent" to their parents.

s216B TCA97 Section 12 Finance Act 2004 introduced a form of "Rent a Room" relief for households in Gaeltacht areas. A scheme known as Scéim na bhFoghlaimeoirí Gaeilge exempts such income from tax with no income limit.

Example 19.9

Margaret Kelly has lived alone for many years. Due to diminishing returns on her investments she finds that her income is not sufficient to meet her day-to-day living needs. Her only recourse is to let part of her own home. She is not happy with the idea of a stranger using her cooking and washing facilities. Therefore she decides to offer accommodation on a full-board basis, which includes providing laundry facilities. She registers with a local college and a student is recommended to her. The guidelines for the weekly provision of accommodation and related services given to her are as follows:

	€
Bed and breakfast only	*85.00*
Lunch and evening meal	*30.00*
Laundry	*5.50*
Total	*120.50*

Margaret Kelly charged the recommended amount of €120.50 per week. In 2018, she received €120.50 per week from Student A for 30 weeks and €120.50 per week from Student B for 25 weeks. The related costs amounted to €2,305

The total gross amount received in 2018 is €6,627.50. Since this is below the exempt threshold of €14,000, Margaret Kelly is not liable to tax under Schedule D Case V.

Had she received €14,700 gross, even though the allowable expenses would reduce the profit figure to under €14,000, she would be liable to tax under Schedule D Case V on the net rental profit.

19.4.7 Taxation of reverse premiums

s98 TCA97 In recent times, it has become more popular for property developers to offer some type of inducement to prospective tenants to encourage them to enter into a lease for a commercial premises. This would especially have been the case with "anchor tenants". Such an inducement usually consisted of a direct payment to the prospective tenant and was not subject to income tax in the hands of the tenant.

s98A(2) TCA97 Section 18 Finance Act 2002 was introduced to redress this position. Where an inducement to enter into a lease is made to a prospective tenant, such inducement is treated as a taxable receipt under Case V Schedule D (or Case I or II where the prospective tenant carries on a trade or profession). Section 98A(2) TCA97 treats a reverse premium as a receipt of a revenue nature and hence, the amount is taxed as if it were an amount of rent.

However, where the person enters into such a transaction for the purpose of a trade or profession either carried on or shortly to be carried on by that individual, then the reverse premium is treated as a taxable receipt of the profession or trade and is assessed to tax under Schedule D Case I or II.

19.4.8 Exemption of income from leasing of farmland

s664 TCA97 Exemption from income tax is granted in respect of certain leasing income obtained by a lessor of agricultural land. The conditions attaching to the relief are:

(a) the income must arise from the leasing of farmland;

(b) the lease must be in writing and for a definite term of five years or more;

(c) the land may be leased to an individual or company. However the lessee must not be connected with the lessor and the leased farmland must be used for the purpose of a trade of farming;

(d) (i) The land may not be leased from a connected person on terms which are not at arm's length.

For any qualifying leases entered into on or after 1 January 2006, the limits are:

Up to 2014:

- €15,000 for a lease of seven years or more;
- €12,000 for a lease of between five and seven years;
- €20,000 for a lease exceeding ten years duration.

From 2015 onwards

- €18,000 for a lease of five years
- €22,500 for a lease of at least seven years duration
- €30,000 for a lease of at least ten years duration;
- €40,000 for a lease of fifteen years or more.

The leasing income of a husband and wife/civil partners is treated separately for the purposes of the relief, whether they are jointly assessed or not. There are anti avoidance measures to prevent connected parties entering into leases where both parties would otherwise qualify for the exemption.

19.4.9 Property-based tax incentives

Position up to 31/12/2010

Various incentive measures applied under many property schemes, which were introduced over the course of the last 20 years. A detailed analysis of the various schemes is outside the scope of this publication. However, a short resumé of one measure, which is commonly known as "Section 23" relief, is included.

Expenditure on rented accommodation

Expenditure incurred on the construction, refurbishment or conversion of a house or flat for letting was allowable as a deduction against the rental income from the property or other properties.

The relief applied to new, refurbished or converted properties measuring between 35 sq.m. and 125 sq.m. in the case of a house and 30 sq.m. to 90 sq.m. in the case of a flat which, without having been used for owner-occupation, is let by its owner to a tenant on an arm's length basis.

A clawback of relief arose where the property ceases to be a qualifying premises or the lessor's interest passes to another party (including on death) within ten years of the first letting of the premises under a qualifying lease.

In calculating the relief, the site cost together with a proportion of the builder's profit was not allowable as qualifying expenditure. Qualifying expenditure was arrived at by applying the following formula:

$$\text{Purchase Price} \times \frac{\text{Builder's Development Cost}}{\text{Builder's Site Cost} + \text{Builder's Development Cost}}$$

Example 19.10

	€
Cost of site	*5,000*
Site development costs	*2,000*
Building costs	*20,000*
Builders profit	*3,000*
Purchase price	*30,000*

Qualifying expenditure is, therefore:

$$30{,}000 \times \frac{(€2{,}000 + €20{,}000)}{(€5{,}000 + €2{,}000 + €20{,}000)} = €24{,}444$$

Assuming the assessable Case V figure in the year in which the above expenditure is incurred is €20,000, the net tax position is as follows:

	€
Case V	*20,000*
"Section 23" relief	*(24,444)*
Case V loss	*(4,444)*

The loss arising may be carried forward to future years.

Finance Act 2011 proposed wide ranging measures to curtail/abolish the use of "property incentives". For example, where capital allowances were used against total Case V income, the proposal was to ring fence the capital allowances to the specific building on which the expenditure was incurred. However the proposals were not be implemented until at least 60 days after an economic impact assessment. Followings the findings of the economic impact assessment, Finance Act 2012 has reversed the Finance Act 2011 proposals.

As stated above a detailed analysis of the various schemes is outside the scope of this publication, however for information purposes only, readers should be aware that FA 2014 proposed the introduction of a new "Living City Initiative" the introduction of which is subject to EU approval.

19.5 Schedule F

19.5.1 Income assessable

s20 TCA97 Tax under Schedule F is charged on dividends and other distributions received from Irish-resident companies. The term "distribution" is widely defined and it includes any distribution out of profits of a company except distributions in respect of a company's share capital on the winding-up of that company. A comprehensive list of items to be treated as a distribution is reproduced at Appendix I.

19.5.2 Basis of assessment

The basis of assessment for Schedule F for any year of assessment is the actual dividends or distributions received in that year of assessment.

19.5.3 Dividend withholding tax (DWT)

s172A TCA97 Withholding tax equal to the standard rate of tax applies to dividends (including scrip dividends and non-cash dividends) and other distributions (referred to as relevant distributions) paid by an Irish-resident company.

Dividends paid to Ministers of Government in their capacity as such Ministers and distributions made by an Irish-resident subsidiary company to its parent in another EU Member State are excluded from the provisions of dividend withholding tax. An Irish resident individual in receipt of distributions from an Irish-resident company is entitled to offset the withholding tax deducted against his/her total tax liability. Where the withholding tax deducted exceeds the recipient's tax liability, the excess may be reclaimed from the Revenue Commissioners. Thus, dividend withholding tax constitutes a refundable tax credit.

Example 19.11

Brian Jones is single and age 45. In 2018 he received €24,000 net dividends from Irish quoted companies. His assessment to tax, PRSI and USC as follows:

	€
Schedule F	*30,000*
Taxed as follows:	
€30,000 × 20%	*6,000*

Less non-refundable credits:	
Single person's credit	*(1,650)*
Tax liability	*4,350*
PRSI	
30,000 × 4%	*1,200*
USC	
12,012 × 0.5% = 60	
7,360 × 2% = 147	
10,628 × 4.75% = 505	
	712
	6,262
Less refundable credits:	
Dividend withholding tax	*(6,000)*
Liability	***(262)***

Dividends may be paid gross (i.e., without the need to deduct DWT) to the following recipients:

(a) other Irish-resident companies;

(b) charities;

(c) pension funds;

(d) certain collective investment undertakings;

(e) certain employee share-ownership trusts;

(f) certain residents of the EU Members States or Tax Treaty countries;

(g) distributions made to designate brokers for the benefit of a holder of a special portfolio investment account;

(h) fund managers of approved retirement fund or approved minimum retirement fund;

(i) savings managers of special savings incentive accounts;

(j) permanently incapacitated individual exempt from income tax on income from investment of compensation awards from personal injury claim;

(k) certain amateur and athletic sports bodies;

(l) trustees of tax-exempt trust funds set up by public funds on behalf of permanently incapacitated individuals and permanently incapacitated individuals in receipt of income from such trusts.

19.5.4 Non-resident individuals

Sch 2A TCA97

An exemption from dividend withholding tax applies to individuals who are neither resident nor ordinarily resident in the State and who are resident in a country with which Ireland has a tax treaty or in another EU Member State. To qualify for the exemption, the individual must make a declaration of entitlement and provide a certificate given by the tax authority in that country confirming that the person is resident in that State.

Non-resident individuals who are in receipt of dividends, but are not resident in either another EU Member State or a country with which Ireland has a tax treaty are only chargeable to income tax on the dividend income at the standard rate of tax.

19.5.5 Shares in lieu of dividend

Dividends are assessable in full on the basis of the gross amount received, i.e., the net dividend received plus dividend withholding tax is subject to tax. The dividend withholding tax is allowed as a credit against the tax liability of the recipient for the year of assessment.

It is common for companies, when declaring dividends, to give their shareholders the option of receiving additional share capital in the company rather than the cash dividend. If the shareholder opts to receive the additional share capital in the company rather than the dividend, the shareholder is assessed to tax under Schedule F on the cash foregone. This tax treatment applies where the paying company is an Irish-resident quoted company. The individual is taxed on an amount equal to the distribution (plus the dividend withholding tax) that he/she would have received had the option to take additional shares not been exercised. Therefore the tax position of shareholders who take a cash dividend and those who take shares is identical.

Readers are referred to paragraph 19.3.3 for an analysis of the tax treatment of the dividend foregone where the paying company is Irish tax resident but is not a quoted company, and to paragraph 19.2 for an analysis of the tax treatment of the dividend foregone where the paying company is not Irish tax resident.

The following diagram summarises the tax treatment of scrip dividends:

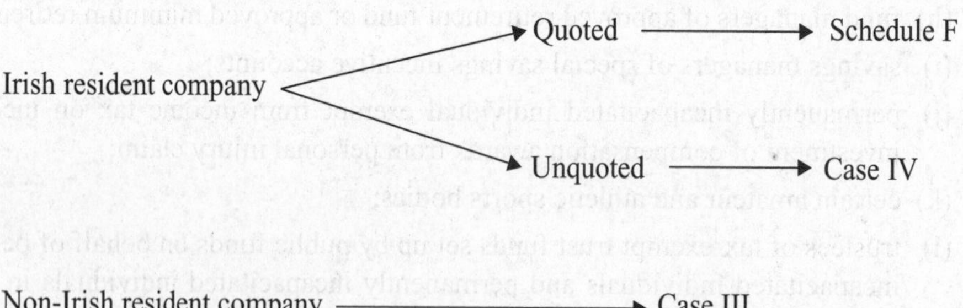

19.5.6 Exempt distributions

Some distributions/dividends are exempt from tax in the hands of the shareholder. Certain types of income preserve their tax-free status when passed on to shareholders in the form of dividends. The following are the types of income from which dividend income is exempt:

s140 TCA97 stallion services;

s140 TCA97 woodlands occupied on a commercial basis, in order to realise a profit;

s140 TCA97 profits from qualifying patents.

Dividend income, which is exempt under any of the above headings, is not regarded as income for any purpose of the Income Tax Acts.

19.5.7 Credit unions

s700 TCA97 Dividends paid by credit unions were exempt from dividend withholding tax up to 31 December 2014. Such dividends were assessable under Schedule D Case III (considered at paragraph 19.2 above). Section 23 F(No. 2)A 2013 introduced the application of DIRT on all dividends payable by credit unions from 1 January 2014.

Tax Facts

The introduction of DIRT for credit union dividends means that from 2015 onwards credit union members under 65 years who are otherwise tax exempt will now suffer a non-refundable tax deduction of 39%.

Appendix I

The following matters are treated as distributions and amounts received by an individual are assessable to income tax in his/her hands under Schedule F:

- any dividend paid by a company, including a capital dividend;
- any distribution out of the assets of the company in respect of shares in the company except so much of the distribution, if any, as represents a repayment of share capital or is made for new consideration;
- scrip dividends (see 19.5.5);
- a redemption of bonus securities insofar as is not referable to new consideration;
- interest paid on bonus securities;
- interest on securities convertible into shares or carrying rights to shares or securities (unless they are quoted securities or securities issued on terms reasonably comparable with those of quoted securities);
- interest which depends on the results of the borrowing company's business;
- the excess of interest over a reasonable commercial rate;
- interest on securities which are connected with shares in the company;
- a bonus issue followed by a repayment of share capital – A bonus issue is not regarded as a distribution if:
  - the company is not a close company,
  - the bonus issue was of shares other than redeemable shares,
  - the repayment takes place more than 10 years after the bonus issue;
- a repayment of share capital followed by a bonus issue – The amount of the repayment is not treated as a distribution if:
  - (i) the company is not a close company,
  - (ii) the bonus issue is of share capital other than redeemable share capital,
  - (iii) the bonus issue takes place more than 10 years after the repayment of share capital;
- transfer of assets at undervalue or liabilities at overvalue by a company to its members;

- any expenses incurred by a close company (see Chapter 32) in providing benefits, or facilities of any kind for shareholders and their associates (other than directors or employees);

- loan interest in excess of 13% paid to a director or to an associate of a director with a material interest in a close company (see Chapter 32):

  – "Material interest" means the ability to control directly or indirectly more than 5% of the ordinary share capital.

  – A close company, broadly speaking, is a company under the control of five or fewer shareholders or under the control of the directors regardless of their number.

20 TAXATION OF INCOME FROM OFFICE AND EMPLOYMENT

Learning Outcomes

On completion of this chapter you will be able to:

- ✓ Describe the scope of the charge to Schedule E
- ✓ Explain the difference between "employed" and "self-employed" and describe the criteria used to make the distinction.
- ✓ Describe the conditions necessary for expenses to be allowed as a deduction under Schedule E.

20.1 Introduction

The purpose of this chapter is to identify the sources of income which are charged to tax under Schedule E.

In general, tax is charged under Schedule E:

- on every individual holding a public office or employment within the State;
- in the case of a resident individual, on profits arising from any employment wherever exercised;
- on employments exercised within the State (regardless of where the individual is resident).

Tax is also charged under Schedule E on pensions, including pensions payable out of the public Revenue of the State, pensions payable under occupational pension schemes and social welfare pensions.

The chapter also considers the difficulties in determining the distinction between an individual who is employed under a contract *of* service and an individual retained under a contract *for* service. Finally, the chapter considers expenses allowable as a deduction under Schedule E.

20.2 Scope of Charge to Schedule E

s112 TCA97 Schedule E charges to tax income from all "salaries, fees, wages, perquisites or profits whatever" arising from an office or employment. The definition also includes occupational pensions and certain social welfare payments. The term "emoluments" is used to cover any such amounts chargeable under this Schedule.

s123 TCA97 In addition, Schedule E extends the charge to include specific types of income, e.g., payments on retirement or removal from office or employment (discussed in Chapter 22).

20.2.1 Meaning of "emoluments"

s112(2)(a) TCA97 The term "emoluments" is used to describe anything assessable to tax under Schedule E. It is defined as including "all salaries, fees, wages, perquisites or profits whatever" arising from an office or employment. Benefits-in-kind and perquisites are considered in Chapter 21.

The terminology "arising from an office or employment" is important. In the case of *Seymour v Reed* (11 TC 625), Lord Cave stated:

> *"It must now (I think) be taken as settled that the words, 'salaries, fees, wages, perquisites or profits whatsoever' include all payments made to the holder of an office or employment as such, that is to say, by way of remuneration for his services, even though such payments may be voluntary, but they do not include a mere gift or present (such as a testimonial) which is made to him on personal grounds and not by way of payment for his services".*

If a payment meets the above criteria, i.e., by reference to the service the employee renders by virtue of his office, and is in the nature of a reward for those services, then the payment is assessable under Schedule E, even if the payment is voluntary.

20.2.2 Office or employment

The first principle of Schedule E is to establish whether an office or employment exists.

There are two types of office and employment within the scope of Schedule E, namely "public" offices and employments and other employments.

There is no statutory definition of an office or employment. In this regard, decisions from a number of cases are relevant.

An "office" was defined by Rowlatt J. in *Great Western Railway Co. v Bater* (8TC 231) as "a subsisting, permanent, substantive position, which had an existence independent of the person who filled it, and which went on and was filled in succession by successive holders; an example of an office holder is a company director".

This definition was quoted with reserved approval in the more recent case of *Edwards v Clinch* ([1981] STC 617), where Lord Wilberforce questioned Rowlatt J.'s use of the word "permanent". However, Lord Wilberforce did say that "the word (office) must involve a degree of continuance (not necessarily continuity) and of independent existence".

In practice, there is no distinction between public offices and other offices.

20.2.3 Basis of assessment

s112 TCA97 Tax is charged under Schedule E on the actual amount of all salaries, fees, wages, perquisites or profits whatsoever derived from the office, employment or pension for the year of assessment. Up to 2017, Schedule E income was taxed on an earnings basis. Finance Act 2017 changed the earnings basis to a payments basis except for proprietary directors and employees respect of whom a PAYE exclusion order has issued (i.e. non Irish resident employees who remain on an Irish payroll).

20.3 Distinction Between "Employed" and "Self-Employed"

The terms "employed" and "self-employed" are not defined in law. It is sometimes difficult to determine whether an individual is:

- employed and consequently chargeable under Schedule E; or
- self-employed and chargeable under Case I or II of Schedule D (considered in Chapter 14).

In this regard, decisions from a number of cases are relevant. The courts have treated as employed, individuals who operate under a contract of service, while self-employed individuals are those who operate under a contract for service.

20.3.1 Relevant case law

Cooke J.'s comment in *Market Investigations v Minister of Social Security* ([1968] 3 All ER 732) has been quoted with approval in subsequent cases:

"the fundamental test to be applied is this: Is the person who has engaged himself to perform these services performing them as a person in business on his own account? If the answer to that question is 'yes', then the contract is a contract for service. If the answer is 'no', then the contract is a contract of service."

There are no established criteria for determining whether a contract is one "of" service or "for" service. Relevant factors include pay arrangements, working hours, the degree of control held by the individual over his/her work, whether the individual may hire other people to do work he/she has undertaken, etc.

Whether a contract of service or a contract for service was in existence was discussed in the case of *Director of Public Prosecutions v Martin McLoughlin* (6 ILRM 493).

In this case, Mr McLoughlin skippered a boat which went on weekly fishing trips. Each weekly trip was a separate venture and although the same crew turned up regularly, no crew member had a contract which entitled him to participate in future trips. No wages were paid to the crew members but each member was entitled to a share of the profits, such share being decided by custom and agreement. If there was no profit, the crew did not suffer a share of the losses. It was held, on the facts of the case, that there was no contract of service between the crew members and the skipper. The profits paid to the crew members were accordingly not assessable under Schedule E.

In a recent Irish case, *Henry Denny & Sons (Ireland) Limited v Minister for Social Welfare* (1997), it was held by the High Court that a supermarket demonstrator was engaged under a contract of service. The case considered the various tests, which may be applied in determining whether a contract of service exists:

1.	control test	–	the demonstrator was subject to control, direction and dismissal by the company;
2.	integration test	–	the supermarket demonstrations were considered an integral part of the company's business;
3.	economic relations test	–	the terms of engagement were consistent with those of a contract of service;
4.	entrepreneurial test	–	the demonstrator was shown not to be in business on her own account.

This decision was upheld by the Supreme Court. In his judgment, Keane J. placed emphasis on the substance of the contract over its form.

20.3.2 Report of the employment status group

The Employment Status Group[1] delivered a report in August 2006. The group had been set up because of a growing concern that there may be increasing numbers of individuals categorised as self-employed when the indicators may be that "employee" status would be more appropriate.

The report was issued as a code of practice and is reported in the Revenue Commissioner's publication *Tax Briefing Issue 43*. While the code of practice does not have legislative effect, it is expected that its contents will be considered by those involved in disputes on the employment status of individuals. The report established the criteria to determine whether an individual is an employee. It advised that whilst all of the following factors may not be applicable, an individual would normally be an employee if he or she:

- is under the control of another who directs as to how, when and where the work is to be carried out;
- supplies labour only;
- receives a fixed hourly/weekly/monthly wage;
- cannot sub-contract the work;

1 This group was set up under the Programme for Prosperity and Fairness (PPF) and consisted of representatives from the Irish Congress of Trade Unions, the Irish Business and Employers Confederation, the Revenue Commissioners, the Department of Employment Affairs and Social Protection, the Department of Jobs, Enterprise and Innovation and the Department of Finance.

- does not supply materials for the job;
- is not exposed to personal financial risk in carrying out the job;
- does not have the opportunity to profit from sound management;
- works set hours or a given number of hours per week; and
- receives expense payments to cover subsistence and/or travel expenses.

20.4 Expenses Allowable as a Deduction under Schedule E

s114 TCA97 For a deduction to be allowed for travelling expenses, "the holder of an office or employment" must have been "necessarily obliged" to incur the expense "in the performance of the duties of the office or employment". A deduction is given for other expenses to the extent that they are incurred "wholly, exclusively and necessarily in the performance of the duties" of the office or employment. In both cases, a test of necessity is imposed and the expense must be incurred in "the performance of the duties" of the office or employment.

Whether an expense is allowable usually hinges on the interpretation of one or more of the following phrases:

- "in the performance of the duties of the office or employment;"
- "necessarily obliged to incur and defray" (travelling expenses);
- "wholly, exclusively and necessarily" (other expenses).

These phrases are now considered in turn.

20.4.1 "In the performance of the duties"

For an expense to be allowable, it must be incurred in the actual discharge or performance of the duties of the office or employment to which it relates. It is an established principle that expenses incurred by an employee in travelling to the place where he/she performs the duties of his/her office or employment are not expenses incurred in the actual performance of those duties, but merely expenses incurred in putting him/her in a position to perform those duties. In this regard, case law is relevant.

In the case of *Ricketts v Colquhoun* (10 TC 118), a barrister who was living and practising in London was appointed to the position of Recorder of Portsmouth. He was obliged to travel to Portsmouth four times a year to hold Court there and he claimed relief for the expenses of travelling to and from Portsmouth and his hotel expenses in Portsmouth. It was held that the expenses were not incurred in the performance of his duties as Recorder but partly before he entered upon his duties and partly after he had fulfilled these duties, and as such they were not allowable.

20.4.2 "Necessarily obliged to incur and defray"

This is a condition of the test which applies to travelling expenses. The full test is that "the holder of the office or employment is necessarily obliged to incur the expenses of travelling in the performance of the duties of the office or employment". The test is an objective one, not a personal one, i.e., the individual must be obliged to incur the expense by the very fact that he/she holds the office or employment and must perform its duties.

Returning to the case of *Ricketts v Colquhoun* (10 TC 118) already referred to above, the hotel expenses failed the objective test on the grounds that if an individual elects to live away from his/her work and must bear the expenses of staying away from home, it is by his/her own choice and not by reason of any necessity arising out of his/her employment.

20.4.3 "Wholly, exclusively and necessarily"

s114 TCA97 This condition is substituted for the phrase "necessarily obliged to incur" in looking at the allowability of non-travelling expenses under s114 TCA97 so that the test becomes: "the holder of the office or employment incurs the expense wholly, exclusively and necessarily in the performance of the duties of the office or employment". The objective test discussed above in connection with travelling expenses applies equally here.

The duties of the office or employment must impose the test of necessity, not the employer. In *Brown v Bullock* (40 TC 1), a bank manager joined a West End club, membership of such a club being virtually a requisite of his appointment. He claimed a deduction for the subscription to the club. It was disallowed on the grounds that the expense was not necessary to enable him to perform the duties of the office of bank manager. If he had not joined the club he could still have performed those duties.

In *Lupton v Potts* (45 TC 643), examination fees paid by a solicitor's apprentice were not allowed as they were not laid out "wholly, exclusively and necessarily" to carry out his duties. The fees could also have been disallowed on the grounds that they were not incurred in the performance of the duties of the employment.

Although the words "wholly and exclusively" might be held to prohibit the deduction of any part of an expense, where the expense as a whole is not incurred in the performance of the duties, in practice, if the nature of an expense is such that a definite part or proportion can be regarded as being expended "wholly, exclusively and necessarily" in the performance of the duties of the office or employment, then that part or proportion will be allowed.

It will be noted for the latter two tests above that the expense must actually be "incurred" by the holder of the office or employment, prohibiting a claim for notional or estimated expenses. The onus is on the taxpayer to prove that expenditure has been incurred.

The following expenses are generally allowable in practice:

- expenditure on special clothing worn in the performance of the duties;
- expenditure on tools used in the performance of the duties;
- expenditure on books and newspapers for journalists;
- expenses incurred by commercial travellers who are required to bear travelling and hotel expenses in the course of performing their duties.

20.5 Expenses of Travel To/From Work

The cost of travel to and from work by employees and directors is taxable as 'pay' if reimbursed by the employer/company. Where such employees/directors have to travel during the course of their work they may be reimbursed tax free for the cost of subsistence and travel either on a vouched basis or using agreed Civil Service rates. Prior to 2016 non-executive directors could not be paid tax free for the travel cost of attendance at board meetings.

From 1 January 2016, travel and subsistence expenses incurred by a **non-resident**, non-executive director to attend board meetings may now be paid tax free. The non-resident, non-executive director must provide receipts for the expenses and the meetings attended must be for the purposes of conducting the business of the company.

From 1 January 2017, the exempt status of travel expenses afforded to non-resident, non-executive directors is now extended to **Irish resident**, non-executive directors. Section 3 FA 2016 introduced a new section; s195D TCA97 to provide for this exemption. Travel expenses to which the exemption applies may not exceed the Civil Service approved rates for mileage and subsistence. Also, the Irish resident, non-executive director's remuneration with the paying company must not exceed €5,000 per annum.

20.6 Share Incentive Schemes

Employee share incentive schemes can be an effective way of encouraging employee participation and loyalty in the employer company. Under employee share schemes, employers allocate free or discounted shares to their employees. An employee participating in a share incentive scheme would (in the absence of any relieving measures) be chargeable to tax under section 112 on any benefit received as a Schedule E taxable emolument.

Irish tax legislation allows for many types of schemes which facilitate employers in allocating shares, or granting options to buy shares, to employees tax efficiently. At the same time the tax incentives/tax expenditures can reward the employee by giving them a share in the capital/underlying ownership of the company rather than just an income therefrom. Depending on the type of scheme, employees may have to hold the shares for a number of years before they receive the tax benefits. Examples of employee share incentive schemes are:

- Share options (approved and unapproved)
- Share awards
- Approved profit sharing schemes (APSS)
- Restricted stock units (RSUs)
- Save as you Earn (SAYE)

A share option is different from a share award. There are in turn different kinds of share option schemes and different kinds of share award schemes with different tax rules attaching to each. The benefits, together with the conditions and restrictions of the different schemes, are outlined below.

20.7 Share Options

A share option, is an option granted by a company to its directors or employees to subscribe for shares in the company (or an associated company) at a pre-determined price at some point in the future. The option must be "exercised" in order for the individual to take beneficial ownership of the shares. Until such time as the option is exercised, the individual does not enjoy any rights relating to the shares which are the subject of the option.

The different events that may occur in the life of an option are as follows:

Grant

The grant of an option means giving the grantee the rights under the option. In relation to employee share options, it means giving the option-holder the right to acquire shares in the future.

Vest

Sometimes when an option is granted, there may be conditions relating to when it may be exercised. An option "vests" when there is an unconditional right to exercise it.

Exercise

The exercise of an option means that the option-holder uses or implements the rights under the option. In the context of employee share options, this means that the option-holder uses the rights under the option to buy shares at the option exercise price.

Sale

In some cases, an option can be sold by the grantee prior to being exercised. The option may or may not be capable of being exercised at the date of its sale, depending on the circumstances.

Forfeiture

There may be an obligation to forfeit an option where the option-holder has failed to meet certain conditions during a set period (called the forfeiture period). The option is lost or surrendered at this time. For example, an employee may be obliged to forfeit their share options if they leave the company to take up employment elsewhere.

Abandonment

An option is abandoned where the option holder is entitled to exercise the option but chooses not to do so. For example, the holder of an employee share option may choose not to exercise it because the current market value of the shares is lower than the exercise price.

Approved share option schemes were a very tax efficient way of rewarding staff however these were discontinued from 24 November 2010. A detailed analysis of the tax treatment of such schemes is therefore outside the scope of this publication. Below is a summary of the tax treatment of 'unapproved' share options only.

20.8 Unapproved Share Option Schemes

20.8.1 Grant

s128(5) TCA97 There is no charge to tax on the grant of a share option unless it is capable of being exercised later than 7 years after the date on which it was granted.

If the share option is capable of being exercised 7 years after being granted, the employee is subject to income tax in the year of grant on the market value of the underlying shares at the date of grant less the exercise price payable to acquire them. An option capable of being exercised 7 years after being granted is usually referred to as a "long option" while an option which must be exercised within the 7 year period is usually referred to as a "short option".

20.8.2 Exercise

Under s128(2) TCA97, there is a charge to income tax under Schedule E on the amount of gain arising on the exercise of a share option. The tax charge is generally on the difference between the price paid (i.e. the exercise price or "option price") and the market value of the shares at the date of exercise. This share option gain can be reduced by any payment made by the employee for the grant of the option (i.e. any payment made in return for being given the right to acquire the shares, rather than the payment to acquire the shares themselves when the option is later exercised).

Where income tax was chargeable on the grant of the option under s128(5)(a) TCA97, (i.e., if it was a 'long option') a credit for this tax may be taken against the tax due on the exercise of the option.

The tax, USC and PRSI due on share option gains is collected through the self-assessment system and deems an individual who realises a share option gain to be a "chargeable person". There is no employer PRSI chargeable on share option gains.

If a cash payment is made to an employee for the release of a share option, PAYE will apply to the gain as the cash payment represents a "normal pay".

20.8.3 Forfeiture

Where an employee forfeits his or her share options there are no income tax or CGT implications. The employee will not be able to obtain loss relief for any consideration paid to the company to acquire the options.

20.8.4 Abandonment

Generally, the abandonment of an option has no income tax consequences unless tax was payable at the date of grant of unapproved share options (i.e. the options were exercisable after more than 7 years). If tax was paid on the long option and the option is abandoned (not subsequently exercised), the individual will not be able to reclaim that income tax.

20.8.5 Sale

A CGT liability may arise on the disposal of the shares acquired on the exercise of a share option. The allowable cost of the shares for CGT purposes is the exercise price plus any amount paid in return for the grant of the option (s540(4)), plus the amount of any share option gain which was subject to income tax on the grant (long option) or exercise of the option. Invariably, this will be equal to the market value of the shares at the date on which the option is exercised.

20.8.6 Filing requirements

For the employee

The marginal rate tax, USC and PRSI due on share option gains is collected through the self-assessment system and deems an individual who realises a share option gain to be a "chargeable person". The employee must file Form RTSO1 within 30 days of the date of exercise of the options along with the relevant payment.

For the employer

There is no employer PRSI chargeable on share option gains.

The employer granting the options must deliver details of this in writing to Revenue on or before 31 March in the following year of assessment. The relevant details should be entered on a form RSS1, which covers details of all unapproved share schemes and must be delivered electronically.

Example 20.1 – Unapproved share option scheme

Roy O'Neill was granted share options on 1 June 2016 to acquire 1,000 at €3 per share (the market value of the shares was €3 each on 1 June 2016). Under the terms of the agreement the share options must be exercised by 1/12/2020. This is a 'short option' as it must be exercised within 7 years of the date of grant. Roy exercised his option to acquire the 1,000 shares on 1 December 2018. The market value per share on 1 December 2018 was €5. There is no income tax implication at the date of grant as the option is a 'short' option (i.e. the tax is due on the exercise rather than on the grant of the option).

Value of each share on exercise €5.00 × 1,000	*= €5,000*
Less :	
Amount paid €3.00 × 1,000	*= €3,000*
Gain	*= €2,000*

Roy must pay 40% rate tax, 4% PRSI and 8% USC on the gain of €2,000 (i.e. by reference to 2018 rates) and file Form RTSO1 within 30 days of 1 December 2018.

20.9 Share Awards

In contrast to share options, which give an employee a right to acquire shares in the future, other share award schemes involve giving employees shares in the employer company upfront, often at a discount. The provision of shares at a discount is a perquisite (i.e. it is capable of being turned into money) and is chargeable to tax as a result.

A significant difference between share options and share awards is that tax on the latter is collected by the employer through the PAYE system, whereas tax on share options is payable through self-assessment by the individual employee. This can have cashflow implications for the employer, given that share awards are non-cash remuneration, and they must fund the tax liability. This can be collected from the employee in future payroll periods provided that the liability is fully paid by the employee by 31 March of the following tax year. If the full liability is not paid by this date, the outstanding balance owed to the employer will be treated as a BIK and a further charge to tax will arise.

20.10 Approved Profit Sharing Schemes (APSS)

s509 – s518 TCA97 An approved profit sharing scheme (APSS) is a Revenue approved scheme that allows employees and directors to convert a profit sharing bonus into shares in their employer company. The shares can be issued to the employees and directors up to a certain value each year income tax free.

The scheme operates within the framework of a trust. The participating employees either apply a percentage of their basic gross salary towards the purchase of shares, or instead can accumulate funds from profit sharing bonuses to purchase the shares. This is known as salary sacrifice.

Revenue's guidance in relation to schemes that include a salary sacrifice provision includes a requirement that the maximum amount of salary that may be foregone does not exceed 7.5% of basic salary. Section 118B(2)(a)(ii) TCA97 provides that the salary sacrificed in this way is exempt from tax. These funds are passed on by the company to the trustees of the trust established for the purposes of the scheme. The trustees use the monies to acquire shares in the company or its parent. The trustees have legal ownership of the shares but must appropriate (allocate) the shares within 18 months of their acquisition to employees participating in the scheme.

No income tax charge arises on the allocation of the shares to the employee by the trustees. A charge to USC and employee PRSI arises on the initial appropriation of the shares. Where USC has been charged on the initial appropriation of the shares, it will not be charged again on a disposal so as to avoid a double charge.

The shares are left in the trust for a minimum of 2 years ("the period of retention") but the employee can only dispose of them, income tax-free after 3 years (i.e. after the "release date"). Between years two and three, the employee can dispose of the shares but this triggers a charge to income tax on 100% of the "locked-in" value of the shares, subject to some exceptions. If the shares are disposed of after the release date (i.e. after the third anniversary of the date they were appropriated to the employee), there is no income tax charge.

The legislation sets a limit on the market value of the shares that each employee can be appropriated in a year of assessment. The current limit is €12,700 per annum.

The company may pay dividends to the trustees on shares held by them. The trustees in turn allocate the net dividend they receive among the employees in proportion to their individual shareholdings.

20.10.1 Filing requirements

- The employee must detail acquisitions and disposals of shares and dividends received on his or her annual tax return
- The company must apply in writing to Revenue for approval of the scheme
- The trustees of an APSS must deliver a return of information to Revenue on or before 31 March in the year following the year of assessment by filing a form ESS1
- The trustees must also make an annual return (Form 1) of any income and capital gains. This is due by 31 October of the following year.

Example 20.2

Tomás is a full time employee of Treedawn Manufacturers Limited. Tomás was allocated 1,000 shares in the company under a Revenue APSS on 17 February 2016. Their market value at the date of appropriation was €4,000. The shares have gone up in value since then and Tomás wants the trustees of the APSS to sell all of the shares appropriated to him under the scheme on his behalf. The shares are sold on 19 February 2018 at a market price of €5.10 per share.

The shares were appropriated to Tomás under the APSS on 17 February 2016 at a market value of €4,000. USC and PRSI was payable on this amount in 2016.

The retention period ends on 17 February 2018 however the shares can only be sold tax-free from 17 February 2019 onwards (the "release date"). As the shares are being sold before 17 February 2019, Tomás is subject to income tax under Schedule E. The amount of the charge is 100% of the locked–in value of the shares, i.e. €4,000.

20.11 Restricted Shares

s128D TCA97

Tax legislation provides for a reduction (abatement) of up to 60% in the taxable value of the share award where a restriction of more than 12 months is placed on the employee's right to dispose of the shares. The enforced retention period is commonly called the "clog" period.

The director or employee must be restricted from disposing of the shares for a period of at least one year (the "specified period"). During that specified period, the shares must be held in a trust in Ireland or the EEA established by the employer for the benefit of employees or directors or in some other structure approved by Revenue.

The amount chargeable to income tax under Schedule E by a percentage as follows:

Number of years of restriction on sale	Abatement Percentage
1 year	10%
2 years	20%
3 years	30%
4 years	40%
5 years	50%
> 5 years	60%

When calculating the charge to tax under Schedule E which is to be reduced/abated, any effect which the restriction may have on the market value of the shares is ignored.

The discounted/abated amount is liable to income tax, USC and PRSI (employee not employer). As the employee is being awarded shares the employer must account for the tax through the PAYE system.

There is a clawback where the restriction on the disposal of the shares is altered or lifted. The clog scheme rules cannot apply to shares acquired by a director or employee under an APSS or a Save As You Earn scheme. However, a clog scheme can be combined with an unapproved share option scheme.

Example 20.3

On 1 January 2017, Jim received ordinary shares in Polish Limited as a benefit of his employment with the company. He only paid €5,000 for the shares even though the shares had a market value of €50,000 at the time. Under the terms of the shareholders' agreement, the shares may not be disposed of for 5 years and are held in an employee trust during this period.

During 2017, Polish Limited suffers trading difficulties. On 1 January 2018, there is an offer made by a third party for the entire share capital of the company. The offer is accepted. Jim's shares are released from the restriction and are sold for cash of €20,000.

2017

Jim has received a taxable benefit from Polish Limited and is subject to tax under s112 TCA97. However, the shares are restricted shares. The amount chargeable to income tax, PRSI and USC (€50,000 less €5,000 = €45,000) will be abated to 50% as the restriction on the disposal of the shares is for 5 years. Accordingly, the amount chargeable to tax under Schedule E for 2017 will be €22,500 (€45,000 × 50%).

2018

On the lifting of the restriction, the abatement of the amount chargeable to income tax is reduced to 10% (the discount which applies when the specified period is only one year). Revenue will adjust Jim's 2017 assessment to reflect the fact that the discounted amount upon which tax is chargeable should have been €40,500 (€45,000 – 10%) and not €22,500.

20.11.1 Filing requirements

Employers granting shares must deliver a return (Form RSS1) on or before 31 March in the year of assessment following the year in which the following occurs:

- restricted shares are awarded to a director or employee,
- the restriction on the shares is varied or removed or the shares are disposed of.

Tax on share awards (other than share options) is paid and collected by the employer through the PAYE system.

20.12 Restricted Stock Unit (RSU)

A restricted stock unit or RSU is a promise to receive shares or cash to the value of those shares in an employer or related company at a future date. Often, there is a delay between the date of grant and vesting. This could be a time-based restriction (e.g. the employee must stay in employment for a stated period) or on the happening of an event (e.g. the company raises external equity or there is an IPO). The units are often forfeitable or cannot be sold prior to vesting.

There is no specific Irish legislation covering RSUs but Revenue, acknowledging that such schemes are becoming more commonplace, issued Tax Briefing 63 to set out their view of the appropriate tax treatment. According to Revenue, the RSUs do not become taxable until the earlier of the RSU vesting date or the date the shares or cash are actually passed to the employee.

Tax Briefing 2/2011 also confirms that if there is a further period between the vesting date and that date that the units are actually settled on the employee (known as a blocking or lock-in period), Revenue will postpone the due payment date of the tax until that settlement date to give the employees the opportunity to sell their shares to fund the tax liability. However, this concession is only given if the blocking period is less than 60 days from the vesting date.

RSUs are chargeable to income tax under Schedule E and are within the scope of PAYE. USC and PRSI are also chargeable on RSUs.

RSUs are fully taxable in Ireland if they vest at a time when the holder is Irish resident, without any apportionment by reference to any part of the vesting period during which the holder was resident elsewhere.

If the RSUs vest and the holder is no longer Irish resident, the RSUs are not taxable in Ireland, regardless of the fact that the holder may have been resident in Ireland at the Jime of the grant. RSUs awarded to a director in his or her capacity as a director of an Irish company who is not tax resident in the State at the time of vesting, are fully taxable in the State at the time of vesting subject to any relieving provisions of an appropriate Double Taxation Agreement.

In the case of individuals who–

- in a tax year are resident but not domiciled in the State,
- have income (including RSUs) arising from a non-Irish employment,
- perform some of the duties of their employment in the State and some of the duties outside the State, and
- have RSUs vesting in that tax year,

Revenue are prepared to accept that the appropriate deductions under the PAYE system should be made at the time of vesting from that proportion of an RSU attributable to the performance of the duties of the foreign employment in the State.

Certain individuals may, in addition to having a liability under the PAYE system in the State, also have a liability to income tax in a foreign State on the RSU or a portion of the RSU. Where this arises, and a double taxation agreement is in place with the other State, the individual may be entitled to a credit in relation to any amount subject to double taxation.

20.13 Save As You Earn (SAYE) Share Schemes

s519A
Sch12A
TCA97

There are two elements to these schemes; an approved savings-related share option scheme and a certified contractual savings scheme. The latter scheme is used to fund the purchase of shares allocated to employees under the former scheme.The SAYE scheme allows employees to save a part of their after-tax pay to purchase shares in their employer's company The savings can be between €12 and €500 per month over a three-year period – and at the end of this period the savings can be used to purchase the shares.

The shares can be purchased at a discount of 25% of their market value at the beginning of the three-year savings period. No charge to income tax arises on the purchase at this discounted price. Where an individual obtains a right to acquire shares in his/her employing company or a group company, no tax will be chargeable in respect of the receipt or exercise of that right except in certain circumstances where the option is exercised within 3 years of being obtained.

Contractual savings schemes must be with "qualifying savings institutions" as listed.

Certain conditions must be complied with in order for a savings-related share option scheme to be approved by the Revenue Commissioners. These conditions govern the type of company eligibility, type of shares, exercise of rights, acquisition of shares and the share price and include:

- The shares must be in a company that is not under the control of another company or must be quoted on a recognised stock exchange.
- The options must be over the ordinary share capital of the grantor, a company that has control of the grantor or a member of a consortium that controls the grantor.
- Employees and full-time directors who have been employees/directors for a specified period not exceeding three years must be eligible to participate on "similar terms".

20.13.1 Taxation

Where the terms of the legislation are met, no income tax, USC or employee PRSI charges arise on the grant and no income tax charge arises on the exercise of the option. USC and employee PRSI will be charged on the option gain on the date of exercise. Unlike unapproved share options, the employer is required to remit the USC and PRSI liability via the PAYE system. Where the exercise is by a former employee, the option holder must self-assess for the USC and PRSI liabilities.

The interest or bonus earned on savings can be paid free of income tax, DIRT, USC and PRSI.

20.14 Key Employee Engagement Programme (KEEP)

s128F TCA97

As evidenced above the use of equity based remuneration (unless otherwise exempt) gives rise to income tax/USC/PRSI charges. These charges apply on any gain realised by an individual on the exercise of a share option acquired by the employee or director. These high charges (up to 52%) can make incentives like share option schemes unattractive.

Section 10 FA 2017 introduced 'Key Employee Engagement Programme' (KEEP) to help SMEs attract and retain expertise in a competitive labour market. Unlike share option gains; KEEP options by employees and directors will not be subject to income tax/USC/PRSI where the conditions of s128F TCA97 are satisfied. Capital Gains Tax will arise on a subsequent disposal of the shares, at which time the sales proceeds will be available to discharge the CGT liability. KEEP is applicable in respect of share options granted during the period 1 January 2018 to 31 December 2023.

21 BENEFITS-IN-KIND

Learning Outcomes

On completion of this chapter, you should be able to:

- ✓ Explain the scope of the benefit-in-kind provisions and identify which benefits and expense payments are exempt from tax.
- ✓ Explain how different types of benefit-in-kind are valued.
- ✓ Calculate the amount assessable as benefit-in-kind in the case of employer-provided vehicles, living accommodation, preferential loans, etc.
- ✓ Describe the obligations of employers with respect to reporting the provision of benefits to employees.
- ✓ Describe the proposed parking levy
- ✓ Exempt benefits-in-kind

21.1 Introduction

This chapter covers the charge to tax on the provision of various employer-provided assets, expense allowances and other benefits. The analysis is concerned with how such benefits are valued for assessment purposes. The typical types of employer-provided assets, expense allowances and benefits are as follows:

Company cars/vans

A tax charge is not confined to the provision of a company car. A tax charge may also arise on the provision of vans. This chapter explains how to calculate the amount assessable for both types of vehicle and also considers amounts that may be deducted to reduce the amount assessable to tax.

Living accommodation

This chapter explains how to value accommodation and also identifies the circumstances where accommodation can be provided tax-free.

Preferential loans

Where loans are provided by an employer at a rate of interest that is lower than that in the market place, a charge to tax arises. This chapter explains how to calculate the amount assessable to tax.

Expenses paid by employers

In addition to the above benefits, it is common for employers to pay certain expenses on behalf of employees, e.g., medical insurance (VHI/Quinn Healthcare/Aviva Healthcare) and golf subscriptions. This chapter explains how to value these expenses for assessment purposes.

21.1.1 General

Tax is charged under Schedule E on every person having or exercising an office or employment in respect of "all salaries, fees, wages, perquisites or profits whatsoever arising from the office or employment". Income tax under Schedule E is therefore charged on the emoluments of an employment, which are paid either in cash or in a form which can be converted into money. Accordingly, benefits received by an employee, which cannot be converted into money, such as free accommodation, free travel or the use of certain company assets, cannot be assessed to tax under general principles. In order to counter this situation, the legislation contains special provisions to bring within the scope of Schedule E, expense allowances and benefits-in-kind (BIK), which are not otherwise chargeable to tax. The BIK legislation also applies to directors and office holders, references hereafter to "employee(s)" should be taken to include directors and office holders unless otherwise stated.

Where the benefit to the employee derives from the transfer of ownership of an asset (previously used by the employer) from the employer to the employee, the prevailing market value of the asset at the time of transfer (and not the original cost to the employer of acquiring the asset) is taken to be the benefit-in-kind.

Where the benefit involves the free use of property without the transfer of ownership, the annual value of the property is generally taken to be the benefit-in-kind. However, very specific rules exist for valuing benefits arising on the provision of living accommodation, motor cars and preferential loans and these are discussed in detail below.

Where the benefit derives from the provision of some service by the employer or from the payment of some expenses by the employer on behalf of the employee, the costs incurred by the employer are generally taken to be the benefit-in-kind. In Ireland, marginal cost as opposed to average cost is taken to be the normal measure of the BIK assessment. The precedent in the following UK case is interesting in this regard.

The UK case of *Pepper v Hart* ([1992] STC 898) raised an important point in relation to the valuation of "in-house" benefits where the employer permits employees to acquire goods or use facilities at a reduced price. The case concerned a number of schoolmasters who were entitled to have their sons educated at the college in which they were employed in return for a payment equal to 20% of the normal fees.

The schoolmasters contended that this payment covered all the additional costs incurred by the college in educating these boys and as such no BIK charge would arise. The Revenue took a different view, contending that the true cost to the college in providing this benefit had to be ascertained by taking the total cost to the college in educating all its pupils and dividing this cost rateably between all those pupils (i.e., the average cost). On this basis the benefit to the schoolmasters exceeded the amount reimbursed by them and a BIK charge arose on the excess.

The Revenue's view was upheld by the Court of Appeal. However, the taxpayers won a subsequent appeal to the House of Lords. In arriving at their decision, the Law Lords referred to statements made in Parliament during the passage of the relevant legislation (UK Finance Act 1976, s63, the equivalent of s118), which indicated that the intent of the legislation was to charge only the marginal cost as a BIK rather than the average cost. Lord Browne-Wilkinson, in the course of his judgment, remarked that were it not for the fact that such reference was permitted, the Revenue view would have to be upheld. The basis of the House of Lords' decision is essentially a point of UK constitutional law. Its applicability in this jurisdiction is doubtful. However, Irish Revenue practice continues to be that marginal cost is the normal measure of the BIK assessment in such cases.

21.1.2 Exemption from tax of certain benefits-in-kind

s118 TCA97 Not all benefits are liable to tax. The following are exempt from tax:

- The provision by the employer of any accommodation, supplies or services for use by a director or employee in any of its business premises, where used by that director or employee solely in performing the duties of the employment;
- The provision of living accommodation for an employee (other than a director), who is required to live on the business premises, provided that such accommodation:
  - is necessary for employees of that class because of the nature of their employer's trade, or
  - has commonly been provided in trades of that kind since before 1948;
- The provision of canteen meals, which are provided for all staff generally;
- The provision of any pension, annuity, lump sum, gratuity or other like benefit accruing on the death or retirement of a director or employee;
- Expenses incurred by an employer in providing a monthly or annual bus, Luas or train pass issued by or on behalf of CIE or any of its subsidiaries, or by holders of licenses to provide public bus passenger services or passes for travel on commuter ferries which operate in the State;
- Employer-provided security services/assets are exempt where there is a risk to the personal safety of the employee/director while carrying out the duties of their employment;
- Employer provided new bicycles and related safety equipment to a maximum value of €1,000 tax-free. The bicycles must be used mainly for 'qualifying journeys' i.e. from home to work or between places of work while carrying out the employment duties;

- Employer provided voucher which does not exceed €500 (the voucher cannot be redeemed in whole or in part for cash). This exemption is applicable from 22 October 2015.

Employer provided electric cars and vans during 2018. The exemption also applies to the provision of charging points on site by the employer. Note this exemption does not apply to hybrid vehicles.

21.2 Application of PAYE/PRSI to Benefits-in-Kind

Non-cash benefits and perquisites provided by an employer to an employee are effectively deemed to be emoluments to which the PAYE rules apply. Employers are obliged to deduct income tax, PRSI and the USC from an employee's salary each month/week for any taxable benefits-in-kind[1].

Readers are referred to Chapter 23 for details of how PAYE and PRSI applies to such benefits.

21.2.1 The Valuation of benefits-in-kind

The following are considered:

- Valuation of company car;
- Valuation of company van;
- Valuation of employer-provided accommodation and land;
- Valuation of an employer-provided asset other than a car, van or accommodation;
- Valuation of a preferential loan from an employer;
- Discharge by an employer of employee personal expenses;
- Proposed introduction of a parking levy.

21.3 Company Vehicles

The tax treatment varies depending on whether the employee is provided with exclusive use of a motor car or commercial vehicle, or simply has the use of a pooled car.

21.3.1 The valuation of a company car

s121 TCA97 An employee is charged to tax on the "cash equivalent" of the benefit of an employer-provided motor vehicle, otherwise known as a "company car". The BIK is calculated at 30% of the Original Market Value (readers are referred to 21.3.2 for proposed higher

1 Employer PRSI contributions must also be paid on all taxable benefits-In-kind, through the PAYE system.

rates in certain circumstances). "Original market value" (OMV) is defined as the price including any customs or excise duty or value-added tax chargeable on the car which the car might reasonably have been expected to fetch if sold in Ireland singly in a retail sale on the open market immediately before the date of its first registration. If the car was first registered abroad, the OMV is still taken as the price it would have retailed for if sold on the open market in Ireland and not the country of registration. In practice, the Revenue take the list price and allow a deduction (normally 10%) representing a cash discount.

If an employee is provided with a second-hand car, the original market value of the car when new is used in calculating the benefit-in-kind and not the amount paid by the employer. If an employee is supplied with a company car for only part of the year of assessment, the cash equivalent is reduced proportionately.

The 30% rate is reduced where business travel exceeds 24,000 kilometres per annum. The extent of the reduction is set out in the table below:

Business kilometres	**Taxable % of OMV**
24,000 kms or less	30%
24,001 to 32,000 kms	24%
32,001 to 40,000 kms	18%
40,001 to 48,000 kms	12%
over 48,000	6%

Finally, the resulting figure may be further reduced where the employee bears the costs of private fuel, servicing and repairs, road tax and/or insurance.

Refer to 21.3.2 for proposed higher rates on certain categories of cars supplied from 1 January 2009.

Example 21.1

Jim McDonald pays income tax at the marginal rate. In 2013, he was supplied with a company car with an OMV of €40,000. Mr McDonald pays for his car insurance and also for private fuel costs.

BIK 2018 (ignoring PRSI + USC)

	€
€40,000 @ 30% =	*12,000*
Tax due @ 40% =	***4,800***

If the employer incurred the expenditure on insurance and fuel and Jim McDonald reimbursed his employer, (say €2,000), the calculation for 2018 would be as follows:

BIK 2018 (ignoring PRSI + USC)

	€
€40,000 @ 30% =	*12,000*
Less employee contribution	*(2,000)*
Assessable	*10,000*
Tax due @ 40% =	***4,000***

Example 21.2

Thomas Wilson is a top-rate taxpayer whose company car supplied to him in 2013 has an OMV of €40,000. He completed 50,000 business kilometers in the year and his employer bears all running costs on the car.

BIK 2018 (ignoring PRSI + USC)

	€
€40,000 @ 6% =	*2,400*
Tax due @ 40% =	***960***

Car not available for full year

Where an individual does not have the use of the company car for the full tax year, the business mileage is annualised. The annualisation process is provided for by legislation and is calculated as follows:

(a) Adjust the 24,000 kms threshold by reference to the number of days in the year the car was available for use; and

(b) Adjust all the figures in the five categories by reference to the following percentage:

<u>Result of (a)</u>
24,000

The reason for annualising the business mileage is that the table which reduces the BIK percentage is based on annual mileage. Accordingly, if the business mileage was not annualised, we would not be comparing like with like.

The simplest method of annualising the business mileage is to apply the following formula:

Business mileage × 365 / A
where A = days in which the company car was made available

Having applied the appropriate percentage, it is then necessary to reduce the resulting figure to take into account that the car was only made available for part of the year.

The above is best explained by the following example.

Example 21.3

Michael Ryan is provided with a fully expensed company car for nine months each year. For the months of June, July and August, the car in not available to Mr Ryan. The OMV is €50,000 and his business mileage in each nine-month period is 30,000 km.

1. *Annualise the business mileage: 30,000 km × 365/273 = 40,110 km*
2. *Select appropriate percentage: 12%*
3. *Calculate cash equivalent: €50,000 × 12% = €6,000*
4. *Reduce cash equivalent to reflect actual use of car: €6,000 × 273/365 = €4,488*

Calculating company car BIK, step by step.

The following is a step-by-step guide to calculating the car BIK:

Step 1

Calculate the annual business mileage.

Step 2

Select the appropriate percentage, based on the annual business mileage.

Step 3

Calculate the cash equivalent (i.e. OMV appropriate percentage)

Step 4

Adjust the cash equivalent to reflect actual use in year (e.g., if car is only provided on 1 July 2018, cash equivalent is reduced by 6/12).

Step 5

Deduct any of contribution by employee.

Example 21.4

Michael Jones is provided with a company car on 1 March 2018. The OMV is 48,000 and his business mileage to 31 December 2018 is 42,000 km . He contributed €900 in respect of insurance.

Steps:

1. *Annualise the business mileage: 42,000km × 12/10 = 50,400km*
2. *Select appropriate percentage: 6%*
3. *Calculate cash equivalent: €48,000 × 6% = €2,880*
4. *Reduce cash equivalent to reflect actual use of car: €2,880 × 10/12 = €2,400*
5. *Deduct any contribution by employee: €2,400 – €900 = €1,500*

Taxable BIK : €1,500

Alternative relief

There is an alternative relief for extensive use of a car for business purposes where an employee does not have significantly high business mileage. This relief is appropriate for employees who regularly use their cars for business purposes, but who are unable to avail of the conventional high business mileage relief (i.e., business mileage does not exceed 24,000 kms per annum) because, for example, they operate mainly in urban areas.

The alternative relief provides that the employee may elect to have the BIK charge on the company car reduced by 20% provided all of the following conditions are met:

- He/she must spend at least 70% of his/her time working away from his/her employer's premises;
- Annual business mileage must exceed 8,000 kms;

- He/she must work on average at least 20 hours per week; and
- A detailed logbook to record daily business travel must be maintained.

Example 21.5

Robbie Brown has the use of a company car. The car had an original market value of €30,000 when purchased new by his employer in 2016. All expenses relating to the car are borne by the employer with the exception of petrol for private use, which is borne by Robbie Brown. His business mileage in the tax year is 10,000 kms, however he satisfies all the criteria for the alternative BIK calculation. He reimburses his employer €1,000 towards his private use of the car each year.

	€
Original market value (OMV)	*30,000*
Relevant percentage	*30%*
	9,000
Less:	
20% reduction	
	(1,800)
	7,200
Less reimbursement	*(1,000)*
Assessable benefit	***6,200***

21.3.2 Pooled cars

Where an employee has the use of a car from a car pool no liability to tax arises provided that:

- The car is made available to, and actually used by, more than one employee and is not ordinarily used by one to the exclusion of the others;
- Any private use by the employees of the car is incidental to other use; and
- The car is not normally kept overnight in the vicinity of any of the employees' homes.

21.3.3 The valuation of a company van

s121A TCA97

A van is defined as follows:

"A mechanically propelled road vehicle which:

(a) is designed or constructed solely or mainly for the carriage of goods or other burden;

(b) has a roofed area to the rear of the driver's seat; and

(c) has no side windows or seating fitted in that roofed area."

The rules provide that the BIK valuation is 5% of the original market value ("OMV") of the van. The OMV is defined in the same manner as that applicable to a company car, which in effect means the VAT-inclusive amount is relevant.

Section 8 Finance Act 2004 provides that incidental private use of a van will be exempt from tax where:

- The vehicle is necessary in the performance of the duties of employment
- The employee is required to keep the van at his/her residence while not in use
- Apart from business travel, private travel is prohibited
- The employee spends at least 80% of his/her time away from the employer's premises

The section is therefore intended to exempt the private use of the van in travelling to/from work, which would otherwise be taxable.

21.4 The Valuation of an Employer-Provided Accommodation and Land

s118 TCA97 The provision of living accommodation by an employer to an employee, such as the use of a house rent-free or at a reduced rent, is a taxable benefit unless the provision of such accommodation is within the exemptions outlined above at 21.1.2.

The BIK assessable on the employee is the annual open market rent for the house (together with any expenses connected with the house which are borne by the employer and not reimbursed by the employee), less any rent payable by the employee. In practice, where the employer owns the premises, Revenue takes the annual value of the accommodation provided as 8% of its current market value. This can often be higher than the "annual letting value". Otherwise, the value of the BIK is an amount equal to the actual rent payable by the employer.

Example 21.6

Peter McCartney is provided with a house by his employer for his private use. The employer pays a gardener €5,000 per annum to maintain the house's grounds. The employer does not own the house and pays rent of €10,500 a year. Mr McCartney pays rent of €2,500 to his employer. Mr McCartney is liable to pay tax on a benefit-in-kind arising from his use of the house and the provision by the company of a gardener for the tax year, as follows:

	€
Rent payable by employer	*10,500*
Gardener's wages	*5,000*
	15,500
Less: rent paid	*(2,500)*
Benefit-in-kind	*13,000*

With effect from 1 January 2005, where an employee enjoys the use of employer-provided land, the BIK is calculated at 5% of the market value of the land.

21.5 The Valuation of an Employer-Provided Asset other than a Car, Van or Accommodation

s122 TCA97 The annual value of the use of an asset is 5% of its market value when first applied for the benefit of the employee.

Example 21.7

John McCarthy is provided with a computer for his private use. It was purchased on 1 January 2018 at a cost of €1,500 to his employer and was supplied to him on the same date. The amount assessable 2018 is:

€1,500 × 5% = €75

21.6 Preferential Loan from an Employer

s122 TCA97 Where an employer provides a "preferential" loan to an employee (or former employee), a charge to tax may arise on the benefit to the employee of the low or nil rate of interest on the loan. A "preferential" loan is one in respect of which no interest is payable or interest is payable at a rate less than the "specified rate". For the tax year 2018, the specified rate is:

- 4% where the loan is used to fund the cost/repair of the employee's principal private residence;
- 13.5% in other cases.

The BIK charge is on the difference between the interest on the loan at the specified rate, and the interest actually paid on the loan for the year.

Where the loan is used to fund the cost/repair of the employee's principal private residence, the employee will obtain tax relief for the notional interest paid.

Example 21.8

Paul Gill received an interest-free loan of €26,000 from his employer on 1 January 2018, which he used to finance an extension to his house. He has no borrowings on his house. He repaid €3,000 off the loan on 1 April 2018 and a further €3,000 on 1 July 2018. The BIK charge for the 2018 tax year is as follows:

	€
€26,000 at 4% × 3/12	*260.00*
€23,000 at 4% × 3/12	*230.50*
€20,000 at 4% × 6/12	*400.00*
BIK charge	*890.00*

A charge to tax also arises where a loan to an employee is released or written off by the employer. The loan in such a case need not be a preferential one.

Example 21.9

Jeff Best borrowed €20,000 from his employer, Big Bank plc. The rate of interest charged was the market rate (i.e., the loan was not at a preferential rate). Therefore no BIK arose on the provision of the loan. The balance of the loan outstanding at 31 December 2017 was €18,200. In recognition of the valuable contribution of Mr Best to his employer's business it was decided that the loan should be written off on 1 January 2018.

The amount assessable in the tax year 2018 is €18,200, being the amount written off.

21.7 The Discharge by an Employer of Employee Personal Expenses

The BIK assessable is the actual amount discharged by the employer. Examples of such expenditure are:

- Telephone rental,
- Club subscriptions, and
- Medical expenditure.

21.8 Expense Payments

Where an employee or director receives a payment in respect of expenses from his/her employer, he/she is charged to tax as if that payment were part of his/her salary, subject to the right of claiming deductible expenditure under general rules.

Where an employee incurs expenses in the course of carrying out the duties of his/her employment and is reimbursed by his/her employer based on individual vouchers submitted by him/her, no liability in practice arises on receipt of the payments from his/her employer. Note that vouched reimbursed expenses must be incurred "wholly, exclusively and necessarily" in the performance of the duties of the employment.

The legislation is designed to assess "round sum" expense allowances, which are paid to employees even though the expenses are designed to cover business expenses. Round sum expenses paid to employees are taxable as if they were another component of salary.

An example would be an employer paying €500 per month to an employee to cover travel and other "out of pocket" business expenses. Even though the employee may very well incur costs of approximately €500 per month, the payment by the employer must be taxed at source as it is a round sum expense and not specific to a vouched allowable claim. There are certain exceptions to the taxation of such amounts, e.g., the Revenue will in certain instances grant approval for the payment of tax-free round sum expense allowances. Such tax-free payments are discussed in further detail in 21.8.1 below. In general, this treatment only applies where the amounts are agreed in writing with the Revenue in advance.

21.8.1 "Tax-free" payments

The Revenue Commissioners permit the payment of certain expenses tax-free, provided they refer solely to expenses incurred in the actual performance of the employee's duties and do no more than reimburse the employee for the actual expense incurred. These expenses include:

- Motoring expenses,
- Subsistence expenses,
- Removal expenses.

Motoring and subsistence expenses

Historically, the Revenue Commissioners required prior approval for the payment of these expenses tax-free. It is now possible to pay specific amounts tax-free without prior Revenue approval. Revenue has issued leaflets (IT51 for motor expenses and IT54 for subsistence expenses), which set out amounts that employers may pay to staff tax-free without the need for staff to provide receipts. All the conditions set out in the leaflets must be adhered to – otherwise the employer may not pay the amounts tax-free. The rates covered in the leaflets reflect the expense amounts payable to civil servants.

Removal expenses

The Revenue Commissioners have issued a Statement of Practice (SP IT/1/91) in relation to expenses incurred by an employee in moving home to take up a new employment either within the same organisation or with a new employer. Such expense payments may be made without deduction of tax provided they are within the guidelines set down in the Statement of Practice. The types of expense covered include auctioneer's fees and legal fees, removal and storage of furniture and effects and the payment of temporary subsistence allowances to the employee while he/she is looking for accommodation at the new location.

21.9 Parking Levy

The Finance (No. 2) Act 2008 proposed the introduced parking levy in designated areas where employers provide free car parking spaces to employees. The levy is a stand-alone levy and the amount is €200.

The designated areas are in the following five city councils:

- Dublin
- Cork
- Galway
- Limerick
- Waterford

There are exemptions to the imposition of the levy and the €200 charge is reduced for employees who are job sharing, work part time or are on maternity leave.

Implementation of the proposed levy is subject to a Commencement Order which at the time of writing is still awaited.

22 TERMINATION PAYMENTS

Learning Outcomes

On completion of this chapter you will be able to:

- ✓ Identify the different elements of a termination package, separating taxable payments from non-taxable ones.
- ✓ Calculate the amount of the tax-free lump sum.

22.1 Introduction

The termination of an employment can occur for various reasons:

- Redundancy;
- Dismissal;
- Death of the employee;
- Resignation;
- Retirement.
- In cases of redundancy (whether voluntary or compulsory), it is quite common for employees to receive "termination payments". In these cases the payments are intended to represent a compensation for loss of office. Termination payments are sometimes made to employees who have been dismissed (known as a "golden boot" payment) and to employees on resigning or retiring in recognition of past performance (known as a "golden handshake" payment). The payments can therefore be put into two categories:
- (a) compensation for loss of office (whether on dismissal or redundancy); and
- (b) *ex gratia* payments in recognition of past performance.

The tax treatment for both types of payment is the same and hereinafter will be referred to only as termination payments.

This chapter examines the circumstances in which termination payments may be paid tax-free by the granting of exempt amounts. The analysis focuses on how the exempt amounts are calculated and also on how the final liability to tax on the taxable portion of a termination payment can be reduced in certain circumstances.

22.2 Elements of a Severance Package

A payment made to an employee in connection with the termination of an employment may be made up of the following components:

- Lump sums on retirement from Revenue-approved pension schemes;
- Payments on account of injury, disability or death in service;
- Statutory redundancy;
- *Ex gratia* termination payments;
- Pay in lieu of notice;
- Holiday pay.
- Retraining costs

In addition, an employer may agree to write off an outstanding loan or transfer an asset (e.g., a company car) to the employee as part of an agreed severance package.

Pension lump sums

Lump sums paid from Revenue-approved pension schemes are generally not taxable where the amount received:

- is no more than 1.5 times the salary of the employee in his or her final year of employment; and
- does not exceed the lifetime cap of €200,000

Whilst such amounts might not be taxable, they can have the effect of reducing the tax-free component of any *ex gratia* payment. In this regard, readers are referred to the analysis at 22.4 below.

Compensation for injury, disability or death in service

Payments received on account of injury, disability or death in service were completely exempt from tax regardless of the size of the payment. FA 2013 introduced a lifetime cap of €200,000 on the exempt portion of the payment. Any excess over €200,000 is taxable as normal. There is a reporting requirement, whereby details of such payments must be delivered to the Revenue Commissioners not later than 46 days after the end of the year of assessment in which the payments were made.

Statutory redundancy payments

These are payments an employee is entitled by law to receive provided certain conditions are met. They are, as the name suggests, only payable where the termination of the employment arises as a result of redundancy (whether voluntary or compulsory). These payments are exempt from tax.

Ex gratia termination payments

These are amounts, which the employer is not obliged to pay to the employee. The tax treatment of such '*ex gratia*' payments is covered in detail in paragraph 22.4 below.

Pay in lieu of notice

An employer is obliged by law to give notice in advance that an employment is to be terminated. The length of the notice depends on the employee's number of years of service and can range from one week to eight weeks. An employment contract usually states what the required period of notice is. It may happen that an employer will not want the employee to work out the notice period. In these circumstances, the employer must pay the employee in lieu of notice. The treatment of pay in lieu of notice is similar to that of *ex gratia* payments and accordingly, it may be paid tax-free provided it does not exceed a certain tax-free amount (covered in 22.4.1 below).

Holiday pay

Such pay is treated as forming part of normal salary and is taxed under general rules. It is not treated as a "termination payment" for tax purposes.

Loans written off or assets transferred

Where these form part of a severance package, they must be taken into account. They are valued and added to any other termination payments for the purposes of determining whether or not they are subject to tax. For loans, the cash value is the amount of the loan written off. Assets transferred are valued at their market value at the time of transfer.

Retraining costs

Section 201(1A)(b) TCA97 provides for an additional exemption of up to €5,000 for 'eligible employees' where an employer bears the cost of retraining such employees. The retraining must be part of a redundancy package and be designed to improve skills or knowledge used in obtaining employment or setting up a business. The course must be completed within 6 months of the employee being made redundant. An 'eligible employee' is one who has more than 2 years continuous full time service or is deemed for the purposes of the redundancy acts to have 2 years continuous service. The exemption does not apply to spouses or dependants of the employer, and the employees must avail of the retraining rather than receive cash.

22.3 Calculation of the Tax-Free Amount of *Ex Gratia* Payments

s112, s123, s201 TCA97

A payment made to an employee in connection with the termination of an employment is assessable as normal pay under the ordinary Schedule E rules (i.e., s112 TCA97) if it represents a payment under the terms of a contract of employment, or if it is in consideration for services rendered by the employee in his/her capacity as such. However, a payment not made by virtue of a contract of employment but as a voluntary or *ex gratia* payment by the employer is treated as not having the nature of emoluments taxable under general Schedule E rules. Instead such payments are assessed under s123 TCA97 and afforded certain exemptions and reliefs under s201 TCA97 and Schedule 3, TCA97.

Case law is often considered in determining whether a payment is to be assessed as an emolument under s112 or as a termination payment within s123. It is important to note at this stage that it is only payments specifically brought within the charge to tax by the termination payments provisions which may qualify for relief or exemption under s201 or Schedule 3. Other payments, such as holiday pay, are taxable under the general Schedule E rules and may not qualify for the exemptions and reliefs available for termination payments.

Case law

In *Henley v Murray* (31 TC 351), the Managing Director of a company was employed under a service agreement which was not terminable before a certain date. However, it became desirable from the company's point of view that he should leave the service of the company. The Managing Director subsequently left the company before the service agreement expired and was paid an amount equal to that to which he would have been entitled had his employment continued until the expiry of the service agreement. It was held that the payment was in consideration of the abrogation of his contract of employment and was not a payment under that contract and, as such, it was not assessable as an emolument of the employment.

In *Mairs v Haughey* [1993] STC 569, in advance of the privatisation of Harland & Wolff, employees were offered a lump sum to give up the enhanced redundancy rights which they had enjoyed as a condition of their employment with a nationalised company. The lump sum comprised two elements:

- Element A: – a payment amounting to 30% of the amount the employee would have received under the scheme if he or she were made redundant at the time of the privatisation.
- Element B: – an additional payment negotiated by the unions to obtain the consent of employees to the changed conditions of their employment.

The Inland Revenue contended that the lump sum was taxable in full as an emolument of the taxpayer's employment, or alternatively as an inducement to take up new employment with the privatised company. It was held that if the enhanced redundancy payment had been made, it would not have been an emolument assessable under Schedule E even though it formed part of the taxpayer's conditions of employment. Therefore the element of the lump sum which bought out the right to the redundancy payment (i.e., Element A) was equally not an emolument. However, Element B was held to be taxable on the grounds that it was an inducement payment to enter into employment with the privatised company.

22.3.1 Exemptions for payments within s123

s201 TCA97 Payments which fall within the definition of this section qualify for exemption if they are less than certain "tax-free amounts" under s201 TCA97 as follows:

- Basic exemption;
- Increased exemption; and
- Standard Capital Superannuation Benefit (SCSB).

Basic exemption

The basic exemption is €10,160 plus €765 for each complete year of service.

Example 22.1

Jane Fitzsimons was made redundant after three years and 11 months of service with her employer. The amount which she can receive tax-free is:

€10,160 + (€765 × 3) = €12,455

Note: Only complete years of service are taken into consideration. Thus, the period of 11 months is ignored.

Increased exemption

The basic exemption may be increased by a maximum of €10,000 if:

(i) No claim for relief (other than the basic exemption) has been made in respect of a previous lump sum payment within the previous 10 years; and

(ii) No tax-free lump sum has been received or is receivable under an approved superannuation scheme relating to the office or employment. If a tax-free lump sum of less than €10,000 has been received or is receivable from the scheme, the increased exemption will be the basic exemption plus €10,000, less the tax-free lump sum or, in the case of deferred benefits, the actuarial value of that amount. Thus, the following formula summarises the position:

Increased basic exemption = basic exemption + (€10,000 – pension lump sum entitlement).

Example 22.2

Assume the same facts as above except that Jane Fitzsimons was entitled to receive €3,000 of a tax-free lump sum pension payment. She had never made a previous claim for an increased exemption. The amount which she can receive tax-free is:

€10,160 + (€765 × 3) + (€10,000 – €3,000) = €19,455

Standard Capital Superannuation Benefit (SCSB)

The Standard Capital Superannuation Benefit (SCSB) may be substituted for the basic or increased exemption, if it produces a higher figure. The SCSB is calculated by the formula:

$$A \times \frac{B}{15} - C$$

where

A = the average for 12 months of the emoluments of the employment for the last 36 months of service up to the date of termination. Emoluments for this purpose include salary, benefit-in-kind, etc., before deduction of superannuation contributions.

B = the number of complete years of service in the office or employment.

C = any tax-free lump sum received or receivable under an approved superannuation scheme.

The term "lump sum received or receivable" as used in the calculation of the increased exemption and SCSB does not include amounts received by an employee as refunds of personal contributions from a pension fund, which have borne tax at 20%.

Example 22.3

Jean Flood was made redundant on 31 October 2018 after 22 years' service with Jack Weldon Products Limited. On leaving, she was paid a lump sum of €50,000 comprised as follows:

	€
Statutory redundancy	*14,600*
Ex gratia payment	*35,400*

In addition, she is entitled to a tax-free lump sum from the pension fund of €3,000. Her average pay for the three years ending 31 October 2018 was €27,000.

Basic exemption

€10,165 × (€765 × 22) = €26,995

Increased exemption

€26,995 + (€10,000 − €3,000) = €33,995

Calculation of SCSB:

$$(€27{,}000\ (A) \times \frac{22\ (B)}{15}) - €3{,}000\ (C) = €36{,}600$$

The tax-free amount is €36,600. Since this exceeds the termination payment of €35,400, the latter can be paid tax-free.

Since 1 January 2011, there is a lifetime tax free cap of €200,000 for termination payments.

22.4 "Top-Slicing Relief"

Schedule 3, paragraph 10 TCA97 gave an additional measure of relief to an employee by limiting the rate of tax payable on the taxable portion of a termination payment to the average rate of tax (i.e., tax paid/taxable income) borne by the individual over the previous three tax years. This is more commonly known as "top-slicing relief".

For the year 2013, top-slicing relief no longer applied where a termination payment made on/after this date *equaled* €200,000 or greater. The removal of the relief did not just apply to the excess over €200,000 but to the total taxable amount. Section 4 F(No. 2)A 2013 removed top slicing relief for any payments made after 1 January 2014, irrespective of the amount. Students are referred to previous editions of this publication for detailed analysis of the operation of top-slicing relief.

Tax Facts

Tax Free Limit on Termination Payments

The Finance Act 2011 introduced for the first time ever a lifetime tax free cap of €200,000 for termination payments. Finance Act 2013 introduced a lifetime tax free cap of €200,000 for disability and death in service payments, the Act abolished Foreign Service Relief and curtailed Top Slicing Relief. Finance (No. 2) Act 2013 abolished top slicing relief altogether.

23 OPERATION OF PAYE/PRSI SYSTEM

Learning Outcomes

On completion of this chapter you will be able to:

- ✓ Explain how the PAYE system operates and describe its implications for an employer.
- ✓ Describe the difference between the "Cumulative", "Month 1", "Temporary" and "Emergency" basis of taxation.
- ✓ Explain how PRSI operates and describe the different classes of PRSI.
- ✓ Describe the rules for determining the valuation of benefits-in-kind and how such benefits are taxed through the payroll system.

23.1 Introduction

The Pay As You Earn (PAYE) system is a method of tax deduction at source, which applies in the case of annuities, salaries, wages, certain benefits and pensions, etc. This chapter examines:

- The types of income which are specifically within the PAYE system;
- The obligations of an employer in relation to employees and the Revenue Commissioners;
- How the PAYE system works; and
- How Pay Related Social Insurance (PRSI), which is not a tax but a social security contribution, must be collected through the PAYE system.

With effect from 1 January 2019, 'PAYE Modernisation' will come into effect. This will impact on how employers interact with Revenue. Under the current system Revenue have no visibility on the level of employee pay and deductions until after the end of the tax year in which the pay/deductions are made. PAYE Modernisation will change that to a 'real time' accounting system. More detailed coverage of PAYE Modernisation will be covered in next year's publication.

23.2 Operation of PAYE

s986 The authority governing the operation of PAYE is contained within the Income Tax (Employments) (Consolidated) Regulations 2001. Such Regulations were made by the

TCA97 powers conferred on the Revenue Commissioners by s986 TCA97 (No.39 of 97).

Tax is charged under Schedule E on the actual amount of all salaries, fees, wages, perquisites or profits whatsoever derived from the office, employment or pension for the year of assessment. The Pay As You Earn (PAYE) system is a method of tax deduction at source by the payer (usually the employer) whereby income tax is paid by deduction at source on amounts which come within the scope of the PAYE system. PAYE applies to all income chargeable under Schedule E except emoluments upon which the Revenue Commissioners consider the operation of PAYE to be "impractical", e.g.,

- Emoluments paid from outside the State;[1]
- Certain taxable social welfare benefits.

As discussed in chapter 21, PAYE/PRSI also applies to all benefits-in-kind (considered in detail at 23.9) with deductions being made at source through the PAYE system.

Where tax is collected under the PAYE system, the taxpayer effectively pays tax each week or month as he/she receives his/her wages or salary. It is also a method of collecting Pay-Related Social Insurance (PRSI) contributions (considered in more detail at 23.6 below) and USC.

The PAYE system is designed so that, as far as is possible, the correct amount of tax is deducted from an employee's pay, to meet his/her tax liability for the year. Therefore, the PAYE system removes, in the majority of cases, the necessity for raising formal assessments on employees in respect of Schedule E income. However this does not prevent the raising of an assessment on an employees in certain situations, such as:

- Where underpayments of tax cannot be recovered by adjusting the tax credits and standard rate cut-off point (tax credits and standard rate cut-off point are considered below);
- Where the employee has other income (e.g., investment income or rental income), which has not been effectively taxed by reducing the tax credits and standard rate cut-off point; or
- Where an assessment is requested by the taxpayer.

To ensure that the correct amount of tax is deducted for the year, PAYE is normally computed on a "cumulative basis". This means that when an employer computes the total tax of an employee, he/she actually calculates the total tax due from the beginning of the tax year to the date on which the payment is being made. The tax deducted in the particular week/month is the cumulative tax due to that date from the beginning of the tax year, reduced by the amount deducted up to the previous pay period. It also ensures that refunds can be made to an employee, where a revised Certificate of Tax Credits and Standard Rate Cut-Off Point is received, increasing the employee's tax credits and standard rate cut-off point.

1 Refer to 23.2.2 for Finance Act 2006 changes for foreign employers.

23.2.1 Certificate of tax credits and standard rate cut-off point

A Certificate of tax credits (and standard rate cut-off point) is a document which the Inspector of Taxes issues on behalf of an employee. At the start of each year, the Inspector of Taxes issues a certificate of tax credits (and standard rate cut-off point) to each employee. A shortened version of the certificate is issued to the employer.

There are two main components within the certificate:

Tax credits

The certificate sets out (based on the information available to Revenue) the tax credits which the taxpayer is entitled to in the tax year, and which will be taken into account in calculating his/her PAYE (Tax credits are considered in detail in Chapter 11).

As already stated, tax credits are non-refundable; they are used to reduce tax on gross pay for each pay period. However, any unused tax credits are carried forward on a cumulative basis and can be used in a subsequent pay period(s) in the same tax year. Tax refunds arise when the cumulative tax due and paid for the last pay period exceeds the cumulative tax due for the current pay period. Readers are referred to Appendix I for a worked example.

Standard rate cut-off point

The certificate sets out the taxpayer's standard rate cut-off point, i.e., the amount of the personal standard rate tax band as adjusted for any non-PAYE income, benefits-in-kind or tax reliefs due at the higher rate of tax. Tax rates and tax bands are considered in detail in Chapter 11.

The details contained in the certificate are based on the information available to Revenue. Therefore, it is important for each taxpayer to review the certificate to ensure all of his/her entitlements are taken into account when calculating his/her PAYE and to inform Revenue where this is not the case.

Since 2012, the certificate also contains relevant details for USC purposes. Since USC is calculated on a cumulative basis since 2012, the employer or pension provider needs to know what USC rates to apply. For example, an employee might have two employments; in Employment 1, the full bands for the 1%/3% and 5.5% rates are allocated to that employment which means that for Employment 2, all pay will liable at 8% and Employer 2 must be advised of this via the certificate of tax credits.

23.2.2 Adjustments to the certificate for non-PAYE income

Some employees may have other taxable income on which tax may be collected through the PAYE system (depending on the figures involved) rather than through the self-assessment system.

Under the PAYE system other income is taxed by reducing:

- The tax credits by the amount of the income at the standard rate of tax; and
- The standard rate band by the amount of the income.

Reducing the tax credits ensures the non-PAYE income is taxed at the standard rate. Reducing the standard rate band ensures the income is taxed at the difference between the standard rate and the higher rate of tax, if appropriate. The combined effect is to collect tax due on the non-PAYE income at the higher rate of tax, when due.

23.2.3 Adjustments to the certificate for deductions/reliefs

Some employees may have deductions or reliefs on which tax relief is due at the higher rate of tax. The relief in respect of non-standard rated deductions is granted by increasing:

- The tax credits by the amount of the relief at the standard rate of tax; and
- The standard rate band by the amount of the relief.

Increasing the tax credits ensures relief is obtained at the standard rate of tax, while increasing the standard rate band ensures relief is obtained at the difference between the standard rate and the higher rate of tax. The combined effect ensures relief is obtained in full at the higher rate of tax, if applicable.

23.2.4 Obligation on employer to deduct PAYE

A person (or corporate body) who intends hiring staff for the first time must register as an employer with the Revenue Commissioners. The Revenue Commissioners allocate a tax registration number specific to the operation of PAYE and PRSI. Each employer who pays remuneration exceeding €8 per week to a full-time employee (or exceeding €2 per week where the employee has other employments) is obliged to register with the Revenue Commissioners and operate PAYE on all emoluments paid to the employee. The threshold is increased to €40 per week for employers with only one domestic employee. The Revenue Commissioners have the power to compulsorily register an employer who has neglected to register for PAYE.

Section 16 Finance Act 2006 imposed an obligation on foreign employers to deduct PAYE from individuals working in the State. Where the employee is carrying out duties in Ireland for someone other than the employer (e.g. an Irish subsidiary of a USA parent) there is an obligation to operate PAYE on the amount of emoluments which are applicable to the Irish duties.

Where the foreign employer fails to deduct PAYE, the Irish entity is held accountable.

Example 23.1

John, an American citizen, has worked for JB (USA) Corp for many years. JB (USA) Corp's Irish subsidiary, JB (Irl) Ltd needs expertise in setting up a new computer system which they cannot source in Ireland. John is sent to Ireland to assist with the project. He spends six months in Ireland in 2018. He remains on the USA payroll for the duration of the time in Ireland.

If JB (USA) Corp fail to register for and account for PAYE on John's emoluments, JB (Irl) Ltd, will be accountable for the PAYE due for John.

23.3 Calculation of Tax

s123 TCA97 "Pay" for the purposes of PAYE includes salary, wages, benefits, pensions, fees, arrears of pay, bonuses, overtime, commissions, holiday pay, pay during illness, etc. It also covers termination payments chargeable under s123 TCA97 (considered at Chapter 22) and expenses payments (to the extent that agreement has not been reached with the Inspector of Taxes to make the payments gross). PAYE must be operated on all emoluments (as set out above), which are paid during the tax year. This is so even if the emoluments were actually earned, but not paid, in a prior year, and therefore assessable in that prior year.

Example 23.2

Mary Guinness is paid commissions based on quarterly sales. For the quarter ended 31 December 2017 she earned €2,000 which is payable with her salary on 31 January 2018. PAYE must be operated on the €2,000 by reference to 2018 tax, USC and PRSI rates and not by reference to 2017 rates.

The calculation of tax for each pay period is made by applying the information supplied in the certificate of credits (and standard rate cut-off point) for the employee supplied to the employer. The certificate of tax credits which issues to the employer contains the following information:

- The total amount of tax credits (but not itemised);
- Standard rate cut-off point; and
- Rates of tax prevailing for the year of assessment.

The information supplied in the certificate is applied against the employee's pay as follows:

- Gross pay (less superannuation deductions) is taxed at the appropriate tax rates to give gross tax;
- The standard rate of tax is applied to gross pay up to the standard rate cut-off point for that week or month. Any balance of pay over that amount in the pay period is taxed at the higher rate;
- The gross tax is reduced by the tax credit as advised in the certificate of tax credits to arrive at the net tax payable.

Example 23.3

The Inspector of Taxes issues a certificate of tax credits to John's employer containing the following information:

tax credits of €275.00 per month;

SRCOP €2,816.67 per month;

standard rate of tax 20%, higher rate 40%.

John earns €4,158.00 per month and pays €158 pension.

The tax, PRSI & USC calculations for each month are as follows:

		€	€
Gross pay			*4,158.00*
Less superannuation			*(158.00)*
Pay for tax purposes			*4,000.00*
Tax on €2,816.67 × 20%		*563.34*	
Tax on €1,183.33 × 40%		*473.33*	
Gross tax due		*1,036.67*	
Less tax credits		*(275.00)*	
Tax due for the month		*761.67*	
PRSI			
4,158.00 × 4%		*166.32*	
USC			
1,001.00 × 0.5%	*5.01*		
613.33 × 2%	*12.27*		
2,543.67 × 4.75%	*120.82*		
4,158.00		*138.10*	
Total deductions		***1,066.09***	

Tax credits are non-refundable, i.e., where the gross tax due is less than the tax credit, the difference is not refundable. In this case the employee has no liability for the period and any excess tax credit is carried forward for offset against future tax due on a cumulative basis. However, tax refunds arise when the cumulative tax due and paid for the last pay period exceeds the cumulative tax due for the current pay period. Readers are referred to Appendix I (months four and nine) for an example of a refund in these circumstances.

The cumulative basis also applies to the SRCOP. Where an individual's SRCOP exceeds the gross pay in a pay period, the unused amount is carried forward on a cumulative basis for use in the following pay period(s) in the same tax year. Again, readers are referred to Appendix I for an example of how the cumulative basis operates.

23.4 Temporary Basis/Emergency Basis

Where an employee remains with the same employer from year to year, there are seldom problems in relation to the issue of a certificate of tax credits. Problems can arise where an employee changes employment mid-year. On joining a new employer, if PAYE is to be operated on a cumulative basis, the new employer will require the following:

1. Form P45 (considered at 23.8 below) from the employee's previous employer, and

2. Certificate of tax credits.

In the absence of a form P45, the Inspector of Taxes may issue a statement advising the new employer of the employee's previous pay, tax, PRSI, tax credits and SRCOP details.

23.4.1 Week 1/Month 1 (non-cumulative) basis

A certificate of tax credits usually applies on a cumulative basis from the previous 1 January. However, there are occasions when the certificate is issued on a non-cumulative basis known as a Week 1/Month 1 certificate. If the Week 1/Month 1 basis applies, neither the pay, tax credits, nor the standard rate cut-off point are accumulated for tax purposes. The pay for each income tax week or month is dealt with separately. The tax credits and standard rate cut-off point for Week 1 (or Month 1) are used in the calculation of tax due, each week (or each month). No refunds may be made in such cases. Readers are referred to Appendix II for a worked example.

23.4.2 Temporary basis

Another method of operating PAYE is by using the "temporary basis". This is very similar in principle to the Week 1/Month 1 basis. An employer is obliged to operate this basis where a new employee joins, provides a form P45 but a certificate of tax credits has not yet been issued. The tax credits and SRCOP details on the P45 may be used on a non-cumulative basis.

23.4.3 Emergency basis

An individual must be taxed on the "emergency basis" if:

- The employer has not received, in respect of the employee, either a certificate of tax credits (or TDC) or a form P45 for the current year; or

- The employee has given the employer a completed form P45 indicating that the emergency basis applies; or

- The employee has given the employer a completed P45 without a PPS number and not indicating that the emergency basis applies.

Tax is calculated on the gross pay (after deduction of pension contributions where relevant). Different rules apply depending on whether or not the employee provides the employer with a PPS number.

Where an employee provides a PPS number

The table below outlines the tax credits and standard rate cut-off points applicable where the employee provides a PPS number:

	SRCOP	Tax Credit
Weekly paid:	€	€
Weeks 1 to 4	665.00	32.00
Weeks 5 to 8	665.00	0.00
Week 9 onwards	0.00	0.00
Monthly Paid:		
Month 1	2,880.00	138.00
Month 2	2,880.00	0.00
Month 3	0.00	0.00

Where an employee does not provide a PPS number

If the employee does not provide a PPS number, tax is calculated on all gross pay:

- At the higher rate (40%); and
- With no deduction for a tax credit.

23.5 Pensions

Tax is charged under Schedule E on the actual amount of all salaries, benefits, fees, wages, perquisites or profits whatsoever derived from the office, employment or pension for the year of assessment. The same PAYE rules apply equally to occupational pensions as they do to salary/wages. The application of PAYE does not apply to pensions payable by the State. Such pensions are paid without the deduction of tax at source.

23.6 Application of PAYE/PRSI to Benefits-in-Kind

The Finance Act 2003 introduced new provisions, which came into force on 1 January 2004. From that date, non-cash benefits and perquisites provided by an employer to an employee are effectively deemed to be emoluments to which PAYE rules apply.

Prior to 1 January 2004, calculation of and payment of the tax due on non-cash benefits and perquisites provided by an employer was the responsibility of the employee.

An example of some of the more common benefits which are subject to PAYE/PRSI since 1 January 2004 are as follows:

- Preferential loans;
- Medical insurance premia;
- Company cars;
- Company vans.

It should be noted that benefits in respect of shares and/or contributions to personal retirement savings accounts (PRSAs) are specifically excluded from these new provisions.

s985A(3) TCA97

Employers have the onerous task of having to calculate the benefit-in-kind (BIK) figure assessable on each employee. This point is recognised by the new legislation which states that employers should operate PAYE on an amount, which is the "best estimate that can reasonably be made" of the amount "likely" to be chargeable under Schedule E. Having calculated the value of the BIK, the figure is then added to "normal" salary and PAYE and PRSI is applied. The BIK figure is known as "notional pay".

Where an employer is unable to withhold the full amount of tax due from the employee's cash salary (e.g., due to insufficiency of income in any particular pay period), the employer is responsible for remitting the full amount of the tax to the Revenue Commissioners. Where the employee does not make good the tax owing before the end of the tax year in question, the amount outstanding is treated as an emolument in the following year of assessment. This leads to an additional tax charge for employees. However, Revenue practice is to allow the employee up until 31 March in the following tax year to reimburse the employer before the additional BIK arises.

Example 23.4

Jonny Laidlaw receives a holiday voucher worth €3,500 from his employer in December 2018. His gross pay each month is €1,000, he has a monthly standard rate cut-off point of €2,950 and a tax credit of €305. The calculation is as follows:

			€	€
Pay				*1,000.00*
Notional pay				*3,500.00*
				4,500.00
Tax thereon:				
€2,950	×	*20%*	*590.00*	
€1,550	×	*40%*	*620.00*	
			1210.00	
Less tax credit			*(305.00)*	
Tax due				*905.00*
PRSI				
€4,500	×	*4%*		*180.00*

USC			
€1001.00	×	*0.5%*	*5.01*
€613.33	×	*2%*	*12.27*
€2885.67	×	*4.75%*	*137.07*
			154.35
Total deductions			*1,239.35*

Since the cash amount is only €1,000, the full liability of €1,239.35 cannot be collected:

	€
Cash	*1,000.00*
Less PRSI	*(180.00)*
Cash available to pay tax & USC	***820.00***
Actual tax & USC due	*(1,059.35)*
Balance uncollected	***(239.35)***

The €239.35 not collected from Jonny Laidlaw in 2018 becomes a further BIK in 2018.

Revenue practice is to allow the employee up until 31 March in the following year to reimburse the employer before the additional BIK arises. Therefore, if Jonny Laidlaw reimburses his employer the outstanding amount of €239.35 by 31 March 2019, no further liability will arise.

The employer must pay the following to the Revenue Commissioners by 14/23 January 2019:

	€
As above	*1239.35*
Employer PRSI €4,500 × 10.85%	*488.25*
Total	*1,727.6*

Valuation of benefits-in-kind

The employer must value the particular BIK using stated rules and then add that value to salaries/wages as notional pay.

The following are considered in detail in Chapter 21:

- The valuation of an employer-provided car;
- The valuation of an employer-provided van;
- The valuation of employer-provided accommodation and land;
- The valuation of an employer-provided asset other than a car, van or accommodation;
- The valuation of a preferential loan from an employer;
- The discharge by an employer of employee's personal expenses.

References and Recommended Further Reading

MAGUIRE, T. (2018), *Direct Tax Acts*, Irish Tax Institute.

DEEGAN, G., G. REDDIN, A. BOLSTER (Ed.), 2010, *Income Tax*, Irish Tax Institute.

MARTYN, J., D. SHANAHAN, T. COONEY (Ed.), 2018, *Taxation Summary*, Irish Tax Institute.

Appendix I

Tax Calculation 2018
Cumulative Basis

Standard Rate	20%
Higher Rate	40%
Total Tax Credit	€3,300 per annum
Total SRCOP	€34,550 per annum

	Gross Pay this month	Cum Gross Pay to Date	Cum SRCOP	Cum Tax due 20% SR	Cum Tax 40% HR	Cum Gross Tax	Cum Tax Credit	Cum Tax	Tax Ded this Month	Tax Refund this Month
Month No.	**€**	**€**	**€**	**£**	**€**	**€**	**€**	**€**	**€**	**€**
1	3200.00	3200.00	2879.17	575.83	128.33	704.17	275.00	429.17	429.17	0.00
2	3000.00	6200.00	5758.33	1151.67	176.67	1328.33	550.00	778.33	349.17	0.00
3	2900.00	9100.00	8637.50	1727.50	185.00	1912.50	825.00	1087.50	309.17	0.00
4	1000.00	10100.00	11516.67	2020.00	0.00	2020.00	1100.00	920.00	0.00	−167.50
5	2900.00	13000.00	14395.83	2600.00	0.00	2600.00	1375.00	1225.00	305.00	0.00
6	2900.00	15900.00	17275.00	3180.00	0.00	3180.00	1650.00	1530.00	305.00	0.00
7	2900.00	18800.00	20154.17	3760.00	0.00	3760.00	1925.00	1835.00	305.00	0.00
8	2900.00	21700.00	23033.33	4340.00	0.00	4340.00	2200.00	2140.00	305.00	0.00
9	500.00	22200.00	25912.50	4440.00	0.00	4440.00	2475.00	1965.00	0.00	−175.00
10	2900.00	25100.00	28791.67	5020.00	0.00	5020.00	2750.00	2270.00	305.00	0.00
11	2900.00	28000.00	31670.83	5600.00	0.00	5600.00	3025.00	2575.00	305.00	0.00
12	2900.00	**30900.00**	34550.00	6180.00	0.00	6180.00	3300.00	**2880.00**	305.00	0.00

Glossary of abbreviations:

SR	Standard Rate
HR	Higher Rate
Cum	Cumulative
SRCOP	Standard Rate cut off Point
Ded	Deducted

Appendix II

Tax Calculation 2018
Week 1/Month 1 Basis

	Gross Pay this month	SRCOP	Tax due 20% SR	Tax 40% HR	Gross Tax	Tax Credit	Tax	Tax Ded this Period	Tax Refund this Month
Month No.	**€**	**€**	**€**	**€**	**€**	**€**	**€**	**€**	**€**
1	3200.00	2879.17	575.83	128.33	704.17	275.00	429.17	429.17	0.00
2	3000.00	2879.17	575.83	48.33	624.17	275.00	349.17	349.17	0.00
3	2900.00	2879.17	575.83	8.33	584.17	275.00	309.17	309.17	0.00
4	1000.00	2879.17	200.00	0.00	200.00	275.00	0.00	0.00	0.00
5	2900.00	2879.17	575.83	8.33	584.17	275.00	309.17	309.17	0.00
6	2900.00	2879.17	575.83	8.33	584.17	275.00	309.17	309.17	0.00
7	2900.00	2879.17	575.83	8.33	584.17	275.00	309.17	309.17	0.00
8	2900.00	2879.17	575.83	8.33	584.17	275.00	309.17	309.17	0.00
9	500.00	2879.17	100.00	0.00	100.00	275.00	0.00	0.00	0.00
10	2900.00	2879.17	575.83	8.33	584.17	275.00	309.17	309.17	0.00
11	2900.00	2879.17	575.83	8.33	584.17	275.00	309.17	309.17	0.00
12	2900.00	2879.17	575.83	8.33	584.17	275.00	309.17	309.17	0.00
	30900.00							**3,251.67**	
	Tax per Cum TDC							2880.00	
	Difference							371.67	

Glossary of abbreviations:

SR	Standard Rate
HR	Higher Rate
SRCOP	Standard Rate Cut-Off Point
Ded.	Deducted

24 BASIC PRINCIPLES OF CAPITAL GAINS TAX

Learning Outcomes

On completion of this chapter you will be able to:

- ✓ Identify issues/transactions which give rise to a disposal of an asset for CGT purposes.
- ✓ Appreciate the importance of the timing of disposal and ascertain the correct timing of a disposal.
- ✓ Identify non-chargeable assets, i.e., those that are exempt from CGT.
- ✓ Explain the CGT treatment of wasting and non-wasting movable assets.
- ✓ Explain the implications of the residence, ordinary residence and domicile status of an individual on the scope of CGT.
- ✓ Discuss the remittance basis of taxation and identify the taxable portion of a gain where only a portion of the sales consideration is remitted to Ireland.
- ✓ Describe the scope of CGT for companies.
- ✓ List the bodies which are not chargeable persons for the purposes of CGT.
- ✓ Describe the CGT treatment of transactions between connected persons.
- ✓ Describe the CGT treatment of married persons.
- ✓ Identify the due dates for payment of CGT and for filing of returns.
- ✓ Describe the general rules and procedures in relation to CGT withholding tax.

24.1 Introduction

Capital gains tax (CGT) was introduced in 1975 by the Capital Gains Tax Act 1975. CGT applies to capital gains arising on the disposal of chargeable assets made on or after 6 April 1974. The legislation has been amended by subsequent Finance Acts and it is now contained in the Taxes Consolidation Act 1997 (TCA97). CGT was introduced as a means of collecting tax from persons disposing of assets, where the assets being disposed of have increased in value during the period of ownership. Therefore, it is the increase in the value of the asset that is subject to CGT. It is important to note that CGT only applies to realised gains; no CGT arises in respect of assets which are not disposed of, albeit that those assets may have risen substantially in value since the date of acquisition. Furthermore, not all assets and not all persons are subject to CGT; certain exemptions and reliefs may apply. These matters are discussed in some detail in the paragraphs that follow. The final section of this chapter is concerned with some of the administrative requirements in relation to CGT, i.e., payment and filing dates and procedures relating to CGT withholding tax. Detailed rules regarding the computation of CGT liabilities are addressed in Chapter 25.

24.2 The Charge to Capital Gains Tax

s28 TCA97 Section 28 TCA97 provides that CGT:

> *"...shall be charged in accordance with the Capital Gains Tax Acts in respect of capital gains, that is, in respect of chargeable gains computed in accordance with those Acts and accruing to a person on the disposal of assets."*

Therefore, the principle for charging CGT is that the following must occur:

- a disposal,
- of an asset,
- by a chargeable person,
- triggering a chargeable gain.

Consequently, a charge to CGT only arises where these four elements are present. The first three elements, i.e., the "disposal" of an "asset" by a "chargeable person" are considered in detail in the paragraphs that follow.

24.3 Disposal of an Asset

In order for a liability to CGT to arise, there must be a disposal of an asset. The term 'disposal' is not defined in the legislation. For CGT purposes, a disposal is generally taken to arise when a person gives up the rights which he/she has in relation to certain assets. While in practice this usually involves a transfer of the ownership of an asset from one person to another, this is not always the case. Furthermore, the transfer of ownership of an asset may occur in different ways and does not necessarily require the physical disposal of the asset. For example, an individual may receive a capital sum in exchange for the surrender of their rights to shares held at a fixed price at a fixed date in the future. The receipt of the capital sum constitutes the disposal of a right and so is deemed to be a disposal of an asset for capital gains tax purposes. With regard to the disposal of an asset, there are two main issues to be aware of and these are the types of disposal and the timing of the disposal.

24.3.1 Types of disposal

In order for a charge to CGT to arise, a disposal or deemed disposal of an asset must take place. There are many types of transactions which constitute an actual disposal of an asset for CGT purposes. Some examples are as follows:

- the sale of an asset;
- the sale of part of an asset (a 'part-disposal'), for example, where 10 acres of land are disposed out of a holding of 100 acres;
- the gift of an asset or part thereof;
- a compulsory purchase order;
- the receipt of a capital sum for the surrender of rights or for not exercising rights – an example of this is where a payment is made for the release of a person from a contract or restrictive covenant;
- an option ceasing to exist;
- the creation, sale or assignment of a leasehold interest;
- the purchase by a company of its own shares;
- the receipt of a capital sum as consideration for the use or exploitation of assets;
- the transfer of an asset by an individual to a trust or a corporate body;
- the exchange of assets in a barter transaction;
- the repayment or forgiveness of a debt.

The analysis in this book is concerned mainly with the sale and gift of assets and parts of assets. For commentary on the CGT treatment of other transactions referred to above, readers are referred to *The Taxation of Capital Gains* by O'Hanlon, F. and McCleane, J. (2018), Irish Tax Institute.

In addition to the actual disposals referred to above, certain transactions can be classified as "deemed" disposals for CGT purposes, albeit that there is no actual surrender of any right in relation to any asset. For example, a deemed disposal takes place when a company, which is resident in Ireland becomes non-resident on or after 21 April 1997.

s534 TCA97 A part-disposal of an asset is also chargeable to CGT. Section 534 TCA97 provides that references to disposal of an asset in the CGT legislation include references to a part-disposal of an asset. A part-disposal of an asset occurs where, on a person making a disposal, any description of property derived from the asset remains undisposed of. There are special rules to calculate the part of the cost of the asset which is allowable as a deduction when calculating the chargeable gain or loss arising on the part-disposal of the asset. These rules are considered in detail at 25.13.

24.3.2 Death

Death does not give rise to a disposal for CGT purposes. Accordingly, any gain accruing up to the date of death is not subject to CGT. In this case, the ownership of the deceased's assets transfers to the beneficiaries and they are deemed to acquire the assets at their market value on the date of death of the original owner. Therefore, for subsequent disposal purposes, the date of acquisition of the assets for CGT purposes is the date of death of the original owner and the base cost of the assets is their market value at the original owner's date of death.

Example 24.1

Mr Boyle acquires 1,000 shares in December 1979 for €800. He dies in January 2001 and the market value of the shares at that date is €5,000. Mr Boyle's wife inherits the shareholding and subsequently disposes of the shares in March 2018 for €7,000. There is no CGT liability in respect of the gain accruing from December 1979 up to January 2001. When preparing Mr Boyle's wife's CGT computation for the disposal of the shares in 2018, the sales proceeds are €7,000 and the date of acquisition and the cost of the shares for inclusion in the calculation are January 2001 and €5,000 respectively.

24.3.3 Timing of a disposal

The timing of a disposal of an asset for CGT purposes is important because it determines the tax year in which the disposal of an asset takes place and details of the disposal must be returned to the Revenue for that tax year. In addition, the timing of the disposal has implications for the actual calculation of the gain. Firstly, the rate of CGT and the amount of gains exempt from CGT vary between tax years. Secondly, inflation relief applies to assets acquired before 2003 and the level of relief available varies with the period of ownership of the asset and accordingly with the date of disposal. These issues are considered in further detail in Chapter 25.

s542 TCA97 Section 542 TCA97 sets out the basic rules to determine the date of disposal in certain types of transactions. These are set out as follows:

1. Unconditional Contract

   Where an asset is disposed of by unconditional contract, the date of disposal is the date of the contract.

2. Conditional Contract

   Where a contract is conditional, the date of disposal for CGT purposes is the date the condition is satisfied. For example, where the sale of a property is dependent on planning permission being granted, the date of disposal is the date the stipulated condition is satisfied, i.e., the date planning permission is granted.

3. Compulsory Purchase Order (CPO)

   Where an interest in land is acquired by a local authority by means of a CPO, the date of disposal is:

   – the date on which the compensation for the acquisition of the land is received; or

– at a time immediately prior to the person's death if the consideration has not been received at the date of his or her death.

This applies to disposals by means of a CPO made on or after 4 February 2010. There are exceptions to this rule in the case of certain CPOs.

Section 38 Finance Act 2015 amended s542 TCA97 by inserting s542(1A) and (1B). The new section provides that notwithstanding s542(1)(c) TCA97, the time of disposal of land compulsorily acquired will be the time when the compensation proceeds are received where they are received after 1 January 2016. Revenue have confirmed that the later date of disposal will apply in situations where compensation amounts have been agreed or an authority has entered onto the land before 1 January 2016 but the proceeds are not paid until after that date.

4. A Capital Sum Derived from an Asset

   Where a capital sum is derived from the ownership of an asset, the date of disposal is the date the capital sum is received.

5. Gifts

   In the case of gifts, the date of disposal is the date on which the asset passes to the beneficiary/recipient.

6. Receipt of a Compensation Payment

   The date of disposal is generally the date of receipt of the compensation payment.

24.4 Assets

There must be a disposal of a chargeable asset in order to incur a charge to CGT. Section 532 TCA97 defines a chargeable asset for CGT purposes. In general, a chargeable asset for CGT purposes includes all forms of property, whether situated in Ireland or not, with the exception of assets specifically exempt from CGT under the legislation. These non-chargeable assets are discussed in 24.4.1.

s532 TCA97

Specifically included in the legislative definition of assets are:

- options and debts;
- any currency, other than Irish currency (which is now the Euro); and
- intangible property, e.g., goodwill, patents, copyrights.

It is worth noting that an ordinary debt owed by a debtor to a person is not an asset for CGT purposes unless the debt is sold by the person to a third party.

Where there is indeed a disposal of a chargeable asset, it is also worth noting that the legislation provides exemptions and reliefs from a charge to CGT where qualifying conditions are satisfied. Examples include retirement relief and principal private residence (PPR) relief. Retirement relief is, in general, a relief granted to an individual on the sale of all or part of the qualifying assets of his/her business provided he/she is 55 years of age or more at the date of disposal. PPR relief provides for an exemption from CGT in respect of any gain arising on the disposal of an individual's principal private residence. These reliefs are discussed in more detail in Chapter 27.

24.4.1 Non-chargeable assets

The legislation specifically exempts certain types of assets and certain bodies from CGT. The following assets are generally not subject to CGT:

- government securities, i.e., those issued by the government, local authorities, semi-State bodies and other similar organisations;
- life assurance policies and contracts for deferred annuities, or interests therein, except where the disposer is not the original beneficial owner of the policy;
- any gain accruing to a body with charitable status, provided the asset disposed of was applied for charitable purposes;
- any gain arising on approved superannuation funds;
- any gain on the disposal of growing timber;
- any gain arising on the disposal of a debt by an original creditor;
- prize bond winnings, national lottery winnings and sums received by way of compensation for or damages for any wrong or injury suffered by an individual in his/her person or in his/her profession;
- wasting chattels, except those used for the purposes of a trade and qualifying for capital allowances;
- non-wasting chattels sold for €2,540 or less.
- s613 TCA97 any compensation received under the cessation of turf cutting compensation scheme (introduced by s62 FA 2012).

Where an asset is not a chargeable asset for CGT purposes, there is no relief for any loss arising on the disposal of such an asset. Readers are referred to 25.14 for commentary on the relief available for losses arising on chargeable assets.

24.4.2 Chattels

The definition of a chattel is "tangible, movable property", i.e., it is an asset, which can be touched and which is capable of being moved from one place to another. Examples include a car, a painting, a piece of furniture, etc. Goodwill is not a chattel as it is intangible, nor are buildings or land as these are immovable. There are two types of chattel – wasting and non-wasting.

Wasting chattels

s603 TCA97 A wasting chattel is defined as an asset that wastes away over its life and is taken to have a predictable life of less than 50 years. Examples include livestock, motor vehicles and plant and machinery. Section 47 Finance Act 2014 excludes 'work of art' which might otherwise be considered "plant" from being considered a wasting chattel. 'Work of art' includes a picture, print, book, manuscript, sculpture, piece of jewellery, furniture or similar object. Section 603 TCA97 provides an exemption from CGT for any item of tangible movable property, which is a wasting asset (excluding 'work of art'). The exemption applies to all taxpayers irrespective of the sales proceeds received on the disposal of the asset. However, wasting chattels which are used for business purposes and which qualify for capital allowances do not qualify for the exemption from CGT. Where capital allowances have not been claimed but could have been claimed, the CGT exemption will not apply.

Accordingly, a gain arising on the disposal of a motor vehicle by a private individual is not subject to CGT. However, a gain arising on the disposal of a motor vehicle used by an individual for the purposes of his/her trade is subject to CGT to the extent that the motor vehicle qualifies for capital allowances.

No relief under CGT is available for losses arising on the disposal of wasting assets. Such losses are dealt with at 25.14.7.

Non-wasting chattels

s602 TCA97 Conversely, a non-wasting chattel is defined as tangible, movable property, which has a predictable life of more than 50 years when acquired. Examples of non-wasting chattels include antique furniture, paintings and jewellery. In relation to non-wasting chattels, s602 TCA97 provides an exemption from CGT where the consideration received on the disposal of the asset does not exceed €2,540. It is important to note that the CGT exemption for non-wasting chattels applies only to individuals.

Example 24.2

Mr X disposes of jewellery for €2,000. He had acquired this jewellery for €400 three years earlier. As this is the disposal of a non-wasting chattel for less than €2,540, the exemption from CGT applies. Therefore, the gain arising on the disposal is not liable to CGT.

The CGT exemption is not an annual exemption applying to the collective disposal of all non-wasting chattels in the tax year. The exemption applies to each separate non-wasting chattel disposed of in a year of assessment. Therefore, the number of non-wasting chattels disposed of in a tax year is irrelevant. Provided that the consideration received on each disposal does not exceed €2,540, each disposal is exempt (see 25.15.3 for rules regarding sets of chattels).

Where a non-wasting chattel is disposed of resulting in a capital loss, special rules apply to determine the allowable loss for CGT purposes. In addition, where a non-wasting chattel is sold for an amount slightly in excess of the exemption threshold of €2,540, marginal relief may apply. The application of these special rules and marginal relief is considered in greater detail in Chapter 25 (25.15.1 and 25.15.2).

24.4.3 Location of assets

s533 TCA97 To determine whether a charge to Irish CGT arises on the disposal of a chargeable asset, it is necessary to know where the asset is located. This is an important factor when considered in conjunction with the territorial scope of CGT (see paragraph 24.5 below). Section 533 TCA97 stipulates the location of certain assets where the location of the assets may not be self-evident. These provisions relating to the deemed location of various assets are as follows:

- rights or interests in or over immovable or tangible movable property are situated where the property is situated;
- debts (secured or unsecured) are situated in Ireland only if the creditor is resident in Ireland;
- shares or securities issued by a municipal or governmental authority are situated in the country where the authority is established;
- s56 FA 2012 other registered shares and securities are situated where they are registered; however, s56 FA 2012 amended s533 TCA97, stating that shares in an Irish incorporated company will always be regarded as located in Ireland for CGT purposes.
- a ship or aircraft is situated in Ireland only if the owner is resident in Ireland;
- goodwill of a trade, business or profession is situated in the place where that trade, business or profession is carried on;
- patents, trademarks and designs are situated in the country where they are registered;
- copyrights and licenses to use any copyright material, patents, trademarks or designs are situated in Ireland if the rights derived from them are exercisable in Ireland;
- a judgment debt is situated where the judgment is recorded.

24.4.4 Specified assets

An individual who is neither resident nor ordinarily resident in Ireland is only chargeable to Irish CGT on the disposal of "specified" assets. Readers are referred to paragraph 24.5 below for further commentary on the territorial scope of CGT.

s29 TCA97 Specified assets comprise:

(a) land and buildings in Ireland including any interest in land (such as leases);

(b) minerals or any rights, interests or other assets in relation to mining or minerals or the searching for minerals in Ireland. Exploration or exploitation rights within the Irish Continental Shelf are also deemed to be assets situated in Ireland for CGT purposes;

(c) assets situated in Ireland, which were used in, or acquired for use for the purposes of a trade carried on in Ireland;

(d) unquoted shares deriving the greater part of their value from (a) or (b) – the greater part of their value is taken to be greater than 50%.

24.5 Chargeable Persons

At this stage, we have addressed the issues relating to two of the four elements necessary for a charge to CGT to arise, i.e. where there is a 'disposal' of a 'chargeable asset'. Therefore, issues involving the third element - the person making the disposal - must now be considered. CGT is assessed on chargeable gains realised by individuals, partnerships and trusts. In limited cases it also applies to companies.

24.5.1 Individuals

An individual's residence, ordinary residence and domicile status impact on his/her exposure to Irish CGT. The terms residence, ordinary residence and domicile have the same meaning as for income tax purposes. Readers are referred to Chapter 9 for a detailed explanation of these concepts.

Irish resident and/or ordinarily resident and domiciled individual

Where an individual is resident, and/or ordinarily resident, and domiciled in Ireland, he/she is liable to CGT on chargeable gains arising on the disposal of all assets wherever they are situated and whether or not the gains on the disposals are remitted to Ireland.

Irish resident and/or ordinarily resident but non-domiciled individual

s29 TCA97 Where an individual is resident and/or ordinarily resident but not Irish-domiciled, he/she is liable to CGT on chargeable gains arising on the disposal of assets situated in Ireland and on gains arising on the disposal of assets situated outside Ireland to the extent that the proceeds of such gains are remitted to Ireland, i.e., transferred to Ireland. Where the gains are remitted to Ireland, the remitted gains are taxed in the year of assessment in which they are remitted to Ireland, as opposed to in the tax year in which the disposal of the asset takes place. However, the CGT liability is calculated by reference to the rules applying in the tax year in which the disposal of the asset has taken place.

It is important to note that where an individual is assessed to CGT on the remittance basis, he/she will not receive relief for a capital loss realised on the disposal of an asset situated outside of Ireland.

Where only a portion of the sales proceeds in respect of an asset (subject to CGT on the remittance basis) is remitted to Ireland, the gain arising on the disposal is deemed to be remitted first. Accordingly, each euro of sales proceeds remitted will trigger €1 of a chargeable gain, until the full amount of the gain has been remitted. Section 45 of Finance Act 2013 made an amendment to the 'remittance rules', dealing with situations where a non-Irish domiciled individual makes a gain from assets situated outside Ireland, but transfers the gain (or any amounts derived from it) to his/her spouse/civil partner who then remits the funds into Ireland. Prior to the amendment in FA 2013, the remittance by the spouse/civil partner may not have given rise to CGT. However, from 13 February 2013, the non-domiciled individual who originally disposed of the asset will be treated as having remitted the gain to Ireland, and so will be liable to CGT.

Example 24.3

John is resident in Ireland but domiciled in Germany. During the 2018 tax year, John disposed of his German shareholdings. The proceeds of disposal amounted to €10,000 and the chargeable gain arising on the disposals was €4,000.

Firstly, John transferred the €10,000 to his wife Mary and she remitted €2,000 of the sales proceeds to Ireland on 1 August 2018. John is chargeable to CGT in 2018. Albeit that John did not remit the proceeds to Ireland, he is still chargeable as he transferred the proceeds to his wife and she remitted them to Ireland.

Secondly, even though Mary has only remitted 20% of the proceeds, John is taxable in full on the amount remitted. This is because the gain arising on the disposal is deemed to be remitted first. If Mary had remitted sales proceeds of €4,000 he would have been chargeable to CGT on all of the gain, despite the fact that only a portion of the proceeds had been remitted.

Individual not resident and not ordinarily resident in Ireland

Where an individual is neither resident nor ordinarily resident in Ireland, irrespective of domicile, he/she is assessed to CGT on chargeable gains realised on the disposal of certain specified assets, as defined in paragraph 24.4.4 above. However, Section 34 FA 2015 amends section 29 of the Taxes Consolidation Act 1997, the amendment counters a scheme whereby cash is transferred to a non-resident company prior to a disposal of shares by that company so that at the time when the shares are disposed of, the value of those shares is derived mainly from cash rather than land or buildings situated in this country. The amendment applies to disposals made on or after 22 October 2015.

Summary

The following chart summarises the scope of CGT for individuals.

Individual	Liable to CGT
Resident/ordinarily resident and domiciled	On worldwide gains (irrespective of whether the assets are situated in Ireland or not and irrespective of whether the gains are remitted to Ireland)
Resident/ordinarily resident but non-domiciled	On Irish gains as they arise and on foreign gains only to the extent that they are remitted to Ireland
Non-resident/non-ordinarily resident, irrespective of domicile	Gains on specified assets only (subject to anti avoidance measure above)

Temporary non-residents

s29A TCA97 Where an individual ceases to be resident in 2003 or later years, they are deemed for capital gains tax purposes to have disposed of certain assets on the last day of the year in which they were resident. This charge will only arise where the individual:

- is non-resident for a period of five years of less before becoming resident again
- the assets are disposed of during that period of temporary non residence
- was domiciled in Ireland prior to becoming non-resident
- the assets disposed of consist of at least 5% shareholding of the issued share capital of a company or the shares have a value exceeding €500,000

This section is designed to counter the avoidance of CGT by Individuals by becoming temporarily non-resident.

Section 46 Finance Act 2014 amended s29A TCA97 by providing that where there is an increase or decrease in the market value of those assets between the last day in the year where they were resident and the date of disposal, the market value at the date of disposal will be used for the purposes of CGT calculation. This amendment applies to disposal made on or after 23 December 2014.

24.5.2 Companies

An Irish-resident company is liable to CGT but only on gains arising on the disposal of development land (see Chapter 26). With regard to the disposal of other assets by a company, any chargeable gains realised on the disposal are subject to corporation tax and not CGT.

Readers are referred to Chapter 29 (29.6) for further commentary on the tax treatment of chargeable gains realised by companies.

24.5.3 Trusts and Partnerships

In the case of partnerships, gains are attributable not to the partnership or firm as a separate entity but rather to the individuals who form that partnership. For more detailed commentary on the CGT treatment of partners in partnership and for an analysis of the position in relation to trusts, readers are referred to the commentary in *The Taxation of Capital Gains* by Appleby, T. and O'Hanlon, F. (2018), Irish Tax Institute. This text is concerned primarily with the scope of CGT for individuals and companies. In general, the scope of CGT varies with the residence status of the chargeable person.

24.5.4 Exempt persons

The following bodies are not chargeable persons for the purposes of CGT:

- Registered Trade Unions;
- Friendly Societies;
- Local Authorities;
- County Councils;
- The Health Service Executive;
- Vocational Educational Committees and Committees of agriculture;
- Regional tourism bodies;
- Various government agencies, e.g., IDA, Enterprise Ireland, etc.;
- The Commission for Communications Regulation (Comreg);
- The Digital Hub Development Agency (effective from 1 January 2008).

Therefore, any gains realised by these bodies are exempt from a charge to CGT.

In addition, we have already identified that gains accruing to Revenue-approved pension funds and charities are exempt from CGT.

24.5.5 Connected persons

s10 TCA97 It is important to know whether or not a disposal is taking place between connected persons, as it will result in certain restrictions for CGT purposes. Where there is a transaction between connected persons, the proceeds received (or 'consideration') are deemed to equal the open market value of the asset being disposed of. Therefore, any consideration agreed between connected persons is replaced by the open market value of the asset for the purpose of calculating the chargeable gain or allowable loss arising on the transaction. In addition, where a capital loss arises on the disposal of a chargeable asset to a connected person, the loss is available only for offset against chargeable gains arising on the disposal of other assets to the same connected person (CGT losses are dealt with in detail in 25.14. Section 10 TCA97 set out the types of relationships that will lead to persons being "connected". These relationships are set out below:

Spouses and blood relatives

A husband, wife, or relative is a "connected" person. Relative includes brother, sister, uncle, aunt, niece, nephew, lineal ancestor, lineal descendant, step child or a person adopted under the Adoption Acts 1952 to 1991, including foreign adoptions.

The use of the term lineal descendant would include most children. It clearly includes a child born naturally to a couple. The question of a legally adopted child (under the specific Acts mentioned) is also clear.

"In-laws"

The following will all be treated as being "connected" with an individual:

- The spouse of a relative of the individual;
- A relative of the individual's spouse;
- The spouse of a relative of an individual's spouse.

Example 24.4

Peadar has just sold shares in Confussed plc. for €12.50 per share (well below their current market value of €20) to the following individuals:

- *His brother Jim;*
- *Jim's wife, Hannah;*
- *Olivia, Peadar's wife's aunt;*
- *Oisin, Olivia's husband.*

In all instances, each individual will be considered as "connected" to Peadar.

Accordingly, when calculating any gain arising on the disposals, the market value of €20 per share will be treated as the proceeds, rather than the actual proceeds of €12.50 per share.

Trustees

A trustee of a trust is connected with the settlor (i.e the person transferring assets to the trust) and any person connected with that settlor. However, this will only apply if the settlor is an individual.

A trustee of a settlement will be connected with a body corporate, if the body corporate is connected with the settlement. A body corporate is connected with a settlement in any year if it is a close company (or would be so if Irish resident) and the shareholders include either the trustees or a beneficiary of the settlement. Close companies are considered in Chapter 32.

Partners

A person is connected with any business partners of his/hers and with the husband, or wife, or relatives of any of his/her partners. However, there is one important exception to this rule. A person is not connected with another person solely by reason of being that person's partner, where the transaction in question is the acquisition or disposal of partnership assets pursuant to *bona fide* commercial arrangements.

Company

A person is connected with any company he/she controls either on his/her own or together with other persons connected with him/her. In addition, companies under common control are connected persons.

24.5.6 Married persons

s1028 TCA97 Section 1028 TCA97 deals with married persons for CGT purposes. In general, the CGT arising on chargeable gains accruing to a married person living with their spouse in any year of assessment are assessed and charged on the assessable spouse. It is possible, however, to have the CGT assessment issued in the wife's name if both spouses jointly elect in writing by 1 April in the year of assessment in respect of which the assessment is to be raised in the wife's name. The gains and losses realised by each spouse are calculated separately as if they were single persons and then assessed on a joint basis. Each spouse's residence status must be examined individually to determine whether that individual is chargeable to Irish CGT.

Separate assessment

An election for separate assessment can be made by either spouse by giving written notice to the Inspector of Taxes before 1 April following the end of the year of assessment in respect of which the separate assessment basis is to apply. The effect of the separate assessment election is that both spouses will be assessed separately in respect of any chargeable gains accruing to them. The election for separate assessment continues to have effect until it is withdrawn. In the event that a married couple wish to revert to the joint assessment basis at any time after they elect for separate assessment, an election must be made by the spouse who initially lodged the claim for separate assessment. The notice of withdrawal must be made before 1 April following the end of the year of assessment in which the joint assessment basis is to be effective.

Transactions between spouses

Broadly speaking, transactions between spouses are not subject to CGT. The manner in which this relief is applied and the CGT implications of disposing of an asset originally acquired from one's spouse are considered in greater detail in Chapter 25 (25.10).

24.6 Administration of CGT

24.6.1 Self-assessment system

The year of assessment for CGT purposes is the same as the year of assessment for income tax purposes. Therefore, the CGT year of assessment runs from 1 January to the following 31 December. For example, where an asset is disposed of in March 2018, the year of assessment for CGT purposes is the tax year 2018.

s913, s959I TCA97 The self-assessment system applies to CGT. Section 913 TCA97 stipulates that the provisions of the Income Tax Acts relating to the making or delivery of any return, statement, declaration, list, etc., subject to any necessary modification, apply to capital gains tax as the provisions apply to income tax. Section 959I TCA97 imposes an obligation on all chargeable persons disposing of assets in a tax year to file a return of capital gains realised in the tax year. The return must be made in a form prescribed by the Revenue. In general, the capital gains tax return is made on the same form used to file an income tax return. It is the responsibility of the chargeable person to submit details of any chargeable gains realised in the tax year and to pay the CGT liability by the due date, irrespective of whether or not the Revenue has requested it. In addition, any person requested by the Revenue to file a return is required to do so. The obligation to file a return to include details of the chargeable assets disposed of in the relevant period extends not only to individual taxpayers and trustees, but also to companies.

Return filing date

s1084 TCA97 The return filing date for CGT is the same as for income tax. Therefore, the due date for filing a return of capital gains realised in a tax year is 31 October following the year of assessment in which the disposal of the asset occurs. Therefore, for capital gains realised in the tax year 2018, the due date for filing the 2018 return is 31 October 2019. For individuals who file through Revenue's online service ROS, the date of filing for 2018 returns is extended to 15th November 2019. As the return filing date for income tax and CGT is the same, the CGT reporting requirement is simplified by the inclusion of a section on the taxpayer's return for chargeable gains realised in the tax year. Forms 11 and 12 contain a section on which chargeable gains may be returned by a taxpayer. Where a taxpayer is not liable to income tax, he/she must file a form CG1 to return details of chargeable assets disposed of during the year of assessment. Where a taxpayer fails to submit a return of chargeable assets disposed of in the tax year, or alternatively, submits an incorrect return, Revenue has the power to impose a surcharge on the relevant amount of CGT due. The surcharge is treated as part of the total CGT liability for the year, and therefore, interest charges for late payment of the tax due will be applied to the CGT liability and the surcharge. The surcharge is calculated on the total CGT liability before taking into account any CGT payment on account. Section 1084 TCA97 provides that the surcharge to be applied where a tax return is filed late is as follows:

- Where the return is filed within two months of the due date, a surcharge of 5% of the tax, or €12,695, if lower, is applied.
- Where the return is filed more than two months late, the surcharge to be applied is 10% of the tax, or €63,485, if lower.

Payment of CGT liability

Payment of a CGT liability is also determined under the self-assessment provisions. The adoption of the pay and file system, effective for the year of assessment 2001 and subsequent tax years, removed the application of preliminary tax to CGT.

The legislation stipulates that for 2009 and subsequent tax years, CGT is payable on the following dates:

- 15 December in the current year of assessment in respect of the disposal of chargeable assets made between 1 January and 30 November inclusive (described as the *initial period*); and
- 31 January in the following year of assessment in respect of the disposal of chargeable assets made between 1 December and 31 December (described as the *later period*).

Tax Facts

The government estimate the total Tax Revenue in 2018 to be €53.7 billion, of which capital gains tax will account for €843 million - a 6% increase on 2017. (Source: www.budget.gov.ie)

Example 24.5

Mary disposes of shares in ABC Limited on 1 April 2018 and she realises a gain of €10,000 on the disposal of the shares. On 1 December 2018, Mary disposes of more shares in ABC Limited, and this time, due to a significant increase in the company's share price, she realises a gain of €25,000.

Mary must file a return no later than 31 October 2019 to include details of the chargeable assets disposed of in the tax year 2018. With regard to paying the CGT liability arising on the disposals of the shares, she must make CGT payments by the following dates:

- *15 December 2018 in respect of the disposal made on 1 April 2018;*
- *31 January 2019 in respect of the disposal of shares made on 1 December 2018.*

s1080 TCA97 The relevant amount of CGT due must be paid by the due date to avoid an exposure to interest charges. The interest rate charged from 1 July 2009 onwards is 0.0219% per day or part of a day (s1080 TCA97) where the CGT liability is not fully settled by the due date. Interest is charged from the due date and will continue to accrue until the relevant tax is paid.

24.6.2 Withholding tax

s980 TCA97 Section 980 TCA97 provides that where certain types of asset are disposed of, the person by or through whom payment is made is obliged to withhold an amount from the sales proceeds and remit it to the Revenue. The requirement to withhold tax from the sales proceeds applies to certain types of asset as specified in the legislation where the consideration received for the disposal of the asset exceeds €1,000,000 (s39 FA 2016 increased this limit from €500,000 to €1,000,000 for disposals of houses and apartments only). The aim of this is to collect tax from a non-resident in the event that later collection of the tax due may prove impossible. However, the legislative provision with regard to the operation of withholding tax also applies to the disposal of specified assets by an Irish resident. The withholding tax requirement applies to the following types of asset:

(a) land and buildings in the State;

(b) minerals in the State or any rights, interests or other assets in relation to mining or minerals or the searching for minerals;

(c) exploration or exploitation rights in a designated area;

(d) unquoted shares in a company deriving their value or the greater part of their value directly or indirectly from assets specified in (a), (b) or (c) above; s28 FA 2017 amended s980 TCA97 by ensuring that the exclusion for shares quoted on a stock exchange will apply only to shares that are actively and substantially traded on the stock exchange and that money or other assets transferred to a company prior to a disposal of shares in that company will not be taken into account in determining whether the value of the shares disposed of is derived from those assets. This amendment applies to disposals made on or after 19 October 2017.

(e) unquoted shares accepted in exchange for shares deriving their value, or the greater part of it, from (a), (b) or (c) above;

(f) goodwill of a trade carried on in the State.

The current rate of withholding tax is 15% and it is chargeable on the full consideration. Where the consideration exceeds the limit (currently €1,000,000), the full proceeds are subject to the 15% withholding tax, not just the excess over the specified limit. The onus to withhold tax rests with the purchaser, who is required to return the amount of tax withheld to the Revenue under the self-assessment rules within 30 days of the acquisition of the asset. If payment has not been made within 30 days, Revenue can assess the purchaser for that amount. A form CG50B should be provided to the individual disposing of the asset confirming the amount of tax deducted. The vendor can then use this form to obtain a refund of the tax withheld, if necessary, when the correct CGT liability has been agreed.

The purchaser need not withhold tax where the consideration for the disposal does not exceed €1,000,000 or where the vendor provides a form CG50A. A form CG50A is a clearance certificate from the Revenue authorising the purchaser to pay over the full proceeds to the vendor. The vendor can obtain a clearance certificate from the Revenue by completing an application form CG50. The application form should be accompanied by a copy of the contract of sale.

Revenue will issue a CG50A to the vendor where:

- the vendor is resident in the State, or
- no amount of CGT is payable in respect of the disposal, or
- the CGT chargeable has already been paid.

Where the consideration is not for cash and the vendor has not provided a form CG50A, the purchaser is obliged to provide the following details to the Revenue within 30 days of the acquisition:

- the asset acquired;
- the consideration for acquiring the asset;
- market value of the consideration;
- name and address of the person making the disposal.

The purchaser must also pay over 15% of the estimated market value of the consideration to the Revenue within 30 days of the acquisition. The purchaser then has a right to recover this amount from the person from whom he/she acquired the asset.

Where the amount is recovered from the vendor, the vendor is entitled to a credit for this amount against his/her possible capital gains tax liability, provided the amount required to be deducted is paid within the 30 days.

25 COMPUTATION OF GAIN OR LOSS

Learning Outcomes

On completion of this chapter you will be able to:

- ✓ Identify the amount of consideration or "deemed" consideration and the amount of the allowable cost for CGT purposes.
- ✓ Describe the CGT treatment of enhancement expenditure and calculate CGT liabilities where enhancement expenditure has been incurred.
- ✓ Calculate gains after inflation relief on disposals and part-disposals of chargeable assets.
- ✓ Calculate losses arising on the disposal of chargeable assets and show how loss relief may be utilised.
- ✓ Describe the CGT treatment of married couples and the CGT implications of transfers between spouses.
- ✓ Calculate marginal relief from CGT on non-wasting chattels and calculate losses arising on the disposal of non-wasting chattels.
- ✓ Describe the implications of the €2,540 exemption limit for disposals of non-wasting chattels, which form part of a set.

25.1 Introduction

In general, the chargeable gain or allowable loss arising on the disposal of an asset is calculated as the difference between the consideration received for the disposal of the asset and the cost of acquisition of the asset. Therefore, when preparing a capital gains tax computation, it is necessary to identify both the consideration and the costs that may be taken into account.

Where any part of the consideration received for the disposal of the asset is included as income for income tax or corporation tax purposes, it is excluded from the consideration figure for CGT purposes. Consequently, a taxpayer will never be liable to tax twice on the same income or gains. Similarly, any expenditure incurred on the acquisition of an asset or on enhancing the value of the asset will only be allowable as a deduction under one tax head. Hence, expenditure allowed as a deduction for income tax or corporation tax purposes will not be an allowable deduction for CGT purposes. The purpose of this chapter is to set out the rules used to determine the consideration or deemed consideration received on the disposal of an asset and also to identify the allowable cost of an asset for CGT purposes. Having established these elements, the remainder of the chapter is concerned with the general rules and basic reliefs applied in calculating CGT liabilities and allowable losses. More detailed rules unique to the disposal of certain types of asset, namely shares and development land, are the subject matter of Chapter 26. Chapter 27 is concerned with some additional more complex reliefs, which may apply in certain circumstances.

25.2 Consideration

s547 TCA97 The legislation does not define "consideration". The general rule is that the actual consideration received for the disposal of an asset is included in the CGT computation. However, in certain circumstances, the legislation (s547 TCA97) substitutes market value as the consideration for CGT purposes in place of the actual consideration received on the disposal of a chargeable asset (see 25.6). Other legislative provisions substitute base cost for the consideration received in certain scenarios, e.g., on the transfer of chargeable assets between spouses (see 25.10).

s563 TCA97 Where the legislation does not substitute deemed consideration for actual consideration received, then the consideration to be taken into account is the actual consideration received by a person disposing of an asset.

25.3 Allowable Expenditure

s552 TCA97 Section 552 TCA97 sets out the deductions allowable in calculating the chargeable gain or allowable loss arising on the disposal of an asset. The legislation provides that *inter alia*, the following expenditure is allowable for CGT purposes:

- the amount or value of the consideration in money or money's worth given by the individual wholly and exclusively for the acquisition of the asset, together with the incidental costs of acquisition;
- expenditure wholly and exclusively incurred on the asset for the purpose of enhancing the value of the asset (consequently, expenditure on repairs is not allowable) – the expenditure must be reflected in the state or nature of the asset at the time of disposal to be allowable for CGT purposes;
- expenditure wholly and exclusively incurred in establishing, preserving or defending title to, or to a right over, the asset;
- the incidental costs of making the disposal.

In respect of assets acquired prior to the introduction of CGT, i.e., pre-6 April 1974, such assets are deemed to have been disposed of and immediately reacquired at 6 April 1974. Therefore, the market value of the asset at 6 April 1974 is taken to be the cost of the asset for CGT purposes, irrespective of the actual acquisition cost pre-6 April 1974.

This effectively ensures that the gain, which accrued prior to the introduction of CGT, is not taxed when the asset is ultimately sold. The deemed disposal of the asset at 6 April 1974 does not give rise to a disposal for CGT purposes.

Example 25.1

Mr Boyle acquired a property in 1963 for €5,000. The market value of the property was €15,000 on 6 April 1974. Mr Boyle disposes of the property in 2018 for €90,000.

As the property was acquired pre-6 April 1974, the cost is taken to be €15,000, i.e., the market value of the property at 6 April 1974. Hence, the gain of €10,000 that had accrued between 1963 and 1974 will not be taxed when the asset is disposed of in 2018.

Additional rules in relation to the substitution of market value on 6 April 1974 for base cost are considered in 25.9.

25.3.1 Expenditure Using Borrowed Funds

Section 40 F(No. 2)A 2013 imposes a restriction on the amounts that can be included as acquisition or enhancement costs, where those costs were funded via borrowed monies. The restriction arises where the costs of acquisition of an asset or enhancement expenditure is defrayed out of borrowed money and the debt in respect of such expenditure is released in whole or in part (whether on or after the disposal of the asset). In such instances the allowable base cost used in calculating the gain on the disposal is reduced by the amount of the debt which is released.

Even where the taxpayer attempts to circumvent the restriction and the debt is released in whole or in part in a year of assessment after the year of assessment in which the disposal of the asset takes place (and therefore the release of the debt is not taken into account in the computation of the gain or loss on the disposal of the asset), a chargeable gain equal to the amount of the debt released shall be deemed to accrue to the debtor on the date on which the debt is released.

The restrictions apply to debt releases on or after 1 January 2014.

Example 25.2

Bevin bought a rental property in 2011 for €150,000. The property was financed via a bank loan. Bevin sold the property in June 2018 for €300,000. In August 2018, he managed to negotiate with the bank to have €50,000 of the 2011 loan written off.

Applying the FA (No.2) 2013 restriction, the gain arising on the disposal amounts to €200,000, i.e. €300,000 less (€150,000 - €50,000).

If Bevin was able to arrange for the write-off to occur in 2019, the full amount of the acquisition costs would be allowed in calculating the gain on the disposal of the rental property in 2018. However, a gain of €50,000 (i.e. the amount of the debt released) would be deemed to arise in 2019.

25.4 Incidental Costs

The legislation stipulates that incidental costs of acquisition or disposal must be incurred wholly and exclusively for the purpose of the acquisition or the disposal of the asset. Examples of incidental costs include:

- fees, commission or remuneration paid for the professional services of any surveyor, valuer, auctioneer, accountant, agent or legal adviser;
- costs of transfer or conveyance (including stamp duty);
- costs of advertising to acquire the asset;
- in the case of a disposal, costs of advertising to find a buyer and costs reasonably incurred in making a valuation necessary to compute the gain or loss arising on the disposal.

In effect, the allowable incidental costs will either:

(a) increase the cost of the asset – the incidental costs on acquisition are added to the original purchase price of the asset; or

(b) reduce the amount of consideration received – the incidental costs of disposal are deducted from the consideration received on the disposal.

Thus, when calculating the chargeable gain or allowable loss arising on the disposal of an asset, the amount of consideration paid by the taxpayer to acquire the asset, inclusive of any expenses of acquisition, is deducted from the proceeds received on disposal net of any selling expenses. An exception to this arises where incidental costs are incurred on the acquisition of an asset pre-6 April 1974. In this case, the incidental costs incurred on acquisition of the asset are deemed to be included in the market value of the asset at 6 April 1974.

s554 TCA97 Section 554 TCA97 provides that any expenditure allowable as a deduction for income tax purposes, or expenditure which would be allowed if the asset were used as a fixed asset for trade purposes, is not allowable for CGT purposes.

Example 25.3

John purchased a rental property in January 2018 for €240,000. Legal expenses in connection with the acquisition amounted to €2,950. In February 2018, he spent €20,000 on structural improvements to the property. In March 2018, he agreed to lease the property to a tenant for six months for €1,000 per month. Estate agent's fees in connection with the letting amounted to €300. Legal fees relating to the draft of this lease amounted to €350. Repairs to the property during the period of the lease amounted to €1,000. In December 2018, John sold the property for €320,000. Estate agent's fees (inclusive of advertising) in connection with the sale amounted to €4,300. Legal fees on selling amounted to €3,800.

John has also informed you that he was billed €3,200 by his tax advisors in connection with the property. This comprises €1,500 in respect of the calculation of taxable Case V rental income and €1,700 in respect of tax advice regarding the disposal of the property.

John's capital gains computation is as follows:

	€	€
Sales proceeds		*320,000*
Less selling expenses: – estate agent's fees		*(4,300)*
– legal fees		*(3,800)*
– tax fees		*(1,700)*
		310,200
	€	€
Cost – acquisition	*240,000*	
– acquisition expenses	*2,950*	
– enhancement	*20,000*	*(262,950)*
		47,250)

Note: There is no deduction for the expenses which relate to the letting of the property, i.e., estate agent's fees of €300, legal fees of €350, repairs of €1,000 and tax fees of €1,500. As these expenses are non-capital in nature, they are deductible from Case V income for income tax purposes.

Example 25.4

Michael purchased land in January 1970 for €30,000. Legal fees on acquisition amounted to €3,500. The market value of the land on 6 April 1974 was €45,000.

The legal fees incurred on acquiring the property in 1970 are deemed to be reflected in the value of the property on 6 April 1974, i.e., €45,000. Accordingly where market value on 6 April 1974 is substituted for original cost, there is no relief for expenses of acquisition.

25.5 Capital Grants

Where part of the acquisition cost of an asset is met by means of a capital grant or other type of subsidy, no deduction is available for that part. For example if an asset is acquired in June 1990 for €25,000 and qualifies for a grant of €3,000, the amount of the acquisition cost allowable for CGT purposes is €22,000.

Where an asset is acquired prior to 6 April 1974, the asset is deemed to have been disposed of and immediately reacquired at market value on that date, i.e., 6 April 1974. The market value of any asset on that date is to be reduced by any capital grant received in respect of the acquisition of that asset.

Example 25.5

Pat acquired a factory in July 1969 for €45,000. He received a grant from the IDA in the amount of €10,000 in respect of this factory. Expenses of acquisition amounted to €3,500. The market value of the factory on 6 April 1974 was €62,500.

Where market value on 6 April 1974 is substituted for original cost, the amount of the grant received on acquisition is deducted in full. Accordingly, in this case, the deemed base cost is €52,500.

25.6 Application of Market Value

s547 TCA97 Section 547 TCA97 provides that, in certain circumstances, the actual consideration received on the disposal of a chargeable asset is ignored and the market value of the asset is imposed in place of the actual proceeds received. The legislation sets out the rules to determine the type of transactions where the market value of an asset must be substituted for the actual consideration. In general, market value means the amount which the asset might reasonably be expected to fetch if sold on the "open market". A person is deemed to acquire an asset for a consideration equal to its market value where:

- the person acquires the asset otherwise than by way of a bargain made at arm's length (e.g., assets acquired as gifts, assets acquired on a death);
- the person acquires the asset by way of a distribution from a company in respect of shares in the company, e.g., by way of a distribution on a winding-up of a company;
- the asset is acquired wholly or partly for a consideration that cannot be valued, e.g., in a barter situation;
- the asset is acquired from a connected person (other than a spouse), e.g., an acquisition from a sibling, parent, etc. The concept of connected persons has already been dealt with in Chapter 24 (24.5.5);
- the asset is acquired in connection with loss of employment or diminution of emoluments or in recognition for services or past services.

In the above transactions, market value is deemed to equal the consideration for the purpose of calculating the chargeable gain or allowable loss for CGT purposes. It is important to note that transfers between spouses are not deemed to take place at market value. In this regard, readers are referred to the analysis at 25.10 below.

Example 25.6

Mr Crowley acquired 10,000 shares in ABC Ltd for €5,000 in 1988. In 2018, Mr Crowley gifted the entire shareholding with a market value of €60,000 to his daughter. For CGT purposes, Mr Crowley has made a disposal of a chargeable asset. The market value of the shares, i.e., €60,000 is deemed to be the consideration for inclusion in the CGT computation.

Where his daughter subsequently disposes of the shares in ABC Ltd, the base cost of the shareholding for CGT purposes is €60,000, i.e., the market value of the shares at the date of acquisition.

25.7 Indexation Relief

s556 TCA97 Indexation relief was originally legislated for in the Capital Gains Tax Amendment Act 1978. It was introduced retrospectively to 6 April 1974, the date CGT was introduced. Section 556 TCA97 provides that indexation relief operates by adjusting the acquisition cost of a chargeable asset for inflation by reference to the Consumer Price Index (CPI) over the period of ownership of the asset. Accordingly, the objective of indexation relief was to ensure that only real gains (i.e., gains on assets that appreciated in value by more than the cumulative rise in CPI throughout the period of ownership) were subject to capital gains tax. Where the relief is available, it may be claimed by all taxpayers irrespective of their residency position.

Section 556 TCA97 has been amended by Finance Act 2003. The amendment provides that the application of indexation relief is now restricted to assets which were acquired prior to 1 January 2003. Thus, for assets acquired in 2003 and subsequently, indexation relief is no longer available. For assets acquired prior to 2003, indexation relief only eliminates the part of the gain attributable to inflation in the years up to and including 2003. Thus, there is no relief for inflation attributable to subsequent periods of ownership.

The relief operates by applying a multiplier to the base cost of the asset inclusive of expenses of acquisition. This results in the allowable base cost of the asset being increased in line with inflation, and accordingly, the gain (calculated as the difference between the sales consideration and the increased base cost) is lower. A table of multipliers issued by the Revenue Commissioners indicates the rate of relief to be applied to deductible acquisition costs for different periods of ownership. This table has been reproduced below to facilitate an understanding of the examples that follow.

INDEXATION FACTORS FOR CAPITAL GAINS TAX

Tax Year Expenditure Incurred	Indexation Factor for Disposals in Tax Year																	
	1987/88	1988/89	1989/90	1990/91	1991/92	1992/93	1993/94	1994/95	1995/96	1996/97	1997/98	1998/99	1999/00	2000/01	2001	2002	2003	2004 *et seq.*
1974/75	4.756	4.848	5.009	5.221	5.355	5.552	5.656	5.754	5.899	6.017	6.112	6.215	6.313	6.582	6.930	7.180	7.528	7.528
1975/76	3.842	3.916	4.046	4.217	4.326	4.484	4.568	4.647	4.764	4.860	4.936	5.020	5.099	5.316	5.597	5.799	6.080	6.080
1976/77	3.309	3.373	3.485	3.633	3.726	3.863	3.935	4.003	4.104	4.187	4.253	4.325	4.393	4.580	4.822	4.996	5.238	5.238
1977/78	2.837	2.892	2.988	3.114	3.194	3.312	3.373	3.432	3.518	3.589	3.646	3.707	3.766	3.926	4.133	4.283	4.490	4.490
1978/79	2.621	2.672	2.760	2.877	2.951	3.059	3.117	3.171	3.250	3.316	3.368	3.425	3.479	3.627	3.819	3.956	4.148	4.148
1979/80	2.365	2.410	2.490	2.596	2.663	2.760	2.812	2.861	2.933	2.992	3.039	3.090	3.139	3.272	3.445	3.570	3.742	3.742
1980/81	2.047	2.087	2.156	2.247	2.305	2.390	2.434	2.477	2.539	2.590	2.631	2.675	2.718	2.833	2.983	3.091	3.240	3.240
1981/82	1.692	1.725	1.782	1.857	1.905	1.975	2.012	2.047	2.099	2.141	2.174	2.211	2.246	2.342	2.465	2.554	2.678	2.678
1982/83	1.424	1.451	1.499	1.563	1.603	1.662	1.693	1.722	1.765	1.801	1.829	1.860	1.890	1.970	2.074	2.149	2.253	2.253
1983/84	1.266	1.290	1.333	1.390	1.425	1.478	1.505	1.531	1.570	1.601	1.627	1.654	1.680	1.752	1.844	1.911	2.003	2.003
1984/85	1.149	1.171	1.210	1.261	1.294	1.341	1.366	1.390	1.425	1.454	1.477	1.502	1.525	1.590	1.674	1.735	1.819	1.819
1985/86	1.082	1.103	1.140	1.188	1.218	1.263	1.287	1.309	1.342	1.369	1.390	1.414	1.436	1.497	1.577	1.633	1.713	1.713
1986/87	1.035	1.055	1.090	1.136	1.165	1.208	1.230	1.252	1.283	1.309	1.330	1.352	1.373	1.432	1.507	1.562	1.637	1.637
1987/88	–	1.020	1.054	1.098	1.126	1.168	1.190	1.210	1.241	1.266	1.285	1.307	1.328	1.384	1.457	1.510	1.583	1.583
1988/89	–	–	1.034	1.077	1.105	1.146	1.167	1.187	1.217	1.242	1.261	1.282	1.303	1.358	1.430	1.481	1.553	1.553
1989/90	–	–	–	1.043	1.070	1.109	1.130	1.149	1.178	1.202	1.221	1.241	1.261	1.314	1.384	1.434	1.503	1.503
1990/91	–	–	–	–	1.026	1.064	1.084	1.102	1.130	1.153	1.171	1.191	1.210	1.261	1.328	1.376	1.442	1.442
1991/92	–	–	–	–	–	1.037	1.056	1.075	1.102	1.124	1.142	1.161	1.179	1.229	1.294	1.341	1.406	1.406
1992/93	–	–	–	–	–	–	1.019	1.037	1.063	1.084	1.101	1.120	1.138	1.186	1.249	1.294	1.356	1.356
1993/94	–	–	–	–	–	–	–	1.018	1.043	1.064	1.081	1.099	1.117	1.164	1.226	1.270	1.331	1.331
1994/95	–	–	–	–	–	–	–	–	1.026	1.046	1.063	1.081	1.098	1.144	1.205	1.248	1.309	1.309
1995/96	–	–	–	–	–	–	–	–	–	1.021	1.037	1.054	1.071	1.116	1.175	1.218	1.277	1.277
1996/97	–	–	–	–	–	–	–	–	–	–	1.016	1.033	1.050	1.094	1.152	1.194	1.251	1.251
1997/98	–	–	–	–	–	–	–	–	–	–	–	1.017	1.033	1.077	1.134	1.175	1.232	1.232
1998/99	–	–	–	–	–	–	–	–	–	–	–	–	1.016	1.059	1.115	1.156	1.212	1.212
1999/00	–	–	–	–	–	–	–	–	–	–	–	–	–	1.043	1.098	1.138	1.193	1.193
2000/01	–	–	–	–	–	–	–	–	–	–	–	–	–	–	1.053	1.091	1.144	1.144
2001	–	–	–	–	–	–	–	–	–	–	–	–	–	–	–	1.037	1.087	1.087
2002	–	–	–	–	–	–	–	–	–	–	–	–	–	–	–	–	1.049	1.049
2003 *et seq.*	–	–	–	–	–	–	–	–	–	–	–	–	–	–	–	–	–	1.00

NOTE: No indexation is available for expenditure made within 12 months prior to the date of disposal.

When using the table of multipliers, the year in which the asset was acquired must be identified. This is located in the table in the column headed "Tax Year Expenditure Incurred" (A). The tax year in which the disposal of the chargeable asset took place must subsequently be identified. This is located at the top of the table under the heading "Indexation Factor for Disposals in Tax Year" (B).[1] To identify the indexation factor applicable to the disposal, trace from (A) to (B) to the point of intersection.

Example 25.7

Assuming that all of the following disposals took place in the tax year 2018, identify the relevant indexation factors:

1. *Asset acquired in March 1979.*
   Indexation factor: 4.148.
2. *Asset acquired in December 1983.*
   Indexation factor: 2.003.
3. *Asset acquired in May 2001.*
   Indexation factor: 1.087.
4. *Asset acquired in February 2003.*
   No Indexation.

On careful consideration of the table, a number of issues (some already addressed) become obvious. These are as follows:

- There are no indexation factors for expenditure incurred prior to 1974/75, i.e., prior to 6 April 1974. This is because there is no capital gains tax on gains accruing prior to this date. Where assets were acquired prior to 6 April 1974, the market value of the asset on 6 April 1974 is substituted and indexed in calculating the deductible expenditure for CGT purposes.
- The column of multipliers for 2003 applies for "2003 *et seq*" i.e., it applies for all years after 2003 also. Therefore, the multipliers for 2018 are the same as those in 2003. In fact, the column of multipliers for all future years will be identical to that for 2003. This is because inflation relief has effectively been terminated for inflation attributable to subsequent periods. The Finance Act 2003 provides that there is no inflation relief for expenditure incurred on or after 1 January 2003.
- There is no inflation relief for assets acquired and disposed of in the same income tax year. In fact, the legislation states that there is no indexation relief for expenditure incurred in the 12 months prior to disposal. This was an important point to note prior to 2003, as the multiplier table does not highlight this matter in cases where the acquisition and disposal take place in different income tax years. For example, assume an asset is acquired in December 2002 and disposed of in February 2003.

---

1 Where the table refers to a tax year by making reference to two calendar years, e.g., 1988/89, it is referring to the period from 6 April to the following 5 April, in this case, the period from 6 April 1988 to 5 April 1989. With effect from 6 April 2001 onwards, the tax year-end coincided with the calendar year-end. Prior to this, the tax year ended on 5 April (this gave rise to a transitional 'short tax year' in 2001, starting on 6 April 2001 and ending on 31 December 2001).

No indexation relief can be applied to the cost of this asset because the cost was incurred less than 12 months prior to the date of sale. However, the table correctly indicates that a factor of 1.049 can apply to disposals in 2003 of assets acquired in 2002 and readers may find the table deceptive in such cases.

25.8 Indexation and Enhancement Expenditure

The acquisition cost of an asset together with any allowable incidental acquisition costs are indexed from the tax year in which the expenditure is incurred up to the tax year in which the asset is disposed of. Indexation relief may also be applied to enhancement expenditure. In general, enhancement expenditure is expenditure wholly and exclusively incurred on an asset for the purpose of enhancing the value of the asset. In addition, the expenditure must be reflected in the state or nature of the asset at the time of disposal of the asset. Therefore, to qualify as a deduction for CGT purposes, enhancement expenditure must increase the value of the asset and be reflected in the asset at the date of disposal. Enhancement expenditure is indexed from the date on which it is incurred. Thus, where there is a disposal of a chargeable asset and enhancement expenditure is incurred in some year or years subsequent to the original year of acquisition, two or more indexation factors may be applied when calculating the chargeable gain arising on the disposal.

Example 25.8

Joe acquired a rental property in 1970 for €16,000. Expenses of acquisition amounted to €1,000. He began letting the property immediately. In 1980, an extension was built at a cost of €8,000. In 1982, the local authority forced Joe to take down this extension as proper planning permission had not been obtained. In June 1985, Joe paid a builder €15,000 to construct another extension. Planning and design expenses paid to an architect in connection with this extension amounted to €4,000. In August 1990, the property was vandalised by the tenants and Joe spent €10,000 repairing broken fittings and windows and €2,000 on legal fees in an effort to recover costs from the tenants. In September 2003, Joe added a conservatory to the property at a total cost of €18,500. In February 2018, he sold the property for €550,000. Legal expenses and auctioneer's fees on sale amounted to €4,000 and €6,800 respectively. The market value of the property on 6 April 1974 was €22,000.

Joe's capital gain is calculated as follows:

	€	€
Sales proceeds		*550,000*
Deduct selling expenses (€4,000 + €6,800)		*(10,800)*
		539,200
M.V. 6/4/1974	*22,000*	
Indexed @ 7.528		*(165,616)*
Enhancement 1985/1986	*15,000*	
Expenses	*4,000*	
	19,000	
Indexed @ 1.713		*(32,547)*
Enhancement 2003		*(18,500)*
Gain		*322,537*

Notes:

1. *The expenses of acquisition were not added to the market value on 6 April 1974 on the basis that they are already deemed to be included therein.*

2. *There is no relief for costs incurred on the first extension which was taken down, on the basis that this expenditure was not reflected in the asset at the time of disposal.*

3. *There is no relief for the expenditure incurred on repairs on the basis that these repairs did not constitute improvements/enhancement expenditure and would in any event have been allowable against Case V rental income for income tax purposes.*

4. *There is no indexation of the enhancement expenditure incurred on the conservatory in 2003 as indexation does not apply to expenditure incurred on or after 1 January 2003.*

25.9 Restrictions on the Use of Indexation and the Market Value 1974 Rule

The rationale for indexation and the market value 1974 rule is to ensure that only real gains accruing from 1974 onwards are taxable and only real losses are allowable. A number of exceptions ensure that the application of these rules cannot:

1. increase the actual monetary loss suffered;
2. increase the actual monetary gain realised;
3. turn an actual monetary gain into a book or paper loss;
4. turn an actual monetary loss into a book or paper gain.

Examples of the restrictions on the use of indexation and the market value 1974 rule are set out below.

(1) Where the effect of the rules is to increase the actual loss arising on the disposal of an asset, the rules are ignored and the actual loss is taken as that arising on the disposal.

Example 25.9

An asset acquired in March 1988 for €40,000 is disposed of in December 2018 for €35,000. The gain/loss arising on the disposal is calculated as follows:

	€	€
Proceeds		*35,000*
Cost	*40,000*	
Indexation factor	*1.583*	
Indexed cost		*(63,320)*
Indexed loss		*(28,320)*

The actual monetary loss on this transaction is €5,000. In this case the application of indexation has had the effect of increasing the loss from €5,000 to €28,320. Accordingly, the allowable loss available for offset against any chargeable gains arising in the tax year 2018 and subsequent years is restricted to the monetary loss of €5,000.

(2) Similarly, for a gain, if after applying the rules, the resultant gain is higher than the actual gain arising, the effect of the rules is ignored. The actual gain replaces the indexed gain in the computation.

Example 25.10

An asset purchased in 1973 for €48,000 is disposed of in October 2018 for €50,000. The market value of the asset on 6 April 1974 was €6,000. The gain/loss arising on the disposal is calculated as follows:

	€	€
Proceeds		*50,000*
Cost	*6,000*	
Indexation factor	*7.528*	
Indexed cost		*(45,168)*
Indexed gain		***4,832***

The actual monetary gain is €2,000. Therefore, the taxpayer will be assessed to CGT on the lower actual gain of €2,000.

(3) If the effect of the rules is to turn a monetary gain into an indexed loss, this is treated as if neither a gain nor a loss arose on the transaction. This situation is known as a "no gain/no loss" situation.

Example 25.11

An asset purchased in June 1985 for €50,000 is disposed of in May 2018 for €70,000. The gain/loss arising on the disposal is calculated as follows:

	€	€
Proceeds		*70,000*
Cost	*50,000*	
Indexation factor	*1.713*	
Indexed cost		*(85,650)*
Indexed loss		***(15,650)***

In this example, there is an indexed loss even though a monetary gain arises on the transaction. Accordingly, this is treated as a "no gain/no loss" situation. The monetary gain is not assessable to CGT and the indexed loss is not available for offset against any chargeable gains.

(4) If the effect of the rules is to turn an actual monetary loss into an indexed gain, again this is deemed to be a "no gain/no loss" situation.

Example 25.12

An asset acquired in 1963 for €40,000 is disposed of in July 2018 for €30,000. The market value of the asset at 6 April 1974 was €2,500. The gain/loss arising on the disposal is calculated as follows:

	€	€
Proceeds		*30,000*
Cost	*2,500*	
Indexation factor	*7.528*	
Indexed cost		*(18,820)*
Indexed gain		***11,180***

In this example, there is an indexed gain. However, a monetary loss of €10,000 arises on the transaction. Accordingly, this is treated as a "no gain/no loss" situation. The indexed gain is not assessed to CGT and the monetary loss is not available for offset against any chargeable gains.

In addition to the restrictions outlined above, there is a restriction on the amount of indexation relief available on a disposal of development land. This will be dealt with in detail in Chapter 26 (26.2).

25.10 Transactions between Spouses

s1028(5) TCA97 Section 1028(5) TCA97 provides that the disposal of an asset between spouses is treated as having been made at a price which gives no gain and no loss to the spouse making the disposal. Therefore, the disposal does not give rise to a charge to CGT, nor does it create an allowable loss for the spouse who effects the transfer. Where the asset was acquired by the transferring spouse prior to 6 April 1974, the transfer is treated as being at market value on 6 April 1974. The couple must both be Irish resident and living together. Depending on the circumstances, difficulties may arise in availing of the favourable treatment if one of the spouses is non-resident at the date of transfer.

The spouse who has acquired the asset from his/her partner takes over the period of ownership and the base cost from that partner. For subsequent disposals outside of the parties to the marriage, the acquiring spouse is deemed to have acquired the asset at the same cost and on the same date as the spouse who had originally acquired the asset. Enhancement expenditure incurred by either spouse is taken into consideration and attributed to the spouse making the disposal to the third party. (However, assets acquired from a spouse on death are acquired at market value, see 24.3.2.)

Example 25.13

Mr A acquires a painting in June 1989 for €5,000, which he gives to his wife in July 1993. Mrs A subsequently disposes of the asset for €15,000 in May 2018. At the date of the transfer of the painting in July 1993, the market value of the painting was €10,000.

The effects of the transactions are as follows:

The transfer by Mr A to Mrs A in July 1993 gives rise to a "no gain/no loss" transaction. For subsequent disposals, Mrs A is deemed to have acquired the asset on the original date of acquisition and at the original cost, i.e., in June 1989 for €5,000.

The gain by Mrs A on the subsequent disposal of the asset is calculated as follows:

	€	€
Proceeds		*15,000*
Less:		
Cost 1989/1990	*5,000*	
Indexation factor	*1.503*	
Indexed cost		*(7,515)*
Indexed gain		***7,485***

25.11 Annual Exemption

s601 TCA97 Section 601 TCA97 provides that the first €1,270 of chargeable gains realised by an individual in a year of assessment is exempt from CGT. The annual exemption of €1,270 is only available to individuals. Companies, trustees and partnerships cannot claim the annual exemption. Where an individual does not utilise his/her annual exemption in a year of assessment, the exemption is effectively lost, as it cannot be carried forward. An individual is entitled to claim the annual exemption irrespective of his/her residence position in a year of assessment.

Each spouse is entitled to a separate annual exemption.

25.12 Capital Gains Tax Rate

s28 TCA97 The CGT rate to be applied to the disposal of chargeable assets made on or after the 6 December 2012 is 33%. It should be noted that a rate of 30% applied to the disposal of chargeable assets disposed of between 7 December 2011 and 5 December 2012[2]. The rate of 33% now applies to the disposal of all assets with the exception of foreign life policies and certain offshore funds, where the CGT rate applicable is 40%.

Tax Facts

The CGT rate has increased steadily from 20% in 2008 to its current rate of 33%.

25.13 Part-Disposal of an Asset

The disposal of part of an asset is deemed to be chargeable to capital gains tax. A part-disposal occurs where a portion of an asset is sold. Where a part-disposal of an asset occurs, the sales proceeds are known. However, the cost of the portion of the asset disposed of must be determined to calculate the chargeable gain or allowable loss arising on the transaction.

s557 TCA97 Section 557 TCA97 provides that the portion of the original expenditure, which is allowed as a deduction against the sales proceeds received on the part-disposal, is restricted to the proportion of the original cost of the asset, which the value of the part being disposed of bears, at the date of disposal, to the market value of the full asset. The formula to calculate the acquisition cost of an asset part disposed of is as follows:

2 Between 8 April 2009 and 6 December 2011, the CGT rate was 25%. Between the 15 October 2008 and 7 April 2009, the CGT rate was 22%. Prior to 7 April 2009, the CGT rate was 20%.

$$\text{Original Cost of Asset} \times \frac{A}{A+B}$$

Where:

A = the amount of sales proceeds received on the part-disposal of the asset (or market value if appropriate), and

B = the market value of the remaining part of the asset retained after the disposal.

Incidental costs of acquisition are also apportioned using the above formula where a part-disposal of an asset occurs.

The base cost of the remainder of the asset for the purposes of subsequent disposals is the full original cost less the portion attributed to the previous part disposal.

Where there is a disposal of shares, as each share is identical and of equal value, the fraction applied in the part-disposal formula may be modified to mean the following:

$$\frac{\text{Number of shares sold}}{\text{(Number of shares sold + number of shares retained)}}$$

However, this modification is relevant only in the case of disposals of shares. For other assets, the component parts are not identical and use of a unit basis as opposed to a value basis for apportioning the original cost may yield an incorrect result.

Example 25.14

Paul purchased 10 acres of farmland in December 1990 for €30,000. Incidental costs of acquisition amounted to €2,000. In 2018, he disposed of five acres from this holding for €25,000. The market value of the remainder of the farm at the date of disposal was €75,000. Paul's gain arising on the 2018 part-disposal is calculated as follows:

	€
Sales proceeds	*25,000*
*Costs: (€30,000 + €2,000) * €25,000/(€25,000 + €75,000) = €8,000*	
Indexed @ 1.442	*(11,536)*
	13,464

Note 1: Albeit that half of the land has been sold, only 25% of the original costs are attributed to the part-disposal.

Note 2: The base cost of the remaining five acres for the purposes of subsequent disposals is €24,000, comprising actual acquisition cost of €22,500 and expenses of acquisition of €1,500.

Where a part-disposal of an asset occurs and enhancement expenditure has been incurred in respect of the asset in its entirety, the enhancement expenditure must also be apportioned for CGT purposes. The above formula is also used to apportion enhancement expenditure incurred between the part of the asset disposed of and the asset remaining.

Where enhancement expenditure relates only to a specific part of the asset, which is readily identifiable, no apportionment of the enhancement expenditure is necessary. In this instance, the enhancement expenditure attaches to that part of the asset in respect of which it is incurred. Accordingly, it is only taken into account for disposal purposes when that part of the asset is disposed of.

Example 25.15

Helen purchased an old period residence in Rathmines for €60,000 in March 1994. In June of 1995, she spent €45,000 on converting the entire property into four separate residential units. In August 2002, she sold the two ground-floor units for €600,000. The market value of the remaining first-floor units at this time was €800,000. In September 2018, she sold the remaining two first-floor units for €950,000. She had no other disposals in 2002 and 2018. Helen's capital gains tax liability for 2002 is calculated as follows:

		€
Sales proceeds		*600,000*
Cost 1993/1994:	*€60,000 * €600,000/(€600,000 + €800,000)* *= €25,714* *Indexed @ 1.27*	*(32,657)*
Enhancement 1995/1996:	*€45,000 * €600,000/(€600,000 + €800,000)* *= €19,286* *Indexed @ 1.218*	*(23,490)*
		543,853
Annual exemption		*(1,270)*
		542,583
CGT at 20% (2002)		*108,517*

Helen's capital gains tax liability on the disposal of the remainder of the property in 2018 is calculated as follows:

		€
Sales proceeds		*950,000*
Cost 1993/1994:	*€60,000 – €25,714 = €34,286* *Indexed @ 1.331*	*(45,635)*
Enhancement 1995/1996:	*€45,000 – €19,286 = €25,714* *Indexed at 1.277*	*(32,837)*
		871,528
Annual Exemption		*(1,270)*
		870,258
CGT at 33%		*287,185*

25.14 Losses

s546(2) TCA97 Section 546(2) TCA97 provides that "the amount of a loss accruing on a disposal of an asset shall be computed in the same way as the amount of a gain accruing on a disposal is computed". Therefore, when calculating the gain/loss arising on the disposal of an asset, the same rules apply as to the consideration and the allowable expenditure.

25.14.1 Indexation

There are restrictions on the use of indexation in calculating an allowable loss for CGT purposes. In effect, indexation cannot create or augment a loss.

Example 25.16

Tom purchased shares at a cost of €4,000. He disposed of them for €5,000. Assume that the effect of indexation is to increase the cost of acquisition by €2,000. The computation is as follows:

	€
Acquisition cost	*4,000*
Indexation increase	*2,000*
Deductible cost	*6,000*
Consideration for sale	*(5,000)*
Loss	*1,000*

This is not an allowable loss because it arises entirely due to indexation. The sales proceeds of €5,000 exceed the acquisition cost of €4,000, so there was in fact a gain, but for indexation. The indexation is allowed to eliminate the gain but it cannot create a loss. Therefore, the transaction gives rise to neither a chargeable gain nor an allowable loss.

25.14.2 Use of losses

Losses are relieved in the tax year in which the disposal takes place. They are offset against a chargeable gain prior to the deduction of the annual exemption (Therefore, the offset of capital losses in priority to the annual exemption may sometimes result in the loss of the benefit of the annual exemption). Where the loss (or any portion of it) remains unutilised in the year of disposal, it can be carried forward for offset against the earliest future chargeable gains. Relief cannot be given more than once for capital losses. For example, a taxpayer cannot utilise the losses in the year they arise and carry them forward for relief in subsequent tax years.

Losses cannot be carried back for offset against chargeable gains arising in earlier years of assessment. The restriction on the carry-back of losses, however, does not preclude the offset of losses against gains, which arise earlier than the losses, but where both arise in the same year of assessment.

Example 25.17

John realises a gain on the disposal of an asset in June 2018 and then incurs a loss on a subsequent disposal in December 2018. The loss is available for offset against the gain. This results in only the net gain being assessed to CGT. The offset is available because both the gain and the loss arise in the same year of assessment.

Losses arising in the year of death

There is an exception to the rule that losses cannot be carried back to previous year. It applies to losses arising in the year of the death of a taxpayer. In such cases, the losses can be carried back and offset against any gains arising in the three years of assessment preceding the year of assessment in which the death of the taxpayer arises. This is known as Terminal Loss Relief.

For example, if a taxpayer dies in June 2018, any capital losses arising in the tax year 2018, to the extent unutilised in that year, are available to be carried back and offset against gains arising in any of the three preceding tax years: 2017, 2016 and 2015.

It is important to note that it is only the current year losses (i.e., the losses arising in the year of death) that can be carried back. Any aggregated losses carried forward from earlier years of assessment are not available for relief in this way.

For example, if capital losses arose in 2012 and remain unutilised, they will be carried forward and aggregated with any subsequent losses until they are relieved. However, if the taxpayer dies in the tax year 2018, the aggregated losses carried forward are lost and the only losses available for relief by means of carry-back under a Terminal Loss Relief claim are the losses arising in the year of death.

25.14.3 CGT – initial period (1 January 2018 to 30 November 2018)

For the initial period of 1 January 2018 to 30 November 2018, allowable capital losses incurred in the eleven-month period ended 30 November 2018 and/or any such losses carried forward from 2017 (together with the annual exemption of €1,270) may first be deducted from the chargeable gains accruing in the period.

Example 25.18

Mary disposes of shares in March 2018 and realises a chargeable gain of €4,000. She has unutilised capital losses carried forward of €1,500.

She is due to pay CGT in respect of the chargeable gain she made in March 2018 by 15 December 2018. The capital losses carried forward of €1,500 are first offset against the chargeable gain of €4,000, and her annual exemption of €1,270 is set against the balance of the gain of €2,500. Therefore, Mary is due to pay CGT on the net gain of €1,230 (i.e., €1,230 @ 33% = €406) by 15 December 2018. She will include details of the disposal on the 2018 tax return, which is due to be filed by 31 October 2019.

25.14.4 Connected persons

Where a capital loss arises on the disposal of a chargeable asset to a connected person, the loss is available only for offset against chargeable gains arising on the disposal of other assets to the same connected person.

25.14.5 Non-wasting chattels

Where a non-wasting chattel is disposed of resulting in a capital loss, special rules apply to determine the allowable loss for CGT purposes. This is discussed in detail in paragraph 25.15.2.

25.14.6 Wasting chattels

As noted at 24.4.2, gains on disposals of wasting chattels are exempt, except where the wasting chattel has been used for business purposes and qualified for capital allowances. Losses on wasting chattels are never allowable losses, even in cases where a gain would be taxable. Where a wasting asset that qualifies for capital allowances is disposed of, any loss arising is not allowable for CGT purposes, as relief will have been given for the loss through the capital allowances system and relief cannot be given twice.

25.14.7 Married persons

The general rule is that where a married couple is jointly assessed, surplus losses of one spouse are offset against chargeable gains accruing to the other spouse in a year of assessment. The surplus losses taken into account include current year losses and losses carried forward from prior tax years. The exception to the general rule is where the married couple are separately assessed. In the latter case, it is not possible to transfer any surplus losses between spouses. In this case, the unutilised losses of the spouse are carried forward for offset against any future chargeable gains accruing to the spouse who incurred the losses.

It is possible to elect not to have losses transferred between spouses, where the couple are jointly assessed. The election must be made before 1 April following the end of the year of assessment in which the losses are incurred.

25.14.8 Loss or destruction of an asset

s538 TCA97 Section 538 TCA97 provides that the entire loss, destruction, dissipation, or extinction of an asset constitutes a disposal of that asset for CGT purposes, which may give rise to a loss claim.

25.14.9 An asset of negligible value

In general, only a realised loss is allowable for CGT purposes. However, if the Revenue is satisfied that the value of an asset has become negligible, they may allow loss relief as if the asset had been sold and reacquired at market value, and the loss in fact realised. (s538(2) TCA97).

Where an inspector allows the loss relief claim, the loss arises not on the date at which the asset lost its value, but rather on the date on which the claim for the loss relief is made.

25.14.10 Non-allowable losses

No loss relief is available for losses arising on the disposal of assets which are not chargeable assets for CGT purposes, e.g., government stock. In effect, where a gain arising on the disposal of an asset is not liable to CGT, then a loss incurred on the disposal of such an asset is not available for offset.

Losses available for relief against profits liable to income tax or corporation tax cannot be offset against chargeable gains. Conversely, capital losses are not available for offset against income taxable under corporation tax or income tax.

In relation to a person who is either resident or ordinarily resident in Ireland but not Irish domiciled, he/she is liable to Irish CGT on Irish gains, and foreign gains to the extent the proceeds of such gains are remitted to Ireland.

Where a loss arises on the disposal of an asset situated outside Ireland, no loss relief is available in respect of that loss irrespective of whether the sales proceeds are remitted to Ireland or not.

In the case of an individual liable to Irish CGT on the disposal of specified assets, loss relief is available only in respect of gains arising on the disposal of specified assets.

The Finance Act 2010 introduced a new measure which disallows capital losses if they arise from arrangements whose main purpose is to secure a tax advantage.

The Finance Act 2010 also introduced a further measure which disallows ordinary capital losses from being set against windfall gains. Section 644AB provides that ordinary losses cannot be deducted from a rezoning disposal so the only loss that can be set against a rezoning profit is a loss arising on a rezoning.

25.15 Chattels

The concept of chattels was initially dealt with in Chapter 24. Readers should refer to Chapter 24 (24.4.2) to refresh themselves on the definition of a wasting chattel and a non-wasting chattel. Having considered the calculation of CGT liabilities, the treatment of losses and the part-disposal rules in detail, we are now in a position to revisit the CGT treatment of chattels and to consider each of these issues in turn.

25.15.1 Marginal relief – Non-wasting chattels

The legislation provides for an exemption from CGT where the consideration received on the disposal of a non-wasting chattel does not exceed €2,540. Where the consideration received on the disposal of a non-wasting chattel is slightly in excess of the €2,540 limit, marginal relief exists to restrict the tax payable to 50% of the excess of the consideration over the €2,540 limit. Where the actual CGT liability is lower than the CGT liability after applying the marginal relief, the lower amount will be payable.

Example 25.19

In February 2018, Mr Z disposes of a painting for €3,100. The painting cost €1,600 in the 1993/94 tax year. The CGT liability arising on the transaction is calculated as follows:

	€	€
Sales proceeds		*3,100*
Cost 1993/94	*1,600*	
Indexation factor	*1.331*	
Indexed cost		*(2,130)*
Gain		***970***

CGT at 33% (ignoring the annual exemption): €320.

Marginal relief works to restrict the CGT liability to 50% of the excess of the consideration over the €2,540 limit,

i.e., 50% × (€3,100 – €2,540) = €280.

The actual CGT liability is €320, therefore, the marginal relief provisions would operate to restrict the CGT liability payable to €280.

25.15.2 Losses – non-wasting chattels

Where a non-wasting chattel is disposed of resulting in a capital loss, special rules apply to determine the allowable loss for CGT purposes. Where the consideration is less than €2,540, for the purpose of determining the allowable loss, the consideration is deemed to equal €2,540. In this respect, the loss relief is restricted and is limited to the excess of the cost of the asset over the €2,540 limit. In such cases, it is important to note that any incidental costs incurred on the disposal of the asset are added to the allowable loss and are not deducted from the consideration.

Example 25.20

Mr X acquired a painting for €2,800 in 2018 and he disposed of it in the same tax year for €2,400. A monetary loss of €400 arises on the disposal. However, as the asset disposed of is a non-wasting chattel and the consideration received on the disposal is €2,400, i.e., less than the €2,540 limit, the consideration is deemed to be €2,540, thus creating an allowable loss for CGT purposes of €260, i.e., €2,800 – €2,540.

If, in the above example, €50 of incidental costs were incurred on the disposal of the painting the allowable loss would be €310, i.e., the incidental disposal costs would increase the allowable loss and would not reduce the consideration as normal.

Where a loss arises on the disposal of a non-wasting chattel, a monetary loss will not be converted into a notional gain by virtue of deeming the consideration received on the disposal of the asset to equal €2,540. The purpose of imposing the €2,540 limit in such loss scenarios is to reduce the amount of allowable loss available for offset against chargeable gains.

Example 25.21

Mr Y disposes of a painting for €1,200, which he acquired for €1,800 a number of years ago.

The transaction results in a monetary loss of €600. However, as the asset is a non-wasting chattel and the consideration is less than €2,540, the consideration received on the disposal is deemed to equal €2,540. By imposing the €2,540 limit, a gain of €740 arises and theoretically converts the actual monetary loss of €600 to a notional gain of €740.

As the imposition of the €2,540 limit as consideration converts the monetary loss arising on the disposal to a notional gain, no relief is available for the actual loss suffered, i.e., the loss cannot be offset against any chargeable gains. However, no assessment to CGT will be raised on the notional gain of €740. In effect, this transaction will be treated as a "no gain/no loss" situation.

25.15.3 Sets of non-wasting chattels

Where the non-wasting chattels form a set (e.g., four antique chairs), the exemption from CGT cannot be gained by disposing of each asset separately for less than €2,540 to the same person or connected persons. In such circumstances, the disposal of each of the assets is treated as part of a single transaction for the purpose of applying the CGT exemption for non-wasting chattels. The consideration on each separate disposal is aggregated to determine whether the €2,540 limit applies and whether a CGT liability arises.

The exemption from CGT on the disposal of a non-wasting chattel is only available on the part-disposal of a chattel (i.e., the disposal of a right or interest in the chattel) if, at the time of the disposal, the consideration received together with the value of the interest remaining is less than €2,540. Where the combined value of the consideration and the interest remaining does not exceed €2,540, no charge to CGT arises on the part-disposal. However, where the combined value exceeds €2,540, the normal part-disposal rules apply. Where the combined value does not exceed €2,540 and a loss arises, the loss is restricted.

For the purposes of the operation of the exemption, marginal relief and loss relief provisions, the consideration is taken to be the actual consideration received on the part-disposal together with the value of the interest remaining.

Example 25.22

Mr A sells an interest in a non-wasting chattel for €1,000. The value of the interest remaining in the chattel is €1,300. As the combined value of the consideration and the interest remaining is less than €2,540, the relief applies in full to the part-disposal, i.e., the part-disposal is exempt from CGT.

Example 25.23

Mr B sells an interest in a non-wasting chattel for €1,650. The value of the interest remaining is €1,100. In this example, the aggregate value of the consideration and the interest remaining is €2,750. It is this value that is used in the marginal relief calculation. Accordingly, the maximum tax payable ordinarily would be €105, i.e., ((€2,750 – €2,540) × 50%).

However, as the consideration figure used in the calculation above comprises a value relating to an interest in the asset not disposed of, the maximum tax payable, as calculated, must be divided between the asset disposed of and that remaining. The maximum tax payable on the part-disposal is arrived at by apportioning the amount calculated above by reference to the consideration received on the part-disposal as a percentage of the combined value of the consideration and the interest remaining, i.e., €105 × (€1,650/€2,750) = €63.

26 ADVANCED COMPUTATIONAL ISSUES

Learning Outcomes

On completion of this chapter you will be able to:

- ✓ Explain what is meant by development land and describe the onerous CGT provisions that apply to disposals of development land.
- ✓ Calculate gains arising on the disposal of development land.
- ✓ Apply loss relief where there are disposals of development land.
- ✓ Calculate gains arising on the disposal of shares, whether acquired by direct purchase, under a rights issue, a bonus issue or a scrip issue.
- ✓ Calculate gains arising on the sale of rights under a rights issue.
- ✓ Describe what is meant by a "bed-and-breakfast" transaction and apply the relevant anti-avoidance rules.

26.1 Introduction

The analysis so far has been concerned with the computational rules which generally apply to disposals of chargeable assets. This chapter is concerned with certain refinements to these rules and certain additional considerations, which need to be taken into account in calculating gains and losses on the disposal of specific chargeable assets. The particular assets considered here are development land and shareholdings in companies.

Development land is defined as land, the consideration for the disposal of which exceeds the current use value (normally the agricultural value) of the land, i.e., land with development potential. Where land falls within this category, certain restrictions apply to the normal rules regarding the application of indexation relief and the use of losses. These restrictions and certain other issues relevant to transactions in development land are considered at 26.2.

With regard to disposals of shares, as with all assets, it is necessary to identify the date of acquisition and the cost of the shares for the purposes of preparing a capital gains tax computation. However, shares are unique in that each share of the same class in any company is identical despite the fact that the shares may have been acquired on different dates over a period of time. The most common method by which an individual acquires shares is through a purchase. However, an individual can also increase a shareholding by means of a bonus issue or a rights issue. Special computational rules exist to enable us to identify which shares are the subject matter of the disposal, thereby facilitating the calculation of the base cost of the shares for CGT purposes. The remaining paragraphs in this chapter are concerned with those special rules and also with certain anti-avoidance legislation which applies in the case of disposals of shares.

26.2 Disposals of Development Land

26.2.1 Development land

In general, where there is a disposal of land and the consideration received for the disposal of the land exceeds the current-use value (CUV) of the land, it is development land.

The meaning of development land is not related in any way to the use to which the land is put. It is defined only in terms of its value on disposal.

s648 TCA97 Section 648 TCA97 defines development land as "land in the State, the consideration for the disposal of which, or the market value of which at the time at which the disposal is made, exceeds the current-use value of that land at the time at which the disposal is made, and includes shares deriving their value or the greater part of their value directly or indirectly from such land, other than shares quoted on a Stock Exchange."

The meaning given to current-use value differs in relation to land and shares deriving value from land.

Section 648 TCA97 defines current-use value:

(a) Land:

"in relation to land at any particular time means the amount which would be the market value of the land at that time if the market value were calculated on the assumption that it was at that time and would remain unlawful to carry out any development (within the meaning of Section 3 of the Act of 1963 or, on or after 21 January 2002, within the meaning of Section 3 of the Act of 2000) in relation to the land other than development of a minor nature."

The Acts referred to are the Local Government (Planning and Development) Act 1963 and the Planning and Development Act 2000.

(b) Shares deriving their value from land:

"in relation to shares in a company (being shares deriving their value ... from land other than shares quoted on a Stock Exchange) at any particular time, means the amount which would be the market value of the shares at that time if the market value were calculated on the same assumption, in relation to the land from which the shares so derive value, as is mentioned in paragraph (a)."

Thus, the definition of development land requires the current-use value of the land to be compared with the consideration for the disposal or the market value of the land at the time of disposal. Where the market value of the land which is the subject matter of the disposal exceeds the current-use value of the land, the land constitutes development land and certain onerous restrictions apply.

26.2.2 Rate of charge

Gains accruing on the disposal of development land on or after 6 December 2012 are chargeable at the rate of 33%. Finance Act 2010 introduced s649B to the TCA97, which charged gains on disposal of development land to the extent to which they are attributable to rezoning, to CGT at a special rate of 80% windfall tax. The provision applies to disposals on or after 30 October 2009. Section 31 of Finance Act 2014 abolished this "windfall tax" with effect from 1 January 2015.

26.2.3 Restriction on indexation

In computing a gain or loss on the disposal of development land, on or after 28 January 1982, the relief due in respect of indexation of expenditure incurred is restricted. The effect of the restriction is that indexation is only allowed in respect of the part of the cost (or market value at 6 April 1974) attributable to the current use value at the date of acquisition or 6 April 1974 (if later). In addition, no indexation is allowed on enhancement expenditure in the computation of a gain arising on the disposal of development land.

Example 26.1

Land was acquired in 1972 at a cost of €25,395. Planning permission was obtained in 1973. Market value at 6 April 1974 was €253,947. Enhancement expenditure incurred in 1976 was €76,184. Current-use value at 6 April 1974 was €38,092. The land was sold in March 2018 for €900,000, when its current use value was €350,000.

The gain is calculated as follows:	€	€	€
Sales proceeds (March 2018)			*900,000*
Market Value at 6 April 1974	*253,947*		
CUV at 6/4/1974	*38,092*		
Indexed @ 7.528		*286,757*	
Development Value	*€253,947 – €38,092*	*215,855*	
Enhancement Expenditure		*76,184*	
			(578,796)
Gain			*321,204*

26.2.4 Restriction on use of losses

s653 TCA97 Section 653 TCA97 provides for a restriction on the offset of losses against development land gains where the gain arises on or after 28 January 1982. The only losses which can be offset against gains arising on the disposal of development land are losses accruing on the disposal of development land. Other losses cannot be offset against such gains.

Losses arising on the disposal of development land are not required to be offset against development land gains in priority to other gains.

Students are referred to Section 25.14.2 on the restriction of losses against windfall gains.

26.2.5 Scope of restrictions

Certain other restrictions in the context of "rollover relief" and "principal private residence relief" also apply to development land and these are considered in Chapter 27.

The restrictions relating to development land do not apply to an individual in a year of assessment if the total consideration from disposals of development land in that year do not exceed €19,050.

It should be noted that this exception to the normal rules is given by reference to the amount of the consideration for the disposal. The amount of the actual gain or loss is not relevant.

In applying this rule, husband and wife are treated separately.

26.3 Disposals of Shares

In order to calculate the correct amount of CGT on the disposal of shares, it is of vital importance to firstly identify the make-up of shares being disposed of. This will ensure that the correct cost and indexation is applied.

26.3.1 Share identification rules

Each shareholding acquired in a company on a separate date is treated as the acquisition of a separate asset for capital gains tax purposes.

s580 TCA97 Section 580 TCA97 provides that the principle of first in/first out (FIFO) applies to the disposal of shares of the same class, i.e., the shares acquired on the earliest date are deemed to be sold first.

Example 26.2

Details of Ann's dealings in shares in XYZ Limited are as follows:

Date		*Number*	*Cost*
June 1984	*Acquired*	*100*	*€200*
August 1986	*Acquired*	*200*	*€400*
December 1989	*Sold*	*(50)*	*–*
May 1992	*Acquired*	*150*	*€300*
September 1995	*Sold*	*(300)*	*–*

The 50 shares disposed of in December of 1989 were sold for €600, i.e., €12 per share. The 300 shares disposed of in September 1995 were sold for €900, i.e., €3 per share.

Applying the FIFO rules, the disposals are dealt with as follows:

- *December 1989 disposal – The 50 shares disposed of are deemed to be out of the shares purchased in June 1984. This results in a remaining holding of June 1984 shares in the amount of 50 shares.*
- *September 1995 disposal – The 300 shares disposed of are deemed to be out of different blocks of shares and are deemed to be separate disposals as follows:*
  - *50 shares remaining out of the June 1984 purchase.*
  - *200 shares purchased in August 1986.*
  - *50 shares out of the purchase made in May 1992. This results in a remaining holding of May 1992 shares in the amount of 100 shares.*

For the purpose of tracking the share acquisitions and disposals, it may be easier to draw a table to follow the share transactions. Each shareholding acquired on a separate date is treated as a separate asset and is included in a separate row in the table.

Date	***Original***	***Disposal 1989***	***Subtotal***	***Disposal 1995***	***Subtotal***
June 1984	*100*	*(50)*	*50*	*(50)*	–
August 1986	*200*	–	*200*	*(200)*	–
May 1992	*150*	–	*150*	*(50)*	*100*
				(300)	

Using the table to track what happens to each of these shareholdings in chronological order enables us to clearly identify which asset is being disposed of at each particular point in time.

26.3.2 Part-disposals of shareholdings

The acquisition of each shareholding on a separate date constitutes a separate asset for capital gains tax purposes. Therefore, in Example 26.2, the disposal of 50 shares in 1989 is a part-disposal of the asset acquired in June 1984 and the disposal in 1995 of 300 shares out of three separate shareholdings is deemed to be three separate disposals as follows:

- the disposal of the remainder of the asset acquired in 1984;
- the disposal of all of the asset acquired in 1986;
- the part-disposal of the asset acquired in May 1992, i.e., the disposal of 50 shares out of a total of 150 shares.

We have already considered the CGT treatment of part-disposals in Chapter 25. This commentary merits revisiting in the context of part-disposals of shares.

s557 TCA97 Section 557 TCA97 provides that the portion of the original expenditure which is allowed as a deduction against the sales proceeds received on the part-disposal is restricted to the proportion of the original cost of the asset, which the value of the part being disposed of bears, at the date of disposal, to the market value of the full asset. The formula to calculate the acquisition cost of an asset part-disposed of is as follows:

$$\text{Original Cost of Asset} \times \frac{A}{A + B}$$

Where:

A = the amount of sales proceeds received on the part-disposal of the asset (or market value, if appropriate), and

B = the market value of the remaining part of the asset retained after the disposal.

The base cost of the remainder of the asset for the purposes of subsequent disposals is the full original cost less the portion attributed to the previous part-disposal.

Where there is a disposal of shares, as each share is identical and of equal value, the fraction applied in the part-disposal formula may be modified to mean the following:

$$\frac{\text{Number of shares sold}}{\text{(Number of shares sold + number of shares retained)}}$$

On this basis, Ann's capital gains on each of the relevant disposals in Example 26.2 are as follows:

Capital Gains Computation 1989/1990

Disposal of 50 shares acquired in June 1984

	€
Sales proceeds	*600*
Less:	
*Allowable Cost: €200 * (50/100) = €100*	
Indexed @ 1.210	*(121)*
Chargeable gain	*479*

Capital Gains Computation 1995/1996

(1) *Disposal of remaining 50 shares acquired in June 1984*

	€
Sales proceeds (50 @ €3)	*150*
Less:	
Allowable Cost: €200 – €100 = €100	
Indexed @ 1.425	*(143)*
Chargeable gain	*7*

It is important to note that the 50 shares remaining from the June 1984 acquisition are disposed of in September 1995. Therefore, the disposal of 50 shares involves the disposal of the remainder of an asset, which has been subjected to a previous part-disposal. Readers are referred to Chapter 25 for additional examples on this issue.

(2) Disposal of 200 shares acquired in August 1986

	€
Sales proceeds (200 @ €3)	*600*
Less:	
Allowable Cost: €400	
Indexed @ 1.283	*(513)*
Chargeable gain	*87*

(3) Disposal of 50 shares acquired in May 1992

	€
Sales proceeds (50 @ €3)	*150*
Less:	
Allowable Cost (Note 1): €100 indexed @ 1.063	*(106)*
Chargeable gain	*44*
Total Chargeable Gain	*138*

Note 1:

Cost of 50 shares disposed of is calculated as follows:

€300 × 50/(50 + €100) = €100

26.3.3 Bonus issues

A bonus issue is also known as a scrip issue or a capitalisation. A bonus issue occurs when a company allocates shares to existing shareholders and no consideration is paid by the shareholders for the bonus shares. The issue of the shares is made in direct proportion to the existing shareholdings. For example, a bonus issue of one for two means that a shareholder will receive one new share for every two shares already held.

For the purposes of the FIFO rule, shares acquired by means of a bonus issue are deemed to have been acquired on the same date as the original holding in respect of which they are issued. The bonus shares form part of this holding for subsequent disposal purposes and accordingly, the cost per share of the original holding is diluted as a result of the bonus issue. The reason for this is that the total number of shares has increased while the original cost of the shares remains the same.

Example 26.3

Ann acquired 1,000 shares in ABC Ltd in July 1995 at a cost of €2 per share, i.e., €2,000 in total. In December 1998, ABC Ltd made a bonus issue of one for five (i.e., one new share for every five shares held at that date). As a result of the bonus issue, Ann now holds 1,200 shares at a cost of €2,000, i.e., €1.67 per share. In October 2003, Ann purchases 800 shares at a cost of €4,000. Ann subsequently disposes of 1,500 shares in May 2018 for €6 each.

Prior to Ann's disposal in May 2018, her shareholding was made up as follows:

Deemed Date of Acquisition	*Number*	*Cost*
July 1995	*1,200**	*€2,000*
October 2003	*800*	*€4,000*

** Includes the bonus issue of 200 shares.*

The disposal of the 1,500 shares is deemed to come out of the following holdings:

- *1,200 shares acquired in July 1995 for €2,000; and*
- *300 shares out of the holding of 800 shares acquired in October 2003 for €4,000.*

The disposal of 1,500 shares gives rise to two separate disposals of two separate assets, and therefore, two separate computations must be prepared, as each acquisition of shares in ABC Ltd is treated as the acquisition of a separate asset.

Date	*Original*	*Bonus*	*Subtotal*	*Disposal*	*Subtotal*
July 1995	*1,000*	*200*	*1,200*	*(1,200)*	–
October 2003	*800*	–	*800*	*(300)*	*500*
				(1,500)	

Capital Gains Computation 2018

	€
Sales proceeds (1,200 @ €6)	*7,200*
Less:	
Allowable cost: €2,000 indexed @ 1.277	*(2,554)*
Chargeable gain	*4,646*
Sales proceeds (300 @ €6)	*1,800*
Less:	
*Allowable cost: €4,000 × 300/800 = €1,500**	*(1,500)*
Chargeable gain	*300*
Total Chargeable Gain	*4,946*

** No indexation is available, as indexation does not apply to expenditure incurred on or after 1 January 2003.*

26.3.4 Rights issues

Disposals of shares acquired under a rights issue

s584 TCA97 Section 584 TCA97 deals with the capital gains tax treatment of re-organisations of share capital including rights issues. A rights issue occurs when a company offers its existing shareholders the opportunity to purchase additional shares at a discount on the market value of the shares. A rights issue is similar to a bonus issue in that it is offered in proportion to the shareholders' existing holdings. However, it differs in that the shareholders must subscribe some amount for the shares offered under the rights issue; in the case of a bonus issue, the bonus shares are granted without requiring any additional outlay from the shareholders. A rights issue generally takes place when a company is seeking to raise funds; it gives the company the necessary cash injection.

For the purposes of the FIFO rule, the treatment of shares acquired under a rights issue is the same as for a bonus issue, i.e., the shares are deemed to be part of the original holding in respect of which they are allocated. Therefore, for disposal purposes, the shares acquired under a rights issue merge with the shares of the original holding. The price paid by the shareholders for shares acquired under a rights issue is treated as enhancement expenditure incurred in respect of the original shareholding.

We have already observed, in Chapter 25 (25.8) that enhancement expenditure is indexed upwards from the date on which it is incurred. Thus, for the purposes of indexation, the enhancement expenditure (i.e., the cost of the rights issue) is indexed up from the date which the enhancement expenditure is incurred (i.e., the date of the rights issue). Where such enhancement expenditure is incurred on or after 1 January 2003, no indexation will apply.

It is important to repeat the use of the different dates when it comes to the treatment of shares acquired under rights issue:

- For FIFO purposes, the rights issue shares are deemed to have been acquired on the same date as the original holding;
- For indexation purposes, the expenditure on the rights issue shares is treated as enhancement expenditure, and the appropriate indexation to apply is the indexation that relates to the date on which the expenditure was actually incurred.

Example 26.4

Mary acquired 2,000 shares in XYZ Ltd in July 1996 for €4,000, i.e., at a cost of €2 per share. In January 1998, Mary acquired a further 1,000 shares for €500, i.e., €0.50 per share. In February 1999, XYZ Ltd made a rights issue of one for two (i.e., one new share for every two shares held) at €1 per share. Mary takes up the rights issue, and she acquires 1,500 shares at a cost of €1,500. Mary disposes of 4,000 shares in June 2018 for €3 each.

Mary's shareholding is made up as follows (prior to the disposal):

Date	***Original***	***Rights***	***Subtotal***	***Disposal***	***Subtotal***
July 1996	*2,000*	*1,000*	*3,000*	*(3,000)*	–
January 1998	*1,000*	*500*	*1,500*	*(1,000)*	*500*
				(4,000)	

The shares acquired under the rights issue are split between the original shareholdings. The disposal of 4,000 shares is treated as two separate disposals. The disposal is deemed to come out of the following holdings:

- *3,000 shares acquired in July 1996; and*
- *1,000 shares out of the holding of 1,500 shares acquired in January 1998 (leaving 500 shares of this holding remaining).*

Capital Gains Computation 2018

Capital Gain on Disposal of 1996 Holding

	€
Sales proceeds (3,000 × €3)	*9,000*
Less:	*2,784*
Original cost: €4,000 indexed @ 1.251	*(5,004)*
Rights issue: €1,000 indexed @ 1.212 (enhancement expenditure)	*(1,212)*
Chargeable gain	*2,784*

Capital Gain on Part-Disposal of 1998 Holding

		€
Sales proceeds (1,000 × €3)		*3,000*
Less:		
Original cost €500 ×	*1,000 = 333* *1,500*	
	Indexed @ 1.232	*(410)*
Rights issue €500 × (enhancement expenditure)	*1,000 = 333* *1,500*	
	Indexed @ 1.212	*(404)*
Chargeable gain		*2,186*
Total Chargeable Gain		*4,970*

Scrip dividends

A company may offer its shareholders the option to take additional shares in the company in lieu of a cash dividend. Dividends taken in this way are known as scrip dividends. The capital gains tax treatment of disposals of shares acquired in lieu of dividends is the same as for disposals of shares acquired under a rights issue. Therefore, for FIFO purposes, the shares acquired attach to the original holding of shares in respect of which they are issued, and the cost of the shares, i.e., the dividend foregone, is treated as enhancement expenditure.

Example 26.5

Bernadette acquired 1,000 shares in Setel Limited on 1 January 2000 for €2,000. On 30 June 2003, a dividend of €0.50 per share is proposed or alternatively, a scrip dividend of one share for every four shares held is offered. Bernadette opts for the scrip dividend and the shares are issued in July. On 30 May 2018, Bernadette sells 625 shares for €3,000.

Prior to the disposal, Bernadette's shareholding is comprised as follows:

Date	*Original*	*Scrip*	*Subtotal*	*Disposal*	*Subtotal*
January 2000	*1,000*	*250*	*1,250*	*(625)*	*625*

The scrip issue increases the size of the original holding to 1,250 and Bernadette sells half of this holding on 30 May 2018.

The cost of the scrip issue, i.e., the enhancement expenditure laid out at the date of issue, is the dividend foregone, i.e., €500 (1,000 × €0.50 per share).

Assuming no other disposals in 2018, Bernadette's chargeable gain for 2018 is as follows:

	€
Sales proceeds	*3,000*
Cost: €2,000 × (625/1,250) = €1,000 Indexed @ 1.193	*(1,193)*
Scrip: €500 × (625/1,250) (Note)	*(250)*
Chargeable gain	*1,557*

Note: There is no indexation of the cost of the scrip issue (i.e., the enhancement expenditure), as indexation does not apply to expenditure incurred on or after 1 January 2003.

Disposal of rights

Shareholders entitled to subscribe for rights issues may elect to sell their rights. In such circumstances, the cash sum received in respect of the sale of the rights is a capital distribution and the original holding is deemed to have been disposed of in part. This will require the application of the formula A/(A + B) to the original cost of the Shareholding. In this case,

A = proceeds of the sale of rights, and

B = market value of the remainder of the holding, i.e., ex-rights price of the shares.

Example 26.6

Tom acquired 5,000 shares in ABC Limited on 1 May 2000 for €10,000. In July 2018, the company makes a rights issue of two for five, which may be exercised at a cost of €3.00 per share. Tom sells all of his rights for €1 per share. The ex-rights price per share is €4.

Tom's capital gains computation for 2018 is as follows:

	€
July 2018 Consideration: 5,000 × 2/5 × €1	*2,000*
Cost 2000/01: €10,000 × 2,000/(2,000 + (5,000 × 4)) = 909 Indexed @ 1.144	*(1,040)*
Gain	*960*

26.3.5 Bed-and-Breakfast transactions

Loss relief is only available for realised capital losses, i.e., there is no relief available unless the asset which has fallen in value is actually sold. In the absence of anti-avoidance legislation, losses on shareholdings could be realised without, in substance, disposing of the shares, by simply putting in place a succession of paper transactions. Such transactions are known as "bed-and-breakfast" transactions and are very restricted by anti-avoidance legislation. The anti-avoidance legislation is two-fold: it targets situations where shares are reacquired within four weeks of their disposal and also situations where shares are disposed of within four weeks of acquisition. The provisions also apply where shares disposed of by one spouse are reacquired by the other.

Acquisition of shares within four weeks of disposal

s581 TCA97 Section 581 TCA97 was introduced to prevent individuals from using "bed-and-breakfast" transactions to create artificial losses for offset against chargeable gains. An example best illustrates the anti-avoidance provisions where there is an acquisition of shares within four weeks of disposal.

Example 26.7

Sharon acquired 10,000 shares in ABC plc on 1 December 2000 for €20,000, i.e., €2 per share. On 1 March 2018, the shares are quoted at €1 each. Sharon is confident that the share price will rise, and therefore, she does not wish to dispose of her shareholding in ABC plc. However, she would like to claim loss relief for the "paper loss" she has suffered as a result of the share price movement. The only way to realise a loss is for her to dispose of the shareholding. She makes an arrangement with her stockbroker whereby she disposes of the shares on 1 March 2018 for €1 per share and she repurchases 10,000 shares in ABC plc within the next few days.

As a result of this, Sharon realises an "artificial loss" of €10,000 on the disposal of her shareholding in ABC plc which, in the absence of anti-avoidance legislation, would be available for offset against any chargeable gains she realises in the 2018 tax year. In addition, she will still own 10,000 shares in the company.

The legislation stipulates that where a disposal and reacquisition of the same class of shares takes place within four weeks, the loss arising on the disposal of the shares can only be set against a subsequent gain arising on the disposal of the shares that have been reacquired. Therefore, the loss cannot be offset against other chargeable gains realised in the tax year. Thus, in Example 26.7 above, Sharon may not claim relief for the artificial loss of €10,000 against gains on other assets disposed of in 2018.

Disposal of shares within four weeks of acquisition

Section 581 TCA97 also provides that the FIFO rule does not apply where shares of the same class are bought and sold within a period of four weeks. Where shares are sold within four weeks of the date of acquisition, for capital gains tax purposes, the shares disposed of are identified with the shares of the same class acquired within the preceding four-week period. This is known as the last in/first out (LIFO) rule.

This provision effectively covers situations where the "buy-back" for the purposes of "bed-and-breakfast" transactions precedes the disposal.

Example 26.8

Mary acquired 1,000 ordinary shares in DEF Limited in May of 1997 for €5,000. On 1 August 2000, she bought 500 shares for €1,250. On 15 July 2018, she bought 1,000 shares for €500. On 1 August 2018, she sold 1,000 shares for €495.

If we apply the normal FIFO rules in this case, Mary will be deemed to be selling the 1,000 shares, which she acquired in May of 1997 and she will have a loss of €4,505 (i.e., €495 – €5,000). However, because the shares are being sold within four weeks of their acquisition, the LIFO rules apply and Mary is deemed to be selling the shares acquired most recently. Accordingly, the loss is restricted to €5 (€495 – €500) and there is no benefit in engaging in such bed-and-breakfast transactions.

The usual FIFO rules will apply to disposals of the balance of the 1,500 shares.

There is no restriction on the losses arising in Example 26.8 above. The loss is limited by the LIFO rules to €5 and this may be used in the normal way. The provision which provides that the loss arising on the disposal of shares can only be set against subsequent gains arising on the disposal of the shares reacquired only applies where the sale precedes the repurchase.

27 CGT RELIEFS

Learning Outcomes

On completion of this chapter you will be able to:

- ✓ Identify the circumstances in which principal private residence relief applies.
- ✓ Calculate the partial principal private residence relief which applies when a residence has not been occupied by the claimant for all of the period of ownership.
- ✓ Understand the restrictions which apply when a principal private residence has development potential.
- ✓ Describe the relief available on the transfer of a site by a parent to a child.
- ✓ Explain how the relief on the transfer of a site to a child may be clawed back in certain circumstances.
- ✓ Describe the conditions that need to be satisfied to qualify for rollover relief and explain the form that this relief takes.
- ✓ Explain why the rollover relief provisions will continue to have implications for a number of years and identify any deferred gains as they become payable in future years.
- ✓ Describe the conditions that need to be satisfied to qualify for relief from CGT on incorporation.
- ✓ Calculate the amount of any gain deferred as relief from CGT on incorporation.
- ✓ Calculate the gain arising on a subsequent disposal of shares where relief from CGT on incorporation had previously been claimed.
- ✓ Describe the conditions that need to be satisfied to avail of retirement relief in respect of disposals of both business assets of an unincorporated entity and shares in an incorporated entity.
- ✓ Explain the form that retirement relief takes and calculate the amount of any marginal relief in the case of disposals of both business assets of an unincorporated entity and shares in an incorporated entity.
- ✓ Explain the retirement relief measures that apply on disposals to a child of the claimant and describe how this relief may be clawed back in certain circumstances.
- ✓ Describe the circumstances in a disposal of a 5% or greater shareholding can be exempt from Corporation Tax.

27.1 Introduction

In Chapter 24, we observed that the gains on disposals of certain assets are exempt from CGT. The exemptions that we have already considered are very straightforward and in general, do not involve special computational rules. A number of additional reliefs are available in certain circumstances where detailed conditions are satisfied. These reliefs frequently involve exemption of only a portion of the gain from CGT and the calculation of the amount of relief available is generally quite complicated. The purpose of this chapter is to consider these more advanced reliefs in some detail as follows:

- paragraph 27.2 is concerned with principal private residence relief;
- paragraph 27.3 considers the relief available on the transfer of a site to a child of the owner;
- paragraph 27.4 deals with rollover relief,[1] i.e., relief from CGT on the disposal of certain assets where the proceeds are reinvested in replacement assets;
- paragraph 27.5 considers the relief available on conversion of a sole trade operation to a limited company;
- paragraph 27.6 deals with retirement relief; and
- paragraph 27.7 deals with relief on the disposal of shares in other companies by holding companies.

27.2 Principal Private Residence Relief

s604 TCA97 Broadly speaking, the legislation provides for an exemption from CGT on the gain arising on the disposal by an individual of his or her principal private residence together with gardens or grounds of up to one acre. A person may not have more than one principal private residence at any one time. Furthermore, where a married couple are living together, they may only have one principal private residence for the purposes of the relief. Individuals and married couples who own two dwelling houses must therefore nominate which one should qualify for relief by giving notice to the Inspector of Taxes in writing within two years of acquiring the second property. Such an election is only valid with the agreement of the Inspector. The relief extends to properties owned by the taxpayer and occupied by a dependent relative of the taxpayer free of charge. The dependent relative must be the widowed parent of either the taxpayer or his or her spouse. Other dependent relatives may also qualify provided they are incapacitated by old age or infirmity.

The principal private residence exemption only applies where the property has been occupied by the individual as his or her main residence throughout the period of

1 Although rollover relief was effectively terminated by Finance Act 2003, it may continue to have implications for the calculation of CGT liabilities for a number of years.

ownership. There are some exceptions to this requirement and these are considered in greater detail in 27.2.1 to 27.2.3.

27.2.1 Period of ownership

Where an individual has not occupied the property as his principal private residence during his entire period of ownership, part of the gain may be chargeable. In such cases, the exempt part of the gain is arrived at using the following formula:

$$\text{Chargeable gain} \times \frac{\text{Total period of occupation}}{\text{Total period of ownership}}$$

When working out the above formula, it is important to bear in mind a few issues. Firstly, in making the calculations for total period of occupation and total period of ownership, any period of occupation or ownership before 6 April 1974 is ignored.

Secondly, in arriving at the total period of occupation (after 5/4/1974), the legislation sets out certain circumstances in which the property is deemed to be so occupied. These are as follows:

Foreign employment

s604(5)(b)(i) TCA97 "Any period of absence (after 5/4/1974) throughout which the individual worked in an employment or office all the duties of which were performed outside the State", may be deemed to be a period of occupation for principal private residence relief purposes.

Condition of employment

s604(5)(b)(ii) TCA97 Any period (after 5/4/1974) of absence, not exceeding four years (or periods of absence which together do not exceed four years), throughout which the individual was prevented from residing in his/her house because of any condition imposed on him/her by his/her employer requiring him/her to reside elsewhere may be deemed to be a period of occupation of the property as a principal private residence provided the condition was reasonably imposed to secure the effective performance of his/her duties.

S604(5) TCA97 Note that in both the above instances, the word 'may' was used, signifying that it is not enough to satisfy the criteria set out above in order for the periods to be deemed periods of occupation. Both of the above periods of absence will only be treated as a period during which the house was occupied by the individual as a principal private residence "if both before and after the period, the dwelling house (or the part in question) was occupied by the individual as his or her only or main residence".

In addition, for both of the above periods to qualify as periods of deemed occupation, it is a requirement that the taxpayer should have no other residence eligible for the relief at the time.

Last 12 Months

The last 12 months of ownership is deemed to be a period of residential occupation for the purpose of calculating the relief. The "last 12 months" deemed residence applies without any other conditions provided the property is, or was, (at some time), the taxpayer's main residence.

However, it is important to note the interaction between this deemed period of occupation and the criteria for the previous two deemed periods of occupation mentioned above. As already observed, to avail of the deemed period of residence during an absence caused by employment, it is necessary for the taxpayer to reside in the premises after the absence. The "deemed" period of residence in the last twelve months of ownership is not sufficient in itself to satisfy this condition; there must be an actual period of residence.

In summary, "period of ownership" and consequently "period of occupation" cannot include any period prior to 6 April 1974 and certain periods are deemed periods of occupation albeit that the individual does not actually reside in the house during those periods. Consequently, the formula used to calculate the exempt portion of the gain can be expanded:

$$\text{Chargeable gain} \times \frac{\text{Total period of actual and "deemed" occupation after 5 April 1974}}{\text{Total period of ownership after 5 April 1974}}$$

The following example should illustrate how the exempt portion of the chargeable is calculated:

Example 27.1

John is unmarried. He bought a house in Dublin for IR£10,000 on 1 January 1970. It was his home until 30 September 1981 when he was required to move to Cork to set up a new branch of his employer's business. He stayed in a rented house in Cork until 31 December 1983 and during that period let his Dublin home. On his return, he reoccupied his Dublin home. On 31 March 1994, he moved to Limerick permanently and let the house in Dublin. On 31 March 2018, he sold the house for €360,000. He has no other chargeable gains for 2018.

The market value of the property at 6 April 1974 was IR£25,000 (€31,743).

The chargeable gain is calculated as follows:

Period of Ownership	***Years***
6/4/1974 to 31/3/2018	*44*
Period of Occupation as residence	***Years***
Actual – 6/4/1974 to 30/9/1981	*7.50*
Deemed – 30/9/1981 to 31/12/1983	*2.25*
Actual – 1/1/1984 to 31/3/1994	*10.25*
Deemed – 1/4/2017 to 31/3/2018 (last year)	*1.00*
Total	*21.00*

CGT – 2018	*€*
Sale price	*360,000*
Market value 6 April 1974 (as indexed)	
€31,743 indexed @ 7.528	*(238,961)*
Total gain	*121,039*
Less: Principle private residence relief: €121,039 × 21/44	*(57,769)*
Chargeable gain	*63,270*
Less: Annual exemption	*(1,270)*
Taxable gain	*62,000*
CGT @ 33%	*20,460*

Note: In calculating the principal private residence relief, all periods of both occupation and ownership prior to 6 April 1974 are ignored.

27.2.2 Not wholly used as principal private residence

In addition, principal private residence relief may be lost in whole or in part where the building or a portion of it is/was used for trade or professional purposes. In these circumstances, it may be necessary to apportion the gain between the exempt and non-exempt elements. This issue is illustrated in the example below.

Example 27.2

On 1 July 2018, Grace sold a house in Dublin for €500,000. The house, which is on a 0.5-acre site, was purchased on 1 October 1988 for €60,000. Throughout Grace's period of actual occupation, she used a portion of the house (25% of the total area) exclusively for the purposes of a trade.

Details of the use of the house during the period of ownership are as follows:

1/10/1988 – 30/6/1995	*It was Grace's only private residence, with 25% used for the purposes of her trade.*
1/7/1995 – 31/12/1998	*It was let to a third party. During this period, Grace was employed by a company in France and lived in rental accommodation.*
1/1/1999 – 31/12/2001	*It was Grace's only private residence and 25% of the house was again used for the purposes of her trade.*
1/1/2002 onwards	*The house was again let to a third party and Grace purchased another property which became her principal private residence.*

The chargeable gain is calculated as follows:

Period of ownership	***Years***
1/10/1988 to 30/6/2018	*29.75*
Period of occupation as principal private residence	***Years***
Actual – 1/10/1988 to 30/6/1995	*6.75*
Deemed – 1/7/1995 to 31/12/1998	*3.50*
Actual – 1/1/1999 to 31/12/2001	*3.00*
Deemed – 1/7/2017 to 30/6/2018 (last year)	*1.00*
Total	*14.25*

CGT – July 2018	**€**	**€**
Sale price		*500,000*
Cost	*60,000*	
Indexed @ 1.553		*(93,180)*
		406,820
Deduct principal private residence relief (Note 1)		*(146,148)*
		260,672
Less annual exemption		*(1,270)*
Taxable gain		*259,402*
CGT at 33%		*85,603*
(Note 1)		
Total gain		*406,820*
Less: Gain attributable to office (25%)		*(101,705)*
Gain attributable to residence		*305,115*
Principal private residence relief: €305,115 × (14.25/29.75)		*146,148*

27.2.3 Restriction in the case of development land

S604(12) TCA97

The relief given to an individual on the sale of his/her residence does not apply to the part of the gain reflecting "development value". In such instances, the gain on the disposal of the property is calculated in the normal way (taking into account any restrictions in the calculations appropriate to development land), and the resulting gain is reduced by a restricted principal private residence relief. The relief is calculated only by reference to the gain which would have arisen if the property was both bought and sold for its value solely as a residence (i.e., ignoring its development value).

Example 27.3

Claire bought a property on 31 January 1987 for its residence value of €88,882. Incidental costs of acquisition amounted to €10,745. The asset was sold to a developer on 28 February 2018 for €900,000. Its value as a residence at that time was €300,000. The incidental costs of disposal were €15,000. Throughout her period of ownership of the property, it was her principal private residence.

The gain chargeable for February 2018 is calculated as follows:

		€	**€**
Sale proceeds (development land)			*900,000*
Cost (current-use value)		*88,882*	
Indexed @ 1.637		*145,500*	
Incidental costs	*– acquisition €10,745*		
	indexed @ 1.637	*17,590*	
	– disposal	*15,000*	*(178,090)*
GAIN			*721,910*
Less principal private residence relief	(See below)		*(131,910)*
Chargeable gain			*590,000*

Principal private residence relief:	*€*	*€*
Sale price as residence		*300,000*
"Residence" cost (as indexed above)	*145,500*	
Incidental cost of acquisition (as indexed above)	*17,590*	
Incidental cost of disposal (apportioned – see Note)		
€15,000 × €300,000/€900,000	*5,000*	*(168,090)*
"Residence" gain (qualifying for full relief)		*131,910*

Note: In calculating the gain that would arise on the sale solely as a residence, the incidental costs of a disposal are apportioned proportionately.

Example 27.4

If, in Example 27.3, the cost price of the residence in January 1987 was €177,764, of which the residential current-use value was €88,882, the computation would be as follows:

Development land computation:	*€*	*€*
Sales proceeds (development land)		*900,000*
Indexed current-use value €88,882 @ 1.637	*145,500*	
Indexed incidental acquisition costs – €10,745 × (€88,882/€177,764) @ 1.637	*8,795*	
Development potential (no indexation relief) (177,764 − 88,882)	*88,882*	
Acquisition costs referable to development potential (no indexation) − €10,745 × (€88,882/€177,764)	*5,372*	
Incidental costs of disposal	*15,000*	*(263,549)*
Gain		*636,451*
Less principal private residence relief (see below)		*(140,705)*
Gain taxable		*495,746*
Principal private residence relief:		
Sale price as residence		*300,000*
"Residence" cost (indexed) €88,882 @ 1.637	*145,500*	
Incidental cost of acquisition proportionate to residence cost − €10,745 × (€88,882/€177,764) @ 1.637	*8,795*	
Incidental cost of disposal €15,000 × (€300,000/€900,000)	*5,000*	
		(159,295)
(Residence) gain (qualifying for full relief)		*140,705*

27.3 Transfer of a Site to a Child

s603A TCA97 s93FA 01 s53FA 07 A CGT exemption applies on the transfer by a parent to a child (or certain foster children) of land, provided certain conditions are met. The exemption applies in respect of disposals on or after 6 December 2000.

The conditions that must be met are:

- the open market value of the land being transferred must not exceed €500,000 (€254,000 for disposals prior to 5 December 2007) at the date of transfer;

- the area of the site must not exceed 1 acre;
- the transfer must be for the purpose of enabling the child to construct on the land a dwelling house to be occupied by the child as his/her only or main residence.
- the €500,000 limit applies where both parents make a simultaneous disposal of a site to their child.

There is a claw-back of the relief if the child disposes of the land at a time when a dwelling house has not been built on it. The claw-back also applies where the dwelling house has been built but has not been occupied by the child as his or her only or main residence for a period of three years. In these circumstances, the gain, which would have arisen to the parent on the transfer, accrues instead to the child and is levied on the child at the time of his or her disposal of the property. This claw-back could result in the child suffering a 'double hit' to CGT.

Note that this relief is normally a 'once-off' relief. However, if the child suffers a claw-back of the relief, a subsequent transfer of a site to the child could also then qualify for relief (assuming the criteria are satisfied).

Example 27.5

Joe Smith owns a farm of land in Galway. On 1 January 2007, he transferred a one-acre site to his son to enable the son to build a house on the site for use as a principal private residence. At the date of transfer, the site was worth €70,000. Joe's CGT allowable cost of the site was €8,000.

The child, Peter, built a house upon the site and lived in it as his principal private residence for ten years from 2008. As his family was growing, he felt he needed a larger house and wished to build a new house rather than extending the existing house. Accordingly, he sold the site for a taxable gain of €50,000 and purchased a further site from his father in 2018. The market value of the second site at the date of its purchase by Peter from Joe in 2018 was €160,000. Peter built a new house on it and resided in it as his principal private residence.

The transfer of the first site from Joe to Peter satisfies all the criteria for CGT relief. In addition, because Peter occupied the house as his main residence for more than three years, no claw-back arises on his sale of the house in 2018. As no claw-back arose on the disposal of the first site, there is no CGT relief available on the disposal of the second site from Joe to Peter in 2018.

Example 27.6

If, in Example 27.5. Peter had disposed of the property in 2010, before it had been occupied by him for a three-year period as his principal private residence, a claw-back of the relief originally claimed by Joe would arise. As a result, Peter in effect would suffer a 'double hit' to CGT. The gain on which Joe received relief in 2007 (a chargeable gain of €62,000) would have been treated as accruing to Peter. In addition, he would be liable to the CGT arising on the gain from his disposal (€50,000).

However, because of the claw-back of the relief on the first disposal, relief under s603A TCA97 is now available to Joe in relation to the second transfer in 2018. Depending on values, it might be a better result all around to have crystallised the first gain, and make the relief available in respect of the second gain.

27.4 Rollover Relief

In certain circumstances the legislation gave relief from an immediate charge to tax which would otherwise occur on the disposal of an asset where the consideration for the disposal of the asset was reinvested. Broadly speaking, the relief was available in respect of trading assets, certain shares, certain rental properties and compulsory purchase orders. The relief generally applied to sole traders and companies, but public authorities, bodies promoting games or sports (e.g., the GAA), farmers, persons occupying woodlands on a commercial basis with a view to profits, trade associations, non-profit-making bodies, employees and persons carrying on a profession were also eligible. In general, no relief was available in respect of gains on the disposal of "development land". However, there was an exception in the case of disposals of such land by bodies promoting amateur games or sports (e.g., the GAA) and also in the case of certain compulsory purchase orders.

Finance Act 2003 restricted the relief to disposals before 4 December 2002 (with limited transitional provisions). However, as the relief simply involved a deferral of the payment of the CGT liability, CGT liabilities relieved under the rollover relief provisions will continue to arise for some time into the future and accordingly, an understanding of the provisions that applied prior to 4 December 2002 is very important. The analysis here is concerned only with the rollover relief which applied to business assets.

27.4.1 Conditions

In order for the relief to apply, certain conditions had to be met. These were as follows:

- The old and the new asset, i.e., the asset sold and the replacement had to belong to one of the following classes:

  (i) land and buildings occupied as well as used only for the purpose of the trade, generally excluding development land;

  (ii) plant and machinery;

  (iii) goodwill.

  Financial assets also qualified for the relief where the assets were disposed of by a body established for the purposes of promoting amateur sports.

  It was not necessary for the old and the new asset to belong to the same class of asset, e.g., a reinvestment in plant and machinery could qualify the owner for rollover relief on a disposal of land.

- The new assets had to be used in the same or in a similar trade carried on concurrently in a different locality. An exception existed where a person had been trading for 10 years or longer and ceased to trade but recommenced a different trade within two years. In these circumstances, both trades were regarded as the same for the purposes of rollover relief. Thus, gains arising on the disposal of the old trade could be deferred by investing in qualifying assets in the successor trade.

- In general, the reinvestment of the proceeds had to take effect within the period beginning 12 months before and ending three years after the date of the disposal or within such longer time as otherwise allowed at the discretion of the Revenue Commissioners.

27.4.2 Form of relief

Unlike some other reliefs that give relief by deeming "no disposal" of the asset with a corresponding adjustment to the qualifying cost of the replacement asset, with rollover relief, the gain was calculated in the normal way and simply held in abeyance until the happening of a specified future event. The gain on the "old" assets is deferred until the "new" replacement assets cease to be used for the trade. The relief only applies where the old assets are disposed of before 4 December 2002 (with, depending on the facts, an extension of the period up to 31 December 2003).

Where only a portion of the disposal proceeds was reinvested, deferral of any gain arising was restricted to the amount by which the gain exceeded the proceeds not reinvested. Where the disposal proceeds not reinvested was equal to, or exceeded the gain, no relief could be claimed. In effect, each euro of proceeds not reinvested triggered €1 of chargeable gains, up to the amount of the gain.

Example 27.7

Alan disposed of his factory premises for €470,000 on 1 December 2002 giving rise to a chargeable gain of €60,000. He spent €450,000 on a new premises.

As only part of the sales proceeds was reinvested, the gain deferred on the 2002 disposal is restricted to the amount by which the gain exceeds the amount not reinvested:

	€
Chargeable gain arising	*60,000*
Proceeds not reinvested	*(20,000)*
Deferred gain	*40,000*
Taxable gain 2002 (€20,000 – annual allowance €1,270)	*18,370*
Taxed at 20% (the CGT rate applicable in 2002)	*3,674*

The deferred gain of €40,000 will be chargeable when the new premises ceases to be used by Alan for the purposes of the trade.

27.4.3 Significance in future years

Section 597(4)(b) TCA97 extends the deferral further where the "new" replacement assets were themselves sold and the sale proceeds were used to acquire "further new" replacement assets. Thus, if the sales proceeds of the new premises were invested in further new qualifying assets, the gain of 40,000 might be further deferred, and so on.

Finance Act 2003 did not change this part of the relief, allowing the continued deferral where the original gain arose on a qualifying asset disposal before 4 December 2002.

The rollover relief provisions will be relevant for some years yet, as the time allowed for reinvestment extends to three years after the qualifying disposal and the continuing rollover for existing deferrals could continue indefinitely. In addition, understanding the rollover relief provisions is key to identifying the crystallisation of any deferred gain and the amount of any such gains in future years.

Example 27.8

Peter carries on a manufacturing trade. In March 1972, he acquired his factory premises for IR£60,000 (market value on 6/4/1974 was IR£80,000). In June 1999, he sold the premises for IR£680,000 and purchased another for IR£750,000. In March 2000, he decided to change the location of his operation. He sold the 1999 premises for IR£800,000 and used the proceeds towards the cost of new plant costing IR£150,000 (€190,461) and a unit in a new industrial estate costing IR£650,000 (€825,330). The old plant was scrapped and a balancing allowance obtained for the loss.

In 2018, his health deteriorated and in September of that year he retired, selling the plant for €240,000 and the building for €990,000.

Peter's liability to tax on these transactions is calculated as follows:

Disposal June 1999	***IR£***
Sale proceeds (March 1972 factory)	*680,000*
MV 6/4/1974 (indexed) IR£80,000 6.313	*(505,040)*
Gain IR£	*174,960*
Gain (€ equivalent)	*222,153*

The full proceeds of IR£680,000 were invested in 1999 in a new factory so that the gain is deemed not to arise until the 1999 factory ceases to be used for the purposes of the trade.

Disposal March 2000	***IR£***
Sale proceeds (March 1999 factory)	*800,000*
Cost (no indexation – 12-month rule)	*(750,000)*
Gain IR£	*50,000*
Gain (€ equivalent)	*63,487*

Again, however, the full proceeds were invested in 2000 in new plant and factory buildings so that the gain arising in 2000, and that arising in 1999 are deferred.

Disposals September 2018			***€***	***€***
Sales proceeds		*Plant (2000)*	*240,000*	
		Buildings (2000)		*990,000*
Cost:	*Plant*	*IR£150,000*		
		€190,461 @ 1.193	*(227,220)*	
	Buildings	*IR£650,000*		
		€825,330 @ 1.193		*(984,619)*
			12,780	*5,381*
Total gain on both assets			*18,161*	

As the sale proceeds are not reinvested, all deferred gains (i.e., €222,153 from 1999 and €63,487 from March 2000) are now deemed to arise in addition to the €18,161 gain in September 2018.

Although the "plant" is a wasting chattel, and would normally have a life not exceeding 50 years, it is not treated as an exempt wasting chattel because it qualifies for capital allowances – see Chapter 24 (24.4.2).

It is important to note that if Peter had not retired in 2018 and if he had invested the full proceeds of the 2018 disposals in other qualifying assets, he would not have been able to claim rollover relief in respect of the 2018 gains of €18,161. However, the gains of €222,153 from 1999 and €63,487 from 2000 would continue to be deferred until such time as the new replacement assets ceased to be used for the trade.

Example 27.9

John carries on a manufacturing trade. He sold his factory premises in 2001 for €4m, realising a gain of €1m. On 31 January 2002, he reinvested the entire proceeds in a new factory premises costing €5m, deferring the full gain on disposal of the "old" asset. He found the new factory premises unsatisfactory, and on 18 January 2018 he sold it for €6m, and bought a further new premises for €6.5m in December 2018.

The gain on disposal of the "old" factory of €1m is deferred as it was sold before 4 December 2002 and the full consideration for the sale was reinvested. On disposal of the "new" 2002 premises in January 2018 the "old" gain of €1m is further deferred, as the sale proceeds of the "new" property have been reinvested (in full) in "further new assets". The "old" gain will remain deferred until the "further new assets" cease to be used for the trade.

The gain of €500,000 on the 2018 disposal cannot be deferred as the property was disposed of after 4 December 2002.

27.5 Relief from CGT on Incorporation

s600 TCA97 Where a non-corporate person (i.e., an individual, trust, or partnership) transfers a business (as a going concern) to a company, a measure of relief is given to the extent that the sale proceeds are taken by way of shares in the company. In the absence of this relief, capital gains tax would be payable in full on the gains arising on the disposal of the assets of the business to the company. The relief, in effect, consists of a deferral of the tax payable on the amount of the consideration taken in the form of shares in the company.

27.5.1 Conditions for relief

All of the following conditions must be complied with before the relief applies:

(a) there must be a transfer of a business to a company from a person who is not a company;

(b) the business must be transferred as a going concern;

(c) the whole of the assets of the business or all of those assets other than cash must be transferred;

(d) the transfer must be wholly or partly for shares in the company;

(e) the transfer must be for *bona fide* commercial reasons and must not form part of any arrangement or scheme of which the main purpose or one of the main purposes is avoidance of tax.

There is no requirement that the person making the transfer should have worked in the business. A sleeping partner is as entitled to this relief on the incorporation of a business as is a full-time worker in the business.

27.5.2 Calculation of relief

Calculation of the relief involves the following process:

- The gain is calculated on the normal basis, ignoring any relief, which may be available under this provision.
- The gain is then apportioned (on the basis of market value) between:
  - the value of shares taken in consideration of the transfer, and
  - the value of other consideration (i.e., cash, assets, loan account, etc.).

Where the acquiring company takes over the liabilities of the business (on the transfer of the business to the company) the value of the liabilities taken over represents consideration other than shares, for the transfer. This is on the basis that the discharge of liabilities of the transferor by the transferee is equivalent to the payment of cash by the transferee to the transferor. Concessionally, the Revenue Commissioners may treat the transfer of *bona fide* trade liabilities as not being consideration for the purpose of calculating the relief, provided that the individual transfers the business in exchange for shares only and assets exceed liabilities.

- The relief applies by deferring the amount of the gain apportioned to the value of the shares taken in the company. This amount is calculated using the following formula:

$$\text{Gain} \times \frac{\text{Value of shares taken in consideration}}{\text{Total consideration}}$$

- The balance of the gain (i.e., the part of the gain apportioned to the other consideration) is assessed in the normal manner.

- The deferral is achieved by deducting the deferred gain the element of the gain not assessed, is deducted from the base cost of the shares taken in the company, thereby reducing the allowable cost of the shares for the purposes of calculating a gain or loss on their ultimate disposal. Unlike rollover relief, the gain is not merely held in abeyance; the cost of the shares is reduced. On a subsequent sale of the shares, with a reduced cost, the gain (if any) on the disposal of those shares will be increased, and the tax may, in effect, be payable at that stage. If, however, the value of the shares fell substantially before the disposal, the tax on the gain deferred on the transfer of the business may never be collected.

Example 27.10

Michael, who started in business on 30 June 1965, transferred his business (all of its assets) to "Aztec Limited" in exchange for 10,000 ordinary shares of €1 each in Aztec Limited and €30,000 cash on 31 March 1995.

Michael's assets as shown by his balance at 31 March 1995 were:

			MV 6/4/1974
		€	€
Premises (at cost 30/6/1965)		*7,000*	*15,000*
*Goodwill (*Michael's estimate at 1995)*		*12,000**	*3,000*
Debtors		*4,000*	*N/A*
Stock in trade		*10,000*	*N/A*
Cash		*3,000*	*N/A*
		36,000	
Less creditors: bank loan	*€6,000*		*N/A*
Taxation due	*€2,000*	*(8,000)*	*N/A*
		28,000	

During the negotiations with Aztec Limited, the following market values (at 31 March 1995) were agreed:

	€
Premises	*100,000*
Goodwill	*20,000*
Debtors	*3,000*
Stock in trade	*10,000*
Agreed value of business and assets at 31/3/1995	*133,000*

The following were to be paid by Aztec Limited, on behalf of Michael:

	€	€
Creditors: bank loan	*6,000*	
Taxation	*2,000*	*8,000*
Net consideration due to Michael		*125,000*

On 30 November 2018, Michael sold his €10,000 ordinary shares in Aztec Limited to Takeover Limited for €200,000.

The first matter to be looked at is the 1995 transfer of the business to the company. Firstly, we need to calculate the gains that would have arisen in the absence of any relief

Premises:			
Sales proceeds		*100,000*	
		€	€
6/4/1974 value indexed	*€15,000 5.754*	*(86,310)*	*13,690*
Goodwill:			
Sales proceeds		*20,000*	
6/4/1974 value indexed	*€3,000 5.754*	*(17,262)*	*2,738*
Debtors	*– no chargeable gain*		
Stock	*– no chargeable gain*		
Cash	*– no chargeable gain*		
TOTAL GAIN			*16,428*

Secondly, we need to work out the value of the shares on incorporation. We know that Michael would expect to receive consideration equal to the value of the assets transferred to the company, i.e. €133,000. This consideration is comprised of the following:

Total	*133,000*
Taken in cash	*(30,000)*
Debts paid on behalf of William 8,000 + 30,000	*(38,000)*
Value of shares (balance)	*95,000*

We can now work out how much of the gain is going to be deferred:

DEFERRED GAIN

$$\text{Gain} \times \frac{\text{Value of shares taken in consideration}}{\text{Total consideration}} \quad €16{,}428 \times €95{,}000/€133{,}000 \quad \underline{11{,}734}$$

For the purposes of calculating any gains arising on the future disposal of the shares, the base cost of the shares is reduced by the deferred gain.

	€
i.e.,	
Base cost (i.e. market value at date of incorporation)	*95,000*
Less: deferred gain	*(11,734)*
"Cost"	*83,266*

CGT Computation for 1994/1995:

Total gain	*16,428*
Relief from CGT on incorporation	*(11,734)*
CHARGEABLE GAIN (i.e., the gain attributable to the 'other' consideration):	*4,694*

This part of the gain was taxed in the normal manner, at the appropriate rate.

The final step to complete the picture is the calculation of the gain on the subsequent sale of the shares in November 2018. Remember, the base cost of the shares has been reduced by the amount of the deferred portion of the gain arising on incorporation:

	€
Sale proceeds (November 2018)	*200,000*
March 1995 – cost €83,266	
Indexed @ 1.309	*(108,995)*
GAIN	*91,005*

Tax is calculated in the normal way on this gain.

27.6 Retirement Relief

Retirement relief is something of a misnomer in that there is no actual requirement that the taxpayer retire. Broadly speaking, the relief provides for an absolute exemption from CGT on the disposal of certain qualifying assets (in general, business assets) by individuals who are aged 55 years or more on the date of disposal. The relief is available even though the owner, who disposes of all or part of his/her business assets, remains actively engaged in the business after the disposal. Where all conditions are met, the relief takes the form of a reduction in the tax (CGT) payable on gains accruing on the disposal of the qualifying assets. In most circumstances, the relief reduces the tax payable to nil. The relief is absolute in the sense that the gain relieved is not held in abeyance, as in the case of rollover relief. However, it is important to note that the relief may only be temporary, and could, in effect, be withdrawn by reference to certain events happening subsequent to the relieved disposal.

Retirement relief only applies to individuals. A company, or person holding the business in a fiduciary or representative capacity (who would be deemed not to be an individual in that capacity) does not qualify for this relief. The relief extends to an individual sole trader, a farmer, an individual partner in a partnership, or an individual who holds his/her business interests through a company (on the disposal of all or part of the shares in his/her family company). Where the relief is being claimed in respect of a disposal of shares held in the claimant's family company, additional conditions apply and the computation can be more complicated. For this reason, disposals of assets held in an unincorporated entity and disposals of shares in an incorporated entity are considered separately below in 27.6.1 and 27.6.2 respectively.

Note: Where an individual disposes of qualifying assets before his/her 55th birthday, the Revenue will consider a claim for relief where the individual is within 12 months of his/her 55th birthday and is disposing of qualifying assets due to chronic ill health.

27.6.1 Unincorporated business

The relief is available for disposals by qualifying individuals of "qualifying assets", i.e., "chargeable business assets" of an unincorporated business. A number of detailed conditions must be met. (Note: the relief also applies to certain farm related assets of farmers that do not satisfy the normal conditions.)

Conditions

- The claimant must be an individual and must be at least 55 years of age. The claimant need not actually retire.
- The relief is available in respect of disposals of "chargeable business assets". Chargeable business assets are assets (including goodwill but not including shares or securities or other assets held as investments), which are used by sole traders or partners in a partnership for the purposes of a trade, profession or farming. The relief also extends to assets used for the purpose of an employment.
- The claimant must have owned the chargeable business assets for at least 10 years prior to the date of disposal. This condition does not apply to movable chattels, (e.g., plant and machinery), which qualify for relief irrespective of the period of ownership. In determining the period of ownership for the purposes of this condition, the following rules apply:

1. Where the claimant acquired the qualifying assets from his or her spouse, the latter's period of ownership is aggregated with his or her own period of ownership.
2. Where assets (which qualified for rollover relief) were sold, and the proceeds were reinvested in further qualifying assets, the period of ownership of the assets that were sold is taken into account as if it were a period of ownership of the new assets.
3. Where the assets consist of land, which the individual had farmed for at least 10 years and subsequently rented the land for a period not greater than 25 years (amended by Section 50 Finance Act 2014, previously 15 years), to a "child" (s599 TCA97), relief will apply.
4. Where land is acquired under a compulsory purchase order for the purposes of road widening, the relief is extended provided the land has not been leased for more than 5 years and had been farmed for a minimum of 10 years prior to renting.
5. Section 43 of Finance (No. 2) Act 2013 amended s598 TCA97 to include disposals of leased land where the land is leased for a minimum of 5 years and a maximum of 25 years to a person other than a child of the individual disposing of the land. Section 50 of Finance Act 2014 states that the land must be either disposed of prior to 31 December 2016 or is leased before that date for a minimum of 5 years (maximum 25 years) ending with the disposal of the land. Prior to renting, the land must have been farmed for a minimum of 10 years by the person making the disposal. The purpose of this measure is to encourage older farmers who do not have children interested in farming to lease the land to younger farmers. Section 34 FA 2017 amended s598 TCA97 by including the leasing of agricultural land for solar energy production where 50% or less of the total area of the leased land was used for that purpose. This amendment applies to disposals made on or after 1 January 2018.

Computation of relief

Before calculating the relief, any losses arising on chargeable business assets should be netted off against gains on chargeable business assets.

The annual allowance of €1,270 cannot be claimed by an individual in the same year of assessment in which he/she benefits from retirement relief.

s598(2)(b) TCA97 Full relief from CGT payable on the disposal of qualifying assets to parties other than a child of the claimant is available provided the aggregate sale proceeds of such assets do not exceed a current threshold of €750,000. Section 59 FA 2012 amended s598 by reducing the proceeds limit for individuals aged 66 or over from €750,000 to €500,000. The current threshold of €750,000 will continue to apply to disposals by individuals aged 55 or over but who have not yet attained the age of 66. This reduction is to incentivise the timely transfers of qualifying assets. This reduction of the relief will apply to disposals on or after 1 January 2014. (s59 FA 2012)

For the position with regard to disposals of assets to a child of the claimant, readers are referred to 27.6.3.

Example 27.11

John sold a building used by him for the purpose of his business at arm's length to a total stranger. He had owned the building and used it for business purposes for the past seventeen years. He also sold a painting, which was not a business asset. The relevant details are as follows:

	Sale Price	*Gain*
	€	€
Building	*260,000*	*20,000*
Painting	*10,000*	*2,000*

John is unmarried, and has no other gains or losses to be taken into account in calculating the tax payable for that year. He is fifty-six years of age, and has never sold any other qualifying assets. Both sales took place during 2018.

The gain on the disposal of the building is exempt since the sales proceeds do not exceed €750,000 and the building is a chargeable business asset.

The gain of €2,000 on the disposal of the painting is taxable in full and since John is claiming retirement relief in 2018, he is not entitled to the annual exemption. Accordingly, the CGT payable is €2,000 @ 33%, i.e., €660.

s598(2) TCA97 Marginal relief may be available where the aggregate sales proceeds exceeds the current limit. The effect of this marginal relief is to restrict the maximum CGT payable to a sum equal to half the difference between the limit of €750,000 (or €500,000, as appropriate) and the consideration.

Example 27.12

If in example 27.11 above, the sales proceeds of the business premises were €751,000, and the gain remained the same at €20,000, the tax payable on the disposal of the premises would be reduced from €6,600 to a maximum of one-half of (€751,000 – €750,000), i.e., €500.

To this would be added the tax payable on the disposal of the painting of €660, making a total CGT payable by John for 2018 of €1,160.

Where an individual makes two or more disposals of qualifying assets, the consideration for all the disposals is aggregated for the purposes of considering whether they fall within the €750,000 limit and whether they qualify for marginal relief. Thus, the €750,000 limit is a lifetime limit. Both the full and marginal reliefs are potentially subject to re-computation in the future if the taxpayer makes further disposals of qualifying assets, and increases the aggregate of such disposal proceeds. The revised sale proceeds aggregate applies to current and also to past years. Applying this revised aggregate to earlier years may result in a full or partial claw-back of relief already granted in those earlier years.

The €750,000 threshold is available to each spouse. It is important to note that disposals of qualifying assets to a spouse, although exempt in themselves, erode the €750,000 threshold.

27.6.2 Incorporated business

Where the subject matter of the disposal is shares in a "family company", retirement relief can also apply. Again, it is necessary for the claimant to be an individual aged 55 years or over. A number of additional conditions are relevant with regard to the shares in the "family company".

Conditions

Additional conditions where the subject matter of the disposal is shares in a "family company" are as follows:

- At least 25% of the voting rights in the company must be controlled by the claimant or alternatively at least 10% of the voting rights must be controlled by the claimant and not less than 75%, including his/her 10%, must be controlled by his/her family. "Family" in this context includes spouses, direct relatives (brothers, sisters, ancestors or lineal descendants) and direct relatives of spouses (brothers-in-law, etc.).

- The family company must have been engaged in either trading or farming for at least ten years ending with the date of disposal. Relief is also extended to holding companies of trading or farming companies.

- The claimant must have owned the shares in the family company for a period of at least 10 years ending with the date of disposal. Where the claimant had previously transferred his trade to the company and obtained incorporation relief, the shares will be treated as having been acquired on the same date as the original trade.

- The claimant must have been a working director for a period of at least ten years and a full-time working director for at least five of those years. A "full-time working director" is one who is "required to devote substantially the whole of his time to the service of the company in a managerial or technical capacity" (s598(1) TCA97). Where the claimant's spouse has previously died, the deceased's period of ownership and period of service as a full-time working director is attributed to the claimant. Where shares are disposed of to a spouse, while the transferor is alive, the period of ownership of the transferor is attributed to the spouse receiving the shares. However, this period of service as a working director is NOT attributed to the spouse receiving the shares. In accordance with s600 TCA97, where the individual transferred a business, carried on by him as a sole trader, to the company within the last ten years, the period during which he operated as a sole trader is deemed to be a period during which he owned the shares and during which he was a full-time working director. This rule only applies where capital gains tax relief for transferring the business to the company was claimed.

Computation of relief

Where the disposal consists of shares in a family company, then relief is only available for the portion of the gain on the shares arrived at using the following formula:

$$\text{Gain} \times \frac{\text{Market value of chargeable business assets}}{\text{Market value of total chargeable assets}}$$

Similarly, the consideration taken into account for the purposes of the determining whether or not the disposal is within the €750,000 threshold is restricted by reference to the ratio of chargeable business assets to total chargeable assets owned by the company (taken again at current market values).

Example 27.13

Joe is aged 60 years, and has decided to sell the shares in his family trading company. He has owned the shares in the company for the past 20 years and worked as a full-time working director of the company for the first 15 years of that period. He has been a part-time director for the last five years. Joe has had no previous disposals of qualifying business assets since his fifty-fifth birthday. Immediately prior to the disposal of the shares, the assets of the company were as follows:

	€
Land and buildings	*350,000*
Plant and machinery	*20,000*
Goodwill	*250,000*
Government stocks (investments)	*50,000*
Quoted shares (investments)	*55,000*
Trade stocks	*30,000*
Trade debtors	*40,000*
Cash at bank	*160,000*
TOTAL ASSETS	*955,000*

The total liabilities of the company amount to €155,000.

The agreed sale price of the shares in the company is €800,000. Joe paid the IR£ equivalent of €10,000 for the shares in May 1983.

The trade debtors, trade stocks and cash at bank are neither chargeable business assets nor chargeable assets.

The government stocks are not chargeable business assets and neither are they chargeable assets because they are exempt from CGT.

The quoted shares are chargeable assets since they are assets upon whose disposal a chargeable gain can arise, but they are not chargeable business assets since they have not been used for the purpose of a trade but rather were held for investment purposes.

The land and buildings, plant and machinery, and goodwill are all chargeable assets and also chargeable business assets being both chargeable to CGT and used in the trade.

The value of the chargeable business assets therefore in total amounts to €620,000 (€350,000 + €20,000 + €250,000).

The value of the chargeable assets amounts to €675,000 (the same as above, with the addition of the quoted shares of €55,000).

The gain on the disposal of these shares is calculated as follows:

CGT Computation for September 2018:

	€
Sales proceeds	*800,000*
Cost €10,000	
Indexed @ 2.003	*(20,030)*
	779,970
Retirement relief (Notes 2 & 3)	*(716,417)*
Taxable gain	*63,553*
CGT @ 33% (Note 1)	*20,973*

Note 1:

The annual exemption is not available, as retirement relief is claimed.

Note 2:

Is retirement relief available? Is the portion of the consideration referable to chargeable business assets less than or equal to €750,000?

$$Proceeds \times \frac{Market\ value\ of\ chargeable\ business\ assets}{Market\ value\ of\ total\ chargeable\ assets}$$

€800,000 × €620,000/€675,000 = €734,815; therefore retirement relief is available on the portion of the gain referable to the chargeable business assets.

Note 3:

The element of the gain eligible for retirement relief is calculated as:

$$Gain \times \frac{Market\ value\ of\ chargeable\ business\ assets}{Market\ value\ of\ total\ chargeable\ assets}$$

$$€779{,}970 \times \frac{€620{,}000}{€675{,}000} = €716{,}417$$

Company redeems its own shares

From 4 February 2010, a technical amendment to retirement relief for disposals of interests in family business assets to third parties means that where the retiring individual who is disposing of shares in his family company receives payment in exchange for that disposal from a company on the redemption, repayment or purchase of its own shares (which is not treated as a distribution), the payment will be taken into account in determining whether the €750,000 retirement relief threshold is exceeded.

27.6.3 Disposals to a child of the claimant

s599 TCA97 Where the disposal is to a child of the claimant, in most instances there is no limit on the proceeds of disposal, or gain, which may qualify for relief. However, s60 FA 2012 amended this relief by introducing an upper limit of €3 million on the relief in the case of disposals by individuals aged 66 or over. Unrestricted relief continues to apply to individuals aged 55 or over but who have not attained the age of 66. The upper limit of €3 million applies to disposals made or after 1 January 2014. Again, this amendment is to incentivise the timely transfers of qualifying family businesses.

Such disposals do not erode the €750,000 threshold (or €500,000, where appropriate) for the purposes of disposals to third parties. A child for the purposes of this section includes the child of a deceased child, certain foster children and a nephew or niece who has worked substantially on a full-time basis for at least five years prior to the disposal in carrying on or assisting in carrying on the trade.

However, there may be a claw-back of the relief granted to the parent if the child does not retain the assets for a period of six years. This claw-back involves the tax, which would have arisen if the original relief under s599 TCA97 had not applied, being levied on the child. Thus, the child may well suffer a 'double hit' to CGT, being liable to account for CGT on his or her own actual disposal and also for the CGT that would otherwise have been payable on the original transfer.

It should be noted that there is no relief from this claw-back on a subsequent transfer by the child of his business to a company within the six-year period. The relief for such transfers (as set out in paragraph 27.5) applies only to the child's own gain on the transfer of assets. It does not prevent the claw-back of the parent's gain, which is chargeable on him by virtue of the disposal of the assets to a company.

Example 27.14

William, who is entitled to retirement relief, transferred all his qualifying assets by way of gift to his son George in January 2012. The assets were valued at that time at €5,300,000. William's base cost of those assets to be deducted in computing the gain on the disposal was €100,000 (including indexation). In July 2018, George sold the assets (which were transferred to him by his father) for a total consideration of €6,000,000.

Because George disposed of the qualifying assets within six years of the transfer from his father, he is now liable to:

- *any CGT arising on his own disposal of those assets; and*
- *pay the CGT his father would have paid on the 2012 disposal if relief under s599 TCA97 did not apply to the transfer.*

It is therefore necessary to calculate what amount of tax his father would have paid if no relief was available under s599 TCA97 at the time of the transfer.

If retirement relief had not been available to William at the date of transfer to his son George, CGT of €1,559,619, i.e., (30% × (€5,300,000 – €100,000 – €1,270)) would have been payable. This amount now becomes payable and is levied on George.

Additionally, George has of course to compute his own CGT liability by reference to the base cost of €5,300,000 (and any enhancement expenditure which may have arisen in the five-year period) and the consideration of €6,000,000 on the disposal.

27.6.4 Relief on Disposal of Asset Used by Company

A taxpayer claiming retirement relief in respect of the disposal of shares in a family company may also claim retirement relief in respect of land and buildings and machinery and plant which the individual has owned for a period of at least ten years ending on the date of the disposal provided that:

(i) the asset(s) was used by the company throughout the taxpayer's period of ownership, and

(ii) the asset(s) is disposed of at the same time and to the same person as the shares in the family company.

27.6.5 Retirement Relief and Decommissioning of Fishing Vessels

The Finance Act 2008 introduced retirement relief under s598 in respect of compensation payments made under the scheme for decommissioning fishing vessels. For retirement relief to apply, the person who received the compensation payment must have owned and used the fishing vessel for a period of six years prior to receipt of that payment and must have been at least 45 years of age at the time.

27.7 Relief on the Disposal of Shares in Other Companies

s626B TCA97

Finance Act 2004 introduced a number of new exemptions/reliefs in order to make Ireland an attractive location for headquarter operations and holding companies. One of these exemptions is an exemption from corporation tax on gains on certain disposals of shares and assets related to shares.

In order for this exemption to apply, the following conditions must be satisfied:

- First, the investor company must have a minimum shareholding of 5% in the investee company. The investor is required to have the minimum 5% holding in the investee company for a continuous period of at least 12 months in the three years prior to the disposal.
- Second, the investee company must carry on a trade, or else the business of the investor company, its investee company and their "10 per cent" investee companies, taken as a whole, must consist wholly or mainly of the carrying on of a trade or trades.
- Finally, at the time of the disposal, the investee company must be resident in an EU Member State or a country with which Ireland has a tax treaty. (This includes the Irish State, i.e., disposals of shares in Irish companies where the Irish company owns at least 5% of the other Irish company, and the trading test is satisfied, are exempt from Irish corporation tax.)

The exemption does not apply where the shares are part of a life assurance company's life business fund. Nor does it apply to shares which derive the greater part of their value from land in the State or from minerals, or rights or interests in relation to mining or minerals or the searching for minerals or deemed gains on change of residence.

The exemption also applies to gains on disposal of assets related to shares, e.g., an option to acquire or dispose of shares.

This exemption applies from 2 February 2004.

Section 27 FA 2017 amended s626B TCA97 by ensuring that money or other assets which are transferred to a company prior to a disposal of shares in that company in order that the value of shares will be derived mainly from those assets will not be taken into account in determining whether the value of the shares disposed of is derived from those assets.

This amendment applies to disposals made on or after 19 October 2017.

Example 27.15

Irish Limited sells its shares in Maith Limited, an Irish trading company, in which it has owned 10% of the shares for the last five years. Irish Limited also sells its shares in Paris Limited, a French trading company in which it owns 8% of the shares for the last four years.

The gains on disposal of shares in both of these companies are exempt from corporation tax.

Example 27.16

Holdco Limited is an Irish resident holding company and wholly owns two Irish resident subsidiary companies one of which is trading and one of which is a property management company (X and Y Limited).

Holdco Limited has agreed to sell 100% of its holding in X Limited to a third-party purchaser on 1 December 2017.

X Limited's balance sheet is carrying high value commercial properties valued at €1 million.

The shares in X Limited derive the main part of their value from land & buildings in Ireland. Therefore, any gain arising on the disposal of shares in X Ltd should not qualify for the Participation Exemption under s626B TCA97.

In order to avail of the s626B exemption, the directors of Holdco Limited decide to transfer cash of €3 million from Y Limited to X Limited in advance of the sale in order to inflate the value of non-relevant assets on the balance sheet. This will mean that the value of the shares in X Limited will derive the greater part of their value from assets other than "relevant assets".

The new anti-avoidance measure introduced through s27 FA 2017 counteracts this exact situation.

As Y Limited would transfer the cash immediately prior to the sale of the shares in X Limited, this transfer of money will not be taken into account in determining if the value of the shares in X Limited being sold are derived from relevant assets.

It is worth noting that there is no limit in how far back Revenue could look in ascertaining whether a transfer of assets from a connected person took place.

Example 27.16 is taken from *FINAK – Finance Act 2017 Explained*, published by the Irish Tax Institute 2018.

27.8 Relief for Certain Disposals of Land or Buildings

s604 TCA97 Section 64 FA 2012 introduces a new relief from CGT. Up to 31 December 2017, full relief from CGT was given for the first seven years of ownership for properties bought between 7 December 2011 and the 31 December 2014, where the property is held for more than seven years. The deadline of 31 December 2014 was not extended by Finance Act 2014. Section 33 of Finance Act 2017 amends s604A TCA97 by granting the relief in full for land or buildings disposed of in the period commencing 4 years from the date of purchase and ending 7 years after that date. This amendment applies to disposals made on or after 1 January 2018. This is to encourage individuals who acquired land in 2013/2014 to sell the land now (to enable more houses to be built) as opposed to waiting for the 7 years to elapse to avail of the relief.

The relief will apply to all land or buildings (whether residential or commercial) situated in the EU, Norway, Iceland and Liechtenstein. The relief will not apply if a property is sold within four years of its acquisition. If it is sold more than seven years after acquisition and a gain is made on the sale, relief will be given for the initial seven-year holding period. For example, if the property was bought in January 2014 and sold in January 2023, the property would have been held for nine years, so 7/9 of any gain will be relieved from CGT and 2/9 is taxable. If the property was sold in February 2018, the full gain would be exempt.

In addition, the relief will only be given if the income or profits (if any) arising from the property in question in the first seven years of ownership is liable to income tax or corporation tax, as appropriate.

27.9 Relief for Restructuring of Farm Lands

s604B TCA97 Section 48 FA 2013 introduces a new relief which allows farmers restructure their farm lands without triggering a liability to capital gains tax, where the restructuring has been certified by Teagasc . The first sale, purchase or exchange of farm land must take place between 1 January 2013 and 31 December 2019, (amended by s29 Finance Act 2016, previously 31 December 2016) and the subsequent sale, exchange or purchase must take place within two years of the initial transaction. The relief only applies to agricultural land and does not apply to buildings on the land.

Full relief from CGT is available provided the full consideration for the purchase or exchange of the new farm land is at least equal to or greater than the sales proceeds from the sale or exchange of the original farm land disposed of. Where the consideration for the purchase or exchange of the new farm land is less than the consideration from the sale or exchange of the land disposed of, relief will be given in the same proportion that the consideration for the new land bears to the consideration of the land disposed of. The new land must be retained for a period of five years to avoid a clawback of the relief. Section 29 FA 2017 amended s604B TCA97 by providing that individuals who have obtained exemption under the section are required to provide Revenue with certain information on the amount of CGT that would have been payable if the exemption had not been applied. This is to enable Ireland comply with State Aid publication requirements.

This amendment applies to disposals made on or after 1 July 2016.

Example 27.17

Michael is a farmer and on 1st April 2018 he sold qualifying farm land for €400,000 which would have triggered a capital gain of €100,000. On 1st October 2018 he purchased qualifying land for €300,000. As the consideration for the purchase of the new land is less than the consideration for the land sold, only partial relief is available. The relief is restricted to 75% (€300,000/€400,000) of the capital gain, therefore only €25,000 of the €100,000 gain is taxable.

27.10 Revised Entrepreneur Relief

s597AA TCA97 Introduced in FA 2016 this section provides that a reduced rate of CGT of 10% (previously 20% from 1 January 2016 to 31 December 2016) will apply in respect of a chargeable gain or chargeable gains in the case of a disposal or disposals of chargeable business assets made by an individual on or after 1 January 2017 up to a lifetime limit of €1m.

The chargeable business assets must have been owned by that individual for a minimum period of 3 years prior to the disposal of those assets.

The relief will not apply to disposals of chargeable business assets by companies or to disposals of development land or a business consisting of dealing in or developing land, a business consisting of the letting of land or buildings or holding investments. Where the business is carried on by a private company, individuals seeking to qualify for the relief must own at least 5% of the shares in the company or at least 5% of the shares in a holding company which owns 100% of the company. The shareholder must have been a full-time working director of the company for a minimum period of 3 years prior to the disposal of the chargeable business assets.

Example 27.18

An individual disposed of chargeable business assets in 2017 for consideration of €750,000, realising a capital gain of €300,000. He had owned the assets since 2012 and had not previously claimed entrepreneur relief. As the consideration is less than €1 million lifetime limit and he had owned the chargeable assets for more than 3 years, he will be liable to CGT at the reduced rate of 10% and will have a CGT liability of €30,000. If he had sold the chargeable assets for €1,100,000 he would not have been eligible for the relief and the entire gain would have been liable to CGT at 33%.

27.11 Reconstructions and Amalgamations

Reconstructions and Amalgamations are very common practice in today's challenging environment. In some cases two companies merge together to become one or alternatively a company may hive off some of its trade to another company in exchange for shares. We must look at the tax implications of both and any reliefs available.

Generally a reconstruction or amalgamation will take the form of:

(i) Share for Share exchange, OR

(ii) Share for Undertaking exchange.

(i) Share for Share Exchange

This occurs where a shareholder in a target company surrenders their shares to an acquiring company in return for shares in the acquiring company. There is deemed to be no disposal for capital gains tax purposes and the shares received in the acquiring company take the same date of acquisition and cost incurred in the target company. It is a condition of the relief that the acquiring company acquires control of the target company. Section 625 TCA97 provides that the transferor will be subject to CGT on the initial transfer by way of clawback if the target company leaves the group within ten years.

Example 27.19

Share for Share Exchange

Before

Mr A *Mr B*

A Ltd *B Ltd*

Mr B and his company B Ltd (takeover company) want to acquire the shares in A Ltd (target company). Mr A will surrender his shares in A Ltd to B Ltd and in turn acquire shares in B Ltd

After

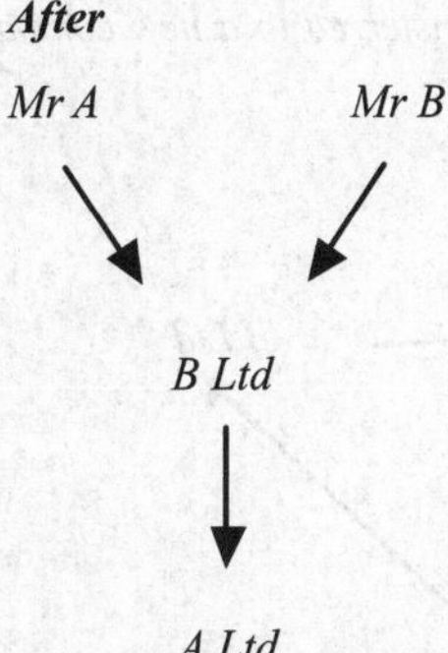

Mr A will not be subject to Capital Gains Tax on the disposal of A Ltd as he is merely receiving shares in B Ltd.

(ii) Share for Undertaking

This transaction involves transferring an undertaking (broadly a trade) to a new company and issuing shares in that new company back to the original owners. The most important aspect of this transaction is that the disposal of an undertaking would involve CGT (and corporation tax) for the company transferring the trade. Any capital gains accruing in the transferring company are exempt from Capital Gains Tax under Section 615 TCA97. The new company receiving the trade/undertaking assumes all assets at the costs and date of acquisition of the transferor. The primary condition required to avail of Section 615 relief is that the transferring company receives no consideration other than the transferee company assuming the liabilities of the undertaking. Sections 40 and 41 amended s615 of the Taxes Consolidation Act 1997 which provides relief from CGT for any scheme of reconstruction or amalgamation involving the transfer of the whole or part of a company's business to another company. The amendment counters arrangements where the section is used as part of a scheme to avoid CGT on the ultimate disposal of assets in respect of which relief had been granted. With effect from 22/10/2015 relief is only available where the reconstruction/amalgamation is shown to be effected for bona fide commercial reasons and not for tax avoidance purposes.

Example 27.20

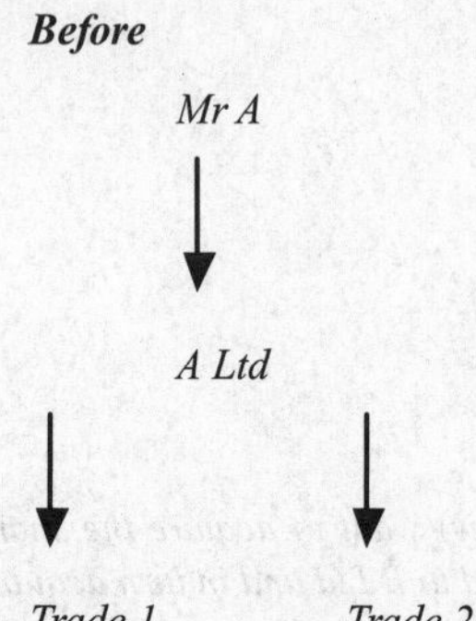

This transaction involves an undertaking being transferred to a new company and shares being issued back to the existing shareholders.

After

Mr A

B Ltd

A Ltd

Trade 1 *Trade 2*

Trade 2/undertaking 2 is transferred to B Ltd and B Ltd issues shares back to Mr A. The transfer of assets from A Ltd to B Ltd would normally involve a CGT charge on A Ltd. The capital gains tax charge does not arise in A Ltd under Section 615 TCA97 as long as consideration received from B Ltd only constitutes liabilities being taken over and it is shown to be effected for bona fide commercial reasons and not tax avoidance scheme.

References and Recommended Further Reading

MAGUIRE, T. (2018), *Direct Tax Acts,* Irish Tax Institute.

MARTYN, J., D. SHANAHAN, T. COONEY (Ed.), 2018, *Taxation Summary,* Irish Tax Institute.

O'HANLON, F., J. McCLEANE (Ed.) (2012), *The Taxation of Capital Gains*, Irish Tax Institute.

28 GENERAL PRINCIPLES OF IRISH CORPORATION TAX

Learning Outcomes

On completion of this chapter you will be able to:

- ✓ Describe the scope and territoriality of Irish corporation tax and identify sources of income which are subject to Irish corporation tax
- ✓ Explain the rules and factors to be taken into consideration in determining a company's residence status
- ✓ State the due dates for filing of corporation tax returns and payment of corporation tax
- ✓ Describe the requirements to pay preliminary tax and identify the amount payable
- ✓ Describe the consequences of late filing and late payment or under-payment of corporation tax.
- ✓ Identify the rate of corporation tax appropriate to different classes of taxable profit.

28.1 Introduction

Companies in Ireland pay corporation tax on their "profits" and have done so since 1976. It was in that year that the Corporation Tax Act 1976 was passed and "corporation tax" introduced.

The legislation behind our corporation tax regime is contained in the Taxes Consolidation Act 1997 (TCA97). This legislation is based on the original Corporation Tax Act 1976. Prior to the introduction of corporation tax, companies were liable to income tax, corporation profits tax and capital gains tax. Much of the corporation tax legislation is based on the original Income Tax Act and Capital Gains Tax Act, the rules of which are still used primarily to compute taxable income and gains for corporation tax purposes.

Corporation tax is not the only tax which a company may be liable to pay – the following taxes may also apply depending on the company's circumstances and the transactions it carries out:

The Irish Tax Institute would like to acknowledge the use of some material from *Corporation Tax* by Julie Herlihy, Paul Moore and Helen O'Sullivan and edited by Michael Ryan in this section and published by the Irish Tax Institute in 2010. Such material has been adapted specifically for students, with the addition of focused commentary and examples.

- Income tax;
- Capital gains tax;
- Dividend withholding tax;
- Value-added tax;
- Stamp duty;
- Capital acquisitions tax;
- Deposit interest retention tax;
- Encashment tax;
- Professional services withholding tax (F45);
- Relevant contracts tax (RCT);
- Local Property Tax (LPT);

However, the focus of this part of the book is to examine the extent of a company's corporation tax liability and, to a very limited extent, any possible income tax and capital gains tax liabilities that may arise. Withholding taxes such as professional services and relevant contracts are discussed in the income tax module.

28.2 The System of Corporation Tax in Ireland

Corporation tax systems in general are built around one of two models, namely the classical system or the imputation system. Some countries may operate systems which have features of both, applying an imputation system which is not a "full" imputation system, i.e., a partial imputation system. The difference between the two systems is basically that the classical system does not give credit to shareholders for the underlying corporation tax paid by the company, whereas the imputation system does.

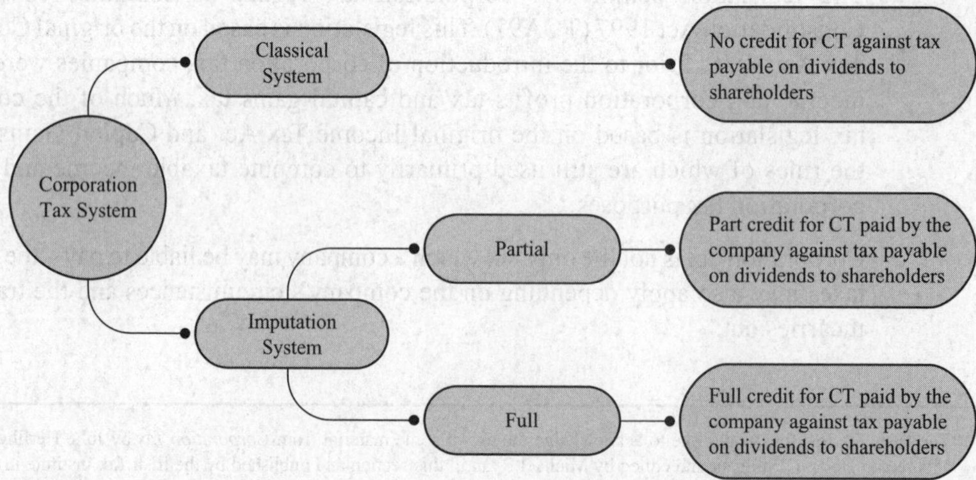

28.2.1 Classical system of corporation tax

Tax is assessed on an Irish resident company under a regime having the full characteristics of a classical corporation tax system. Corporation tax is levied at the company level on profits, i.e., income plus chargeable gains. When those profits are withdrawn by way of a distribution, a further tax levy will generally arise on the shareholders. No credit is given for any element of the underlying tax paid by the company.

The payment of such a distribution is subject to withholding tax at the standard income tax rate, currently 20%. Where the recipient is another Irish resident company, or a company or individual resident in another EU country or a Tax Treaty country (or a company under the control of such persons), then withholding tax does not arise. Where the recipient is an Irish resident individual, he/she will be subject to income tax on the gross dividend (i.e., the net dividend amount plus the withholding tax) and credit will be given for the tax withheld. In essence, the position for the individual, under the withholding tax system, is similar to that which applies for a credit system.

28.2.2 The imputation system

The classical system of corporation tax is a system where no credit is given to shareholders for underlying tax paid at the company level. This differs from an imputation system which gives credit for the underlying corporation tax paid against any further income tax liability of the shareholder arising on the dividend. A system of full imputation or partial imputation may operate to give shareholders either some credit or full credit for underlying tax paid by the company on the profits out of which the dividend is paid.

A full imputation system makes no distinction between distributed and undistributed profits and charges all company profits at the same rate of corporation tax. Part of the company tax is "imputed" to the shareholder by granting credit for tax paid by the company to the shareholder. This credit attaches to the dividend paid. The shareholders receive a net dividend from the company plus a tax credit. They are then subject to income tax on the gross amount received (the net dividend plus the tax credit amount), with credit granted for the tax already paid by the company.

The tax is imputed in terms of the rate applicable to corporate profits. If a company distributes all of its profits, with a tax rate of 12.5% and a personal tax rate of 40%, the effective rate of tax is 47.50% (12.5% + [40% of 87.5%]), whereas under a full imputation system the effective rate of tax is 40% regardless of the company rate. It should be noted that the 47.50% does not include the universal social charge or PRSI. Depending on the individuals personal circumstances these taxes may also be levied on dividend income.

28.2.3 History of the Irish tax system

Prior to 6 April 1999, Ireland operated an imputation system of corporation tax. The payment of tax on dividends was by way of a payment of "advance corporation tax" (ACT). This system was abolished in April 1999, effectively bringing the Irish system of imputation to an end, replacing it with a classical system and introducing dividend withholding tax (DWT). Withholding tax does not operate to impute any tax payment to the shareholder. It applies to dividends only after the profit out of which the dividend is paid has been subject to full corporation tax and is analogous to an advance payment of income tax as opposed to an advance payment of corporation tax.

The Irish corporation tax system effectively doubly taxes dividends which are distributed, while at the same time providing for a surcharge on the undistributed income of close companies. Most Irish companies are close companies (see Chapter 32 for a detailed discussion on close companies). The total effective rate of tax for such companies on distributed income is 47.50%, i.e., 12.5% + [40% of 87.5%], plus the possible additional personal taxes noted in 28.2.2. The total effective rate of tax on undistributed income is dependent on the company's sources of income. For a professional company, in receipt of trading income only, it is 19.06% [12.5% + (15% of 50% × 87.5%)].

28.3 Scope of Corporation Tax

s26 TCA97

Corporation tax is generally applied to a company's profits. The term "profits" means income and chargeable gains. The extent to which a company's profits are liable to corporation tax will depend largely on whether or not the company is resident in Ireland. This is discussed in detail in paragraph 28.5.

The basic principle in calculating income and chargeable gains for corporation tax purposes is that, apart from certain specific provisions of the Corporation Tax Act 1976, the principles of income tax and capital gains tax law and practice apply. The calculation of such income and chargeable gains is discussed in detail in Chapter 29.

While members of groups of companies, consortia and associated companies are each dealt with separately as stand-alone entities for the purposes of calculating corporation tax, special rules governing their association or relationship exist and certain reliefs may apply depending on the nature of the relationship (see Chapter 31 for a discussion on groups).

There are also special rules governing the taxation of close companies (see Chapter 32).

28.3.1 Gains not treated as 'profits'

Certain gains realised by a company will not be treated as forming part of a company's profits for corporation tax purposes, but instead will be subject to capital gains tax instead of corporation tax. These are as follows:

1. Gains on development land (including gains from unquoted shares deriving the greater part of their value from development land) are separately assessed to capital gains tax. It is important therefore that a distinction is made between development

land and non-development land. Students are referred to Chapter 26 for further discussion on this issue.

Such gains do not form part of a company's profits and are assessed separately to capital gains tax, rather than to corporation tax on chargeable gains. There are restrictions on the reliefs that can be claimed against development land gains. The rate of capital gains tax on all development land gains is 33%.

2. Non-resident companies are liable to capital gains tax on disposals of certain specified assets including land in the State, minerals in the State or any rights, interest or other assets in relation to mining or minerals or the searching for minerals in the State.

It is important to make these distinctions, in order to ensure that the correct rate of tax (indeed, the correct tax!) is applied to a company's income/gains. In addition, certain reliefs (such as loss relief) are only available against a company's profits. Thus, incorrectly including income/gains as part of a company's profits could result in excessive amounts of relief from corporation tax being claimed. Tax payment obligations (in terms of amounts and deadlines) also differ greatly between corporation tax, income tax and capital gains tax.

28.3.2 Dividend withholding tax

s29(3)(a), (b) TCA97

In addition to the tax on a company's profits, dividend withholding tax is also *prima facie* (on first glance) payable by a company on distributions or dividends paid from its "after tax profits". Dividend withholding tax applies at the standard rate of income tax, which is currently 20%.

28.4 Who Can Expect to Pay Corporation Tax?

s4(1) TCA97

All companies resident in Ireland are liable to corporation tax, with some exceptions. For corporation tax purposes, a company means any body corporate, including a Trustee Savings Bank within the meaning of the Trustee Savings Bank Act 1989. The term therefore includes companies governed by the Companies Act 2014, whether those companies are limited by shares, designated activity companies, limited by guarantee or unlimited.

The term also includes societies registered under the Industrial and Provident Societies Act, friendly societies and companies established by statute or incorporated by charter, e.g., ESB, RTÉ, etc.

The most important concept to appreciate when dealing with companies is that their identity is separate from the identity of the owners of the company, i.e., the shareholders. The term "company" does not include partnerships even in circumstances where the partnership is limited. Each partner is assessed personally on his/her share of profits. However, a company may form a partnership with a number of individuals, or with another company. Where a share of partnership profits is earned by a company, then that share of profits is liable to corporation tax.

As a company is a separate legal entity from its shareholders, the responsibility for the activities and actions of a company normally rests with the directors of a company and the company secretary. This is the case unless a liquidator has been appointed to the company.

Certain bodies (e.g., health boards, Vocational Educational Committees, and local authorities) are specifically excluded from the meaning of a company and accordingly will not pay corporation tax. In addition, certain companies (e.g., The Custom House Docks Development Authority, The Pensions Board, and The Irish Horse Racing Authority) have been granted exemption from corporation tax on certain or all sources of income.

All companies will be exempt from corporation tax on specific sources of income (e.g., certain grants, profits from commercially managed woodlands), which are excluded by reason of a statutory income tax exemption, which extends to corporation tax.

28.5 Territoriality

The scope of corporation tax will depend largely on whether or not a company is tax resident in Ireland. The charge to corporation tax by reference to a company's residence is fundamental.

The residence of a company, for taxation purposes was, prior to 11 February 1999, determined broadly by where central management and control were exercised. This has now been extended so that all companies incorporated in Ireland are also automatically considered resident here, with certain exceptions. This "incorporation test" as it is known, has been used in a number of other tax jurisdictions for many years. For a fuller discussion of company residence, see 28.5.4 to 28.5.7 below.

28.5.1 Irish resident company

s26 TCA97

A company resident in the State is chargeable to corporation tax in respect of its total profits. This covers the company's worldwide profits irrespective of where they arise and whether or not they are remitted to the State.

Example 28.1

Celtic Tiger Limited is an Irish resident company and has the following income and gains in 2018:

		Jurisdiction	€	Extent of Corporation Tax Charge
	Trading Income			
a)	*Profits from trading*	*(Ireland)*	*440,000*	*Liable on total profits*
b)	*Profits from trading*	*(Rest of Europe)*	*210,000*	*Liable, with credit for foreign tax paid on the branch/agency profits (may be subject to limitations).**
	Capital Profits			
c)	*Sale of premises*	*(Ireland)*	*48,000*	*Liable to corporation tax on chargeable gains*
d)	*Sale of investments*	*(Ireland)*	*75,000*	*Liable to corporation tax on chargeable gains*
e)	*Sale of development land*	*(Ireland)*	*120,000*	*Liable to capital gains tax (see 28.3)*
f)	*Sale of premises*	*(Hungary)*	*92,000*	*Liable to corporation tax on chargeable gains with relief under the treaty for Hungarian tax paid (may be subject to limitations)**
	Investment Income			
g)	*Deposit accounts*	*(Ireland)*	*10,000*	*Liable on total income*
h)	*Deposit accounts*	*(Rest of Europe)*	*15,000*	*Liable with offset for local tax paid (may be subject to limitations)**
i)	*Dividends*	*(Irish subsidiaries)*	*148,000*	*Not liable to corporation tax (with exceptions, see below)*
j)	*Dividends*	*(Hungary)*	*134,000*	*Liable with offset for tax credit or underlying tax depending on terms of the treaty or by reference to unilateral relief (may be subject to limitations)**

** Limitations can arise where the Irish tax liability on the income is lower than the overseas tax suffered, subject to pooling with tax paid in other foreign branches with tax lower than the Irish effective rate, A detailed discussion of this is beyond the scope of this publication, see 28.5.9. See also 29.7.1 regarding the taxation of certain foreign dividends.*

Distributions - Franked Investment Income

s129 TCA97 Specifically excluded are distributions received from Irish resident companies. As Irish dividends are simply an appropriation of profits already subjected to Irish corporation tax, there is no tax deduction for the paying company and therefore no charge to tax for the company receiving the dividend. This form of income is known as "franked investment income"[1].

1 Distributions received by a close company (as defined) may in certain circumstances attract a surcharge or additional levy of corporation tax of 20% (see Chapter 32).

s129A TCA97 Section 129A TCA97 contains an anti-avoidance mechanism aimed at non-resident companies that are connected to Irish resident companies. Normally, where a non-resident company pays a dividend to an Irish resident company, the Irish company would suffer corporation tax on those dividends at either 12.5% or 25% (see 29.7.1). This legislation prevents non-resident companies becoming resident and paying dividends to other Irish resident companies (which would otherwise be treated as franked investment income) tax-free.

If a non-resident company becomes resident from either 3rd April 2010 or 10 years before the distribution was paid to its resident parent, whichever is the later, any dividend paid out of its after-tax accounting profits earned while it was non-resident, will be taxed in the hands of the receiving company under Schedule D Case IV. The section affects connected companies or companies which are party to a scheme, of which the main purpose is to avoid the taxation of foreign distributions. The section does not apply if the paying and receiving companies were not connected while the paying company was non-resident.

Example 28.2

France Ltd, a wholly owned non-resident subsidiary of Irish Resident Ltd moved its residency to Ireland from France on 1st October 2018. France Ltd's profit after tax as per its accounts for the year ended 31st December 2018 is €400,000. It declares and pays a dividend of €250,000 in March 2019, which is due to Irish Resident Ltd.

25% of the €400,000 earnings, €100,000, is treated as coming from France Ltd's Irish earnings, i.e., during the three month period October – December 2018. In the corporation tax computation of Irish Resident Ltd for 2019 therefore €100,000 of the dividend is treated as Franked Investment Income with the balance (€250,000 less €100,000 = €150,000) deemed to have been earned when the company was non-resident , and so taxed under Schedule D Case IV, under Section 129A TCA97.

28.5.2 Non-resident company

Where a company is not resident in Ireland, the extent of its Irish corporation tax liability is limited to:

s25(2) TCA97

- Trading income arising directly or indirectly through a branch or agency, in the State; and
- Any income from property owned or used by, or held by or for, a branch or agency in the State, e.g., deposit interest.

It should be noted that:

- The exclusion from tax for distributions received from companies resident in the State also applies to non-resident recipient companies carrying on a trade in the State through a branch or agency; and
- Income received by a non-resident company which is not attributable to a branch or agency (such as rental income or deposit interest) is liable to Irish income tax. The specific provisions of any appropriate double taxation treaty should be considered.

s29(3)(a)-(c) TCA97 Non-resident companies are liable to corporation tax on chargeable gains arising from disposals of assets used by the branch or agency and to capital gains tax on disposals of non-branch assets or any disposal of specified assets (including land in the State, minerals in the State or any rights, interest or other assets in relation to mining or minerals or the searching for minerals in the State).

Example 28.3

Rostock Ltd, a German resident company, has the following income and gains:

	Trading Income	**Jurisdiction**	**€**	**Extent of Corporation Tax Charge**
(a)	*Profits from trading*	*(Germany)*	*580,000*	*Not liable as trade not carried on in the State*
(b)	*Profits from trading*	*(Ireland)*	*180,000*	*Liable to Irish corporation tax, with credit or other relief for Irish tax paid under the terms of the appropriate treaty against its German tax liability*
	Capital Profits			
(c)	*Sale of trade premises*	*(Ireland)*	*48,000*	*Liable to corporation tax on chargeable gains*
(d)	*Sale of investments*	*(Ireland)*	*75,000*	*Liable to capital gains tax*
(e)	*Sale of development land*	*(Ireland)*	*120,000*	*Liable to capital gains tax*
(f)	*Sale of premises*	*(Germany)*	*92,000*	*Not liable – company not resident in the State, nor is the asset situated in the State*
	Investment Income			
(g)	*Deposit accounts*	*(Ireland)*	*10,000*	*Liable to corporation tax. Note: if the company had no trade in the State, it would be liable to income tax on this deposit income*
(h)	*Deposit accounts*	*(Germany)*	*15,000*	*No liability – not an Irish source of income*
(i)	*Dividends*	*(German subsidiaries)*	*148,000*	*Not liable to Irish tax*
(j)	*Dividends*	*(Ireland)*	*134,000*	*Once the company has filed the necessary documentation with the Irish company, it will receive the dividends gross (see 19.5.6)*

28.5.3 Summary

The territorial scope of Irish corporation tax can be summarised diagrammatically as follows:

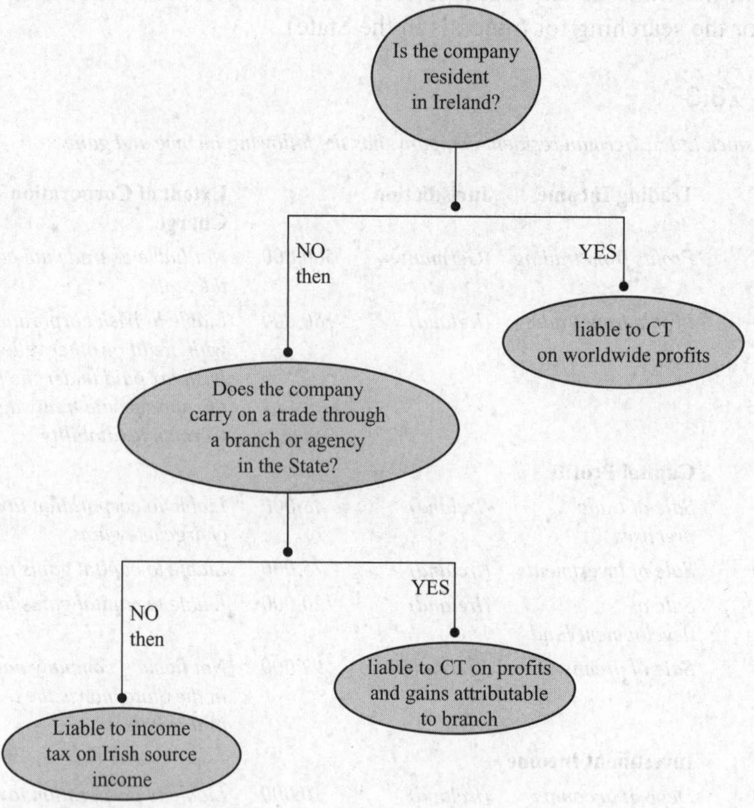

28.5.4 Company residence

Until 11 February 1999, the question of where a company resides was one of fact. The Courts, by examining all of the evidence, attempted to ascertain "where the central management and control actually abides". This dictum, taken from Lord Loreburn's judgement in *De Beers Consolidated Mines v Howe* [1906] STC 198 was the guiding principle in deciding such cases. The place of incorporation, while a factor, was very much subsidiary to other considerations.

The site of management and control is still the most important factor in determining residence status in many instances. Accordingly, the meaning of the term merits further commentary.

Control is concerned with where the directors hold their meetings and whether real decisions affecting the company are taken at those meetings.

This latter point is of importance where a foreign subsidiary is concerned. If the real control of the company and the guiding decisions are taken by the parent company, then the subsidiary may be resident where the parent company resides.

Factors which Determine Central Management and Control

In deciding where a company's central management and control resides, the following points should be considered:

List of factors

- Where are the directors' meetings held?
- Where do the majority of directors reside?
- Where are the shareholders' meetings, both general and extraordinary, held?
- Where is the negotiation of major contracts undertaken?
- Where are the questions of important policy determined?
- Where is the head office of the company?
- Where are:
  - the books of account kept?
  - the accounts prepared and examined?
  - the accounts audited?
  - minute book kept?
  - company seal kept?
  - share register kept?
- From where are dividends, if any, declared?
- Where are the profits realised?
- Where are the company's bank accounts on which the secretary, etc., draws?

A combination of these factors will normally indicate the place of central management and control.

28.5.5 Irish registered non-resident companies

s23A TCA97

Under the system of case law precedent, if the central management and control of a company is located in Ireland, the company is treated as Irish tax resident and until 1999, no other criterion was relevant.

Many offshore activities were structured by companies or individuals who acquired an Irish registered company as the trading entity. Since these companies typically were not, until the publication of the Finance Bill 1999, resident in the State or carrying on a trade in Ireland, they were not liable to tax within the State.

Then a major legislative change was introduced which treated an Irish incorporated company as resident for tax purposes.

s23A TCA97

As a result of this legislation, all companies incorporated after 11 February 1999 (the date of publication of the Finance Bill 1999) are regarded as Irish resident irrespective of the location of their central management and control. Companies incorporated prior to that date came within the provisions as and from 1 October 1999.

28.5.6 Companies incorporated on or after 1 January 2015

Following on from the amendments introduced by Finance (No. 2) Act 2013 that affected certain "stateless companies" (see 28.5.7) Finance Act 2014 replaced s23A TCA97 in its entirety for certain companies from 1 January 2015.

S23A TCA97 states that all companies incorporated in Ireland are deemed to be tax resident here, s23A(1) TCA97, unless they are resident in another country under a double tax treaty, s23A(2) TCA97. Section 23A(3) confirms that the legislation is in addition to the existing central management and control test (see 28.5.4).

The section effects companies incorporated on or after 1 January 2015 and for companies incorporated before this date, it comes into effect from 1 January 2021.

As an anti-avoidance measure the section applies to companies incorporated before 1 January 2015 if there is both a change in ownership and nature of the trade before the 1 January 2021 implementation date, these changes occurring within a period of up to six years. This will bring this date forward to the date of the change. This measure was primarily aimed at restricting the incorporation of companies between the date of the Finance Bill, 23 October 2014 and 31 December 2014 in order to avail of the extension to 1 January 2021 for existing companies.

28.5.7 Companies incorporated before 1 January 2015

In reading this part it should be borne in mind that references to s23A TCA97 are to the legislation as it existed up to Finance (No. 2) Act 2013. As noted in 28.5.6 s23A TCA97 was replaced in its entirety by Finance Act 2014.

For companies incorporated before 1 January 2015 and not subject to the anti-avoidance rules noted above the amendments introduced by Finance (No. 2) Act 2013 will still apply until 1 January 2021.

The amendments were introduced to address concerns in relation to the taxation of multinationals incorporated in Ireland which were not tax resident in any country, due to anomalies between Irish tax laws and those of other jurisdictions. These are commonly known as "stateless companies".

The amendment ensured that if a company is incorporated in Ireland but is not currently tax resident here or in an EU Member State or in a country with which Ireland has a double tax treaty, it will be tax resident in Ireland. The amendment applies to companies managed and controlled in an EU Member State or a double tax treaty country and who were not tax resident in that country and who would, if managed and controlled in Ireland, be resident here, s23A(5) TCA97.

The original 1999 legislation provided for two exemptions to the general residency through incorporation rule and these are still available for companies incorporated before 1 January 2015 (and not subject to the anti-avoidance rules noted above):

The "trading exemption" applies (s23A(3) TCA97)

- The company, or a related company, carries on a trade in the State, and
- Either (a) the company is ultimately controlled by persons resident in an EU Member State or in a country with which Ireland has a double tax treaty, or (b) the company or a related company is a quoted company;
  - This exemption is subject to not being deemed resident under the Finance (No.2) Act 2013 amendment, s23A(5) TCA97.

or

The "Treaty exemption" applies (s23A(4) TCA97)

- The company is not regarded as resident in the State under the provision of a double taxation treaty between Ireland and another country.

Where either of these exemptions apply, the site of management and control remains the fundamental principle in determining residence status.

28.5.8 Summary

The various tax residence tests can be summarised as follows:

A. Overview of the tax residence tests – incorporated from 1 January 2015

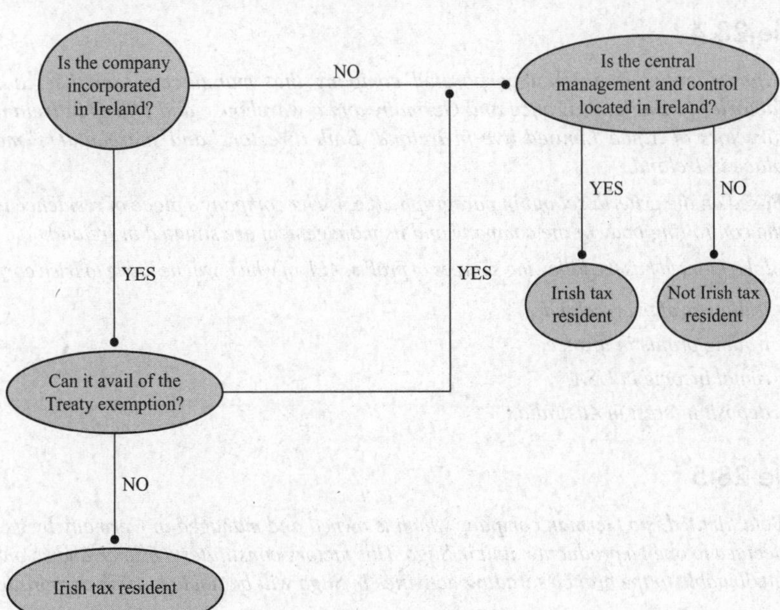

B. Overview of the tax residence tests – incorporated before 1 January 2015

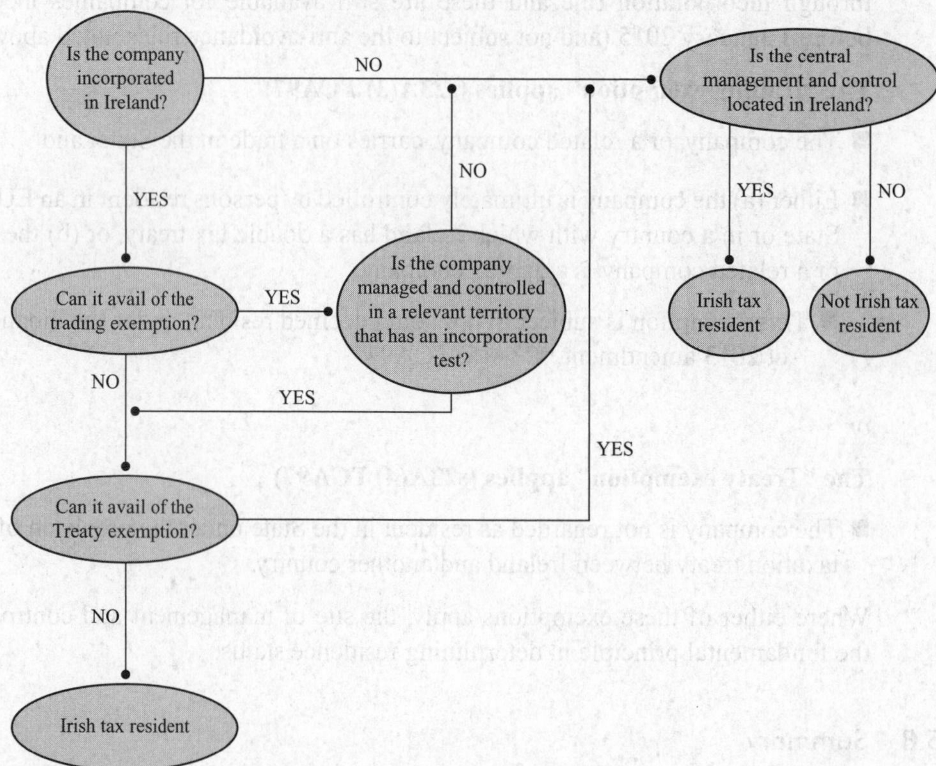

The following additional examples illustrate the residence rules and the territorial scope of Irish corporation tax.

Example 28.4

Alpha Limited is a UK incorporated company that manufactures clothes. It has several factories in England, France and Germany and a warehouse and offices in Ireland. All of the directors of Alpha Limited live in Ireland. Both directors' and shareholders' meetings take place in Ireland.

Based on the criteria set out in paragraph 28.5.4, The company's place of residence is Ireland, as the controlling body of the company and its management are situated in Ireland.

Alpha Limited has the following sources of profits, ALL of which will be liable to Irish corporation tax:

- *trading profits in Ireland;*
- *trading profits in France;*
- *rental income in USA;*
- *deposit interest in Australia.*

Example 28.5

Beta Limited is a German company which is owned and managed in Germany by its directors. It decided to open a production unit in Sligo. This factory constitutes a branch and so only the profits attributable to the branch's trading activities in Sligo will be liable to Irish corporation tax.

Example 28.6

Delta Limited is a company incorporated in Ireland since 2010. Last year, all of the company directors moved to a newly built modern factory and offices in Rotterdam but still kept the factory in Ireland open. The directors managed the operations of the Irish factory from Rotterdam.

Based on the criteria set out in paragraph 28.5.4, Delta Limited's centre of management and control is now The Netherlands. However, as the place of incorporation is Ireland the company will remain Irish resident unless it claims exemption under s23A(3) & (4) TCA97, as set out in paragraph 28.5.7.

Example 28.7

Gamma S.A. is a company resident in France. It owns a valuable greenfield site in Naas. It decides to sell this land to an Irish developer and a gain arises on this disposal. Gamma S.A. is liable to Irish capital gains tax on this gain as it arises on the disposal of a "specified asset".

Example 28.8

Sure Limited is a Dublin based trading company incorporated in Ireland since 2000. It is owned and controlled from Los Angeles. Sure Limited would satisfy the trading exemption test; as a result, it would not be treated as being Irish resident under s23A(3) TCA97 (company incorporated before 1 January 2015). However, as the US only operates an incorporation test to determine corporate residence, Sure Ltd would also not be tax resident in the US. It is therefore treated as being tax resident in Ireland under s23A(5) TCA97, as set out in paragraph 28.5.7.

Example 28.9

Madison Limited is a company incorporated in Ireland in March 2016. The company operates a Brazilian mine and their board of directors hold all of their meetings in that country. The company undertakes no activities in Ireland. Under the management and control test the company is not deemed to be tax resident in Ireland. However, Section 23A(1) TCA97 (company incorporated on or after 1 January 2015) deems the company to be tax resident in Ireland and it cannot avail of the double tax treaty exemption as Ireland does not currently have a treaty with Brazil.

28.5.9 Foreign branches and subsidiaries of Irish companies

While a detailed discussion on the tax implications of foreign tax paid and double taxation relief is outside the scope of this publication, a brief introduction to the topic is discussed below.

The accounts of an Irish company with a foreign branch will include the results of the branch. The combined profits will be taxed as though earned in Ireland and a credit will be allowed for the tax paid by the branch in the foreign country in accordance with Irelands double taxation credit rules. In general if the foreign effective tax rate is higher than Irelands, no additional tax is payable in Ireland. In a situation where the foreign effective tax rate is lower, an incremental tax may be payable in Ireland.

If the Irish company trades through a subsidiary this is a separate legal entity and its results are not included in the Irish company's tax return as Ireland does not operate a system of preparing consolidated group tax returns. Dividends paid by the foreign subsidiary to the Irish parent will be taxed in the parent's tax return subject to double tax relief for the underlying tax paid. See also 29.7.1 for the taxation of certain foreign dividends.

As noted above, an Irish branch of a foreign company will prepare an Irish tax return and pay tax on its Irish source income. If the foreign company has an Irish subsidiary it is subject to the rules of residency as noted above.

28.6 The Pay and File System

28.6.1 General

The self-assessment system was introduced for companies for accounting periods ending on or after 1 October 1989. As a result, the onus for determining the amount and timing of corporation tax payable and the responsibility for the making of a timely and accurate return are placed firmly and fully on the taxpayer. Part 41A TCA97 contains the legislation which deals with the self-assessment system that applies for income tax, corporation tax and capital gains tax and imposes the pay and file system for corporation tax.

The obligations of a company with regard to paying corporation tax and filing its return are as follows. A company must:

- Compute and pay its preliminary tax liability on or before the appropriate due dates;
- Calculate its tax liability and lodge its return of income (including accounts extract or iXBRL and computations) with the Inspector within eight months and twenty-one days (twenty three days if filing and paying the return on ROS) of the end of the accounting period (companies filing accounts via IXBRL have a further 3 months to file after the return of income is filed); and
- Pay any balance of tax due by the return filing date.

A percentage of the returns made will be selected by the Revenue Commissioners for audit. The same Revenue audit procedures apply to both companies and individuals and students are referred to Chapter 10 for commentary on these procedures.

28.6.2 Payment of corporation tax

s959AS TCA97

The timetable and percentage payments for companies which are not deemed to be "small companies", known as companies with relevant accounting periods (see 28.6.3) are as follows:

Initial instalment – this payment is due on the 23rd day of the sixth month of the accounting period. The payment due is the lower of 50% of the previous period's corporation tax liability or 45% of the current year's liability.

Final instalment – this payment is due on the 23rd day of the eleventh month of the accounting period. It must be of sufficient amount to ensure that, when taken together, the initial instalment and the final instalment are equal to at least 90% of the current period's corporation tax liability. Note that the figure for the current year's liability upon which the final instalment is based may well differ from the figure that may have been used to calculate the initial instalment. This is because the figure now includes the tax due on any chargeable gains made between the initial instalment date and the final instalment date).

Note also that if the accounting period is less than seven months the initial instalment is not payable and the final instalment is the only preliminary payment required before the period end.

Chargeable gains top-up – if the company makes a chargeable gain between the final instalment date and the period end, it must pay 90% of the tax due on the chargeable gain within 31 days of the accounting period end.

The company must pay any remaining balance of its corporation tax liability by the 23rd day of the ninth month after the period end.

The above payment requirements are set out in the example below.

Example 28.10

A Limited's accounting year end is 31 December. Its corporation tax liability for the year ended 31 December 2017 was €500,000. In June 2018 it is estimated that its corporation tax for the year ended 31 December 2018 will be €750,000. It makes two chargeable gains in the subsequent months, giving rise to tax liabilities of €50,000 on a July 2018 gain and €80,000 on a December 2018 gain.

Therefore its total tax liability for the year ended 31 December 2018 is €880,000.

A Limited's pay and file requirements are as follows:

23.06.18 Initial instalment: Lower of €750,000 × 45% or 500,000 € 50%	*€250,000*
23.11.18 Final instalment: ((€750,000 + €50,000) × 90%) – €250,000	*€470,000*
31.01.19 Chargeable gains top-up: €80,000 × 90%	*€72,000*
At this stage A Limited has now paid 90% (€792,000) of its overall liability	
23.09.19 Lodge CT1 corporation tax return and pay €880,000 × 10%	*€88,000*

At this stage A Limited has now paid its total corporation tax liability of €880,000 in four instalments.

From a practical perspective, these payment requirements can give rise to considerable difficulties. For example, when calculating the amount of the initial instalment, a company must either base the amount on the corporation tax liability of the current accounting period - which still has over six months left to run - or on the prior year's liability - which may not yet be fully calculated, as the return would not be due for a further three months.

Similarly, when calculating the amount of the final instalment, the current accounting period still has one month left to run. As a result, calculating the correct payment - especially where the activities of the company are subject to seasonal variations - can be quite a challenge.

This issue becomes all-the-more worrying because if the company underpays any of its preliminary tax, it may be subjected to an interest charge on the underpayment (see section 28.6.5). Consequently, companies often find themselves weighing up the cashflow implications of overpaying preliminary corporation tax with the potential interest arising on failing to satisfy its preliminary corporation tax obligations.

28.6.3 Small companies (known as companies other than with relevant accounting periods)

To ease the difficulties that "small companies" (i.e., companies where the tax liability for the preceding chargeable period does not exceed €200,000) may have in assessing their preliminary tax obligations, special rules apply. A small company can opt to base its preliminary tax payment on 100% of the prior year's corresponding corporation tax liability.

It should be noted that the status of a "small" company may change from time to time. A company that is regarded as a "small" company in one period may be treated as a "large" company for the next period and indeed revert to a "small" company again at a later point.

s959AR TCA97

Calculating a company's previous period's corporation tax liability can prove difficult where the current and prior periods are not the same length. In such instances, the €200,000 limit is adjusted to factor in the differences in the length of accounting periods. Readers are referred to Appendix I for further commentary on this matter.

Finally, a new company is entitled to make a nil preliminary payment if its final liability is not expected to exceed €200,000 (this figure is proportionately reduced where the company's first accounting period is less than 12 months).

28.6.4 Group preliminary tax

Section 959AT TCA97 provides for the concept of group preliminary corporation tax. If a group company (see 31.2.1) overpays its preliminary corporation tax it can elect to have the overpayment (known as the "relevant balance") treated as being part of a preliminary payment of a group company which has underpaid its preliminary tax.

To qualify for this relief the following conditions must be complied with:

(a) Both companies must be members of the same corporate group.

(b) Both companies must inform the Collector-General of the transfer.

(c) Neither company qualifies for treatment as a small company.

(d) The company receiving the transfer must pay the balance of any tax owing on or before the due date.

(e) The surrendering company cannot claim the "relevant balance" as a deduction against its tax liability.

28.6.5 Failure to pay preliminary tax

s1080 TCA97

There are interest penalties for a corporate body which has failed to meet its preliminary tax obligations due to non-payment, insufficient payment or late payment of preliminary tax.

Interest charges will apply at the rate of 0.0219% per day (8% p.a.) on late and insufficient payment of preliminary tax.

28.6.6 Filing of corporation tax return

s959I TCA97

A company must file a return of its income, i.e., a Corporation Tax Return Form (CT1) within eight months and twenty-three days of the accounting period end. Failure to do so will lead to surcharges (see 28.6.7 below). In addition, claims to use certain losses are restricted where corporation tax returns are submitted late. Full details of these restrictions are set out in Chapters 30 and 31.

s917EA TCA97

All companies must file their tax returns via ROS (as provided for by regulations under s917EA TCA97). Manual filing is only available at the discretion of the Inspector of Taxes, based on the personal circumstances of the filer (for example, age, access to the internet, etc.). For these cases the return date remains at the 21st of the month.

28.6.7 Late filing surcharge

s1084 TCA97

A surcharge penalty (not to be confused with the surcharge payable by close companies in certain circumstances – see Chapter 32) applies when a company fails to deliver a return of income on or before the specified return date. The surcharge is to be treated in all respects as part of the company's corporation tax liability.

s1084 TCA97

The surcharge is levied as follows:

(a) Where the delay in filing is less than two months, the surcharge is 5% of the company's corporation tax liability for the period in question, subject to a cap of €12,695.

(b) Where the delay in filing is greater than two months, the surcharge is 10% of the company's corporation tax liability for the period in question, subject to a cap of €63,485.

The amount of corporation tax on which the surcharge is calculated is reduced by:

- Any tax deducted by virtue of any of the provisions of the Tax Acts from any income, profits or chargeable gains, charged in the assessment to tax insofar as that tax has not been repaid or is not repayable to the chargeable person and insofar as the tax so deducted may be set off against the tax contained in the assessment to tax;
- The amount of any tax credit to which the chargeable person is entitled in respect of any income, profits or chargeable gains charged in the assessment to tax; and
- Any other amounts which are set off in the assessment to tax against the tax contained therein.

The following examples set out the calculation of the late filing surcharge. Note that preliminary corporation tax is not deducted in arriving at the surchargeable amount.

Example 28.11

A Ltd has an accounting year-end of 31 December 2017. Its corporation tax liability is €21,000 and its CT1 return is sent to the Inspector of Taxes on 14 November 2018. The return should have been filed on or before 21 September 2018 (the ROS extension to 23rd is ignored is cases of late filing). As it is filed less than two months late, the surcharge is 5% or €12,695, whichever is less.

The surcharge is calculated as the corporation tax assessed €21,000 × 5%, i.e., €1,050. This surcharge is not deductible against future income.

Example 28.12

B Limited has an accounting year-end of 31 July 2018. Its corporation tax liability is €311,000 and its CT1 return is sent to the Inspector of Taxes on 14 June 2019. The return should have been filed on or before 21 April 2019 (the ROS extension to 23rd is ignored is cases of late filing). As it is filed less than two months late, the surcharge is 5% or €12,695, whichever is less.

The surcharge is calculated as the corporation tax assessed of €311,000 × 5%, i.e., €15,550. As this exceeds €12,695 the surcharge is limited to €12,695. This surcharge is not deductible against future income.

Example 28.13

C Limited has a trading year-end of 30 September 2018. Its corporation tax liability is assessed at €150,000. It has suffered Deposit Interest Retention Tax (DIRT) on its Schedule D Case IV income of €5,000 and received Professional Services Withholding Tax (PSWT) certificates (F45s) totalling €8,000. Its CT1 return is sent to the Inspector of Taxes on 14 September 2019. The return should have been filed on or before 21 June 2019 (the ROS extension to 23rd is ignored is cases of late filing). As it is filed more than two months late, the surcharge is 10% or €63,485, whichever is less.

	€
Corporation tax	*150,000*
Less DIRT	*(5,000)*
PSWT	*(8,000)*
Surchargeable amount	*137,000*
Surcharge at 10%	*13,700*

If a company makes a fraudulent or negligent return of income on or before the specified date, it is treated as having failed to make a timely return for the purposes of the surcharge unless the error in the return is remedied on or before the specified date. If the return is incorrect (but not fraudulently or neglectfully so) and it comes to the company's notice, the company will be regarded as having failed to make a timely return unless the error is corrected without unreasonable delay. These latter two points often arise in the context of a Revenue audit. The surcharge will not apply in cases where the company pays a penalty.

28.7 Rates of Corporation Tax

The current standard rate of corporation tax is 12.5%, which applies for the financial years 2003 and onwards.

28.7.1 Introduction of the 12.5% rate

With effect from 1 January 2003, Ireland boasts of having effected the smooth transition to a 12.5% standard rate of corporation tax, which was announced by the Minister for Finance in his Budget speech of 3 December 1997. The reduction in rate has been achieved by an annual 4% cut from 1998–2003. The table below indicates the dramatic reduction in the standard corporation tax rate since 1995.

Standard Corporation Tax Rates 1991–2003

Accounting Period	*Standard Rate**
1/4/1991 to 31/3/1995	*40%*
1/4/1995 to 31/3/1997	*38%*
1/4/1997 to 31/12/1997	*36%*
1/1/1998 to 31/12/1998	*32%*
1/1/1999 to 31/12/1999	*28%*
1/1/2000 to 31/12/2000	*24%*
1/1/2001 to 31/12/2001	*20%*
1/1/2002 to 31/12/2002	*16%*
1/1/2003 onwards	*12.5%*

* Lower rates applied to certain companies with "small" profits from 1 April 1995.

Ireland has historically used corporation tax incentives to attract foreign direct investment. However, due to EU pressure, certain specific incentives could not be maintained in the long term. This has resulted in the withdrawal of earlier incentives aimed at encouraging inward investment. Some examples include:

- Export sales relief (0%), which was considered incompatible with the Treaty of Rome;
- Manufacturing relief, which applied until 31 December 2010; and
- The IFSC regime and the Shannon Free Airport Zone under which a 10% rate applied to 31 December 2005.

These reliefs had to be withdrawn prematurely as a result of action by the Commission in 1998 under the State Aid provisions of the EU Treaty. Ireland's response to this was to introduce a uniform low rate of corporation tax of 12.5%. As this rate applies to all trading companies and is not focused on a particular industry sector, it is not regarded as a State Aid from an EU perspective.

The move to a lower tax rate without specific incentives should continue to encourage long-term inward investment in Ireland.

Ireland has managed to achieve national fiscal autonomy with regard to corporation tax rates while adhering to the common framework recommended by the EU for its tax system generally. At the same time as introducing the 12.5% rate, Ireland has taken a number of steps to comply with the "code of conduct" signed up to by Finance Ministers of the Member States in December 1997. The code of conduct was drawn up as a result of a report produced in 1996 by Commissioner Monti entitled *Taxation in the European Union*, which was commissioned in order to examine tax-based incentives and to develop greater tax co-ordination across the EU.

Finance Act 2015 introduced the Knowledge Development Box (KDB) which saw Ireland becoming the first country to legislate for this relief in line with the OECD approved guidelines. The aim of the relief is to provide for an effective tax rate of 6.25% on certain income, see 29.9 for a background discussion to this relief.

28.7.2 Classification of profits by corporation tax rate

The rate of corporation tax that applies to a company's profits is largely dependent on the type of profits earned by the company. At present, there are two rates of corporation tax.

	Rate	Applicable to:
(i)	*12.5%*	***Schedule D Case I and II income***
		Profits taxable 25% are excluded from qualifying under this rate.
		See 29.7.1 for a discussion regarding treatment of foreign dividends paid from trading profits.
		Chargeable gains (exception of foreign life assurance policies where the rate is 40%).
		Chargeable gains are adjusted for the purposes of inclusion in the corporation tax computation such that effective tax at a rate of 33% is collected on the actual gain by applying the 12.5% rate to the adjusted amount. See 29.8 for further details.
(ii)	*25%*	***Passive non-trading income***
		Applicable to Schedule D:
		Case III: interest paid gross, dividends (unless included under s21B TCA97, see 29.7.1), discounts, foreign income
		Case IV: interest paid net, royalties and other miscellaneous income
		Case V: Irish rental income.
		Income from "excepted trades", i.e., income from:
		– land-dealing profits (including residential land from 1st January 2009) other than profits from construction operations,
		– working minerals, and
		– petroleum activities.

28.7.3 Summary

If it is established that different sources of income exist that are liable to corporation tax, further classification will be necessary between those sources of income in order to determine the appropriate corporation tax rate applicable to each source. The level of complexity in income classification is a relatively recent development in corporation tax. In the past, once a decision was made as between income and capital, the only further distinction that was necessary from an income perspective was between manufacturing and non-manufacturing activities.

However, it is now also necessary to distinguish between trading income (taxable at 12.5%) and passive income (taxable at 25%). The lack of clarity regarding the distinction between 'trading' and 'non-trading' can in certain circumstances make the classification of income very difficult. This arises largely due to the fact that there is no statutory definition of trading income. The absence of a definition of trading income in legislation means that we are forced to rely on case law precedent and Revenue guidelines in making this distinction.

The Knowledge Development Box (KDB) also requires the classification of qualifying income.

With regard to capital gains, there are two effective rates of tax applicable to chargeable gains (though the actual rate of corporation tax will be 12.5% - see 29.8): a 33% rate and a 40% rate, which applies to disposals of life assurance policies.

The chart below illustrates the inherent complexity in segregating income into its various classes.

Rates of tax

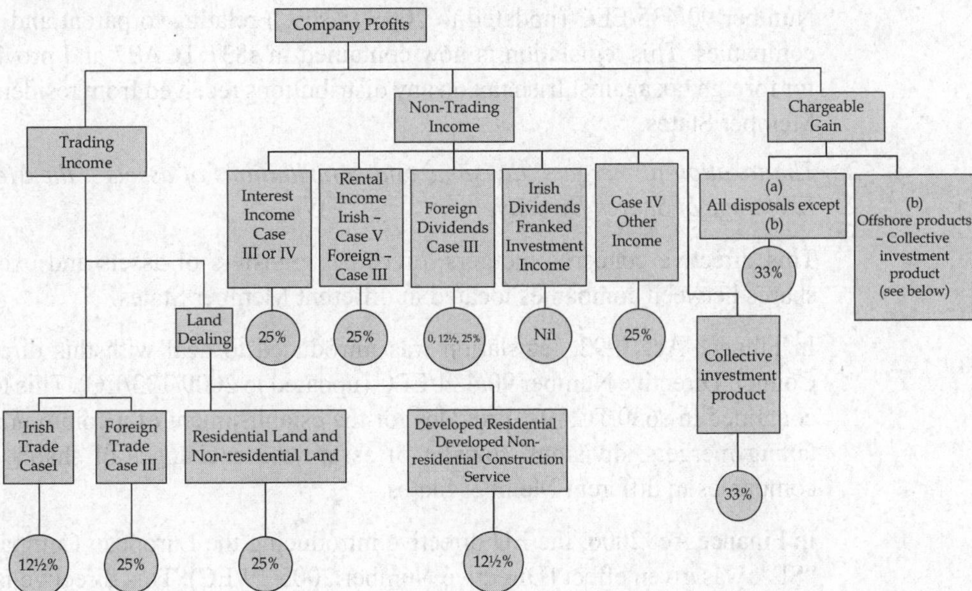

The above chart illustrates the classification process which must be considered when deciding the appropriate rate of tax applicable to a company's profits.

28.8 Other International Influences

28.8.1 European Union

The political debate in terms of the proposed Common Consolidated Corporate Tax Base (CCCTB) continues to be discussed at EU level, especially following the recent bailout programs undertaken by various EU member states, including Ireland. In addition, Ireland continues to vigorously defend the 12.5% corporation tax rate following increasing pressure from some of its fellow EU member states, notably France and Germany. The Department of Finance has cited research figures which show that a considerable number of EU states have effective corporate tax rates (after allowing for various tax reliefs etc) lower than our rates. A report from the Worldbank-PwC, *Paying Taxes 2013* indicates that Ireland's effective corporation tax rate of 11.9% is higher than France's, at 8.2%.

However, as regards other aspects of our corporation tax legislation, Ireland must comply with EU directives and EU case law.

EU Directives

To date, there have been four directives agreed by the EU which affect direct taxation of Irish corporations. These relate to:

1. *The taxation of parent and subsidiary companies – the Parent/Subsidiary Directive*

   This directive is concerned with a common system of taxation where parent companies and subsidiaries operate in different Member States.

   Section 31 Finance Act 1991, implemented this directive, i.e., Council Directive Number 90/435/EEC (updated to 2003/123/EC) relating to parent and subsidiary companies. This legislation is now contained in s831 TCA97 and provides credit for foreign tax against Irish tax on any distributions received from residents of other Member States.

2. *The taxation of mergers, divisions and contributions of assets – the Mergers and Exchange of Shares Directive*

   This directive concerns mergers, divisions, transfers of assets and exchanges of shares between companies located in different Member States.

   In Finance Act 1992, legislation was introduced to deal with this directive, i.e., Council Directive Number 90/434/EEC (updated to 2009/133/EC). This legislation, contained in s630 TCA97, provides for the establishment of a common method of taxing mergers, divisions, transfer of assets and exchanges of shares, involving companies in different Member States.

   In Finance Act 2006, the EU directive introducing the European Company model, "SE", was given effect (Directive Number 2005/19/EC). This directive is designed to provide tax neutrality in relation to the activities covered by directive 90/434/EEC, for these new companies.

3. *Interest and royalty payments between associated companies – the Withholding Tax Exemption Directive*

   Finance Act 2004 amended the withholding tax rules to incorporate EU Council Directive 2003/49/EC regarding interest and royalty payments within the EU to associated companies. An associated company is one in which one company can control 25% of the voting power of the other, or both companies are 25%-owned by a third, for a continuous period of two years. If these conditions are met, there is no obligation to withhold income tax on interest and royalty payments. On 11 November 2011 the Commission published proposals to reduce the 25% holding to 10%.

   A condition of the regime is that any royalties paid in excess of an arm's length rate and any interest which is payable on loans in excess of 50 years will not qualify for exemption.

4. *Exchange of information between EU Member States*

   Directive 2014/107/EU ensures the automatic exchange of information on transactions and assets such as property ownership, employments, pensions between EU tax authorities. This is known as DAC2. In addition Ireland also participates in the Common Reporting Standard (CRS) exchange of information between tax authorities both in the EU and outside the EU, including a large number of so called "tax haven" countries.

   In future years, it is expected that EU legislation and corresponding developments will be reflected in further tax changes, which will form an increasing part of our taxation code.

EU Case Law

From your study of Section II (Value-Added Tax), you should be aware that decisions of the European Court of Justice (ECJ) are becoming increasingly important for Irish legislation. The European Courts are prepared to overrule national Courts where there is a breach of fundamental freedoms. It is likely, going forward, that European case law will impact even more significantly on Irish legislation. The two cases which have impacted most significantly in the area of corporation tax are *ICI v Colmer* and the *St. Gobain* case. More recently, cases brought by Marks & Spencer and *FII Group Litigation v CIR* in the UK and referred to the ECJ are also significant. These cases have implications for Irish companies and are considered briefly in Chapters 29 and 31.

28.8.2 Organisation for Economic Co-operation and Development

On 5 October 2015, the Organisation for Economic Co-operation and Development (OECD) released the final package of measures under the Base Erosion and Profit Shifting (BEPS) project. The aim of the project was to support countries' efforts to shape fair, effective and efficient tax systems. The package provides a comprehensive framework of international standards and recommendations to help address the BEPS concerns identified by the OECD in their 15 point Action Plan of July 2013. The package, which consists of 13 Reports in total, can be found on the OECD's website.

Many countries (Ireland included) have commenced introducing changes to their domestic law to implement the BEPS measures.

Country-by-Country Reporting

Finance Act 2015 introduced country-by-country reporting for accounting periods beginning on or after 1 January 2016.

This legislates requires multinationals whose ultimate parent is tax resident in Ireland to provide certain financial information to Revenue within 12 months of its year end. The information required includes, among other items, sales, profits, tax and employee numbers and is required in total for each country that the multinational operates in.

It is also obliged to provide the group structure and the tax residency of each company in the group.

The requirements are for multinationals whose consolidated turnover exceeds €750 million per annum.

The legislation is based on the OECD BEPS action plan (specifically number 13) and can be shared with other taxation authorities who Revenue enter in information sharing arrangements with.

28.8.3 Foreign Account Tax Compliance Act (FATCA)

FATCA is an information sharing agreement between the United States tax authority, IRS, and numerous countries around the world, including Ireland. The legislation governing the agreement in Ireland is contained in s891E TCA97.

In summary the agreement ensures that all Irish based financial institutions who have customers resident in the US or entities linked to the US must report details of accounts held to Revenue by 30th June of each year. Revenue in turn then furnish this information to the IRS by 30th September of that year. The IRS reciprocate with reports gathered from US financial institutions.

The financial institutions are required to report details of their customers tax numbers, controlling persons of the entity, as well as certain transactions including gross dividends and interest credited to the accounts, asset sales and closing balances. This information is provided to the financial institution by the customer under a self-certification process.

Appendix I

Preliminary Tax Payments for Small Companies

Similar to the facility afforded to individuals in paying preliminary income tax, small companies are entitled to base their corporation tax preliminary payments on the final tax liability for the previous year.

Where the company has a current 12-month period and a similar previous period of equal length, it is defined as small if its final corporation tax liability for the prior period is less than €200,000. If either period is less than 12 months, the following formulae must be used:

Current period less than 12 months – calculate relevant period limit:

$$\text{€}200{,}000 \times \frac{\textit{No. of days in current accounting period}}{365}$$

Prior period less than 12 months or of different length from current period – calculate corresponding corporation tax:

$$\textit{Prior period CT liability} \times \frac{\textit{No. of days in current accounting period}}{\textit{No. of days in prior accounting period}}$$

Example

X Limited has a year end to 31 August 2017 (tax liability of €30,000) followed by a 10-month period to 30 June 2018 (tax liability of €300,000). To help with cash flow, X Limited wants to base its 2018 preliminary tax liability on its 2017 accounts. As one period is not of 12 months' duration, we must utilise the above formulae:

$$\textit{Relevant limit} = \text{€}200{,}000 \times \frac{304}{365} = \text{€}166{,}575$$

$$\textit{Corresponding CT} = \text{€}30{,}000 \times \frac{304}{365} = \text{€}24{,}986$$

As the relevant limit is higher than the corresponding corporation tax, the company qualifies as a small company. The company will base its preliminary payment on €24,986.

29 CALCULATING THE CORPORATION TAX LIABILITY

Learning Outcomes

On completion of this chapter you will be able to:

- ✓ Describe the differences between the adjusted profits calculation for a sole trader and for a limited company
- ✓ Calculate the tax-adjusted Case I figure for a company
- ✓ Identify a period of account for corporation tax purposes
- ✓ Identify the period of account in which various sources of income are taxable
- ✓ Calculate the adjusted chargeable gain of a company
- ✓ Calculate the corporation tax liability of a company
- ✓ Identify corporation tax reliefs such as R&D, intellectual property, start-up relief

29.1 Introduction

The purpose of this chapter is to provide a methodology for calculating total profits subject to corporation tax.

As you will be aware from your study of Section III, calculating the income tax liability of any individual taxpayer comprises two elements:

- calculating taxable income, i.e., the net income on which the taxpayer must pay tax; and
- applying the relevant income tax rates to that income in the hands of the taxpayer.

Broadly speaking, the same principle applies to companies. However, individuals are subject to income tax only on sources of income. Capital gains, which accrue to individuals, are subjected to a separate tax, i.e., capital gains tax. As we saw in Chapter 28, companies pay corporation tax, not on "total income", but on "total profits", which comprises both income and the majority of chargeable gains.

Aside from this major difference in the tax base for companies, there are also subtle differences in the rules for classifying and calculating the taxable income of a company. Unless otherwise stated, the Taxes Consolidation Act 1997 provides that income of a company is to be computed in accordance with income tax principles. Similarly, when calculating a company's chargeable gains, capital gains tax principles are used, with a few adjustments to take into account the difference between the corporation tax and capital gains tax rates.

The overall corporation tax computation identifies the various components of a company's taxable profits. Taxable income is broken down into the same classifications that apply for income tax purposes and calculations are in accordance with the laws applicable to those classifications. Any chargeable gains realised by the company are then added to taxable income to arrive at the company's taxable profits.

This chapter is concerned with revisiting those rules, which are common to both income tax and corporation tax and with developing a methodology for calculating the taxable profits of a company. Emphasis is placed on highlighting issues that are unique to corporation tax. In addition, we will look at the calculation of a company's chargeable gains.

29.2 The Layout of a Corporation Tax Computation

The Taxes Consolidation Act specifies that different types of income must be taxed under specified "Schedules". Each schedule applies different rules for calculating the amount of income taxable under that Schedule. Income taxable under Schedule D is further classified under specified "Cases". Section 18(2) TCA97 sets out the various cases under which income is to be assessed. This classification system has already been outlined in Chapter 8 but it is useful to revisit the subject as companies will typically earn income across a number of these cases. They are critical to the correct computation of a company's tax and it is essential that readers fully understand them.

The relevant categories affecting companies are as follows:

Schedule D Case I

Income from Irish trades, e.g., retail trades, manufacturing trades, etc.

Schedule D Case II

Income from the provision of professional services, e.g., accountancy services, legal services, etc.

Schedule D Case III

Interest received gross, foreign income.

Schedule D Case IV

Interest received net of deposit interest retention tax, any other miscellaneous sources of income not included under another Case or Schedule.

Schedule D Case V

Income from the letting of Irish property.

It should be clear from the above list that companies are only chargeable to tax on Schedule D income. As a company is not an individual, it cannot earn employment income and therefore it cannot be charged to tax under Schedule E.

The receipt of Irish dividends by a company (taxable in the hands of an individual under Schedule F) is treated as franked investment income and so are exempt from corporation tax. Accordingly, a company cannot be charged to tax under Schedule F, subject to the exception as set out in section 28.5.1. Dividends received in respect of shareholdings in non-Irish resident companies are taxable under Schedule D, as in the case of individuals.

The sum of the amounts of income under each of the relevant categories or Cases is the "**total income**" of the company. Chargeable gains are added to this amount to calculate "**total profits**" subject to corporation tax. It is important to note that the terminology used for these total amounts is very relevant. The terms "income" and "profit" should not be confused. The analysis can be summarised with the following equation:

TOTAL INCOME + CHARGEABLE GAINS = TOTAL PROFITS

Corporation tax is then applied to the total profits figure at the rates identified in Chapter 28 and certain reliefs may be claimed against specific sources of income, total profits and the corporation tax liability. A pro forma corporation tax computation is set out in Appendix I.

29.3 Basis of Assessment and Accounting Periods

s27 TCA97 The purpose of this section is to outline the importance of an accounting period in the context of the charge to corporation tax.

The income tax concept of tax years and the charge to tax of the profits of an accounting period ending in an income tax year does not apply for corporation tax purposes. Similarly, the complicated commencement and cessation rules addressed in Chapter 14 are not relevant.

A company is chargeable to corporation tax in respect of its taxable profits for an accounting period irrespective of how it falls in the income tax year. Thus, a company is chargeable on an "actual basis" in respect of accounting periods rather than in respect of tax years.

A number of key features of corporation tax are fixed by reference to accounting periods, e.g., assessments to tax and filing of corporation tax returns (on form CT1), due dates for payment of tax, loss relief claims, etc.

29.3.1 Length of accounting periods

Usually an accounting period for corporation tax purposes corresponds to the company's period of account, i.e., the period for which the company prepares its annual accounts.

However, for tax purposes an accounting period cannot exceed 12 months. If a company's period of account extends beyond this maximum, it will then be necessary for tax purposes to split the period of account into two (or more) accounting periods; the first will relate to the first 12 months of the period while the second will relate to the remainder of the period.

Example 29.1

A company prepares accounts for an 18-month period to 30 June 2018. The corresponding accounting periods used to calculate the CT liability are:

1. *Twelve months to 31 December 2017.*
2. *Six months to 30 June 2018.*

The Revenue Commissioners strictly enforce the legislation in this area and will reject returns that contain periods of longer than 12 months, even if the period is only a small number of days over a year. The author of this chapter has personal experience of a company which incorporated and commenced trading on 31 March 2000. The client requested a 31 March annual accounting period end and therefore the first financial statements, together with a corporation tax return, were prepared for the period 31 March 2000 to 31 March 2001. The return was rejected by the Inspector of Taxes on the basis that the period exceeded one year. The company was required to prepare two separate returns: one for the period 31 March 2000 to 30 March 2001 and a second for the 31st March 2001, a one day period.

29.3.2 Commencement and cessation of an accounting period

An accounting period commences on the occasion of any of the following:

1. the end of the preceding accounting period;
2. a company commences to carry on a trade;
3. a company becomes resident in the State;
4. a company acquires its first source of income (including interest on deposit);
5. a company commences to be wound up.

An accounting period ceases on the occasion of the first of any of the following:

1. expiration of 12 months from beginning of an accounting period;
2. accounting date of the company;

3. a company beginning or ceasing to trade;
4. a company beginning or ceasing to be within charge to corporation tax in respect of its trade or (if more than one) of all the trades carried on by it;
5. a company beginning or ceasing to be resident in the State;
6. commencement or completion of a winding-up.

Example 29.2

AP Limited was incorporated in Ireland on 1 February 2017. The shareholders, who are also the company directors, subscribed for share capital on 1 April 2017 for cash of €100,000, which was put on deposit. The company commenced trading on 1 July 2017 and made its first set of accounts for a 15-month period to 30 September 2018.

Accounting Period		*Explanation*
1 April to 30 June 2017	*Commence*	*AP Limited acquires a source of income as the cash deposit creates interest income.*
	Cease	*AP Limited commences trading.*
1 July 2017 to 30 June 2018	*Commence*	*AP Limited commences trading.*
	Cease	*Expiration of 12 months from the beginning of the accounting period.*
1 July 2018 to 30 September 2018	*Commence*	*End of preceding accounting period.*
	Cease	*Accounting date of AP Limited.*

29.3.3 Allocation of profits between accounting periods

Where only one set of financial accounts covers more than one accounting period for tax purposes, profits will need to be allocated between two or more periods. For example, in Example 29.2 above, AP Limited has only one set of accounts for the period from 1 July 2017 to 30 September 2018, which comprises two accounting periods for tax purposes.

s4(6) TCA97

In these circumstances, the accounting profits of the "long" period are adjusted in the normal way and the resulting tax-adjusted trading profits of the company are apportioned to the different accounting periods on a time basis, according to the respective lengths of those periods.

The legislation specifically provides that the tax-adjusted Case I income figure should be split on a time basis in the manner described above, notwithstanding that the company may have management accounting information at its disposal, which would allow the figure to be split on an actual basis.

Example 29.3

Rocky Road Limited normally prepares accounts to 30 June but, resulting from its decision to change this accounting period to 30 September, it prepares financial statements for the 15 months to 30 September 2018. Since the company is accustomed to a 30 June year-end, it may provide actual results both for the 12 months to 30 June 2018 and for the balance of the three months to 30 September 2018. This "actual" split should NOT be used as s4(6) TCA97 tells us we must apportion on a time basis. We must therefore disregard the information provided for the two distinct accounting periods and split the total 15-month adjusted Case I profits, etc., on a time basis, i.e., 12:3.

Not all items are allocated on a time-apportioned basis. While trading profits, as adjusted for tax purposes, are time apportioned, the legislation provides that other items, such as other sources of income, charges and chargeable gains, should be allocated to the specific period in which they actually arise. Similarly, capital allowances can only be claimed by companies on plant/machinery in use at the end of the appropriate accounting period. In this regard, readers are referred to the analyses in 29.5.3 and 29.7 below.

29.4 Calculation of Tax-Adjusted Case I/II

29.4.1 First step: calculating taxable profits

In the vast majority of cases, the audited accounts of a company will not show the final figure to be taxed for the period. While the Revenue Commissioners require GAAP (generally accepted accounting practice) to be used in the computation of taxable profits, there are certain core tax principles and specific legislative sections, which give rise to differences between the accounting and taxable profits.

The figure used as a starting point is the profit before tax and before any appropriations of profit such as dividends, distributions, etc. Dividends and distributions are simply appropriations of the company's profit to the company's shareholders and accordingly, are not deductible in arriving at taxable profits.

29.4.2 Next step: Case I/II income

Having established the correct starting point, the next step is to adjust the "profit before tax" figure in order to determine the various components of company's taxable profits, namely:

- Case I/II income;
- Case III income;
- Case IV income;
- Case V income;
- Chargeable gains.

This is normally achieved by firstly focusing on calculating the company's Case I/II income. As we saw in Chapter 15, identifying and excluding income/expenditure not allowable under Case I/II will indirectly identify items of income/expenditure taxable under another Case. Similarly, identifying and excluding capital items from being taxed under Case I/II will provide us with the figures necessary to calculate the company's chargeable gains (or losses).

Always bear in mind that you will be stripping out figures that are in the profit and loss account or IFRS income statement. You can only strip out amounts that are already in the profit and loss account or IFRS income statement. If something is not booked to the profit and loss account or IFRS income statement you do not need to adjust profit before tax for that item.

In determining whether or not individual items in the profit and loss account or IFRS income statement need to be adjusted for in arriving at the company's Case I/II income figure, it is necessary to consider the four criteria identified in Chapter 15 for the purposes of calculating tax-adjusted Case I/II for income tax purposes. A brief synopsis of these criteria has been reproduced below as follows:

"1. It is necessary to consider whether the item is capital in nature or income/ revenue related. In general, an adjustment is required for capital items. A number of Irish and UK decisions help to clarify the distinction between "capital" and "revenue". It is important to bear in mind that some capital expenses, which are disallowed for the purposes of calculating Case I, may be deductible in calculating chargeable gains.

2. The item must be "trade" related. In general, items that do not relate to the trade are adjusted for in arriving at taxable Case I. The legislation specifically requires that for amounts to be deductible under Case I, the expenditure must be incurred "wholly and exclusively" for the purposes of carrying on the trade. This concept of "wholly and exclusively" is a complex area and has been the subject of much case law in Ireland and the UK over many years.

3. In general, items of expenditure must have been incurred in the period. An adjustment will be required if an item relates to a movement on a general provision. Movements in provisions are only allowable where they relate to specific items, the amount of which can be determined with exactitude. Rough estimates of future expenditure are not allowable.

4. Certain specific items of expenditure are disallowed by statute notwithstanding that they are revenue in nature and may have been incurred wholly and exclusively for the purposes of the trade. The main provisions disallowing specific types of expenditure are addressed in 15.3.4 below."

Taken from Chapter 15 – paragraph 15.3.

29.5 Issues Arising in Calculating a Company's Case I/II Income

Broadly speaking, the methodology in calculating trading income is the same for both individuals and companies and in general, the analysis and examples included in Chapter 15 also apply in calculating the Case I/II income of a company. However, there are certain exceptions to this rule and a number of issues unique to the calculation of the adjusted profits of a company merit further commentary.

29.5.1 Salaries and private expenses of owner-directors

It is important that you should understand the legal difference between a sole trader and the shareholders of a company. A sole trader is taxable under Case I/II on all his trading/professional income in the taxable period. In calculating tax-adjusted Case I/II, he receives no deduction for his drawings or for his personal expenses during the period. To reclassify drawings as salary on the basis that it is referred to as such in the accounts would involve incorrectly classifying trading income as Schedule E income for tax purposes. The owner cannot employ himself and accordingly is taxed under Case I/II on all his earnings in the period irrespective of whether or not he spends or draws down these amounts. He must also add back the private element of any expenditure booked to the accounts, e.g., the private element of any motor expenses.

Companies, on the other hand, are separate legal entities distinct from their owners and they are taxed on their income accordingly. The vast majority of companies in Ireland are family controlled; they will usually have two shareholders of which either one or both work in the company as full-time directors. The directors will draw a salary from the company, upon which they will pay tax under Schedule E and the company will get a deduction for this cost. The company is then taxed on the profits after the deduction for directors' salaries. Similarly, where the company funds personal or private expenses of the shareholder directors, such amounts are allowable in full on the basis that the expenditure is a cost of rewarding employees and the shareholder directors will be taxed on these amounts under the benefit in kind (BIK) rules (see Chapter 21). The following example illustrates the position where a company pays a salary to a shareholder director and funds personal expenses of that shareholder director. To facilitate an understanding of the distinction between Case I/II computations for sole traders and companies, readers should compare this example with Example 15.1 in Chapter 15.

Example 29.4

John is the majority shareholder in X Limited and works full-time for the company as managing director. The profit and loss account of X Limited for the year ended 31 December 2018 is as follows:

	€	€
Sales		*300,000*
Cost of sales		*(100,000)*
Gross profit		*200,000*

Less expenses:		
Depreciation	*20,000*	
Salaries and wages	*65,000*	
Light and heat	*1,000*	
Telephone	*1,500*	
Motor expenses	*3,000*	
Miscellaneous	*4,000*	*(94,500)*
Profit before tax		*105,500*

The salaries and wages include a salary of €25,000 paid to John.

X Limited operates from a room in John's home. The light and heat expense included in the accounts relates to the expenses for the house as a whole for the year. John pays the bill using the company cheque book. John has agreed with his Inspector of Taxes that one-fifth of this amount is business related.

The telephone expense relates to a separate line, which John has put in place exclusively for the purposes of the company's business.

The motor expenses relate to petrol and insurance expenses incurred by X Limited. The amount comprises an amount of €1,000 in respect of John's car, which is used 50% for business purposes (as agreed with the Inspector of Taxes), and €2,000 in respect of a salesman's car, which is used 60% for business purposes.

The miscellaneous expenses are all allowable.

The Case I computation of X Limited is as follows:

	€
Profit before tax	*105,500*
Add back:	
Depreciation	*20,000*
Tax-adjusted Case I	*125,500*

Note:

The salary of the managing director is a normal trading expense and is deductible in full in calculating Case I. Accordingly, no adjustment is necessary. John is taxable on the amount of this salary under Schedule E.

He is also taxed under Schedule E on other benefits accruing from his involvement in the company. Thus, the private elements of the light and heat and motor expenses are allowable for Case I purposes on the basis that they are costs of rewarding an employee. The benefits accruing to him would be taxable in his hands under Schedule E as a BIK. Thus, he would be taxable on a BIK of €800 in respect of the light and heat and €500 in respect of the motor expenses. In this regard, readers are referred to Chapter 21.

29.5.2 Dividends and distributions

Any distributions or dividends made by a company are not allowed for tax purposes as they are not incurred "wholly and exclusively" for the purposes of the trade; they are paid to shareholders as a reward for taking the financial risk of investing in the company. Thus, they are treated as an appropriation of profits rather than as an expense incurred in earning the profit.

It is a common misconception among shareholders of Irish companies that as they own the company they can do what they wish with its assets and funds. However, any drawings by the shareholders may be classified as distributions and can give rise to onerous consequences under close company legislation (see Chapter 32)[1].

The definition of distributions in the legislation is very wide and seeks to cover all possible payments made to a shareholder. The most common examples are:

- Dividends;
- Any amount received for the redemption of bonus shares (s130(2)(c) TCA97);
- Interest on securities convertible into shares (s130(2)(d)(ii) TCA97);
- Transfer of assets to a shareholder for consideration less than the worth of the assets (s130(3)(a) TCA97);
- Transactions within the provisions of close company legislation (see Chapter 32).

As mentioned in 29.4.1, the figure used as a starting point is the profit before tax and before any appropriations of profit such as dividends, distributions, etc. However, some distributions may be "buried" under expense headings in the profit and loss account and because such amounts will have been deducted in arriving at "profit before tax", they should be added back for tax purposes. For example, under close company legislation, expense payments to shareholders and certain "excess" interest payments to directors (on loans advanced to the company) may be regarded as distributions for tax purposes and accordingly must be added back if deducted in arriving at the profit before tax figure. In this regard, readers are referred to the commentary in Chapter 32.

Companies are generally not taxed on dividends received from Irish resident companies (see 28.5.1 for further discussion). Franked investment income is deducted in calculating a company's tax-adjusted Case I/II. Dividends received from foreign companies are also deducted for the purposes of calculating tax-adjusted Case I/II, as they are usually taxable under Case III (however, it may be possible that such dividends are taxable under Case I or II, depending on the source of the profit - see 29.7.1).

---

1 Incidentally, use of company assets and funds by shareholders may also impact upon company law and may lead to possible indictable offences, which would be reported to the Office of the Director of Corporate Enforcement by the company's auditor.

29.5.3 Company capital allowance claims

The legislation governing the claim for capital allowances on capital expenditure incurred by individuals as discussed in Chapter 16 applies equally for companies. The main difference between a sole trader's capital allowance claim and a company's claim is that for income tax purposes, a capital allowance is treated as a relief, which is deducted from the taxable income, whereas for corporation tax purposes, the capital allowance is treated as a deduction in arriving at the taxable income. Therefore, in calculating the charge to corporation tax, it is included with deductions such as exempt income, profit on sale of fixed assets, non-taxable employment grants, etc., in arriving at tax-adjusted Case I.

Capital allowances and accounting periods

As already emphasised at 29.3.3 above, companies must calculate a separate capital allowance claim for each accounting period in order to ensure that capital allowances are only claimed on assets in use at the end of the accounting period in question. Where an accounting period is shorter than 12 months in duration, the wear and tear allowance otherwise available is reduced proportionately.

Example 29.5

Converse Limited commenced to trade on 1 December 2017 as a retail unit. The directors of the company decided on a December year-end for stock-taking purposes and made up accounts from the date of commencement to 31 December 2018, a period of 13 months.

It purchased qualifying plant on 17 December 2017 for €10,000 and also purchased further plant in November 2018 for €5,000. In December 2018, it purchased qualifying plant for €6,000. All purchases were put in use immediately.

It is necessary to calculate two capital allowance claims as there are two accounting periods for tax purposes and it is necessary to time-apportion any claim relating to a period of less than 12 months in duration.

	12 months ended 30 Nov 2018	*1 month ended 31 Dec 2018*
	€	*€*
Cost of assets in use at start of accounting period	*Nil*	*15,000*
Additions	*15,000*	*6,000*
Cost of assets in use at end of accounting period	*15,000*	*21,000*
Wear and tear (Notes 1 & 2)	*1,875*	*219*

Note 1:

€15,000 × 12.5% = €1,875

Note 2:

€21,000 × 12.5% × 1/12 = €219.

Capital allowances for energy efficient equipment

In order to encourage energy-efficient equipment, 100% capital allowances are available to companies who incur expenditure on 'green' capital items. In addition, an intangible assets capital allowances scheme is also available which helps improve Ireland's attractiveness as a corporate location for holders of patents (see Appendix II) and other intangible assets (see 29.9.2). The energy efficient scheme runs to 31 December 2020. The scheme was historically only available to companies but from 1 January 2017 it was extended to sole traders and partnerships.

29.6 Case I/II and Accounting standards

29.6.1 Introduction

Section 76A TCA97 states that the trading profits of a company will form the basis of its taxable profits subject to any adjustments as required under tax legislation.

The two main accounting standards currently in operation are:

(1) IFRS (International Financial Reporting Standard) - this is used by all publicly quoted companies and by any other company which voluntarily chooses to use it

(2) FRS (102) (Financial Reporting Standard) - this is used by non-publicly quoted company

It should be noted that FRS 102 (which commenced from 1 January 2015) and IFRS (which was introduced in 2005) are all considered to be GAAP (Generally Accepted Accounting Practice) for the purposes of TCA97. GAAP is the term used in the legislation for an acceptable accounting standard.

29.6.2 Accountancy interaction with taxation

From a taxation point of view both standards are similar.

The only major common difference between the standards is the treatment of goodwill. Under FRS 102 Section 19 it will generally be amortised over 10 years whereas IFRS allows impairment only, IAS 36, 38 and IFRS 3.

Goodwill is not recognised under Irish corporation tax legislation and therefore, the write-off or impairment of goodwill is not deductible for tax purposes. Any amortisation or impairment costs are added back in the tax computation. The one exception to this is goodwill related to specified intangible assets, see 29.9.2.

Section 76A TCA97 provides for the following when preparing financial standards in line with generally accepted accounting practice:

(A) - Subsection (2) - Transition from FRS (the old standard to 31 December 2014) to FRS 102/IFRS, see Appendix III

(B) - Subsection (3) - Change of an Accounting Policy - following the change in an accounting policy, any amount that is adjusted against prior year reserves will be deductible or taxable in the current year

(C) - Subsection (4) - Adoption of a new Accounting Standard - following the adoption of a new standard a procedure similar to subsection (2) above will occur, see Appendix III. This subsection is designed to allow for the updating and changing of accounting standards over time and gives certainty to companies in how to treat any amendments for tax purposes. As explained in Appendix III, following such a changeover, income or expenses which were previously debited or credited in the prior year may be similarly debited or credited in the current year under the new standard. In this case the current year debit or credit will be spread over 5 years

(D) - Subsection (5) - Correction of Errors - the subsection states that it is necessary to amend the year in which the error occurred by re-opening the corporation tax return

29.7 Other Sources of Income

Having calculated a company's Case I/II income, the next step is to establish the company's total taxable income for the accounting period by calculating the company's other income under Cases III, IV and V.

Unlike trading income, which is apportioned on a time basis, income under each of the cases listed above is computed on an actual basis. Therefore, in the case of an 18-month set of accounts which contains interest income, it will be necessary to ascertain the actual interest received in each period to arrive at the taxable income for each period (contrast this with the calculation of trading income as detailed in 29.3.3).

In addition, unlike trading income, these other sources of income will be classified as "passive income" (see 28.7.2) and will be liable to tax at 25% rather than 12.5%.

29.7.1 Case III income

Included in this case is foreign income (of any type - trading income, dividends, rents, etc.) and gross interest received from banks, i.e., interest income received without deduction of deposit interest retention tax (DIRT).

Foreign trading income

Whether trading income should be taxed under Case I or Case III depends on the level of independence the foreign trade has from the Irish company. Case law precedent would suggest that if the foreign trade is managed or controlled from the State, it should be taxed under Case I, whereas if the trade is carried on entirely abroad, it should be taxed under Case III. Any income from the foreign trade included in the accounts of the main company should be deducted in arriving at Case I income and taxed under Case III. Similarly, any expenses relating to the foreign trade should be added back in the main Case I computation and deducted against the Case III trading income.

Foreign dividends

s21B TCA97 Up to Finance Act 2008, dividends from foreign companies received by an Irish company were automatically taxable under Case III (as opposed to dividends received from Irish companies, which are exempt). As a result of the *FII Group Litigation Case (C-446/04)* certain dividends received by Irish companies from EU/Tax Treaty resident companies will be taxed at trading rates (12.5%) rather than Case III (25%).

While a detailed discussion of the legislation is beyond the scope of this publication, broadly speaking, when a foreign qualifying company pays a dividend to an Irish company and that foreign qualifying company's trading profits account for more than 75% of its total profits, that dividend is taxed at 12.5% in the hands of the Irish company. Where the dividend is paid out of specified profits, then the portion taxable at 12.5% is in proportion to the percentage of specified profits compared to trading profits.

The company paying the dividend does not have to be resident in the EU or a tax treaty state. It can also trade on any stock exchange which is recognised by the Minister.

Dividends from companies in countries that have ratified the OECD Convention on Mutual Administrative Assistance in Tax Matters are also included.

For Irish companies who have made portfolio investments in a foreign qualifying company the 12.5% rate will always apply, regardless of the source of the foreign company's profits. A portfolio investment is one in which the total shareholding of the investor is not more than 5%.

The most recent ruling in the FII Group Litigation Case (C-35/11) in November 2012 came after the UK Courts referred the original case back to the ECJ for further clarification. The court held that the general exemption from corporation tax for resident company dividends as distinct from the corporation tax credit system for non-resident company dividends was not compatible with EU law.

To reflect this ruling, Finance Act 2013 amended Schedule 24 TCA97 to allow the granting of an Additional Foreign Tax Credit (AFTC) to increase the foreign tax credit allowable when calculating the tax due on the dividend to ensure that it equates to the 12.5% or 25% corporation tax that the dividend is liable to. This ensures that no additional tax is due in the corporation tax return.

The AFTC is only granted to dividends from companies resident in a relevant member state (EU, Iceland and Norway). It will not apply when the dividend has not been subject to tax in the company of the relevant member state and it has been received from a connected company outside of a relevant member state and has not been subjected to tax in the non-relevant member state.

A further credit is available in situations where the Irish parent receives dividends from an EU subsidiary which in turn has received dividends from its own EU subsidiary and this sub-subsidiary's income is subject to corporation tax in its own country. The credit available to the Irish company is based on the rate technically payable in its subsidiary's sub-subsidiary.

Foreign rents

Foreign rents are taxed under Case III, unlike rent from property in the State, which is taxed under Case V. However, when calculating the amount of taxable foreign rental income, the same deductions are available as when calculating the taxable rental income of an Irish property.

Gross deposit interest

s256 TCA97 Irish companies are entitled to receive interest on bank deposits and similar investments without deduction of DIRT. However, the interest is still fully liable to corporation tax under Case III, as no tax is deducted at source. To avail of the DIRT exemption, the investing company must file the necessary "DIRT-free declaration" and must furnish the relevant deposit-taker with its tax reference number.

Companies are only taxable on the actual interest received in the period, therefore any interest receivable which is accrued in the accounts should be deducted and taxed in the period in which it is actually received.

29.7.2 Case IV income

The main charge to tax under Case IV is interest received after deduction of DIRT. As noted above, companies who make the necessary declaration can have the interest paid to them without deduction of DIRT at source. However, even if a company suffers DIRT at source, the amount deducted will be credited against its overall corporation tax liability and any excess will be refunded (in contrast, DIRT is non-refundable in the case of most individuals).

As the interest under Case IV is paid net of DIRT (at a 2018 deduction rate of 37%) it will be necessary to re-gross the income for the Case IV computation.

Example 29.6

X Ltd receives €63 (net of DIRT) in August 2018 for the year ended 31 December 2018. In the corporation tax computation, the €63 will be deducted from the taxable Case I income and re-grossed (€63/63%) to €100 and charged to tax under Case IV. The DIRT suffered of €37 is credited against the company's total tax liability.

29.7.3 Case V income

A charge to corporation tax under Case V arises where a company receives rental income from Irish property and receipts from easements. Therefore, the following types of income are assessable under Case V of Schedule D:

- Rents in respect of any premises or lands in the Republic of Ireland, i.e., offices, shops, factories, land, etc.;
- Receipts in respect of an easement, i.e., any right, privilege or benefit in, over or derived from a premises, e.g., a right of way;
- Certain premiums received for the granting of a lease.

It is important to remember that rental income derived from foreign property is assessable under Case III of Schedule D as **foreign** income (see 29.7.1).

Case V is assessed on the full amount of rental income receivable in an accounting period. Thus, if a company is entitled to receive rental income in the accounting period ended 31 December 2018, the income will be assessed on the company for that accounting period, even if the income was not received in the period.

The relevant date to create a commencement of a source of rental income for a company is the date on which income first arises from the Case V source and not when the Case V source is acquired. Income "arises" to the company when it becomes entitled to receive such rents, even though the income may not necessarily be received as yet.

The relevant date to trigger a cessation of a source of rental income for a company is the date on which the source is disposed of and not the date on which the income ceases. Thus, there is no cessation where a source continues to exist but does not produce income in a particular accounting period.

Capital allowances are available against rental income where companies acquire and fit out certain properties. Depending on the tenants, allowances are available for the renting of industrial buildings or for the fit-out of residential properties. These are discussed in Chapter 18.

Each property should be dealt with separately and a computation prepared for each premises.

In the main computation any rental income received should be deducted from the taxable Case I income and any rental expenses should be added back and deducted from the gross rental income to arrive at the taxable Case V income. The main rental expenses allowable are covered in Chapter 18.

Companies which own Irish residential property are liable to the Local Property Tax (LPT), which is not allowable as a deduction against corporation tax.

29.8 Chargeable Gains and Losses

As noted in 29.2, corporation tax is a tax on the profits of a company which arise in a specific accounting period. 'Profits' in the context of corporation tax means total income (trade, professional, interest, foreign, rental, etc.) plus chargeable gains. Therefore, any capital gains generated by a company in an accounting period will be subject to corporation tax and NOT capital gains tax as is the case for individuals.

A chargeable gain/loss arises for tax purposes when a company sells assets held for the purposes of its trade or held as investments. The accounting profit or loss on the disposal of the asset is included in the company's profit before tax (the starting point for calculating corporation tax). However, for corporation tax purposes, the profit/loss is capital in nature and therefore should be deducted/added back (depending on whether it is a profit or loss) for the purposes of calculating tax-adjusted Case I/II. Note also that any costs incurred on the disposal of the asset are not trade-related and so must be added back to the accounting profit/loss in calculating a company's Case I/II income.

A separate calculation of the capital gain/loss must be computed in accordance with CGT rules. Unutilised capital losses incurred in previous accounting periods can be carried forward and offset against current capital gains less current capital losses.

The net gain is eventually taxed using the applicable CGT rate, currently 33% (30% to 5th December 2012).

At this point it might seem that a company suffers less of a tax liability than an individual, as its gains are liable to corporation tax (at 12.5%) rather than capital gains tax (at 33%). However, to ensure a level playing field, the gain to be taken into the corporation tax computation must be adjusted so as ensure that the amount of corporation tax on the gain will not differ from the amount of tax that would have arisen under CGT. The gain is adjusted using the following formula:

$$\text{Gain under CGT rules} \times \frac{33\%}{12.5\%}$$

Example 29.7

Company A acquired a premises in October 1990 for €100,000. This was subsequently sold in August 2018 for €273,000. The accounting profit on disposal shown in the profit and loss account is €173,000. A Ltd prepares accounts to 31 December 2018.

Adjustments for corporation tax purposes:

1. *Deduct the profit on disposal of €173,000 from "profit before tax" in the computation of tax-adjusted Case I income.*
2. *Calculate the capital gain on the disposal in the tax year to 31 December 2018.*

			€
Sales proceeds			*273,000*
Less cost of acquisition			
October 1990	*100,000*		
Indexed @ 1.442		=	*(144,200)*
			128,800
Less capital losses (current and brought forward)			*Nil*
			128,800

The theoretical CGT on this gain is: €128,800 × 33% = €42,504. Therefore the chargeable gain required to give a corporation tax liability of €42,504, using the CT rate of 12.5% is as follows:

$$€128{,}800 \times \frac{33\%}{12.5\%} = €340{,}032$$

3. *Therefore, the amount of €340,032 is included as a chargeable gain in the company's corporation tax computation. Taxed at the standard rate of 12.5% this will give tax payable of €42,504.*

29.8.1 Exceptions

It is important to note that there are two exceptions to the rule that a company's gains are taken into the corporation tax computation; these are development land gains and certain gains accruing to foreign companies (see 28.3.1). Gains by companies on such disposals are always calculated separately and the resultant liability is paid as capital gains tax, not as corporation tax. In addition, losses on such disposals are not available against gains which are liable to corporation tax.

Example 29.8

In January 1984 B Limited acquired the freehold interest in a factory for €75,000, together with two acre greenfield site for €60,000. It subsequently sold these items on 20 December 2018. The factory sold for €350,000, while the site sold for €800,000, well in excess of its current use value. The accounting profit on the disposal of these fixed assets shown in the profit and loss account is €311,000 and €740,000 respectively. Legal costs incurred in relation to the disposals were €2,000 and €4,000 respectively.

B Limited prepares its accounts to 31 December each year. Assess the corporation tax implications of these transactions for B Limited.

Adjustments for corporation tax purposes

1. *As they are capital in nature, the profits of the disposal of the building and the greenfield site of €311,000 and €740,000 must be deducted from the profit per the accounts in the Case I tax-adjusted profit computation.*
2. *As they are capital in nature, the legal costs of the disposal of the building and the greenfield site of €2,000 and €4,000 must be added back to the profit per the accounts in the Case I tax-adjusted profit computation.*
3. *The greenfield site satisfies the criteria of development land, and so the company will be liable to capital gains tax on the gain from its disposal.*
4. *The capital gain on disposal in the tax year ended 31 December 2018 is as follows:*

	€
Sales proceeds	*350,000*
Less: legal costs	*(2,000)*
Net proceeds	*348,000*
Less cost of acquisition	
€75,000 × 2.003	*(150,225)*
Capital gain	*197,775*

5. *The theoretical CGT on this capital gain is €197,775 × 33% = €65,266. Therefore the chargeable gain required to give a tax liability of €65,266 using the CT rate of 12.5% is as follows:*

$$€197{,}775 \times \frac{33\%}{12.5\%} = €522{,}126$$

6. *Therefore, €522,126 is included as a chargeable gain in B Limited's corporation tax computation for the accounting period ended 31 December 2018. Taxed at the standard rate of 12.5% this will give tax payable of €65,266.*

29.8.2 Restriction of chargeable losses by capital allowances

Losses on the disposal of trade assets are always restricted by capital allowances claimed during ownership. This ensures that the loss arising cannot be relieved twice, i.e., once under the capital allowances system and again under the CGT rules.

In contrast, Gains on the disposal of trade assets are not restricted by capital allowances previously granted. This is the case because in general, any such capital allowances previously granted are clawed back on disposal by way of a balancing charge.

Example 29.9

C Limited sold plant in March 2018 for €10,000. It had purchased this in January 2015 for €30,000. For CGT purposes, there is an apparent loss as follows:

	€
Sales proceeds	*10,000*
Cost	*(30,000)*
Loss	*20,000*

The capital allowances claimed during the period of ownership are as follows:

	€
Cost in January 2015	*30,000*
W&T × 12.5% 2015	*(3,750)*
W&T × 12.5% 2016	*(3,750)*
W&T × 12.5% 2017	*(3,750)*
TWDV 1/1/2018	*18,750*
Sales proceeds	*(10,000)*
Balancing allowance	*8,750*

Total capital allowances and balancing allowance for the plant amount to €20,000. This is set against the loss of €20,000 thereby reducing it to nil.

29.9 Other Issues

So far, we have looked at the initial steps involved in calculating the various elements of a company's taxable profits, in order to be able to calculate the company's corporation tax liability for the accounting period in question. Unfortunately, if you have glanced even briefly at the *pro forma* corporation tax computation in Appendix I, you will see that computations can involve additional adjustments in order to finalise a company's corporation tax liability. Such adjustments include taking account of losses incurred by the company (dealt with in Chapter 30), taking account of various transactions with other companies in a corporate group (dealt with in Chapter 31), or taking into account that the company may satisfy the criteria of a 'close company' (dealt with in Chapter 32).

29.9.1 Credit for R&D expenditure

Ireland's current research and development (R&D) was introduced in 2004. The relief is calculated by allowing a tax credit of 25% of the qualifying expenditure against the corporation tax liability of the company. The relief is in addition to the normal deduction for expenditure incurred against Case I income.

For the years up to 2014 the qualifying expenditure incurred in 2003 (if any) was deducted from the annual claim prior to the calculation of the 25% credit. This was known as the base year adjustment. For the years 2012 to 2014 a certain level of alleviation had been introduced to this adjustment. Finance Act 2014 removed this requirement for accounting periods beginning on or after 1 January 2015.

The company is entitled to claim credit for any R&D undertaken by a university in the EEA on its behalf (subject to a maximum of 5% of the total R&D spend or €100,000, whichever is the greater) in addition to expenditure incurred prior to the commencement of the company to trade (see paragraph 15.3.4.13 for commentary on pre-trading expenditure).

It can also claim credit for any R&D subcontracted to a third party (subject to a maximum of 15% of the total R&D spend or €100,000, whichever is the greater). The company must notify the subcontractor in writing that it is not to make its own R&D claim on the expenditure it incurs.

Relief is not available for any expenditure covered by grants from any Irish or EEA bodies.

The claim for the R&D expenditure must be made within 12 months of the end of the accounting period in which the expenditure was incurred. Ideally it would be made with the corporation tax return of the period.

Operation of the scheme

The operation of the refundable tax credit scheme in relation to qualifying expenditure is best explained by way of an example.

Example 29.10

X Limited incurred R&D expenditure of €900,000 in the year ended 31 December 2018. Its corporation tax liabilities are as follows:

	€
2017	*50,000*
2018	*60,000*
2019	*12,500*
2020	*8,000*

Total credit available: €900,000 × 25% = 225,000

s766(4A) TCA97

Step 1: The credit is firstly set against the current period's corporation tax liability. Any excess is then set against the tax liability of prior period(s) of corresponding length.

	€
Total credit	*225,000*
Used in 2018	*(60,000)*
Available	*165,000*
Used in 2017	*(50,000)*
Balance	*115,000*

s766(4B) TCA97

Step 2: Any remaining excess is then carried forward. Under s766(4B) TCA97 33% of the amount carried forward will be refunded after the due date of the filing of the corporation tax return for the period in which the R&D claim arose. Any remaining excess is then set against the corporation tax liability of the next accounting period after the R&D claim, subject to allowing the subsequent R&D claim for that period take priority.

	€	
Balance	*115,000*	
Refund 33%	*(37,950)*	*Payable after 21 September 2019*
Carried forward to 2019	*77,050*	
Used in 2019	*(12,500)*	
Balance	*64,550*	

Step 3: *Any remaining excess is then halved. The first half is refunded after the due date of the filing of the corporation tax return of the period immediately after period that gave rise to the original claim. The remaining half is then set against the next period's corporation tax liability.*

	€	
Balance	*64,550*	
Refund 50%	*(32,275)*	*Payable after 21 September 2020*
Carried forward to 2020	*32,275*	
Used in 2020	*(8,000)*	
Balance	*24,275*	

Step 4: *Any final remaining excess is refunded after the filing of the corporation tax return for the second period after the period that gave rise to the original R&D credit. In the case of X Ltd, the remaining credit of €24,275 would be refunded after the return for 2020 was filed on 21 September 2021.*

s766B TCA97 The maximum credit which may be refunded is the greater of:

(A) The total corporation tax paid in all accounting periods for the ten years prior to the period in which relief is claimed, or

(B) The total PAYE/PRSI liability of the company in the period in which the R&D expenditure is incurred and the previous period.

Criteria for relief

The company claiming the relief must carry on a trade in the State, engage in R&D activities in the period and keep a record of all expenditure incurred.

The expenditure must be incurred in the areas of science and technology, and involve research and developmental activities. It must seek to achieve scientific or technological advancement or solutions to scientific or technological uncertainties. Expenditure on R&D buildings is excluded, as it has its own separate relief noted below.

Expenditure will qualify if it is incurred in a country of the European Economic Area (EEA) in the relevant year. The expenditure must qualify for relief in the State and, in the case of an Irish resident company, must not qualify for tax relief outside the State. No relief is available for royalty payments which are exempt in the hands of the recipient.

Expenditure on a specified intangible asset within the meaning of s291A TCA97 (see 29.9.2) will not qualify as research and development expenditure.

In situations where relief will be claimed for expenditure on plant and machinery, the assets must be used "wholly and exclusively" for R&D purposes. For practical reasons, this is not normally the case as the machinery is usually put to commercial use after the R&D process has finished. It is open to the company's Inspector of Taxes to determine (presumably after representations from the company) the "just and reasonable" portion of plant and machinery to be allowed in the R&D claim[2]. There is also a provision to allow the revision of the R&D claim if the plant and machinery usage differs from that forecasted originally.

R&D buildings

Section 766A TCA97 grants relief for expenditure incurred on R&D buildings. To qualify, the company must be entitled to claim industrial buildings capital allowances on the building. The cost of the site is excluded, as is any expenditure covered by grants. The relief will be clawed back if the building is sold or ceases to be used within 10 years. Therefore all expenditure qualifies.

The conditions are as follows:

A. To be a qualifying building it must be used at least 35% of the time as an R&D building over a 4 year period (from the time it is first brought into use after being built or refurbished).

B. The credit will be 25% of the relevant expenditure. Relevant expenditure is determined by the percentage of time it is used as an R&D building, which must be at least 35%. For example a building which costs €1,000,000 and is used for 40% of the time over the four year period would have an R&D credit as follows: €1,000,000 × 40% × 25% = €100,000.

C. If the building ceases to be used within 10 years of the commencement of the 4 year period noted in A, the relief is clawed back.

R&D credit and groups of companies

From 1 January 2012 a company in a group ceasing to trade can transfer its unutilised R&D tax credits to another group company provided that this company carries on the original company's trade.

29.9.2 Intangible Assets

s291A TCA97 In recent years Ireland had been lagging behind in the provision of tax relief for the acquisition of intangible assets in relation to other European countries, which was having an effect on the attractiveness of Ireland as a holding company location for companies with worldwide patents, brands etc.

An intangible assets capital allowances scheme was introduced in 2009 and as noted in 29.9 is now also included in the Knowledge Development Box (KDB) relief.

2 "Just and reasonable" is not defined in the legislation.

Specified Intangible Assets

Under the provisions, companies can claim capital allowances for "specified intangible assets", as defined in s291A TCA97.

These include costs incurred on intangible assets such as patents, registered designs, trademarks and names, brand names, domain names, copyrights, know-how (s768 TCA97), licences etc. and any goodwill related to these assets.

To be an intangible asset it must come within the definition under GAAP. Under IAS 38 an intangible asset is defined as "an identifiable non-monetary based asset without physical substance".

This would generally be an asset that has been created or purchased by the company and from which an income stream or reduced costs are proposed.

The scheme applies to any qualifying expenditure incurred on or after 7th May 2009.

The assets will be treated as qualifying for capital allowances under the normal rules, therefore they will be subject to balancing allowances/charges, etc.

Rates of Claim

The company will have two options in relation to relation to the wear and tear rate:

(1) 7% straight line for 14 years followed by 2% straight line in the 15th year

(2) An amount equivalent to the depreciation/amortisation/impairment charge in the income statement

The company can claim either option at its own discretion for each individual asset. It should be noted that under IAS 38, assets with an indefinite useful life are generally not depreciated/amortised and therefore the company will choose option (1) above, in order to obtain tax relief.

There will be no clawback if the asset is sold more than 5 years (10 years from 4th February 2010 to 13th February 2013 and 15 years prior to that) after the first accounting period in which it was capitalised, s288(3C) TCA97. Finance Act 2014 introduced a flat five year period for all disposals on or after 23 October 2014. It also amended the rules re sales to connected parties and from 23 October 2014 the purchasing party can claim capital allowances on the lower of the purchase price paid or the selling parties tax written down value.

Restrictions on Claim – Relevant Trade

Unlike ordinary capital allowances, there is a restriction on the amounts of allowance that can be offset. In the first instance the capital allowances can only be offset against income from relevant activities, s291A(5) TCA97.

These activities include the managing, developing and exploiting of intangible assets.

These activities are treated as a separate trade for offset purposes, known as a relevant trade.

For expenditure incurred between 8 May 2009 and 10 October 2017 only income from a relevant trade can be sheltered by the relief. For expenditure incurred from 11 October 2017 only 80% of income from a relevant trade can be sheltered by the relief. It is necessary to track the income from each asset in order to ensure that the correct pre and post October 2017 split is in place. This should be done on a just and reasonable basis.

Section 291A(5)(b) TCA97 states that if the company has other trade income, the income from the relevant trade should be split on a just and reasonable basis.

The restriction also applies to interest borrowed to acquire or develop intangible assets.

Given the restriction a loss can never be created and set against non-IP trade income.

Any unutilised capital allowances or interest is carried forward. The capital allowances are restricted in priority to the interest in arriving at the overall claim.

Calculation of IP Relief:

(1) Calculate relevant trading income

(2) Calculate capital allowances on specified intangible assets

(3) Calculate interest on relevant borrowings

(4) Set interest against the relevant trading income, carrying any excess forward

(5) Set capital allowances against any remaining income from (4), carrying any excess forward

Example 29.11

IP Limited incurred expenditure on specified intangible assets of €500,000 for the year ended 31st December 2018.

The company borrowed €400,000 to fund the expenditure and paid €40,000 in interest. The company has chosen the 7% over 14 years option.

Trade results before interest for the year ended 31st December 2018 are €140,000. This is €60,000 for IP management and €80,000 for other trading activities.

Calculate the usage of intangible assets relief under s291A TCA97.

	€		€
Total Income	*140,000*	*Capital Allowances 500,000 × 7%*	*35,000*
Income from relevant trade	*60,000*	*Interest*	*40,000*
		Total Claim	*75,000*

Max Claimable (80%)	*54,000*	
Income from Relevant Trade	*60,000*	
Interest Allowable	*(40,000)*	*(Claimed first)*
Capital Allowances	*(14,000)*	*(after restriction)*
Taxable Relevant Trade	*6,000*	

Add: Non Relevant Trade	*80,000*
Total Income	*86,000*
Corporation Tax @ 12.5%	*10,750*

The restricted capital allowances of €21,000 (€35,000 – €14,000) are carried forward to be offset against future years relevant trading income.

When an intangible asset is included in the purchase of a trade, allowances can be claimed provided the company can show that its valuations are reasonable.

In all cases Revenue can engage experts (subject to not prejudicing the company's entitlement to trade secrecy) to assist in deciding whether the values or claims are just and reasonable.

In relation to the current relief for know-how under section 768 TCA97 and patents under section 755 TCA97, these types of expenditure are included in the new scheme but if the company wishes, it may continue to claim relief under these original sections on expenditure incurred to 7th May 2011.

Section 291A TCA97 does not affect capital allowances for software under s291 TCA97. A company using software as part of its trade will claim under s291A TCA97 whereas a company using end-user type software (e.g. accounting packages) will claim under s291 TCA97.

29.9.3 Knowledge Development Box

As noted in 28.7.1, Finance Act 2015 saw the introduction of the Knowledge Development Box (KDB) which is linked to the R&D tax credit discussed below in 29.9.1 and intellectual property relief (IP) which is covered in 29.9.2.

While the R&D tax credit and the relief for IP are two separate reliefs they are linked for the purposes of the KDB and a claim under this new scheme.

A detailed discussion of the KDB is outside the scope of this publication, however the following commentary is provided to give a background to the provisions.

Ireland was the first country to introduce a KDB which is in full compliance with the OECD's modified nexus approach. This essentially means linking the relief to IP and R&D. The aim of the relief is to effectively tax qualifying income at a rate of 6.25%. It achieves this by deducting 50% of the qualifying income from taxable profits, therefore effectively halving the 12.50% rate.

In order to qualify for relief under the KDB the company must earn income from its IP assets, such as through their exploitation or management/licensing. In order to have income from IP assets it must incur qualifying expenditure on their development.

In essence therefore a company will incur qualifying expenditure (which in the legislation is identical to the definition of qualifying expenditure for R&D purposes) in creating an IP asset from which it will then earn qualifying income upon which it will then claim KDB relief.

In ascertaining the portion of IP income that qualifies for the relief the legislation provides for the formula as shown below:

$$\frac{QE + UE}{OE} \times QA$$

QE (Qualifying Expenditure) is the qualifying R&D expenditure that leads to the creation/improvement etc of the IP asset. The legislation excludes outsourcing to related parties, for example outsourcing to a group company would not be within the definition.

UE (Uplift Expenditure) allows the QE to be increased by a lower of 30% of the QE or the amounts paid to group companies (excluded in QE) and the cost of actually purchasing IP assets.

OE (Overall Expenditure) is the overall expenditure on the qualifying assets and will include acquisition costs, qualifying expenditure and non-qualifying outsourcing expenditure.

QA is the income stream from IP assets less any normal costs incurred in earning this income on a just and reasonable basis.

As can be seen from the above the formula seeks to restrict purchases costs of IP (already allowed under s291A TCA97, see 29.9.2) and group outsourcing – this makes it more beneficial to Irish companies who do the majority of the development work in house rather than multinationals who would outsource elements to group companies.

The above formula will need to be used for every separate IP asset, however grouping is allowed in certain situations, known as "family assets". The legislation also contains provision for transitional measures in relation to assets and certain costs incurred prior to 1 January 2016, interaction with the R&D refundable credits, the effect of a claim which gives rise to a loss and certain relieving measures for SME's.

Claims must be made within 24 months of the period end. The legislation is contained in Part 29 Chapter 5 s769G – s769Q TCA97 and is to run from accounting periods beginning on or after 1 January 2016 and ending before 1 January 2021.

Example 29.12

KDB Limited is a company involved in providing technology services. The following information is provided in respect of the year ended 31 December 2018:

Expenditure on acquisition of a qualifying patent	*€50,000*
Outsourcing costs relating to R&D carried out by a US group company	*€75,000*
Qualifying expenditure on patents and computer software	*€90,000*
Overall expenditure on qualifying assets	*€200,000*

Profit of specified trade relating to the patents and computer software	*€450,000*
Profit of non-specified trade	*€100,000*

The relief is calculated as follows –

$$\frac{QE + UE}{OE} \times QA$$

$$\frac{€90{,}000 + €30{,}000^*}{€200{,}000} \times 450{,}000 = €270{,}000 \text{ qualifying profits}$$

**Uplift expenditure is calculated as the lower of:*

- *30% of €90,000 and*
- *€125,000 (being the acquisition and outsourcing costs)*

Lower of which is €30,000

The qualifying profits of €270,000 will be liable to tax at an effective lower rate of 6.25%. The manner in which the deduction operates to yield the lower effective rate is demonstrated below:

Taxable profits from non-qualifying assets	*€100,000*
Taxable profits from qualifying assets	*€450,000*
Total taxable profits	*550,000*
Less KDB deduction (€270,000 × 50%)	*(€135,000)*
Taxable profits	*€415,000*
Tax at 12.5%	*€51,875*

Equivalent to (€280,000(€100,000 + €450,000-€270,000) × 12. 5%) + (€270,000 × 6. 25%)

29.10 Corporation Tax Exemption for Start-Up Companies

In an attempt to encourage business activity and to maintain the economic recovery this exemption is from certain taxes for new start-up companies. Ireland has always had a very high proportion of small businesses and it is hoped that this incentive can encourage further activity in this sector.

The intention of the relief is straightforward. If the corporation tax of the company in any one year is equal to or lower than €40,000 and the trade is a qualifying trade, the company is exempt from corporation tax in that year. The complications begin when the company has other income or more than one trade, etc.

The legislation is contained in s486C TCA97. It commenced on 15 December 2009 following EU approval and was backdated to 1 January 2009.

The exemption operates as follows:

1. The company must be incorporated within the EEA and can only have been in existence from 14 October 2008.
2. The trade can only have commenced on or after 1 January 2009 and before 31 December 2018. Any relief will apply for the three years from the date of commencement.
3. The relief is available for income of a qualifying trade and gains on the sale of trade assets from that qualifying trade. A qualifying trade is a trade which is *not* one of the following:
   A. A trade that was carried on previously by another person (this rules out sole traders incorporating their trade into a limited company).
   B. An existing trade (this rules out forming a new company and acquiring a new trade).
   C. An excepted trade (see 28.7.2).
   D. A trade which would come within the s441 TCA97 close company surcharge, i.e., a service company (see 32.4.3).
4. In order to qualify for the relief, the company's total corporation tax for the period must be equal to or lower than €40,000. Total Corporation Tax is defined as all corporation tax that is chargeable for the period but excluding income tax. Therefore it would include corporation tax on passive income and the close company surcharge but exclude income tax withheld, for example from a patent royalty payable under s239 TCA97.

   The relief is linked to employers PRSI paid in the period. The total tax relief is the lower of €40,000 or the employers PRSI paid by the company for all employees, subject to a maximum PRSI payment of €5,000 per employee.
5. If the company transfers part of its qualifying trade to another connected company the relief will be unavailable to both companies. This anti-avoidance legislation prevents companies sharing income to avail of the €40,000 limit in group situations, where there has not been a genuine company incorporation to commence a new trade.

   In order to counter some perceived abuse of the €40,000 limit in relation to associated companies' trades, (an associated company is as defined in s432 TCA97 - see 32.2.6) s486C TCA97 states that if a new company is formed to carry on a trade which an associated company also carries on, the new company will not qualify for relief if the associated company could have carried on the trade. This is aimed at preventing companies increasing their operations by starting new companies rather than operating through a branch structure. It will mainly affect retail chains which carry on similar trades in multiple sites. For example, if a chain of coffee shops decides to open a new shop and incorporates a company to operate the trade, the new company will not qualify as the original company could have carried on the trade.

6. To quantify the relief available the company must firstly calculate its 'Relevant Corporation Tax'. Relevant Corporation Tax is a company's total corporation tax as calculated above, less the following:
   A. Tax on income at the 25% corporation tax rate
   B. Close company surcharges
   C. Tax on chargeable gains
7. The legislation requires that amounts which can be set against total profits (typically expenses of management and non-relevant trading charges) must be set against income in priority to chargeable gains. Whilst this would be the most common approach in an ordinary situation, the taxpayer does have the option of offsetting against a chargeable gain in priority to income; however this option is now unavailable if a claim is being made under this legislation.
8. The Relevant Corporation Tax is then applied to the qualifying trade income over total income (defined as total income excluding income charged at the 25% corporation tax rate - essentially trade income). This will then give the amount to be deducted from the corporation tax charge.
9. The relief for the disposal of qualifying trade assets (assets used directly in the operation of the qualifying trade, including goodwill) is operated in the same method as Relevant Corporation Tax at 8 above. The corporation tax on chargeable gains is applied to net gains (profits less losses) on qualifying assets over net gains on all chargeable assets. This amount is then deducted from the corporation tax payable.

   No relief is available for assets transferred under s617 TCA97 (see 31.4.3).
10. Any unutilised relief from the first three years of trading (the period the relief applies for) can be carried forward. The unutilised relief will be the employer PRSI paid during the first three years less any corporation tax sheltered in that same period. This can be carried forward to the fourth and subsequent years and set against future corporation tax of the qualifying trade. This applies to accounting periods ending on or after 1 January 2013.

Example 29.13

New Co Ltd commenced trading on 1st January 2018. Mr. A. incorporated his architectural practice which had been trading for many years and opened a new café. The company's total employer PRSI charge for the year was €15,000 for all employees.

Calculation of Corporation Tax Liability:

	€
Case I – Café	*50,000*
Trade Charges	*(5,000)*
Case II – Architect	*40,000*
Case V – Rent	*10,000*
Income:	*95,000*
Chargeable gain on shares	*15,000*
Non-Trade Charges	*(7,000)*
Profits	*103,000*

Case I: 50,000 – 5,000 × 12.5%	*5,625*
Case II: 40,000 × 12.5%	*5,000*
Gain 15,000 × 12.5%	*1,875*
Passive 10,000 – 7,000 × 25%	*750*
s239 TCA97 5,000 × 20% (income tax)	*1,000*
Tax Payable	*14,250*
Relief (Note 1)	*(5,625)*
Relief (Note 2)	*(0)*
	8,625

Does the company qualify for relief?

Total Corporation Tax = €14,250 – €1,000 = €13,250. As total corporation tax is less than €40,000, relief is available.

Note 1: Calculation of Relief:

Relevant Corporation Tax = Total corporation tax, less tax @ 25%, less tax on chargeable gains = €13,250 – €750 – €1,875 = €10,625, (equivalent to corporation tax on net trading income, i.e., €85,000 × €12.5%).

$$\text{Relief} = \text{Relevant Corporation Tax} \times \frac{\text{Qualifying trade income}}{\text{Total trade income}}$$

$$€10{,}625 \times \frac{(€50{,}000 - €5{,}000)}{(€50{,}000 + €40{,}000 - €5{,}000)} = €5{,}625$$

Note 2: Calculation of Relief for corporation tax on chargeable gains

$$\text{Relief} = \text{Corporation Tax on chargeable gains} \times \frac{\text{Gains on qualifying assets}}{\text{Total chargeable gains}}$$

$$€1{,}875 \times \frac{€0}{€15{,}000} = €0$$

As the employers PRSI is greater than €5,625 this relief is allowable in full.

The company can carry forward the unutilised relief of €9,375 (€15,000 employer PRSI paid less the €5,625 relief claimed) and set it against corporation tax payable on the qualifying trade from 1 January 2016 (after the three year exemption period has expired).

29.10.1 Marginal Relief

As noted above, the full exemption from corporation tax on the qualifying trade is only available if the Total Corporation Tax is equal to, or lower than €40,000.

Marginal relief is available if the Total Corporation Tax is between €40,000 and €60,000. The corporation tax chargeable is reduced by an amount calculated by the following formula:

$$3 \times (T - M) \times \frac{(A+B)}{T}$$

The letters signify the following amounts:

T = Total Corporation Tax

M = €40,000

A = Corporation Tax on the Qualifying Trade (see above)

B = Corporation Tax on the disposal of Qualifying Assets of the Qualifying Trade (see above)

Example 29.14

New Co Ltd commences trading on the 1 January 2018. Its total corporation tax liability for the year ended 31 December 2018 is €53,000. The charge can be analysed as follows:

Tax on qualifying trade	*€25,000*
Tax on rental income	*€20,000*
Tax on qualifying assets sales	*€8,000*

The company's total employer PRSI charge for the year was €20,000 for all employees.

As the total corporation tax is in excess of €40,000 it cannot claim the full exemption. However, as the total corporation tax is lower than €60,000 marginal relief applies as follows:

3 × (€53,000 – €40,000) × (€25,000 + €8,000)/€53,000 = €24,283.

Under section 486C (4)(b) TCA97 the tax payable on the qualifying trade and assets is the greater of the formula (€24,283) or qualifying tax less the prsi (€13,000 (€33,000 - €2,000).

There is also marginal relief available for the carry forward of any unutilised relief in any period when the Total Corporation Tax is between €40,000 and €60,000, using the following formula:

$$(C - (3 \times (T - M) \times C/T) - R$$

The letters signify the following amounts:

C = Total employer PRSI paid in the period

T = Total Corporation Tax

M = €40,000

R = Marginal relief granted in the period

Appendix I

Pro forma Corporation Tax Computation

Corporation tax computation for the twelve-month accounting period to 31/12/2018

		€	€
Case I			
Tax-adjusted trading profits y/e 31/12/2018 after capital allowances		*X*	
Less	Allowable Case I losses forward	*(X)*	
	Trade losses – current period and carried back	*(X)*	
	Allowable trade charges	*(X)*	X
Case III			
Foreign source income (trade/rental, etc.)		*X*	
Interest on Irish Government securities		*X*	
Foreign bond deposit interest		*X*	
Irish building society interest		*X*	
Irish commercial bank deposit interest		*X*	X
Case IV			
Income subject to Irish tax at source		*X*	X
Case V			
Income from the letting of property in the Republic of Ireland		*X*	
Less capital allowances		*X*	X
Total income			X
Chargeable gains (as adjusted)			X
"Total profits" = income + chargeable gains			X
Deduct Allowable non-trade charges paid during y/e 31/12/2018			(X)
Other losses, i.e., excess capital allowances			
Profits liable to corporation tax			X
Corporation tax liability			
Charge at appropriate rate (12.5%, 25%, etc.)			X
			X

Deduct Trade charges and losses on a value basis	(X)
Add Close company surcharges from previous period	X
Income tax deducted by Company Limited on annual payments	X
Deduct Income tax suffered by deduction	(X)
Withholding tax for professional services	(X)
R&D tax credit	(X)
Net corporation tax liability payable	X

Appendix II

Details of Capital Allowances on Green Equipment

s285A TCA97

'Green' capital allowances

To encourage "green" capital spending, capital allowances at a rate of 100% are available for the acquisition of energy-efficient equipment as follows:

1 Motors and drives – minimum spend – €1,000

2 Lighting – minimum spend – €3,000

3 Building energy management systems – minimum spend – €5,000

4 Information and communications technology – minimum spend – €1,000

5 Heating and electricity provision – minimum spend – €1,000

6 Ventilation and air conditioning controls – minimum spend – €1,000

7 Electric and alternative fuels vehicles – minimum spend – €1,000

In relation to vehicles at 7 above, this scheme will apply in priority to the carbon emissions-based capital allowances for motor vehicles as set out in 16.2.9.

8 Refrigeration and cooling systems – minimum spend – €1,000

9 Electro-mechanical systems – minimum spend – €1,000

10 Catering and hospitality equipment – minimum spend – €1,000

The scheme commenced on 9 October 2008 and will run until 31 December 2020.

Appendix III

Transitional Arrangements for the Changeover from FRS to FRS 102/IFRS

Transitional Arrangements – Schedule 17A TCA97

Schedule 17A TCA97 deals with the transitional measures to be adopted during the move from FRS to FRS 102. There are two main parts to the schedule, one dealing with the effect of the transition on financial instruments (including bad debts) and the other with all other matters.

Transitional measures for bad debts – Schedule 17A para 3 TCA97

As noted above financial instruments are beyond the scope of this publication but the following is an example of how bad debts are dealt with during the transitional period. Bad debts are included as a financial instrument under IFRS.

Example

New Co. closed its books as at 31 December 2014 with the following bad debt provisions:

	Opening 01.01.14	***Movement***	***Closing 31.12.14***
	€	**€**	**€**
General Bad Debt Provision	*75,000*	*(25,000)*	*50,000*
Specific Bad Debt Provision	*125,000*	*50,000*	*175,000*
	200,000	*25,000*	*225,000*

For the year ended 31 December 2014 the company would deduct €25,000 from the accounting profit figure in arriving at tax adjusted Case I. There would have been no adjustment in respect of the movement in the specific reserve.

New Co. is obliged to commence implementing FRS 102 for the period beginning 1 January 2015. Under FRS 102 it reviews its bad debt provisions for trade accounts where there is objective evidence that certain amounts are not fully collectible. After the review its opening bad debt provision is €200,000, a decrease of €25,000 in the overall reserve.

For taxation purposes the general bad debt provision is ignored as the entire €50,000 has been disallowed since it was first created. The company will not however receive an allowance for the change in the specific provision from €175,000 to €200,000 (an amount of €25,000) until the annual FRS 102 reserve has fallen below the opening FRS 102 reserve by €25,000.

For the next four years the closing provisions are as follows:

– 31 December 2015 bad debt provision of €230,000

– 31 December 2016 bad debt provision of €195,000

– 31 December 2017 bad debt provision of €185,000

– 31 December 2018 bad debt provision of €100,000

	Balance Sheet	Income Statement	Tax Adjust
	€	€	€
Opening provision as at 01.01.15	*200,000*		
Closing provision as at 31.12.15	*230,000*	*30,000 Note 1*	
Closing provision as at 31.12.16	*195,000*	*(35,000) Note 2*	*5,000*
Closing provision as at 31.12.17	*185,000*	*(10,000) Note 3*	*10,000*
Closing provision as at 31.12.18	*100,000*	*(85,000) Note 4*	*10,000*
Total transitional adjustment			*25,000*

Note 1 – As the reserve has increased, no allowance for the original €25,000 increase due to the FRS 102 changeover is allowed under the transitional arrangements.

Note 2 – As the reserve has fallen below the opening provision under FRS 102 by €5,000, this amount can be deducted from taxable income under the transitional arrangements. Note that there is a further €20,000 left to be adjusted for, providing the provision is reduced sufficiently.

Note 3 – The provision has fallen below the opening provision by a further €10,000, which is deducted from the taxable income, leaving a further €10,000 of a potential deduction.

Note 4 – The closing 2018 reserve has fallen €100,000 below the opening FRS 102 adjusted reserve of 1 January 2015, therefore the final €10,000 can now be claimed.

Transitional measures for other items – Schedule 17A para 2 TCA97

If the change in accounts results in items other than bad debts and financial instruments falling out of the taxable accounts (either income or expenditure), then Sch 17A paragraph 2 spreads the item equally over five years.

There are two items which need to be dealt with for taxation purposes:

(a) – Deductible amount:

This is an expense which would ordinarily have been allowed against taxable income but because of the move from FRS to FRS 102 has not been included. Also any income which has been taxed twice, once under FRS and once under FRS 102 is a deductible amount.

(b) – Taxable amount:

This is a receipt which would ordinarily have been taxed as taxable income but because of the move from FRS to FRS 102 has not been included. Any expenditure which has been deducted twice, once under FRS and once under FRS 102 is also a taxable amount. The amount by which the taxable amount exceeds the deductible amount is taxed equally over five accounting periods and vice versa.

Example

New Co. entered into a four-year contract on 1 January 2014. It received €180,000 as an upfront payment which it included in its profit and loss account for the year ended 31 December 2014 and was taxed accordingly,

New Co. is obliged to commence implementing FRS 102 for the period beginning 1 January 2015. Under FRS 102 it reviews its income recognition policies and notes that under FRS Section 23 it should release €45,000 of the upfront contract receipt each year to its income statement.

Without the transitional measures afforded by Schedule 17A TCA97 the following scenario would arise:

	2014	2015	2016	2017	Total
	€	€	€	€	€
Revenue under FRS	180,000				180,000
Revenue under FRS 102 (Note 1)		45,000	45,000	45,000	135,000
Total amount taxable					315,000

Note 1 – Under FRS 102 it would restate the 2014 accounts for comparison purposes by releasing the first €45,000 and remove the €180,000 from the income statement. The restatement however would not have any impact on the 2014 or 2015 corporation tax computations.

New Co. would be left in a situation of being taxed twice on the same contract during the changeover in standards.

Under Schedule 17A paragraph 2 TCA97 the "deductible amount" is €135,000 and the allowance is spread over five years at €27,000 per annum.

	2014	**2015**	**2016**	**2017**	**2018**	**2019**	**Total**
	€	€	€	€	€	€	€
FRS	180,000						180,000
FRS 102		45,000	45,000	45,000			135,000
Deductible amount		(27,000)	(27,000)	(27,000)	(27,000)	(27,000)	(135,000)
Total amount taxable							180,000

The above treatment will also apply to the adoption of new accounting standards as provided for under Section 76A (4) TCA97, see 29.6.2.

30 LOSSES

Learning Outcomes

On completion of this chapter you will be able to:

- ✓ The categorisation of losses
- ✓ The utilisation of Case I/II losses as allowances and as credits on a value basis
- ✓ The utilisation of trade and non-trade charges
- ✓ The order of set-off under the various Case I/II loss provisions
- ✓ Treatment of non-trade losses
- ✓ Restriction of losses on late filing
- ✓ Compute corporation tax computations

30.1 Introduction

This chapter will consider how losses incurred by a company may be used by it against any other sources of income, either in its current accounting period, its previous accounting period or future accounting periods. Certain losses may also be surrendered to a fellow group or consortium member and this is discussed in greater detail in Chapter 31.

Having adjusted the accounting profit/loss figure for tax purposes, it may well be that losses arise under various cases, rather than profits. The chart below illustrates the various categories of losses that may arise. The manner in which losses are utilised depends firstly on whether or not they are capital losses. If they are not capital losses, the manner in which they are utilised is dependent on the case from which they are derived.

Summary Chart

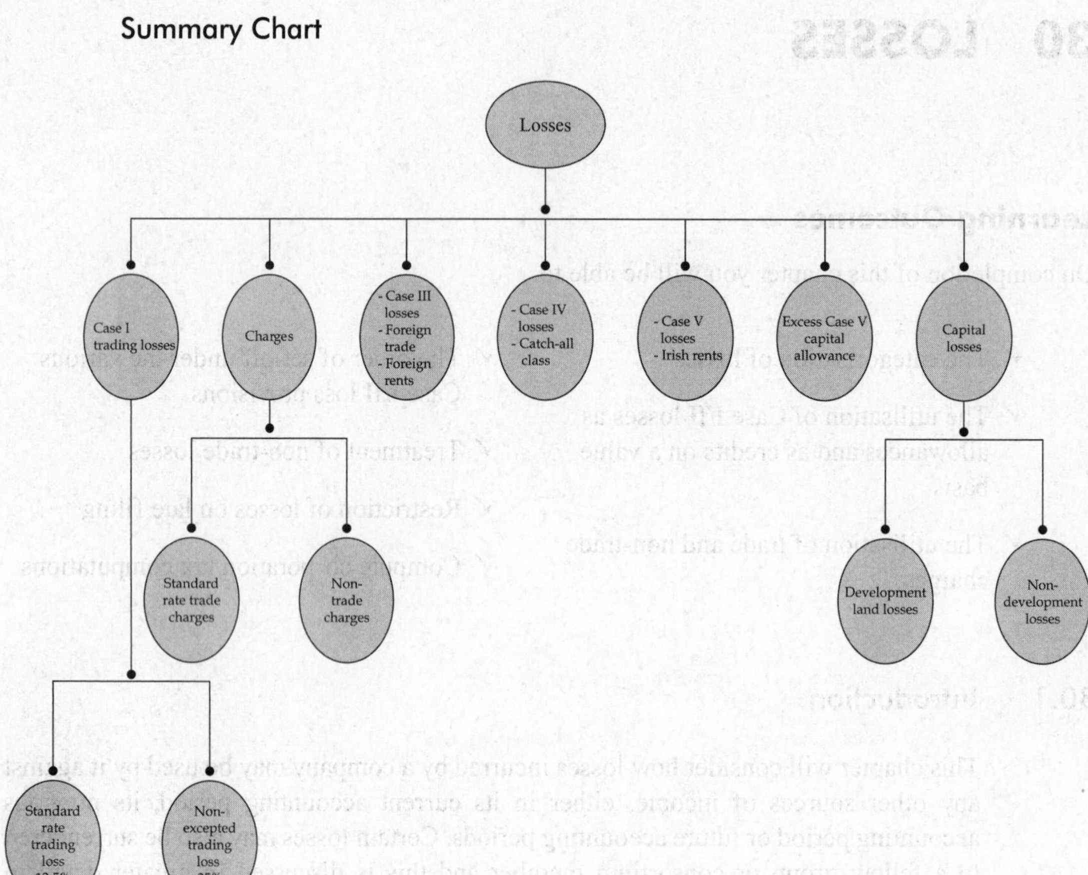

* You will note that the separation of Losses/Charges into different categories is a function of the rate at which the Losses/Charges are taxed, or the manner in which the Losses/Charges are calculated.

30.2 Categorisation of Losses

The main focus of this chapter is the use of trading losses. Since the introduction of the standard 12.5% rate, and the 25% rate for "excepted" trades, a subsequent series of legislative amendments has made what used to be relatively straightforward loss relief provisions very complex. Prior to these amendments, the disparity in the rates meant that Case I/II losses could effectively be relieved at a rate which was 50% higher than the rate at which profits of the same trade would be taxed.

The first part of this chapter considers the use of trading losses and trading charges. The second part of the chapter focuses on non-trade losses. The final section discusses the impact of late filing on losses.

30.3 Trading Losses – Case I

30.3.1 Computation

Trading losses are computed using the same rules as for trading profits, i.e., under the rules of Schedule D Case I. Capital allowances of a company are treated as a trading expense deductible in arriving at Case I profit, and hence are automatically included in the computation of losses. There is no distinction between the portion of the loss attributable to trading and the portion attributable to capital allowances.

30.3.2 Excepted Trade Losses

s396(2) TCA97

For excepted trades, a trading loss may be:

(1) set off against **other profits** before charges in the same accounting period;

(2) set off against **other profits** before charges of the preceding accounting period of corresponding length, if the company carried on the trade in that period;

(3) set off against **future profits of the same trade** unless the loss has otherwise been utilised.

Remember that 'Profits' include chargeable gains but exclude gains on development land.

See 28.7.2 for commentary on the meaning of excepted trades.

30.3.3 Loss relief – Relevant Trades

There are three important terms concerning general trade losses:

1. relevant trading income;
2. relevant trading loss;
3. relevant trading charge.

Relevant trading income

This is a company's trading income other than income from "excepted trades" (see 30.3.2) and Case III income, i.e., income from foreign trades. In essence, it is income taxable at 12.5%.

Relevant trading loss

This is a trading loss incurred in a company apart from losses of excepted trades (see 30.3.2). In essence, these are losses available at the 12.5% rate.

Relevant trading charge

These are charges on income paid by a company which are incurred wholly and exclusively for the purposes of a trade, again excluding charges paid for excepted trades.

Set-off of trade losses against other income

s396A TCA97 Under s396A TCA97 losses incurred in a relevant trade may be set sideways (i.e against income from another relevant trade carried by the company) in the current accounting period or back to the previous accounting period of the same length, but only against "relevant" trading income. The overall intention is to ensure that relevant trading losses (12.5%) are not offset against income taxable at 25%.

The following example illustrates how relief may be claimed under s396A TCA97.

Example 30.1

Loss Limited's results for the last two accounting periods are as follows:

	Year ended 31/12/2017	*Year ended 31/12/2018*
	€	€
Case I (Trade 1)	*50,000*	*(800,000)*
Case I (Trade 2)	*25,000*	*50,000*
Case III	*5,000*	*2,000*
Case V	*7,000*	*4,000*

The s396A relief would operate as follows:

Year ended 31/12/2018:

	€
Case I (Trade 1)	*Nil*
Case I (Trade 2)	*50,000*
s396A	*(50,000)*
Trading income	–
Case III	*2,000*
Case V	*4,000*
Total income	*6,000*

Year ended 31/12/2017:

	€
Case I (Trade 1)	*50,000*
Case I (Trade 2)	*25,000*
s396A	*(75,000)*
Trading income	–

Case III	*5,000*
Case V	*7,000*
Taxable income	*12,000*

The company can carry the trade loss incurred in 2018 back against the corresponding previous period (12 months) and set €75,000 of its 2018 relevant trade loss against its 2017 relevant trading-income. This leaves €675,000 of unutilised relevant trade losses.

In the above example, after utilising s396A the company has €675,000 of losses available for relief under s396B and s396(1) (see below).

The length of the preceding period against which the loss may be set off is a period equal in length to the current accounting period in which the loss is incurred. For more complex examples involving accounting periods of less than 12 months in duration, readers are referred to paragraph 30.3.4 below.

Set-off of trade losses against non-trade profits

s396B TCA97 Where a company has unutilised losses after claiming s396A TCA97, these losses may be offset on a 'value basis', against the company's corporation tax for the current accounting period and the previous accounting period of the same length. The value of the losses is computed by applying the tax rate in the year the loss **arises** (not the rate applicable in the year in which the losses are used)[1]. The losses are then given as a credit against corporation tax.

Loss relief under s396B will only be granted to the extent that losses may not be relieved under other provisions. Accordingly, claims for loss relief under s396B may only be made when maximum loss relief has been claimed under s396A. The practical effect of this is that relevant trading losses are first restricted for offset against relevant trading income and if there is an excess unused amount of losses, they may be set against the corporation tax payable on other profits by way of a credit on a value basis.

Approach to calculating s396B relief

The best way to calculate s396B relief is to answer the following three questions:

1. What is the maximum amount of relief the company could possibly use under s396B?

   The legislation provides a formula to calculate this figure:

   $$L \times \frac{R}{100}$$

   where:

   L = the amount of the relevant trading loss available after relief under s396A, and

   R = the rate of corporation tax for the accounting period in which the loss arises.

1 This would have been important in times past when the rate of corporation tax applicable to trading profits differed from year to year. For example, if a 2003 loss were being carried back to 2002, the credit given was at the rate of 12.5% and not 16%.

2. What amount of credit does the company need to get full relief?

   This is the amount of corporation tax still unrelieved.

3. What amount of credit will the company actually use?

   This is the lesser of the two figures calculated at 1 and 2 above.

4. What amount of losses are available for relief following s396B relief?

   This figure is arrived at by reducing the amount of the relevant trading loss available after relief under s396A by the gross loss used under s396B relief, calculated using the following formula:

   $$T \times \frac{100}{R}$$

   where:

   T is the tax saved (or the amount of credit used), and

   R is the rate of corporation tax for the accounting period in which the loss arises[2].

The position is best illustrated by examining the s396B claim that would apply in the case of Loss Limited in Example 30.1 above.

Example 30.2

Loss Limited's results for the last two accounting periods are as follows:

	Year ended 31/12/2017	*Year ended 31/12/2018*
	€	**€**
Case I	*50,000*	*(800,000)*
Case I (Trade 2)	*25,000*	*50,000*
Case III	*5,000*	*2,000*
Case V	*7,000*	*4,000*

The s396B relief would operate after the utilisation of the s396A relief as follows (numbers in bold signify order of use of losses):

Corporation Tax computation for year ended 31/12/2018

	€	**€**
Case I (Trade 1)		*Nil*
Case I (Trade 2)		*50,000*
s396A	*(1)*	*50,000*

2 R in both of the above formulae may well be a composite rate. Again, this would have been important when the rate of corporation tax on trading income differed from year to year. For example, for the accounting year ended 31 March 2003,

$$R = \left(16\% \times \frac{275}{365}\right) + \left(12.5\% \times \frac{90}{365}\right) = 15.13\%.$$

Case III		*2,000*
Case V		*4,000*
Total income		*6,000*
Corporation tax × 6,000 € 25%		*1,500*
s396Bcredit	*(3)*	*(1,500*)*
Tax payable		

**1. Maximum credit available: €675,000 × 12.5% = €84,375*

2. Credit required for full relief: €1,500

3. Actual credit claimed €1,500 (lesser of 1 and 2 above)

4. Loss available following s396B relief: €675,000 – (€1,500 / 12.5%) =€663,000.

Corporation tax computation for period ended 31/12/2017

		€
Case I (Trade 1)		*50,000*
Case I (Trade 2)		*25,000*
s396A	*(2)*	*(75,000)*
Trade income		*–*
Case III		*5,000*
Case V		*7,000*
Total income		*12,000*
Corporation tax €12,000 × 25%		*3,000*
*s396B credit €24,000** × 12.5%*	*(4)*	*(3,000)*
Tax payable		*–*

***1. Maximum credit available: €663,000 × 12.5% = €82,875*

2. Credit required for full relief: €3,000

3. Actual credit claimed €3,000 (lesser of 1 and 2 above)

4. Loss available following s396B relief: €663,000 – (€3,000 / 12.5%) = €639,000.

Loss Memo	€
Trading loss 31 December 2018	*800,000*
s396A claim 31 December 2018 (1)	*(50,000)*
	750,000
s396A claim 31 December 2017 (2)	*(75,000)*
Loss available for relief under s396B	*675,000*
s396B claim 31 December 2018 (3)	*(12,000)*
	663,000
s396B claim 31 December 2017 (4)	*(24,000)*
Loss available for carry forward	*639,000*

Carry forward of losses

s396(1) TCA97

Unrelieved trading losses may be carried forward for set-off against the trading income of the same trade in which the loss was incurred. A claim to carry forward a loss for set-off in succeeding accounting periods against income from the same trade may be made provided relief has not been claimed for an earlier year, i.e., under s396A or s396B. There is no time limit for making such a claim and the loss can be carried forward indefinitely provided the company continues to carry on the same trade. A loss forward must be set off against the first available income of the same trade for an earlier period in priority to a later period.

However, care needs to be exercised in calculating losses forward to ensure that the correct value of losses used has been taken into account.

Example 30.3

Loss Limited's results for the last three accounting periods are as follows:

	Year ended 31/12/2016	*Year ended 31/12/2017*	*Year ended 31/12/2018*
	€	€	€
Case I (Trade 1)	*50,000*	*(800,000)*	*100,000*
Case I (Trade 2)	*25,000*	*50,000*	*75,000*
Case III	*5,000*	*2,000*	*8,000*
Case V	*7,000*	*4,000*	*15,000*

You will note that the figures for 2016 and 2017 are the same as those used in Example 30.2. As a result, we already know that the loss carried forward as at 31 December 2017 (following relief under s396A and s396B) was €639,000. Part of this can be utilised under s396(1) as follows:

Corporation tax computation for year ended 31/12/2018:

	€
Case I (Trade 1)	*100,000*
s396(1)	*(100,000)*
Case I (Trade 2)	*75,000*
Case III	*8,000*
Case V	*15,000*
Income	*98,000*

Note that the loss carried forward can only be set against income of the same trade. The loss is not available for offset against the income of Trade 2. The remaining loss as at 31 December 2018 of €539,000 (€639,000 – €100,000 used in 2018) is carried forward for set-off against income from Trade 1 in future years.

Displacement of trading losses carried forward by non-trading charges claimed

Section 396B(5) TCA97 requires an amount of unutilised trade loss that is to be carried forward under s396(1) TCA97, to be reduced by the amount of trading losses which would have been utilised except that the company had non-trade charges available to set against profits. If the company made a s396B TCA97 claim and also used non-trade charges such as protected interest, it would have to reduce the loss carried forward by the tax saved as a result of using the charges.

Example 30.4

Charges Limited's results for the year ended 31 December 2018 are as follows:

	€
Case I	*(100,000)*
Case V	*10,000*
Non-trade charges	*5,000*
(qualifying interest on loan borrowed to invest in subsidiary)	

Corporation tax computation for the year ended 31 December 2018

	€
Case I	*0*
Case V	*10,000*
Non-trade charges	*(5,000)*
Profits	*5,000*
Corporation tax €5,000 × 25%	*1,250*
*s396B credit**	*(1,250)*
Tax payable	*0*

***1. Maximum credit available: €100,000 × 12.5% = €12,500*

2. Credit required for full relief: €1,250

3. Actual credit claimed €1,250 (lesser of 1 and 2 above)

Loss Memo	€
Trading loss 31 December 2018	*100,000*
*s396B claim * €1,250/12.5%*	*(10,000)*
	90,000
s396B(5) deemed loss usage claim (Note)	*(10,000)*
*Trade losses forward s396**	*80,000*

Note: as the company utilised both non-trade charges and s396B relief in the same period the trade losses carried forward must be reduced by the corporation tax saved in using the non-trade charges in preference to the trade losses.

The non-trade charges of €5,000 utilised saved tax at 25%, a saving of €1,250. The trade loss carried forward is deemed to be reduced by the extra s396B that would have been utilised but for the non-trade charges, that is €10,000 (€1,250/12.5%).

The additional restriction does not amend the actual computation for the period, only the amount of losses carried forward.

30.3.4 Summary

In summary, the way in which a company can claim relief for trading losses is as follows:

1. Loss as an allowance, s396A TCA97

Where a company has incurred a relevant trading loss which would have been taxable at the standard rate of corporation tax if a profit were made, then on making a claim, it may set that loss against other relevant trading income of the current accounting period, and if the claim so provides, against trading income of the preceding accounting period of corresponding length.

This applies to trading losses calculated by reference to Case I of Schedule D. It does not extend to trading losses calculated by reference to Case III of Schedule D, i.e., losses from a trade carried on abroad.

2. Excess loss as a credit, s396B TCA97

Any excess losses are then available for offset on a credit and value basis against relevant corporation tax payable for either the current accounting period, or if the company was then carrying on a trade, the previous accounting period of corresponding length. Losses available for s396B claims (i.e., those based on value and credit) are the losses as reduced by amounts already offset under s396 or s396A (i.e., those losses used as an allowance).

3. Loss as an allowance against trading income of future periods, s396(1)TCA97

Trading losses may be carried forward against future Case I income from the same trade. Readers should be aware that loss relief under this section is not contingent on maximum claims having been made under s396A and s396B. A formal claim in writing must be made by the company in order to claim relief under either s396A or s396B (see paragraph 30.3.5). However, loss relief under s396(1) is automatic and no claim within a specified time frame is required. It is listed here as the third alternative for claiming relief for trading losses because in practice, most companies prefer to claim maximum relief in the earliest possible accounting period.

A series of practical examples best illustrate how these sections operate in practice.

Example 30.5

Izna Ltd had the following results for the accounting period ended 31/12/2018:

	€
Case I loss	*(200,000)*
Case V income	*120,000*

Ignoring other years and group relief, the corporation tax computation is as follows:

Case V €120,000 @ 25%	*30,000*
*Loss as a credit on a value basis**	*(25,000)*
CT payable	*5,000*

**1. Maximum credit available: €200,000 × 12.5% = €25,000*

2. Credit required for full relief: €30,000

3. Actual credit claimed €25,000 (lesser of 1 and 2 above)

4. Loss available following s396B relief: €200,000 – (€25,000 / 12.5%) = €0.

Note that the trading loss may not be set against the Case V income, but can be used against corporation tax payable thereon as a credit on a value-only basis.

Example 30.6

Abacus cimited's results for the last three accounting periods are as follows:

	Year ended 31/12/2016	*Year ended 31/12/2017*	*Year ended 31/12/2018*
	€	**€**	**€**
Case I	*(500,000)*	*200,000*	*400,000*
Case III	*5,000*	*10,000*	*20,000*
Case V	*10,000*	*20,000*	*40,000*

Corporation tax computation for year ended 31/12/2016:

	€
Case I	*Nil*
Case III	*5,000*
Case V	*10,000*
Total income	*15,000*

Corporation tax computation for year ended 31/12/2017:

	€
Case I	*200,000*
s396(1)	*(200,000)*
	–
Case III	*10,000*
Case V	*20,000*
Total income	*30,000*

Corporation tax computation for year ended 31/12/2018:

	€
Case I	*400,000*
s396(1)	*(300,000)*
	100,000
Case III	*20,000*
Case V	*40,000*
Total income	*160,000*

Loss utilisation table

	€
Trade loss 31 December 2016	*500,000*
s396(1) claim 31 December 2017	*(200,000)*
s396(1) claim 31 December 2018	*(300,000)*
Loss available for carry forward	*–*

Note: The solution to this example is based on the assumption that Abacus Limited did not make a claim under s396A or s396B.

Example 30.7

Loss Leaders Limited had the following results:

	Year ended 31/12/2017	*Six months ended 30/06/2018*
	€	€
Case I	*40,000*	*(60,000)*

The company has no other income and wishes to claim immediate loss relief.

Taxable Case I calculation:

	Year ended 31/12/2017	*Six months ended 30/06/2018*
	€	€
Case I	*40,000*	*Nil*
*Less: s396A**	*(20,000)*	
Taxable	*20,000*	*Nil*

** The loss can only be carried back against a period of equal length. Therefore the profit for offset in the year ended 31/12/2016 is restricted to €40,000 × 6/12 = €20,000. The balance of loss available for relief is €60,000 − €20,000 = €40,000*

Example 30.8

Loser Limited had the following results:

	15 months ended 30/06/2017	*Year ended 30/06/2018*
	€	€
Case I	*20,000*	*(25,000)*

The 15-month period of account is divided into two accounting periods, one of 12 months and the other three months. Note the three-month period falls after the first 12-month period so that relief would be available as follows:

	Year ended 31/03/2017	*Three months ended 30/06/2017*	*Year ended 30/06/2018*
	€	€	€
Case I	*16,000**	*4,000***	*Nil*
*Less: s396A****	*(12,000)*	*(4,000)*	
Taxable	*4,000*	*Nil*	*Nil*

** €20,000 × 12/15*

***€20,000 × 3/15*

**** The loss can only be carried back against a period of equal length (i.e., 12 months). Therefore the Case I in the three-month period can be relieved in full, while only 9/12 for the Case I for the year ended 31/03/2017 can be relieved.*

The loss carried forward is therefore calculated as follows:	*€*
Total loss	*25,000*
Less used in preceding 12 months:	
3 months	*(4,000)*
9 months	*(12,000)*
Loss available for carry forward	*9,000*

Example 30.9

The results of Loss Makers Limited for three accounting periods are as follows:

	Year ended 31/03/2017	*Nine months ended 31/12/2017*	*Year ended 31/12/2018*
	€	*€*	*€*
Case I	*20,000*	*100,000*	*(600,000)*
Case III	*75,000*	*60,000*	*0*

Loss Makers Limited's corporation tax position would be as follows:

	Year ended 31/03/2017	*Nine months ended 31/12/2017*	*Year ended 31/12/2018*
	€	*€*	*€*
Case I	*20,000*	*100,000*	*Nil*
*Less: s396A**	*(5,000)*	*(100,000)*	
Net Case I	*15,000*	*Nil*	*Nil*
Case III	*75,000*	*60,000*	*0*
Taxable Profits	*90,000*	*60,000*	*Nil*
Corporation tax as follows:			
	15,000 × 12.5% = 1,875	*0 × 12.5% = 0*	
	75,000 × 25% = 18,750	*60,000 × 25% = 15,000*	
Less: s396B	*(4,688)*	*(15,000)*	
Final Corporation tax	*15,937*	*0*	

s396B relief for Nine months ended 31/12/2017

1. Maximum credit available	*495,000 × 12.5% = 61,875*
2. Credit required for full relief	*15,000*
3. Actual credit claimed	*15,000*

4. Loss remaining *495,000 – (15,000 / 12.5%) = 375,000*

s396B relief for Year ended 31/03/2017

1. Maximum credit available *375,000 × 12.5% = 46,875*

2. Credit required for full relief *18,750 × 3/12 = 4,688*

3. Actual credit claimed *4,688*

4. Loss remaining *375,000 – (4,688 / 12.5%) = 337,500*

Note: The company must claim loss relief under s396A(3) TCA97 prior to making a claim under s396B TCA97. In addition, full relief is not available in respect of the 12 months to 31 March 2017 as only three of these months fall within the period which is equal in length to the accounting period in which the trading loss arose.

The unused trading losses of €337,500 are available for carry forward by Loss Makers Limited under s396(1)TCA97.

Example 30.10

Tough Times Limited's results for the last two accounting periods are as follows:

	Year ended 31/12/2017	*Period ended 30/06/2018*
	€	€
Case I	*100,000*	*(300,000)*
Case V	*50,000*	*20,000*

Corporation tax computations are as follows:

	Year ended 31/12/2017	*Period ended 30/06/2018*
	€	€
Case I	*100,000*	*Nil*
*Less: s396A**	*(50,000)*	
Net Case I	*50,000*	*Nil*
Case V	*50,000*	*20,000*
Taxable Profits	*100,000*	*20,000*

Corporation tax as follows:

	50,000 × 12.5% = 6,250	*0 × 12.5% = 0*
	50,000 × 25% = 12,500	*20,000 × 25% = 5,000*
Less: s396B	*(6,250)*	*(5,000)*
Final Corporation tax	*12,500*	*Nil*

s396B for Period ended 30/06/2018

1. Maximum credit available *250,000 × 12.5% = 31,250*

2. Credit required for full relief *5,000*

3. Actual credit claimed *5,000*

4. Loss remaining *250,000 – (5,000 / 12.5%) = 210,000*

s396B for Year ended 31/12/2017

1. Maximum credit available	*210,000 × 12.5% = 26,250*
2. Credit required for full relief	*12,500 × 6/12 = 6,250*
3. Actual credit claimed	*6,250*
4. Loss remaining	*210,000 – (6,250 / 12.5%) = 160,000*

Note 1: The loss is only available for offset against 6/12 of the preceding year as the loss was incurred in a period of only six months' duration.

30.3.5 Time limit for claims

The time limit for making claims for loss relief under s396A and s396B TCA97 is two years from the end of the accounting period in which the loss was incurred. Relief under s396(1) is granted automatically, i.e., a formal claim for relief within a specified time frame is not required.

30.4 Relief for Trading Charges

30.4.1 Relief in current period

s243A & s243B TCA97

Charges comprise interest, annuities and other annual payments, patent royalties, etc. These payments are treated as "pure income" receipts in the hands of the recipient. This effectively means that no expenses have been incurred in generating the income. Such payments, known as "charges on income" are set against the total profits of the company and not against the particular source of income with which the payment is actually connected.

Unlike losses, relief for charges is given on a paid basis. In the case of trading charges (i.e. charges incurred wholly and exclusively for the purposes of the trade) s243A TCA97 and s243B TCA97 operate in the same manner as s396A TCA97 and s396B TCA97 respectively, with the exception that there is no carry back to prior period(s).

Accordingly, where trading charges exceed the Case I income in respect of which they are paid, they may be offset against relevant trading income for the period in which they are paid under s243A TCA97. Where trading charges exceed relevant trading income for the period in which they are paid, they may be used under s243B on a value or credit basis against the corporation tax liability for the period in which they are paid. It should also be noted that the following may not be reduced by the excess charges:

- Withholding tax; or
- Close company surcharge on undistributed income (see Chapter 32).

Finally, there is no relief for excess non-trade charges, i.e., non-trade charges, to the extent that they exceed total profits, will remain unrelieved. The following example best illustrates how charges can be relieved in the year in which they are paid.

Example 30.11

Z Limited's results for the year ended 31 December 2018 are as follows:

	Year ended 31/12/2018
	€
Case I	*50,000*
Case V	*100,000*
	€
Trade charges	*(100,000)*
Non-trade charges	*(30,000)*

Corporation tax computation for year ended 31/12/2018

	€
Case I	*50,000*
s243A	*(50,000)*
	–
Case V	*100,000*
Non-trade charges (s243)	*(30,000)*
Taxable profits	*70,000*

Corporation tax liability

	€	
Case V: €70,000 × 25%	*17,500*	
s243B: 50,000 × 12.5%	*(6,250)*	*[(€100,000 – €50,000) × 12.5%]*
Corporation tax payable	*11,250*	

Trade charges utilisation memo

	€
Trade charges paid	*100,000*
Utilised s243A	*(50,000)*
Utilised s243B	*(50,000)*
Unutilised	*–*

Example 30.12

Passive Limited's results for the year ended 31 December 2018 are as follows:

	€
Case I	*25,000*
Case V	*10,000*
Trade charges	*(5,000)*
Non-trade charges	*50,000*

Corporation tax computation for the year ended 31 December 2018

	€
Case I	*25,000*
Trade charges	*(5,000)*
	20,000
Case V	*10,000*
Non-trade charges	*(30,000)*
Profits	*–*

The non-trade charges not utilised €20,000 (€50,000 – €30,000), similar to trade charges, cannot be carried back to a previous period. However, whereas trade charges unutilised can be carried forward with s396(1) TCA97, unutilised non-trade charges cannot and are effectively lost if not relieved in the period.

30.4.2 Carry forward of unused trade charges

s396(7) TCA97

A company may add unused excess trade charges to trading losses for carry forward under s396(1) TCA97. Excess charges are only available for use in the current accounting period or for carry forward as a trading loss. They may not be carried back.

The formulae for calculating the amount of charges that have been used on a value and credit basis and the amount available for carry forward are exactly the same as the formulae used for losses (see paragraph 30.3.3).

30.5 Order of Loss Relief Claims

The order in which losses may be utilised is as follows:

Table 1

Section	*Provision*
396(1) TCA97	*Trading losses forward from an earlier period against trading income of the same trade*
396A TCA97*	*Trading losses against non-25% income - current and prior corresponding period*
243A TCA97	*Relevant trade charges against non-25% income - current period*
243B TCA97	*Relief for charges on a value basis - current period*
396B TCA97	*Relief for losses on a value basis - current and prior period*
420A TCA97	*Group relief for relevant losses and charges - current period*
420B TCA97	*Group relief on a value basis for relevant losses and charges - current period*
396(1) TCA97	*Carry any remaining trade losses forward to future trade income of the same trade*

* The allowance under s396A TCA97 must be claimed before claiming the following:

- Non-trade charges; and
- Management expenses; and
- Other amounts claimable against profits,

with the exception of excess Case V allowances (see 30.10 below).

Section 243B TCA97 and s396B TCA97 can only be claimed when s243A TCA97 and s396A TCA97 respectively have been claimed.

Group relief on a value and credit basis can only be claimed where all other reliefs available to the loss making company have been claimed first. The group relief provisions are considered in Chapter 31.

30.6 Trading Losses – Case III

Summary Chart

s396(4), s396(6) TCA97

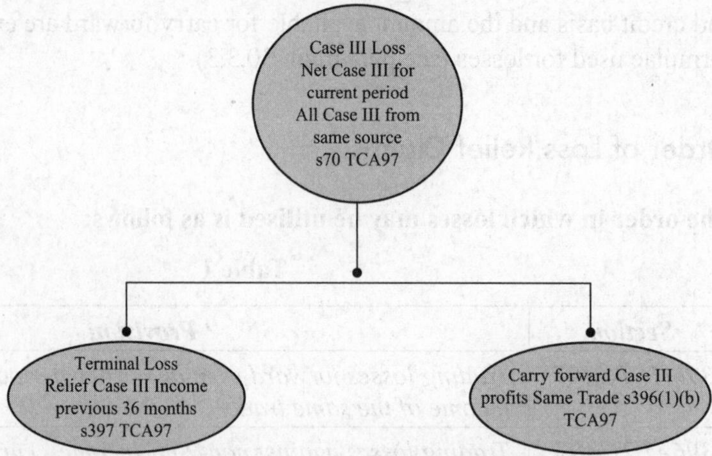

A trade is assessed under Case III if it is carried on wholly abroad. Profits from a trade carried on wholly abroad are taxable at 25%. Case III trading losses can only be used by way of carry forward for offset against future profits of the same trade. However, this includes interest or dividends on investments which would be taken into account as trading receipts, except for the fact that they were taxed under some other section. A claim for terminal loss relief may also be made. Case III losses may not be offset against other profits in the same accounting period or carried back to the preceding period in the same manner as losses calculated under Case I of Schedule D.

Legislation arising from the ECJ decision in the *Marks & Spencer v Halsey* case, which gives limited relief for losses incurred in non-resident EU companies is discussed in section 31.2.

The basis for calculating a liability to tax for income assessable under Case III of Schedule D is to treat all income as arising from a single source s70 TCA97. Therefore if foreign trading losses arise they will effectively be netted against other sources of Case III income, which might include, for example, foreign rents, foreign securities and possessions, deposit interest etc. This netting will effectively give relief for the trading losses where there is another source of Case III income.

Example 30.13

Euro Limited has a trade carried on wholly abroad. It has incurred losses in this trade of €10,000 for the period ended 31 December 2018. For the same period it has earned deposit interest of €15,000, which is assessed to tax under Case III. The net amount assessable to tax under Case III Schedule D is €5,000.

30.7 Case IV Losses

s399(1) TCA97

Summary Chart

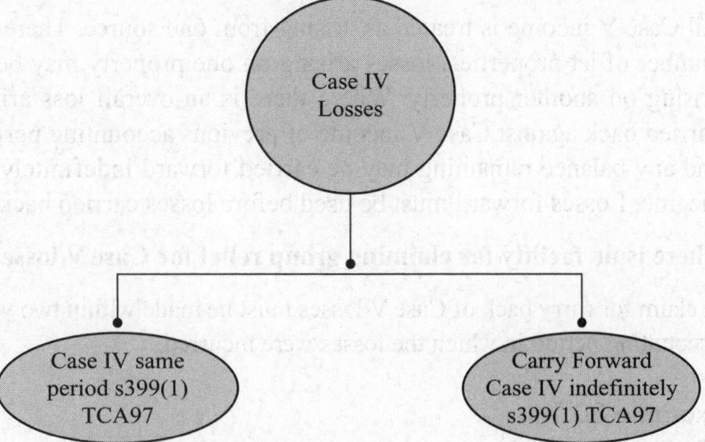

Case IV losses may only be set against other Case IV income of the same period and then carried forward indefinitely against future Case IV income. There is no time limit within which the claim to carry forward the losses may be made.

There is no facility to claim group relief for Case IV losses.

30.8 Case V Losses

s399(2), (3),(4) TCA97

Summary Chart

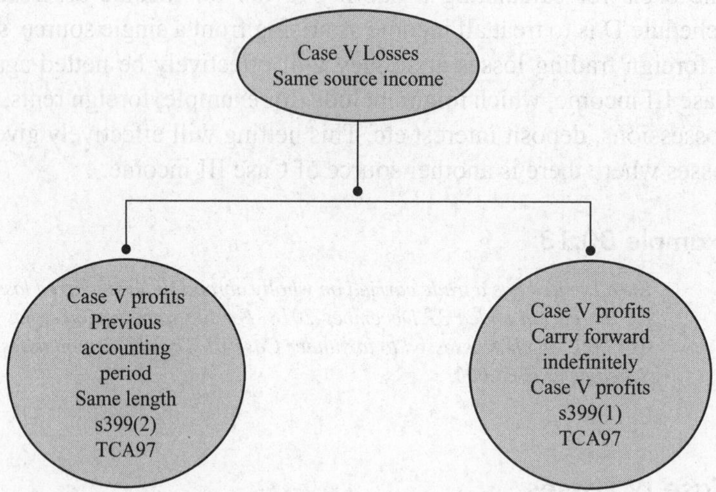

Case V losses are those arising from Irish rents and are specifically described as "the aggregate of the deficiencies computed in accordance with s97(1), which exceed the aggregate of the surpluses as so computed."

All Case V income is treated as arising from one source. Therefore, where there are a number of let properties, losses arising on one property may be netted against profits arising on another property. Where there is an overall loss arising, this loss may be carried back against Case V income of previous accounting periods of an equal length and any balance remaining may be carried forward indefinitely against future Case V income. Losses forward must be used before losses carried back.

There is no facility for claiming group relief for Case V losses.

s399(4) TCA97

A claim for carry back of Case V losses must be made within two years from the end of the accounting period in which the losses were incurred.

Example 30.14

Rack Rent Ltd had the following results:

	€
Accounting period year ended 31/12/2017: Case V profit	*5,000*
Accounting period year ended 31/12/2018: Case V loss	*(7,000)*
There was a loss forward at 1/1/2017 of	*(2,000)*

Loss relief is given as follows:

Case V: year to 31/12/2017	€
Profit	*5,000*
Less loss forward	*(2,000)*
	3,000
Loss carried back from year ended 31/12/2018	*(7,000)*
Loss available for carry forward	*(4,000)*

Example 30.15

Landlord Limited's results for three accounting periods are as follows:

	Year ended 31/12/2016	*Year ended 31/12/2017*	*Period ended 30/06/2018*
	€	€	€
Case I	*5,000*	*12,000*	*20,000*
Case III	*3,000*	*6,000*	*6,500*
Case V	*(2,000)*	*5,000*	*(4,000)*

Corporation tax computation for the year ended 31 December 2016

	€
Case I	*5,000*
Case III	*3,000*
Case V	*0*
Profits	*8,000*
Corporation tax €5,000 × 12.50%	*625*
Corporation tax €3,000 × 25%	*750*
Tax payable	*1,375*

The Case V loss of €2,000 is carried forward under s399 TCA97.

Corporation tax computation for the year ended 31 December 2017

	€	€
Case I		*12,000*
Case III		*6,000*
Case V	*5,000*	
less s399 forward from 31/12/16	*(2,000)*	
	3,000	
less s399 back from 30/6/17 (1)	*(1,500)*	

	1,500
Profits	*19,500*
Corporation tax €12,000 × 12.50%	*1,500*
Corporation tax €7,500 × 25%	*1,875*
Tax payable	*3,375*

Corporation tax computation for the period ended 30 June 2018

	€	
Case I	*20,000*	
Case III	*6,500*	
Case V	*0*	
Profits	*26,500*	
Corporation tax €20,000 × 12.50%	*2,500*	
Corporation tax €6,500 × 25%	*1,625*	
Tax payable	*4,125*	
Loss Memo		
Case V loss 30 June 2018	*4,000*	
s399 claim (1)	*(1,500)*	*Note 1*
s399 TCA97 forward	*2,500*	

Note 1 – as the loss originated in a six-month period it is carried back against a corresponding prior period, 50% of the year ended 31 December 2017 and set against that period's taxable Case V income, €1,500 (€3,000 × 50%).

30.9 Excess Case V Capital Allowances

s308(3), (4) TCA97

Summary Chart

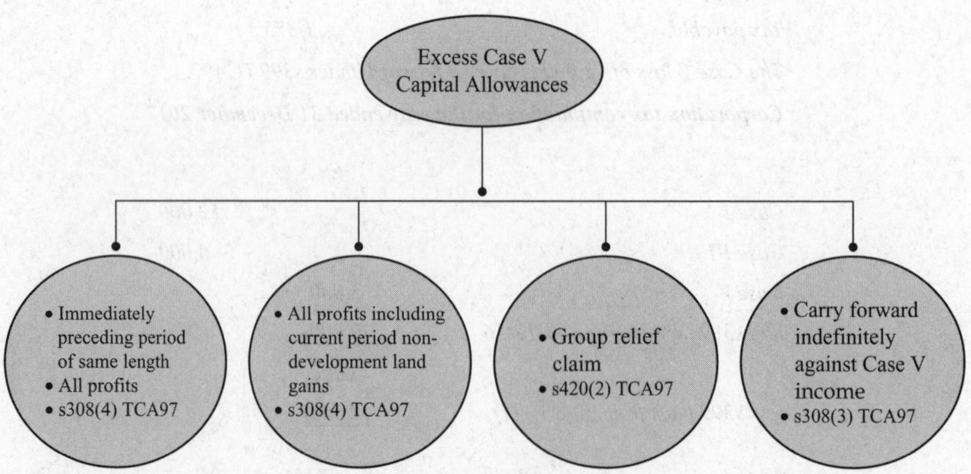

The narrow treatment of "ordinary" Case V losses must be contrasted with the more favourable treatment available for excess Case V capital allowances. The excess may be:

- Deducted from the profits of the accounting period (other income, plus non-development land capital gains); and/or
- Deducted from profits of the immediately preceding accounting period (of equal length); and/or
- Carried forward indefinitely against Case V income in future accounting periods.

A claim for group relief may be made for excess Case V capital allowances, see Chapter 31.

As excess Case V capital allowances are effectively relieved at 25%, none of the earlier value and credit restrictions, etc., apply to the offset of these allowances.

A claim for carry back of excess Case V capital allowances must be made within two years of the end of the accounting period in which the excess Case V capital allowances arise.

Example 30.16

Rent Excess Limited had the following results:

Year-end	*Case I*	*Case III*	*Case V*	*Case V Capital Allowances*
	€	€	€	€
31/12/2016	*1,000*	*1,000*	*1,000*	*500*
31/12/2017	*500*	*500*	*1,000*	*6,000*
31/12/2018	*2,000*	*2,000*	*1,000*	*500*

Accounting period year ended 31/12/2017	€	€
Case I		*500*
Case III		*500*
		1,000
Less Case V excess capital allowances		
Case V	*1,000*	
Capital allowances	*(6,000)*	
Excess	*5,000*	*(5,000)*
Excess available for carry back or forward		*(4,000)*
Accounting period year ended 31/12/2016		
Case I		*1,000*
Case III		*1,000*
Case V	*1,000*	
Capital Allowances	*(500)*	*500*
		2,500
Less excess capital allowances carried back		*(4,000)*
Excess available for carry forward		*(1,500)*

Note: one alternative solution would be to set €1,000 of the excess capital allowances from 2017 against the rental income first and set the capital allowances for 2016 against other income, along with the remaining €3,000 of capital allowances from 2017. This would however give the same amount of losses to be carried forward as under the above method.

Accounting period year ended 31/12/2018

Case I		*2,000*
Case III		*2,000*
		4,000
Case V	*1,000*	
Excess	*(500)*	
Excess brought forward	*(1,500)*	
*Excess carried forward**	*(500)*	
Profits taxable		*3,500*

**The excess Case V capital allowances are available for carry forward against future Case V income under S399(1).*

Example 30.17

Maria Limited's results for three accounting periods are as follows:

	Year ended 31/12/2016	*Year ended 31/12/2017*	*Year ended 31/12/2018*
	€	€	€
Case I	*7,000*	*10,000*	*13,000*
Case III	*2,500*	*3,000*	*3,500*
Case V	*5,500*	*6,000*	*10,000*
Case V capital allowances		*(56,000)*	
Chargeable gains	*6,000*		*90,000*

Corporation tax computation for the year ended 31 December 2016

	€	
Case I	*7,000*	
Case III	*2,500*	
Case V	*5,500*	
Income	*15,000*	
Chargeable gain	*6,000*	
Excess Case V capital allowances	*(21,000)*	*(3)*
Profits	*0*	

Corporation tax computation for the year ended 31 December 2017

	€	€
Case I		*10,000*
Case III		*3,000*
Case V	*6,000*	

Less Case V capital allowances	*(6,000)*	*0*	*(1)*
		0	
Less excess capital allowances		*(13,000)*	*(2)*
Profits		*0*	

Corporation tax computation for the year ended 31 December 2018

		€	
Case I		*13,000*	
Case III		*3,500*	
Case V	*10,000*		
Less Case V loss forward	*(10,000)*		*(4)*
Case V		*0*	
Income		*16,500*	
Chargeable gain		*90,000*	
Profits		*106,500*	
Corporation tax €13,000 × 12.50%		*1,625*	
Corporation tax €90,000 × 12.50%		*11,250*	
Corporation tax €3,500 × 25%		*875*	
Tax payable		*13,750*	

Loss Memo

	€	
Case V capital allowances 31/12/17	*56,000*	
set against Case V 31/12/17	*(6,000)*	*(1)*
Excess Case V capital allowances	*50,000*	
s308(4) claim	*(13,000)*	*(2)*
s308(4) claim	*(21,000)*	*(3)*
s399 Case V losses forward	*16,000*	
s399 claim	*(10,000)*	*(4)*
s399 TCA97 forward		
s399 TCA97 forward	*6,000*	

30.10 Capital Losses

s78(2)(4), s31, s653 TCA97

Summary Chart

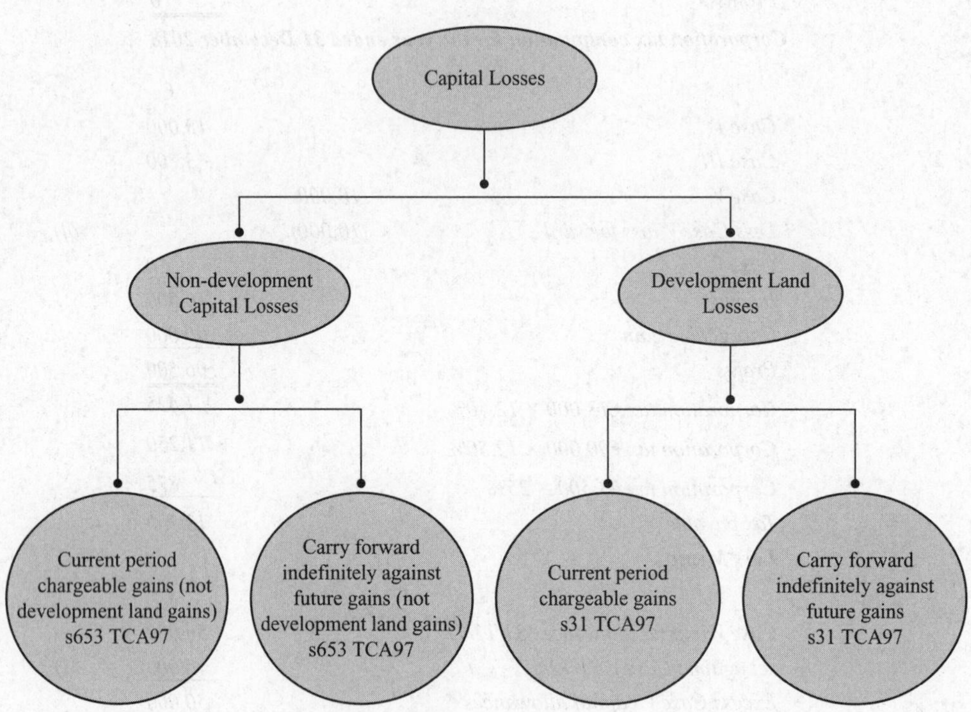

Where a company makes a gain on a disposal of an asset, the gain is regarded as profit of the company for the purposes of corporation tax. Section 649 provides that where a company disposes of development land, the company is liable to capital gains tax on the disposal. The distinction between the two methods of taxing the gains has implications for how losses on disposal are relieved.

Section 31 allows the offset of current period losses against current period gains and allows for the offset of losses forward. Therefore capital losses on non-development land assets may be set against chargeable gains (other than capital gains on development land) in the current accounting period and any balance unused can be carried forward indefinitely with no time limit set for making a claim. Capital losses on development land can be set off against capital gains on any other kind of asset.

Section 653 TCA97 restricts the offset of capital losses on ordinary disposals against develop-ment land disposals.

30.11 Restrictions on Loss Relief

30.11.1 Late filing

s1085 TCA97 Claims over the utilisation of the following "loss" reliefs and certain other set-offs are restricted where corporation tax returns for accounting periods are submitted late.

The claims affected are:

Section	***Provision***
308(4)	*Excess Case V capital allowances*
396(2)	*Current period and prior period losses*
396A(3)	*Relevant trading losses*
399(2)	*Case IV and Case V losses*
396B	*Value and credit basis for claiming loss relief*
420	*Group relief*
420A	*Ring-fenced group relief*
420B	*Value and credit basis for claiming group relief*

Losses forward under s396(1) TCA97 are not restricted

Where returns are submitted more than two months late, there is a 50% restriction on the amount of relief which would otherwise have been available. This restriction is limited to a total of €158,715.

Where the corporation tax return is submitted late but is filed within two months of its due date, a 25% restriction on the utilisation of losses arises. This is subject to a maximum restriction of €31,740.

Example 30.18

Disorganised Limited has the following results:

Year ended 31/12/2018	€
Case I loss	*(10,000)*
Case V profit	*20,000*

The company's liability to corporation tax for the accounting period ended 31/12/2018 is computed as follows:

		€
Case V	*€20,000 @ 25%*	*5,000*
s396B relief	*€10,000 × 12.5%*	*(1,250)*
CT payable		*3,750*

The amount of the loss of €10,000 available for set-off against the profits of accounting period ended 31/12/2018 on a value and credit basis is worth €1,250. However, Disorganised Limited fails to submit its return on time but plans to submit it within a month of its due date. They ask for advice on the revised amount of tax due.

The company's liability to corporation tax for accounting period ended 31/12/2018 is now computed as follows:

		€
Case V	*€20,000 @ 25%*	*5,000*
s396B relief	*€10,000 × 12.5% × 75%*	*(938)*
CT payable		*4,062*

Despite best intentions, the return is not filed until three months after its due date, Disorganised Limited asks for advice on the final amount due:

The company's liability to corporation tax for accounting period ended 31/12/2018 is revised as follows:

		€
Case V	*€20,000 @ 25%*	*5,000*
s396B relief	*€10,000 × 12.5% × 50%*	*(625)*
CT payable		*4,375*

The remaining Case I loss of €5,000 (€10,000 – €625/12.5%) is carried forward for offset against future income of the same trade.

Summary Chart – Treatment of Losses

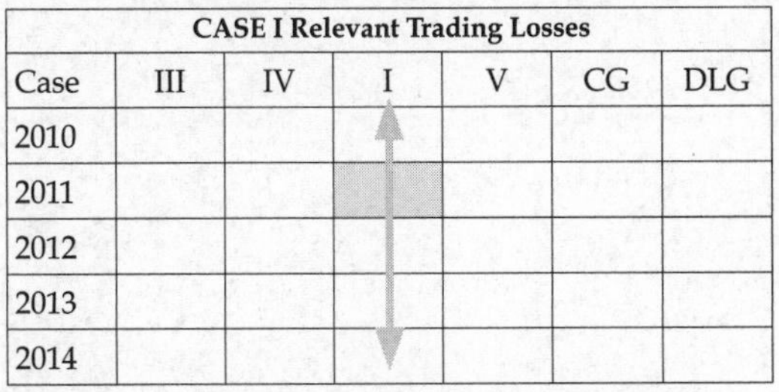

CASE I Relevant Trading Losses						
Case	III	IV	I	V	CG	DLG
2010						
2011						
2012						
2013						
2014						

s396(1) Relevant Trading Losses as deduction
s396A(3) do
Time Limit: Carry back – two years from end of AP in which loss incurred
Time Limit: Carry forward: None

CASE I Excess Relevant Trading Losses on a Value Basis						
Case	III	IV	I	V	CG	DLG
2010						
2011						
2012						
2013						
2014						

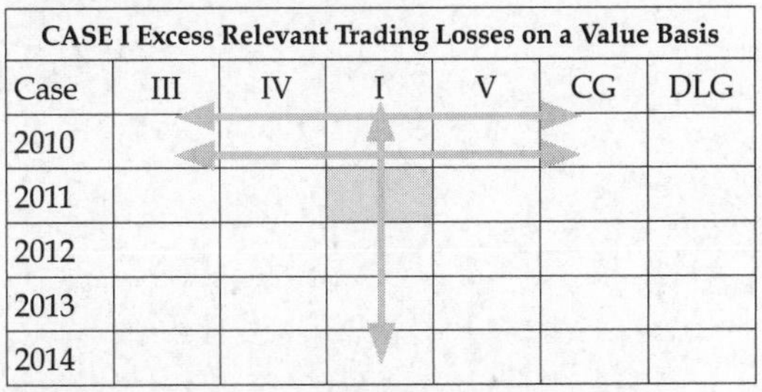

s396B TCA97. Time Limit: Current. Carry back: two years from end of AP. Set off: against relevant corporation tax of current preceding AP

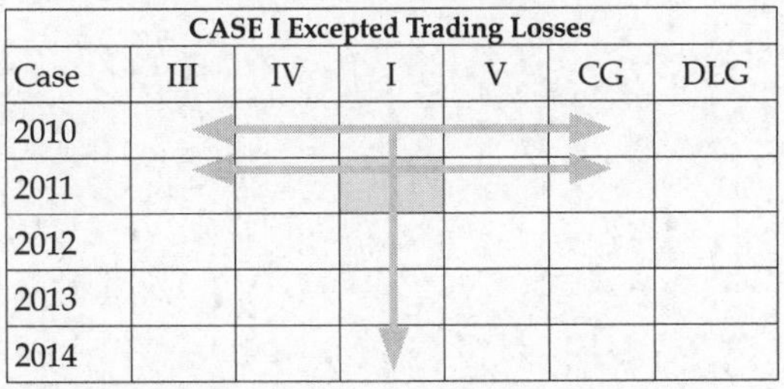

CASE I Excepted Trading Losses						
Case	III	IV	I	V	CG	DLG
2010						
2011						
2012						
2013						
2014						

s399(1), (2)
Time Limit: Carry back – two years from end of AP in which loss incurred
Time Limit: Carry forward: None

CASE IV Losses						
Case	I	III	IV	V	CG	DLG
2010						
2011						
2012						
2013						
2014						

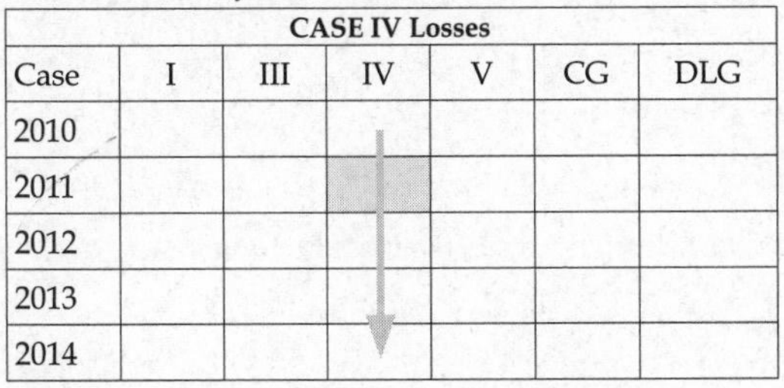

s399(1)
Time Limit: None. Carry forward indefinitely

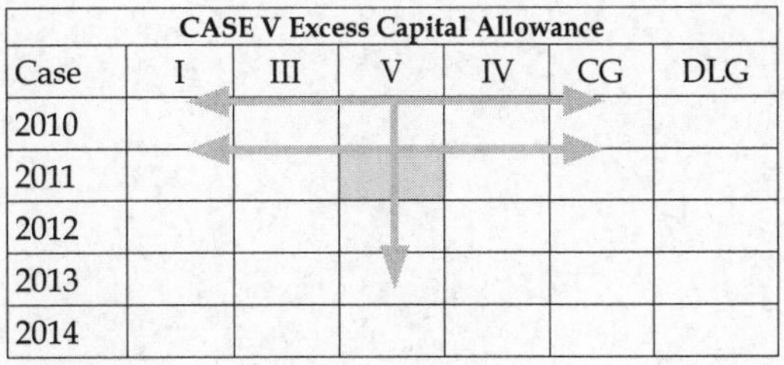

CASE V Excess Capital Allowance						
Case	I	III	V	IV	CG	DLG
2010						
2011						
2012						
2013						
2014						

s307
Time Limit: Carry back – two years from the end of the AP in which the excess arises
Time Limit: Carry forward – None

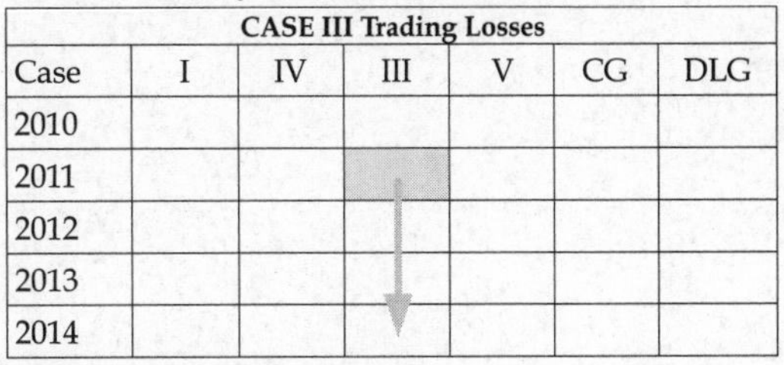

CASE III Trading Losses						
Case	I	IV	III	V	CG	DLG
2010						
2011						
2012						
2013						
2014						

s399(1), (4). Time Limit: none

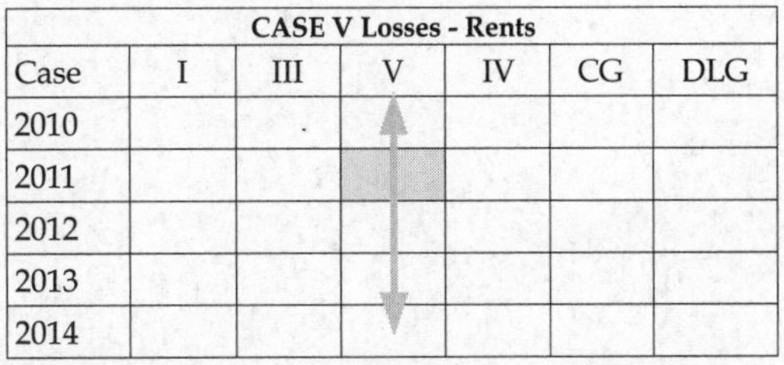

CASE V Losses - Rents						
Case	I	III	V	IV	CG	DLG
2010						
2011						
2012						
2013						
2014						

s399(2), (3), (4). Time Limit: Carry back – two years.
Time Limit: Carry forward - none

Capital Losses (i)						
Case	I	III	CG	DLG	IV	V
2010						
2011						
2012						
2013						
2014						

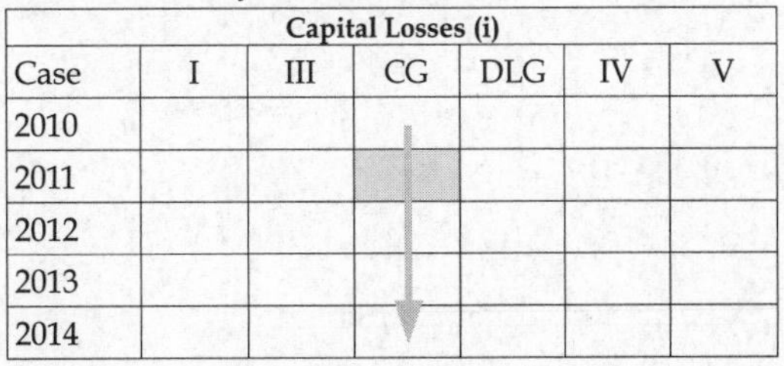

s78(4). Time Limit: None
See FA99 s57 (New Schedule 18A TCA97) which restricts the use "pre-entry losses" where a company joins a group

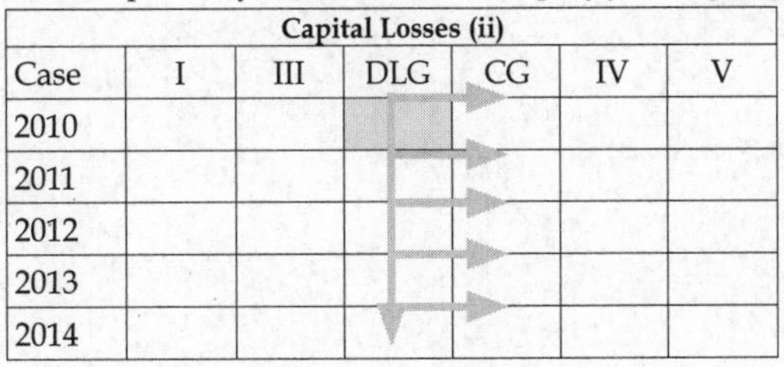

Capital Losses (ii)						
Case	I	III	DLG	CG	IV	V
2010						
2011						
2012						
2013						
2014						

31 GROUPS: PAYMENTS, LOSSES AND TRANSFERS OF ASSETS

Learning Outcomes

On completion of this chapter you will be able to:

- ✓ The meaning of a group for:
  - – losses
  - – capital gains
  - – intra-group payments
- ✓ The utilisation of group loss relief
- ✓ The meaning of a consortium
- ✓ Relief from withholding tax on intra-group payments
- ✓ Relief for intra-group asset transfers
- ✓ Implications of leaving a capital gains group
- ✓ Transfer pricing

31.1 Introduction

A company forms a separate legal entity for tax purposes. However, the relationships that exist between certain companies allow them to avail of reliefs that are not available to companies which operate on a stand-alone basis. This chapter examines the reliefs available to groups of companies and the conditions that are required to be satisfied in order to avail of those reliefs. A group relationship facilitates the offset of losses incurred by one company against profits of another, payments of interest and charges without the necessity to withhold tax and also the ability to transfer assets between group companies without incurring corporation tax on any gains arising.

Unfortunately, the rules associated with group relief in its various formats as outlined are not straightforward. When considering group relief, it is necessary to take account of other sections of the legislation (such as the loss relief provisions) in conjunction with group relief. In addition, there are different definitions of groups and consortia depending on the type of relief claimed, as well as different requirements for availing of relief. For this reason, the discussion is broken down into three sections: the first deals with losses in a group context; the second with relief for different payments made between groups; and the third with intra-group transfers of assets.

31.2 Group Relief for Losses

This section will consider the surrender of losses, excess capital allowances and charges between members of a group of companies.

31.2.1 Introduction

s411 TCA97

Chapter 30 dealt with losses incurred by a company and illustrated how these may be used within that same company. This chapter deals with losses which have not otherwise been relieved within the company, and how they may be transferred within a group of companies. The discussion deals with the relationship that is required in order to allow a claim for group relief (paragraph 31.2.2 below) and also with the type of reliefs that are available to a group of companies.

The scheme of relief operates to permit one company in a group to surrender current year losses and certain other amounts including excess capital allowances and charges to another member of the group that has profits. The relief applies to **current trading losses and excess charges only;** trading losses forward cannot be surrendered.

The company transferring the loss is called the "surrendering company" and the company receiving the loss is called the "claimant company".

31.2.2 Definition of a group for the purposes of loss relief

In order to qualify for group relief, both the claimant company and the surrendering company must be members of the same group.

s412(1) TCA97

Section 412(1) TCA97 states that: "*Two companies shall be deemed to be members of a group of companies if one company is a 75% subsidiary of the other or both are 75% subsidiaries of a third company.*"

31.2.2.1 Shareholding test and anti-avoidance legislation

For the purposes of group relief, the parent company, in addition to owning 75% (directly or indirectly) of the ordinary share capital of a subsidiary, must also be beneficially entitled to not less than:

- 75% of any profits available for distribution to the "equity-holders" of the subsidiary company; and
- 75% of any assets of the subsidiary company available for distribution to its "equity-holders" on a winding-up.

These anti-avoidance provisions (i.e., requirements regarding profit or asset distribution) are designed to defeat situations where ownership of ordinary share capital does not reflect one company's interest in its so-called subsidiary, and where a temporary group is established merely to avail of the relief.

Example of Shareholding Test

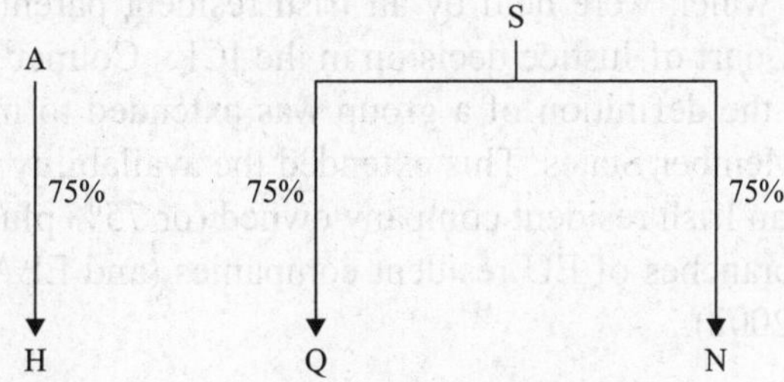

A Ltd and H Ltd form a group as do S Ltd, Q Ltd and N Ltd.

Shareholdings may also be held indirectly provided the 75% test is satisfied.

Group – Example indirect shareholding

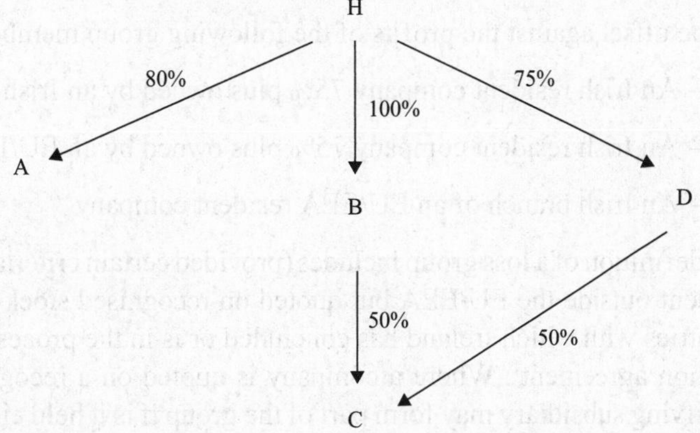

All the above companies are members of the same group because:

- H Ltd owns 80% of A Ltd;
- H Ltd owns 100% of B Ltd;
- H Ltd owns 75% of D Ltd;
- H Ltd owns 87.5% of C Ltd*

* 100% of 50%	=	50%
and		
75% of 50%	=	37.5%
Total		87.5%

31.2.2.2 Residence

s411(1)(c) TCA97 In addition to the shareholding test and the stringent anti-avoidance provisions, there are requirements in relation to residence that need to be satisfied. It is important to note that membership of a group is not restricted to Irish resident companies.

Why is this important? Up to 30 June 1998, group relief was restricted to Irish resident companies which were held by an Irish resident parent. However, resulting from the European Court of Justice decision in the ICI v Colmer case ([1996] STC 352; [1999] STC 874), the definition of a group was extended to include subsidiaries resident in other EU Member States. This extended the availability of group relief within a group to include an Irish resident company owned (or 75% plus owned) by an EU parent and also Irish branches of EU resident companies (and EEA companies, with effect from 1 January 2002).

As a result, Irish trading losses incurred by the following group members:

- An Irish resident company 75% plus owned by an Irish resident parent
- An Irish resident company 75% plus owned by an EU/EEA resident parent
- An Irish branch of an EU/EEA resident ompany

can be offset against the profits of the following group members:

- An Irish resident company 75% plus owned by an Irish resident parent
- An Irish resident company 75% plus owned by an EU/EEA resident parent
- An Irish branch of an EU/EEA resident company

The definition of a loss group includes (provided certain criteria are satisfied) companies resident outside the EU/EEA but quoted on recognised stock exchanges or resident in countries with which Ireland has concluded or is in the process of concluding a double taxation agreement[1]. Where a company is quoted on a recognised stock exchange its qualifying subsidiary may form part of the group if is it held either directly or indirectly.

31.2.2.3 Non-Irish losses

Finance Act 2007 legislated for the ECJ decision in *Marks & Spencer v Halsey* (see Appendix I for a discussion on this case). Prior to this, it was not possible for a non-Irish resident company to surrender its losses to Irish resident companies within the same group.

For accounting periods beginning on or after 1 January 2006 losses incurred in qualifying 75% EU resident subsidiaries will be available for set-off against the profits of the Irish resident parent, but only in very restricted circumstances.

To qualify for this relief the following conditions must be complied with:

(a) Both companies must be members of the same corporate group, with a 75% subsidiary relationship.

(b) The subsidiary must be resident in an EU/EEA state, other than Ireland.

1 This amendment applied from 1 January 2012 and partly arises from the outcome of the FCE Bank case discussed in Appendix I.

(c) The company claiming the loss relief must be the parent and must be resident in Ireland. Only the parent can receive the surrendered losses.

(d) The loss is to be calculated in accordance with the legislation of the state of which the subsidiary is a resident. In addition, the loss must be a 'trapped loss', i.e., the loss is not available for surrender in that country, either in the current period, prior period or by being carried forward. Nor can it be allowable for use in another EU/EEA country.

(e) The claim must be made within two years of the accounting period in which the loss is incurred. In cases where it only becomes apparent that the loss cannot be carried forward, for example due to a cessation of the trade, the two-year period commences from date that the loss can no longer be carried forward.

(f) The loss transfer will not be allowable if arrangements have been entered into with a view to creating the loss in order to claim the relief and for no valid commercial reason.

(g) The Inspector of Taxes may request evidence of the claim prior to allowing the relief.

The *Lidl Belgium Gmbh & Co. KG v Finanzant Heilbronn* shows how far the European Court of Justice will permit utilisation of these losses.

31.2.3 Group relief for trading losses

s396A TCA97 s396B TCA97 A claim for group relief may be made for a trading loss computed for the purposes of the TCA97. By definition, this will include any capital allowances claimed for the period and consequently losses which may be surrendered by way of group relief will include capital allowances.

s420A TCA97 The loss reliefs available under s396A TCA97 and s396B TCA97 operate for groups under s420A TCA97 and s420B TCA97, respectively.

s420B TCA97 Accordingly, relevant trading losses of the "surrendering" company are first grouped against relevant trading income of the "claimant" company as an allowance under s420A. If there is an excess amount of unused losses after claiming such allowances, the excess may be grouped against the corporation tax payable on passive income/gains of the claimant company by way of a credit and value basis under s420B. (Readers are referred to Chapter 30 for a discussion on relevant trading losses and the value basis for claiming loss relief.) Where the excess after claiming losses against relevant trading income consists of relevant losses or charges, the credit under s420B is calculated by valuing those losses or charges at the standard rate of corporation tax for the accounting period in which they arise.

A straightforward example will illustrate the points involved.

Example 31.1

Two members of a qualifying group have results as follows for corresponding accounting periods:

	***Sam Limited* Accounting period ended 31/12/2018**	***Oisin Limited* Accounting period ended 31/12/2018**
	€	**€**
Case I (trade 1) profit (loss)	*40,000*	*(250,000)*
Case I (trade 2) profit (loss)	*Nil*	*80,000*
Case V income	*100,000*	*20,000*

This example ignores previous years.

After claiming all allowances due to it, Oisin Limited wishes to surrender and Sam Limited wishes to claim the optimum amount of losses available.

Oisin Limited – Corporation Tax Computation

		€
Case I income		*80,000*
Less loss relief under s396A(3) (relief as an allowance)		*(80,000)*
		Nil
		€
Case V income		*20,000*
CT @ 25%		*5,000*
Less loss relief under s396B(3) (value and credit)		*(5,000)*
Net CT payable		*Nil*
Loss available for surrender:		€
Case I loss		*250,000*
Loss used: s396A(3) allowance	*80,000*	
s396B(3) credit €5,000/12.5%	*40,000*	*(120,000)*
Loss available for surrender		*130,000*
Sam limited - corporation tax computation		
Case 1		*40,000*
Less group relief + s420A(3)		*(40,000)*
Net Case 1		*Nil*
Case V		*100,000*
CT @ 25%		*25,000*
Less group relief s420B €90,000 @ 12.5%		*(11,250)*
CT payable		*13,750*

Comment on example

As the example shows, there are two ways of getting relief for group losses: one is as an allowance, and the other is as a credit.

Only relevant losses can be set against relevant income as an allowance under s420A(3). Losses not used as an allowance may be granted as a credit under s420B(3), thus giving relief on a value basis. As with relief under s396B, the credit is calculated by multiplying the loss remaining after any allowance claimed, by the standard rate of corporation tax for the accounting period. Where the credit exceeds the amount of corporation tax, it is restricted to the amount of such tax.

31.2.4 Restrictions and other relevant issues

A number of other relevant points in relation to claims for group relief merit further discussion. These are as follows:

1. Only current year losses may be surrendered, therefore losses carried forward or back may not be surrendered.

Example 31.2

Irish Losses Limited had the following results over two years:

	Year ended 31/12/2017	*Year ended 31/12/2018*
	€	**€**
Case I	*100,000*	*(250,000)*

The company had losses forward under s396(1) as at 31/12/2016 of €40,000.

The company's 100% subsidiary, Irish Profits Limited, had the following results over the same period:

	Year ended 31/12/2017	*Year ended 31/12/2018*
	€	**€**
Case I	*50,000*	*100,000*

Irish Losses Limited's computation for the year ended 31/12/2017 is as follows:

	31/12/2017
	€
Case I income	*100,000*
Less s396(1)	*(40,000)*
Less s396A(3)	*(60,000)*
	Nil

The balance of the 2018 loss, i.e., €190,000 (€250,000 less €60,000) is available to be surrendered to Irish Profits Limited. However, it can only set the loss against its income of €100,000, as this is the same year in which the loss was incurred in Irish Losses Limited. The loss cannot be set against the prior year's income of €50,000.

The balance of the loss is retained by Irish Losses Limited (€190,000 – €100,000) and carried forward against future income of the same trade.

2. Capital losses may not be surrendered. However, relief from corporation tax on chargeable gains arising on the inter-group transfers of assets is available and this is discussed in further detail at paragraph 31.4 below.

Example 31.3

In January 2018, Albion Limited makes a gain of €250,000 on the sale of a warehouse. In February 2018, Pendle Limited disposes of a warehouse, which results in a loss of €250,000. Both companies are 100% subsidiaries of Trent Limited and have a December 2018 year-end.

Pendle Ltd cannot transfer its loss to Albion Limited. Therefore Albion Limited will incur a corporation tax liability and Pendle Limited must carry its capital loss forward to shelter future gains (excluding gains on development land which are ring-fenced).

3. A surrendering company can surrender all, or part only, of its losses in an accounting period. However, it cannot surrender more losses to a claimant company than that claimant company is capable of absorbing.

Example 31.4

In Example 31.2 concerning the position of Irish Losses Limited and Irish Profits Limited, the surrendering company, Irish Losses Limited, had a loss of €190,000 available to transfer. However, as Irish Profits Limited could only absorb €100,000, the amount that could be transferred was limited to this amount.

4. Losses can only be grouped against profits of a corresponding accounting period. Where the accounting periods of two companies claiming and surrendering losses are not co-terminous, the losses and profits of each company must be apportioned, usually on a time basis. This is calculated by:
   - time-apportioning the profit attributable to the corresponding accounting period; then
   - time-apportioning the loss attributable to the corresponding period; and
   - allowing group relief on the lower of the two.

Example 31.5

Company A with a year-end of 31 December 2018 has a trading loss of €100,000.

Company B with a year-end of 30 June 2018 has a trading profit of €50,000.

The corresponding accounting period for A and B is 1 January 2018 to 30 June 2018 and is of six months' duration. Taking the lower figure of €50,000 × 6/12, €25,000 of loss relief can be surrendered from A Limited to B Limited.

5. Group relief will only be given if the surrendering company and the claimant company are members of the same group throughout the whole of:
   - the surrendering company's accounting period in question; and
   - the claimant company's corresponding accounting period.

The impact of this is that where a company joins or leaves a group or consortium, the company joining or leaving is assumed to have an accounting period beginning or ending (as appropriate) on the date on which they join or leave the group. Therefore in claiming group relief, the concept of notional accounting periods is introduced and profits and losses must be time-apportioned.

Example 31.6

Cain Limited has a trading profit of €90,000 for the year ended 31 December 2018. On 1 October 2018, it acquired the entire share capital of Able Limited. Able Limited incurred a loss of €60,000 in the year ended 30 November 2018.

The maximum relief that can be claimed or surrendered is the lower of each company's adjusted corresponding period profit or loss:

Cain Limited: €90,000 × 2/12 = €15,000

Able Limited: €60,000 × 2/12 = €10,000

Therefore Able Limited can surrender €10,000 of its loss to Cain Limited.

6. Both the claimant company and the surrendering company must consent to the group relief claim. While this is normally done with the submission of the CT1, a group relief claim may be made at any time within two years from the end of the accounting period of the surrendering company to which it relates. For example, if the surrendering company's accounting period was the year ended 31 December 2016, the claim must be made before 31 December 2018.

7. Losses incurred by a leasing company arising from excess capital allowances cannot be offset against non-leasing income. Section 403 TCA97 allows leasing losses to be set against leasing profits of another group company.

   The income from leasing includes ancillary services such as asset financing, services of leasing experts, profits on lease disposals etc.

   This definition ensures that where 90% of the activities are from leasing, the company will be able to offset its capital allowances against all leasing income (including items included under ancillary services).

8. A payment for group relief (to a maximum of the amount surrendered) is not taken into account in computing profits or losses of either company for corporation tax purposes. In practice, payment will most probably be made where there are minority interests and payments are generally valued at an amount equal to the tax saved by the claimant company.

9. Excess trading charges may be group-relieved in exactly the same manner as trading losses.

10. Any claim for group relief must be looked at in the context of a claim for other reliefs. Section 421 TCA97 sets out how group relief interacts with other claims for losses and charges. Current year Case I losses and charges, and losses forward from a previous period must be used by the claimant company in priority to group relief. However, group relief may be claimed before claiming losses under s396A TCA97 or s396B TCA97 carry back of losses, or excess capital allowances s308(4) TCA97 in subsequent periods. At a practical level this facilitates looking

at the group position at a point in time without having to rely on having results for subsequent periods.

The sections listed below should all be considered and claimed where appropriate in the order listed prior to making a claim for group losses on a value and credit basis.

Section	Provision
396(1) TCA97	*Trading losses forward from an earlier period against trading income of the same trade*
396A TCA97	*Trading losses against non-25% income - current and prior corresponding period*
243A TCA97	*Relevant trade charges against non-25% income - current period*
243B TCA97	*Relief for charges on a value basis - current period*
396B TCA97	*Relief for losses on a value basis - current and prior period*
420A TCA97	*Group relief for relevant losses and charges - current period*
420B TCA97	*Group relief on a value basis for relevant losses and charges - current period*
396(1) TCA97	*Carry any remaining trade losses forward to future trade income of the same trade*

The following comprehensive example illustrates the operation of group relief in practice.

Example 31.7

Two members of a qualifying group have results as follows for corresponding accounting periods:

	John Ltd Year-end 31/12/2017	*Jack Ltd Year-end 31/12/2017*
	€	€
Case I	*50,000*	*(60,000)*
Case V	*40,000*	*15,000*

	John Ltd Year-end 31/12/2018	*John Ltd Year-end 31/12/2018*
	€	€
Case I	*(100,000)*	*180,000*
Case V	*20,000*	*25,000*

Jack Limited – Computation for year ended 31/12/2017

	€
Case I	*Nil*
Case V	*15,000*
	15,000

	€
€15,000 × 25%	*3,750*
s396B: €30,000 × 12.5%	*(3,750)*
	Nil

Loss Memo – Jack Limited:

	€
Case I loss	*60,000*
s396B	*(30,000)*
s420A	*(30,000)*
	Nil

John Limited – Computation for year ended 31/12/17

	€
Case I	*50,000*
s420A (above)	*(30,000)*
s396A (from 31/12/2017)	*(20,000)*
	Nil
Case V	*40,000*
	€
€40,000 × 25%	*10,000*
€40,000 × 12.5% (from 31/12/2018)	*(5,000)*
	5,000

John Limited computation for 31/12/2018

	€
Case I	*Nil*
Case V	*20,000*
€20,000 × 25%	*5,000*
s396B: €40,000 × 12.5%	*(5,000)*
	Nil

Loss Memo – John Ltd:

	€
Case I loss	*100,000*
s396A (to 31/12/2017)	*(20,000)*
s396B (to 31/12/2018)	*(40,000)*
s396B (to 31/12/2017)	*(40,000)*
	Nil

Jack Ltd computation for 31/12/2018

	€
Case I	*180,000*
Case V	*25,000*
	205,000
€180,000 × 12.5%	*22,500*
€25,000 × 25%	*6,250*
	28,750

31.2.5 Excess Case V capital allowances

s420(2) TCA97

Excess Case V capital allowances may also be group-relieved. The most usual example met in practice is excess Case V capital allowances in the case of let industrial buildings and capital allowances for plant or machinery leased otherwise than in the course of a trade.

The amount of allowances available for surrender is the excess of those allowances over the related income for the period in question. This does not include losses or capital allowances carried forward or back. As is the case with trading losses, the accounting period of the surrendering company and the claimant company must correspond with one another in order to make a claim for group relief.

The surrendering company is under no obligation to utilise the excess Case V capital allowances against its other income in priority to surrendering it by means of group relief to an associated company. As a result, through careful planning it may be possible to maximize the use of the excess Case V capital allowances by ensuring that they are offset against profits taxable at 25%.

Example 31.8

A Limited and B Limited are members of a group and have the following results:

	A Ltd Year-end 31/12/2018	*B Ltd Year-end 31/12/2018*
	€	**€**
Case I	*60,000*	*50,000*
Case V	*20,000*	*60,000*
Case V capital allowances	*(40,000)*	*(10,000)*

A Ltd – Computation for year end 31/12/2018:

	€	**€**
Case I		*60,000*
Case V	*20,000*	
Case V capital allowances	*(20,000)*	
	Nil	–
		60,000
€60,000 × 12.5%		*7,500*

Loss Memo – A Limited:	**€**
Case V capital allowances	*40,000*
against Case V income	*(20,000)*
s420(2) B Limited 2018	*(20,000)*
	Nil

B Limited – Computation for year end 31/12/2018:

	€	€
Case I		*50,000*
Case V	*60,000*	
Capital allowances	*(10,000)*	
s420(2) (above)	*(20,000)*	
		30,000
		80,000
€50,000 × 12.5%		*6,250*
€30,000 × 25%		*7,500*
		13,750

Note: A Ltd could easily have offset the excess Case V capital allowances against its Case I trading income, resulting in a reduction in corporation tax of €2,500 (i.e. €20,000 × 12.5%). However, by surrendering the allowances to B Ltd, they are offset against Case V income, resulting in a reduction in corporation tax of €5,000 (i.e., €20,000 × 25%).

31.2.6 Restriction of group relief

s1085(2) TCA97 Where a claimant company or a surrendering company fails to file a return of income on time, group relief is restricted. The restriction is calculated by reference to the length of delay in filing the return.

Where the filing delay is less than two months, the group relief claimable is reduced by 25% subject to a maximum restriction of €31,740.

Where the delay in filing exceeds two months then a restriction of 50% applies, subject to a maximum restriction of €158,715.

Similar restrictions apply to companies surrendering losses for group relief.

Example 31.9

Slug Ltd is a 75% subsidiary of Snail Ltd for the whole of the accounting period of 12 months ended 31 December 2018. The return of the company for the 12 months to 31 December 2018 shows the following:

	€
Snail Ltd	
Trading profits	*100,000*
Losses forward	*(20,000)*
Rental income	*10,000*
Capital allowances in rental property	*25,000*
Charges paid	*10,000*
Slug Ltd	
Trading loss	*(30,000)*

Snail Ltd claims relief in respect of excess capital allowances under s308(4) TCA97, and also with the consent of Slug Ltd, the maximum amount of group relief which can be surrendered by Slug Ltd under s420A. The group companies failed to deliver their returns until 31 December 2019.

Corporation Tax Computation Snail Ltd	€
Case I	*100,000*
Relief s396(1)	*(20,000)*
Case V	*Nil*
Charges	*(10,000)*
	70,000
Relief s308 excess capital allowances	
Restricted (€25,000 – €10,000) × 50%	*(7,500)*
	62,500
Group Relief s420A	
Restricted (€30,000 × 50%)	*(15,000)*
Amount chargeable to CT	*47,500*
CT due × 12.5%	*5,938*

Slug Ltd	€
Case I loss available for surrender (€30,000 × 50%)	*15,000*
Amount surrendered	*15,000*
Loss forward (€30,000 – €15,000)	*15,000*

31.2.7 Consortium loss relief

s411(3) TCA97

Consortium relief is very much an extension of group relief, if somewhat more restrictive, whereby losses can only be surrendered up from a trading company to the members of the consortium.

A qualifying consortium exists where the following conditions are met:

1. The company surrendering the relief is a trading company, and 75% or more of the ordinary share capital of the company is owned by five or fewer companies. There is no minimum shareholding requirement. However, there is effectively a maximum shareholding as the consortium company must not be a 75% subsidiary of any one company.

2. All the companies making up the 75% ownership must be resident in a Member State of the EU, or in a Member State of the European Economic Area (EEA) with which Ireland has concluded a double tax treaty. Companies quoted on recognised stock exchanges or companies resident in countries with which Ireland has concluded or is in the process of concluding a double taxation agreement can also be included in the consortium.

A typical consortium structure is illustrated below.

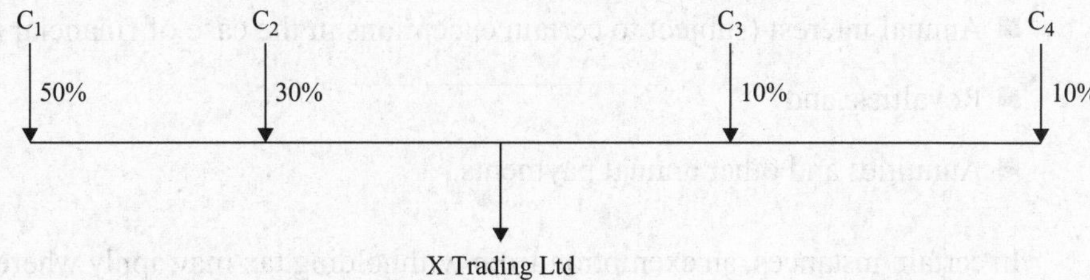

The following points are relevant:

- Loss relief may only be surrendered upwards from the consortium company to the member companies. There is no provision for the surrender of losses from a member company to a consortium company or any other member company.
- The loss that can be surrendered to any member company is limited to that member company's percentage share in the consortium company.
- Losses may also be surrendered by a holding company and by a 90% subsidiary of a holding company where the holding company is owned by a consortium.

Example 31.10

A Limited, B Limited, C Limited, D Limited and E Limited own 25%, 12%, 23%, 16% and 24% of F Limited respectively. F Limited incurred trading losses in the year-ended 31 December 2018 of €100,000.

Assuming all five consortium members have a December year-end, the following amounts can be surrendered from F Limited to each consortium member:

	€
A: €100,000 × 25%	*25,000*
B: €100,000 × 12%	*12,000*
C: €100,000 × 23%	*23,000*
D: €100,000 × 16%	*16,000*
E: €100,000 × 24%	*24,000*
Losses claimed	*100,000*

31.3 Intra-Group Payments

31.3.1 Introduction – obligation to deduct income tax

A company is obliged to deduct income tax at the standard rate (currently 20%) on certain payments. The income tax must be paid as part of the company's corporation tax liability. Details of the payments made under deduction of tax must be included in the company's corporation tax return. The payment is subject to corporation tax rules for preliminary tax payments and return filing deadlines.

s246 TCA97

The payments to which withholding tax applies are:

- Annual interest (subject to certain exceptions in the case of financial institutions),
- Royalties, and
- Annuities and other annual payments.

In certain instances, an exemption from withholding tax may apply where payments are made within the EU. Readers are referred to the commentary at 28.8.1 in relation to EU Council Directives. In all other instances, existing domestic legislation ensures that withholding tax will not apply where a 51% group relationship exists.

Under s242A TCA97 commercial royalty payments can be paid free of withholding tax if it is made from an Irish resident company or any company carrying on a trade in Ireland, to a company resident in a Double Tax Agreement (DTA) country, who will pay tax on the royalty in their own country.

DTA countries include those whose agreements with Ireland have not yet come into force.

Similar provisions apply in relation to interest payments.

31.3.2 Group payments – relief from withholding tax

s410(4)(5) TCA97

The existence of a 51% group relationship or a consortium allows the aforementioned payments to be made without the necessity to deduct income tax.

31.3.3 Definition of a group

s410(3)(4) TCA97

The group relationship and conditions that must be fulfilled in order to avoid withholding tax are as follows:

- Both companies must be resident in an EU Member State or an EEA State with which Ireland has a double tax treaty. Where the recipient is not resident in the State the payment received must be taken into account for taxation purposes.
- The company making the payment must be a 51% subsidiary of the company receiving the payment; or
- Both companies must be 51% subsidiaries of a company resident in a relevant EU Member State, or a relevant Member State of the European Economic Area, EEA (this basically adds Norway, Iceland and Lichtenstein to the EU States); or
- A consortium relationship must exist.

A company is owned by a consortium if 75% or more of the ordinary share capital is beneficially owned by between five or fewer companies resident in the EU where the percentage shareholding by any of the companies can be as low as but not lower than 5%. The company paying the interest must be a trading or holding company owned by a consortium whose members include the company receiving the payment.

The 51% relationship may be either direct or indirect. The following examples illustrate some qualifying group relationships.

Example 30.11

A "51% Group"

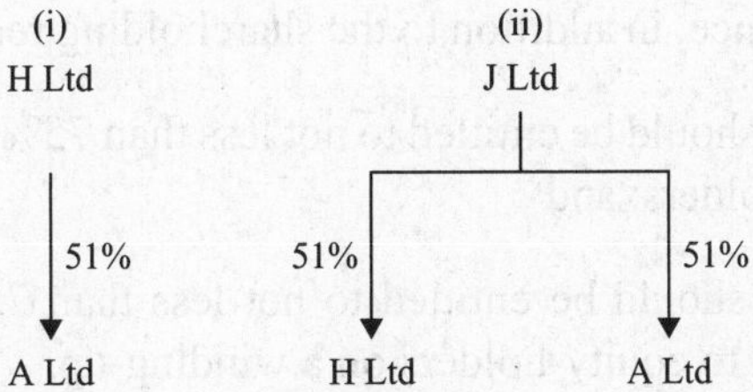

(i) H Ltd can pay interest gross to A Ltd and vice versa.

(ii) H Ltd can pay interest gross to J Ltd and to A Ltd. A Ltd can pay interest gross to J Ltd and to H Ltd.

It is not necessary that a company be a direct 51% subsidiary of another for payments to be made gross.

Example 30.12

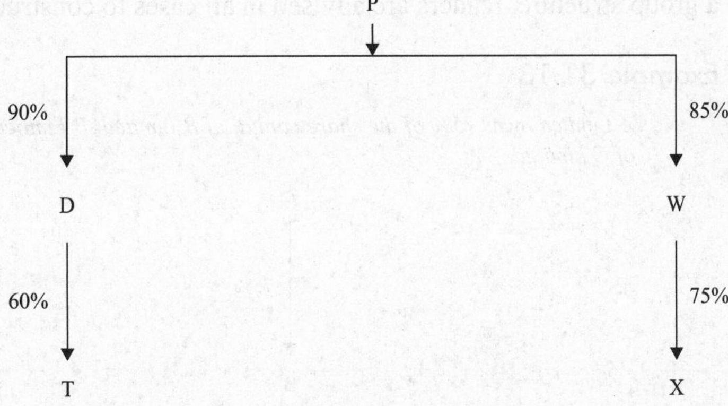

T Ltd is a 54% subsidiary of P Ltd, X Ltd is a 64% subsidiary of P Ltd. It follows that annual payments can be paid gross by all the members of the group.

31.4 Intra-Group Transfers of Assets

31.4.1 Introduction

Relief from corporation tax on chargeable gains arising on the intra-group transfer of assets is available where a qualifying "Capital Gains Group" relationship exists. The structure required for a capital gains group is somewhat different from that which is required for a corporation tax loss group and this is discussed in further detail in paragraph 31.4.2 below. The nature of the relief is considered in paragraph 31.4.3.

31.4.2 What constitutes a capital gains group?

s616 TCA97

Section 616 TCA97 states that a group shall consist of "a principal company and all its effective 75% subsidiaries". A principal company would be known in common parlance as "a parent company".

The anti-avoidance provisions found in the definition of a corporation tax loss group also apply. Hence, in addition to the shareholding requirement, it is also necessary that:

- The parent should be entitled to not less than 75% of profits available for distribution to equity-holders; and
- The parent should be entitled to not less than 75% of the assets and available for distribution to equity-holders on a winding-up.

However, an additional consideration in the case of capital gains groups ensures that there is a clear distinction between the capital gains groups structure and the loss group structure. For capital gains group purposes, where a member of a group has itself got an effective 75% subsidiary, that subsidiary is also a member of the group. In order to be a principal company, or to be an effective 75% subsidiary, and therefore in order to be a member of a capital gains group, it is necessary that a company should be resident for tax purposes in an EEA State.

The following examples best illustrate this point (note: to fully understand the nature of a group structure, readers are advised in all cases to construct a diagram of the group).

Example 31.13

A Limited owns 75% of the share capital of B Limited. B Limited owns 75% of the share capital of C Limited.

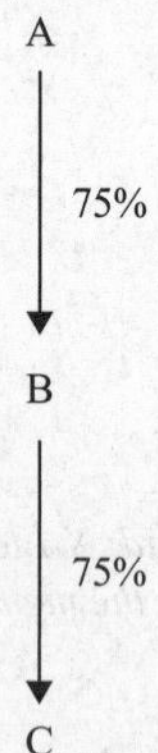

For capital gains group purposes, A and B Limited are members of a group. B and C Limited are also members of a capital gains group. Therefore, C Limited is also a member of A and B's capital gains group as it is a 75% subsidiary of B Limited.

For losses, however, C Limited cannot be a member of A and B's group as A through B only holds 56.25% (75% × 75%) of C Limited. Therefore, A and B Limited and B and C Limited form separate loss groups.

Example 31.14

Fire Limited has the following holdings:

Wind Limited – 75% (Wind Limited in turn owns 80% of Sun Limited).

Water Limited – 75% (Water Limited in turn owns 60% of Earth Limited).

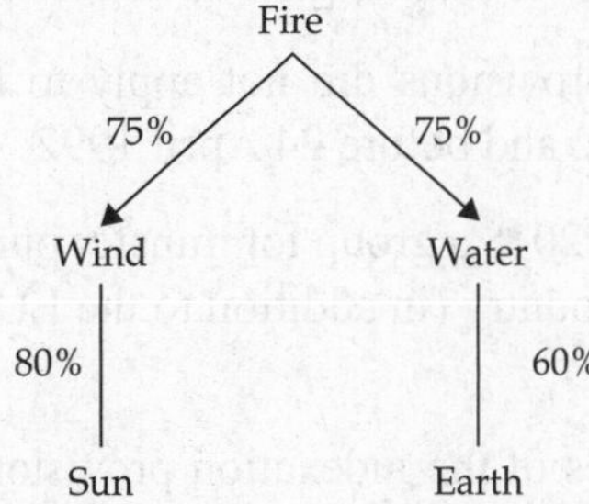

For capital gains group purposes, Fire Limited, Wind Limited and Water Limited are in a group as Wind Limited and Water Limited are both 75% subsidiaries of Fire Limited. Sun Limited is also part of this group as it is a qualifying subsidiary of Wind Limited. Earth Limited is not part of the group, however, as Water Limited owns less than 75% of it.

For losses, the group can only include Fire Limited, Wind Limited and Water Limited. Fire Limited's holding in Sun is only 60% (75% × 80%). It should be noted that Wind Limited and Sun Limited can form their own separate losses group as they have an 80% relationship.

Example 31.15

Pluto Limited owns 90% of the share capital of Mars Limited, which in turn owns 75% of the share capital of Mercury Limited. Both Pluto and Mercury own 55% and 40% of the share capital of Jupiter Limited respectively.

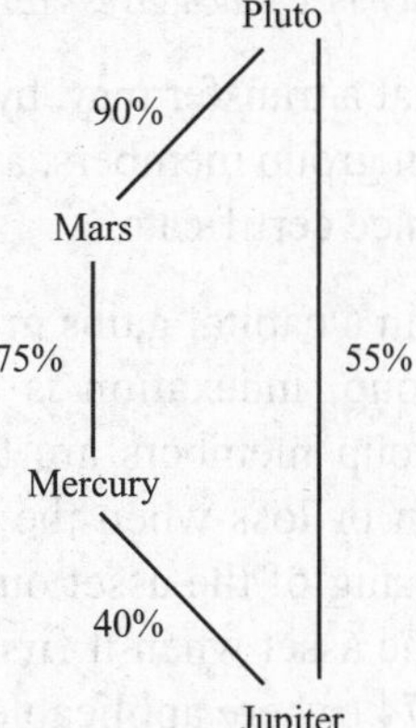

For capital gains purposes, all companies are in a group. Mars and Mercury are members through Pluto's 90% holding in Mars and the fact that Mercury is a 75% subsidiary of Mars. Pluto holds 55% of the shares in Jupiter directly and 27% through Mercury (90% × 75% × 40%). This gives it a holding in Jupiter of 82%.

For losses, all companies are part of the group except for Mercury Limited. Mars is a 90% subsidiary and Jupiter is an indirect subsidiary with 82%. However, Pluto's holding in Mercury (through Mars) is only 67.50% (90% × 75%) therefore it cannot be a member of the group. It is however in a loss group with Mars.

31.4.3 Transfers between group companies

s617, s648 TCA97

Broadly speaking, the effect of the capital gains group relief is to ensure that no chargeable gain arises on a transfer of assets between group members. Where an asset is transferred from one group member to another, it is deemed to be transferred at a price which ensures that no gain or no loss arises to the company making the disposal.

The relieving provisions did not apply to transfers of development land on or after 28 January 1982 and before 24 April 1992.

From 1 January 2018 a group for transfer purposes will also include companies resident in a tax treaty country (in addition to the EU/EEA) as long as the asset is chargeable to Irish tax.

s619, s589 TCA97

For the purposes of the indexation provisions, all members of the group are regarded as one person, so that the group member acquiring the asset takes over the same base acquisition date (and acquisition cost) as the member from which the asset was acquired. Accordingly, when arriving at the deemed transfer price which would give rise to no gain/no loss for the company making the disposal, indexation is not applied.

Example 31.16

HEN LTD acquired an asset in 2005 for €40,000. In 2012, it incurred enhancement expenditure of €30,000 on the asset and then sold it to CHICKEN LTD in December 2018 for €80,000, which was its market value at that time.

If the two companies were not within the same group, HEN LTD would calculate its gain by deducting from the sale price, the cost and the enhancement expenditure.

However, if they are both members of the same group for CGT purposes, the asset is deemed to be transferred at a figure which gives HEN LTD no gain/no loss, i.e., €70,000.

Notwithstanding that a transfer may, by reason of s617, not give rise to a gain or a loss when made between group members, a withholding tax obligation may still exist in the absence of a clearance certificate.

Where a company in a capital gains group disposes of an asset acquired from another member of the group, indexation is applied as if all members of the group were one person. All group members are treated as the same person for the purpose of calculating the gain or loss when the asset is finally disposed of outside the group. The member disposing of the asset outside the group is deemed to be the one which initially acquired the asset when it first came into the group. Accordingly, the market value at 6 April 1974 (where applicable) and the indexation rules are preserved within a group.

Example 31.17

James Limited acquired an asset in June 1994 for €20,000. The asset was transferred to Flynn Limited, another company in the CGT group, in 1998 for €75,000. Flynn Limited sold the asset in June 2018 for €175,000. Flynn Ltd makes up accounts to 31 December in each year.

The amount to be included in the profits of Flynn Limited is calculated as follows:

	€
Consideration received by Flynn Limited	*175,000*
Cost to James Limited (indexed) €20,000 × 1.309	*(26,180)*
Gain	*148,820*
Chargeable to corporation tax: €148,820 × 33% / 12.5%	*392,885*

The CT payable on the gain is €392,885 at 12.5% = €44,911

Example 31.18

Michaels Ltd owns all the issued share capital in Jones Ltd and 65% of the share capital in Flood Ltd.

In June 1996 Michaels Ltd bought a property for €100,000. In December 2001 the property was sold to Jones Ltd for €160,000. Jones Ltd extended the property in March 2015 at a cost of €40,000. Flood Ltd purchased the property from Jones Ltd for €350,000 in May 2018.

The corporation tax position for the year ended 31 December 2018 is as follows (assuming it is not development land):

In December 2001, Jones Ltd is deemed to have acquired the property for €100,000, i.e., an amount which results in no gain and no loss for Michaels Ltd. The sale of the property to Flood Ltd is a sale outside the group and accordingly, a taxable gain arises to Jones Ltd calculated as follows:

Jones Ltd – taxable gain		€
Sales proceeds		*350,000*
Cost (to group) indexed		
	€100,000 indexed @ 1.251	*(125,100)*
Enhancement expenditure		
	€40,000 (not indexed)	*(40,000)*
Gain		*184,900*
Chargeable to CT	*€184,900 × 33% / 12.5%*	*488,136*
CT on chargeable gain	*€488,136 × 12.5%*	*61,017*

Example 31.19

Head Ltd owns all the shares in Nose Ltd and Mouth Ltd. In 1990, Nose Ltd acquired an asset for €12,697. In 1995, it sold the asset to Mouth Ltd for €63,487. In March 2000, Mouth Ltd sold the asset to Head Ltd for €126,974. Head Ltd sold the asset to a non-group member on 2 May 2018 for €150,000.

No chargeable gain arises to Nose Ltd or Mouth Ltd under the group provisions. In calculating the gain of Head Ltd, it is treated as acquiring the asset in 1990 for €12,697; its gain will be calculated by deducting that cost (indexed from 1990) from the sales proceeds of €150,000

		€
Consideration received by Head Ltd		*150,000*
Cost to Nose Ltd (indexed)	*€12,697 × 1.442*	*(18,309)*
Gain		*131,691*
Chargeable to corporation tax:	*€131,691 × 33% / 12.5%*	*347,664*

The CT payable on the gain is €347,664 at 12.5% = €43,458.

Example 31.20

BLACK LTD acquired a building in May 1992 for €50,790. On 31 March 1994, BLACK LTD sold the building to its wholly owned subsidiary, SOOT LTD for €126,974. SOOT LTD sold the building outside the group on 12 April 2018 for €350,000.

Chargeable gains are calculated as follows:

BLACK's disposal		€
Cost		*50,790*
Deemed sale price		*50,790*
Gain/loss		*Nil*

SOOT'S disposal		€
Sale price		*350,000*
Cost as indexed	*€50,790 × 1.356*	*(68,871)*
Gain		*281,129*
Chargeable to corporation tax:	*€742,181 × 33% / 12.5%*	*742,181*

The CT payable on the gain is €742,181 @ 12.5% = €92,773.

s615 TCA97

In addition to the relief for transferring assets to group companies under s617 TCA97, relief is also allowable for amalgamation and reconstructions under s615 TCA97 and is considered in more detail in 27.11.

In brief, an amalgamation is where two or more companies transfer their businesses to a new company and those transfers are deemed to result in a transfer by the original companies at no gain/no loss. In effect the new company steps into the shoes of the original companies.

A reconstruction is generally where an existing company's assets/business is split into separate companies, for example a property holding and trading company is transferred to a property company and a separate trading company. As with an amalgamation, the new company takes the original base cost of the transferring company.

Relief for the shareholders in both of these situations is generally as a "share for share transaction" and no capital gains tax is due as there is deemed to be no sale at the point of transfer, the shareholder has transferred their original shares for new shares. The claims are generally available under s586 and s587 TCA97.

Layout of a reconstruction

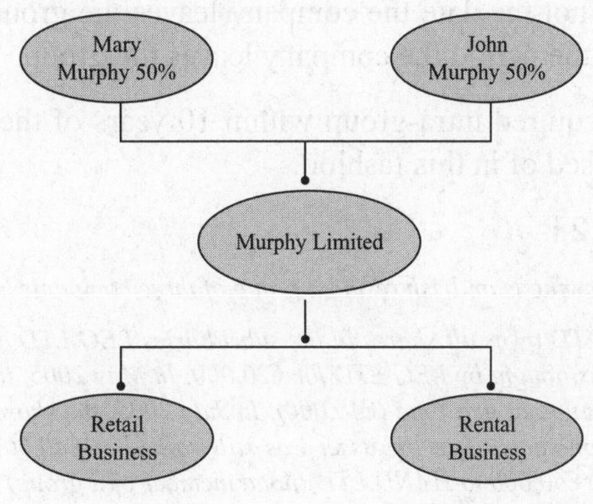

Restructure
Transfer retail business to new company

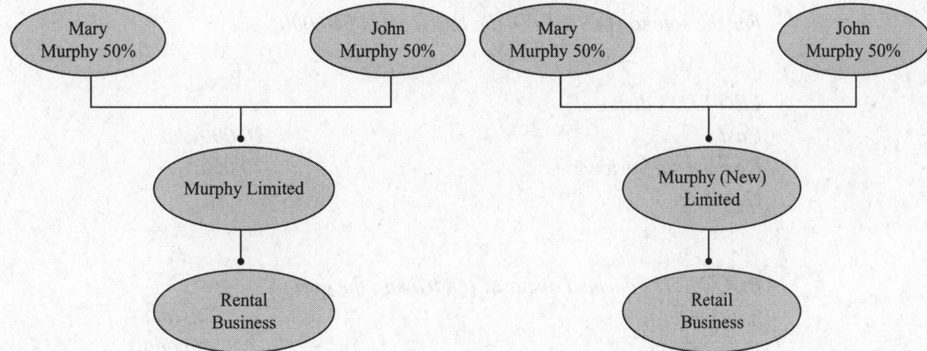

31.4.4 Company leaving group

s623 TCA97 In the case of most relieving provisions, there will normally be anti-avoidance provisions to prevent abuse of the relief and the CGT group relief provisions are no exception.

Provisions are made to effectively charge the tax foregone on a transfer within a group if the group company which acquires the asset leaves the group with that asset. The gain accrues to the company leaving the group, but in some cases, the parent of the group, or the group company from which the asset was acquired can also be held responsible for the tax involved.

Where a company ceases to be a member of a group, any asset which it acquired from other group members while it was a member of the group is deemed to be sold, and immediately reacquired by the company leaving the group at market value, at the date of acquisition from the other group company.

This has the effect of realising the gain, which was deferred on the original inter-company transfer within the group, and making it chargeable on the company leaving the group. It is a chargeable gain arising on the date of acquisition of the asset by that company and not the date the company leaves the group. Any tax due on the deemed gain is due in the period the company leaves the group.

Only assets acquired intra-group within 10 years of the date of leaving the group are deemed disposed of in this fashion.

Example 31.21

The following is an Irish resident group of three companies:

HEAD LTD owns all shares in the subsidiaries LEG LTD and FOOT LTD. In January 2005, an asset was bought by LEG LTD for €20,000. In May 2005, it was transferred to FOOT LTD at its market value at that time (€40,000). In July 2005, the shares in FOOT LTD were sold to a non-group company, when the asset was still valued at €40,000. FOOT LTD subsequently sold the asset for €60,000 to HAND LTD (not a member of a group) in August 2018.

Under the group provisions, LEG LTD is treated as transferring the asset to FOOT LTD at no gain/no loss, i.e., the cost to FOOT LTD of acquiring the asset is deemed to be €20,000.

As soon as FOOT LTD leaves the group, it is deemed to have sold the asset in May 2005 for its market value at that date, i.e., €40,000. The gain therefore accrues to FOOT LTD in July 2005. The normal provisions for charging a gain on an asset acquired in January 2005 at a cost of €20,000 will apply.

For the sale to HAND LTD, the base cost is €40,000.

	€
LEG LTD's disposal	
Cost	*20,000*
Deemed sale price	*20,000*
Gain/loss	*Nil*

	€	
FOOT LTD's deemed disposal (on leaving the group)		
Sale price	*40,000*	
Cost €20,000	*(20,000)*	
Gain	*20,000*	
Notional CGT €20,000 at 20%	*4,000*	
Chargeable to corporation tax: €4,000/12.5%		
Gain chargeable to corporation tax		
€20,000 × 20% / 12.5%*		*32,000*
**The CGT rate in 2005*		

The CT payable on the gain is €32,000 at 12.5% = €4,000

	€	
FOOT LTD's disposal (on sale to HAND LTD)		
Sale price	*60,000*	
Cost €40,000	*(40,000)*	
Gain	*20,000*	
Chargeable to corporation tax:		*52,800*
€20,000 × 33% / 12.5%		

The CT payable on the gain is €52,800 at 12.5% = €6,600.

The legislation provides for any adjustment necessary to assess and collect the tax (i.e., additional assessments, etc.) to be within the time limit allowed for assessing and collecting the tax up to a period of 10 years after the date the company ceased to be a member of the group.

The gain will not crystallise in the following circumstances:

- Transactions between associated companies that leave a group at the same time are ignored and accordingly, any gain on such transactions will not crystallise.

Example 31.22

A Limited, B Limited and C Limited are all members of a capital gains group. A Limited owns 100% of B Limited which in turn owns 100% of C Limited. In March 2010, C Limited sold an asset it had purchased for €30,000 in 2009 to B Limited for €50,000. No chargeable gain arose on this transaction due to group relief.

In June 2018, A Limited sold B Limited to D Limited. Despite the sale, the conditions for capital gains group relief are still in place and there is no chargeable gain on B Limited for the 2010 disposal by C Limited as both are still within their own group (and have now joined a group with D Limited).

- A company that is wound up for bona fide commercial reasons, and not as part of a tax-avoidance scheme, is not to be treated as leaving a group.

- If a company goes into liquidation, it is not deemed to have left a group for the purposes of the exit charge.

- If the transfer under s617 took place more than 10 years previously, the gain will not crystallise.

Example 31.23

A Limited, B Limited and C Limited are all members of a capital gains group. A Limited owns 100% of B Limited which in turn owns 100% of C Limited. In March 1999, B Limited sold an asset it had purchased for €30,000 in 1999 to C Ltd for €50,000. No chargeable gain arose on this transaction due to group relief under s617.

In June 2018, B Limited sold C Limited to D Limited. As the original disposal took place over 10 years ago, there is no claw-back.

- If the company which originally disposed of the asset under s617 leaves the group, the gain will not crystallise. The gain only crystallises when the company which currently owns the asset leaves the group.

Example 31.24

A Limited, B Limited and C Limited are all members of a capital gains group. A Limited owns 100% of both B Limited and C Limited. In March 2010, B Limited sold an asset it had purchased for €30,000 in 2009 to C Limited for €50,000. No chargeable gain arose on this transaction due to group relief.

In June 2018, A Limited sold B Limited to D Limited. Despite the sale, the conditions for capital gains group relief are still in place as the asset has not left the group (A and C are still in a capital gains group and C holds the asset).

31.4.5 Tax on company recoverable from other members of group

Assessed corporation tax which has not been paid within six months of the due date by a group company may, within two years of the due date, be charged:

(a) to the principal company of the group at the time the gain accrued; and

(b) to any other company that was a group member in the two years ending on the date the gain accrued, that previously owned or had an interest in the asset, the disposal of which gave rise to the tax charge.

Such tax, if paid by the principal company or a previous owner of the asset, may be recovered from the company to which the gain accrued.

31.4.6 Group capital losses

There is no provision for transferring capital losses between group members. However, there is scope for tax planning so as to effectively benefit from capital losses in another group company.

Example 31.25

In January 2018, Florence Limited makes a gain of €250,000 on the sale of a warehouse. In February 2018, Rome Limited disposes of a warehouse which results in a loss of €250,000. Both companies are 100% subsidiaries of Bologna Limited and have a December 2018 year-end.

Rome Ltd cannot transfer its loss to Florence Ltd. Therefore, Florence Limited will incur a chargeable gains tax liability and Rome Ltd must carry its capital loss forward to shelter future gains (excluding gains on development land which are ring-fenced).

However, Rome Limited could have transferred the asset to Florence Limited prior to its disposal (this would have no capital gains implications as both companies are in a group). Florence Limited could then have disposed of both properties and set its chargeable loss against the chargeable gain, resulting in a nil liability.

31.4.7 Replacement of business assets by members of group

s620 TCA97 For the purposes of rollover relief (see Chapter 27), all trades carried on by a capital gains tax group are treated as a single trade. Other group members may therefore be treated as having reinvested the disposal proceeds in new assets.

Consequently, if the company which purchased the replacement asset leaves the group, the gain which was rolled over will crystallise.

Example 31.26

A Limited and B Limited are members of a capital gains group. In July 2003, A Limited disposes of a trading asset for €100,000, which results in a gain of €20,000. B Limited purchased an asset for use in its trade in October 2002 for €120,000.

The investment by B Limited is deemed to have been made by A Limited. A Limited qualifies for rollover relief and can defer the gain arising on the sale of its asset until B's asset is sold and the proceeds not reinvested.

With the termination of rollover relief provided for by the 2003 Finance Act, this relief will be of much less significance in the future.

31.4.8 Provisions where companies cease to be resident in the State

s627 TCA97 A company ceasing to be Irish resident on or after 21 April 1997 is treated as having disposed of, and immediately reacquired at market value on the departure date, all of its assets, apart from assets which, after the departure date, are situated in the State, or are used by a branch in the State. This exit charge effectively prevents companies from avoiding corporation tax on chargeable gains by disposing of assets during temporary periods of non-residence.

In the Dutch case, National Grid Indus (C-371/10), the European Court of Justice ruled that this type of exit tax is contrary to the principle of EU freedom of movement and s628A TCA97 gives legislative effect to this ruling. This section gives the company the option of:

1. Paying the exit tax in six annual instaments
2. Paying the exit tax within 60 days of selling the assets (subject to a maximum deferral of 10 years)

A company may also cease to be a member of a group on the occasion of going non-resident, in which case, the provisions of s623 TCA97 (exit charge) will also apply. A simple example best illustrates the two deemed disposals that may arise.

Example 31.27

Clan Limited and Hugh Limited are members of a capital gains group. In July 2009, Clan Limited bought an asset for €50,000 which it sold to Hugh Limited in October 2011 for €60,000 (its market value at the time was €75,000). Hugh Limited operates two trades, one is a manufacturing trade in Bolivia which cost €200,000 in July 2011 and the other is a retail trade in Leitrim which cost €185,000 in August 2012. In August 2018, Hugh Limited was sold to a group of Bolivian investors, which results in Hugh Limited becoming non-resident. At that time, the manufacturing trade was valued at €400,000 and the retail outlet at €375,000.

This has the effect of making the company liable on the inter-group disposal in 2011 under s617 TCA97 and liable to a chargeable gain on the deemed disposal of the Bolivian manufacturing trade. As the Leitrim retail outlet is in the State, there is no chargeable gain until it is sold.

Hugh's deemed disposal of 2011 transfer (on leaving the group)	€	€
Sale price	*75,000*	
Cost (no indexation)	*(50,000)*	
Gain	*25,000*	
Chargeable to corporation tax: €25,000 × 33% / 12.5%		*66,000*

The CT payable on the gain is €66,000 @ 12.5% = €8,250

Hugh's disposal (on ceasing to be resident)

Sale price	*400,000*	
Cost no indexation	*(200,000)*	
Gain	*200,000*	
Chargeable to corporation tax: €200,000 × 33% / 12.5%		*528,000*

The CT payable on the gain is €528,000 @ 12.5% = €66,000.

31.5 Transfer Pricing

31.5.1 Introduction

Until recently Ireland had been unusual among OECD members in not having official transfer pricing legislation. Allied to the fact that our trade corporation tax rate of 12.5% is causing 'dissatisfaction' in some other developed economies (who have been concerned about the migration of multinational headquarters to Ireland), it was decided to introduce legislation that would allow Ireland take its place among developed countries in terms of taxation rules.

The legislation is contained in Part 35A s835A–H TCA97. The legislation commenced for accounting periods beginning on or after 1 January 2011 in relation to any transfer pricing agreements entered into on or after 1 July 2010.

31.5.2 Meaning of transfer pricing

Transfer pricing can be described as the process by which related parties assess the price that will be set for any arrangement, whether in writing and whether legally enforceable, that provides for:

1. The sale of goods,
2. The provision of services,
3. Money (assumed to mean access to finance),
4. The sale/transfer of intangible assets.

s835D TCA97

Section 835D states that companies should use Article 9(1) of the OECD Model Tax Convention on income and capital together with their Transfer Pricing Guideline for Multinational Enterprises and tax administrations when ascertaining the correct transfer price. The legislation also lists other OECD documents together with any future guidelines.

The basic premise is to treat the transaction on the "arms length amount" principle and to identify what a similar price would be between two independent parties on the open market. Each level of service between the related parties should add an ascertainable level of value.

s835B TCA97

Section 835B TCA97 states that transfer pricing only affects associated companies. Companies are associated when one participates in the management, control or capital of another or both are under the management, control or capital of the same person. The legislation uses the s11 TCA97 definition of control, which is more than 50%. Transfer pricing can affect transactions between an individual and a company, but the legislation will only affect the company.

Each of Ireland's Double Taxation Agreements takes precedence over the legislation, where applicable.

31.5.3 Transfer pricing adjustments

s835C TCA97

Section 835C sets out the adjustments required in a company's tax return if the transfer price used is not within the OECD guidelines.

The legislation only affects Irish companies whose trade is chargeable under Schedule D Case I or II. Therefore it does not affect passive income or capital activities. As there is no explicit definition of trade under taxation legislation, guidance must be taken from the UK Badges of Trade Commission and from Revenue trading precedents etc. Trades such as the exploitation of intellectual property would therefore come under the transfer pricing rules (see section 29.3.3). Only one of the parties to the arrangement must be within the charge to tax under Schedule D Case I/II.

The legislation affects not just multinationals dealing with foreign subsidiaries but also domestic groups.

There are two charging sections as follows:

1. Section 835C(2)(a) TCA97 - If the amount payable exceeds the arms length amount in the books of the purchasing company, its profits will be considered to be understated and an adjustment to its taxable income will be required to reduce the amount payable to the arms length amount.
2. Section 835C(2)(b) TCA97 - If the amount receivable is less than the arms length amount in the books of the selling company, its profits will be considered to be understated and an adjustment to its taxable income will be required to increase the amount receivable to the arms length amount.

It follows therefore, that there is no amendment to taxable income if the adjustment would lead to a reduction in profits.

Example 31.28

Irish Subsidiary Ltd (a trading company) licences intellectual property to its US parent for €1,000,000. The OECD arms length amount is ascertained at €750,000, which indicates that the Irish company's profits are overstated by €250,000. Under s835C(2)(b) TCA97, as the amount receivable is not less than the arms length amount, there is no adjustment to the Irish tax computation.

The US company may suffer consequences under its own transfer pricing legislation.

Example 31.29

Irish Holdco Ltd (a non-trading company) sells an intangible asset to a German subsidiary for €1,000,000. The OECD arms length amount is ascertained at €2,000,000, which indicates that the Irish company's capital gains tax proceeds are understated by €1,000,000. As the Irish company is not liable to tax under Schedule D Case I or II, s835C(2)(b) TCA97 does not apply.

However, the company will be charged to capital gains tax on the €2,000,000 due to capital gains tax anti-avoidance rules in relation to disposals to connected persons.

Example 31.30

Irish Subsidiary Ltd (a trading company) purchases goods from UK Parent Ltd for €125,000. The OECD arms length amount is ascertained at €75,000, which indicates that the Irish company's profits are understated by €50,000. Under s835(2)(a) TCA97 as the amount payable is overstated the company's taxable trade income is increased by €50,000.

31.5.4 Relief for 'Irish only' transfer pricing

As the rules apply equally to both international and domestic transfers, s835G TCA97 provides a measure of relief for companies forced to adjust upwards their taxable income due to transfer pricing legislation[2].

In a situation where an Irish company has come within the provisions of either s835C(2)(a) or (b) TCA97 and its taxable income has been adjusted upwards, relief is available to the other associated company, provided that company is within the charge to Irish tax, Schedule D Cases I – V (and not just Case I/II). The relief operates by adjusting downwards the second company's taxable income with the same amount as the company affected by the transfer pricings income rose.

The full tax must be paid by the first company prior to the second company claiming the relief.

Example 31.31

A Ltd (a trading company) provides services to its subsidiary Rent Ltd (a non-trading rental company) for €100,000. The OECD arms length amount is ascertained at €200,000, therefore the taxable income of A Ltd is increased by €100,000 under s835C(2)(b) TCA97.

Under s835G(1) TCA97 Rent Ltd can claim relief for the full €200,000, but only when A Ltd has paid all taxes due.

2 There is also a provision for adjusting the foreign tax credit of a foreign branch affected by the legislation.

31.5.5 Documentation required

Under s835F all companies affected by the legislation must keep sufficient documentation that can support the transfer pricing used in each arrangement. This would show how the company arrived at its conclusion that the transfer was charged on the arms length amount. This would include evidence of similar open market transactions, for example sales with non-related parties or sales by competitors.

Given that many of the large multinationals based in Ireland deal with jurisdictions that already impose transfer pricing legislation, e.g. USA, UK, Australia etc there is generally no need to redraft documentation which have already been prepared. The additional administration may fall on wholly Irish based groups or companies that deal with associated companies in countries that have yet to impose their own transfer pricing legislation.

Once the documentation is in line with the OECD guidelines noted above, it should be sufficient for Revenue inspection and audit purposes. The same rules that apply to normal trading records e.g. 6 year retention etc., also apply to transfer pricing documentation. Under 891GA TCA97 Revenue share information on advance cross-border rulings and pricing arrangements as well as certain information from company accounts, such as turnover, with tax authorities in other EU countries.

31.5.6 Exemptions

The following are excluded from transfer pricing legislation:

1. Section 835E TCA97 - Small and Medium Enterprises "SMEs" (EU definition 2003/36/EC). These are groups with less than 250 staff and one of (a) less than €50m turnover and/or (b) less than €43m in total assets (gross assets with no allowances for liabilities). These limits are group wide and must be reviewed annually.
2. Section 835G(5) TCA97 - Arrangements involving the excepted trade of dealing in or developing land (s21A TCA97) - by election only.
3. Section 835H TCA97 - Wear and tear balancing allowances and charges - these are already covered under s312 TCA97.

Appendix I

ICI v Colmer – 30 June 1998

This case is hugely important in the context of the residence of group companies and merits a separate discussion.

ICI owned 49% of the share capital of a UK resident holding company with 23 subsidiaries, four of which were resident in the UK. One of the UK companies had losses and ICI wished to claim consortium relief. The Inland Revenue denied relief on the basis that such relief could only apply to companies resident in the UK.

All of the relevant companies were actually resident in the UK, i.e., ICI, the holding company and the loss-making subsidiary. However, Revenue argued that the holding company must "mainly" hold UK companies.

The Court of Appeal found that the definition of one section could not be applied to another, unless, of course, legislated for. However, the House of Lords upheld the Revenue appeal.

ICI won the case – the European Court of Justice ruled that the provision of the legislation which required a holding company's 90% trading subsidiaries to be resident in the UK was discriminatory against companies that had exercised their right to the freedom of establishment under Article 52 of the Treaty of Rome. Consequently national legislation was prevented from linking an accountable person's entitlement to a form of tax relief to its tax residency.

The case very much focused on the place of establishment and allowed relief on the basis that, if the majority of the subsidiaries were established in the UK, loss relief would have been allowed but as the majority of the subsidiaries were based outside the UK, loss relief had been denied.

This case resulted in an amendment to the legislation provided by s79 Finance Act 1999. This had the effect of allowing a parent company to include indirect holdings in any company for the purposes of determining 51% ownership, provided the shares were held through a company resident for tax purposes in any Member State of the EU.

The amending legislation allows an Irish company form a group with an Irish branch of a non-resident company under common control for the purposes of group relief. The practical impact for the purposes of this discussion is to allow:

- Surrender of losses between two Irish resident subsidiaries of an EU parent;
- Surrender of losses between an Irish resident subsidiary and Irish branch of an EU parent.

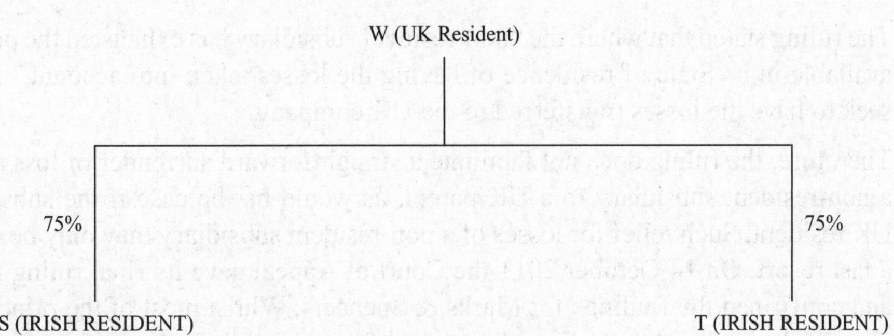

Marks & Spencer case – 1 January 2002

The other case worthy of note with regard to developments in the area of group loss relief is the UK Special Commissioners' decision in the *Marks & Spencer* case. *Marks & Spencer* claimed relief for losses incurred by French, German and Belgian subsidiaries against its UK profits.

The foreign subsidiaries were not resident in the UK in the relevant years and no part of the subsidiary activities were carried on in the UK. Consequently the losses at issue were outside the scope of UK tax. The Inspector of Taxes refused the claim for group relief on the basis that the foreign subsidiaries were not resident in the UK as required under domestic UK legislation. *Marks & Spencer* appealed the case on the basis that the denial of loss relief constituted an infringement of Article 43 of the Treaty of Rome, which concerns freedom of establishment. In this respect, in all its recent case law the European Court of Justice has noted that although direct taxation is a matter for the Member States, they must nevertheless exercise their direct powers consistently with Community Law.

The Special Commissioner, Dr. John Jones, ruled that *Marks & Spencer* was not entitled to the relief. He stated that the relevant principles established by the case law of the ECJ are clear on the matter and found it unnecessary to refer the case to the ECJ for guidance. The Appeal Commissioner distinguished this case from *ICI v Colmer* stating that the discriminatory rule did not relate to the identity of the subsidiaries but rather concerned ICI's right to establish subsidiaries in other Member States. If ICI exercised its right to do so it would no longer be among the category of eligible claimants for the losses in question. In this case, by contrast, the domestic legislation prevents the foreign subsidiaries from surrendering their losses. The inability to claim loss relief is as a consequence of UK restrictions on losses.

The case was appealed to the European Court of Justice to overturn the Special Commissioner's decision. The Advocate-General issued a preliminary ruling on 7 April 2005 stating that Marks & Spencer's claim was justified. He stated that the "principle of territoriality cannot justify the current restriction". The European Commission supported Marks & Spencer, while seven states (including Ireland) supported the UK Inland Revenue.

The European Court of Justice gave its ruling on 13 December 2005, Case C-446/03.

While recognising the right of the UK Revenue to formulate its own internal tax legislation in this area, especially to prevent tax avoidance, the ECJ felt that the legislation went too far in its aims and breached the rights to freedom of establishment.

The ruling stated that where the "non-resident subsidiary has exhausted the possibilities available in its State of residence of having the losses taken into account," it can then seek to have the losses transferred to the UK company.

Therefore, the ruling does not facilitate a straightforward surrender of loss relief from a non-resident subsidiary to a UK parent, as would be the case if the subsidiary was UK resident. Such relief for losses of a non-resident subsidiary may only be claimed as a last resort. On 14 October 2011 the Court of Appeal gave its final ruling in the case and confirmed the findings for Marks & Spencers. Whilst most of the principles were already decided it did confirm that a qualifying subsidiary company may submit its claim only when it has no possibility of claiming loss relief in its own country.

Finance Act 2007 legislated for the ECJ decision, see 31.2.2.3 for a detailed review of the legislation.

The legislation puts a very strict interpretation on the ECJ ruling as regards the actual claiming of the relief, the main point being that the subsidiary would apparently have to cease trading in order to surrender any relief to the Irish parent, as the relief is only available if the subsidiary can never claim relief for its own loss.

In its most recent ruling on this case (February 2015, Case C-172/13) the ECJ confirmed that the UKs own loss relief legislation and its narrow definition of how the non-resident loss could be utilised was ruled to be acceptable and not an infringement on the principles of freedom of establishment.

Due to Ireland's low corporation tax rates it is unlikely that any major multinational would be interested in having the relief surrendered to a parent based in the state.

In the Lidl Belgium Gmbh & Co. KG v Finanzamt Heilbronn case the European Court of Justice set out how far they believe cross border loss relief can be taken (Case C-414/06).

In this ruling, losses in a Luxembourg branch of Lidl were prohibited from being transferred to the parent company in Germany on the basis that they would be allowable against future years Luxembourg profits. They stated that to allow the company's claim may give rise to a double allowance, once in Germany and once in Luxembourg against future income. The European Court of Justice recognised that the treatment was not in keeping with the principle of freedom of establishment (as losses in a German branch could be set against the German parent company's profit) but that the prohibition was important to preserve the tax system in both countries.

One of the most recent tax cases on group losses was FCE Bank v HMRC (2011 UKUT 420 TCC). In this case two UK resident companies could not transfer losses to each other because their parent was US resident and therefore the required ownership could not be followed through to ensure that the two UK companies were in the same losses group. The case predated changes in the UK law in 2000. The taxpayer won the case and was granted loss relief on the basis that the UK/US double taxation agreements non-discrimination clause granted the relief. This case was one of the factors in the change in loss relief discussed in 31.2.1.

32 CLOSE COMPANIES

Learning Outcomes

On completion of this chapter you will be able to:

- ✓ Explain the rationale for close company legislation and discuss its increasing significance in the context of modern tax rates
- ✓ Define a "close company" and identify "close companies" when given key information relating to shareholdings
- ✓ Describe the tax implications for participators/directors and close companies of engaging in certain transactions
- ✓ Calculate the surcharges on undistributed profits for close companies in receipt of both trading income and professional service income

32.1 Introduction

The purpose of this chapter is to explain the reasoning behind the close company legislation and to define the numerous terms in the legislation. The chapter also sets out in detail the disadvantages to a company and its shareholders/directors when it is deemed to be a close company.

The legislation was enacted to ensure that shareholders of (mainly) owner-managed companies could not use their dominant position in the company to withdraw funds or have expenses paid by the company in a manner which eroded the tax base. The vast majority of companies in Ireland are owned and managed by families. An analysis of a section of accounts filed with the Companies Office shows that in a large percentage of cases, a company may have an issued share capital of between €1 and €2,000 and that these shares would usually be held between husband or wife, brothers, etc.

The following example shows just how the tax base could be eroded without close company legislation.

Example 32.1

John Murphy is a self-employed practising architect with an annual tax-adjusted net profit of €100,000. John is single and apart from the annual single tax credit has no other tax credits or reliefs.

John's income tax liability is as follows:

		€
Profit from profession		*100,000*
Taxed at 20%	*€34,550 × 20%*	*6,910*
Taxed at 40%	*€65,450 × 40%*	*26,180*
PRSI	*€100,000 × 4%*	*4,000*
USC	*€12,012 × 0.5%*	*60*
USC	*€7,360 × 2.5%*	*147*
USC	*€50,672 × 4.75%*	*2,407*
USC	*€29,956 × 8%*	*2,396*
Earned income credit		*(1,150)*
Single tax credit		*(1,650)*
Total income tax liability		*39,300*

Therefore from gross income of €100,000, John has after tax cash of €60,700 (€100,000 – €39,300).

John expects to have a similar income in the following year and decides to set up John Murphy Ltd. The company's annual tax liability would be as follows:

	€	
Profit from company	*100,000*	
Taxed at 12.5%	*100,000*	*× 12.5% = 12,500*

The company would have after tax cash reserves of €87,500. John then decides to take this from the company as an interest-free loan. This leaves him better off in cash terms by €26,800 (€87,500 – €60,700). (Note 1)

It is the above type of scenario that the close company legislation seeks to prevent. Now that the gap between income tax and corporation is as wide as it has been for the last 20 years, a greater focus can be expected on the anti-avoidance aspects of the legislation. The particular scenario above is prevented by s438 TCA97, which is covered later in the chapter.

Note 1: This example ignores the possible Company Law implications regarding loans.

32.2 Close Company Definitions

32.2.1 Close company

s430 TCA97 A close company is defined as an **Irish resident company**, which is CONTROLLED by:

(a) five or fewer participators and their associates; or

(b) participators who are directors, without any limitation on the number.

32.2.2 Participator

s433 TCA97 A participator is any person having an interest in the capital or income of a company. The term includes:

(a) a shareholder (the most common example you will come across);

(b) any person who possesses or is entitled to acquire share capital or voting rights in the company, e.g., an option-holder;

(c) any loan creditor of a company (defined below);

(d) any person entitled to receive or participate in distributions from the company or any amounts payable by the company to loan creditors by way of premium on redemption; or

(e) any person who can secure income or assets (whether present or future) of the company, which will be applied either directly or indirectly for his/her benefit, i.e., position of power.

32.2.3 Associate of a participator

s433 TCA97 An associate means, in relation to a participator:

(a) any relative or business partner of the participator

(Relative includes husband, wife, ancestor, lineal descendant, brother or sister. Therefore all "in-laws" are excluded as are nieces and nephews);

(b) the trustees of any settlement of which a participator or any relative of his/hers (living or dead) is the settlor.

Where the participator is interested in shares of the company which are subject to any trust or are part of the estate of a deceased person, an associate would be any other person interested therein, e.g., trustees, executors and beneficiaries. In this definition trusts for employees, directors and their dependents and approved pension funds are specifically excluded.

An associate of an associate cannot be linked to a participator, e.g., a person's wife's/husband's sister's shareholding cannot be added to his/her shareholding if he/she is taken as the participator. However, if it is the wife/husband who is treated as the participator, then the shareholdings of her husband/his wife and her/his sister would be added to her/him shareholding as her husband/his wife and her/his sister are two different associates in their own right.

32.2.4 Director

s433(4) TCA97 This term includes:

- Any person occupying the position of directors by whatever name called;
- Any person in accordance with whose directions or instructions the directors are accustomed to act;
- Any person who is a manager of the company and is either on his own or with one or more associates the beneficial owner of or able to control (directly or indirectly) 20% or more of the ordinary share capital of the company.

Remember that the definition specifically refers to directors. Once a company is controlled by directors, it is a close company regardless of the number of directors included in the "control".

32.2.5 Loan creditor

s433(6) TCA97

A detailed discussion of the term loan creditor is outside the scope of this publication, suffice to say that the term generally means a creditor in respect of any debt incurred by the company apart from ordinary trade debts or bank borrowings.

32.2.6 Associated company

s432(1) TCA97

A company is to be treated as another's associated company at any given time if, at that time or any time within the previous year, one of the two has control of the other or both are under the control of the same person or persons.

32.2.7 Control

s432(2) TCA97

A person is regarded as having control of a company if he/she exercises OR if he/she is able to exercise OR if he/she is entitled to acquire control (whether direct or indirect) over the company's affairs and in particular, if he/she possesses or is entitled to acquire the greater part of:

(a) the ordinary (voting) share capital of the company; or

(b) the total share capital of the company (including preference shares); or

(c) the income of the company on a full distribution among participators (ignoring the rights of loan creditors); or

(d) the assets of the company on a full distribution to shareholders in the event of a winding-up.

"Control" in the above situation means more than 50% (this could be 50.001%). Therefore, five or fewer participators who own 50.001% or more of the voting share capital of a company have control of the company and the company would thus be deemed to be a close company. If eight directors control the company, it is also deemed to be a close company (remember, the second part of the close company definition does not place a maximum number on the amount of directors needed to ensure close company status).

32.2.8 Exceptions

Certain companies are specifically excluded from close company status:

(1) companies not resident in Ireland;

(2) companies controlled by or on behalf of the State, which would NOT be close if the State's interest were ignored. This exemption includes companies controlled by EU Member States or States with which Ireland has a tax treaty;

(3) some public/quoted companies which satisfy certain conditions. A detailed discussion on this point is beyond the scope of this publication and exemptions under this section are relatively uncommon in practice;

(4) companies controlled by one or more other companies, which are "open companies" provided they cannot be treated as "close" except by including as one of the five or fewer participators a company which is not close (an open company is a company which itself is not a close company). A non-resident company which holds shares in the company in question is deemed to be a close company for the purpose of this exception if it would be a close company if it were Irish resident.

32.2.9 Chart to determine whether a company is a close company

The following chart is useful in determining whether or not a company is a close company.

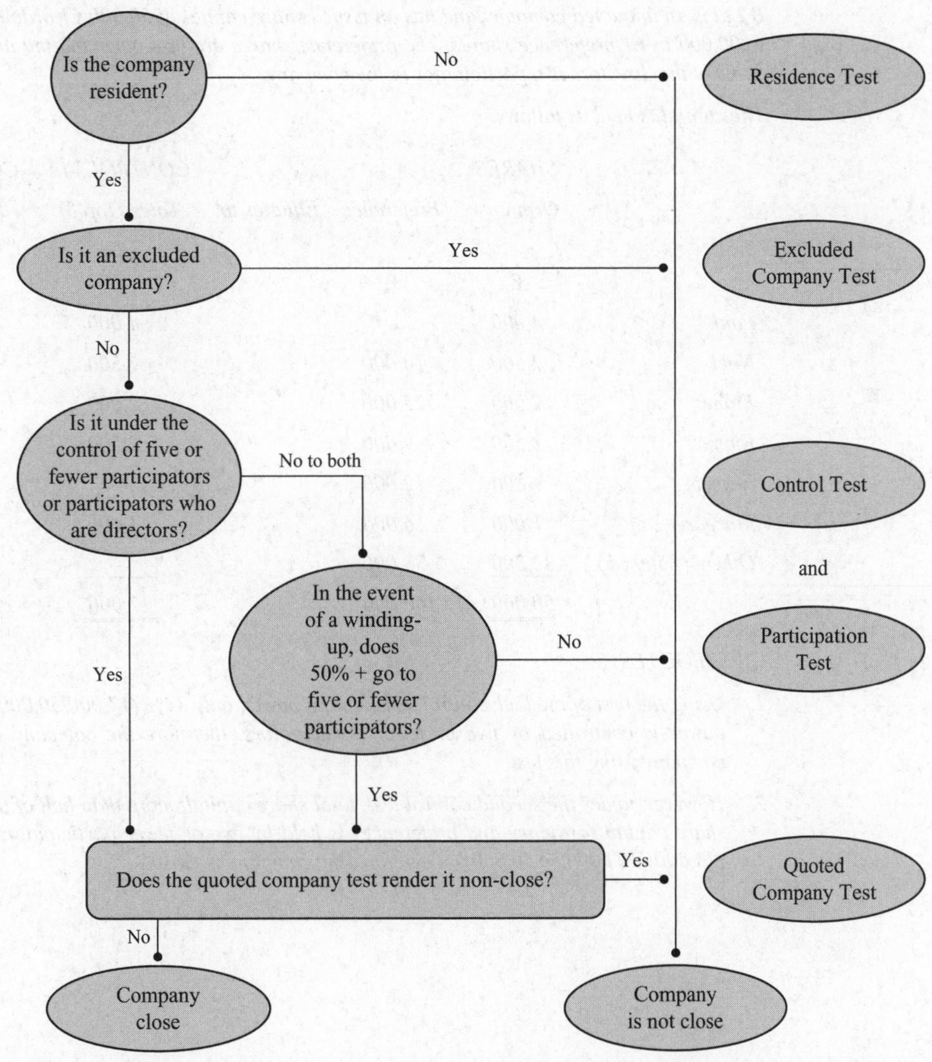

Example 32.2

A Ltd has an issued share capital of €100,000 held as follows:

	€
Mr. Kennedy (Manager)	*45,000*
Mrs. Kennedy	*6,000*
Ten other unrelated shareholders	*49,000*
	100,000

Mr. Kennedy and Mrs. Kennedy are associates. Therefore, they are treated as one participator. As five or fewer participators control 51% of the company's share capital, the company is regarded as close. It should also be noted that Mr. Kennedy is deemed to be a director of the company as he owns 20% or more of the company's ordinary share capital (even though his title is Manager).

Example 32.3

B Ltd is an unquoted company and has an issued share capital of 50,000 €1 ordinary shares and €100,000 in €1 preference shares. The preference shares are non-participating and non-voting. None of the directors is a participator in the company.

The capital is held as follows:

	SHARES			*CONTROL VIA*	*CONTROL VIA*
	Ordinary	*Preference*	*Equates to*	*Votes (Top 5)*	*Issued share capital (Top 5)*
	€	€		€	€
Paul	*4,000*	–		*4,000*	–
Noel	*7,500*	*10,000*		*7,500*	*17,500*
Fiona	*2,000*	*25,000*		*2,000*	*27,000*
Emma	*2,500*	*9,000*		*2,500*	*11,500*
Francis	*800*	*12,000*		–	*12,800*
Margaret	*1,000*	*6,000*		*1,000*	*7,000*
Others (<500 ea.)	*32,200*	*38,000*		–	–
	50,000	*100,000*		*17,000*	*75,800*

CONTROL TESTS

1. *Using the first of the four control tests, voting power, only 34% (17,000/50,000) of the voting power is controlled by five or fewer participators, therefore the company is not a close company using this test.*
2. *However, under the second control test, total share capital, more than half of the total issued share capital (ordinary and preference) is held by five or fewer participators, i.e., 50.53% (75,800/(100,000 + 50,000)). Therefore, the company is close.*

Example 32.4

C Limited has an issued share capital of €100,000 held by the following directors:

		€
Paul	*Director*	*12,000*
Martin	*Director*	*10,000*
Colleen	*Director*	*4,000*
Bríd	*Director*	*5,000*
Aidan	*Director*	*6,000*
Justin	*Director*	*12,000*
Kenneth	*Director*	*9,000*
Others (each owning <5,000)	*Director*	*42,000*
		100,000

The company is not under the control of five or fewer participators as the top five participators only control 49% of the company (Paul, Martin, Aidan, Justin and Kenneth). However, it is under the control of its directors (58%) and is therefore a close company irrespective of the number of directors.

If we revise the facts of the above example, such that Justin is a manager and not a director, the position is as follows:

- *As Justin does not hold 20% or more of the ordinary share capital he does not rank as a director;*
- *The company's directors then hold 46% of the issued share capital which means that it is not director-controlled and is therefore an "open" company.*

Example 32.5

D Limited has an issued share capital held as follows:

	%
Paul	*6*
Joanne (Paul's wife)	*5*
Noel (Paul's brother)	*6*
Marie (Paul's daughter)	*3*
Fiona (Paul's sister)	*5*
George (son of Noel, i.e., Paul's nephew)	*9*
Emma (Paul's sister)	*15*
Rogan Limited (Company controlled by Paul)	*6*
Margaret (Paul's mother)	*5*
5 others, unconnected to Paul or each other, each holding 8%	*40*
	100

Paul's own interests are aggregated with those of his associates, i.e., Joanne, Noel, Marie, Fiona, Emma, Rogan Limited and Margaret. Note that George, who is Paul's nephew, is not an associate as he is not within the scope of the definition of relative. However, even if we only take Paul's and George's interests, they control 60% of the issued share capital. Therefore, D Limited is treated as a close company.

32.3 Impact of Close Company Status on Individuals and Companies

The purpose of this unit is to summarise the disadvantages, which flow from a company having a "close company" status and also to explain what the anti-avoidance measures aim to prevent.

32.3.1 Benefits to participators and associates

s436 TCA97 Any expenses incurred by a close company in providing benefits or facilities of any kind for a participator or an associate will be treated as a distribution made by the company. This means that the amount of the expense is "added back" in the tax-adjusted profits of the Case I computation and the recipient is treated as if the value of the benefit is income received under Schedule F. The company is obliged to account for dividend withholding tax (DWT) and pay this over to the Collector-General based on the **actual value of the benefit.** The company has a right to demand repayment of this withholding tax at 20% from the participator, although in practice this may prove difficult[1]. The individual is liable to income tax on the gross value of the benefit actually received.

The company has a DWT liability equal to the tax credit attaching to the distribution. Expenses incurred on such items as living accommodation, entertainment, domestic and other services would all be classed as benefits to the participator.

Section 436A TCA97 treats the transfer of any asset to a trust held for the benefit of a participator (excluding a loan creditor) or a relative of a participator as a distribution by the company to the trustees of the settlement.

When a participator or relative of a participator receives a benefit from the settlement, either directly or indirectly they will be subject to a charge to tax under Schedule D Case IV. This applies to transactions on or after 21 January 2011.

The following expense payments are not treated as distributions:

(1) any expense made good, i.e., reimbursed, to the company by the participator;

(2) any expense incurred in providing benefits or facilities to directors or employees, which are already assessable as benefit in kind under Schedule E (s118 TCA97); (From 1 January 2004 these benefits are taxed at source through the company's payroll.)

(3) any expense incurred in connection with the provision for the spouse, children or dependants of any director or employee of any pension, annuity, lump sum or gratuity to be given on his/her death or retirement.

1 There may be a technical argument under s172B(3) TCA97 that if the DWT withheld is not repaid by the participator to the company a further benefit arises, as the participator has now received his full benefit and a DWT tax credit - see note to example 32.6.

Example 32.6

In March 2018, Gormally Limited incurred an expense of €1,500 in providing a luxurious Caribbean cruise for a shareholder, who is neither an employee nor a director. The shareholder is an associate of a participator in Gormally Limited, which is a close company. Accounts are prepared to 31/12/2018.

IMPLICATIONS:

A) Corporation Tax

1. *The expense of €1,500 is disallowed and is added back in the adjusted Case I profit computation as it is treated as a distribution.*
2. *The company must account for DWT as it is deemed to have made a distribution. The expense paid is treated as the distributed amount.*

   DWT of €300 (€1,500 × 20%) is payable. This amount is payable to the Collector-General on or before the fourteenth day after the month the benefit was paid, in this case 14 April 2018.
3. *The net effect of 1. and 2. above is that the company has paid €1,500 for the holiday and also €300 withholding tax. In this situation, it could seek recovery of €300 from the shareholder as it only intended to give a benefit of €1,500.*

B) Income Tax

The shareholder is not assessed under Schedule E as he is not an employee or Director but is treated as having received a distribution liable under Schedule F. The amount is €1,500 and the related dividend withholding tax is €300. If the shareholder pays income tax at the marginal rate, then the additional income tax payable (ignoring the impact of PRSI and the USC) would be as follows:

	€
Schedule F	*1,500*
Income tax payable at 40%	*600*
Less DWT	*(300)*
Additional income tax payable by shareholder	*300*

The company is entitled to demand repayment from the shareholder of the tax credit[2]*.*

32.3.2 Interest paid to directors and their associates

s437 TCA97 This piece of legislation is concerned with any interest on loans paid by a close company to, or to an associate of, a person who:

(a) is a director of the close company or of any company which controls or is controlled by the close company; AND

(b) has a material interest in the company. A director has a material interest in a close company if he/she, either on his/her own or with any one or more of his/her associates, is the beneficial owner of, or is able to control, directly or indirectly more than 5% of the ordinary share capital, or of any other company that controls it.

2 Note to example - if the s172B(3) TCA97 argument as noted above is used, the taxpayer would be taxed on €1,875 (€1,500 regrossed at 80%) with a credit for €375 (€1,875 × 20%). This would not apply if the DWT tax credit was repaid to the company.

Such interest payments in excess of a prescribed limit will be treated as a distribution. The practical effect of this treatment is as follows:

(1) For the company, excess interest is added back in the tax-adjusted Case I profit computation. The company must also account for dividend withholding tax (DWT) at the standard rate of income tax, i.e., 20% on the excess amount treated as a distribution[3]. The company is also obliged to withhold tax at the standard rate on the interest allowed under s239 TCA97. This tax is payable with the company's corporation tax liability.

(2) For the recipient, excess interest is treated as a distribution received and is taxable under Schedule F. The recipient director is also taxed on the interest allowed, but in this case, under Schedule D Case IV. He or she will get credit for the DWT withheld on the excess interest and also for the tax withheld on the allowable interest.

The prescribed limit mentioned above is calculated firstly as an "overall" limit. The overall limit is then apportioned between the various directors affected (those with a material interest) on the basis of the amounts of interest paid to each of them.

The overall limit is 13% per annum on the LOWER of:

(a) the total of ALL loans on which interest to directors (or their associates) with a "material interest" was paid by the company in the accounting period; OR

(b) the nominal amount of the issued share capital of the close company PLUS the amount of any share premium account, taken at the BEGINNING of the accounting period.

For the purposes of (a) above, where the total of all loans varies during the accounting period, the average total over the period is to be taken.

In practice a company is usually in financial difficulty when its directors are required to invest in the company and therefore a return on the investment is not generally an issue.

If a return is required it is recommended that a director's fee or increased salary be processed through payroll in preference to the complicated calculation of allowable interest and the implications of overpaying interest.

Example 32.7

Rogan Limited is a close company whose issued share capital is €10,000 (10,000 €1 ordinary shares). The company has no share premium account. In the accounting period ended 31/12/2018, it received the following loans:

3 The argument advanced in 32.3.1 regarding re-grossing the benefit for unpaid DWT by the participator would not apply here as the distribution is in cash and therefore the DWT would have been withheld prior to paying the distribution, s172B(1) TCA97.

	Shareholding	Loans	Interest Paid
	€	€	€
1/1/2018 Philip (Director)	*3,333*	*30,000*	*4,500*
1/1/2018 George (Director)	*300*	*20,000*	*3,000*
1/1/2018 Elizabeth (wife of George)	*300*	*–*	
1/1/2018 Joanne (Director)	*500*	*10,000*	*1,500*

The corporation tax and income tax consequences for Rogan Limited are as follows:

The following Directors are affected by the provisions of s437 TCA97:

1. *Philip is a Director and holds 33% of the ordinary share capital.*
2. *George is a Director and together with his associates, i.e., his wife Elizabeth, he holds over 5% of the ordinary share capital.*
3. *Joanne does not come within this provision as she holds exactly 5% of the ordinary share capital and does not therefore have the necessary "material interest".*

The overall limit is the lower of:

	€	€
(a) 13% of (€30,000 + €20,000)	*6,500*	
(b) 13% of €10,000	*1,300*	*1,300*

Interest paid to Directors with a material interest is:

Philip	*4,500*
George	*3,000*
	7,500
Overall limit	*(1,300)*
Excess (treated as a distribution)	*6,200*

This excess of €6,200 is added back in Rogan Limited's tax-adjusted Case I profit computation.

The overall limit is apportioned among the relevant Directors according to the interest paid to each:

	INTEREST PAID	LIMIT			EXCESS TREATED AS DISTRIBUTION
	€			€	€
Philip	*4,500*	*4,500 × 1,300 / 7,500*	=	*780*	*3,720*
George	*3,000*	*3,000 × 1,300 / 7,500*	=	*520*	*2,480*
	7,500			*1,300*	*6,200*

The dividend withholding tax liability of Rogan Limited for the accounting period ended 31/12/2017 is as follows:

Philip: €3,720 × 20% = €744

George: €2,480 × 20% = €496

The company is also obliged, under s239 TCA97 to deduct tax at the standard rate from the allowable interest paid:

Philip €780 × 20% = €156

George €520 × 20% = €104

The income tax implications (ignoring PRSI and the USC) for Philip and George are as follows (assuming they are taxed at 40%):

	Philip	***George***
	€	**€**
Schedule F	*3,720*	*2,480*
Schedule D Case IV	*780*	*520*
Income	*4,500*	*3,000*
Income tax at 40%	*1,800*	*1,200*
Less DWT credit	*(744)*	*(496)*
Less interest tax credit	*(156)*	*(104)*
Net income tax payable	*900*	*600*

32.3.3 Loans to participators

s438 & s439 TCA97

Where a close company makes a loan to an individual who is a participator or an associate of a participator, the company will be required to pay income tax in respect of the amount of the loan re-grossed at the standard rate (i.e., 20%) as if this re-grossed amount were an annual payment under s239 TCA97 (and not Schedule F, which applies to expenses or excess loan interest paid by the company).

The income tax due cannot be set off against the company's corporation tax liability. When the loan, or part of the loan, is repaid by the participator (or associate), the tax paid or a proportionate part of it will be refunded to the company (without interest), provided a claim is made within 10 years of the year of assessment in which the loan is repaid.

There are three exceptions to the above treatment of loans to participators:

(a) Where the business of the company is or included the lending of money and the loan is made in the ordinary course of that business, the provisions do not apply.

(b) Loans made to directors or employees of the company (or an associated company) are outside of the scope of the provisions if:

1. the amount of the loan together with all other loans outstanding made by the company (or an associated company) to the borrower (or his/her spouse) does not exceed €19,050; *and*

2. the borrower works full-time for the company; *and*

3. the borrower does not have a material interest (as defined previously – more than 5% of ordinary share capital) in the company or an associated company. If the borrower subsequently acquires a material interest, the company will be requested to pay income tax in respect of ALL loans outstanding to the borrower at that time.

(c) The provisions do not apply where the debt is incurred for the supply of goods or services in the ordinary course of business, _unless_ the period of credit given exceeds six months or is longer than credit terms normally given to customers.

It is important to note that the loan is not regarded as income in the individual's hands unless and until the loan is forgiven by the company. In this case, the income tax is not recoverable by the company and the re-grossed loan is assessed on the participator for income tax purposes. The loan is re-grossed at the standard income tax rate applicable in the year of forgiveness and not at the rate for the year it was advanced. Also, the write-off is not deductible against the company's Case I profits.

The income tax payable in respect of loans to participators is payable at the same time as the company's preliminary corporation tax. However, Revenue will not normally require the tax to be paid if the loan has been repaid in full within six months of the end of the accounting period in which the loan was originally made.

Example 32.8

Griffiths Limited makes an interest-free loan of €40,000 to a full-time working Director, Chris Griffiths, in the accounting period ended 31/12/2018. Mr. Griffiths holds 10% of the close company's ordinary share capital. The loan is subsequently forgiven in the accounting period ended 31/12/2019.

NOTE: This loan to a participator does not qualify for the exception at (b) above because Mr. Griffiths has a material interest in the company and the amount of the loan exceeds €19,050.

What are the corporation tax and income tax consequences?

1. ***Corporation tax implications for Griffiths Limited:***

   (a) *Accounting period ended 31/12/2018: income tax of €40,000 × 20/80, i.e., €10,000 is payable by the company with its corporation tax under s239 TCA97. No deduction is allowed in the company's accounts for the loan or the tax paid.*

   (b) *Accounting period ended 31/12/2019: the income tax paid is now irrecoverable and the write-off is not a tax-deductible expense in the adjusted Case I profit computation.*

2. ***Income tax implications for Mr. Griffiths:***

   (a) *Year of assessment 2018: Mr. Griffiths is charged to income tax on the notional benefit in kind on an interest-free loan, currently at 13.50%.*

   (b) *Year of assessment 2019: the loan write-off is treated as Schedule D Case IV income in the amount of €40,000 × 100/80, i.e., €50,000. Credit is given for the €10,000 suffered by the company so that only a higher rate liability arises (i.e., the marginal rate in force in 2019). It is important to bear in mind that if Mr. Griffiths has insufficient income tax payable to fully utilise this credit, the balance is not repayable.*

32.4 Calculation of Close Company Surcharges

32.4.1 Introduction

The disadvantages discussed above mainly affect participators and directors of close companies personally. Legislation was also enacted to narrow the gap between income tax rates for individuals (up to 55% – income tax, USC and PRSI for the self-employed) and corporation tax rates for companies (12.5% on trading income and 25% on passive income). The legislation levies a surcharge on undistributed income at either 20% or 15%, depending on the type of company (see below). This surcharge is in addition to the corporation tax charge that the company would have paid on its income and therefore has the result of bringing the effective rate of corporation tax closer to income tax levels.

As the surcharge is only charged on undistributed income, the chief method of avoiding a surcharge is to distribute the income in the form of a dividend. However, by declaring a dividend, the shareholders will be charged to tax under Schedule F, normally at the marginal rate of income tax.

The two surcharge types affect passive income and professional income and both are discussed below. It can be seen therefore that the surcharge legislation is an effective tool for ensuring that certain types of income cannot be sheltered in a company to avail of Ireland's low corporation tax rates. Despite much media speculation in recent years regarding the extension of the surcharge to all undistributed income (i.e., to include Case I trading income), no major changes have been made in this respect.

32.4.2 Close company surcharge on undistributed income

s440 TCA97 The purpose of this commentary is to set out the provisions relating to an additional surcharge of 20%, which is levied on the undistributed rental and investment income of a close company.

An additional 20% corporation tax surcharge is levied on a close company, which does not distribute income derived from investments or rental property (termed "investment" and "estate" income respectively).

Companies which would be entitled to avail of the participation exemption under s626B TCA97 (which allows holding companies resident in Ireland to sell shares in 5% subsidiaries free of capital gains tax) are not required to include in their surchargeable income dividends received from its non-resident qualifying subsidiaries.

In relation to Irish dividends, the companies paying and receiving the dividend can jointly elect to have it ignored for close company surcharge purposes[4]. Where both the payee and recipient jointly elect, the recipient is not surcharged on the dividend and the payee does not receive a deduction against its own surchargeable income. This applies to distributions payable on or after 31 January 2008.

---

4 Note that even though a company may be exempt from corporation tax on dividends received from Irish resident companies (franked investment income – see 28.5.1), it may still suffer a close company surcharge on such dividends.

The surcharge is paid with the following year's corporation tax. Thus, for a company with a year-end of 31 December 2018, the surcharge is paid with the corporation tax for the year ended 31 December 2019 (unless the company has paid sufficient dividends for 2018).

As noted above a company may declare a dividend in order to reduce its undistributed income and therefore its exposure to the surcharge. Any dividend declared by the company must be paid within 18 months of the period end. Therefore, to reduce the surcharge for year ended 31 December 2018 the dividend must be declared and paid on or before 30 June 2020.

In addition to ordinary dividends declared and paid, deemed distributions such as participators' expenses (32.3.1), settlements (32.3.1), excess interest to directors (32.3.2) and distributions under s130 TCA97 are also included in reducing a company's undistributed earnings for surcharge purposes.

Step-by-step surcharge calculation for trading company.

s440 TCA97

The following step-by-step procedure facilitates calculation of the close company surcharge in accordance with s440 TCA97.

	€
(i) Calculate "Income"	X
Income from Case I, III, IV and V	(X)
Deduct current losses, i.e., s396A, s399 TCA97	(X)
Deduct relevant trade charges, i.e., s243A TCA97	(X)
	X
(ii) Calculate "Estate and Investment Income"	
Answer from (i) × Passive Income/Total Income	X
Add Franked Investment Income (FII)	X
Deduct relevant charges (charges deductible against all profits, i.e., s243 TCA97).	(X)
	X
(iii) Calculate "Distributable Estate and Investment Income"	
Answer from (ii)	X
Less corporation tax on passive income as reduced by relevant charges	(X)
Less 7.5% trading deduction on above sum	(X)
	X

(iv) Calculate surcharges – deduct distributions from distributable estate and investment income (answer from (iii)) and multiply answer by 20%.

Example 32.9

Troy Ltd, a close company, has the following income, chargeable gains and charges on income for its 12-month accounting period ended 31 December 2018.

	€
Trading income (non-professional)	*40,000*
Rental income	*10,000*
Bank interest (Gross)	*6,000*
FII (Gross)	*4,000*

The company paid charges of €5,000 in respect of its trading activities and claimed €10,000 of loss relief in respect of loss relief under s396(1) for a loss that arose in the accounting period ended 31/12/2017.

The company incurred expenses on behalf of a participator of €400 under s436 TCA97 (the participator was neither a director nor an employee of the company) and the final dividend of €2,000 for the year ended 31/12/2018 was declared and paid on 1 February 2019.

1. Calculate the "income" of the company

		€
Schedule D	*Case I*	*40,000*
	Case III	*6,000*
	Case V	*10,000*
		56,000
Less relevant trading charges		*(5,000)*
		51,000

Note that no allowance is given for the loss carried forward. The surcharge calculation is on current year activity only.

2. Calculate the "Estate and Investment Income"

First calculation	€	€
FII		*4,000*
$€51{,}000 \times \frac{€16{,}000}{€56{,}000}$		*14,571*
		18,571
Deduct:		
Relevant charges (against all profits)		*Nil*
"Estate and Investment Income"		*18,571*

3. "Distributable Estate and Investment Income"

Estate and Investment Income	*18,571*
Less corporation tax (€14,571 × 25%)	*(3,643)*
	14,928
Less trading discount at 7.5%	*(1,120)*
	13,808

*4. **Surchargeable amount***

Distributable Estate and Investment Income		*13,808*
Less distributions for the period		
Expenses of participator	*(400)*	
Final dividend declared and paid	*(2,000)*	
		(2,400)
Surchargeable amount		*11,408*
Surcharge at 20%		*2,282*

This surcharge is treated as part of the corporation tax liability for the accounting year ended 31/12/2019. As the company has 18 months to declare and pay dividends, it has until the following year to actually pay the surcharge. If no further distributions are made by the company, by 30/06/2020, the surcharge will be payable with the corporation tax for 31/12/19. The first payment will be due on 23/06/2019 (45% (of the current year) or 50% (of the prior year)) with the second payment due on 23/11/19 (to bring the total of the two payments to 90% of the current year) with the third payment (10%) being due when the return is filed, at the latest by 23/9/20. If the company pays the first and second preliminary payments and subsequently pays a dividend in March 2020 in respect of the year ended 31/12/2018, it will receive a refund or a set-off against its other CT liabilities when it files it return for the year ended 31/12/2019.

32.4.2.1 De minimus relief

Section 440(1)(b) TCA97 provides that no surcharge is imposed in any case where the excess of the "distributable estate and investment income" for an accounting period over the distributions made for that accounting period is €2,000 or less.

There is also an element of marginal relief where the "excess" to which the 20% surcharge is applied exceeds €2,000 by a small amount. This limits the amount of the surcharge so as not to be higher than 80% of the amount by which the "excess" is greater than €2,000. Thus, the marginal relief applies if the "excess" is between €2,001 and €2,665.

Thus, if the "excess" or the surchargeable amount is €2,500, the surcharge is calculated as €2,500 × 20%, i.e., €500.

However, marginal relief limits the amount of the surcharge to: (€2,500 – €2,000) × 80%, i.e., €400.

32.4.2.2 Reduction if accumulated undistributed income is less than excess

Section 440(2) TCA97 provides for a reduction in the amount (the "excess") on which the surcharge is levied for an accounting period if the "excess" is more than the "accumulated undistributed income" of the company at the end of that accounting period. If this occurs, the 20% surcharge is calculated on the amount of that accumulated undistributed income (subject to the same €2,000 *de minimus* exclusion mentioned above).

The accumulated undistributed income at the end of the accounting period is taken as per the accounts of the company plus any transfer to capital reserves, bonus issues or other transactions which would reduce the accumulated income available for distribution.

Example 32.10

Take the case of Troy Ltd, the close company dealt with in Example 32.9. If the financial accounts at period end December 2018 show reserves available for distribution of €7,000, this figure would be surchargeable instead of the €11,408 as previously calculated.

Surcharge: €7,000 × 20% = €1,400.

32.4.3 Surcharge on service companies, s441 TCA97

32.4.3.1 Meaning of service company

Section 440 TCA97 is concerned with surcharging undistributed passive income. Given, however, the wide variance between marginal income tax for self-employed professionals (up to 55%) and the lower rate of corporation tax for incorporated professional companies (12.5%), the s441 TCA97 surcharge on service company income seeks to narrow that gap. The surcharge applies to "active" income where professional persons incorporate in an effort to avoid paying the top rate of personal tax on their fee income. This surcharge is known as the professional services surcharge and is levied on 50% of the annual professional income at a rate of 15%. Passive income is still subject to a surcharge at 20%.

A service company is defined as a close company:

(a) whose business consists of or includes the carrying on of a profession or the provision of professional services;

(b) which holds or exercises an office or employment;

(c) whose business consists of or includes the provision of services or facilities of whatever nature to or for:

(i) a company within the categories (a) and (b) described above,

(ii) an individual or partnership which carries on a profession,

(iii) a person who holds or exercises an employment,

(iv) a person or partnership connected with any of the above.

The term "service company" applies only where the principal part of the company's income which is chargeable under Schedule D Case II is derived from the profession, the provision of professional services, an employment, the provision of certain services or facilities or a combination of these activities. Examples of such companies would include companies established by professionals such as auctioneers, journalists, opticians, etc.

As the legislation provides no definition of a profession, it has fallen upon the Courts to interpret its meaning. In the Irish case of *Mac Giolla Mhaith (Inspector of Taxes) v Cronin & Associates Ltd* ((1984) 3 ITR 211), the Inspector of Taxes imposed a surcharge under s441 TCA97 on the basis that the company's advertising business was a profession. The company appealed this decision and after losing the appeal before the

Appeal Commissioners and winning before the Circuit Court, the case appeared before the High Court in July 1984.

The High Court found in favour of the company. The following extract from the judgement is relevant:

> *"Having read these meanings, I am left in the position that the statute has provided a conundrum which I cannot solve. If the addition of the word 'vocation' does include all occupations, callings, businesses, habitual employments and professions, it seems unnecessary to have the word 'profession' at all. The word 'profession' even as extended by the word 'vocation' must have some limitations. Similarly, it must have been intended to effect some extension but, as I cannot guess what this extension was intended to be I am not in a position to state that the inference drawn by the President of the Circuit Court was not correct."*

See Tax Briefing 48 for a list of activities described by Revenue as being chargeable services.

"Professionals" are taken to include architects, auctioneers, surveyors. In the following tax cases, the listed activities were also held to constitute a profession:

- an optician – *CIR v North and Ingram* ([1918] 2 KB 705);
- a journalist – *CIR v Maxse* ((1919) 12 TC 41);
- an actress – *Davies v Braithwaite* ((1931) 18 TC 198);

In the case of *Barker and Sons v CIR* ([1919] 2 KB 222), a stock-broker was held not to be a professional

One guiding principle regarding whether a company is carrying on a professional service can be taken from how the income of the company is earned. Are the employees who earn fees for the company members of professional organisations? Have they sat exams for their profession? Are they employed by the company on the basis of their qualifications and membership of these bodies? A company who earns the majority of its income from its professional staff would generally be considered to be a professional service company and therefore within the scope of the s441 TCA97 surcharge.

The key point to remember is that a surcharge applies to both passive and active income in the case of service companies. The passive income surcharge is calculated in a manner identical to that provided for by s440 TCA97 (see the four-step process outlined above). The addition of a surcharge on 50% of the active income of service companies is provided for by s441 TCA97.

Step-by-step surcharge calculation for service company, s441

1. Calculate the **"distributable trading income"** (trading income less relevant trade charges and after standard rate corporation tax).

2. Calculate half of the **"distributable trading income"**.
3. Add to amounts at 2 above the **"distributable estate and investment income"** (net of the 7.5% trading discount). This is the same calculation as used for the s440 surcharge and is calculated as follows:

   (i) Calculate "Income":

   Income from Case I, III, IV and V

   Deduct current losses, i.e., s396A, s399 TCA97

   Deduct relevant trade charges, s243A TCA97

   (ii) Calculate "Estate and Investment Income":

   $$\text{Answer from (i)} \times \frac{\text{Passive Income}}{\text{Total Income}}$$

   Add Franked Investment Income (FII)

   Deduct relevant charges (charges deductible against all profits, s243 TCA97

   (iii) Calculate "Distributable Estate and Investment Income":

   Answer from (ii)

   Less corporation tax on passive income as reduced by relevant charges

   Less 7.5% trading deduction on above sum

Steps (i)–(iii) are the same steps as (i)–(iii) for s440 TCA97, as both surcharges calculate the net undistributed passive income in the same manner.

4. From the figure at 3 above, deduct all distributions declared for the accounting period and paid during or within 18 months of the end of the accounting period to give the total surchargeable amount. This figure is required for the purposes of step 7 (see below).
5. Deduct the distributions made from the total of "distributable estate and investment income" (the figure calculated at 3. (i)–(iii) above).
6. Apply a 20% surcharge to the resulting figure at 6. which represents the excess of the total of distributable estate and investment income over the distributions made.
7. Apply a 15% surcharge to the total surchargeable amount at 4., minus the excess figure calculated at 5. above.

Example 32.11

This example uses amounts identical to those in Example 32.9 above (for s440 TCA97 surcharge) except that the company is now a professional company.

Troy Ltd, a close company, has the following income, chargeable gains and charges on income for its 12-month accounting period ended 31 December 2018.

	€
Trading income (professional)	*40,000*
Rental income	*10,000*
Bank interest (Gross)	*6,000*
FII (Gross)	*4,000*

The company paid charges of €5,000 in respect of its trading activities and claimed €10,000 of loss relief under s396(1) for a loss, which arose in the accounting period, ended 31/12/2017.

The company incurred expenses on behalf of a participator of €400 under s436 TCA97 (the participator was neither a Director nor an employee of the company) and the final dividend of €2,000 for the year ended 31/12/2018 was declared and paid on 1 February 2019.

1. *The distributable trading income of the company is calculated as follows:*

	€
Case II	*40,000*
Less relevant trade charges	*(5,000)*
	35,000
CT at 12.5%	*(4,375)*
Distributable trading income	*30,625*

2. *Calculate half of the distributable trading income, €30,625/2, i.e., €15,312.*
3. *Add to amount at point 2, the distributable investment and estate income (net of trading discounts).*

Distributable Estate and Investment Income:

	€
Schedule D Case II	*40,000*
Case III	*10,000*
Case V	*6,000*
	56,000
Less relevant trading charges	*(5,000)*
	51,000
$€51{,}000 \times \frac{€16{,}000}{€56{,}000}$	*14,571*
Franked Investment Income	*4,000*
Estate and Investment Income	*18,571*
Less corporation tax (€14,571 × 25%)	*(3,643)*
	14,928
Less trading discount at 7.5%	*(1,120)*
	13,808
"Distributable Estate and Investment Income"	*13,808*
Half of distributable trading income	*15,312*
Total	*29,120*

4. *Less distributions made*	*(2,400)*
Total surchargeable amount	*26,720*

5. *Excess of Distributable Estate and Investment Income over distributions made.*

	€
Distributable Estate and Investment Income	13,808
Less distributions made	*(2,400)*
	11,408

6. *Surcharge at 20% on €11,408 = €2,282*
7. *Surcharge at 15%*

	€
Total surchargeable amount	*26,720*
Less excess levied at 20%	*(11,408)*
Total	*15,312*

Surcharge at 15% = €2,297

Therefore, the total surcharge assessed on the company is €2,282 + €2,297 = €4,579.

33 BASIC PRINCIPLES OF CAPITAL ACQUISITIONS TAX

Learning Outcomes

On completion of this chapter, you should be able to:

- ✓ Define a number of legal terms that feature prominently in CAT legislation.
- ✓ Describe the territorial scope of CAT and identify the circumstances in which benefits will be taxable.
- ✓ Identify the appropriate group threshold for various relationships and circumstances.
- ✓ Calculate the CAT liability where a number of benefits have been received since 5 December 1991.
- ✓ Describe the main exemptions and reliefs from CAT provided for by legislation.
- ✓ Calculate the taxable value of various benefits, including annuities and limited interests.
- ✓ Define 'agricultural property' and 'business property'.
- ✓ Describe and identify the circumstances in which agricultural relief and business property relief will apply.
- ✓ Apply agricultural relief and business property relief in calculating CAT liabilities.
- ✓ Describe the system of administration and payment of CAT.
- ✓ Complete Assignments and Questions in the corresponding chapter in *Irish Taxation: Law and Practice*, Volume 2.

33.1 Introduction

Capital Acquisitions Tax (CAT) provides for both gift and inheritance tax on assets passing from one individual to another. As the name suggests, it is a tax on acquisitions and accordingly, liability for payment generally rests with the recipient of the gift or inheritance.

CAT was first legislated for in the CAT Act 1976 and its introduction coincided with the abolition of estate duties, arising on legacies and under succession law. It was originally intended to complement an annual wealth tax; however, the annual wealth tax was short-lived and was, in fact, abolished with effect from 5 April 1978, i.e., within three years of its original introduction. The provisions of the CAT Act 1976 and subsequent Finance Acts were consolidated in 2003 and can now be found in the CAT Consolidation Act 2003 (CATCA 2003).

33.2 Terminology

Before considering the provisions of CAT legislation in detail, a number of terms merit definition. In many instances, the definitions provided for by legislation differ from the common sense meaning anticipated by non-professionals. For example, it is possible to acquire an 'inheritance' from an individual who is still living, while in certain circumstances, a 'gift' may be taken from someone who is deceased.

s5 CATCA 2003
s10 CATCA
s3 CATCA

For CAT purposes, a "**gift**" or "**inheritance**" is deemed to be taken whenever there is a "**disposition**" by a "**disponer**" whereby a "**donee**" or "**successor**" becomes "**beneficially entitled in possession**" to a "**benefit**", otherwise than for full consideration. We will now look at each of these terms to determine their meaning.

33.2.1 Parties involved

s2 CATCA 2003

The "disponer" may be defined as the individual who is the source of the benefit, while the "donee" (if the benefit is a gift) or "successor" (if the benefit is an inheritance) is the person who ultimately receives the benefit. Correctly identifying the disponer and the donee or successor is imperative as the relationship between the two is a key determinant in calculating the level of CAT payable.

Example 33.1

If Tom owes Eileen €50,000 and Eileen agrees to waive this debt provided Tom pays Sean €10,000, then in these circumstances, two separate benefits are taken. Tom takes a benefit of €40,000 being the amount of the debt that is waived less the consideration that he is required to pay Sean. Sean takes a benefit of €10,000, being the cash received from Tom. Eileen is the ultimate source of both benefits and accordingly, is the disponer. This is the case notwithstanding that the benefit to Sean is indirectly provided through Tom. Tom and Sean are the donees.

33.2.2 Types of benefit

s2 CATCA 2003

"Benefit" as defined in CAT legislation, includes any "estate, interest, income or right". Thus, it would include any interest in a property, either absolute or limited (see 33.5.5), and it would also include any annuity or other periodic payment (see 33.5.4).

The valuation of benefits for CAT purposes is considered at section 33.5 below. In addition, certain benefits and certain dispositions are exempt from CAT and these are considered at Section 33.6 below.

33.2.3 Gift v Inheritance

An "**inheritance**" is taken "**on a death**". The legislation outlines the circumstances where a benefit constitutes an inheritance. In addition to covering the situation where property passes directly from the deceased to a successor under the terms of a will or under intestacy (i.e. where the disponer died without a will), the term also includes a benefit where the disponer dies within two years of the "**date of disposition**". Accordingly, where an individual dies within two years of making a gift, the property transferred constitutes an inheritance.

An inheritance is also taken where a life interest is terminated on the death of a life tenant.

Example 33.2

If John settles property on his brother Mike for life with the remainder to his niece Helen absolutely, then Helen takes an inheritance from John on Mike's death. This is the case albeit that John may still be living when Helen becomes entitled to her remainder interest.

Conversely, a **"gift"** arises otherwise than **"on a death"** and accordingly, it is possible to envisage a situation whereby a "donee" takes a gift from someone who is deceased.

Example 33.3

If John grants a limited interest of 10 years duration to his brother Mike with the remaining interest in the property to his niece Helen absolutely, then Helen takes a gift from John on the expiry of the intervening limited interest. This is the case albeit that John may have died in the interim period.

33.2.4 Disposition

A "disposition" may be defined as any act or omission or failure by an individual, as a result of which, the value of the individual's estate is reduced. Thus, it would include not only the transfer of property otherwise than for full consideration, but also the provision of any benefit or the waiver of any debt. In addition, a 'disposition' can include any reciprocal arrangement whereby the disponer binds a third party to the provision of a benefit to a donee or successor (see example 33.1).

33.2.5 Beneficially entitled in possession

s2 CATCA 2003

In order to come within the scope of CAT, a done/successor must become beneficially entitled in possession to the benefit in question. "Beneficially entitled in possession" is defined as having a current (as opposed to a future) right to enjoy the property comprising a gift or inheritance.

Example 33.4

By deed of conveyance, Emma gifts her son Emmet a limited interest in a particular property for a period of five years with absolute ownership transferring to her granddaughter Dervla, thereafter. In these circumstances, Emmet becomes beneficially entitled in possession to his benefit immediately, i.e., when the deed is executed. In contrast, when the deed is executed, Dervla merely has a future interest in the property. Her gift does not fall within the scope of CAT until she becomes beneficially entitled in possession to her remainder interest, i.e., until five years have elapsed.

33.3 Territorial Scope

s6 CATCA 2003
s11 CATCA 2003

Prior to 1 December 1999, the scope of CAT depended on the domicile of the disponer. Where the disponer was Irish domiciled on a date of disposition prior to 1 December 1999, the property comprising the disposition was taxable in full irrespective of where it was situated. Where the disponer was non-Irish domiciled, only so much of the gift or inheritance as was situated in the State was subject to CAT.

Finance Act 2000 introduced changes such that the scope of CAT is now based on residence or ordinary residence. Thus, for dispositions on or after 1 December 1999, the entire property comprising a gift or inheritance is within the scope of CAT where:

- the disponer is resident or ordinarily resident in the State, or
- the donee or successor is resident or ordinarily resident in the State, or
- the property is situated in the State.

Thus, Irish property (property situated in the Republic of Ireland) is always within the scope of CAT. With effect from 2 February 2006, this would include shares in a private company incorporated outside of the State to the extent that these shares derive their value from property situated in the State. Foreign property is only within the scope of CAT if the disponer is resident or ordinarily resident in the State or if the donee or successor is resident or ordinarily resident in the State. Where a gift or inheritance passes between individuals who are neither resident nor ordinarily resident in the State, then to the extent that the gift or inheritance comprises only a portion of property situated in the State, then only a similar proportion of the gift or inheritance will be within the scope of CAT.

In general, the Income Tax rules for determining residence and ordinary residence apply (see Chapter 9, section 9.3). However, in order to ensure that foreign domiciled individuals, who are only in Ireland for a short period of time, will not trigger an Irish CAT liability, additional rules apply. A non-domiciled individual will not be considered resident or ordinarily resident in the State for CAT purposes until 1 December 2004 and then only when he or she has been resident in the state for five consecutive tax years prior to the date of disposition (in the case of the disponer) or the date of the gift or inheritance (in the case of the donee/successor).

It should be borne in mind that the above rules apply in general and not necessarily in the case of discretionary trusts, which are beyond the scope of this analysis. In addition, just because a particular disposition is within the scope of CAT does not necessarily mean that a CAT liability will arise. Because of the method of calculation (see Section 33.4 below), the particular gift or inheritance may not be sufficient to give rise to a CAT liability. Alternatively, the gift or inheritance may be exempt from CAT (see Section 33.5 below).

33.4 Method of Calculation

Schedule 2 CATCA

The basic concept behind calculating the CAT liability on a gift/inheritance is relatively straightforward. If the **"taxable value"** of the gift/inheritance is less than the **"group threshold"**, no CAT arises. Where the taxable value exceeds the group threshold, the excess is taxed at 33% (for benefits received on or after 6 December 2012).

33.4.1 Group thresholds

There are three group thresholds available. However, the choice of threshold will depend on the relationship between the disponer and the donee/successor, as follows:

Group A: Broadly speaking, this applies to dispositions from a parent/civil partner of a parent to a child.

Group B: This applies to dispositions to lineal ancestors and descendants (other than those included in Group A above), brothers, sisters, nephews and nieces/child of the civil partner of a brother or sister.

Group C: This applies to dispositions not covered under Group A or B above.

The group thresholds for 2011, 2012 to 2014, 2015 and 2016 onwards are set out in the table below.

Group	Relationship to Disponer	Group Threshold			
		07/12/2011–05/12/2012*	06/12/2012–13/10/2015	14/10/2015–11/10/2016	on or after 12/10/2016
A	Son/Daughter	€250,000	€225,000	€280,000	€310,000
B	Lineal Ancestor / Descendant/Brother/ Sister/Niece/Nephew	€33,500	€30,150	€30,150	€32,500
C	Relationship other than Group A or B	€16,750	€15,075	€15,075	€16,250
*Finance Act 2012 abolished the indexation of the tax-free group thresholds.					
Source: www.revenue.ie					

Example 33.5

On 1 July 2018, Helen's uncle dies and leaves her a cash sum of €30,000. She has received no other benefits since 5 December 1991.

As the taxable value is less than the group threshold of €32,500, no CAT arises.

Example 33.6

On 1 July 2018, Anne's nephew dies and leaves her a cash sum of €40,000. She has received no other benefits since 5 December 1991.

		€
Taxable value		*40,000*
Group threshold:	*€16,250 @ Nil*	
Balance:	*€23,750 @ 33%*	*7,838*
CAT liability		*7,838*

33.4.1.1 Group A - preferential treatment

In determining which group threshold applies to particular dispositions, preferential treatment is given to some relationships in certain circumstances.

Group A applies not only to dispositions to a natural child, but also to a step child, an adopted child and a foster child, subject to certain conditions. This threshold also applies to certain grandchildren of the disponer who take a benefit under a marriage settlement, and also, to dispositions to a minor child of a deceased child/a minor child of a deceased child's civil partner, i.e., dispositions from a grandparent to a grandchild under the age of 18, whose parent is deceased (see example 33.10 below). Furthermore, a parent taking an inheritance (but not a gift) from a child can qualify for the Group A threshold.

Example 33.7

On 1 July 2018, June's son dies and leaves her a cash sum of €600,000. She has received no other benefits since 5 December 1991 and had not previously gifted her son any benefits.

		€
Taxable value		*600,000*
Group threshold:	*€310,000 @ Nil*	
Balance:	*€290,000 @ 33%*	*95,700*
CAT liability		*95,700*

Example 33.8

On 1 July 2018, Sophie's son gave her a cash sum of €500,000. She has received no other benefits since 5 December 1991.

		€	
Taxable value net of annual gift exemption		*497,000*	*(See section 33.4.3 below for commentary on annual gift exemption)*
Group threshold:	*€32,500 @ Nil*		
Balance:	*€464,500 @ 33%*	*153,285*	
CAT liability		*153,285*	

Certain nephews/nieces will be treated as 'favoured' nephews/nieces and accordingly, will be treated, in certain circumstances, as sons/daughters qualifying for the Group A tax-free threshold. This preferential treatment applies only to gifts/inheritances of trading or business assets to a niece or nephew/child of a civil partner of a brother or sister who has worked substantially on a full-time basis in the business, trade or profession for a period of five years. The 'full-time' requirement is satisfied where the niece or nephew/child of a civil partner of a brother or sister works more than 24 hours a week in the business. Where the business is exclusively carried on by the disponer, his spouse and the favoured niece or nephew/child of a civil partner of a brother or sister, then this requirement is relaxed to 15 hours a week. Where the disponer carries on his business through the medium of a limited company, the Group A threshold is extended to gifts and inheritances consisting of shares in that company.

Example 33.9

On 1 May 2018, Michael White dies and leaves his farm worth €900,000 and publicly quoted shares worth €150,000 to his nephew John who has worked full-time on the farm for the last 10 years.

As the farm is a trading asset and as John has worked full-time on the farm for the requisite period of five years, the group threshold applicable to the inheritance of the farm is €310,000. The normal group threshold applicable to dispositions to a nephew (i.e., €32,500) applies in respect of the shares as these do not constitute business assets. (Note: agricultural relief may apply to farm – see Section 33.7 below.)

33.4.1.2 Group thresholds and surviving spouse

The legislation also provides for a relaxation of the normal group threshold rules in respect of dispositions to the surviving spouse/civil partner of a deceased person. In these circumstances the surviving spouse/civil partner is deemed to 'stand in the shoes' of the deceased spouse/civil partner and vis-à-vis the deceased spouse's relationship with the disponer, the surviving spouse/civil partner may qualify for a more favourable tax threshold in computing any CAT liability due.

Example 33.10

John and Mary are married and have one child, Grace. Michael is Mary's father.

In 2013, Michael gave John €50,000 and Grace (aged 8) €80,000.

In 2014, Mary died.

In 2018, Michael gave John 100,000 and Grace (aged 11) €150,000.

John qualifies for the Group C threshold in respect of the gift from Michael in 2013. He is effectively treated as stranger as he is not a blood relative of the disponer.

Grace qualifies for the Group B threshold in respect of the gift from Michael in 2013. She is a lineal descendant of the disponer.

John qualifies for the Group A threshold in respect of the gift from Michael in 2018, given that his deceased spouse was a daughter of the disponer.

Grace qualifies for the Group A threshold in respect of the gift from Michael in 2018, as she is the minor child of a deceased child of the disponer.

33.4.2 Computation

As seen in examples 33.7 to 33.10, calculating the CAT liability in respect of the first benefit taken since 5 December 1991 is very straightforward. If the taxable value is less than the group threshold, no CAT arises. Where the taxable value exceeds the group threshold, the excess is taxed at 33% (for benefits received on or after 6 December, 2012).

However, where other benefits have been received since 5 December 1991, calculating the CAT liability on the current benefit involves a three-step process.

'Step 1' involves calculating the CAT on the current aggregate (Aggregate A), i.e., the aggregate of the current benefit and all previous benefits from within the same group threshold taken on or after 5 December 1991.

'Step 2' involves calculating the CAT on the previous aggregate (Aggregate B), i.e., the aggregate of all previous benefits from within the same group threshold taken on or after 5 December 1991, excluding the taxable value of the current benefit.

'Step 3' involves calculating CAT on the current benefit, being the excess of the CAT on Aggregate A over the CAT on Aggregate B.

Example 33.11

On 1 August 2018, Bernadette received an inheritance of €400,000 from her father. She had previously received the following benefits:

15 January 1991, a gift of €30,000 from her mother

25 December 1997, a gift of €6,000 from her brother

1 March 2002, an inheritance of €140,000 from her mother

16 February 2013, an inheritance of €20,000 from her aunt

Step 1: Calculation of Tax on Current Aggregate – Aggregate A

Note: *The gift from her mother on 15 January 1991 is not aggregated as it was received prior to 5 December 1991.*

The gift from her brother and the inheritance from her aunt are not aggregated as these are not covered by the Group A threshold applicable to the current benefit.

Thus, the only prior benefit to be aggregated is the inheritance from her mother on 1 March 2002.

		€
Aggregate A:	*Current inheritance from father*	400,000
	Inheritance from mother 1/3/'02	140,000
		540,000
Group threshold:	*€310,000 @ Nil*	
Balance:	*€230,000 @ 33%*	75,900
CAT liability on Aggregate A		75,900

Step 2: Calculation of Tax on Aggregate B

Aggregate B:	*Inheritance from mother 1/3/'02*	140,000
Group threshold:	*€310,000 @ Nil*	
Balance:	*@ 33%*	0

Step 3: Calculation of Tax on Current Benefit

	€
CAT on Aggregate A	75,900
CAT on Aggregate B	(Nil)
CAT on current benefit	75,900

Example 33.12

Philip received the following benefits in 2018:

1 May 2018, a cash gift of €10,000 from his friend John

7 August 2018, a cash gift of €50,000 from his uncle

13 October 2018, a gift of shares from his father worth €200,000

Philip had previously received the following benefits:

25 December 1990, a gift from his mother of €100,000,

10 March 1991, a gift from his father of €200,000,

6 April 2009, an inheritance of publicly quoted shares worth €60,000 from his cousin,

6 May 2012, an inheritance of €20,000 from his aunt.

Cash gift from John:

		€
Aggregate A:	*Current gift net of exemption (see 33.4.3)*	7,000
	Inheritance from cousin 6/4/'09	60,000
		67,000
Group threshold:	*€16,250 @ Nil*	
Balance:	*€50,750 @ 33%*	16,748
CAT liability on Aggregate A		16,748
Aggregate B:	*Inheritance from cousin 6/4/'09*	60,000
Group threshold:	*€16,250 @ Nil*	
Balance:	*€43,750 @ 33%*	14,438
CAT liability on Aggregate B		14,438
Tax on current benefit	*(€16,748 – €14,438)*	2,310

Cash gift from uncle:

Aggregate A:	*Current gift net of exemption (see 33.4.3)*	*47,000*
	Inheritance from aunt 6/5/'12	*20,000*
		67,000
Group threshold:	*€32,500 @ Nil*	
Balance:	*€34,500 @ 33%*	*11,385*
CAT liability on Aggregate A		*11,385*
Aggregate B:	*Inheritance from aunt 6/5/'12*	*20,000*
Group threshold:	*€32,000 @ Nil*	
Balance:	*€0 @ 33%*	
CAT liability on Aggregate B		*Nil*
Tax on current benefit		*11,385*

Gift of shares from father:

There were only two previous benefits covered by the Group A threshold and as both of these were taken prior to 5 December 1991, they are ignored. As the taxable value of the current benefit (€197,000 – see 33.4.3) is less than the Group A threshold of €310,000, no CAT is payable on the gift from the father.

33.4.3 Small gift exemption

s69 CATCA 2003

With effect from 1 January 2003, an annual exemption of €3,000 applies in respect of gifts taken by any one donee from any one disponer. Thus, in computing the amount of a gift to be aggregated, the first €3,000 of the taxable value (see section 33.5) taken from the same disponer in any calendar year is disregarded. For gifts taken before 1 January 1999, the annual small gift exemption was €635 and for gifts taken between 1 January 1999 and 1 January 2003, the annual small gift exemption was €1,270.

This exemption does not apply to inheritances. However, there is no claw-back of the exemption where a gift subsequently becomes an inheritance following the disponer's death within two years of the date of the gift.

Example 33.13

On 2 June 2018, John's father died leaving him the residue of his estate, valued at €390,000.

John had previously received the following benefits:

On 1 June 2004, an inheritance from his mother of €280,000

On 1 August 2007, a gift from his stepmother of €5,000

On 25 December 2007, a gift from his stepmother of €3,000

On 1 June 2009, a gift from his sister of €50,000

On 25 December 2009, a gift from his stepmother of €3,000

		€
Aggregate A:	*Current inheritance*	*390,000*
	Gift from stepmother in 2009 (Note 1)	*Nil*
	Gift from stepmother December 2007 (Note 2)	*3,000*
	Gift from stepmother August 2007	*2,000*
	Inheritance from mother in 2004	*280,000*
		675,000
Group threshold:	*€310,000 @ Nil*	
Balance:	*€365,000 @ 33%*	*120,450*
CAT liability on Aggregate A		*120,450*
Aggregate B:	*Gift from stepmother in 2009*	*Nil*
	Gift from stepmother December 2007	*3,000*
	Gift from stepmother August 2007	*2,000*
	Inheritance from mother in 2004	*280,000*
		285,000
Group threshold:	*€310,000 @ Nil*	
Balance:	*€0 @ 33%*	
CAT liability on Aggregate B		*Nil*
Tax on current benefit (€120,450 – €0)		*120,450*

Note 1: *As this gift was received in 2009, the relevant annual exemption is €3,000. The fact that John has already qualified for an annual exemption of this amount in respect of a gift taken from his sister in 2009 does not preclude him from getting the annual exemption in respect of a gift from a separate disponer.*

Note 2: *The annual small gift exemption is not available as it has already been claimed against an earlier gift from this disponer in this calendar year.*

33.5 Taxable Value

s28 CATCA 2003

In general, the taxable value of a gift or inheritance is calculated by firstly deducting any liabilities and expenses payable out of the gift or inheritance from the market value of the property comprising the gift or inheritance. The resulting figure (known as the 'incumbrance-free' value) is then reduced by the market value of any consideration payable by the donee or successor. Thus, a pro-forma computation of taxable value can be presented as follows:

	€
Market value	*X*
Less: liabilities, cost and expenses	*(X)*
Incumbrance-free value	*X*
Less: consideration payable by beneficiary	*(X)*
Taxable value	*X*

Note that if the benefit is a gift, the taxable value may be further reduced by the small gift exemption (as discussed in section 33.4.3).

The approach is somewhat different in the case of agricultural property and business property (see Section 33.7) and further refinements are also necessary in valuing limited interests (see 33.5.5 below).

33.5.1 Market value and valuation date

s26 CATCA 2003 Market value may be defined as the price which the property would secure if sold on the open market on the 'valuation date'. Certain provisions, which apply in valuing shares in a private company, are beyond the scope of this analysis.

In the case of a gift, the 'valuation date' is normally the date of the gift. In the case of inheritance, the valuation date is normally the earlier of:

- the earliest date on which any person becomes entitled to retain the subject matter of the inheritance on behalf of the successor; or
- the actual date of retainer; or
- the actual date of delivery or payment to the beneficiary.

The valuation date is an important concept, not only because it is the date on which the property is valued for CAT purposes, but also because it is the date on which certain tests are applied for the purposes of ascertaining entitlement to agricultural relief and business property relief (see section 33.7) and it is the date on which CAT becomes payable (see section 33.8).

33.5.2 Deductible liabilities, costs and expenses

s28 CATCA 2003 Most costs associated with the transfer of property, e.g., legal costs and stamp duties, are fully deductible in arriving at the incumbrance-free value of a gift or inheritance. In the case of inheritances, any debts of the deceased, funeral expenses and costs of administering the estate are fully deductible. In general, expenses and liabilities of the deceased are deductible from the residue of the estate (i.e., the remainder of the estate following the disposition of specific benefits). However, in some instances, specific property may be charged with the payment of a liability and such liabilities must be deducted in arriving at the incumbrance-free value of the particular property.

Liabilities that are contingent on the happening of some future event, and liabilities that may be reimbursed from some source, are not deductible. In addition, liabilities associated with exempt assets may not be deducted for the purposes of ascertaining the taxable value of non-exempt property.

Furthermore, the amount of any CAT liability or interest or penalty payable under the legislation is not deductible.

33.5.3 Consideration paid by the donee/successor

s28 CATCA 2003 To arrive at the taxable value, the incumbrance-free value is reduced by any consideration payable by the donee/successor. The payment of consideration can take the form of the done/successor undertaking to discharge a liability of the disponer, or indeed an undertaking to pay an amount to, or discharge a liability of, some third party.

Example 33.14

Mr. X owes Mr. Y €20,000 and Mr. Y agrees to waive this debt provided Mr. X pays Mr. Z €5,000. In these circumstances, the incumbrance-free value of the benefit taken by Mr. X is €20,000. The taxable value is calculated as €15,000, i.e. €20,000 less the consideration of €5,000 payable to the third-party Mr. Z. Incidentally, Mr. Z also takes a benefit from Mr. Y, in this case valued at €5,000 – see commentary on Example 33.1 above.

Where consideration is payable in respect of a gift or inheritance which comprises both taxable and non-taxable property, then the amount of the consideration deductible needs to be apportioned on a pro-rata basis.

33.5.4 Valuation of annuities

s5(5) CATCA 2003 Where a gift or inheritance involves the provision of an amount to a beneficiary an annual basis, special rules are applied in determining the market value of such dispositions. The method of valuation depends on whether or not the annuity is charged on a specific property. Where an annuity is charged or secured on a particular property, it is valued using the following formula:

$$\text{Market value of property} \times \frac{\text{annual value of benefit}}{\text{annual value of property}}$$

Example 33.15

Tom gives an annuity of €10,000 to his daughter Kate. The annuity is secured on a rental property which Tom owns in Dublin. The rental property is valued at €420,000 and it produces annual rental income in the amount of €30,000.

The annuity is valued as: $€420{,}000 \times \frac{€10{,}000}{€30{,}000} = €140{,}000$

s5(2)(b) CATCA 2003 Where an annuity is not secured on any particular asset, the value of the benefit is taken to be the market value of the capital sum which must be invested in Government stock to acquire an amount of income equivalent to the annuity. The relevant Government stock is the latest issue prior to the date of disposition, which is not redeemable within 10 years. A list of appropriate Government securities may be obtained from the Department of Finance or from the Capital Taxes Division of the Revenue Commissioners.

Example 33.16

Michael covenants to pay an annuity in the amount of €15,000 to his mother Mary, aged 60, for the remainder of her life. The latest Government stock issue which was not redeemable within 10 years was a 6% government bond. The price per stock unit (valued at €1.00) on the valuation date was €0.95.

In order to produce an annual income of €15,000 by investing in Government stock, it would be necessary to purchase €250,000 worth of Government bonds, i.e., €15,000/6%. At a discount of €0.95 on the valuation date, it would cost €237,500 (€250,000 × 0.95) to purchase the appropriate amount of Government stock. Thus, the market value of Mary's benefit is calculated as €237,500.

33.5.5 Valuation of limited interests

Where an annuity or any other benefit is taken for a period certain, which is of less than 50 years in duration, or alternatively, where an annuity is granted for the duration of the life of an individual or where property is granted to an individual for life, further adjustment is necessary to reflect the fact that the beneficiary does not have a permanent or absolute interest in the subject matter of the disposition.

s2 CATCA 2003 A limited interest may be defined as an interest which is not an absolute interest. It may be an interest for a period certain or it may be an interest for the duration of a life or for the lives of specified individuals.

s28(4) CATCA 2003 As a limited interest is less than a full or absolute interest, CAT legislation provides for the application of a limiting factor to the incumbrance-free value so as to ensure that the taxable value is reduced accordingly. The shorter the duration or the expected duration of the limited interest, the smaller the taxable value.

Thus, the pro-forma computation of taxable value can now be refined as follows:

	€
Market value	*X*
Less: liabilities, cost and expenses	*(X)*
Incumbrance-free value	*X*
Adjustment for limited interest	
(Multiplication by limited interest factor)	*X*
Less: consideration payable by beneficiary	*(X)*
Taxable value	*X*

The appropriate limited interest factor is taken from Table A or Table B as set out in Parts II and III of the First Schedule to the CAT Consolidation Act 2003 and as reproduced in Appendix I to this chapter.

Table A is concerned with the factors to be applied in valuing a life interest.

Example 33.17

Tom transfers a farm for life to his son Pat on 1 July 2018, with the remainder on Pat's death transferring to Pat's son Martin. The farm is valued at €500,000 on 1 July 2018 and Pat was 58 years old at this time. Legal fees on the transfer of the limited interest amounted to €8,000. The taxable value of Pat's benefit is calculated as follows:

	€
Market value	*500,000*
Less: liabilities, cost and expenses	*(8,000)*
Incumbrance-free value	*492,000*
Adjustment for limited interest (Multiplication by .6129 – Table A)	*301,547*
Less: consideration payable by beneficiary	*(Nil)*
Taxable value	*301,547*

Martin will take an inheritance from Tom on the date of Pat's death (irrespective of whether or not Tom is still living). This will be valued as an absolute interest on the basis of the open market value of the farm on the date of Pat's death.

Example 33.18

Michael covenants to pay an annuity in the amount of €15,000 to his mother Mary, aged 60, for the remainder of her life. In consideration, Mary agrees to transfer publicly quoted shares to Michael. These are valued at €10,000 on the grant of the annuity.

The latest government stock issue, which was not redeemable within 10 years was a 6% government bond. The price per stock unit (valued at €1.00) on the valuation date was €0.95.

In order to produce an annual income of €15,000 by investing in Government stock, it would be necessary to purchase €250,000 worth of Government bonds, i.e., €15,000/6%. At a discount of €0.95 on the valuation date, it would cost €237,500 (€250,000 × 0.95) to purchase the appropriate amount of Government stock. Thus, the market value of Mary's benefit is calculated as €237,500.

The taxable value of Mary's benefit is calculated as follows:

	€
Market value	*237,500*
Less: liabilities, cost and expenses	*(Nil)*
Incumbrance-free value	*237,500*
Adjustment for limited interest (Multiplication by .6475 – Table A)	*153,781*
Less: consideration payable by beneficiary	*(10,000)*
Taxable value	*143,781*

Special rules for valuing interests for the lives of more than one person are beyond the scope of this analysis.

Table B deals with the valuation of interests for a period certain of less than 50 years in duration. (It is reproduced in Appendix I to this chapter.) Where an interest is for a period of 50 years or more in duration, no adjustment is necessary. Thus, in Example 33.15 above, no further adjustment is necessary if Tom grants the annuity to Kate for a period of 50 years or more. Where an amount is provided for a period of less than 50 years, the relevant factor from Table B must be applied to the incumbrance-free value.

Example 33.19

Tom gives an annuity of €10,000 to his daughter Kate for a period of 5 years. In consideration, Kate agrees to waive a debt in the amount of €2,500 owed to her by her brother Jack.

The annuity is secured on a rental property which Tom owns in Dublin. The rental property is valued at €420,000 and it produces annual rental income in the amount of €30,000.

The annuity is valued as: $€420{,}000 \times \frac{€10{,}000}{€30{,}000} = €140{,}000$

The taxable value of Kate's benefit is calculated as follows:

	€
Market value	*140,000*
Less: liabilities, cost and expenses	*(Nil)*
Incumbrance-free value	*140,000*
Adjustment for limited interest (Multiplication by .2869 – Table B)	*40,166*
Less: consideration payable by beneficiary	*(2,500)*
Taxable value	*37,666*

If this is Kate's first gift from a disponer to which the Group A threshold applies, no CAT will arise on this benefit.

Jack receives a benefit from Tom in the amount of €2,500. On the assumption that this is Jack's first benefit from Tom in the current calendar year, the benefit will be exempt on the basis that it is less than €3,000, the annual gift exemption.

33.6 Exemptions

A number of other exemptions exist for specific benefits/dispositions. These are summarised as follows:

s70–71 CATCA 2003

- Gifts and inheritances taken by spouses/civil partners are exempt from CAT and are not aggregated for the purposes of calculating CAT on other benefits. For the purposes of this exemption, separated spouses/civil partners (whether formally or informally separated) are also considered spouses. Transfers between divorced persons are chargeable to CAT. However, where property is transferred at dissolution of a marriage, under orders from the Family Law Act 1995 and Family Law (Divorce) Act 1996, a CAT exemption applies. No CAT is chargeable on the transfer of assets under a civil partnership dissolution order.
- Finance (No. 3) Act 2011 did not give opposite-sex or same-sex cohabiting couples the same tax treatment as married couples or civil partners. However, it does provide that where one of the former cohabiters is granted redress by the Courts through the transfer of an asset, the individual acquiring the asset will not be liable to CAT on the transfer (this mirrors the capital gains tax treatment).

s79 CATCA 2003

- Inheritances taken by a parent from a child, where the child had taken a non-exempt benefit from either parent in the preceding five years, are exempt from CAT.

s81 CATCA 2003

- In order to encourage non-nationals to invest in Irish Government stock, certain Government securities are exempt from CAT where the donee or successor is neither domiciled or ordinarily resident in the State at the date of the gift or inheritance, and;
  - the disponer is neither domiciled or ordinarily resident in the State at the date of disposition, or;
  - the disponer was the beneficial owner of the securities for fifteen years previously (six years where the disponer acquired the securities prior to 24 February 2003).

s72 CATCA 2003

- The proceeds of qualifying insurance policies are exempt from CAT where the policy is taken out for the purposes of paying CAT. Thus, the proceeds of such policies must be used to pay any CAT arising on the death of the insured. In the absence of this relief, the proceeds of a life assurance policy taken out for the purposes of paying CAT would be aggregated with other benefits and would thus result in an increased tax liability. These policies are historically known as Section 60 (s60) policies. The relief has been extended to also cover policies effected for the purposes of paying CAT arising on gifts in certain circumstances.

s77 CATCA 2003

- Certain objects of national interest are exempt from CAT provided they are not disposed of by the beneficiary within six years of the valuation date. This relief applies to works of art, scientific collections, libraries, stately houses and gardens, etc. and also to shares in companies holding such heritage property. The relief only applies where the property is kept permanently in the State and where there are facilities for public viewing.

s82 CATCA 2003

- Certain payments made during the lifetime of the disponer, for the support, maintenance or education of children of the disponer/civil partner of the disponer, are exempt from CAT. The exemption applies to normal and reasonable payments. Finance Act 2014 has introduced an age limit to the exemption and as a consequence, the relief will now only apply to payments made to children (including orphaned children) under the age of 18, or those between the age of 18 and 25 who are in full-time education, and to children, regardless of age, who are permanently incapacitated.

s86 CATCA 2003

- A gift or inheritance of a dwelling house (and grounds of up to one acre) is exempt from CAT where certain conditions are met. Prior to Finance Act 2016, there was a complete exemption from CAT on the gift or inheritance of a dwelling house that had been occupied by a beneficiary for a period of three years prior to the date of a gift or inheritance. Finance Act 2016 completely replaced section 86 CATCA 2003, providing for a dwelling house exemption in the case of inheritances, and only in limited circumstances in the case of gifts to dependent relatives. The conditions are as follows:
  - In general, the beneficiary must have occupied the dwelling house continuously, as his or her only or main residence, for a period of three years prior to the date of the inheritance. Where the inherited house replaced another dwelling house, that was the beneficiary's only or main residence, a

combined period of three out of four years of occupation of both houses will be sufficient to satisfy the condition.

- A "relevant dwelling house" is one that is occupied by the disponer as his or her main residence at the date of their death.
- The dwelling house must be owned by the disponer for the three-year period prior to the gift.
- At the date of the inheritance, the beneficiary must not have an interest in, and must not be beneficially entitled to, any other dwelling house.
- In general, where the beneficiary is under the age of 65, he or she must continue to occupy the dwelling house for a period of six years commencing on the date of the gift or inheritance.
- The only circumstances that a gift of a dwelling house will qualify for exemption, is when the gift is to a dependent relative. A dependent relative is someone who is permanently and totally incapacitated by reason of mental or physical infirmity from maintaining themselves or someone 65 years of age or more. The requirement that the disponer has resided in the dwelling house before the benefit is provided does not apply to a gift of a dwelling house to a dependent relative. Finance Act 2017 clarifies that no liability to CAT will be triggered where a gift to a dependent becomes an inheritance due to the disponer passing away within two years of making the gift.

A claw-back of the exemption applies in certain circumstances.

s76 CATCA 2003 Gifts or inheritances taken for public or charitable purposes are generally exempt from CAT.

In addition, superannuation payments to employees, certain retirement benefits, compensation, redundancy, gambling winnings, prizes, and certain benefits taken by permanently incapacitated individuals are exempt from CAT. For further commentary on these exemptions, readers are referred to the Irish Tax Institute publication "The Taxation of Gifts and Inheritances" by Whelan, J. and A. Williams.

33.7 Advanced Reliefs

33.7.1 Agricultural relief

s89 CATCA 2003 Agricultural relief has existed since the introduction of Capital Acquisitions Tax in 1976. The relief operates by reducing the market value of specified **"agricultural property"** in calculating the taxable value of a gift or inheritance taken by a qualifying **"farmer"**.

"Agricultural property" includes the following:

agricultural land, pasture and woodlands situated in the State or in the EU;

crops, trees and underwood growing thereon;

houses and other farm buildings situated on the property;

livestock, bloodstock and farm machinery thereon; and

the EU single farm payment entitlement.

Finance Act 2017 confirmed that agricultural land on which solar panels are installed will remain agricultural land for the purposes of agricultural relief, provided that the area on which the solar panels are installed does not exceed 50% of the total land qualifying for agricultural relief. The relief will also apply where a beneficiary leases land for the installation of solar panels, provided that the area on which the solar panels are installed does not exceed 50% and the beneficiary actively farms the land not occupied by solar panels, or alternatively leases it to a lessee who actively farms the land.

Shares deriving their value from agricultural property do not qualify for agricultural relief. However, such shares and certain other assets may qualify for business relief – see section 33.7.2 below.

In order to obtain agricultural relief on a gift or inheritance of agricultural property (other than trees or underwood), the donee/successor must be a "farmer". A farmer is defined as any individual whose assets are represented mainly by agricultural property. Finance Act 2006, removed the requirement that the individual be domiciled in the State, while Finance Act 2012 removed the requirement that the individual be resident in the State for three years after the gift or inheritance.

For the purposes of determining whether or not an individual's assets are represented mainly by agricultural property, an 80% test applies. Thus, at least 80% of the gross market value of all property to which the individual is beneficially entitled (after taking the gift or inheritance) must consist of agricultural property (as defined above). Note that it is not necessary for the beneficiary to actually farm the agricultural property. Thus, agricultural relief commonly applies in the case of let property.

In general, no deduction is made for mortgages, etc. when calculating the gross value of property for the purposes of the 80% test. However, with effect from 1 February 2007, the value of an "off-farm" principal private residence, which is a non-qualifying asset, is to be determined after deducting any borrowings which have been used to purchase, repair or improve that residence.

Example 33.20

John owns a house in Dublin valued at €360,000 and he has a mortgage of €280,000. His only other assets are as follows:

- *a bank deposit of €3,500; and*
- *publicly quoted shares worth €10,500.*

In June 2018, he inherits farmland worth €720,000 plus an old farmhouse and buildings situated on the farm worth €310,000. His inheritance also includes livestock and farm machinery worth €60,000.

The gross market value of all property, owned by John, after taking the inheritance, is €1,184,000 (after deducting the mortgage of €280,000). The gross value of agricultural property is €1,090,000. Thus, the percentage of John's assets represented by agricultural property is 92% (1,090/1,184). Thus, John is a "farmer".

Example 33.21

In December 2017, Mary's uncle gave her a small farm worth €165,000. At this time, her only other assets were a bank deposit account of €10,000 and a car worth €25,000.

The percentage of Mary's assets represented by agricultural property is 82.5% (165/200). Thus, she is a "farmer" for the purposes of claiming agricultural relief.

Example 33.22

Maria inherited 100 acres of land including buildings from her late uncle, Trevor on 1 February 2018. Maria does not have an agricultural qualification and is a fulltime teacher. 40 acres of the land had been leased to Solar Energy Limited since 2015 under a 10-year lease, who have installed solar panels on the land. The leased land will be regarded as agricultural property for the purposes of calculating whether 80% of her gross assets on the valuation date are agricultural. If the 80% test is met, agricultural relief will apply provided Maria leases the whole or substantially the whole of the remaining 60 acres to a farmer for 6 years.[1]

Finance Act 2014, introduced a number of additional conditions that must be satisfied, in order for agricultural relief to apply to gifts or inheritances taken on or after 1 January 2015. The beneficiary must now either have an agricultural qualification e.g. Green Cert, Agricultural Science degree (or attain such qualification within 4 years of the gift or inheritance) and must farm the land on a commercial basis, with a view to making a profit; or if the beneficiary does not have an agricultural qualification, they must spend not less than 50% of their normal working time farming. "Normal working time" is approximately 40 hours per week and therefore the beneficiary will be required to work a minimum of 20 hours per week, farming.

If the beneficiary does not fulfill either of the above criteria, they can still qualify for agricultural relief if they lease out the farm that has been transferred to them, to a farmer (who fulfills either of the above criteria) for a minimum of 6 years. Where agricultural property is leased, it may be leased on a number of leases, as long as all lessees satisfy the relevant conditions.

Calculation of relief

For gifts and inheritances of agricultural property, the relief is calculated by reducing the market value of the property by a flat rate of 90%.

Example 33.23

On 1 August 2018, Michael transfers agricultural property with a market value of €400,000 to his daughter Ann. Ann qualifies as a farmer. The agricultural value of the property is calculated as follows:

	€
Market value of agricultural property	*400,000*
Relief – 90% reduction of market value	*(360,000)*
Agricultural value of property	*40,000*

1 Example from *FINAK – Finance Act 2017 Explained,* published by Irish Tax Institute 2018.

Given that the full market value of the agricultural property is reduced by 90% in order to arrive at the agricultural value, any liabilities, costs and expenses payable out of the property and any consideration paid for the property must be proportionately reduced before being deducted from the agricultural value.

Thus, the pro-forma computation of taxable value can be refined as follows:

	€
Market value	
Less: Agricultural relief	
Agricultural value	*X*
Less: proportion of liabilities, cost and expenses	*(X)*
Incumbrance-free value	*X*
Less: proportion of consideration payable by beneficiary	*(X)*
Taxable value	*X*

Example 33.24

On 1 August 2018, Michael transfers agricultural property with a market value of €400,000 to his daughter Ann. Ann qualifies as a farmer. The lands are charged with a mortgage of €200,000 and Ann by way of consideration is obliged to pay her brother Conor an amount of €100,000.

The taxable value of the gift is calculated as follows:

	€
Market value of agricultural property	*400,000*
Agricultural relief – 90% reduction of market value	*(360,000)*
Agricultural value of property	*40,000*
Less: proportion of mortgage charged on land	*(20,000)*
Incumbrance-free value	*20,000*
Less: proportion of consideration payable by beneficiary	*(10,000)*
Taxable value	*10,000*

Where a gift or inheritance comprises both, agricultural and non-agricultural property, any expenses, etc. relating to both component parts will need to be apportioned. 10% of expenses, etc. relating to agricultural property will be allowable and expenses relating to the non-agricultural property will be allowable in full. Thus, it is necessary to calculate the taxable value of each component separately.

Example 33.25

Tom transfers the following assets to his grandson Liam on 25 December, 2018:

	Market Value
	€
Farmland in Tipperary	*350,000*
Woodland in Kerry	*100,000*
Farm buildings situated on above farmland	*140,000*

Holiday cottage in Donegal		*100,000*
Farm machinery		*30,000*
Bloodstock		*420,000*
		1,140,000

The farmland is mortgaged for €80,000. In consideration for the transfer, Liam has agreed to pay his grandfather an amount of €250,000.

Legal and other costs associated with the transfer amount to €25,000 and these are payable out of the gift.

Liam has not received any benefits prior to this. Liam's only other assets are his principal private residence worth €140,000 (with a mortgage outstanding of €40,000) and a bank deposit account of €5,000.

Liam is a full-time farmer and has an agricultural qualification from his local agricultural college. After taking the gift from his grandfather, more than 80% of his gross assets comprise agricultural property, calculated as follows:

$$\frac{€1{,}040{,}000^*}{€1{,}245{,}000^{**}} = 83.5\%$$

** (€350,000 + €100,000 + €140,000 + €30,000 + €420,000)*

The holiday cottage in Donegal does not constitute agricultural property.

*** (€1,140,000 + (€140,000 – €40,000) + €5,000)*

Debts charged on the property comprising the gift or inheritance are taken into consideration in apportioning expenses and consideration between agricultural and non-agricultural property.

Step 1: Computation of Taxable Value of Agricultural Property

		€
Market value of agricultural property		*1,040,000*
Relief – 90% reduction of market value		*(936,000)*
Agricultural value of property		*104,000*
Less: Proportion of mortgage charged on land (10%) (relates exclusively to agricultural property)	*(8,000)*	
Legal expenses applicable to agricultural property		
$€25{,}000 \times \dfrac{€1{,}040{,}000 - €80{,}000}{€1{,}140{,}000 - €80{,}000} = €22{,}642$		
Restrict to 10%	*(2,264)*	*(10,264)*
Incumbrance-free value		*93,736*
Less: Consideration applicable to agricultural property		
$€250{,}000 \times \dfrac{€1{,}040{,}000 - €80{,}000}{€1{,}140{,}000 - €80{,}000} = €226{,}415$		
Restrict to 10%		*(22,642)*
Taxable value of agricultural property		*71,094*

Step 2: Computation of Taxable Value of Non-Agricultural Property

	€
Market value of holiday cottage	*100,000*
Less: Legal expenses applicable to non-agricultural property	
$€25{,}000 \times \dfrac{€100{,}000}{€1{,}140{,}000 - €80{,}000} =$	*2,358*
Incumbrance-free value	*97,642*
Less: Consideration applicable to non-agricultural property	
$€250{,}000 \times \dfrac{€100{,}000}{€1{,}140{,}000 - €80{,}000} =$	*(23,585)*
Taxable value of non-agricultural property	*74,057*

Step 3: Calculation of Total Taxable Value of Property

	€
Taxable value of agricultural property	*€71,094*
Taxable value of non-agricultural property	*€74,057*
Total	*145,151*

Step 4: Calculation of CAT

Total taxable value	*145,151*
Less: Small gift exemption	*(3,000)*
Final taxable value	*142,151*
Less: Group threshold	*(32,500)*
Taxable	*109,651*
CAT @ 33%	*36,185*

Clawback of relief in certain circumstances

Agricultural relief will be withdrawn or partially clawed back in the following circumstances:

s89(4)(a) CATCA 2003

- Where the agricultural property is sold (or compulsorily acquired) within six years of the date of the gift or inheritance and is not replaced within one year (or six years where the agricultural property has been compulsory acquired) by other agricultural property, agricultural relief is withdrawn or clawed back. Where only a portion of the sales is reinvested in replacement agricultural property, a partial claw-back arises. The claw-back does not apply in relation to the sale of crops, trees or underwood, or where the beneficiary dies before the sale or compulsory acquisition.
- Where a beneficiary qualifies as a "farmer" under the revised definition of Finance Act 2014, at the date of gift or inheritance, but ceases to qualify as a "farmer" within the six-year claw-back period, any agricultural relief previously granted will be clawed back.

  Finance Act 2010 introduced an anti-avoidance provision to this section of the legislation. The anti-avoidance measure provides that if a spouse acquires replacement agricultural property which he/she has previously transferred to his/her spouse, these assets will not be deemed to be agricultural property for the purposes of the relief, and as such, in these circumstances a claw-back of agricultural relief cannot be avoided. This provision applies to transfers between spouses executed on or after 4 February 2010.

s102A CATCA 2003 The retention period is extended by four years to 10 years in respect of development land, i.e., a claw back applies to agricultural relief granted in respect of the development value of the land where development land is disposed of in the period commencing six years after the date of the gift or inheritance and ending 10 years after that date. For commentary on the meaning of "development land," readers are referred to Chapter 26, section 26.2.1.

s89(4)(c) CATCA 2003

- Prior to 2012, agricultural relief was also withdrawn in circumstances where the beneficiary was not resident in the State for all of the three tax years immediately following the tax year in which the valuation date falls. Finance Act 2012 removed the condition that an individual must be resident in the State for three years after the gift or inheritance. Therefore, agricultural relief will no longer be withdrawn in these circumstances. This applies to gifts or inheritances taken on or after 8 February 2012.

33.7.2 Business property relief

A relief, very similar to agricultural property relief, applies to relevant business property. Agricultural property which fails to qualify for agricultural relief may qualify for business property relief provided the relevant criteria for business property relief are met. Thus, an individual who fails the "farmer" test as described at section 33.7.1 may qualify for business property relief. It should also be noted that certain benefits will qualify as "agricultural property" but will not constitute "business property" as defined below. For example, farmland that has been the subject of a gift/inheritance will qualify for agricultural relief but may not qualify for business property relief.

s94 CATCA 2003 Relief will only apply to property that was held for a minimum period of five years to the date of a gift. If an inheritance is taken, the relevant holding period is two years prior to the date of the inheritance. Ownership by the disponer's spouse is aggregated for the purposes of establishing the duration of the holding period.

"**Business property**" is defined as:

- The business or an interest in the business, in the case of a business carried on by a sole trader or by a partnership. "Business" includes the exercise of a profession, vocation or trade. An interest may include a life interest or an annuity charged on business property.
- Unquoted shares or securities of a company carrying on a business provided that the beneficiary will (after taking the gift or inheritance), either:

- own more than 25% of the voting rights of the company, or
- control the company within the meaning of s27 CATCA 2003, or
- own at least 10% or more of the aggregate nominal value of all the issued shares and securities of the company and have worked fulltime in the company (or in the case of a group, for any company or companies in the group) throughout the period of 5 years ending on the date of the gift or inheritance.

- Individual items of land, buildings, and plant and machinery owned by the disponer or by a partnership but used wholly or mainly for the purposes of a business carried on by a company controlled by the disponer or by a partnership of which the disponer was a partner. The item of property and the partnership interest or shares in the company must be taken as a gift or inheritance by the same beneficiary from the same disponer. Furthermore, the partnership interest or the shares or securities must qualify as relevant business property and the item of property must have been used by the company or by the partnership throughout the minimum ownership period.

Businesses which are involved wholly or mainly in property or share dealing, or in managing investments are specifically excluded from the relief. Individual assets used in the business, will not qualify for the relief if transferred to the beneficiary without the business.

Calculation of relief

s92 CATCA 2003 The relief takes the form of a reduction of 90% in respect of the net market value of the business. This is calculated by reducing the market value of the assets used in the business (including goodwill) by the market value of any business liabilities. The value of any asset not being used for the purposes of the business is ignored. Readers are referred to the example at 33.26 below.

Clawback of relief

s101 CATCA 2003 Where the business ceases to trade within a period of six years after the valuation date, the relief will be clawed back unless the business is replaced within one year by other relevant business property. There will be no clawback of the relief where the business ceases as a result of bankruptcy or insolvency. The relief will also be clawed back if, within a six-year period after the valuation date, business property is sold or compulsorily acquired and not replaced within one year by other relevant business property.

s102A CATCA 2003 The retention period is extended by four years to 10 years in respect of development land, i.e., a clawback applies to business property relief granted in respect of the development value of property where the property is disposed of in the period commencing six years after the date of the gift or inheritance and ending 10 years after that date. For commentary on the meaning of 'development land', readers are referred to Chapter 26.

33.8 Administration and Payment of CAT

33.8.1 Filing of returns

s46 CATCA 2003 Traditionally a return showing details of any gift or inheritance received would have been filed within four months of the valuation date. However, Finance Act 2010 introduced a fixed pay and file date of 31 October, to align CAT with the Income Tax pay and file deadline. The additional time given for filing Income Tax returns online, through the Revenue online system (ROS), will also now apply to the filing of CAT returns. All gifts and inheritances with a valuation date in the 12-month period ending on the previous 31 August must be included in the return to be filed by 31 October in that year, and where the valuation date falls in the period between 1 September and 31 December, the pay and file deadline will be 31 October of the following year[2]. On this basis the return in respect of a gift which has a valuation date of say 31 July 2018 must be filed by 31 October 2018 (subject to the additional ROS extension). The return in respect of a gift with a valuation date of say 30 November 2018 must be filed by 31 October 2019 (subject to the additional ROS extension).

An obligation to file a return is imposed on both the donee/successor and on the donor of gifts. A return must be filed by the donee/successor when the aggregate value of all taxable benefits taken from disponers within the same group threshold (since 5 December 1991) exceeds 80% of the group threshold amount. In relation to gifts, a return must also be filed by the donor where gifts amounting to more than 80% of the group threshold have been made to a particular beneficiary.

The return must show details of the property comprising all benefits to be aggregated. An estimate of the market value of all such property must also be provided.

s53 CATCA 2003 A surcharge of up to 30% may be imposed on, an accountable person who underestimates the market value of any property included in a return for CAT purposes.

33.8.2 Payment of CAT

s51 CATCA 2003 Traditionally, CAT became due for payment on the valuation date. Following the introduction of a pay and file regime for CAT, the due date for the payment of CAT is the same date as the due date for the filing of an individual's CAT return. Again, all gifts and inheritances with a valuation date in the 12-month period ending on the previous 31 August the relevant CAT must be paid by 31 October in that year, and where the valuation date falls in the period between 1 September and 31 December, the relevant CAT must be paid by 31 October of the following year. On this basis the CAT in respect of a gift which has a valuation date of say 31 July 2018 must be paid by 31 October 2018 (subject to the additional ROS extension). The CAT in respect of a gift with a valuation date of say 30 November 2018 must be paid by 31 October 2019 (subject to the additional ROS extension).

2 Finance Act 2011 brought forward the pay and file dates by 1 month, i.e. to 30 September; however, Finance Act 2012 returned the pay and file deadline to 31 October.

Where CAT is paid late, simple interest accrues at a rate of 0.0219% per day for the period from 1 November to the date of actual payment.

s54 CATCA 2003 An accountable person; may elect to pay tax on real property and on limited interests by means of five equal yearly instalments, subject to the payment of interest at the normal daily rate on unpaid tax. Such interest must be added to each instalment and paid at the same time as the instalment.

s55 CATCA 2003 In the case of agricultural or business property, the daily interest rate is reduced to 0.0164% i.e., 75% of the normal rate.

s56 CATCA 2003 In certain circumstances, inheritance tax may be settled in whole or in part by the surrender of certain government securities at face or par value, albeit that their market value may be less. This effectively facilitates a discount on the payment of inheritance tax. This option is only available where the securities have been part of the estate of the deceased for at least three months.

33.8.3 Late Filing Surcharge

Similar surcharge provisions to that of Income Tax, Corporation Tax and Capital Gains Tax apply where an individual fails to file their CAT return on time. A 5% surcharge applies, subject to a maximum of €12,695, where the return is filed within two months of the filing deadline, while a 10% surcharge, up to a maximum of €63,485, will be applied where the return is not filed within two months of the filing deadline.

The introduction of a pay and file system for CAT (and its associated surcharge provisions) came into effect from 14 June 2010.

33.8.4 Credit for capital gains tax

s104 CATCA 2003 In the case of a gift, a CGT liability and a CAT liability may well arise on the same event, i.e., there will be a CGT liability for the donor and a CAT liability for the donee. CGT paid by the disponer may be credited against the CAT liability of the donee. The credit is limited to the lower of the CAT and CGT arising on the gift.

Where the CGT liability and CAT liability do not arise on the same event, there is no credit for CGT arising. Thus, where an individual, disposes of an asset to a third party and subsequently gifts the sales proceeds to a family member, there is no relief for the CGT arising on the disposal as the CGT and CAT arise separately, as a consequence of two separate transactions. However, in the case of a direct transfer of the asset to a family member, CGT and CAT may arise as a consequence of one single event and in such instances the credit relief may be available.

With effect from 2 February 2006, the credit relief for CGT against the CAT liability will no longer apply where the beneficiary disposes of the property within two years of having acquired it.

Example 33.26

John gifted 100% of the shares in Staples Limited, a trading company, to his daughter Anne on 1 June 2018. The company had been incorporated in March 1996 by John with original share capital valued at €100. John is 60 years old and has worked full-time for the company since incorporation. The shares in Staples Limited were valued at €960,000. The company's net assets (at market value) on this date were as follows:

	€
Factory premises	*450,000*
Investment property	*250,000*
Goodwill	*100,000*
Plant and machinery	*50,000*
Stock	*90,000*
Trade debtors	*80,000*
Trade creditors	*(60,000)*
	960,000

Anne had received no benefits from any disponer previously.

John's CGT liability June 2018
(Assuming John is not entitled to claim entrepreneur relief on the disposal):

	€
Deemed sales proceeds/market value	*960,000*
Cost: €100	
Indexed @ 1.277	*(128)*
Gain	*959,872*
Retirement relief (Note 1)	*(677,574)*
	282,298
CGT @ 33%	*93,158*

Note 1: Relief rate = Chargeable business assets/Total chargeable assets

$$= \frac{450,000 + 100,000 + 50,000}{450,000 + 250,000 + 100,000 + 50,000}$$

$$= 70.59\%$$

*Exempt portion of gain = €959,872 * 70.59% = €677,574*

Anne's CAT liability:

	€
Market value of shares	*960,000*
Value attributable to investment property	*(250,000)*
Value excluding investment property	*710,000*
Business property relief	*(639,000)*
	71,000
Value attributable to investment property	*250,000*
	321,000
Small gift exemption	*(3,000)*
	318,000
Group threshold: €310,000 @ Nil	
balance: €8,000 @ 33%	*2,640*
Deduct: CGT same event credit (Note 2)	*(2,640)*
CAT payable	*Nil*

Note 2: Even though the CGT on the disposal of the shares amounted to €93,158, the maximum credit available equals the CAT arising on the gift, i.e. €2,640. Note also that there is no refund for the 'unused' CGT.

Tax Facts

Did you know that taxes similar to capital acquisitions tax are not a new phenomenon? Death or estate taxes were in fact used by the ancient Egyptians, Greeks and Romans!

Did you know that while most countries operate some form of inheritance tax, not all countries tax the beneficiary? In some countries, for example in the UK, it is the estate that is taxed and not the beneficiaries.

References and Recommended Further Reading

WHELAN, J. and A. WILLIAMS (2012), *The Taxation of Gifts and Inheritances,* Irish Tax Institute.

KEOGAN, A. and E. SCULLY (Eds.) (2018), *Law of Capital Acquisitions Tax, Stamp Duty and Local Property Tax,* Irish Tax Institute.

MARTYN, J., D. SHANAHAN, COONEY, T. (Ed) (2018), *Taxation Summary,* Irish Tax Institute.

Appendix I

TABLE A

Factors to be Applied in Valuing a Life Interest

Years of age (1)	Joint Factor (2)	Value of an interest in a capital of €1 for a male life aged as in column 1 (3)	Value of an interest in a capital of €1 for a female life aged as in column 1 (4)
0	.99	.9519	.9624
1	.99	.9767	.9817
2	.99	.9767	.9819
3	.99	.9762	.9817
4	.99	.9753	.9811
5	.99	.9742	.9805
6	.99	.9730	.9797
7	.99	.9717	.9787
8	.99	.9703	.9777
9	.99	.9688	.9765
10	.99	.9671	.9753
11	.98	.9653	.9740
12	.98	.9634	.9726
13	.98	.9614	.9710
14	.98	.9592	.9693
15	.98	.9569	.9676
16	.98	.9546	.9657
17	.98	.9522	.9638
18	.98	.9497	.9617
19	.98	.9471	.9596
20	.97	.9444	.9572
21	.97	.9416	.9547
22	.97	.9387	.9521
23	.97	.9356	.9493
24	.97	.9323	.9464
25	.97	.9288	.9432

Years of age (1)	Joint Factor (2)	Value of an interest in a capital of €1 for a male life aged as in column 1 (3)	Value of an interest in a capital of €1 for a female life aged as in column 1 (4)
26	.97	.9250	.9399
27	.97	.9209	.9364
28	.97	.9165	.9328
29	.97	.9119	.9289
30	.96	.9068	.9248
31	.96	.9015	.9205
32	.96	.8958	.9159
33	.96	.8899	.9111
34	.96	.8836	.9059
35	.96	.8770	.9005
36	.96	.8699	.8947
37	.96	.8626	.8886
38	.95	.8549	.8821
39	.95	.8469	.8753
40	.95	.8384	.8683
41	.95	.8296	.8610
42	.95	.8204	.8534
43	.95	.8107	.8454
44	.94	.8005	.8370
45	.94	.7897	.8283
46	.94	.7783	.8192
47	.94	.7663	.8096
48	.93	.7541	.7997
49	.93	.7415	.7896
50	.92	.7287	.7791
51	.91	.7156	.7683
52	.90	.7024	.7572
53	.89	.6887	.7456
54	.89	.6745	.7335
55	.88	.6598	.7206
56	.88	.6445	.7069
57	.88	.6288	.6926

Years of age (1)	Joint Factor (2)	Value of an interest in a capital of €1 for a male life aged as in column 1 (3)	Value of an interest in a capital of €1 for a female life aged as in column 1 (4)
58	.87	.6129	.6778
59	.86	.5969	.6628
60	.86	.5809	.6475
61	.85	.5650	.6320
62	.85	.5492	.6162
63	.85	.5332	.6000
64	.85	.5171	.5830
65	.85	.5007	.5650
66	.85	.4841	.5462
67	.84	.4673	.5266
68	.84	.4506	.5070
69	.84	.4339	.4873
70	.83	.4173	.4679
71	.83	.4009	.4488
72	.82	.3846	.4301
73	.82	.3683	.4114
74	.81	.3519	.3928
75	.80	.3352	.3743
76	.79	.3181	.3559
77	.78	.3009	.3377
78	.76	.2838	.3198
79	.74	.2671	.3023
80	.72	.2509	.2855
81	.71	.2353	.2693
82	.70	.2203	.2538
83	.69	.2057	.2387
84	.68	.1916	.2242
85	.67	.1783	.2104
86	.66	.1657	.1973
87	.65	.1537	.1849
88	.64	.1423	.1730
89	.62	.1315	.1616

Years of age (1)	Joint Factor (2)	Value of an interest in a capital of €1 for a male life aged as in column 1 (3)	Value of an interest in a capital of €1 for a female life aged as in column 1 (4)
90	.60	.1212	.1509
91	.58	.1116	.1407
92	.56	.1025	.1310
93	.54	.0939	.1218
94	.52	.0858	.1132
95	.50	.0781	.1050
96	.49	.0710	.0972
97	.48	.0642	.0898
98	.47	.0578	.0828
99	.45	.0517	.0762
100 or over	.43	.0458	.0698

TABLE B

Valuation of Interests: Less than 50 Years

Number of years (1)	Value (2)	Number of years (1)	Value (2)
1	.0654	26	.8263
2	.1265	27	.8375
3	.1836	28	.8480
4	.2370	29	.8578
5	.2869	30	.8669
6	.3335	31	.8754
7	.3770	32	.8834
8	.4177	33	.8908
9	.4557	34	.8978
10	.4913	35	.9043
11	.5245	36	.9100
12	.5555	37	.9165
13	.5845	38	.9230
14	.6116	39	.9295
15	.6369	40	.9360
16	.6605	41	.9425
17	.6826	42	.9490
18	.7032	43	.9555
19	.7225	44	.9620
20	.7405	45	.9685
21	.7574	46	.9750
22	.7731	47	.9815
23	.7878	48	.9880
24	.8015	49	.9945
25	.8144	50 and over	1.0000

Note:
Column (2) shows the value of an interest in a capital of €1 for the number of years shown in column (1).

34 TRUSTS

Learning Outcomes

On completion of this chapter you will be able to:

- ✓ Describe the different elements of a trust
- ✓ Describe the difference between different types of trust, nominee/bare trusts, fixed trusts/interest in possession trusts and discretionary trusts.
- ✓ Describe and calculate the tax implications on the creation of a trust.
- ✓ Describe and calculate the tax implications of the appointment of assets from a trust
- ✓ Describe the administration of trusts.

34.1 Introduction

Historically trusts were used to defer tax liabilities for a number of generations. However, due to anti-avoidance legislation trusts are no longer necessarily tax driven. There are various non-tax reasons that trusts are now used to pass assets from one generation to the next;

- Parents might be reluctant to give their children access to a large amount of income or capital, in circumstances where they believe that their children may not have the maturity to handle the funds sensibly or where one of their children is unable to manage the funds due to being incapacitated.
- Parents might be reluctant to give up control of an asset to their children, where they believe that their children may lack the expertise to exercise control over the property properly.
- When children are young it can be difficult to predict their future needs.

34.1.1 Elements of a trust

A trust is a **relationship** that exists between a **settlor**, who transfers assets into a trust and the **trustee**, the individual who has custodianship of property and the **beneficiaries** who receive (or may receive) a benefit from the trust. A settlor can set up a trust while they are still alive, an inter vivos trust (a gift trust) or a settlor can set up a trust on their death, a will trust. The core obligation of a trustee is to act in a fiduciary capacity for the benefit of the beneficiaries. The trustees are the legal owners of the assets in a trust. Their role is to deal with the assets in a trust in accordance with the settlor's wishes, as set out in the trust deed of the settlor or in the settlor's will. Trustees are responsible for managing the trust on a day to day basis (deciding how to invest or use the trust's assets), for filing any tax returns of the trust and paying any taxation due.

Terminology of Trusts	
Absolute Interest	A beneficiary who has an absolute interest in property can deal with or dispose of that property as he/she pleases.
Limited Interest	Includes life interests and interests for a period certain, beneficiaries cannot dictate to whom the property ultimately goes to.
Life Interest	The beneficiary has use of the property until their death.
Interest for a Period Certain	The beneficiary has use of the property for a fixed period of time.
Remainder Interest	The beneficiary who is entitled to an absolute interest in the property after all limited interests (life/period certain) have expired (referred to as a remainder-man).
Appointment	When trustees transfer property from the trust to the beneficiary.

34.1.2 Main Types of Trust

The main types of trust that are relevant from a tax perspective are nominee/bare trusts, fixed trusts/interest in possession trusts and discretionary trusts.

34.1.3 Nominee/Bare Trusts

The beneficiary of a nominee/bare trust is beneficially entitled in possession to the assets of the trust. The trustees of a nominee/bare trust have no active duties to perform; they simply hold legal title to property. Nominee/bare trusts are often used in the case of children who cannot legally hold property until such time as they are 18 years old.

34.1.4 Fixed Trusts/Interest in Position Trusts

Each beneficiary has a fixed entitlement to a specific share or interest in the trust property. The beneficiary may become entitled to the property after a specific time period ("a period certain"), has passed, or on the death of a person who has an interest in the property for the duration of their life (i.e. on the death of a "life tenant".)

34.1.5 Discretionary Trusts

Under a discretionary trust, no one is entitled to the income or capital of the trust. The trustees (within the terms of the trust deed) have discretion on the distribution of the income or capital. They may accumulate some or all of the income for future use. The settlor may choose to give the trustees a "letter of wishes" setting out the settlor's present and future intentions for the trust property.

34.1.6 Taxation of Trusts

Over the life time of a trust various taxes including capital gains tax, stamp duty, income tax and capital acquisitions tax, may arise, depending on the nature of the trust, the nature of the property settled on trust, what transactions if any that are undertaken by the trustees and the timing of when trustees transfer property to the ultimate beneficiaries of a trust.

34.2 Capital Gains Tax/Stamp Duty

34.2.1 Creation of an inter-vivos (gift) trust

s575 TCA97 The creation of an inter-vivos (gift) trust will involve the transfer of assets or funds from a settlor into the trust. The settlor will typically have a capital gains tax liability when they transfer assets into the trust, as being a transaction between connected parties, market value is imposed on the transaction. This can be mitigated against by transferring assets that qualify for a capital gains tax relief (such as a principal private residence) in to the trust or alternatively transferring assets that have a high base cost into the trust. Again, as the transaction is between connected parties, any capital loss made on the transfer of assets into a trust are ring-fenced.

s30 SDCA 1999 The transfer of assets into a trust also results in a liability to stamp duty, 1% for shares and up to 6% for other assets. This can often lead to a need for a settlor to transfer cash into a trust to cover the stamp duty liability. The transfer of funds (cash) into a trust will not trigger a capital gains tax liability or a stamp duty liability.

Example 34.1[1]

In June 2018, Andrew settles shares worth €800,000 on trust for his wife Jenny for life with the remainder to his son, David, then aged 10, absolutely. The shares had been purchased by Andrew in January 2012, for €460,000 inclusive of incidental costs. Andrew's capital gains tax liability on the disposal will be as follows, (assuming he has not made any other disposals in 2018).

Capital Gains Tax	**€**
Deemed sale proceeds	*800,000*
Less: Total base cost	*(460,000)*
Gain	*340,000*
Less annual exemption	*(1,270)*
Taxable gain	*338,730*
Tax @ 33%	*111,781*
Stamp Duty	
800,000 @ 1%	*8,000*

As the only asset in the trust is the shares, Andrew will need to transfer €8,000 into the trust to cover the stamp duty liability. Alternatively, the trustees would need to dispose of some of the shares to cover the stamp duty.

1 Adapted from *Trust and Succession Law*, Anne Corrigan and Anne Williams, 2003, Irish Tax Institute

34.2.2 Creation of a will trust

Trusts created on the death of a settlor, as a result of their will do not trigger a capital gains tax liability or a stamp duty liability.

34.2.3 Transactions by Trustees

s568 (1) TCA97

The market value of any assets transferred into a trust is the base cost of the assets for future disposals of those assets, by the trustees. Any disposals of assets by the trustees will normally trigger a capital gains tax liability, with no entitlement to reliefs or exemptions (other than the potential to claim principal private residence relief). Furthermore, any assets purchased by the trustees will trigger a stamp duty liability.

However, if the trust is a nominee/bare trust, the beneficiary is treated for capital gains tax and stamp duty purposes as making the acquisitions and disposals made on their behalf by the trustee and any gains or losses attach to the beneficiary, not the trustees.

34.2.4 Appointment of Trust Assets

s576 (1) TCA97

s577 (2) TCA97

s577 (3) TCA97

When a beneficiary becomes beneficially entitled to assets from a trust, the trustees are deemed to have disposed of those assets and immediately re-acquired them for a consideration equal to market value. A capital gains tax liability will arise for the trustees, assuming a capital gain is made. The immediate transfer of the assets to the beneficiary does not trigger a capital gains tax liability. The market value is also the base cost for the beneficiary for any future disposals. However, in circumstances where the beneficiary becomes absolutely entitled to the assets, as a result of the death of a life tenant, no capital gains tax liability will arise, even though the trustees are still deemed to have disposed of and immediately re-acquired the assets for a consideration equal to market value. If a life tenant dies and trust assets remain settled property, i.e. no-one is beneficially entitled to the assets as against the trustees, then a capital gains tax will arise in those circumstances.

No stamp duty arises on the appointment of trust assets to a beneficiary as the appointment by the trustees of assets out of the settlement is simply that, an appointment to the beneficiaries of their beneficial entitlement. A liability to stamp duty does not arise either, on assets leaving a trust as a result of the death of a life tenant.

Example 34.2[2]

Under the terms of a settlement the trustees hold investments in trust for Stephen contingent on his living to the age of twenty-five years.

When he becomes twenty-five years of age, Stephen will be absolutely entitled to the assets as against the trustees. At that time, there is a deemed disposal by the trustees. They are also deemed to reacquire the assets at market value at that date as nominee for Stephen. The trustees will have

2 Adapted from Section 8.3.7 *The Taxation of Capital Gains,* Finola O'Hanlon, Jim McCleane, 2012, Irish Tax Institute.

a capital gains liability, (the transaction is not exempt, as Stephen is not beneficially entitled to the investments as the result of the death of a life tenant).

Stephen will have a deemed "cost" for CGT purposes equal to the market value of each and every separate investment comprised in the trustee's investments to which he becomes "absolutely entitled" at the date on which he becomes so entitled.

Example 34.3[3]

John settled shares in ABC Plc worth €500,000 on a discretionary settlement, on 1st February 2015. John's total base cost was €100,000. John had acquired the shares on 1st February 2008. The trustees sold the shares in ABC Plc on 5th April 2016 for €750,000 and bought shares in XYZ Plc for €750,000. The trustees then appointed a life interest in the shares to John's wife Sarah and a remainder interest in half the shares to John's son Mark, on 1st May 2016 when the shares were valued at €800,000. When John's wife Sarah died on 1st February 2018 the shares were worth €900,000. A month after her death the trustees appointed the remaining half of the shares to Mark's wife Michelle when the remaining half of the shares were worth €500,000. The capital gains tax and stamp duty consequences are as follows, (assuming that John introduces the necessary cash to cover any tax liabilities of the trust).

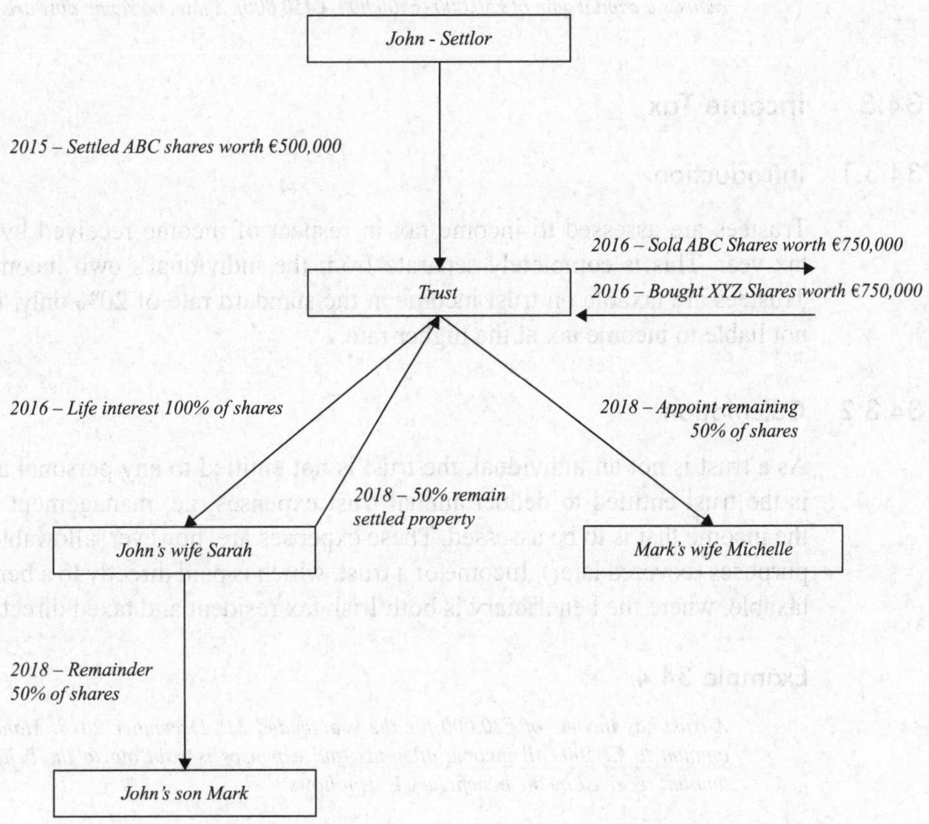

3 Adapted from Section 8.3 *The Taxation of Capital Gains,* Finola O'Hanlon, Jim McCleane, 2012, Irish Tax Institute.

In February 2015, John is treated as realising a capital gain of €400,000 (€500,000–€100,000) on the transfer of the ABC Plc shares into the trust. The trust will also have a stamp duty liability of €5,000, being €500,000 @ 1%. The base cost (ignoring stamp duty) of the shares for the trust will be €500,000.

In April 2016, the trust realises a capital gain of €250,000 (€750,000–€500,000) on the sale of the ABC Plc shares. The trust will also have a stamp duty liability on the acquisition of the XYZ Plc shares of €7,500; being €750,000 @ 1%. The base cost (ignoring stamp duty) of the XYZ Plc shares for the trust will be €750,000.

In May 2016, the creation of life interest to John's wife Sarah and the creation of the remainder interest to John's son Mark are not subject to capital gains tax or stamp duty.

In February 2018, on the death of Sarah, Mark becomes absolutely entitled to one half of the shares. There is a disposal of these shares, but it is exempt as from capital gains tax as Mark becomes absolutely entitled to the shares on the death of a life tenant, his mother Sarah. The transfer of one half of the shares to Mark does not trigger a stamp duty liability.

After the death of the life tenant, Sarah, the other half of the shares (the ones not given to Mark) remain settled property and the trust is deemed to have disposed of and re-acquired them at market value triggering a capital gain of €75,000 (€450,000–€375,000).

In March 2018, on the appointment of the remaining half of the shares to Mark's wife, Michelle, the trust realises a capital gain of €50,000 (€500,000–€450,000). Again, no stamp duty arises on the transfer.

34.3 Income Tax

34.3.1 Introduction

Trustees are assessed to income tax in respect of income received by the trust each tax year. This is completely separate from the individual's own income tax liability. Trustees are taxable on trust income at the standard rate of 20% only, i.e. trustees are not liable to income tax at the higher rate.

34.3.2 Calculation

As a trust is not an individual, the trust is not entitled to any personal allowances, nor is the trust entitled to deduct annual trust expenses, i.e. management expenses from the income that is to be assessed. These expenses are, however, allowable for surcharge purposes (covered later). Income of a trust, which is paid directly to a beneficiary, is not taxable, where the beneficiary is both Irish tax resident and taxed directly.

Example 34.4

A trust has income of €20,000 for the year ended 31st December 2018. Management expenses amount to €1,500. All income after tax and expenses is paid out to the beneficiaries. The net amount received by the beneficiary is as follows:

	€
Gross income of trust	*20,000*
Less: Tax @ 20%	*(4,000)*
	16,000
Less expenses	*(1,500)*
Net distributed	*14,500*

34.3.3 Surcharge on undistributed trust income

s805(3) TCA97 A 20% surcharge applies to undistributed trust income of both accumulated trusts (where income is accumulated within the trust) and discretionary trusts (where the income is paid over to the beneficiaries at the discretion of the trustees). The surcharge applies where the trust income exceeds the trust expenses in the year of assessment, and the income is not distributed within the year or within 18 months of the end of the year of assessment. The surcharge does not apply where the beneficiary is taxed directly or where the income is treated as that of the settlor.

Example 34.5

A trust has €20,000 of income for the tax year ended 31st December 2018. Accountancy fees amounted to €900. Other trustee expenses amounted to €500. The trust distributed €2,500 to the beneficiaries. The surcharge is calculated as follows:

	€
Gross income of trust	*20,000*
Less: Tax @ 20%	*(4,000)*
	16,000
Less expenses	*(1,400)*
Less distributions to beneficiaries	*(2,500)*
Net undistributed income	*12,100*
Re-gross to 100% (12,100 × 100/80)	*15,125*
20% surcharge	*3,025*
Net accumulated income	*9,075*

34.3.4 Beneficiaries

If the trust is taxed first, the beneficiaries will be taxed under Schedule D Case IV on the gross income received and will receive a credit for the tax deducted by the trustees.

34.3.5 Taxation of Settlors

s791(2) TCA97 Provision is made for the taxation of settlors, where income is received under revocable dispositions. In this instance, the income is regarded as the income of the person who can obtain enjoyment of the income, without consent of another (excluding one's spouse).

34.3.6 Trusts in favour of minors

s794(4) TCA97 Income settled on minors is normally taxed in the hands of the settlor. However, this does not apply to settlements made for the benefit of a minor who is permanently incapacitated. The income of settlements on behalf of the minor child of the settlor, are still taxed in the hands of the settlor, regardless of whether or not the minor child is incapacitated.

34.3.7 Administration and accountability

Similar to other taxpayers, trustees must file income tax returns on a self-assessment basis. On this basis, trustees being liable to income tax/capital gains tax, they must file tax returns and pay preliminary tax by the 31st October deadline, just like any other self-assessment taxpayer. It is important to emphasise that it is the trustees that are primarily accountable for the payment of any income tax/capital gains tax due by the trust.

34.4 Capital Acquisitions Tax

34.4.1 Nominee/Bare Trusts

The beneficiary of a nominee/bare trust is beneficially entitled in possession to the assets of the trust. Therefore a CAT event is triggered on the transfer of assets to a bare trust and the beneficiary may have a CAT liability (subject to the possibility of "same event" CGT credit relief).

Example 34.6[4]

Sean owns a commercial property worth €1M. In order to take advantage of low property values, he decides to gift the property to his daughter Aisling who is 13 years old. As Aisling is under 18, she is unable to hold a legal interest in the property herself. Therefore, on 1 June 2018 Sean executes a declaration of trust indicating that from that date onwards, he will hold the property on trust for Aisling. Assuming that Aisling has not received any prior gifts or inheritances Aisling CAT on the gift taken on 1 June 2018 will be as follows:

Market value		*1,000,000*
Less small gift exemption		*(3,000)*
Taxable value		*997,000*
Group threshold:	*€310,000 @ Nil*	*Nil*
Balance:	*€687,000 @ 33%*	*226,710*
CAT liability		*226,710**

* *If Sean pays any CGT on the disposal of the commercial property, Aisling will be able to offset the CGT paid against her CAT liability (it being the same event that triggers both CGT and CAT liabilities).*

34.4.2 Fixed Trusts/Interest in Position Trusts

Each beneficiary has a fixed entitlement to a specific share or interest in the trust property. The beneficiary may become entitled to the property after a specific time period ("a period certain"), has passed, or on the death of a person who has an interest in the property for the duration of their life (i.e. on the death of a "life tenant".) Normal

4 From *Capital Acquisitions Tax & Stamp Duty* – Part 2 CTA Student Manual, Irish Tax Institute.

CAT rules provide that CAT arises when a beneficiary becomes entitled in possession to property. In the case of a trust it is present rights to enjoyment of property that are taxed, not future rights to the enjoyment of property. Thus, a future interest is not taxed until an event happens whereby the future interest becomes a present interest.

Example 34.7[5]

Owen settles shares by deed dated 1 February 2018 on his brother Luke for life and then on to his sister Kate absolutely. A CAT tax charge arises on Luke at 1 February 2018 as he receives a present right to the enjoyment of the shares (i.e. an interest in possession, Luke is entitled to receive the income from the shares); while no tax arises on Kate at this date as she has only received a future interest in the shares. On Luke's death, Kate will be liable to CAT on the value of the shares at that date as she will then have a present right to those shares.

Example 34.8[6]

John by deed dated 1 February 2011, settles shares valued at €200,000 on his brother Tom (who is aged 19) until Tom reaches the age of 25 (on 1 February 2018) with the remainder to John's sister Ann-Marie, absolutely. The shares are valued at €240,000 on 01 February 2018. Their respective CAT liabilities will be as follows;

Tom - 2011

Market value		*200,000*
Adjustment for limited interest (Multiplication by .3335 – Table B)		*66,700*
Less small gift exemption		*(3,000)*
Taxable value		*63,700*
Group threshold:	*€33,208 @ Nil*	*Nil*
Balance:	*€30,492 @ 25%*	*7,623*
CAT liability		*7,623*

Ann-Marie - 2018

Market value		*240,000*
Less small gift exemption		*(3,000)*
Taxable value		*237,000*
Group threshold:	*€32,500 @ Nil*	*Nil*
Balance:	*€204,500 @ 33%*	*67,485*
CAT liability		*67,485*

5 From *Capital Acquisitions Tax & Stamp Duty* – Part 2 CTA Student Manual, Irish Tax Institute
6 Adapted from *Capital Acquisitions Tax & Stamp Duty* – Part 2 CTA Student Manual, Irish Tax Institute

34.4.3 Discretionary Trusts

Under a discretionary trust, no one is entitled to the income or capital of the trust. The trustees (within the terms of the trust deed) have discretion on the distribution of the income or capital. They may accumulate some or all of the income for future use. The settlor may choose to give the trustees a "letter of wishes" setting out the settlor's present and future intentions for the trust property.

No liability to CAT arises when property is initially settled on discretionary trust as no individual has yet to become beneficially entitled in possession to a benefit under the trust. CAT is charged on each benefit, whether of income or capital, taken by a beneficiary of a discretionary trust when an appointment is made from the trust property by the trustees of the trust to that beneficiary. Benefits taken by beneficiaries from discretionary trusts are deemed to be taken from the settlor of the trust (not from the trustees).

34.4.4 Discretionary Trust Tax

s15 CATCA 2003 To discourage the accumulation of property in discretionary trusts for long periods of time, the following discretionary trust taxes apply;

- 6% once off discretionary trust tax
- 1% annual discretionary trust tax

The 6% discretionary trust tax (levied on the market value of trust property) applies on the later of;

- The date that the trust is set up
- The date that the settlor dies, and
- The date that all the principal objects (spouse, civil partner, children, children of a deceased child) reach the age of 21

s18 CATCA 2003 One half of the 6% charge (3%) will be refunded if all property in the trust is appointed within 5 years of it being levied.

s20/23 CATCA 2003 The 1% discretionary trust tax is levied on the market value of the trust property on 31 December each year, thereafter, with the exception of the first 31 December following the imposition of the 6% charge.

s17/22 CATCA 2003 Discretionary trusts set up for the exclusively for the following purposes are exempt from discretionary trust tax;

- public or charitable purposes
- superannuation or unit trust scheme purposes

- for the benefit of improvident or incapacitated Individuals
- for the upkeep of heritage houses or gardens

Example 34.9[7]

Derek Donnelly set up a discretionary trust for the benefit of his wife Mairead and his two daughters Nuala and Niamh on 1 July 2014. Nuala was aged 19 on this date and Niamh was aged 17.

Derek died on 10 July 2016. The value of the trust on this date was €350,000. On 10 January 2018 Niamh turned 21.

The trustees decided to wind up the trust on Niamh's 25th birthday on 10 January 2022 and appoint the property in equal shares to Nuala and Niamh.

Assuming a constant value of €350,000, the discretionary trust tax liabilities will be as follows:

6% initial discretionary trust tax

The initial charge to discretionary trust tax arises on the latest of the following dates:

- *The date the property becomes subject to the discretionary trust (1 July 2014: the date the trust was set up).*
- *The date of death of the settlor (10 July 2016 : Derek's date of death), and*
- *The date on which there are no principal beneficiaries of the trust aged less than 21 years.*

Niamh's 21st birthday on 10 January 2018 is the latest of the three dates and, therefore, the initial charge to discretionary trust tax arises on this date.

10 January 2018 - €350,000 × 6% = €21,000

31 December 2018 = Nil

31 December 2019 - €350,000 × 1% = €3,500

31 December 2020 - €350,000 × 1% = €3,500

31 December 2021 - €350,000 × 1% = €3,500

The trust is wound up on 10 January 2022. As the entire assets of the trust have been appointed within 5 years of the Initial charge to discretionary trust tax, a refund of half the initial tax is available, i.e. €10,500. This amount falls into the trust and must be appointed out to prevent any further charge to tax arising.

34.4.5 Administration and accountability

s45 CATCA 2003

The beneficiary of a trust is the individual primarily accountable for the filing of tax returns and the payment of capital acquisitions tax and the normal self-assessment rules apply, with regard to filing and payment dates. Trustees, however, remain secondarily accountable for any capital acquisitions tax payable on assets appointed out of a trust.

7 From *Capital Acquisitions Tax & Stamp Duty* – Part 2 CTA Student Manual, Irish Tax Institute.

35 INTRODUCTION TO STAMP DUTY & LOCAL PROPERTY TAX

Learning Outcomes

On completion of this chapter, you should be able to:

- ✓ Calculate a stamp duty liability
- ✓ Identify the key reliefs and exemptions
- ✓ Understand the Local Property Tax charge and calculate the liability

35.1 Stamp Duty Introduction

Stamp Duty in Ireland is legislated by Stamp Duties Consolidation Act 1999 (SDCA). It is a tax on the written documents associated with a particular transaction and not on the transaction itself. In order for a stamp duty charge to arise, a written document must be executed in relation to the transaction. If no document is executed with a transaction then no stamp duty is payable. Prior to the introduction of electronic stamping (e-Stamping) on 31 December 2009, stamp duties were denoted by physical stamps affixed or impressed on documents. All documents are now stamped by attaching a stamp certificate, obtained under the e-Stamping system, to the document.

The amount of duty applicable will either be a fixed amount or an *ad valorem* amount. *Ad valorem* is a term commonly applied to taxes on the value of property. Ad valorem is a latin expression meaning "to the value" or "according to value". An ad valorem duty is one determined by assessment or appraisal. *Ad valorem* duty is based on the value of the asset being transferred, whereas nominal/fixed duty is a fixed amount regardless of the value of the transaction.

35.1.1 Key Terms: 'Sale' and 'Conveyance on Sale'

A sale involves a contractual bargain between two or more parties for a price in money or its equivalent. Four elements are essential to a sale, in the absence of any one of these elements, a sale cannot take place. They are:

- a seller or vendor
- a buyer or purchaser
- a thing sold (e.g. property)
- a price

The conveyance on sale is the most important kind of document in stamp duty terms and its definition is set out in the legislation. Essentially a conveyance on sale is a document which, on a sale of property, transfers ownership of the property to the purchaser. Examples are a conveyance of land, a stock transfer form (the standard form for transferring title to shares), or an assignment of a patent.

35.2 The Charge to Stamp Duty

The main charging provisions for Stamp Duty are contained in Schedule 1 of SDCA where over 20 instruments are listed. An instrument is defined in s2 as "every written document." The territoriality provisions are set out in s2, which states that any instrument that

> *"is executed in the State or, wherever executed, relates to any property situated in the State or any matter or thing to be done in the State, shall be chargeable with stamp duty."*

Any instrument not listed in Schedule 1 is not liable to Stamp Duty. Examples of instruments listed in Schedule 1 include

- Conveyance on sale
- Lease
- Policy of insurance
- Cheques
- Stock transfer form

Stamp Duty charges in Ireland fall into two main categories:

1. Duties payable on legal and commercial documents, such as conveyances of property, leases of property, share transfer forms and certain agreements.
2. Duties and levies payable by reference to statements. These duties and levies mainly affect banks and insurance companies and include a duty in respect of financial cards (e.g. Credit, ATM, Laser and Charge cards) and levies on certain insurance premiums and pension schemes.

35.2.1 Payment and Returns

Stamp duty is paid on the VAT exclusive consideration paid for the relevant property. The time limit for filing the Stamp Duty Return (on ROS) and payment of the duties is 30 days from the date of the execution of the document (but in practice within 44 days) before penalties and interest, are imposed.

The "accountable person"; is the person liable to pay the stamp duty due on a particular instrument. The person liable for the duty will depend on the nature of the charge (i.e. the instrument heading specified in Schedule 1 SDCA 1999), e.g.

- The purchaser on a sale;
- The lessee on a lease;
- The mortgagee on a loan;
- Either party on a gift.

35.3 Rates of Stamp Duty and Calculation

Stamp Duty is chargeable at different rates, depending on the nature of the document and on the value of the transaction and is paid by the purchaser.[1]

1. Residential property transactions

Consideration	Rate
First €1,000,000	1%
Excess over €1,000,000	2%

Example 35.1

John O'Brien purchased a residential property for €350,000 from Mark Clancy on 1 June 2018.

John's stamp duty liability on the purchase is €3,500, i.e. €350,000 @ 1%.

Example 35.2

Rachel Hanley purchased a residential property for €1,850,000 from Denis Dunleavy on 5 September 2018.

Rachel's stamp duty liability on the purchase is €27,000, i.e. €1,000,000 @ 1%, plus €850,000 @ 2%.

2. Commercial property transactions

Consideration	Rate
All considerations	6%*

*Finance Act 2017 increased the rate of stamp duty on non-residential property from 2% to 6%. However, in recognition of the potential impact that this might have on the supply of residential property, a simultaneous stamp duty refund scheme was introduced,

1 The rate of Stamp Duty on residential property is based on a sliding scale and was in the past as high as 9%. During the economic downturn and to acknowledge the difficulties in both the residential and commercial property markets stamp duty rates of 1–2% were introduced in Finance Act 2011 and 2012.

for land purchased for the development of housing. The refund mechanism effectively reverts the stamp duty on qualifying disposals to 2%. It should be noted that it does not reduce the stamp duty rate to 2% but instead allows a refund of the differential between 6% and 2% i.e. 4%.

Example 35.3

Daniel Burke purchased a commercial property for €1,500,000 form Richard O'Connor on 7 June 2018.

Daniel's stamp duty liability on the purchase is €90,000, i.e. €1,500,000 @ 6%.

3. Stocks and marketable securities

1% of consideration (rounded down to the nearest zero)

Finance Act 2017 also increased the rate of stamp duty on transfers of shares where the shares derive their value, or the greater part of their value, from Irish property, from 1% to 6%. The increased rate will not apply where the underlying property is residential, nor will it apply where the property in the company is held for long term rental income (as opposed to holding the property for disposal). In addition to these exceptions, the increased rate will only apply if there is a change in control of the underlying assets i.e. the disposal of minority interests should remain at 1%.

4. Leases

Stamp duty is calculated on both the rent (see below) and any premium payable (1%/2% for residential and 6% for commercial leases).

Term	Rate
Less than 35 years	1% of the average annual rent
35 – 100 years	6% of the average annual rent
Over 100 years	12% of the average annual rent

There is no stamp duty on a lease for a residential property if the rent is €40,000 (previously €30,000) or less per annum and the period of the lease is 35 years or less (or for an indefinite period).

Where the consideration cannot easily be established Revenue may charge *ad valorem* duty on the market value of the property conveyed or transferred. Where a sale consists of mixed use e.g. residential and other property, the apportionment must be made on a "*just and reasonable*" basis irrespective of how the consideration is shown on the instrument of transfer. In the case of a sale or lease both parties to the agreement are required to submit separate estimates of the residential element.

A *de minimus* exemption applies where total stamp duty payable on an instrument is €10 or less.

35.4 Stamp Duty on Gifts (Voluntary Disposition Inter Vivos)

Stamp duty is payable at the same rates on a gift of property (a voluntary disposition inter vivos) as for a conveyance on sale. As no consideration is paid, stamp duty is payable on the market value of the gift. Sales at undervalue are treated as gifts and the stamp duty is payable on the full market value.

Example 35.4

James O'Boyle purchased a residential property for €230,000 from his friend Beatrice Carey on 12 July 2018. The market value of the property at the date of transfer was €290,000.

James' stamp duty liability on the purchase is €2,900, i.e. €290,000 @ 1%.

Where a sale is at undervalue, but the purchaser agrees to take over a liability as well as paying some cash, stamp duty is payable on the higher of the liability taken over plus cash, or the equity of redemption (i.e. the market value of the property less the amount of the mortgage).

Example 35.5

Ralph Ward purchased a commercial property for €220,000 from Keith Burns on 28 January 2018. Ralph also agreed to take over the remaining mortgage on the property of €260,000. The market value of the property at the date of transfer was €500,000.

Ralph's stamp duty liability on the purchase is €28,800, i.e. €480,000 (€220,000 + €260,000) @ 6%. Had Ralph paid €470,000 for the property, with the remaining mortgage being €10,000, then Ralph's stamp duty liability on the purchase would be €9,400, i.e. €490,000 (€500,000 − €10,000) @ 6%.

35.5 Reliefs and Exemptions

35.5.1 Introduction

There are a number of reliefs and exemptions available from stamp duty. The most common and noteworthy of these are detailed below.

35.5.2 Transactions between spouses, civil partners and co-habitants

S96/97/97A SDCA 99 There is a total stamp duty exemption for transfers between spouses and civil partners. Unlike capital gains tax there is no requirement to be living together, once the couples remain married the exemption applies. For the purposes of this exemption, separated spouses/civil partners (whether formally or informally separated) are also considered spouses. Transfers between divorced persons are chargeable to stamp duty. However, where property is transferred at dissolution of a marriage, under orders from the Family Law Act 1995 and Family Law (Divorce) Act 1996, a stamp duty exemption applies. No stamp duty is chargeable on the transfer of assets under a civil partnership dissolution order.

Example 35.6

Timothy Reynolds separated from his wife Jane on 2 July 2018. On 17 August 2018 Timothy transferred an investment property worth €230,000 to Jane.

The inter-spousal exemption will apply in this instance and therefore Jane will not incur a stamp duty charge on the transfer.

Finance (No. 3) Act 2011 did not give opposite-sex or same-sex cohabiting couples the same tax treatment as married couples or civil partners. However, it does provide that where one of the former cohabiters is granted redress by the Courts through the transfer of an asset, the individual acquiring the asset will not be liable to stamp duty on the transfer (this mirrors the capital gains tax treatment).

35.5.3 Transactions between related persons

Par 1 Sch 1 SDCA 99

'Consanguinity relief' refers to a special relief for transactions where there is a relationship between the purchaser/donee and the vendor/donor. Where this relief applies, the duty payable is restricted to 50% of the duty that would otherwise be payable. Relationships covered under consanguinity relief included lineal descendants, parents, grandparents, step-parents, civil partners, spouses, uncles, aunts, brothers, sisters, step-brothers/sisters, step-children, nieces/nephews. However, consanguinity relief does not apply on a transfer of residential property (for properties where instruments were executed on or after 8 December 2010), stocks and marketable securities and leases (rent and premium). The relief was to be abolished for non-residential property where instruments are executed on or after 1 January 2015.

However, Finance Act 2014 extended the relief until 1 January 2018, but confines the relief to conveyances or transfers of farmland. The relief was further extended by Finance Act 2017 to 31 December 2020.

The conditions that must be satisfied, in order for consanguinity relief to apply to conveyances or transfers of farmland on or after 1 January 2015, mirror those introduced for CAT. The individual to whom the land is conveyed or transferred to must either have an agricultural qualification e.g. Green Cert, Agricultural Science degree etc, (or attain such qualification within 4 years of the gift or inheritance) and must farm the land on a commercial basis, with a view to making a profit, or if the individual to whom the land is conveyed or transferred to does not have an agricultural qualification, they must spend not less than 50% of their normal working time farming. Again, "normal working time" is approximately 40 hours per week and therefore individual to whom the land is conveyed or transferred to will be required to work a minimum of 20 hours per week, farming.

If the individual to whom the land is conveyed or transferred to does not fulfill either of the above criteria, they can still qualify for consanguinity relief if they lease out the farm that has been transferred to them, to a farmer (who fulfills either of the above criteria) for a minimum of 6 years.

In addition to the above conditions, from 1 January 2016, transferors must be under the age of 67 at the date of transfer in order to obtain the benefit of the relief. This condition was removed by Finance Act 2017.

Example 35.7

George Darcy gifted a small farm worth €190,000 to his niece Beverly on 17 August 2018. Beverly has farmed full-time, since finishing her "green cert" qualification in 2010.

As the transaction is between connected parties, market value is imposed on the transaction. However, Beverly will qualify for consanguinity relief and therefore her stamp duty liability is reduced by 50%. Beverly's stamp duty liability is €1,900, i.e. €190,000 × 2% × 50%.

35.5.4 Transactions involving young trained farmers

s81AA SDCA 99

Transfers of land that take place between 1 January 2000 and 31 December 2018 to "young trained farmers" are exempt from stamp duty. A young trained farmer is a person under 35 years of age and who has met certain educational requirements. The recipient must make a declaration in writing that it is their intention to retain ownership of the land and to spend not less than 50% of normal working time farming the land for 5 years from the date of the transfer.

Relief can also apply where the transfer is to joint owners where both individuals qualify as young trained farmers. Where the transfer is to an individual and their spouse, it is not necessary that the spouse also qualifies as a young trained farmer. If the property is disposed of within 5 years of purchase/gift (and the proceeds are not reinvested in agricultural property within 1 year); or where a declaration is deemed to be untrue (in relation to the 50% working requirement), a claw-back of the relief occurs. A part disposal of the property to one's spouse does not trigger a claw-back.

Finance Act 2017 amended the relief to take account of EU State Aid rules. The young trained farmer must now submit a business plan to Teagasc and must come within the EU definition of a "micro, small or medium enterprise".

Example 35.8

Daniel Cronin gifted land worth €650,000 into the joint names of his daughter, Claire, and her husband, Alan an accountant. Claire (who is aged 27) has worked full-time on the farm with Daniel since she left college 4 years ago (where she attended agricultural college and obtained a "green cert").

Claire should not have stamp duty liability on the transfer as she is less than 35 years of age and has met the educational requirements. This is assuming that she signs the relevant declaration stating that she intends to retain ownership and meet the 50% working requirement for the relevant 5-year period. The fact that Alan is not a "young trained farmer" does not prohibit Claire and Alan from obtaining the exemption.

35.5.5 Farm Consolidation Relief

s81C SDCA 99 Finance Act 2017 re-introduces stamp duty relief for farm consolidation. The purpose of the relief is to encourage the consolidation of farm holdings in order to reduce fragmentation and improve the operation and viability of the farm(s) concerned. The relief provides that where there is a valid consolidation certificate issued by Teagasc in relation to the sale and purchase of lands, occurring within 24 months of each other, stamp duty will only be paid (at 1%) on the purchase to the extent that the value of the lands purchased exceeds the value of the lands sold. The qualifying period is between 1 January 2018 and 31 December 2020.

35.5.6 Leasing Farmland

S81D SDCA 99 Finance Act 2014 introduced a new relief in relation to certain leases of farmland. In order to qualify for the relief, the term of the lease must be for a period of not less than 6 years and not more than 35 years and the land must be used exclusively for farming carried on by the lessee. Again, the majority of the conditions mirror those introduced for CAT purposes, i.e. the lessee must either have an agricultural qualification e.g. Green Cert, Agricultural Science degree etc, (or attain such qualification within 4 years of the gift or inheritance) and must farm the land on a commercial basis, with a view to making a profit, or if the lessee does not have an agricultural qualification, they must spend not less than 50% of their normal working time farming.

The section also provides that the stamp duty that would have been chargeable on the grant of the lease, becomes payable with interest in the event that the conditions of the relief are not fulfilled for the first 6 years of the lease.

35.5.7 Associated companies' relief

s79 SDCA 99 Where there is a 90% shareholding relationship (direct or indirect) between two companies or at least 90% of the issued share capital of each company is owned directly or indirectly by a third party, any transfer of assets between the companies is exempt from stamp duty. The 90% test must also be satisfied in relation to profits and assets available for distribution on a winding up of the company (similar to the 75% test for corporation tax purposes). There is a claw-back of relief if the group relationship is broken within two years of the transfer. The claw-back does not apply, in a merger scenario, provided certain conditions are met.

Example 35.9

Holdco Ltd owns 95% of the share capital of Sub1 Ltd and 90% of the share capital of Sub2 Ltd. The share capital percentages also apply to the profits and assets available for distribution in the event of a winding up of Holdco's subsidiaries. The group relationship has been in place for a number of years. On 5 May 2018 Sub1 Ltd transfers a commercial property worth €390,000 to Sub2 Ltd.

As the 90% relevant relationship is satisfied, the transfer of the commercial property from Sub1 Ltd to Sub2 Ltd will be exempt from stamp duty. To avoid a claw-back of the relief the group relationship will need to stay in place for 2 years after the transfer.

35.5.8 IP Exemption

s101 SDCA 99 The sale, transfer or other disposition of intellectual property e.g. patent, trade mark, inventions etc. are exempt from stamp duty. Goodwill is also included in the exemption to the extent that it is attributable to such intellectual property.

35.6 Local Property Tax (LPT)

A residential property tax was introduced by the Finance (Local Property Tax) Act 2012 and effectively replaces what was known as the 'Household Charge' and 'NPPR' (both of which are outside the scope of this publication).

35.6.1 Charge to LPT

With effect from 1 July 2013, residential property owners are liable to pay local property tax (LPT) based on the market value of their property on 1 May 2013. The valuation placed on the property at 1 May 2013 was to be valid up to and including 2016. The next valuation date was due to be on 1 November 2016 and was to determine the basis for LPT liabilities for 2017, 2018 and 2019. Finance Act 2015 postponed the valuation date for LPT from 1 November 2016 to 1 November 2019. The determination of the market value is on a self-assessment basis. In 2013 property owners were required to only pay a half year's liability with the full amount payable in 2014 and following years.

35.6.2 Exemptions

- Residential properties exempt from LPT include:
- New and previously unused properties purchased from a builder/developer between 2013 and 2016
- Properties purchased by first time buyers in 2013
- Properties affected by pyrite damage
- Residential properties used for recreational activities connected with a charity
- Residential properties occupied by permanently incapacitated individuals.

35.6.3 Calculation of LPT

The property values are grouped into bands. In order to calculate the liability, it is necessary to select the band appropriate to the market value of the property as per the table below.

Valuation band €	2013 LTP (half a year) €	2014–2018 LTP (full year)* €
0 – 100,000	45	90
100,001 – 150,000	112	225
150,001 – 200,000	157	315
200,001 – 250,000	202	405
250,001 – 300,000	247	495
300,001 – 350,000	292	585
350,001 – 400,000	337	675
400,001 – 450,000	382	765
450,001 – 500,000	437	855
500,001 – 550,000	472	945
550,001 – 600,000	517	1,035
600,001 – 650,000	562	1,125
650,001 – 700,000	607	1,215
700,001 – 750,000	652	1,305
750,001 – 800,000	697	1,395
800,001 – 850,000	742	1,485
850,001 – 900,000	787	1,575
900,001 – 950,000	832	1,665
950,001 – 1,000,000	877	1,755
>1m 0.18% on first €1m and 0.25% thereafter		

* Some local authorities have adjusted the LPT rate for 2018 by up to 15%, see revenue.ie for further details.

Example 35.10

Residential property with a market value of €625,000 has a liability of €1,125 in 2018.

35.6.4 Payment dates

The LPT due date depends on the method of payment chosen as property owners have a number of options available to them, they may choose to:

- spread the payments evenly throughout 2018 (commencing in January), by way of monthly direct debit, or deduction from salary, pension or government payment.
- pay by cash payment/debit/credit cards – due date in this case 1 January 2018
- pay online – due date in this case 21 March 2018.

Interest of 8% per annum will be charged on late payment of this tax.

35.6.5 Return filing dates

The 2013 LPT return due date for filing was 7 May 2013 for paper filed returns and 28 May 2013 for returns filed on line. Provided the individual's situation does not change then the next LPT return is not due until 7 November 2019 and every three years thereafter. Individuals who own more than one property must file their LPT returns on line.

If a chargeable person fails to submit their LTP return on time then their income tax return is also deemed late. A 10% surcharge for late filing of an income tax return will apply. Where the LPT return is subsequently filed then this surcharge will not exceed the LPT liability. This rule applies regardless of whether the individual's income tax return is filed on time or not (self-assessment rules are dealt with at Chapter 10).

35.6.6 Deferrals

In certain circumstances LPT liability may be deferred:

- If gross income for an individual does not exceed €15,000 (or €25,000 for a couple)
- Marginal relief may also apply allowing 50% of the LPT be deferred.

Interest will be charged at 4% per annum on amounts deferred.

References and Recommended Further Reading

POWER, T. and E. SCULLY (2013), *The Law and Practice of Irish Stamp Duty,* Irish Tax Institute.

KEOGAN, A. and E. SCULLY (Eds.) (2018), *Law of Capital Acquisitions Tax, Stamp Duty and Local Property Tax,* Irish Tax Institute.

MARTYN, J., D. SHANAHAN, COONEY, T. (Ed) (2018), *Taxation Summary,* Irish Tax Institute.

INDEX

K

L

S